THE YALE EDITION

OF

HORACE WALPOLE'S

CORRESPONDENCE

EDITED BY W. S. LEWIS

VOLUME NINE

HORACE WALPOLE'S
CORRESPONDENCE

WITH

GEORGE MONTAGU

I

EDITED BY W. S. LEWIS

AND

RALPH S. BROWN, JR

NEW HAVEN

YALE UNIVERSITY PRESS

LONDON : HUMPHREY MILFORD : OXFORD UNIVERSITY PRESS

1941

ADVISORY COMMITTEE

LIST OF SUBSCRIBERS

H. M. KING GEORGE VI

ALBERTUS MAGNUS COLLEGE LIBRARY, New Haven, Connecticut
RICHARD S. ALDRICH, Esq., Providence, Rhode Island
ALLEGHENY COLLEGE, THE REIS LIBRARY, Meadville, Pennsylvania
ALL SOULS COLLEGE LIBRARY, Oxford
JOSEPH W. ALSOP, Esq., Avon, Connecticut
AMERICAN UNIVERSITY LIBRARY, Washington, D. C.
AMHERST COLLEGE, CONVERSE MEMORIAL LIBRARY, Amherst, Massachusetts
ATLANTA UNIVERSITY LIBRARY, Atlanta, Georgia
C. C. AUCHINCLOSS, Esq., New York, New York
HUGH D. AUCHINCLOSS, Esq., McLean, Virginia
Mrs HUGH D. AUCHINCLOSS, New York, New York
AVON OLD FARMS, Avon, Connecticut
RICHARD B. BAKER, Esq., Providence, Rhode Island
R. E. BALFOUR, Esq., Cambridge
Sir T. D. BARLOW, K.B.E., London
BATH MUNICIPAL LIBRARY, Bath
BAVARIAN STATE LIBRARY, Munich
C. F. BELL, Esq., Kensington
BERKELEY COLLEGE LIBRARY, YALE UNIVERSITY, New Haven, Connecticut
THEODORE BESTERMAN, Esq., London
Messrs BICKERS AND SON, LTD, London
Mrs NORMAN H. BILTZ, Reno, Nevada
BIRMINGHAM PUBLIC LIBRARY, Birmingham
CHARLES L. BLACK, Esq., Austin, Texas
R. K. BLAIR, Esq., Edinburgh
BOSTON ATHENAEUM, Boston, Massachusetts
BOSTON COLLEGE LIBRARY, Chestnut Hill, Massachusetts
BOSTON PUBLIC LIBRARY, Boston, Massachusetts
BOSTON UNIVERSITY GRADUATE SCHOOL, Boston, Massachusetts
BOWDOIN COLLEGE LIBRARY, Brunswick, Maine
JULIAN P. BOYD, Esq., Princeton, New Jersey
Miss EMMA JEANNETTE BRAZIER, New York, New York

vii

Denver Public Library, Denver, Colorado
Des Moines Public Library, Des Moines, Iowa
Detroit Public Library, Detroit, Michigan
Mrs Robert Cloutman Dexter, Belmont, Massachusetts
Charles D. Dickey, Esq., Chestnut Hill, Philadelphia, Pennsylvania
Dickinson College Library, Carlisle, Pennsylvania
Mrs Frank F. Dodge, New York, New York
Drake University Library, Des Moines, Iowa
Drew University Library, Madison, New Jersey
Duke University Library, Durham, North Carolina
Edinburgh Public Library, Edinburgh
Edinburgh University Library, Edinburgh
Rodney R. Ellis, Esq., Poultney, Vermont
Albert H. Ely, Esq., Coldspring Harbor, New York
Emory University Library, Emory University, Georgia
Enoch Pratt Free Library, Baltimore, Maryland
Farmington Village Library, Farmington, Connecticut
Henry Field, Esq., d.sc., Chicago, Illinois
Maurice Firuski, Esq., Salisbury, Connecticut
Harry Harkness Flagler, Esq., Millbrook, New York
Mrs Margaret Mitchell Flint, Westport, Connecticut
Florida State College for Women Library, Tallahassee, Florida
Forbes Library, Northampton, Massachusetts
Fordham University Library, New York, New York
Franklin and Marshall College Library, Lancaster, Pennsylvania
Free Library of Philadelphia, Philadelphia, Pennsylvania
Donald T. Gammons, Esq., Boston, Massachusetts
Georgetown University, Riggs Memorial Library, Washington,
    D. C.
Glasgow University Library, Glasgow
Howard L. Goodhart, Esq., New York, New York
Philip L. Goodwin, Esq., New York, New York
R. Grant, Esq., Edinburgh
Mrs William Greenough, Newport, Rhode Island
Lauder Greenway, Esq., Greenwich, Connecticut
Mrs Octavia Gregory, Parkstone, Dorset
William V. Griffin, Esq., New York, New York
Farnham P. Griffiths, Esq., San Francisco, California
Maitland F. Griggs, Esq., New York, New York
Grinnell College Library, Grinnell, Iowa

GROSVENOR LIBRARY, Buffalo, New York
GROTON SCHOOL LIBRARY, Groton, Massachusetts
SIDNEY LEWIS GULICK, Jr, Esq., Oakland, California
HACKLEY PUBLIC LIBRARY, Muskegon, Michigan
Mrs CHANDLER HALE, Washington, D. C.
ALFRED E. HAMILL, Esq., Lake Forest, Illinois
ALLEN HAMILTON, Esq., M.D., Fort Wayne, Indiana
KENNETH E. HARTMAN, Esq., Des Moines, Iowa
HARVARD COLLEGE LIBRARY, Cambridge, Massachusetts
LEWIS HATCH, Esq., New York, New York
HAMILTON A. HIGBIE, Esq., Jamaica, New York
EDWIN L. HILDRETH, Esq., Brattleboro, Vermont
FREDERICK W. HILLES, Esq., New Haven, Connecticut
HOBART COLLEGE LIBRARY, Geneva, New York
C. B. HOGAN, Esq., Woodbridge, Connecticut
HOTCHKISS SCHOOL, Lakeville, Connecticut
ELTON HOYT, Esq., Cleveland, Ohio
HUNTER COLLEGE LIBRARY, New York, New York
HENRY E. HUNTINGTON LIBRARY AND ART GALLERY, San Marino,
   California
INCARNATE WORD COLLEGE LIBRARY, San Antonio, Texas
INDIANA STATE LIBRARY, Indianapolis, Indiana
INDIANA UNIVERSITY LIBRARY, Bloomington, Indiana
STUART W. JACKSON, Esq., Montclair, New Jersey
JACKSONVILLE PUBLIC LIBRARY, Jacksonville, Florida
OLIVER B. JENNINGS, Esq., New York, New York
JOHNS HOPKINS UNIVERSITY LIBRARY, Baltimore, Maryland
Professor JARVIS KEILEY, New York, New York
KENYON COLLEGE LIBRARY, Gambier, Ohio
WILLARD L. KING, Esq., Chicago, Illinois
KING'S COLLEGE LIBRARY, Cambridge
YALE KNEELAND, Jr, Esq., M.D., New York, New York
KNOX COLLEGE LIBRARY, Galesburg, Illinois
SEYMOUR H. KNOX, Esq., Buffalo, New York
LAFAYETTE COLLEGE LIBRARY, Easton, Pennsylvania
LEEDS PUBLIC LIBRARIES, Leeds
A. N. LEWIS, Esq., San Francisco, California
CHARLES L. LEWIS, Esq., Puente, California
LIBRARY ASSOCIATION OF PORTLAND, Portland, Oregon
LIVERPOOL PUBLIC LIBRARIES, Liverpool

Loras College Library, Dubuque, Iowa
Los Angeles Public Library, Los Angeles, California
Louisiana State University Library, Baton Rouge, Louisiana
Compton Mackenzie, Esq., Isle of Barra
Reuben McMillan Free Library, Youngstown, Ohio
Mrs W. S. McNeill, Richmond, Virginia
Manchester Public Libraries, Manchester
Anthony F. Marreco, Esq., London
Marywood College Library, Scranton, Pennsylvania
B. I. Messelbrook, Esq., Southampton
Miami University Library, Oxford, Ohio
William Davis Miller, Esq., Wakefield, Rhode Island
Mills College Library, Oakland, California
Minneapolis Athenaeum, Minneapolis, Minnesota
Paul Moser, Esq., Chicago, Illinois
Mount Holyoke College Library, South Hadley, Massachusetts
Mount Union College Library, Alliance, Ohio
A. R. Mowbray and Company, Ltd, Leeds
Municipal University of Omaha Library, Omaha, Nebraska
Merrill Calvin Munyan, Esq., Durham, North Carolina
Colonel H. L. Nathan, London
The National Central Library, London
National Library of Ireland, Dublin
A. E. Neergaard, Esq., m.d., New York, New York
Newberry Library, Chicago, Illinois
New Britain Institute Library, New Britain, Connecticut
New Hampshire State Library, Concord, New Hampshire
New Haven Public Library, New Haven, Connecticut
New Jersey College for Women Library, New Brunswick, New
  Jersey
Charles Newman, Esq., New York, New York
New York Public Library, New York, New York
New York State Library, Albany, New York
New York University Library, New York, New York
North Texas State Teachers College Library, Denton, Texas
Northwestern University Library, Evanston, Illinois
Oberlin College Library, Oberlin, Ohio
Ohio State University Library, Columbus, Ohio
Ohio Wesleyan University, Charles Elihu Slocum Library, Dela-
  ware, Ohio

OKLAHOMA A. AND M. COLLEGE LIBRARY, Stillwater, Oklahoma
ASHLEY W. OLMSTED, Esq., Buffalo, New York
PEABODY INSTITUTE LIBRARY, Baltimore, Maryland
PEMBROKE COLLEGE LIBRARY, Cambridge
PENNSYLVANIA STATE COLLEGE LIBRARY, State College, Pennsylvania
PENNSYLVANIA STATE LIBRARY AND MUSEUM, Harrisburg, Pennsylvania
Miss MARION B. PHILLIPS, San Bernardino, California
PHILLIPS ACADEMY LIBRARY, Andover, Massachusetts
PHILLIPS EXETER ACADEMY, DAVIS LIBRARY, Exeter, New Hampshire
Mrs PORTER'S SCHOOL, Farmington, Connecticut
L. F. POWELL, Esq., Oxford
PRINCETON UNIVERSITY LIBRARY, Princeton, New Jersey
PROVIDENCE ATHENAEUM, Providence, Rhode Island
PRUSSIAN STATE LIBRARY, Berlin
PURDUE UNIVERSITY LIBRARY, Lafayette, Indiana
QUEENS UNIVERSITY OF BELFAST LIBRARY, Belfast
READING UNIVERSITY LIBRARY, Reading
REDWOOD LIBRARY AND ATHENAEUM, Newport, Rhode Island
RHODE ISLAND STATE COLLEGE LIBRARY, Kingston, Rhode Island
RICE INSTITUTE LIBRARY, Houston, Texas
The Reverend T. LAWRASON RIGGS, New Haven, Connecticut
THE ROYAL LIBRARY, Stockholm
RUTGERS UNIVERSITY LIBRARY, New Brunswick, New Jersey
ST. BONAVENTURE COLLEGE, FRIEDSAM MEMORIAL LIBRARY, St. Bonaventure, New York
ST. JOSEPH'S COLLEGE LIBRARY, Emmitsburg, Maryland
ST. LOUIS PUBLIC LIBRARY, St. Louis, Missouri
ST. LOUIS UNIVERSITY LIBRARY, St. Louis, Missouri
ST. MARY'S COLLEGE, Strawberry Hill, Middlesex
ST. MARY'S COLLEGE LIBRARY, Notre Dame, Indiana
ST. OLAF COLLEGE LIBRARY, Northfield, Minnesota
ST. PETERS COLLEGE LIBRARY, Jersey City, New Jersey
Mrs JAMES SALLADE, Ann Arbor, Michigan
SAN BERNARDINO VALLEY JUNIOR COLLEGE LIBRARY, San Bernardino, California
SAN FRANCISCO PUBLIC LIBRARY, San Francisco, California
PAUL S. SCHOEDINGER, Esq., Durham, New Hampshire
SEATTLE PUBLIC LIBRARY, Seattle, Washington
GEORGE SHERBURN, Esq., New York, New York

SMITH COLLEGE LIBRARY, Northampton, Massachusetts
Mrs THEODORE J. SMITH, Geneva, New York
WILLARD SMITH, Esq., Oakland, California
P. H. B. OTWAY SMITHERS, Esq., London
SOUTH AFRICAN PUBLIC LIBRARY, Capetown
SOUTHERN METHODIST UNIVERSITY LIBRARY, Dallas, Texas
SOUTHWESTERN COLLEGE LIBRARY, Memphis, Tennessee
T. M. SPELMAN, Esq., Harrison, New York
STANFORD UNIVERSITY LIBRARIES, Stanford University, California
STATE UNIVERSITY OF IOWA LIBRARIES, Iowa City, Iowa
JAMES STRACHEY, Esq., London
STRATFORD LIBRARY ASSOCIATION, Stratford, Connecticut
SWARTHMORE COLLEGE LIBRARY, Swarthmore, Pennsylvania
HENRY C. TAYLOR, Esq., Coldspring Harbor, Long Island, New York
TEMPLE UNIVERSITY, SULLIVAN MEMORIAL LIBRARY, Philadelphia,
    Pennsylvania
TEXAS STATE COLLEGE FOR WOMEN LIBRARY, Denton, Texas
THACHER SCHOOL LIBRARY, Ojai, California
TRANSYLVANIA COLLEGE LIBRARY, Lexington, Kentucky
TULANE UNIVERSITY LIBRARY, New Orleans, Louisiana
UNION COLLEGE LIBRARY, Schenectady, New York
UNIVERSITY CLUB LIBRARY, New York, New York
UNIVERSITY COLLEGE LIBRARY, Hull
UNIVERSITY COLLEGE LIBRARY, London
UNIVERSITY OF ALABAMA LIBRARY, University, Alabama
UNIVERSITY OF ARIZONA LIBRARY, Tucson, Arizona
UNIVERSITY OF BIRMINGHAM LIBRARY, Birmingham
UNIVERSITY OF BUFFALO, LOCKWOOD MEMORIAL LIBRARY, Buffalo,
    New York
UNIVERSITY OF CALIFORNIA AT LOS ANGELES LIBRARY, West Los An-
    geles, California
UNIVERSITY OF CALIFORNIA LIBRARY, Berkeley, California
UNIVERSITY OF CHICAGO LIBRARIES, Chicago, Illinois
UNIVERSITY OF CINCINNATI LIBRARY, Cincinnati, Ohio
UNIVERSITY OF COLORADO LIBRARY, Boulder, Colorado
UNIVERSITY OF CONNECTICUT LIBRARY, Storrs, Connecticut
UNIVERSITY OF DELAWARE LIBRARY, Newark, Delaware
UNIVERSITY OF DURHAM LIBRARY, Durham
UNIVERSITY OF FLORIDA LIBRARY, Gainesville, Florida
UNIVERSITY OF GEORGIA LIBRARIES, Athens, Georgia

Washington University Library, St. Louis, Missouri
M. E. Weatherall, Esq., North Clifton, Guernsey
Vanderbilt Webb, Esq., New York, New York
Wellesley College Library, Wellesley, Massachusetts
Wells College Library, Aurora, New York
Wesleyan University Library, Middletown, Connecticut
Waldemar Westergaard, Esq., Los Angeles, California
Western College Library, Oxford, Ohio
Western Kentucky State Teachers College Library, Bowling
   Green, Kentucky
Western Reserve University Library, Cleveland, Ohio
Western State Teachers College Library, Kalamazoo, Michigan
Wheaton College Library, Wheaton, Illinois
Henry Wade White, Esq., Waterbury, Connecticut
Thornton Wilder, Esq., Hamden, Connecticut
William and Mary College Library, Williamsburg, Virginia
Williams College Library, Williamstown, Massachusetts
Wittenberg College Library, Springfield, Ohio
Worthy Paper Company, West Springfield, Massachusetts
Yale Club Library, New York, New York
Yale University Library, New Haven, Connecticut
Maurice F. Yorke, Esq., Green Craig, Aberlady
Innis Young, Esq., New Haven, Connecticut

TABLE OF CONTENTS

VOLUME I

LIST OF ILLUSTRATIONS

VOLUMES I AND II

 *Grateful acknowledgment is made to the Duke of Buc-
 cleuch, the trustees of the National Portrait Gallery,
 and the Henry E. Huntington Library and Art Gallery for permission to reproduce illustrations listed
 here.*

INTRODUCTION

OOKS of selections from Walpole's letters show that his
letters to Montagu are of more general interest than are
those written to any other correspondent. This is due
partly, no doubt, to their providing the key, as Saintsbury put it,
to 'society';[1] it is due, also, to their gaiety. Richard West called
Walpole's youthful style *allegro,* and that applies to these letters
even when Walpole is most exasperated with Montagu, for Montagu was 'a good audience'; he stimulated Walpole to do his best,
even when Montagu nodded off during the performance. It is
illuminating to contrast Walpole's letters in this correspondence
with those of the correspondence which followed it, the one with
Lady Ossory. The tone and content of each are similar, the great
figures of politics and society march across the paper, but in the
later correspondence they do so more self-consciously; posterity
has moved in from the next room and is sitting in a nearby chair.

Each correspondence, it is now clear, offers its own peculiar
problems to the editor. The most difficult problem in the Montagu correspondence is to understand its private allusions. They
include standing jokes which began at Eton and which multi-
plied during Montagu's London sojourn in the 'forties when he
was, greatly to our surprise, a Member of Parliament. He and
Walpole invented words and phrases: 'prance-aboutable,' 'touch
a card,' 'greenth,' 'blueth,' 'lilac-hood.' These are immediately
clear, but there are others which are not: 'Cudom,' for example,
which means the Montagu family, and there is one paragraph in
Montagu's letter of 30 Dec. 1765 (ii. 190) which even Walpole
could make nothing of (ii. 193). This sort of thing has always
been common among schoolboys with humorous minds and
bookish tastes, and Montagu and Walpole retained something of
the juvenile to the end of their days. Furthermore, their reading
was wide and varied. Montagu surprises us with allusions to the

1. George Saintsbury, *The Peace of the Augustans,* 1916, p. 230.

Bible and to the less read plays of Shakespeare. There are allusions to out-of-the-way books, a few of which have eluded us altogether, 'Cronk's false cabinet,' may be in one (i. 121). Finally, since both were old and intimate friends, the correspondence is filled with tacit assumptions and obscure allusions to persons and things, even though one of the correspondents was aware of posterity while he was writing. An example of this is in the letter of 2 Feb. 1762 (ii. 6) where Walpole describes going to hear the Cock Lane Ghost: 'We set out from the Opera, *changed our clothes* at Northumberland House' and proceeded *'all in one hackney coach.'* I confess I had read this passage many times without realizing the significance of the words which I have italicized: the fact that if they had gone into Cock Lane in their evening clothes and in their resplendent coaches they would have had mud and insults heaped upon them, as foreign travellers of the period testify. This sort of allusion of course occurs elsewhere in Walpole's intimate correspondences, but it is particularly frequent in the present one.

Montagu's letters are printed here completely for the first time, though extracts from them were included in Cunningham's edition of Walpole's letters and in the *Eighth Report of the Royal Commission on Historical Manuscripts*, App. II, 1881, pp. 112–20.[2] In the introduction to this last, L. Owen Pike states that Montagu 'uses many words that gentlemen of the present day would hardly put upon paper, but there are some at which he stops short, and for which he judiciously leaves a blank' (p. 16). Connoisseurs of erotica, however, will be disappointed by the full text. Incidentally, their disappointment will extend to the deleted passages in Walpole's letters for which Lytton Strachey sighed in vain, and which have also, of course, been restored for the first time in print. One of Walpole's passages (i. 139) has been suppressed in the past, not because of any sexual reference but because it is, by any standard, disgusting. That Walpole could have thought it was amusing, discloses an unsuspected as-

2. See the section 'Bibliography and Method' below.

pect of his personality. It reminds one of Gillray at his most brutal; not too much stress should be put upon it, for no other passage like it has yet been found, but there it is, and its suppression has, to that extent, falsified our view of its writer.

George Montagu owes his posthumous existence entirely to his friendship with Horace Walpole. He was the son of Brigadier-General Edward Montagu and Arabella Trevor and, as Mr Brown has shown in Appendix 7, he was closely connected with all the noble Montagu families. There is some doubt about the year of his birth, but it was probably 1713.[3] He is one of the 'Montagues' who appear in the Eton Lists of 1725 and 1728, and it was at Eton where his intimacy with Walpole, despite the difference in their ages, began. Cunningham saw, presumably at Kimbolton, a memoir drawn up by Montagu in which Montagu described himself as being 'of a tender delicate constitution and turn of mind, and more adapted to reading than exercises, to sedentary amusements than robust play. I had an early passion for poetry: at Eton, when in the fifth form, I presumed to make English verses for my exercise, a thing not practised then.'[4] This passage confirms Walpole's letter of 6 May 1736. Montagu was admitted Fellow Commoner at Trinity College, Cambridge, in 1731. He made the Grand Tour, partly, at least, in the company of George Selwyn, and he met Gray and Walpole at Rheims.[5] He sat for Northampton in the Parliaments of 1741 and 1747; he was Gentleman Usher of the Black Rod in Ireland in the viceroyalty of his cousin Lord Halifax in 1761; he was Deputy Ranger of Rockingham Forest through the interest of his cousin, Lady Beaulieu. When his cousin, Lord North, became Chancellor of the Exchequer in 1767, he offered Montagu the place of his Secretary. 'This office is not troublesome,' North reassured him, 'either from business or confinement; the most diligent secretaries, as far as I can learn, have done little more than attend the Chancellor once or twice a year to the Court of Exchequer,

3. See i. 333 n. 8.   5. *Gray's Corr.* i. 114.
4. Cunningham ix. pp. xxi–xxii.

and at the Declaration of Public Accounts.' These crumbs of preferment fell naturally to agreeable members of the cadet branch
of a great eighteenth-century family. No one deserved them
more than Montagu: his interest in the welfare of the 'Cues' was
so strong that it could even, at times, surmount his interest in
eating and sleeping.

It is remarkable that a man so fortunately placed in life, with
such powerful friends and relations, and with so much wit and
humour, should have sunk into obscurity, but Montagu was
paralyzed by laziness. Gray visited him once at Greatworth;[6]
Cole mentions him in Appendix 4 of the present correspondence
(ii. 333); George Hardinge called him one of Walpole's witty and
effeminate friends;[7] Sylvester Douglas, Lord Glenbervie, heard
of him after his death from Lady Glenbervie who had seen him
often in her youth at her father's, Lord North's, house. She described Montagu as a delightful old man who was not *laudator
temporis acti*.[8] And this is all we know of Montagu outside of this
correspondence. Except for a few excursions to town, he remained 'buried in squireland,' at the three houses he successively
occupied, Roel, Greatworth, and Adderbury, drinking port, nursing the gout, and dozing by his fire in the company of his brother
John who, according to Sir Walter Scott,[9] was still a midshipman
at the age of sixty. The friends of his youth and the active members of his family were far away in the haze of London. Only
rarely would he rouse himself to write a letter to Walpole which
compares favourably with the best he received in return.

In the dozen or so letters where Montagu lets himself go, the
reader will be startled by the similarity to Walpole's best letters.
'*I am shedding my grey hairs one by one; not that I mean to appear the young creature, but that I have youth coming to me
with purple wings and a bag of counters to play with the rest of*

---

6. See H. T. Swedenberg, Jr, 'Thomas
Gray's "Journal for 1754 from the first of
March,"' *The Huntington Library Quar-
terly*, Oct. 1939, p. 100.

7. John Nichols, *Literary Anecdotes*,
1812–15, viii. 526.

8. *The Diaries of Sylvester Douglas*, ed.
Francis Bickley, 1928, ii. 303.

9. *The Quarterly Review*, 1818, xix. 131.

my days' (i. 352). 'We have had cold weather, but I am now writing with my windows up and *violent zephyrs a little warmed over the fire'* (i. 352). 'I know you will say why not come to town and manage your own matters than employ me *to dress up an old doll?'* (i. 355). Anyone familiar with Walpole's style would say that he had written the passages I have italicized. Walpole picked up words and phrases and turns of expressions as he picked up objects of art and curiosities. Much of what in Walpole's style we find most Walpolian can be traced, it now seems clear, to George Montagu.

The two friends shared more than wit and humour. They were equally interested in gossip about great names, those of the dead as well as those of the living. They loved visiting country houses, not to see their owners, for both were shy, but to study the building and its prospects, to pore over the family portraits and to rummage the attics for family papers. Neither ever outgrew his Eton practice of 'sighing some pastoral name to the echo of the cascade under the bridge.' When Montagu was in Ireland, he acquired the pocket book of a young Chevalier de Malte who had been killed at Carricfergus, together with the young man's collection of songs and pictures of his mistresses, and Montagu had him decently buried, 'for they used to take him out of his grave by his fine long hair to show the French enemy.'[10] They were proud of their disinterestedness in an age when virtually every man they knew scrambled for sinecures;[11] their idols were Montagu's ancestors, Algernon Sidney and John Hampden. While they annotated prints at Strawberry Hill or read Lucan at Greatworth, their breasts burned with ardour for the cause of common men against kings. Walpole, on more than one occasion, stood up publicly for liberal opinion and action, but Montagu was content to fold his hands inside a 'grave and warm' muff and sleep away his life.

The correspondence fades into silence. We can see the end ap-

10. See ii. 12.

11. Sinecures came to both, it is true; but Walpole displayed a quixotic indifference to them. Montagu's disinterestedness was alloyed with a human longing for more money, but it was strong enough to keep him from 'scrambling' for preferment.

proaching months before it arrives. Montagu's attachment to Lord North annoyed Walpole, but it was Montagu's apathy which brought the end. Walpole gives him fair warning, Montagu starts up guiltily with a tardy reply which keeps Walpole going; finally Montagu does not reply; they may have met in London after the last letter, but one of the most entertaining of all correspondences is finished. Whatever one may think of Madame du Deffand's complaints of Walpole's severities to her, one cannot deny that his scoldings of Montagu are justified. Each correspondence gives us a somewhat different picture of Walpole. With Cole, for example, he is a brilliant amateur antiquarian; with Montagu he is the man of the world and an amusing, devoted, and much tried friend. When one finishes this correspondence, one must admit that Walpole possessed both generosity and patience.

Walpole wrote to Cole 11 May 1780, 'A much older friend of mine died yesterday, . . . George Montagu whom you must remember at Eton and Cambridge. I should have been exceedingly concerned for him a few years ago—but he had dropped me, partly from politics and partly from caprice, for we never had any quarrel—but he was grown an excessive humourist, and had shed almost all his friends as well as me. He had parts and infinite vivacity and originality till of late years—and it grieved me much that he had changed towards me after a friendship of between thirty and forty years.' Montagu died, oddly enough, in London, but the Duke of Manchester permitted one more crumb of preferment to fall upon his loyal kinsman: Montagu was buried in the ducal vault at Kimbolton, the only Montagu commoner to receive that final condescension.[12]

W. S. L.

12. Cunningham iv. 475 n.

BIBLIOGRAPHY AND METHOD

WALPOLE'S correspondence with George Montagu now consists of 449 letters, of which 262 are Walpole's and 187 are Montagu's. The latter have not previously been published (except those of 28 July 1745 and ca 25 Sept. 1749, printed in the first supplement to Mrs Toynbee's edition of Walpole's letters), but fragments of ten letters[1] were printed by Cunningham in footnotes to his edition of the letters, and considerable fragments of twenty-six letters with shorter quotations from some seventy others were published by the Historical Manuscripts Commission in its calendar of the manuscripts at Kimbolton.[2] A few of Walpole's memoranda on the backs of Montagu's letters were also quoted in this calendar but most of them are here first printed. Cole's description of his journey with Walpole (Appendix 4), Mrs Piozzi's note on the Earl of Salisbury (Appendix 5), and her marginal notes to Walpole's letters are printed here for the first time. Many letters from Montagu and a few from Walpole are obviously still missing; the correspondence as it now stands is very one-sided up to 1760. The missing letters, beginning with 1760, are indicated here by headings, with approximate dates.

Frederick Montagu of Papplewick, Notts, who was George Montagu's second cousin, residuary legatee, and sole executor, came into possession of Walpole's letters to Montagu, which Montagu had once said he intended to bequeath 'with the most solemn trust and precautions to the last Cu of ye Cudoms.'[3] After George Montagu's death in 1780, it seems clear[4] that the letters were returned to Walpole, who half-heartedly essayed to edit them. In some cases he crossed out passages (e.g. in his letter of

1. Those of 27 Nov. 1768, 11 April, ca 25 Aug., 27 Aug., 18 Sept., 22 Oct., and ca 18 Dec. 1769, 18 June, 17 July, and 6 Oct. 1770.

2. *Eighth Report of the Royal Commission on Historical Manuscripts*, App. II, 1881, pp. 112–20.

3. Montagu to Walpole 3 Feb. 1760.

4. Walpole to Frederick Montagu 28 Oct. 1784, printed here at the beginning of the correspondence.

20 May 1736) and he made a correction in his letter of 25 Oct.
1760; he obliterated a few names (those of Gray in the letter of
17 Nov. 1759, and of Bentley in that of 18 June 1764); and he
noted the year on the backs of the last letters of 1768, of 1769,
and of 1770. He then returned them to Frederick Montagu with
the exception of the letter of 30 May 1763. With them, it appears
from his letter to Frederick Montagu, went Montagu's letters to
Walpole, except those of 28 July 1745 and ca 25 Sept. 1749,
which (together with his own letter of 30 May 1763) Walpole
presumably kept and left to Mrs Damer, since they are in the
collection of Sir Wathen Waller, Bt. After Frederick Montagu's
death in 1800, the letters apparently passed to his kinsman, Lord
Frederick Montagu, brother of the fifth Duke of Manchester.
When Lord Frederick died, unmarried, in 1827, the letters must
have come into possession of the Dukes of Manchester at Kimbolton Castle where Cunningham saw them in 1857.[5]

It is to be assumed that all the letters, unless otherwise designated, are printed from photostats which were made from the
originals in the Duke of Manchester's collection (at Kimbolton
or on loan at the Public Record Office). The three letters from
the Waller collection (see above) are likewise printed from photostats of the originals. Those of 28 July 1745 and ca 25 Sept.
1749 are from Montagu and were first printed, as we have seen,
in 1918. The third is Walpole's letter of 30 May 1763. This was
the first letter in the Montagu correspondence to appear in print;
it was included by Miss Berry (Walpole's literary executrix) in
The Works of Horatio Walpole, Earl of Orford, 1798, v. 639, as
one of Walpole's miscellaneous letters. Miss Berry annotated it.

Besides these three letters, two others (from Walpole, 2 May
1736 and 18 May 1748) are not in the Kimbolton collection,
though Cunningham in 1857 apparently saw the earlier one
there.[6] Mrs Toynbee notes the absence of the later one in 1903,
but does not mention the absence of the earlier one. They are
printed here from the text of the first edition of Walpole's letters
to Montagu: *Letters from the Hon. Horace Walpole to George*

5. Cunningham iv. 475 n, ix. p. vi.   6. Cunningham ix. 499.

Montagu, Esq. from the Year 1736, to the Year 1770, London, 1818, 'printed for Rodwell and Martin, New Bond Street and Henry Colburn, Conduit Street' as Volume VI of *The Works of Horatio Walpole, Earl of Orford.* Three of Walpole's letters[7] are omitted, and the letter of 23 July 1763 is printed as two letters. The title-page says, 'Now first published from the originals in the possession of the editor.' The editor was presumably Lord Frederick Montagu, but John Martin the bookseller and bibliographer (junior partner of Rodwell and Martin who published the book) afterwards wrote:[8]

'The letters to George Montagu, first published in quarto, were conducted through the press by the editor of this work [Martin himself] from the originals in the possession of the late Lord Frederick Montagu, brother of his Grace the Duke of Manchester, and for a short period Postmaster-General. So tender was his Lordship of the reputation of those who came under the censure of Walpole, that the editor had great difficulty in persuading him to fill up any of the blanks, even the most harmless, though the parties intended must have been apparent to any one in the slightest degree conversant with the history of those times. In the second edition his Lordship became less fastidious, although too many blanks were still preserved.'

A separately printed table, giving a key to the omitted names, was put at the back of many copies of the first edition; it was 'privately' circulated after the book was printed.[9] Mrs Piozzi (Dr Johnson's Mrs Thrale) was living at Bath, aged seventy-seven, when the first edition appeared; her copy, which she labelled 'Bath 1818' on the flyleaf, is now in the possession of W. S. Lewis. It contains many marginal notes in her hand; those which are merely exclamations, ecstatic and otherwise, we have omitted, the rest are printed here for the first time.

7. Those of ca 11 May 1745, 14 July 1748, and 30 May 1763; the last of these had already been printed. In numbering the letters in the first edition, two numbers were omitted, so that the last letter should be No. 260 instead of No. 262.

8. John Martin, *Bibliographical Catalogue of Books Privately Printed,* 1834, p. 488 n.

9. See *The Quarterly Review* 1818, xix. 130.

A French translation of Walpole's letters to Montagu was published by Charles Malo in 1818 in octavo. The Comte de Baillon describes the translation as 'un amalgame de fragments tronqués et recousus ensemble, sans aucun égard pour l'ordre ni pour les dates et où les noms propres, on ne sait pourquoi, ne sont indiqués que par des initiales.'[10] We have not seen a copy of it.

The 'second edition,' mentioned above by John Martin, is presumably the *Private Correspondence of Horace Walpole, Earl of Orford,* London, 1820, 'printed for Rodwell and Martin, Bond Street, and Colburn and Co., Conduit Street' in four octavo volumes. The subsequent editions of 1822, 1837, 1840, 1857, and 1903–5 are those listed in Cole i. pp. li–lii. The first important one of these is Peter Cunningham's (1857–9). When Cunningham's earlier volumes were already in print, he collated Walpole's letters to Montagu with the originals at Kimbolton, finding many omissions which he added in his last volume. He also found the unpublished letter of 14 July 1748, and another letter (that of 23 Dec. 1756) which he printed as previously unpublished although he had already printed it under another date in his third volume.

Mrs Toynbee likewise collated the text with the originals for her edition (Oxford, 1903–5) and included the previously unpublished letter of ca 11 May 1745. Like all her predecessors, she printed Walpole's letter of 23 July 1763 as two letters. She and Cunningham both condemned the inaccuracy of preceding editors and restored many omitted passages without including the 'improper' bits. She printed Walpole's hitherto unpublished letter to Frederick Montagu as a footnote. Dr Toynbee, in the first supplement (Oxford, 1918) to his wife's edition, added, as notes, Montagu's two letters from the Waller collection.

Biographical notes, without reference, are from the *Dictionary of National Biography* or the *Complete Peerage* or *Complete Baronetage.* Other sources quoted in the biographical footnotes are assumed to be supplemented by those reference works. Members of Parliament who are listed in those works are designated

10. *Lettres de Horace Walpole,* ed. Comte de Baillon, Paris, 1872, p. lxvii.

as M.P. in our index, but their parliamentary membership is not given in our footnotes. In the notes where parliamentary membership is set forth, the dates and constituencies are taken from *Accounts and Papers* lxii (1890–1) *House; Elections*. When artists are given without reference, their names and dates are to be found in Ulrich Thieme and Felix Becker, *Allgemeines Lexikon der bildenden Künstler,* Leipzig, 1907—.

All English books are assumed to be published at London, and all French books at Paris, unless otherwise stated.

Square brackets indicate editorial emendation; angular brackets, the restoration of the manuscript where it has been mutilated.

In all the letters, the hyphenization and capitalization have been modernized here. The spellings have been modernized (a list of Walpole's obsolete ones is given on page xxxiii) but proper names are kept in the original spelling. Walpole's punctuation is retained, but Montagu's letters have been given such punctuation as is essential to intelligibility, since his own punctuation is scanty and erratic.

The numbering and lettering of the postmarks have been retained here although the significance of some of them is not known.

W. H. S.

WALPOLE'S SPELLING

The following are a selection of Walpole's spellings which differ from modern usage. They are included here to supplement the similar list in COLE i. p. xliii.

allum	guitarre	recompence, expence, etc.
base (bass)	hassocs	relicks
bishoprick	higle pigledy	reliques
blew (blue)	inchanted	reperation
bloodied (blooded)	inclosure	rhime
born (borne)	intail	smugle, smugler
carabine (carbine)	jayl	sollicitor
chearfullness	journies	sowed (sewed)
clarinettes	linnen	stroak
clarionets	litterally	stroler
cloyster	litterature	surprize
cotillon	meaned (meant)	taylor
cribbidge	medalions	teize
cristal	memoires	terreen
cyder	peice (piece)	tho, thro, etc.
desart (desert)	philigree	waggon
descendent	pitt	watry
fantom	prophane	wofull
gawze	quarentine	writ (written)

ACKNOWLEDGMENTS

OUR first acknowledgment is to the Duke of Manchester who, as Lord Mandeville, kindly permitted me to have photostats made of Walpole's letters to Montagu at Kimbolton, and of Montagu's letters to Walpole which have been deposited at the Public Record Office. We are also indebted to Sir Wathen A. Waller, Bt, for permission to make photostats of Montagu's letters to Walpole of 28 July 1745 and 25 Sept. 1749 and Walpole's letter of 30 May 1763.

Mr R. W. Chapman has read much of the proof and all of it has been read by Miss E. G. Withycombe, Mr R. W. Ketton-Cremer, Professor L. B. Namier, Professor F. A. Pottle, and Mr Leonard Whibley. They have saved us from errors and have added many helpful notes which would not otherwise have been given. I have kept their corrected proofs so that any scholars of the future who may be interested in the making of this edition can see precisely what and how great has been their contribution. We are under particular obligations to Miss Rose Phelps whose class at the University of Illinois Library School solved many of our problems for us and to the editors of *Notes and Queries* who generously printed 186 of our queries, a substantial part of which were answered by their readers. Through the kind offices of Mr Henry M. Hake, Director of the National Portrait Gallery, permission was obtained from the Duke of Buccleuch to reproduce Van Loo's portrait of George Montagu.

Dr Warren Hunting Smith has contributed the section 'Bibliography and Method' and, with the assistance of Mrs Richard G. Gettell, spent a year on the index. Dr Smith and Dr Monroe C. Beardsley performed the laborious task of checking all the references. Dr Smith and Mr William R. Wray have re-checked the text. Dr Smith's contribution has been so important that Mr Brown and I wanted to include his name on the title-page, but his modesty prevented it. Mrs Nicholas Moseley has kindly read the proofs of the index and so has continued her invaluable service to the edition. Mr William A. W. Krebs assisted in the editing, as did the following, on bursary appointments from Yale College: Harvey S. Bennett, William W. Reiter, Alan B. Spurney, William R. Wray. Mr Wade White began the transcribing.

Mr Brown has spent a considerable part of the past six years on this correspondence. My part in our collaboration has again been largely supervisory.

I should also like to express my thanks to the following: Mr R. A. Austen-Leigh; Dr A. V. Bailie, Dean of Windsor; Mr C. H. Collins Baker of the Henry E. Huntington Library and Art Gallery; Dr Charles H. Bennett of Yale University; Rev. Dr H. E. D. Blakiston, President of Trinity College, Oxford; Mr W. Starling Burgess; Mr G. Catalani; the Rev. Basil G. D. Clarke, Vicar of Horton, Northants; Mr C. T. Clay; Dr W. M. Crittenden of Temple University; Mr E. S. De Beer; Dr Gilbert H. Doane, Librarian of the University of Wisconsin; Mr R. H. Dundas of Christ Church; Mrs K. A. Esdaile; the Rev. N. Evans, Vicar of Horton, Northants; Dr John F. Fulton of Yale University; Mr R. M. Glencross; Sir Ambrose Heal; Prof. George L. Hendrickson of Yale University; the Rev. F. E. Hicks, Vicar of Audlem, Northants; Prof. F. W. Hilles of Yale University; the Earl of Home; Prof. Helen Sard Hughes of Wellesley College; the Earl of Ilchester; Prof. Claude Jenkins of Christ Church; Mr G. D. Johnston; Mr Stanley Johnson of Northwestern University; Mr Louis C. Jones of New York State College; Dr James R. Joy of New York City; the King's School, Canterbury; Dr Arnold Klebs of Nyon, Switzerland; Dr T. Loveday, Vice-Chancellor of the University of Bristol; Prof. T. O. Mabbott of Columbia University; Prof. Elizabeth W. Manwaring of Wellesley College; Lord Charles Montagu; Mr Owen F. Morshead; Mr Francis Needham; John L. Nevinson of the Victoria and Albert Museum; Prof. Allardyce Nicoll of Yale University; Prof. C. T. Onions of Magdalen College; Mr James M. Osborn of Yale University; Prof. E. A. Parr of Yale University; the late Mr W. Roberts; Miss Sybil Rosenfeld; Mr John Saltmarsh, Librarian of King's College, Cambridge; the Earl of Sandwich; Mrs Scott-Murray; Dr

Raymond W. Short of Yale University; Mr F. H. Slingsby; Mr Edwin G. Stray, Town Clerk of Twickenham; Mr Francis Thompson; Miss Gladys Scott Thompson; Mr Aubrey P. Toppin, York Herald; Prof. A. S. Turberbille of the University of Leeds; the Rev. A. W. R. Turner, Rector of Greatworth, Banbury; Mr Anthony R. Wagner, Portcullis; the Earl Waldegrave; the late Sir Hugh Walpole; Dr Joseph Lee Walsh of New Haven; Mr A. J. Watson of the British Museum; Mr Harold Williams.

W. S. L.

CUE-TITLES AND ABBREVIATIONS

Anecdotes, Works iii. . . Horace Walpole, *Anecdotes of Painting in England*, in *The Works of Horatio Walpole, Earl of Orford*, 1798, vol. iii.

Army Lists . . . . [Great Britain, War Office], *Army Lists.*

Beauties of England . John Britton and Edward W. Brayley, *The Beauties of England and Wales*, 1801–16, 18 vols.

BM Cat. . . . . British Museum Catalogue, 1881—.

BM *Satiric Prints* . . British Museum, Department of Prints and Drawings, *Catalogue of Prints and Drawings . . . Political and Personal Satires*, 1870–1938, 7 vols.

Boswell, *Johnson* . . *Boswell's Life of Johnson*, ed. George Birkbeck Hill, revised by L. F. Powell, Oxford, 1934—, 6 vols.

Burke, *Landed Gentry* . Sir John Bernard Burke, *A Genealogical and Heraldic History of the Landed Gentry of Great Britain.*

Burke, *Peerage* . . . Sir John Bernard Burke and Ashworth P. Burke, *A Genealogical and Heraldic History of the Peerage and Baronetage.*

Coke, *Journals* . . Lady Mary Coke, *Letters and Journals*, Edinburgh, 1889–96, 4 vols.

COLE . . . . . *The Yale Edition of Horace Walpole's Correspondence; the Correspondence with the Rev. Wm Cole*, New Haven, 1937, 2 vols.

Collins, *Peerage*, 1812 . *Collins's Peerage of England*, ed. Sir [Samuel] Egerton Brydges, 1812, 9 vols.

Country Seats . . . *Horace Walpole's Journals of Visits to Country Seats, &c.*, ed. Paget Toynbee, in *The Walpole Society*, Oxford, vol. xvi, 1928.

Cunningham . . . *The Letters of Horace Walpole, Earl of Orford*, ed. Peter Cunningham, 1857–9, 9 vols.

Delany, *Correspondence* *The Autobiography and Correspondence of Mary Granville, Mrs Delany*, ed. the Right Hon. Lady Llanover, 1861, 3 vols; 2d series, 1862, 3 vols.

Des. of SH . . . Horace Walpole, *A Description of the Villa of Mr Horace Walpole at Strawberry Hill near*

	King George the Third, ed. G. F. Russell Barker, 1894, 4 vols.
Montagu . . .	George Montagu.
MS Cat. . . .	Horace Walpole, 'Catalogue of the Library of Mr Horace Walpole at Strawberry Hill, 1763.' Unpublished MS in possession (1941) of Lord Walpole, Wolterton Park, Norwich.
Musgrave, *Obituary* .	*Obituary Prior to 1800 . . . Compiled by Sir William Musgrave,* ed. Sir George J. Armytage, Harleian Society Publications, 1899–1901, 6 vols.
N&Q	*Notes and Queries.*
Nouv. Biog. Gén. .	*Nouvelle biographie générale,* ed. Jean-Chrétien-Ferdinand Hoefer, Paris, 1852–66, 46 vols.
OED	*New English Dictionary on Historical Principles,* ed. Sir James A. H. Murray, Oxford, 1888–1933, 11 vols.
Scots Peerage .	*The Scots Peerage,* ed. Sir James Balfour Paul, Edinburgh, 1904–14, 9 vols.
SH	Strawberry Hill.
SH Accounts . .	*Strawberry Hill Accounts . . . Kept by Mr Horace Walpole from 1747 to 1795,* ed. Paget Toynbee, Oxford, 1927.
'Short Notes' . .	Horace Walpole, 'Short Notes of the Life of Horatio Walpole, youngest son of Sir Robert Walpole Earl of Orford and of Catherine Shorter, his first Wife,' first printed in Walpole's *Letters* to Mann, 1843, iv. 335–58, reprinted by Mrs Paget Toynbee, *Letters of Horace Walpole,* Oxford, 1903–5, i. pp. xxxiv–lvi.
sold SH . . .	*A Catalogue of the Classic Contents of Strawberry Hill Collected by Horace Walpole, 25 April–21 May 1842.* The roman and arabic numerals which follow these entries indicate the day and lot number: e.g. sold SH v. 2 = sold at the Strawberry Hill Sale, fifth day, lot 2.
Toynbee . . .	*The Letters of Horace Walpole,* ed. Mrs Paget Toynbee, Oxford, 1903–5, 16 vols; Supplement, ed. Paget Toynbee, 1918–25, 3 vols.
Venn, *Alumni Cantab.* .	*Alumni Cantabrigienses,* Part I, to 1751, compiled by John Venn and J. A. Venn, Cambridge, 1922–7, 4 vols.

Vict. Co. Hist.	.	*The Victoria History of the Counties of England* [with name of county].
Works . . .	.	Horace Walpole, *The Works of Horatio Walpole, Earl of Orford,* 1798, 5 vols.
WSL . . .	.	in the possession of W. S. Lewis, Farmington, Conn.

LIST OF LETTERS IN MONTAGU
CORRESPONDENCE

The missing letters are marked by an asterisk after the date. The dates of letters by Montagu are printed in italics. Letters which Cunningham prints in his footnotes are marked 'n.'

		YALE	TOYNBEE	CUNNINGHAM
1784	28 Oct.			
	to Frederick Montagu	i. 1		
1736	2 May	i. 1	i. 10	i. 2
	6 May	i. 2	i. 11	i. 4
	20 May	i. 4	i. 13	i. 5
	30 May	i. 6	i. 17	i. 6
1737	20 March	i. 9	i. 21	i. 14
1745	ca 11 May	i. 11	ii. 96	
	18 May	i. 12	ii. 97	i. 360
	25 May	i. 13	ii. 100	i. 362
	25 June	i. 14	ii. 106	i. 368
	13 July	i. 17	ii. 115	i. 375
	28 July	i. 20	Supp. I. ii. 83	
	1 Aug.	i. 21	ii. 122	i. 380
	17 Sept.	i. 23	ii. 132	i. 388
1746	22 May	i. 25	ii. 195	ii. 22
	5 June	i. 26	ii. 196	ii. 23
	12 June	i. 29	ii. 200	ii. 27
	17 June	i. 31	ii. 202	ii. 28
	24 June	i. 33	ii. 205	ii. 31
	3 July	i. 36	ii. 208	ii. 33
	2 Aug.	i. 38	ii. 223	ii. 43
	5 Aug.	i. 40	ii. 224	ii. 45
	ca 8 Aug.	i. 43	ii. 227	i. 15 misplaced
	11 Aug.	i. 44	ii. 228	ii. 47
	16 Aug.	i. 45	ii. 232	ii. 50
	3 Nov.	i. 48	ii. 248	ii. 63
1747	2 July	i. 49	ii. 285	ii. 90
	1 Oct.	i. 51	ii. 290	ii. 95
	ca 5 Oct.	i. 53	ii. 293	iii. 36 misplaced

		YALE	TOYNBEE	CUNNINGHAM
1748	18 May	i. 54	ii. 310	ii. 109
	26 May	i. 57	ii. 313	ii. 111
	14 July	i. 59	ii. 320	ix. 483
	25 July	i. 63	ii. 323	ii. 118
	11 Aug.	i. 67	ii. 329	ii. 121
	3 Sept.	i. 73	ii. 336	ii. 126
	25 Sept.	i. 77	ii. 342	ii. 130
	20 Oct.	i. 79	ii. 346	ii. 133
1749	18 May	i. 80	ii. 381	ii. 160
	5 July	i. 87	ii. 393	ii. 169
	20 July	i. 91	ii. 396	ii. 172
	26 Aug.	i. 96	ii. 406	ii. 178
	ca 25 Sept.	i. 100	Supp. I. ii. 89	
	28 Sept.	i. 101	ii. 411	ii. 182
1750	15 May	i. 103	ii. 446	ii. 206
	23 June	i. 105	ii. 450	ii. 210
	10 Sept.	i. 111	iii. 14	ii. 225
1751	30 May	i. 112	iii. 53	ii. 255
	13 June	i. 115	iii. 55	ii. 256
	22 July	i. 117	iii. 63	ii. 262
	8 Oct.	i. 122	iii. 69	ii. 267
1752	9 Jan.	i. 125	iii. 79	ii. 275
	12 May	i. 130	iii. 90	ii. 283
	6 June	i. 132	iii. 95	ii. 286
	ca July	i. 136	iii. 98	ii. 288
	30 July	i. 137	iii. 107	ii. 291
	28 Aug.	i. 141	iii. 121	ii. 305
	14 Dec.	i. 144	iii. 140	ii. 314 misdated
1753	22 May	i. 146	iii. 157	ii. 332
	11 June	i. 149	iii. 163	ii. 336
	17 July	i. 151	iii. 170	ii. 341
	16 Aug.	i. 155	iii. 182	ii. 349
	6 Dec.	i. 156	iii. 198	ii. 361
1754	19 March	i. 159	iii. 222	ii. 377
	ca April	i. 160		
	21 May	i. 161	iii. 238	ii. 386
	8 June	i. 162	iii. 243	ii. 390
	29 June	i. 162	iii. 243	ii. 390

		YALE	TOYNBEE	CUNNINGHAM
	29 Aug.	i. 163	iii. 252	ii. 396
	15 Oct.	i. 164		
	17 Oct.	i. 165	iii. 255	iii. 90 misdated
	16 Nov.	i. 165	iii. 263	ii. 405
1755	7 Jan.	i. 166	iii. 277	ii. 415
	13 May	i. 167	iii. 306	ii. 438
	17 July	i. 168	iii. 323	ii. 452
	26 July	i. 170	iii. 325	ii. 452
	20 Sept.	i. 172	iii. 344	ii. 466
	22 Sept.	i. 173		
	7 Oct.	i. 174	iii. 353	ii. 474
	15 Oct.	i. 175		
	8 Nov.	i. 176	iii. 362	ii. 481
	25 Nov.	i. 178	iii. 372	ii. 488
	20 Dec.	i. 180	iii. 378	ii. 493
	30 Dec.	i. 182	iii. 382	ii. 496
1756	20 April	i. 183	iii. 417	iii. 8
	4 May	i. 187	iii. 420	ii. 436 misdated
	19 May	i. 188	iii. 425	iii. 12
	26 May	i. 190		
	ca 6 June	i. 190	iv. 115 misdated	iii. 119 misdated
	ca 21 June	i. 191		
	12 July	i. 192	iii. 438	iii. 22
	ca 13 July	i. 193		
	28 Aug.	i. 195	iii. 449	iii. 25
	7 Oct.	i. 196		
	14 Oct.	i. 197	iv. 1	iii. 35
	28 Oct.	i. 199	iv. 6	iii. 39
	3 Nov.	i. 200		
	6 Nov.	i. 202	iv. 10	iii. 42
	25 Nov.	i. 203	iv. 14	iii. 45
	23 Dec.	i. 204	iv. 24	iii. 120 misdated ix. 488
1757	12 May	i. 205	iv. 53	iii. 11 misdated

		YALE	TOYNBEE	CUNNINGHAM
	19 May	i. 206	iv. 55	ii. 439 misplaced
	27 May	i. 206	iv. 56	iii. 77
	ca 29 May	i. 208		
	2 June	i. 209	iv. 59	iii. 80
	ca 10 June	i. 211		
	18 June	i. 212	iv. 64	iii. 21 misdated
	ca 20 June	i. 212		
	16 July	i. 213	iv. 74	iii. 90
	4 Aug.	i. 214	iv. 81	iii. 95
	25 Aug.	i. 215	iv. 88	iii. 99
	8 Sept.	i. 217	iv. 93	iii. 104
	18 Oct.	i. 217	iv. 106	iii. 113
1758	4 May	i. 218	iv. 133	iii. 133
	6 July	i. 221	iv. 153	iii. 147
	20 Aug.	i. 222	iv. 173	iii. 161
	3 Oct.	i. 225	iv. 195	iii. 177
	24 Oct.	i. 227	iv. 209	iii. 187
	26 Nov.	i. 229	iv. 217	iii. 191
	26 Dec.	i. 230	iv. 224	iii. 197
1759	26 April	i. 231	iv. 256	iii. 219
	16 May	i. 234	iv. 265	iii. 225
	2 June	i. 237	iv. 269	iii. 229
	23 June	i. 239	iv. 276	iii. 233
	19 July	i. 240	iv. 281 misdated	iii. 237
	ca 24 July	i. 242		
	26 July	i. 243	iv. 282	iii. 238
	29 July	i. 245		
	9 Aug.	i. 245	iv. 289	iii. 243
	9 Oct.	i. 247		
	11 Oct.	i. 248	iv. 304	iii. 252
	21 Oct.	i. 250	iv. 314	iii. 258
	ca 25 Oct.	i. 251		
	8 Nov.	i. 253	iv. 317	iii. 261
	ca 15 Nov.	i. 257		
	17 Nov.	i. 258	iv. 323	iii. 265

		YALE	TOYNBEE	CUNNINGHAM
	ca 20 Nov.	i. 260		
	ca 27 Nov.*	i. 261		
	4 Dec.	i. 261		
	23 Dec.	i. 262	iv. 330	iii. 271
	29 Dec.	i. 266		
1760	14 Jan.	i. 267	iv. 340	iii. 277
	28 Jan.	i. 271	iv. 345	iii. 281
	3 Feb.	i. 275		
	27 March	i. 276	iv. 366	iii. 296
	ca 9 April	i. 277		
	19 April	i. 278	iv. 370	iii. 299
	ca 25 April	i. 281		
	5 May	i. 282		
	6 May	i. 283	iv. 377	iii. 303
	4 July	i. 284	iv. 404	iii. 324
	8 July	i. 286		
	10 July	i. 287	iv. 408	iii. 327 misdated
	11 July	i. 287		
	ca 15 July*	i. 288		
	19 July	i. 288	iv. 408	iii. 326
	20 July	i. 290		
	12 Aug.	i. 291	iv. 416	iii. 332
	23 Aug.	i. 292		
	1 Sept.	i. 293	iv. 420	iii. 335
	16 Sept.	i. 300		
	2 Oct.	i. 301	iv. 430	iii. 343
	5 Oct.	i. 302		
	14 Oct.	i. 303	iv. 435	iii. 347
	19 Oct.	i. 308		
	25 Oct.	i. 310	iv. 439 misdated	iii. 350
	28 Oct.	i. 312	iv. 442	iii. 352
	ca 30 Oct.	i. 315		
	31 Oct.	i. 315	iv. 447	iii. 355
	4 Nov.	i. 317	iv. 452	iii. 358
	ca 9 Nov.	i. 319		
	13 Nov.	i. 320	iv. 454	iii. 360

		YALE	TOYNBEE	CUNNINGHAM
	18 June	i. 372	v. 68	iii. 407
	29 June	i. 374		
	ca 3 July	i. 374		
	4 July	i. 375	v. 70 misdated	iii. 408 misdated
	ca 7 July	i. 375		
	10 July	i. 376	v. 74	iii. 414 misdated
	22 July	i. 378	v. 85	iii. 419
	26 July	i. 380		
	28 July	i. 381	v. 92	iii. 424
	15 Aug.	i. 383		
	20 Aug.	i. 384	v. 99	iii. 429
	14 Sept.	i. 385		
	24 Sept.	i. 386	v. 110	iii. 436
	1 Oct.	i. 390		
	8 Oct.	i. 392	v. 125	iii. 447
	8 Oct.	i. 393		
	10 Oct.	i. 394	v. 129	iii. 450
	12 Oct.	i. 395		
	24 Oct.	i. 396	v. 135	iii. 454
	24 Oct.	i. 399		
	4 Nov.	i. 399		
	7 Nov.	i. 401	v. 140	iii. 458
	17 Nov.	i. 402		
	19 Nov.	i. 403		
	23 Nov.	i. 404		
	27 Nov.	i. 404		
	28 Nov.	i. 405	v. 144	iii. 461
	8 Dec.	i. 407	v. 149	iii. 465
	ca 15 Dec.	i. 408		
	ca 20 Dec.*	i. 410		
	23 Dec.	i. 410	v. 154	iii. 469 misdated
	ca 24 Dec.	i. 414		
	ca 26 Dec.*	i. 415		
	30 Dec.	i. 416	v. 160	iii. 473
1762	2 Jan.	ii. 1		

		YALE	TOYNBEE	CUNNINGHAM
1762	23 Jan.	ii. 2		
	26 Jan.	ii. 3	v. 164	iii. 477
	2 Feb.	ii. 5	v. 169	iii. 480
	6 Feb.	ii. 7		
	6 Feb.	ii. 9	v. 171	iii. 482
	18 Feb.	ii. 10		
	20 Feb.	ii. 13		
	22 Feb.	ii. 13	v. 176	iii. 486
	25 Feb.	ii. 15	v. 182	iii. 491
	27 Feb.	ii. 17		
	27 Feb. bis	ii. 19		
	ca 2 March	ii. 19		
	9 March	ii. 20	v. 186	iii. 493
	22 March	ii. 21	v. 191	iii. 497
	12 April	ii. 23		
	26 April	ii. 25		
	29 April	ii. 25	v. 198	iii. 502
	5 May	ii. 27		
	ca 10 May	ii. 28		
	14 May	ii. 29	v. 202	iii. 505
	17 May	ii. 30		
	20 May	ii. 31		
	25 May	ii. 31	v. 206	iii. 507
	27 May	ii. 33		
	8 June	ii. 34	v. 210	iii. 511
	28 July	ii. 35	v. 216	iii. 511
			misdated	misdated
	ca 5 Aug.*	ii. 37		
	8 Aug.*	ii. 37		
	9 Aug.	ii. 37		
	10 Aug.	ii. 38	v. 230	iv. 11
	18 Aug.	ii. 41		
	19 Sept.	ii. 41		
	24 Sept.	ii. 43	v. 246	iv. 23
	14 Oct.	ii. 45	v. 262	iv. 35
	4 Nov.	ii. 45	v. 271	iv. 41
	? Nov.	ii. 46		
	ca 10 Dec.*	ii. 47		

		YALE	TOYNBEE	CUNNINGHAM
	ca 17 Dec.	ii. 47		
	20 Dec.	ii. 48	v. 280	iv. 48
1763	*? Jan.*	ii. 51		
	25 March	ii. 51	v. 293	iv. 58
				misdated
	6 April	ii. 55	v. 296	iv. 60
	8 April	ii. 58	v. 299	iv. 62
	ca 10 April	ii. 60		
	11 April	ii. 61		
	14 April	ii. 62	v. 306	iv. 67
	17 April	ii. 65		
	21 April	ii. 67		
	22 April	ii. 67	v. 310	iv. 70
	17 May	ii. 69	v. 326	iv. 81
	21 May	ii. 74		
	ca 23 May*	ii. 75		
	ca 25 May	ii. 76		
	30 May	ii. 76	v. 335	iv. 88
	4 June	ii. 80		
	14 June	ii. 81		
	16 June	ii. 82	v. 342	iv. 93
	23 June	ii. 83		
	1 July	ii. 84	v. 345	iv. 95
	5 July	ii. 85		
	ca 8 July*	ii. 86		
	ca 12 July	ii. 86		
	23 July	ii. 88	v. 351, 354	iv. 98, 101
	15 Aug.	ii. 92	v. 360	iv. 105
	23 Aug.	ii. 95		
	28 Aug.	ii. 97		
	3 Sept.	ii. 98	v. 369	iv. 111
	5 Sept.	ii. 99		
	7 Sept.	ii. 100	v. 370	iv. 112
	9 Sept.	ii. 101		
	27 Sept.	ii. 102		
	3 Oct.	ii. 103	v. 373	iv. 114
	19 Oct.	ii. 107		
	12 Nov.	ii. 108	v. 383	iv. 122

		YALE	TOYNBEE	CUNNINGHAM
	15 Nov.	ii. 109		
	20 Nov.	ii. 110	v. 396	iv. 133
	26 Nov.	ii. 112		
1764	11 Jan.	ii. 113	v. 427	iv. 159
	14 Jan.	ii. 119		
	ca 23 April	ii. 120		
	ca 26 April*	ii. 121		
	1 May	ii. 121		
	10 May	ii. 123	vi. 62	iv. 233
	13 May	ii. 124		
	ca 20 May*	ii. 125		
	27 May	ii. 125		
	18 June	ii. 126	vi. 85	iv. 250
	27 June	ii. 128		
	16 July	ii. 128	vi. 88	iv. 251
	ca 21 July	ii. 131		
	23 July	ii. 132		
	16 Aug.	ii. 133	vi. 109	iv. 265
	30 Aug.	ii. 133		
	5 Oct.	ii. 134		
	ca 7 Oct.*	ii. 135		
	14 Oct.	ii. 135		
	ca 20 Oct.*	ii. 136		
	25 Oct.	ii. 136		
	26 Oct.	ii. 137		
	16 Dec.	ii. 137	vi. 156	iv. 301
	ca 19 Dec.	ii. 141		
	23 Dec.	ii. 143		
	24 Dec.	ii. 144	vi. 163	iv. 306
1765	*ca 3 Jan.*	ii. 146		
	19 Feb.	ii. 147	vi. 192	iv. 326
	24 Feb.	ii. 148		
	5 April	ii. 149	vi. 208	iv. 338
	ca 15 April	ii. 151		
	26 May	ii. 152	vi. 250	iv. 372
	ca 1 June	ii. 156		
	10 June	ii. 156	vi. 254	iv. 375
	ca 13 June	ii. 157		

	YALE	TOYNBEE	CUNNINGHAM
6 July	ii. 159	vi. 259	iv. 379 misplaced
8 July	ii. 160		
11 July	ii. 160	vi. 264	iv. 382
16 July	ii. 161		
28 July	ii. 162	vi. 268	iv. 385
1 Aug.	ii. 164		
23 Aug.	ii. 165	vi. 277	iv. 391
ca 27 Aug.	ii. 168		
31 Aug.	ii. 171	vi. 282	iv. 395
5 Sept.	ii. 173		
22 Sept.	ii. 174	vi. 299	iv. 406
15 Oct.	ii. 177		
16 Oct.	ii. 179	vi. 326	iv. 421
2 Nov.	ii. 181		
21 Nov.	ii. 183	vi. 357	iv. 440
7 Dec.	ii. 185		
24 Dec.	ii. 188		
30 Dec.	ii. 189		
1766 5 Jan.	ii. 191	vi. 387	iv. 458
8 Jan.	ii. 193		
20 Jan.	ii. 195		
5 Feb.	ii. 197	vi. 415	iv. 474
11 Feb.	ii. 198		
19 Feb.	ii. 199		
23 Feb.	ii. 200	vi. 419	iv. 477
3 March	ii. 201	vi. 428	iv. 482
7 March	ii. 203		
12 March	ii. 205	vi. 442	iv. 488
12 March	ii. 206		
21 March	ii. 207	vi. 443	iv. 489
29 March	ii. 209		
3 April	ii. 211	vi. 447	iv. 491
18 April	ii. 213		
28 April	ii. 213		
ca 1 May*	ii. 214		
5 May	ii. 214		
25 May	ii. 215	vii. 3	iv. 501

liv — LIST OF LETTERS

		YALE	TOYNBEE	CUNNINGHAM
	29 May	ii. 217		
	20 June	ii. 217	vii. 7	iv. 504
	23 June	ii. 220		
	26 June	ii. 221		
	ca 1 July*	ii. 221		
	10 July	ii. 221	vii. 12	iv. 509
	12 July	ii. 222		
	21 July	ii. 223	vii. 26	v. 3
	28 July	ii. 224		
	ca 3 Aug.	ii. 225		
	ca 5 Sept.	ii. 226		
	23 Sept.	ii. 226	vii. 40	v. 11
	27 Sept.	ii. 227		
	5 Oct.	ii. 228	vii. 46	v. 14
	12 Oct.	ii. 229		
	18 Oct.	ii. 230	vii. 50	v. 17
	22 Oct.	ii. 232	vii. 53	v. 19
	27 Oct.	ii. 234		
	10 Dec.	ii. 235		
	12 Dec.	ii. 236	vii. 77	v. 29
	16 Dec.	ii. 238		
	16 Dec.	ii. 239	vii. 79	v. 33
	ca 20 Dec.	ii. 240		
1767	13 Jan.	ii. 241	vii. 80	v. 33
	ca 20 April*	ii. 242		
	ca 28 April	ii. 242		
	24 May	ii. 243		
	31 July	ii. 244	vii. 122	v. 57
	ca 4 Aug.	ii. 245		
	7 Aug.	ii. 247	vii. 126	v. 60
	11 Aug.	ii. 247		
	19 Sept.*	ii. 249		
	8 Oct.	ii. 249		
	13 Oct.	ii. 250	vii. 137	v. 67
	15 Oct.	ii. 251		
	1 Nov.	ii. 252	vii. 145	v. 72
	14 Nov.	ii. 253		
1768	12 March	ii. 253	vii. 174	v. 89

		YALE	TOYNBEE	CUNNINGHAM
	14 March	ii. 255		
	14 April	ii. 257		
	15 April	ii. 258	vii. 179	v. 94
	12 June	ii. 260		
	15 June	ii. 262	vii. 194	v. 104
	8 Aug.	ii. 263		
	13 Aug.	ii. 264	vii. 213	v. 118
	7 Nov.	ii. 265		
	10 Nov.	ii. 266	vii. 236	v. 132
	12 Nov.	ii. 267		
	15 Nov.	ii. 268	vii. 237	v. 133
	27 Nov.	ii. 270		v. 136 n.
	1 Dec.	ii. 271	vii. 240	v. 136
1769	26 March	ii. 273	vii. 262	v. 151
	11 April	ii. 275		v. 158 n.
	15 April	ii. 276	vii. 271	v. 158
	11 May	ii. 277	vii. 273	v. 160
	14 May	ii. 280		
	18 Aug.	ii. 282	vii. 306	v. 181
	ca 25 Aug.	ii. 283		v. 185 n. misdated
	27 Aug.	ii. 285		v. 185 n. misdated
	7 Sept.	ii. 288	vii. 309	v. 184
	17 Sept.	ii. 291	vii. 315	v. 189
	18 Sept.	ii. 295		v. 196 n.
	16 Oct.	ii. 297	vii. 324	v. 196
	22 Oct.	ii. 299		v. 192 n., 197 n.
	14 Dec.	ii. 300	vii. 338	v. 206
	ca 18 Dec.	ii. 302		v. 206 n.
1770	*27 March*	ii. 303		
	31 March	ii. 303	vii. 374	v. 224
	6 May	ii. 304	vii. 381	v. 237
	11 June	ii. 306	vii. 384	v. 240
	18 June	ii. 308		v. 240 n.
	29 June	ii. 310	vii. 388	v. 243
	1 July	ii. 311	vii. 389	v. 243
	7 July	ii. 313	vii. 390	v. 245

To FREDERICK MONTAGU, Wednesday 28 October 1784

Oct. 28, 1784.

MR FREDERICK MONTAGU[1] will do what he pleases with these letters. As mine must be preserved, they may be kept together, as they may serve to explain passages in each other.

HOR. WALPOLE

To MONTAGU, Sunday 2 May 1736

Not with Kimbolton MSS. First printed 1818, in Letters from the Hon. Horace Walpole to George Montagu Esq. *(Works vi), p. 1. See Introduction. From the reference to the royal wedding it is clear that Montagu was in London.*

King's College,[1] May 2, 1736.

Dear Sir,

UNLESS I were to be married myself, I should despair ever being able to describe a wedding so well as you have done: had I known your talent before, I would have desired an epithalamium. I believe the Princess[2] will have more beauties bestowed on her by the occasional poets,[3] than even a painter would afford her. They will cook up a new Pandora, and in the bottom of the box enclose, Hope, that all they have said is true. A great many out of excess of good breeding, having heard it was rude to talk Latin before women, propose complimenting her in English;[4] which she will be much the better for. I doubt most of them, instead of fearing their compositions should not be understood, should fear they should: they write they

---

1. Frederick Montagu (1733–1800), of Papplewick, Notts; politician (DNB). For his possession of this correspondence, see Introduction.

1. HW matriculated at King's 11 March 1735 as a gentleman commoner ('Short Notes').

2. Princess Augusta (1719–1772), youngest dau. of Frederick II, D. of Saxe-Gotha, m. (27 April 1736) Frederick Louis, Prince of Wales.

3. Doubtless a reference to the forthcoming *Gratulationes* presented to the Prince and Princess of Wales by the Universities.

4. At Cambridge, 35 of the poems (including HW's and Gray's) were in Latin, 12 in English, 6 in Hebrew, 5 in Greek, and 1 each in Italian, French, and Hebrew with a Latin translation. At Oxford the tally was: Latin 59, English 16, Greek 5, and Hebrew, Welsh, and German, 1. See *Gratulatio Academiæ Cantabrigiensis Frederici Walliæ Principis et Augustæ Principissæ Saxo-Gothæ nuptias celebrantis,* Cambridge, 1736; *Gratulatio Academiæ Oxoniensis in nuptias . . . Frederici principis Walliæ et Augustæ principissæ de Saxo-Gotha,* Oxford, 1736.

don't know what, to be read by they don't know who. You have made me a very unreasonable request, which I will answer with another as extraordinary: you desire I would burn your letters; I desire you would keep mine. I know but of one way of making what I send you useful, which is, by sending you a blank sheet: sure you would not grudge three-pence for a half-penny sheet, when you give as much for one not worth a farthing. You drew this last paragraph on you by your exordium, as you call it, and conclusion; I hope for the future our correspondence will run a little more glibly, with dear George and dear Horry;[5] not as formally as if we were playing a game at chess in Spain and Portugal; and Don Horatio was to have the honour of specifying to Don Georgio by an epistle whither he would move. In one point I would have our correspondence like a game at chess; it should last all our lives—but I hear you cry check; adieu!

Dear George, yours ever,

Hor. Walpole

To Montagu, Thursday 6 May 1736

Address: To George Mountagu Esq. in Sherard[1] Street near Golden Square London. *Postmark:* Cambridge 7 MA.

King's College, May 6, 1736.

Dear George,

I AGREE with you entirely in the pleasure you take in talking over old stories, but can't say but I meet every day with new circumstances, which will be still more pleasure to me to recollect. I think at our age 'tis excess of joy, to think, while we are running over past happinesses, that 'tis still in our power to enjoy as great. Narrations of the greatest actions of other people, are tedious in comparison of the serious trifles, that every man can call to mind of himself, while he was learning those histories: youthful passages of life, are the chippings of Pit's diamond,[2] set into little heart-rings with mottoes: the

5. 'Harry' in the original printed text.

———

1. Now spelled Sherwood St.

2. The Pitt Diamond was bought for about £20,000 in India by Thomas Pitt (1653–1726), Governor of Madras and grandfather of the first Earl of Chatham.

In 1717 it was purchased from him by the Regent Duc d'Orléans, on behalf of Louis XV, for £125,000. The fragments from it when cut were valued at several thousand pounds (DNB; Sir Cornelius Neale Dalton, *Life of Thomas Pitt,* Cambridge, 1915).

stone itself more worth, the filings more genteel, and agreeable. Alexander at the head of the world never tasted the true pleasure, that boys of his own age have enjoyed at the head of a school. Little intrigues, little schemes, and policies, engage their thoughts, and at the same time that they are laying the foundation for their middle age of life, the mimic republic they live in furnishes materials of conversation for their latter age; and old men cannot be said to be children a second time with greater truth from any one cause, than their living over again their childhood in imagination. To reflect on the season when first they felt the titillation of love, the budding passions, and the first dear object of their wishes! how unexperienced they gave credit to all the tales of romantic loves! Dear George, were not the playing fields at Eton food for all manner of flights? No old maid's gown, though it had been tormented into all the fashions from King James to King George, ever underwent so many transformations, as those poor plains have in my idea. At first I was contented with tending a visionary flock, and sighing some pastoral name to the echo of the cascade under the bridge: how happy should I have been to have had a kingdom, only for the pleasure of being driven from it, and living disguised in an humble vale. As I got farther into Virgil and *Clelia*,[3] I found myself transported from Arcadia, to the garden of Italy, and saw Windsor Castle in no other view than the *capitoli immobile saxum*.[4] I wish a committee of the House of Commons may ever seem to be the senate; or a bill appear half so agreeable as a billet-doux. You see how deep you have carried me into old stories; I write of them with pleasure, but shall talk of them with more to you: I can't say I am sorry I was never quite a schoolboy; an expedition against bargemen, or a match at cricket may be very pretty things to recollect; but thank my stars, I can remember things that are very near as pretty. The beginning of my Roman history was spent in the Asylum,[5] or conversing in Egeria's hallowed grove;[6] not in thumping

3. *Clélie*, the romantic novel by Madeleine de Scudéry (1607-1701). HW's copy does not appear in the MS catalogue of his library or in the SH sale catalogue. *Clélie* was Englished, 1655-8, but HW had learned French at Eton ('Short Notes'; his copy of John Palairet, *A New Royal French Grammar*, 1730, with HW's signature and '1730' is now WSL).

4. *Æn.* ix. 448.

5. The Eton localities HW refers to have not been identified, and they are probably nonce names used by HW and his friends.

6. Numa, the second king, traditionally founder of the religious institutions of Rome, was supposed to have been instructed by the nymph Egeria, with whom he conversed in the sacred grove at Aricia.

and pummelling King Amulius's herdsmen.[7] I was sometimes troubled with a rough creature or two from the plow; one that one should have thought had worked with his head, as well as his hands, they were both so callous. One of the most agreeable circumstances I can recollect is the Triumvirate, composed of yourself, Charles,[8] and

Your sincere friend,

HOR. WALPOLE

To MONTAGU, Thursday 20 May 1736

The letter was sent in a cover (now missing); on the fourth 'side' HW had written 'To the Honourable Lady Walpole' which he crossed through and added: 'Excuse me dear George, for sending you this, but I had made a mistake and could not write it over again now.' No letters from HW to his mother have been discovered of this period.

It appears from HW's reference to masquerades that Montagu was in London.

King's College, May 20, 1736.

Dear George,

YOU will excuse my not having wrote to you, when you hear I have been a jaunt to Oxford.[1] As you have seen it, I shall only say I think it one of the most agreeable places I ever set my eyes on. In our way thither we stopped at the Duke of Kent's[2] at Wrest.[3] On the great staircase is a picture of the Duchess's; I said 'twas very like; 'Oh dear Sir,' said Mrs Housekeeper, 'it's too handsome for my lady Duchess;[4] her Grace's chin is much longer than that.' [5]In an old closet hangs a portrait of one of the old Dame de Greys, in a gown of her own work, embroidered all over with little flowers of all colours, like

7. That is, the herdsmen who rescued Romulus and Remus from the Tiber, in which Amulius, whom they later killed, had ordered them drowned.

8. Charles Lyttelton (1714–68), Bp of Carlisle, 1762.

1. Earlier in May; see Gray to West 8 May 1736, Gray's Corr. i. 38–9; West to HW 1 June 1736.

2. Henry Grey (1671–1740), 12th E. of Kent; cr. (1706) M. and (1710) D. of Kent.

3. Wrest Park, 4 miles SW of Shefford,

Beds. For HW's account of a later visit there, see Country Seats 70–1; see also Thomas Pennant, Journey from Chester to London, 1782, pp. 383–95.

4. Lady Sophia Bentinck (d. 1748), m. (1729, as his 2d wife) Henry Grey, 1st D. of Kent.

5. This passage has been written over in the MS, probably by HW, but is easily decipherable. The portrait is of 'Lady Susanna Grey, daughter to Charles Earl of Kent, and wife to Sir Michael Longueville. She was a celebrated workwoman;

the border of an under-petticoat, round her head, is a kind of hoop-petticoat of gauze, her face is of a dead complexion; with her needle and thread in her hands. She was a great workwoman and died at it.[5] In the garden are monuments in memory of Lord Harold,[6] Lady Glenorchy;[7] the late Duchess;[8]—and the present Duke. At Lord Clarendon's[9] at Cornbury[10] is a prodigious quantity of Vandykes;[11] but I had not time to take down any of their dresses. By the way you gave me no account of the last masquerade.[12] Coming back we saw Easton Neston[13] a seat of Lord Pomfret's,[14] where in an old greenhouse is a wonderful fine statue of Tully,[15] haranguing a numerous assembly of decayed emperors, vestal virgins with new noses, Colossuses, Venuses, headless carcasses, and carcassless heads, pieces of tombs, and hieroglyphics.[16] I saw Althrop[17] the same day; where are a vast many pic-

and the dress in which she is drawn is said to have been a wedding-suit of her own doing. This is the lady who is fabled to have died of the pricking of her finger with the needle, and who is shown as such in Westminster Abbey. She looks as pale as if the fact was true' (Pennant, op. cit. 389). She was dau. of the 10th E. of Kent, m. 1611 and d. 1620 (GEC, *Peerage* vi. 161, n. b). Pennant's allusion to Westminster Abbey has not been explained.

6. Anthony Grey (1696–1723), styled E. of Harold; predeceased the D. of Kent, his father.

7. Lady Amabel Grey (d. 1727), eld. dau. of D. of Kent; m. (1718) John Campbell, Lord Glenorchy; 3d E. of Breadalbane, 1752. Her dau. Jemima succeeded the Duke as Marchioness Grey, and was his heir.

8. Hon. Jemima Crew (d. 1728), m. (1695) Henry Grey, D. of Kent (n. 2 above).

9. Henry Hyde (1672–1753), 4th E. of Clarendon.

10. Cornbury Park, near Charlbury, Oxon. The Clarendon estates in Oxfordshire were sold in 1751 to the second Duke of Marlborough (Vernon J. Watney, *Cornbury and the Forest of Wychwood*, 1910, pp. 190–1).

11. This collection, made by the Lord Chancellor Clarendon, was divided on the death of the fourth Earl (see *Anecdotes of Painting*, ed. James Dallaway, 1828, ii. 200–1). 'Of the so-called Vandykes, some half-dozen only are originals. As a series

of portraits, the collection is highly curious' (Cunningham i. 6). Much of it was reassembled at Cornbury by the late Vernon Watney (see Vernon J. Watney, *op. cit.*, pp. 235–44, for a catalogue of the collection at the time of the sale in 1751).

12. HW's interest in masquerades is reflected in Gray to HW, 14 Jan. 1735. Vandyke costumes were in vogue at this time.

13. Easton Neston, near Towcester, Northants; built ca 1702 chiefly from designs of Nicholas Hawksmoor; see H. Avray Tipping, *English Homes*, Period IV, vol. ii (1928). 119–40.

14. Thomas Fermor (1697–1753), 2d Bn Leominster; cr. (1721) E. of Pomfret.

15. See *post* 22 July 1751.

16. Part of the great collection formed by Thomas Howard (1585–1646), 14th E. of Arundel, cr. (1644) E. of Norfolk, 'the first who professedly began to collect in this country,' *Anecdotes, Works* iii. 206. The vicissitudes which these antiquities underwent are related in Adolf Michaelis, *Ancient Marbles in Great Britain*, Cambridge, 1882, pp. 33–41. Lady Pomfret in 1755 presented them to the University of Oxford; for Montagu's account of the presentation ceremonies see *post* ca 13 July 1756. See also *Marmora Oxoniensia*, ed. Richard Chandler, Oxford, 1763, pt i, and *Anecdotes, Works* iii. 208.

17. Althorp, the seat of Earl Spencer, near Northampton. See *Country Seats* 31–3 for a full account of HW's visit in 1760; and H. Avray Tipping, *English Homes*, Period VI, 1926, pp. 299–320.

tures; some mighty good, a gallery with the Windsor Beauties,[18] and Lady Bridgewalter[19] who is full as handsome as any of 'em. A bouncing head of, I believe Cleopatra; called there the Duchess of Mazarine:[20] the park is enchanting. I forgot to tell you I was at Bleinheim,[21] where I saw nothing but a cross housekeeper, and an impertinent porter; except a few pictures; a quarry of stone, that looked at a distance like a great house, and about this quarry, quantities of inscriptions in honour of the Duke of Marlborough; and I think of her Grace[22] too, for she[23]   herself mentioned, as putting 'em up, in almost all of 'em.

Adieu! dear George,

Yours ever,

Hor. Walpole

The verses[24] are not published yet.

To Montagu, Sunday 30 May 1736

Address: To George Mountagu Esq. in Sherard Street near Golden Square London. *Postmark:* Cambridge 31 MA.

<King's> College, May 30, 1736.

Dear George,

YOU show me in the prettiest manner how much you like Petronius Arbiter;[1] I have heard you commend him, but I am more pleased with your tacit approbation of writing, like him, prose interspersed with verse. I shall send you soon in return some poetry in-

18. Replicas by Lely himself of the eleven portraits of court ladies he painted for the Duchess of York; the originals were taken to Windsor by James II. See *Anecdotes of Painting*, ed. James Dallaway, 1828, iii. 32–3.

19. Lady Elizabeth Churchill (1688–1714), m. (1703) Scroop Egerton, 5th E., cr. (1720) D. of Bridgewater. The portrait is by Charles Jervas (Thomas F. Dibdin, *Ædes Althorpianæ*, 1822, p. 237).

20. Hortense Mancini (1646–99), m. (1661) Armand-Charles de la Porte, Duc de Mazarin (*Nouv. Biog. Gén.*).

21. HW did not admire Blenheim more on a later visit in 1760; see *Country Seats* 26.

22. Sarah Jennings (1660–1744), m. (1678) John Churchill (1650–1722), cr. (1682) Bn Churchill, (1689) E. and (1702) D. of Marlborough.

23. Half a line has been effectually crossed out in MS, probably by HW; the rest of the sentence can be made out.

24. Probably the Cambridge *Gratulatio* (see next letter).

_____

1. HW's acquaintance with Petronius apparently began in his thirteenth year when he wrote his initials and '1730' in a copy of the Amsterdam 1700 ('abridged') edition (now WSL).

terspersed with prose: I mean the Cambridge Congratulation[2] with the notes, as you desired. I have transcribed the greatest part of what was tolerable at the coffee-houses;[3] but by most of what you will find, you will hardly think I have left anything worse behind. There is lately come out here a new piece, called *A Dialogue between Philemon and Hydaspes on false Religion,* by one Mr Coventry[4] A. M. and Fellow, formerly fellow-commoner of Magdalen. He is a young man, but 'tis really a pretty thing. If you can't get it in town, I will send it with the verses. He accounts for superstition[4a] in a new manner, and, I think, a just one; attributing it to disappointments in love. He don't resolve it all into that bottom; ascribes it almost wholly as the source of female enthusiasm: and I dare say there's ne'er a girl from the age of fourteen to four-and-twenty, but will subscribe to his principles, and own, if the dear man was dead, that she loves, she would settle all her affections on heaven,—whither he was gone.

Who would not be an Artemisia, and raise the stately mausoleum to her lord; then weep and watch incessant over it, like—the Ephesian matron, *quando quidem data sunt ipsis quoque fata sepulchris.*[5] I have heard of one lady[6] who had not quite so great a veneration for her husband's tomb, but preferred lying alone in one, to lying on his left hand: perhaps she had an aversion to the German custom of left-handed wives. I met yesterday with a pretty little dialogue on the subject of constancy; 'tis between a traveller and a dove:[7]

Le Passant.
Que fais tu dans ce bois, plaintive tourterelle?

2. The *Gratulatio* of the University of Cambridge on the marriage of the Prince of Wales (*ante* 2 May 1736, n. 4). For HW's Latin verses see *Horace Walpole's Fugitive Verses,* ed. W. S. Lewis, New York, 1931, pp. 99–100.

3. Presumably, local effusions on the marriage, in newspapers.

4. Henry Coventry (d. 1752). This was the first part of his *Dialogue;* four more appeared in 1737, 1738, 1741, 1744.

4a. Changed by HW from 'some superstitions.'

5. Juvenal, *Sat.* x. 146. The line is crossed out in MS.

6. 'Francis Bridges [Frances Brydges (ca 1580–1663), m. (1) Sir Thomas Smith; m.

(2) (1610) Thomas Cecil, cr. (1605) E. of Exeter], daughter of the lord Chandos, and second wife of Thomas Cecil earl of Exeter, on whose left hand she refused to lie on his tomb in Westminster Abbey' (from HW's description of his Van Dyck of her, *Works* ii. 463). She is buried in Winchester Cathedral, though the inscription on the tomb of her husband (who died forty-one years before her) states that both his wives are buried with him (Collins, *Peerage,* 1812, ii. 601–02). See COLE for five references to her.

7. ' 'Tis in Père Bouhours' *Manière de bien penser;* I have often tried to translate it, but never could do it as prettily as this is done. H.L.P.'—MS note by Mrs

La Tourterelle.
Je gémis, j'ai perdu ma compagne fidèle.

Le Passant.
Ne crains tu pas que l'oiseleur
Ne te fasse mourir comme elle?

La Tourterelle.
Si ce n'est lui, ce sera ma douleur.

'Twould have been a little more apposite if she had grieved for her lover. I have ventured to turn it to that view, lengthened it, and spoiled it, as you shall see;

P. Plaintive turtle, cease your moan;
Hence away!
In this dreary wood alone
Why d'ye stay?
T. These tears alas! you see flow
For my mate!
P. Dread you not from net or bow
His sad fate?
T. If, ah! if they neither kill,
Sorrow will!

You will excuse this gentle nothing, I mean mine, when I tell you I translated it out of pure good nature for the use of a disconsolate wood pigeon in our grove, that was made a widow by the barbarity of a gun. She coos and calls me so movingly, 'twould touch your heart to hear her! I protest to you it grieves me to pity her. She is so allicholly[8] as anything. I'll warrant you now she's as sorry as one of us would be. Well, good man, he's gone, and's died like a lamb. She's an unfortunate woman, but she must have patience; 'tis what we must all come to. And so as I was saying, Dear George, Good-bye t'ye.

Yours sincerely,

Hor. Walpole

PS. I don't know yet when I shall leave Cambridge.

Piozzi in her copy of these letters, published as vol. vi of *Works*, 1818. *La Manière de bien penser dans les ouvrages d'esprit*, by Père Dominique Bouhours (1628–1702), was published in 1687 and has been 'souvent réimprimé' (*Nouv. Biog. Gén.*). Chesterfield commended it both to his son (8 Feb. 1750) and to his godson (22 Oct. 1769). The verses translated by HW are on pp. 217–18.

8. Used 'jocosely in Shakespeare for melancholy' (OED).

'But indeed she is given too much to allicholy and musing.'

(*Merry Wives* I. iv. 164.)

TO MONTAGU, Sunday 20 March 1737

Address: À Monsieur Monsieur Mountagu racommandé à Monsieur Alexandre Banquier à Paris. *Postmark:* 21 MR PD. Paid 3ᶜᵉ.

King's College, March 20, 1737.

Dear George,

THE first paragraph in my letter, must be in answer to the last in yours; though I should be glad to make you the return you ask, by waiting on you myself. 'Tis not in my power from more circumstances than one, (which are needless to tell you)[1] to accompany you and Lord Conway[2] to Italy: you add to the pleasure it would give me, by asking it so kindly. You I am infinitely obliged to, as I was capable, my dear George, of making you forget for a minute that you don't propose stirring from the dear place you are now in.[3] Poppies indeed are the chief flowers in love-nosegays, but they seldom bend towards the lady; at least not till the other flowers have been gathered. Prince Volscius's boots were made of love-leather, and honour-leather;[4] instead of honour some people's are made of friendship; but since you have been so good to me as to draw on[5] this, I can almost believe you are equipped for travelling farther than Rheims. 'Tis no little inducement to make me wish myself in France, that I hear gallantry is not left off there; that you may be polite, and not be thought awkward for it. You know the pretty men of the age in England use the women with no more deference than they do their coach-horses,[6] and have not half the regard for 'em that they have for themselves: the little freedoms you tell me you use, take off from formality, by avoiding which ridiculous extreme, we are dwindled into the other barbarous one, rusticity. If you had been at Paris; I should have en-

1. These undoubtedly were circumstances in the Walpole family: Lady Walpole's failing health (she died 20 August 1737), and HW's lack of independent funds (his first places were not given him until later in the year).

2. Francis Seymour Conway (1718–94), 2d Bn Conway; cr. (1750) E. and (1793) M. of Hertford; HW's first cousin and correspondent.

3. Rheims (see below). In the absence of Montagu's letter, HW's meaning cannot be understood.

4. Volscius, in *The Rehearsal,* by George Villiers (1628–87), Duke of Buckingham, while drawing on his boots likens one to honour and the other to love (III. v).

5. HW is perhaps continuing the allusion to drawing on boots invested with human attributes.

6. 'And *we* say how respectful they were in those days' (Mrs Piozzi). HW may be punning on Prince Prettyman in *The Rehearsal.*

quired about the new Spanish ambassadress,[7] who by the accounts we
have thence, at her first audience of the Queen,[8] sat down with her at
a distance that suited respect and conversation: dear woman! You
won't be angry with me I hope if I fill up the remainder of my letter, with transcribing some lines out of a new poem,[9] which will
hardly reach you; 'tis wrote by a man of the Custom House, of little
learning, new ideas, and odd sentiments; 'tis on Spleen.

> Laugh and be well; monkeys have been
> Extreme good doctors for the spleen;
> And kitten, if the humour hit,
> Has harlequin'd away the fit.
> Since mirth is good on this behalf,
> At some partic'lars let us laugh.[10]
>
> *   *   *   *   *
>
> Poor authors worshipping a calf,
> Deep tragedies that make us laugh;[11]
> Folks, things prophetic to dispense,
> Making the past the future tense:[12]
> Disdainful prudes, who ceaseless ply
> The superb muscle of an eye;
> A coquet's April-weather face etc.[13]
>
> Hunting I reckon very good
> To brace the nerves and stir the blood;
> But after no field honours itch,
> Achieved by leaping hedge and ditch;
> While spleen lies soft relax'd in bed,
> Or o'er coal fires reclines the head,
> Hygeia's sons with hound and horn,
> And jovial cry awake the morn:
> These see her in her dusky plight,
> Smear'd by th' embraces of the night,

7. The Spanish ambassador to France
1736–40 was Jaime Miguel (d. 1756?), Marqués de La Mina (*Enciclopedia Universal
Ilustrada*, Barcelona, 1905–30, xxxv. 487);
his wife is described as 'personne fort
douce et fort raisonnable' (Alfred Baudril-
lart, *Philip V et la Cour de France*, 1890–
1901, iv. 360).

8. Marie-Catherine-Sophie-Félicité   Le-
szczyńska (1703–68), m. (1725) Louis XV.
  9. *The Spleen*, by Matthew Green
(1696–1737).
  10. ll. 93–9.
  11. ll. 103–4.
  12. ll. 107–8.
  13. ll. 119–21.

With roral wash redeem her face,
An<d pr>ove herself of Titan's race,
An<d> mounting in loose robe the skies,
Shed light and fragrance as she flies.[14]

Sometimes I dress; with women sit, and chat away the gloomy fit;
Quit the stiff garb of serious sense, and wear a gay impertinence.
Nor think nor speak with any pains, but lay on fancy's neck the reins;
Talk of unusual swell of waist, in maid of honour loosely lac'd;[15]
Of Kitty (aunt left in the lurch by grave pretence to go to church)
Perceiv'd in hack with lover fine, like Will and Mary on the coin. etc.[16]

You see the thoughts are most within the bills of mortality. If you care for any more lines, I will send some in my next; at present

Adieu, dear George,

Yours most heartily,

H.W.

To Montagu, Saturday ca 11 May 1745

The battle of Fontenoy was fought 30 April, O.S. An express with only a vague account of the battle arrived Saturday 4 May, and was published in the *London Gazette* that day. Saturday 11 May a full account arrived, with a list of casualties (HW to Mann 11 May 1745), which was published that night as a *Gazette Extraordinary*. It included Edward Montagu's name among the dead. 11 May seems, therefore, the more likely date for this letter.

[Arlington Street] Saturday night [ca 11 May, 1745].

My dear Sir,

I WENT instantly on my arrival to Mr Pelham,[1] and wish I could tell you anything to give you a ray of comfort.[2] Nothing more is yet come, but on hearing of the two letters from Douglas and Geer-

14. ll. 66–80.
15. ll. 182–9.
16. ll. 194–7.

_____

1. Henry Pelham (1695?–1754), First Lord of the Treasury.
2. On the reported death at Fontenoy of Montagu's next eldest brother, Ed-

ward; the report was correct. Edward Montagu was Lt-Col. in Handasyde's (later 31st) Regiment of Foot (*London Gazette* 11 May 1745), and was commissioned Ensign in 1728 (*The Army List for 1740*, reprinted by the Society for Army Historical Research, Sheffield, 1931).

ing,[3] Mr Pelham mentioned it this morning to the Duke,[4] who replied, they will have him alive, but Legonier's account[5] was so positive that I don't believe a word of the other relation. This is all the light I have been able to get hitherto, but I will stay here till I can send you something more to be relied on, and in the meantime beg my dear Sir, that you will neither flatter yourself too much, nor your sisters[6] in the least, as the support you must give them, must I fear me, be of another sort. I beg my compliments to Mrs and Miss Rice;[7] I have waited on Mrs Boscawen[8] who writes to them tonight.

Yours most sincerely,

H. Walpole

To Montagu, Saturday 18 May 1745

Arlington Street, May 18, 1745.

Dear George,

I AM very sorry to renew our correspondence upon so melancholy a circumstance! But when you have lost so near a friend as your brother, 'tis sure the duty of all your other friends, to endeavour to alleviate your loss, and offer all the increase of affection that is possible, to compensate it. This I do most heartily; I wish I could most effectually!

You will always find in me, dear Sir, the utmost inclination to be of service to you; and let me beg, that you will remember your prom-

3. Unidentified. There were several Douglases in the 1740 *Army List*, the only published list extant for this period. Geering may be a member of the Guerin family, who were regimental agents.

4. Thomas Pelham-Holles (1693–1768), 2d Bn Pelham; cr. (1714) E. of Clare, (1715) D. of Newcastle-upon-Tyne; succeeded his brother, Henry Pelham, as First Lord of the Treasury, 1754.

5. Lt-Gen. John Louis Ligonier (1680–1770), cr. (1757) Vct and (1766) E. Ligonier; field marshal, 1766; commanded the British foot at Fontenoy. His account is probably that given in the *Gazette Extraordinary* for 11 May 1745, which is followed by a list of casualties.

6. Arabella Montagu (d. 1798), m. (1750)

Nathaniel Wettenhall of Hankelow, Cheshire (GM 1750, xx. 380; George Ormerod, *History of the County . . . of Chester*, 1882, iii. 480).

Henrietta Montagu (called Harriet), d. 1755, unmarried.

7. Lucy (b. 1705), dau. of John Morley Trevor of Glynde, Sussex, by Lucy Montagu; Montagu's double first cousin; m. (1722) Edward Rice, of Newton, Glamorganshire (John Comber, *Sussex Genealogies, Lewes Centre*, Cambridge, 1933, p. 292; Collins, *Peerage*, 1812, vii. 507). Their dau. Lucy (ca 1726–1818), was unm. (GM 1818, lxxxviii pt i. 474).

8. Anne (1710–83), dau. of John Morley Trevor (n. 7), m. (1743) Hon. George Boscawen (Collins, *Peerage*, 1812, vi. 69).

ise of writing to me: as I am so much in town and in the world, I flatter myself with having generally something to tell you that may make my letters agreeable in the country: you, anywhere, make yours charming.

Be so good to say anything that you think proper from me to your sisters, and believe me,

Dear George,

Yours most sincerely,

Hor. Walpole

To Montagu, Saturday 25 May 1745

Arlington Street, May 25, 1745.

Dear George,

I DON'T write to you now so much to answer your letter as to promote your diversion, which I am as much obliged to you for consulting me about, at least as much, as about an affair of honour, or your marriage, or any other important transaction, any one of which you might possibly dislike more than diverting yourself. For my part I shall give you my advice on this point with as much reflection as I should if it was necessary for me, like a true friend, to counsel you to displease yourself.

You propose making a visit at Englefield Green,[1] and ask me if I think it right. Extremely so. I have heard 'tis a very pretty place; you love a jaunt; have a very pretty chaise, I believe, and I dare swear, very easy; in all probability you will have a fine evening too; and added to all this, the gentleman[2] you would go to see is very agreeable, and good-humoured. He has some very pretty children,[3] and a

1. Egham, Surrey.

2. Hon. Edward Walpole (1706–84), K.B., 1753; HW's brother, with whom he was on bad terms for some years (see HW to Edward Walpole 17 May 1745).

3. Natural children by Dorothy Clement (ca 1715–ca 1739), a milliner (*Last Journals* i. 93 n):

(1) Laura (ca 1734–1813), m. (1758) Hon. Frederick Keppel, Bp of Exeter, 1762 (GM 1813, lxxxiii pt ii. 298).

(2) Maria (1736–1807), m. (1) (1759) James Waldegrave, 2d E. Waldegrave; m. (2) (1766) William Henry, D. of Gloucester.

(3) Edward (1737–71), Lt-Col. in the army.

(4) Charlotte (1738–89), m. (1760) Lionel Tollemache, styled Lord Huntingtower; 5th E. of Dysart, 1770.

See Violet M. Biddulph, *The Three Ladies Waldegrave*, 1938, pp. 13–17.

very sensible learned man that lives with him one Dr Thirlby,[4] whom I believe you know. The master of the house plays extremely well on the bass-viol, and has generally other musical people with him.[5] He knows a good deal of the private history of a late ministry,[6] and my dear George, you love memoirs—Indeed as to personal acquaintance with any of the court beauties, I can't say you will find your account in him; but to make amends he is perfectly master of all the quarrels that have been fashionably on foot about Handel;[7] and can give you a very perfect account of all the modern rival painters. In short you may pass a very agreeable day with him, and if he does but take to you, as I can't doubt who know you both, you will contract a great friendship with him, which he will preserve with the greatest warmth and partiality. In short I can think of no reason in the world against your going there, but one: do you know his youngest brother? If you happen to be so unlucky, I can't flatter you so far as to advise you to make him a visit, for there is nothing in the world the Baron of Englefield has such an aversion for, as for his brother, and

Your most sincere friend,

Hor. Walpole

PS. Write to me soon, for I love your letters.

To Montagu, Tuesday 25 June 1745

Arlington Street, June 25, 1745.

Dear George,

I HAVE been near three weeks in Essex at Mr Rigby's,[1] and had left your direction behind me, and could not write to you. 'Tis the charmingest place by nature, and the most trumpery by art that ever I saw. The house stands on a high hill on an arm of the sea,

---

4. Styan Thirlby (1686?–1753), critic and theologian (DNB). Sir Edward Walpole (a former pupil) got him a sinecure place in the Customs worth £100 a year. 'While he was in Sir Edward's house, he kept a miscellaneous book of Memorables, containing whatever was said or done amiss by Sir Edward, or any part of his family' (John Nichols, *Literary Anecdotes*, 1812–15, iv. 267).

5. See *Last Journals* i. 102, 104–6, for other references to Sir Edward's musical skill.

6. Sir Robert Walpole's.

7. A vendetta was waged against Handel (1685–1759) by the adherents of Italian opera; for incidents of 1744–5 see Newman Flower, *George Frideric Handel*, 1923, pp. 286–92.

---

1. Richard Rigby (1722–88), politician and political manager for the Duke of

which winds itself before two sides of the house. On the right and left at the very foot of this hill lie two towns, the one, of market quality,[2] and the other with a wharf where ships come up.[3] This last was to have a church, but by a lucky want of religion in the inhabitants who would not contribute to building a steeple, it remains an absolute antique temple with a portico, on the very strand.[4] Cross this arm of the sea, you see six churches, and charming woody hills in Suffolk. All this parent Nature did for this place; but its godfathers and godmothers I believe promised it should renounce all the pomps and vanities of this world, for they have patched up a square house full of windows, low rooms, and thin walls; piled up walls wherever there was a glimpse of prospect; planted avenues that go nowhere, and dug fish ponds where there should be avenues. We had very bad weather the whole time I was there, but however I rode about and sailed,[5] not having the same apprehensions of catching cold, that Mrs Kerwood[6] had once at Chelsea, when I persuaded her not to go home by water, because it would be damp after the rain.

The town is not quite empty yet. My Lady Fitzwalter,[7] Lady Betty Germain,[8] Lady Granville,[9] and the Dowager Strafford[10] have their at-homes, and amass company. Lady Brown has done with her Sundays,[11] for she is changing her house into Upper Brook Street: in the

Bedford. His house, Mistley Hall, built by Richard Rigby the elder (d. 1730), and now pulled down, is described in François de la Rochefoucauld, *A Frenchman in England, 1784*, Cambridge, 1933, pp. 162–9, and illustrated in Thomas Wright, *History . . . of Essex*, 1836, ii. opp. p. 780, q.v. also for a plate of Mistley church (n. 4 below).

2. Manningtree.

3. Mistley.

4. It was built in 1735, and in 1768 was a 'neat edifice' with a tower and five bells (Philip Morant, *History . . . of Essex*, 1768, i. 463). Robert Adam completely changed its appearance in 1776; see Arthur T. Bolton, *Architecture of Robert and James Adam*, 1922, ii. 146–56.

5. Rigby was an 'expert mariner' (ibid. ii. 151).

6. Cornelia, dau. of Mr Hayes of London, m. (1) Galfridus Walpole (d. 1726), brother of Sir Robert; m. (2) (1735) Mr Kyrwood, of Herefordshire (Collins, *Peerage*, 1812, v. 653).

7. Lady Frederica Schomberg (ca 1688–1751), m. (1) (1715) Robert Darcy, 3d E. of Holdernesse; m. (2) (1724) Benjamin Mildmay, 19th Bn Fitzwalter, cr. (1730) E. Fitzwalter.

8. Lady Elizabeth Berkeley (1680–1769), m. (1706) Sir John Germain, Bt (d. 1718); later a friend of HW's.

9. Lady Sophia Fermor (1721–45), m. (1744) John Carteret, 2d E. Granville.

10. Anne Johnson (d. 1754), m. (1711) Thomas Wentworth, 1st E. of Strafford (d. 1739).

11. Margaret Cecil (ca 1698–1782), m. Sir Robert Brown, 1st Bt. 'Her ladyship distinguished herself as a persevering enemy to Handel, and a protectress of foreign musicians in general, of the new Italian style; and was one of the first persons of fashion who had the courage, at the risk of her windows, to have concerts of a Sunday evening' (Charles Burney, *General History of Music*, 1776–89, iv. 671).

meantime she goes to Knightsbridge, and Sir Robert[12] to the woman[13] he keeps at Scarborough. This is the only answer I can give you to your *who lies with who,* for all the women are with child. My Lady Lincoln[14] is cooking up her belly as fast as she can at my Lady Granville's: in short they both teem with rivalship in old love and new politics.[15] Winnington[16] goes on with the Frasi,[17] so my Lady Townshend[18] is obliged only to lie of people, instead of with them.

You have heard of the disgrace of the Archibald,[19] and that in future scandal she must only be ranked with the Lady Elizabeth Lucy,[20] and Madam Lucy Walters,[21] instead of being historically noble among the Clevelands,[22] Portsmouths,[23] and Yarmouths.[24] 'Tis said

12. Sir Robert Brown (d. 1760), Bt, 1732; formerly a merchant at Venice and British Resident there.

13. Not identified.

14. Catherine Pelham (1727–60), m. (16 Oct. 1744) Henry Fiennes-Clinton (later Pelham-Clinton), 9th E. of Lincoln; 2d D. of Newcastle-under-Lyne, 1768. Her son George Clinton, Lord Clinton, was born 26 Nov. 1745.

15. Lady Sophia Fermor had been reported engaged to Lord Lincoln; rather suddenly he married Catherine Pelham, and Lady Sophia, Lord Granville. Lord Granville was in opposition to the Pelhams, whose nephew Lord Lincoln was.

16. Thomas Winnington (1696–1746), politician.

17. Giulia Frasi, opera singer, came to England in 1743 'young, and interesting in person, with a sweet and clear voice' (Charles Burney, *General History of Music*, 1776–89, iv. 449; see also Sir George Grove, *Dictionary of Music*).

18. Etheldreda (or Audrey) Harrison (ca 1703–88), m. (1723) Charles Townshend, 3d Vct Townshend; celebrated for her frank speech and manner; see Erroll Sherson, *The Lively Lady Townshend and her Friends*, 1926.

19. Lady Jane Hamilton (d. 1752), dau. of 6th E. of Abercorn, m. (1719) Lord Archibald Hamilton; Mistress of the Robes to the Princess of Wales, and supposed mistress of the Prince (HW to Mann 27 Jan. 1747; Collins, *Peerage*, 1812, ii. 533). 'Was this my friend Archdeacon Hamilton's mother? The Delamira of the *Tatler* or *Spectator*? I fancy so. Countess Aldborough is no *unworthy* granddaugh-

ter of hers if it is so. 1818' (Mrs Piozzi). According to HW's letter to Mann, 24 June 1745, she became strongly attached to the coalition government, to the displeasure of the Prince, who supported Granville.

20. A mistress of Edward IV. 'Concerning the King's relation with Lady Elizabeth Lucy nothing is known beyond the fact that she was probably the mother of his natural son, Arthur, and also of his natural daughter Elizabeth' (Cora L. Scofield, *Life and Reign of Edward the Fourth*, 1923, ii. 56, 161). 'Elizabeth Lucie is certainly known to have been King Edward's concubine, though nothing so certainly mentioned, whose lady, or of what parentage she was' (John Speed, *Historie of Great Britaine*, edn 1623, p. 896; see also Sir Thomas More, *History of King Richard III*, ed. J. Rawson Lumby, Cambridge, 1924, pp. 61–5).

21. Lucy Walter (1630?–1658), mistress of Charles II, and mother of the Duke of Monmouth.

22. Barbara Villiers (ca 1641–1709), m. (1) (1659) Roger Palmer, cr. (1661) E. of Castelmaine; m. (2) (1705) Robert Feilding; cr. (1670) Duchess of Cleveland; Charles II's mistress.

23. Louise-Renée de Penancoët de Keroualle (ca 1647–1734), cr. (1673) Duchess of Portsmouth; Charles II's mistress.

24. Amalie Sophie Marianne von Wendt (ca 1709–65), m. (1727) Adam Gottlieb Oberhauptman von Wallmoden; cr. (1740) Countess of Yarmouth; George II's mistress (*Allgemeine Deutsche Biographie*, Leipzig, 1875–1912, xl. 756).

Miss Granville[25] has the reversion of her coronet; others say, she won't accept the patent.

Your friend Jemmy Lumley,[26] I beg pardon, I mean your kin, is not he, I am sure he is not your friend; well, he has had an assembly and he would write all the cards himself, and every one of them was to desire *he's* company, and *she's* company;[27] with other curious pieces of orthography.

Adieu! dear George; I wish you a merry farm,[28] as the children say at Vauxhall: my compliments to your sisters.

Yours ever,

Hor. Walpole

To Montagu, Saturday 13 July 1745

Arlington Street, July 13, 1745.

Dear George,

WE are all *Cabob'd* and *Cacofogoed*,[1] as my Lord Denbigh[2] says! We, who formerly you know could any one of us beat three Frenchmen, are now so degenerated that three Frenchmen can evidently beat one Englishman. Our army is running away,[3] all that is left to run, for half of it is picked up by 3 or 400 at a time. In short we must step out of the high *pantoufles* that were made by those cunning shoemakers at Poitiers and Ramillies, and go clumping about perhaps in wooden ones. My Lady Hervey[4] who you know dotes upon

25. Hon. Elizabeth Granville (d. 1790), dau. of 1st Bn Lansdowne; Maid of Honour to the Princess of Wales, 1742–56, and later Bedchamber Woman (Marquis of Ruvigny, *Jacobite Peerage*, 1904, p. 4). See Delany, *Correspondence, passim* (Mrs Delany was her cousin). It is unlikely that she was the Prince's mistress.

26. Hon. James Lumley (d. 1766), 7th son of 1st E. of Scarbrough; M.P. Chichester 1729–34; Arundel 1741–7. His sister married Montagu's uncle, the 1st E. of Halifax, n.c.; see Collins, *Peerage*, 1812, iii. 715.

27. Cards of invitation at this time were thin pieces of paper about 2½ by 3″ and were usually decorated with a printed ornamental design.

28. Possibly an extension of an early meaning of farm—a banquet, a feast, a good time (OED, *sb.* 1), but see *post* 5 June 1746 *ad fin.*

1. Cabob: an oriental dish, of roast meat (OED); cacofogo: from *cacafuego*, a spitfire, or braggart (OED); see also HW to Mann 3 May 1749: 'Cacofogo, the drunken captain in *Rule a Wife and Have a Wife*.'

2. William Feilding (1697–1755), 5th E. of Denbigh.

3. The English position in Flanders was untenable after Fontenoy; see Fortescue, *British Army* ii. 121–2.

4. Mary Lepell (1706–68), m. (1720) Hon. John Hervey, styled (1723) Lord Hervey; cr. (1733) Bn Hervey of Ickworth; she was HW's friend and correspondent.

everything French, is charmed with the hopes of these new shoes, and
has already bespoke herself a pair of pigeon wood.[4a] How did the tapestry at Bleinheim[5] look? did it glow with victory? or did all our glories
look overcast? I remember a very admired sentence in one of my
Lord Chesterfield's[6] speeches, when he was haranguing for this war—
with a most rhetorical transition he turned to the tapestry in the
House of Lords,[7] and said with a sigh, he feared there were no historical looms at work now!—Indeed we have reason to bless the good
patriots who have been for employing our manufactures so historically!

The Countess[8] of that wise Earl, with whose two expressive words
I began this letter, says, she is very happy now that my Lord had
never a place upon the coalition,[9] for then all this bad situation of
our affairs would have been laid upon him!

Now I have been talking of remarkable periods in our annals, I
must tell you what my Lord Baltimore[10] thinks one: he said to the
Prince[11] t'other day, 'Sir, your Royal Highness's marriage will be an
area in English history.'

If it were not for the life that is put into the town now and then
by very bad news from abroad, one should be quite stupefied. There
is nobody left but two or three solitary regents,[12] and they are always
whisking backwards and forwards to their villas; and about a dozen
antediluvian dowagers, whose carcasses have miraculously resisted the
wet, and who every Saturday compose a very reverend catacomb at

4a. 'The wood of various tropical or
sub-tropical trees or shrubs, mostly used
in cabinet-work' (OED, which quotes this
letter as its earliest usage).

5. Probably the tapestries in the state
drawing-rooms, representing the victories
of Marlborough. 'I was looking at them
myself this year 1818—and tho' the tapestry was not faded, it seemed as if the
martial fame of the hero was somewhat
the worse for wear. The man at Windsor
showing the victory of Oudenarde said to
us, "*That*, ladies and gentlemen, is John
Duke of Marlborough; a great warrior,
gentlemen and ladies—*in Queen Anne's
time*" ' (Mrs Piozzi).

6. Philip Dormer Stanhope (1694–1773),
4th E. of Chesterfield; the statesman and
letter-writer.

7. 'The tapestry in the House of Lords,

representing the destruction, in 1588, of
the Spanish Armada, wrought for the Earl
of Nottingham, the Lord High Admiral,
and destroyed with the Houses of Parliament, by fire, in 1834. This historical tapestry was well engraved by Pine' (Cunningham).

8. Isabella de Jong (1683–1769), m. (ca
1718) William Feilding, 5th E. of Denbigh. She lived much at Paris with Lady
Bolingbroke. HW wrote a short account
of his conversations with her (*Anecdotes
Told me by Lady Denbigh, 1768*, ed. W. S.
Lewis, Farmington, Conn., 1932).

9. The ministry formed in 1744.

10. Charles Calvert (1699–1751), 5th Bn
Baltimore.

11. Frederick (1707–51), Prince of Wales;
father of George III.

12. While George II was in Hanover.

my old Lady Strafford's. She does not take money at the door for showing them, but you pay twelvepence apiece, under the denomination of card-money. Wit and beauty indeed remain in the persons of Lady Townshend and Lady Caroline Fitzroy[13]—but such is the want of taste of this age, that the former is very often forced to wrap up her wit in plain English before it can be understood; and the latter is almost as often obliged to have recourse to the same artifices to make her charms be taken notice of. [14]Last Sunday the Viscountess dined at Mr Winnington's; we were several men there when she came in! 'Lord,' says she, 'I have been at Hampstead this morning, and I met Sir John Shelly,[15] who had got a very shabby man with him, but the fellow was handsome: he looked so ashamed, that I fancy it was but just over.'

Of beauty, I can tell you an admirable story: one Mrs Comyns,[16] an elderly gentlewoman, has lately taken a house in St James's Street; some young gentlemen went thither t'other night: 'Well, Mrs Comyns, I hope there won't be the same disturbances here that were at your other house in Air Street.' 'Lord, Sir, I never had any disturbances there: mine was as quiet a house as any in the neighbourhood, and a great deal of good company came to me: it was only the ladies of quality that envied me.'—'Envied you! Why your house was pulled down about your ears.'—'Oh dear Sir! don't you know how that happened?' 'No, pray how?' 'Why, dear Sir, it was my Lady Caroline Fitzroy, who gave the mob ten guineas to demolish my house, because her Ladyship fancied I got women for Colonel Conway.'[17]

My dear George, don't you delight in this story? If poor Harry comes back from Flanders, I intend to have infinite fun with his prudery about this anecdote, which is full as good as if it was true. I beg you will visit Mrs Comyns, when you come to town: she has infinite humour.

Adieu! dear George.

                                        Yours ever,

                                        H. Walpole

13. Lady Caroline Fitzroy (1722–84), m. (1746) William Stanhope, styled Vct Petersham, 2d E. of Harrington, 1756.

14. The remainder of the paragraph has been omitted in previous editions.

15. Sir John Shelley (d. 1771), 4th Bt; brother-in-law of the D. of Newcastle.

16. Unidentified.

17. Hon. Henry Seymour Conway (1719–95), later Secretary of State and field marshal; first cousin of HW, and his lifelong friend and correspondent. At this time there was some likelihood of his marrying Lady Caroline.

From MONTAGU, Sunday 28 July 1745

In the possession of Sir Wathen A. Waller, Bt, Woodcote, Warwick.

Windsor, July[1] 28, 1745.

Dear Horry,

I WAS in Essex with Lady Ann[2] at the Talbots'[3] when your most delightful, agreeable, polite, et cetera, et cetera letter came to Windsor, and I had not the pleasure to read it till my return, or I had returned you before this a thousand thanks for it, for thanks and praises are all I am able to bestow from this place, where I live upon sweet air and save my money. There is not a man to throw to one's dog for society, nor a woman that will throw herself to such a dog as me for pleasure. I dined two days ago and spent the whole day at the Duke of Marlborough's island,[4] which is really a charming little place. I went by the Baron's at Englefeild Green,[5] and saw a covey of children and women before the door, and an old man at six in the evening in a striped satin nightgown and cap I took to be Dr Thirlbey or such a sort of body that does not inhabit our poor earth nor subjects itself to our whims. 'Twas in my way to the Duchess of Manchester's trinket,[6] which she has set in the middle of the green, with a chandler's shop on one side and an inn on the other. 'Twas once a cabinet-maker's shop, but she has so begilt it and bepapered and

1. Montagu first wrote 'Aug.'
2. Montagu's cousin Lady Anne Montagu (ca 1715–66), dau. of 1st E. of Halifax; m. (1750) Joseph Jekyll, of Dallington, Northants (George Baker, *History and Antiquities of the County of Northampton*, 1822–41, i. 132).
3. Henry Talbot (1700–84), brother of 1st Bn Talbot; Commissioner of the Salt Tax (GM 1733, iii. 102); m. (1725) his second wife, Catharine Clopton (d. 1754), dau. of Sir Hugh Clopton, Kt. She was a cousin of HW's mother; a miniature of her by Zincke was sold SH xiv. 73 (Collins, *Peerage*, 1812, v. 233; John Nichols, *History . . . of the County of Leicester*, 1795–1815, iv. 178, n. 7).
4. Monkey Island, in the Thames between Maidenhead and Windsor, where the second Duke of Marlborough had built a sort of summerhouse (*Les Delices de Windsore*, Eton, 1751, p. 104; *Anecdotes*,

Works iii. 449; for a detailed and critical description, see *Correspondence between Frances, Countess of Hartford, and Henrietta Louisa, Countess of Pomfret, 1738–41*, 1805, i. 7–8).
5. Edward Walpole's; see *ante* 25 May 1745.
6. Lady Isabella Montagu (d. 1786), m. (1) (1723) William Montagu, 2d D. of Manchester; m. (2) (1743) Edward Hussey, cr. (1762) Bn Beaulieu, (1784) E. of Beaulieu. 'The Duchess of Manchester has taken a house, no bigger than a nutshell, upon Englefield Green; where the man formerly lived who made the feather dogs, and the bed which the late King of Poland bought. She has added a wooden porch bigger than the house, and furnished all her rooms with paper' (*Correspondence between Frances, Countess of Hartford, and Henrietta Louisa, Countess of Pomfret, 1738–41*, 1805, iii. 279–80).

ornamented with her Grace's own hands that it would please you to see it.

Madame de Bolingbroke[7] goes frequently to Bell Isle's[8] to hold a sabat. He informs himself very particularly of everything that passes, and has made very shrewd remarks on our defenceless state.

Tomorrow we are to have a most famous concert, with the best hands from London. We call it winter here.

Dear Horry, adieu! Believe me ever most cordially yours,

G. Montagu

To Montagu, Thursday 1 August 1745

Dated by the postscript.

[Aug. 1, 1745].

Dear George,

I CAN'T help thinking you laugh at me when you say such very civil things of my letters; and yet coming from you, I would fain not have it all flattery;

> So much the more, as from a little elf
> I've had a high opinion of myself;
> Though sickly, slender, and not large of limb[1]—

With this modest prepossession, you may be sure I like to have you commend me, whom, after I have done with myself, I admire of all men living—I only beg that you will commend me no more; it is very ruinous, and praise like other debts, ceases to be due, on being paid —one comfort indeed is, that it is as seldom paid as other debts.

I have been very fortunate lately; have met with an extreme good print of Monsieur de Grignan;[2] I am persuaded very like, and then it

7. Marie-Claire des Champs de Marcilly (1675–1750), m. (1) Philippe le Valois de Villette, Marquis de Villette; m. (2) (1720) Henry St John, cr. (1712) Vct Bolingbroke.

8. Charles-Louis-Auguste Fouquet (1684–1761), Maréchal-Duc de Belle-Isle, was captured with his brother when he accidentally entered Hanoverian territory en route from Cassel to Berlin, 31 Dec. 1744. He was held at Windsor till 16 Aug. 1745 (*Nouv. Biog. Gén.;* GM 1745, xv. 442; *A Review of the Case of the Marshal Belle Isle,* London, 1745).

1. Dryden, *Fables,* 'The Cock and the Fox,' ll. 655–7. The second line reads 'He had a high opinion of himself.'

2. François de Castellane-Adhémar de Monteil (ca 1629–1714), Comte de Grignan, Mme de Sévigné's son-in-law (*La Grande encyclopédie,* 1885–1902). 'J'embrasse Grignan et le baise à la joue droite, au-dessous de sa touffe ébouriffée' (*Lettres de Madame de Sévigné,* ed. M. Monmerqué, 1862–6, iii. 62).

has his *toufe ébourifée:* I don't indeed know what that was, but I am sure it is in the print: none of the critics could ever make out what Livy's Patavinity[3] is, though they are all confident it is in his writings. I have heard within these few days what for your sake I wish I could have told you sooner, that there is in Belleisle's suite, the Abbé Perrin[4] who published Madame Sevigny's[5] letters, and who has the originals in his hands: how one should have liked to have known him! The Marshal[6] was privately in London last Friday—he is entertained today at Hampton-Court by the Duke of Grafton[7]—Don't you believe it was to settle the *binding the scarlet thread in the window when the French shall come in unto the land to possess it?*[8]—I don't at all wonder at any shrewd observations the Marshal has made on our situation—the bringing him here at all, the sending him away now, in short the whole series of our conduct, convinces me that we shall soon see as silent a change as that in *The Rehearsal* of King Usher and King Physician.[9] It may well be so when the disposition of the drama is in the hands of the Duke of Newcastle. Those hands that are always groping and sprawling, and fluttering and hurrying on the rest of his precipitate person—but there is no describing them but as Monsieur Courcelle[10] a French prisoner did t'other day—'Je ne sais pas,' dit-il, 'je ne saurais l'exprimer, mais il a un certain *tatillonage*'—If one could conceive a dead body hung in chains, always wanting to be hung somewhere else, one should have a comparative idea of him.

For my own part, I comfort myself with the humane reflection of the Irishman in the ship that was on fire, 'I am but a passenger!' If I was not so indolent, I think I should rather put in practice the late Duchess of Bolton's[11] geographical resolution of going to China, when Whiston[12] told her the world would be burnt in three years—Have

3. Patavinity: the dialectal characteristics of Patavium or Padua, as shown in Livy's writings.

4. Denis-Marius de Perrin (ca 1684–1754), Chevalier de St-Louis, published editions of Mme de Sévigné's letters in 1734–7 (6 vols), 1738 (6 vols), 1739 (6 vols), 1751 (1 vol.), and 1754 (6 vols and 8 vols) (*Nouv. Biog. Gén.;* Mme de Sévigné, *Lettres,* ed. Monmerqué, xi. 146, 492–5).

5. Marie de Rabutin-Chantal (1626–96), m. (1644) Henri, Marquis de Sévigné.

6. Belle-Isle.

7. Charles Fitzroy (1683–1757), 2d D. of Grafton.

8. A paraphrase of Joshua ii. 18.

9. In the Duke of Buckingham's comedy *The Rehearsal,* the Gentleman Usher and the Physician usurp the thrones of the two kings of Brentford simply by announcing that they have done so (II. iv).

10. Unidentified.

11. Henrietta Crofts (d. 1730), m. (1697) Charles Powlett, 2d D. of Bolton. Repeated in *Walpoliana,* ed. John Pinkerton [1799], i. 15–16.

12. William Whiston (1667–1752), eccentric divine.

you any philosophy? Tell me what you think—it is quite the fashion to talk of the French coming here—nobody sees it in any other light, but as a thing to be talked of; not to be precautioned against. Don't you remember a report of the plague's being in the City, and everybody went to the house where it was, to see it? You see I laugh about it, for I would not for the world be so un-English as to do otherwise. I am persuaded that when Count Saxe[13] with ten thousand men is within a day's march of London, people will be hiring windows at Charing Cross and Cheapside to see them pass by. 'Tis our characteristic to take dangers for sights, and evils for curiosities.

Adieu! dear George; I am laying in scraps of *Cato*,[14] against it may be necessary to take leave of one's correspondents *à la Romaine,* and before the play itself is suppressed by a *lettre de cachet* to the booksellers.

Yours ever,

HOR. WALPOLE

PS. Lord, 'tis the first of August, 1745,[15] a holiday that is going to be turned out of the almanac!

To Montagu, Tuesday 17 September 1745

Arlington Street, Sept. 17, 1745.

Dear George,

HOW could you ask me such a question, as whether I should be glad to see you? Have you a mind I should make you a formal speech, with *honour, and pleasure and satisfaction,* etc.? I will not, for that would be telling you I should not be glad. However, do come soon, if you should be glad to see me, for we, I mean we old folks that came over with the Prince of Orange in eighty-eight, have had notice to remove by Christmas Day.[1] The moment I have smugged[1a] up a

13. Hermann-Maurice, Comte de Saxe (1696–1750), Maréchal de France, had commanded the abortive invasion of England in 1744 (*Nouv. Biog. Gén.*).

14. Addison's tragedy. HW's copy of Addison's *Works*, 1726, 4 vols, with HW's initials and date of purchase, '1729,' is now WSL.

15. The anniversary of the accession of the House of Hanover.

1. Charles Edward Stuart (1720–88), 'the Young Pretender,' son of James Francis Edward Stuart (1688–1766), 'the Old Pretender,' had landed in Scotland Aug. 2. His forces took Edinburgh the day this letter was written (see *London Gazette* 17–21 Sept. 1745, and *Old England* 28 Sept. 1745).

1a. 'To fit up (a room, etc.) neatly or nicely' (OED, which quotes this passage).

closet or a dressing room, I have always warning given me that my lease is out. Four years ago I was mightily at my ease in Downing Street,[2] and then the good woman Sandys[3] took my lodgings over my head, and was in such a hurry to junket her neighbours, that I had scarce time allowed me to wrap up my old china in a little hay. Now comes the Pretender's boy, and promises all my comfortable apartments in the Exchequer and Custom House[4] to some forlorn Irish peer, who chooses to remove his pride and poverty out of some large old unfurnished gallery at St Germain's. Why really Mr Montagu, this is not pleasant! I shall wonderfully dislike being a loyal sufferer in a threadbare coat, and shivering in an antechamber at Hanover, or reduced to teach Latin and English to the young princes at Copenhagen. The Dowager Strafford has already wrote cards for my Lady Nithisdale,[5] my Lady Tullibardine,[6] the Duchesses of Perth[7] and Berwick,[8] and twenty more revived peeresses to invite them to play at whisk Monday three months: for your part, you will divert yourself with their old taffeties, and tarnished slippers; and their awkwardness the first day they go to court in shifts and clean linen. Will you ever write to me at my garret at Herenhausen?[9] I will give you a faithful account of all the promising speeches that Prince George[10] and Prince Edward[11] make whenever they have a new sword, and intend to reconquer England.—At least write to me, while you may with acts of Parliament on your side: but I hope you are coming. Adieu!

Yours ever,

Hor. Walpole

2. When his father was Prime Minister.
3. Letitia Tipping (d. 1779), m. (1725) Samuel Sandys, cr. (1743) 1st Bn Sandys. He was Chancellor of the Exchequer after Walpole's fall, and lived at No. 10 Downing Street (see HW to Mann 30 June 1742).
4. See 'Account of my Conduct Relative to the Places I Hold,' Works ii. 364–70.
5. Lady Winifred Herbert (d. 1749), m. (1699) William Maxwell, 5th E. of Nithsdale, a Jacobite leader in the '15 uprising.
6. There seems to have been no Lady Tullibardine at this time; see GEC and Scots Peerage, 1904–10, sub Atholl. The Marquis of Tullibardine, Duke of Atholl but for his attainder, died 1746, unmarried.
7. Lady Jean Gordon (ca 1683–1773), m. (1706) James Drummond, 2d titular D. of Perth.
8. Anne Bulkeley (d. 1751), m. (1700) James Fitzjames, D. of Berwick, illegitimate son of James II.
9. The Electoral palace of Hanover.
10. The future George III (1738–1820).
11. Prince Edward Augustus (1739–67), George III's brother, cr. (1760) D. of York.

To Montagu, Thursday 22 May 1746

Arlington Street, May 22, 1746.

Dear George,

AFTER all your goodness to me, don't be angry that I am glad I am got into *brave old* London again: though my cats don't purr like Goldwin, yet one of them has as good a heart as old Reynolds,[1] and the tranquillity of my own closet makes me some amends for the loss of the library, and *toute la belle compagnie célestine;*[2] I don't know whether that expression will do for the azure ceilings, but I found it at my fingers' ends and so it slipped through my pen. We called at Langley,[3] but did not like it, nor the Grecian temple at all; it is by no means *gracious.*[4]

I forgot to take your last orders about your poultry; the Partlets have not laid since I went, for little Chanticleer

> Is true to love, and all for recreation;
> And does not mind the work of propagation.[5]

But I trust you will come yourself in a few days, and then you may settle their route.

I am got deep into the Sidney papers:[6] there are old wills full of bequeathed *owches*[7] and *goblets with fair enamel,* that will delight you; and there is a little pamphlet of Sir Philip Sidney's[8] in defence of his uncle of Leicester,[9] that gives me a much better opinion of his

---

1. Unidentified; possibly cats or servants belonging to Montagu, whom HW had apparently been visiting.

2. If a quotation, not located.

3. Langley Park, Langley Marish, Bucks, a seat of the Duke of Marlborough, 1738–88 (see *Vict. Co. Hist. Bucks* iii. 297).

4. I.e., ducal, with, perhaps, a pun on 'Grecian.'

5. 'Who true to love, was all for Recreation,
   And minded not the Work of Propagation.'
   (Dryden, *Fables,* 'The Cock and the Fox,' ll. 691–2.)

6. *Letters and Memorials of State . . . by Sir Henry . . . Sir Philip . . . Sir Robert Sidney . . .,* ed. Arthur Collins, 2 vols, 1746. HW's copy (MS Cat. F.1.21–2) was sold SH ii. 174, and is now at Northwestern University, Evanston, Ill.

7. Owch or ouch: a clasp, brooch, or buckle (OED).

8. *A Discourse in Defence of the Earl of Leicester,* by Sir Philip Sidney (1554–86), was probably written in 1584 in reply to the bitter anonymous pamphlet generally known as *Leicester's Commonwealth;* the *Discourse* was first published in the collection HW was reading, i. 62. In *Royal & Noble Authors,* where the discussion of Sidney in the article on Fulke Greville parallels the present passage, HW professes to consider the pamphlet 'by far the best presumption of his abilities' (*Works* i. 342).

9. Robert Dudley (1532 or 1533–88), cr. (1564) E. of Leicester; Queen Elizabeth's favourite.

parts, than his dolorous *Arcadia,* though it almost recommended him to the crown of Poland;[10] at least I have never been able to discover what other so great merit he had. In this little tract he is very vehement in clearing up the honour of his lineage; I don't think he could have been warmer about his family, if he had been of the blood of the *Cues.*[11] I have diverted myself with reflecting how it would have entertained the town a few years ago if my cousin Richard Hammond[12] had wrote a treatise to clear up my father's pedigree, when the *Craftsman*[13] used to treat him so roundly with being nobody's son. Adieu! dear George!

Yours ever,

THE GRANDSON OF NOBODY

To Montagu, Thursday 5 June 1746

Arlington Street, June 5, 1746.

Dear George,

YOU may perhaps fancy that you are very happy in the country, and that because you commend everything you see, you like everything; you may fancy that London is a desert, and that *grass now grows where Troy town stood;*[1] but it does not, except just before my Lord Bath's[2] door, whom nobody will visit—so far from being empty and dull and dusty, the town is full of people, full of water, for it has rained this week, and as gay as a new German prince must make any place. Why it rains princes; though some people are disap-

10. According to Sir Robert Naunton's *Fragmenta Regalia,* ca 1630 (Edward Arber, *English Reprints,* 1870, xx. 35) Sidney 'through the fame of his deserts . . . was in the election for the Kingdom of *Pole.*' Mona Wilson, *Sir Philip Sidney,* 1931, p. 319, says, 'The dates make this story difficult of acceptance.'

11. A term frequently used by HW and Montagu to denote the Montagu family.

12. Richard Hamond (d. 1776), eld. son of Anthony Hamond of Wootton and Susan Walpole, Sir Robert's sister (Burke, *Landed Gentry,* 1851, i. 533).

13. A formidable opposition journal, 1726–36, to which Bolingbroke and the Pulteneys were frequent contributors. See William T. Laprade, *Public Opinion and Politics in Eighteenth Century England,* New York, 1936, pp. 292 et seq.

1. 'Iam seges est ubi Troia fuit' (Ovid, *Heroides,* i. 53).

2. William Pulteney (1684–1764), cr. (1742) E. of Bath; statesman.

pointed of the arrival of the Pretender, yet the Duke[3] is just coming, and the Prince of Hesse[4] come. He is tall, lusty and handsome; extremely like Lord Elcho[5] in person, and to Mr Hussey[6] in what entitles him[7] more to his freedom in Ireland, than the resemblance of the former does to Scotland.[8] By seeing him with the Prince of Wales,[9] people think he looks stupid, but I dare say in his own country he is reckoned very lively, for though he don't speak much, he opens his mouth very often. The King has given him a fine sword[10] and the Prince a ball. He dined with the former the first day, and since with the great officers. Monday he went to Ranelagh and supped in the House;[11] Tuesday at the opera he sat with his court in the box on the stage, next the Prince, and went into to theirs to see the last dance, and after it was over to the Venetian ambassadress,[12] who is the only woman he has yet noticed; so he has not put off Lord Petersham's match[13] at all. Tonight there is a masquerade at Ranelagh for him; a play at Covent Garden on Monday and a ridotto at the Haymarket, and then he is to go. His amours are generally very humble, and very frequent, for he does not much affect our daughter.[14] A little apt to be boisterous when he has drank; I have not heard, but I hope he was

3. William Augustus (1721–65), D. of Cumberland, son of George II; at this time highly popular following his defeat of the rebels at Culloden.

4. Friedrich Wilhelm (1720–85), Landgraf of Hesse-Cassel (1760), as Friedrich II (Allgemeine Deutsche Biographie, Leipzig, 1875–1912, vii. 524).

5. David Wemyss (1721–87), styled Lord Elcho. He was attainted after the '45 uprising, in which he took a prominent part, and did not assume the style of Earl of Wemyss on his father's death in 1756.

6. Edward Hussey (after 1749, Hussey-Montagu) (1720–1802), cr. (1762) Bn Beaulieu, (1784) E. of Beaulieu. The reference is probably to the Prince's amatory prowess, since HW considered Hussey, who had married Isabella Duchess of Manchester, an Irish fortune-hunter.

7. The Prince of Hesse.

8. That is, the Prince's resemblance to Elcho, who was a fugitive, would not give him the freedom of Scotland.

9. Frederick, son of George II.

10. 'The Prince of Hesse . . . waited on the King at Kensington [2 June]; when His Majesty was pleased to make him a present of a sword of curious workmanship, set with diamonds of a very great value' (GM 1746, xvi. 324).

11. Presumably, the Rotunda at Ranelagh, not the House of Commons.

12. Elena Albrizzi, m. (1728) Pier Andrea Cappello, Venetian Ambassador at London 1744–8 (G. Catalani in N&Q 1940, clxxviii. 46). She is described as 'extremely young, has the French sort of behaviour,' with 'somewhat of singularity both in her air and dress' (Letters of the First Earl of Malmesbury, ed. the [3d] Earl of Malmesbury, 1870, i. 13, 69); see also HW to Mann 15 April 1744; Lady Mary Wortley Montagu, Letters and Works, ed. Lord Wharncliffe, 3d edn 1861, ii. 381.

13. William Stanhope (1719–79), styled Vct Petersham; 2d E. of Harrington, 1756; m. (11 Aug. 1746) Lady Caroline Fitzroy.

14. Mary (1723–72), 4th dau. of George II; m. (1740) Prince Friedrich of Hesse (n. 4 above) (Burke, Peerage, 1934, p. 39; Mem. Geo. II i. 405). She and the Prince were later separated; see post 5 Aug. 1746, n. 19.

not rampant last night with Lady Middlesex[15] or Charlotte Dives![16] Men go to see him in the morning before he goes to see the lions.[17]

The talk of peace is blown over; nine or ten battalions were ordered for Flanders the day before yesterday; but they are again countermanded; and the operations of this campaign again likely to be confined within the precincts of Covent Garden,[18] where the army surgeons give constant attendance. Major Johnson[19] commands (I can't call it) the corps de *réserve* in Grosvenor Street. I wish you had seen the goddess of those purlieus[20] with him t'other night at Ranelagh; you would have swore it had been the divine Cucumber in person.[21]

The fame of the Violetta[22] increases daily: the sister-Countesses of Burlington[23] and Thanet[24] exert all their stores of sullen partiality in competition for her: the former visits her and is having her picture, and carries her to Chiswick;[25] and she dines at Bedford House,[26] and sups at Lady Cardigan's,[27] and lies—indeed I have not heard where;

15. Hon. Grace Boyle (d. 1763), m. (1744) Charles Sackville, styled E. of Middlesex; 2d D. of Dorset, 1765.

16. Charlotte Dyve (ca 1712–73), m. (1762) Samuel Masham, 2d Bn Masham. Both she and Lady Middlesex were members of the slightly 'shady' household of the Princess of Wales.

17. In the Tower; the menagerie there was long one of the sights of London (see *London Past & Present* iii. 397). HW is doubtless using the lions here for sights in general.

18. The locale of the most famous brothels.

19. James Johnston (ca 1721–97), of the 1st (Royal) Dragoons, which he commanded in the Seven Years' War as Lt-Col.; Gen., 1793; Lt-Gov. of Minorca 1763–74; Gov. of Quebec 1774–; see G. F. R. Barker and Alan Stenning, *Record of Old Westminsters*, 1928; *Marriage, Baptismal, and Burial Registers of the . . . Abbey . . . Westminster*, ed. Joseph L. Chester, 1876, p. 459. In later life he and his wife (Lady Cecilia West) were neighbours and friends of HW's. According to a long memoir of him, by a relative, at the end of vol. vi of Wright's 2d edn (1846) of HW's letters, he was 'considered the handsomest man, and best swordsman, in the army,' and 'Gainsborough requested him,

as a great favour, to sit to him for his portrait, in order to bring himself into vogue —which he did.' He was called 'Irish' Johnston to distinguish him from his namesake, see *post* 9 Aug. 1759, n. 1.

20. Lady Caroline Fitzroy (see *post* 12 June 1746).

21. Hon. Jane Conway (ca 1722–49), half-sister of HW's cousin, H. S. Conway (see *post* 18 May 1749). 'Cucumber' is unexplained.

22. Eva Maria Violette (1725–1822), m. (1749) David Garrick; she was a dancer (GM 1822, xcii pt ii. 468–70).

23. Lady Dorothy Savile (1699–1758), m. (1721) Richard Boyle, 3d E. of Burlington.

24. Lady Mary Savile (1700–51), m. (1722) Sackville Tufton, 7th E. of Thanet.

25. Chiswick House, built by the third Earl of Burlington and William Kent; now owned by the Chiswick District Council. A portrait of 'La Violette . . . by Knapton, in crayons,' hung in Lady Burlington's dressing-room (*Country Seats* 22–3; Findlay Muirhead, *London and its Environs*, 1927, p. 445).

26. In Bloomsbury Square; the town house of the Dukes of Bedford 1704–1800 (*London Past & Present*).

27. Lady Mary Montagu (ca 1711–1775), m. (1730) George Brudenell, 4th E. of Cardigan; cr. (1766) D. of Montagu.

but I know, not at Carlton House,[28] where she is in great disgrace, for not going once or twice a week to take lessons of Denoyer,[29] as he[30] bid her; you know that is politics in a court, where dancing masters are ministers.

Adieu! dear George, my compliments to all at the farm; your cock and hens[31] would write to the poultry, but they are dressing in haste for the masquerade: mind, I don't say that Ashton[32] is doing anything like that; but he is putting on an odd sort of a black gown; but as Di Bertie[33] says on her message cards, *Mum for that!*

Yours ever,

H. Walpole

To Montagu, Thursday 12 June 1746

Arlington Street, June 12, 1746.

MY dear George, don't commend me; you don't know what hurt it will do me; you will make me a painstaking man, and I had rather be dull without any trouble. From partiality to me, you won't allow my letters to be letters—Jesus! it sounds as if I wrote them to be fine and to have them printed, which might be very well for Mr Pope who having wrote pieces carefully,[1] which ought to be laboured, could carry off the affectation of having studied things that have no excuse but their being wrote flying. Therefore if you have a mind I

---

28. Pall Mall; official residence of the Prince of Wales after 1732; torn down 1826 (*London Past & Present*).

29. Dunoyer or Desnoyers, a French dancing-master, was a confidant of the Prince of Wales, and at the same time welcome in the royal household—'a sort of licensed spy on both sides' (Lord Hervey, *Memoirs of the Reign of King George II*, ed. Romney Sedgwick, 1931, iii. 791–2, 867). His name occurs frequently in Chesterfield's letters 1745–69, as both the son and godson were under his tutelage. 'Philip Denoyer had a pension of £100 as Dancing Master to the late Princess Louisa [d. 1768]' MS note by Cunningham in his own copy of his edition, now wsl).

30. The Prince of Wales.

31. Which HW had apparently brought from his visit to Montagu.

32. Rev. Thomas Ashton (1715–75), HW's Eton friend and correspondent; they quarrelled in 1750 (see HW to Mann 25 July 1750). At this time Ashton was rector of Aldingham, Lancs, a preferment he owed to HW, whom he was apparently visiting.

33. Diana Bertie (d. 1754), natural dau. of Hon. Peregrine Bertie by Elizabeth Allen, later wife of William, 5th E. of Coventry; m. (1751) George James ('Gilly') Williams. Mrs Delany says 'she was the *pink of fashion* in the beau monde'; see J. B. Whitmore's solution of her identity in n&q 1937, clxxiii. 206; Delany, *Correspondence* i. 3.

---

1. HW may have meant to write 'carelessly.'

should write you news, don't make me think about it; I shall be so long turning my periods, that what I tell you will cease to be news.[2]

The Prince of Hesse had a most ridiculous tumble t'other night at the opera; they had not pegged up his box tight after the ridotto, and down he came on all four; G. Selwyn[3] says he carried it off with an *unembarrassed* countenance.[3a] He was to go this morning, I don't know whether he is or not. The Duke[4] is expected tonight by all the tallow-candles and faggots in town.

Lady Caroline Fitzroy's match[5] is settled to the consent of all parties; the Duke of Grafton gives them a thousand pound extraordinary to be off their living with him; they are taking Lady Abergavenny's[6] house in Brook Street. The fairy Cucumber houses all Lady Caroline's out-pensioners; Mr Montgomery[7] is now on half-pay with her. Her Major Johnson is chosen at White's[8] to the great terror of the society. When he was introduced, Sir Charles Williams[9] presented Dick Edgcumbe[10] to him, and said, 'I have three favours to beg of you for Mr Edgcumbe; the first, that you would not lie with Mrs Day;[11] the second, that you would not poison his cards; the third, that you would not kill him': the fool answered very gravely, 'Indeed I will not.'

The Good[12] has borrowed old Bowman's[13] house in Kent, and is retiring thither for six weeks; I tell her, she has lived so rakish a life that she is obliged to go and take up.—I hope you don't know any

2. HW made the same complaint to Lady Ossory half a century later.

3. George Augustus Selwyn (1719–91), the wit; HW's lifelong friend and occasional correspondent.

3a. Probably a reference to a political ballad published in April 1746, called *The Unembarrassed Countenance*, possibly written by Sir Charles Hanbury Williams (GM 1746, xvi. 224; Earl of Ilchester, *Life of Sir Charles Hanbury-Williams*, 1929, p. 127).

4. Of Cumberland.

5. With Viscount Petersham.

6. Lady Rebecca Herbert (d. 1758), m. (1732) William Nevill, 16th Bn Abergavenny.

7. Probably Archibald Montgomerie (1726–96), 11th E. of Eglintoun, 1769.

8. [W. B. Boulton], *History of White's*, 1892, ii pt ii, List of Members, p. 50, gives 1745 as the year of his election.

9. Sir Charles Hanbury Williams (1708–59), K.B., 1744; verse-writer, diplomatist, and correspondent of HW.

10. Richard Edgcumbe (1716–61), 2d Bn Edgcumbe, 1758; a frequent visitor at SH.

11. Mrs Ann Franks, alias Day (DNB, *sub* Edgecumbe). Lord Edgcumbe in his will made HW one of her trustees ('Short Notes'). After his death she married Sir Peter Fenouilhet, Kt, Exon of the Guard, but was soon separated from him and lived in France; Selwyn wrote 22 April 1778, 'Milady Fenoulet is in all *beaux cercles* of Calais, painted like the stern of a ship; her daughter married to a Marquis' (S. Parnell Kerr, *George Selwyn and the Wits*, 1909, p. 218). She d. 1790 (*The Times*, 19 Sept. 1790, p. 2). See also DU DEFFAND and *Town and Country Magazine* 1770, ii. 569–70.

12. Not identified.

13. See *post* 28 Jan. 1760, n. 12.

more of it, and that Major Montagu[14] is not to cross the country to her.

There—I think you can't commend me for this letter; it shall not even have the merit of being long.

My compliments to all your contented family!

Yours ever,

H.W.

PS. I forgot to tell you, that Lord Lonsdale[15] had summoned the peers today to address the King not to send the troops abroad in the present conjuncture.[16] I hear he made a fine speech, and the Duke of Newcastle a very long one in answer; and then they rose without a division. Lord Baltimore is to bring the same motion into our House.

To Montagu, Tuesday 17 June 1746

Arlington Street, June 17, 1746.

Dear George,

I WROTE to you on Friday night,[1] as soon as I could, after receiving your letter, with a list of the regiments to go abroad, one of which I hear since is your brother's. I am extremely sorry it is his fortune, as I know the distress it will occasion in your family.

For the politics which you inquire after, and which may have given motion to this step, I can give you no satisfactory answer: I have heard that it is in consequence of an impertinent letter, sent over by Van Hoey,[2] in favour of the rebels; though at the same time I hear we are making steps towards a peace. There center all my politics, all in peace! Whatever your cousin[3] may think, I am neither busy about what does happen, nor making parties for what may. If he knew how

14. Charles Montagu (d. 1777), George Montagu's youngest brother; Eton 1725–8; Lt-Col., 1745; Col. 61st Foot, 1755; 59th Foot, 1756; Maj.-Gen., 1759; Col. 2nd Foot, 1760; Lt-Gen., 1761; K.B., 1771 (Richard A. Austen-Leigh, *Eton College Register, 1698–1752,* 1927; *Army Lists;* Musgrave, *Obituary*).

15. Henry Lowther (1694–1751), 3d Vct Lonsdale.

16. The troops which had been withdrawn from Flanders to crush the rebellion were now returned, and the campaign was resumed there; see Fortescue, *British Army* ii. 146, 149.

———

1. Missing.

2. Abraham Van Hoey (1684–1766), Dutch ambassador at Paris (*Biographisch Woordenboek der Nederlanden,* Haarlem, 1852–78, vi. 276). For the impertinent letter and the repercussions therefrom, see GM 1746, xvi. 302–5, 311, 318.

3. It is not clear which of Montagu's numerous cousins HW considered intriguing or suspicious at this time.

happy I am, his intriguing nature would envy my tranquillity more, than his suspicions can make him jealous of my practices.

My books, my virtu, and my other follies and amusements take up too much of my time, to leave me much leisure to think of other people's affairs; and of all affairs, those of the public are least my concern.

You will be sorry to hear of Augustus Townshend's death;[4] I lament it extremely, not much for his sake, for I did not honour him, but for his poor sister Molly's,[5] whose little heart, that is all tenderness and gratitude and friendship, will be broke with the shock; I really dread it, considering how delicate her health is. My Lady T. has a son with him;[6] I went to tell it her; instead of thinking of her child's distress, she kept me half an hour with a thousand idle histories of Lady Caroline Fitzroy, and Major Johnson, and the new Paymaster's[7] menage, and twenty other things, nothing to me, nor to her, if she could drop the idea of the Pay Office.[8] She said well to the Duchess of Bedford[9] t'other day, who told her the Duke[10] was windbound at Yarmouth; 'Lord,' says she, 'he will hate Norfolk as much as I do!'[11]

The Serene Hessian is gone. Little Brook[12] is to be an Earl; I want[13] to bespeak him a Lilliputian coronet at Chenevix's.[14] Adieu! dear George.

Yours ever,
H.W.

4. Hon. Augustus Townshend, 2d son of 2d Vct Townshend by his marriage with HW's aunt Dorothy Walpole, was a captain in the service of the East India Company, and died at Batavia (Collins, *Peerage*, 1812, ii. 471–2).

5. Hon. Mary Townshend (d. 1776), m. Lt-Gen. Hon. Edward Cornwallis (ibid. ii. 472).

6. Her son apparently accompanied Augustus Townshend. He was probably Hon. Roger Townshend (ca 1731–59), 'entered young into the army' and afterwards killed at Ticonderoga; her other sons were George and Charles (ibid. ii. 477; *post* 9 Oct. 1759; HW to Strafford 13 Sept. 1759).

7. William Pitt (1708–78), cr. (1766) E. of Chatham, became Paymaster 6 May 1746.

8. Pitt's predecessor in the Pay Office was Thomas Winnington, who had been Lady Townshend's lover and who had died 23 April (see HW to Conway 1 July 1745).

9. Hon. Gertrude Leveson-Gower (ca 1719–94), m. (1737) John Russell, 4th D. of Bedford.

10. John Russell (1710–71), 4th D. of Bedford. He was en route to Berwick to review his regiment (*General Evening Post* 5–7 June 1746).

11. Lady Townshend had long been separated from her husband, who lived at Rainham in Norfolk.

12. Francis Greville (1719–73), 8th Bn Brooke; cr. (1746) E. Brooke, (1759) E. of Warwick.

13. 'Went' in previous editions.

14. (?) Mary Roussel (d. 1755) m. Paul Daniel Chenevix (see Gray to HW 11 June 1736). She kept a famous toyshop, and later sublet SH to HW. Her maiden name was perhaps Deard, not Roussel (see *post* 18 May 1749).

To Montagu, Tuesday 24 June 1746

Arlington Street, June 24, 1746.

Dear George,

YOU have got a very bad person to tell you news, for I find I hear nothing before all the world has talked it over and done with it. Till twelve o'clock last night I knew nothing of all the kissing hands that had graced yesterday morning. Arundel[1] for Treasurer of the Chambers, Legge[2] and your friend Welsh Campbell[3] for the Treasury, Lord Duncannon[4] for the Admiralty, and your cousin of Halifax,[5] who is succeeded by his predecessor in the Buckhounds,[6] for Chief Justice in Eyre, in the room of Lord Jersey,[7] who has a pension of twelve hundred a year in Ireland for thirty-one years. They talk of new earls, Lord Chancellor,[8] Lord Gower,[9] Lord Brook and Lord Clinton,[10] but I don't know that this will be, because it is not past.

Tidings are every minute expected of a great sea fight; Martin[11] is got between the coast and the French fleet, which has sailed from Brest. The victory in Italy[12] is extremely big, but as none of my

1. Hon. Richard Arundel (d. 1758), 2d son of 2d Bn Arundel of Trerise; M.P. Knaresborough 1720–58; Treasurer of the Chamber 1746–7; see Collins, *Peerage*, 1768, vii. 92; GM 1758, xxviii. 46.

2. Henry Bilson Legge (1708–64), later Chancellor of the Exchequer (DNB).

3. John Campbell of Calder (ca 1700–77), M.P. Pembrokeshire 1727–47; Nairn 1747–54; Inverness 1754–61; Corfe Castle 1762–68; Lord of the Admiralty 1736–42; Lord of the Treasury 1746–54 (see William Retlaw Williams, *Parliamentary History of the Principality of Wales*, Brecknock, 1895, p. 157). He was probably called 'Welsh' because he represented a Welsh district in Parliament.

4. William Ponsonby (1704–93), styled Lord Duncannon; 2d E. of Bessborough, 1758.

5. George Montagu (1716–71), 2d E. of Halifax, called Montagu-Dunk after his marriage in 1741 to Anne Dunk, heiress of a wealthy clothier. He was Montagu's first cousin, and their relations occupy much space in Montagu's letters. For his political career, culminating in his part with Grenville and Egremont in the 'Triumvirate' of 1763, see DNB.

6. Ralph Jenison (1696–1758), of Els-wick, Northumberland, and Walworth, Durham; M.P. Northumberland 1723–41; Newport 1749–58; Master of the Buckhounds 1737–44, 1746–58 (Robert Surtees, *History . . . of Durham*, 1816–40, iii. 322).

7. William Villiers (ca 1712–69), 3d E. of Jersey. According to a list of pensions on the Irish Establishment in GM 1763, xxxiii. 540, he had £1500 a year.

8. Philip Yorke (1690–1764), cr. (1733) Bn Hardwicke; cr. (not until 1754) E. of Hardwicke; Lord Chancellor 1737–56.

9. John Leveson-Gower (1694–1754), 2d Bn Gower; cr. (8 July 1746) E. Gower.

10. Hugh Fortescue (1696–1751), 14th Bn Clinton; cr. (5 July 1746) E. Clinton. GEC, erroneously, has 1749; see *London Gazette* 1 July 1746.

11. William Martin (1696?–1756), Rear-Admiral, 1744; Admiral, 1747; at this time in command of the North Sea fleet. The great sea fight did not take place.

12. The Austrians under the Prince of Lichtenstein defeated a combined French and Spanish force commanded by the Comte de Gages and Maréchal de Maillebois at Piacenza (Placentia in contemporary reports) 5 June O.S. (GM 1746, xvi. 330; Spenser Wilkinson, *The Defence of Piedmont, 1742–48*, 1927, p. 253).

friends are aide-de-camps there, I know nothing of the particulars, except that the French and Spaniards have lost ten thousand men.

All the inns about town are crowded with rebel prisoners; and people are making parties of pleasure, which you know is the English genius, to hear their trials. The Scotch, which you know is the Scotch genius, are loud in censuring the Duke for his great severities in the Highlands.

The great business of the town, is Jack Spencer's[13] will, who has left Althrop and the Sunderland estate in reversion to Pitt; after more obligations and more pretended friendship for his brother the Duke[14] than is conceivable. The Duke is in the utmost uneasiness about it, having left the drawing of the writings for the estate, to his brother and his grandmother,[15] and without having any idea that himself was cut out of the entail. An additional circumstance of iniquity is, that he had given a bond for Mr Spencer for four thousand pound, which now he must pay, and the will and the bond are dated within three days of one another.

I have heard nothing yet of Augustus Townshend's will; my Lady, who you know hated him, came from the opera t'other night, and on putting off her gloves and finding her hands all black, said immediately,

My hands are guilty, but my heart is free.[16]

Another good thing she said to the Duchess of Bedford, who told her, the Duke was windbound at Yarmouth; 'Lord! he will hate Norfolk as much as I do.'[17]

I wish, my dear George, you could meet with any man that could copy the Beauties in the Castle;[18] I did not care if it were even in

13. Hon. John Spencer (1708–46), 4th son of the 3d E. of Sunderland, whose estates he inherited; his brother, the 3d but eldest surviving son, having succeeded to the Dukedom of Marlborough (n. 14). Their mother, Anne, Countess of Sunderland, was the 2d daughter of the great Duke of Marlborough, and John Spencer was the favourite grandchild of the old Duchess Sarah, who bequeathed him a large part of her estates and probably inspired his attachment to Pitt, to whom she left £10,000 (see the abstract of her will in GM 1744, xiv. 588). Spencer was

M.P. Woodstock 1732–46 (see Collins, Peerage, 1812, v. 42; William Retlaw Williams, Parliamentary History of the County of Oxford, Brecknock, 1899, p. 215).

14. Charles Spencer (1706–58), 5th E. of Sunderland, 1729; 2d D. of Marlborough, 1733 (see n. 13).

15. The Duchess of Marlborough.

16. Dryden and Lee, Oedipus, last line of Act 3.

17. HW repeats himself; see ante 17 June 1746.

18. See ante 20 May 1736, n. 18.

GEORGE MONTAGU, BY VAN LOO, A.D. 1739

Indian ink: will you inquire? Eckardt[19] has done your picture excellently well: what shall I do with the original? Leave it with him till you come?

Lord Bath and Lord Sandys[20] have had their pockets picked at Cuper's Gardens;[21] I fancy it was no bad scene, the avarice and jealousy of their peeresses,[22] on their return.

A terrible *disgrazia* happened to Earl Cholmondeley[23] t'other night at Ranelagh; you know all the history of his letters to borrow money to pay for damask for his fine room at Richmond; as he was going in, in the crowd, a woman offered him roses; '*Right damask,* my Lord!' He concluded she had been put upon it. I was told, apropos, a bon mot on the scene in the opera, where there is a view of his new room, and the farmer comes dancing out and shaking his purse; somebody said, there was a tradesman had unexpectedly got his money.

I think I deal in bon mots today; I'll tell you now another—but don't print my letter in a new edition of Joe Miller's jests.[24] The Duke has given Brigadier Mordaunt[25] the Pretender's coach, on condition he rode up to London in it; 'That I will, Sir,' said he, 'and drive till it stops of its own accord at the Cocoa Tree.'[26]

Adieu! dear George.

Yours ever,

H.W.

19. John Giles Eccardt (d. 1779). Eccardt painted over two dozen portraits of HW's friends and relatives for SH, including those of Gray and HW himself which now hang in the National Portrait Gallery. In July 1746 HW addressed to him a long poem 'The Beauties. An Epistle to Mr Eckardt the Painter' (see *post* 2 Aug. 1746, n. 19; *Works* iii. 448n; Ulrich Thieme and Felix Becker, *Allgemeines Lexikon der bildenden Künstler*, Leipzig, 1907–; HW to Mann 12 Nov. 1746). Eccardt's copy of Montagu's portrait was sold SH xxi. 112. In 1858 it was bought by the Duke of Manchester, who hung it at Kimbolton (Cunningham ix. 525). The original by Van Loo, reproduced here, is now at Boughton House, Kettering, *penes* the Duke of Buccleuch. On the back is written '[J.-B.] Vanloo pinxit George Montagu 1739.' It is No. 66 in the Boughton House catalogue.

20. Samuel Sandys (1695–1770), cr. (1743) Bn Sandys.

21. On the south side of the Thames, opposite Somerset House; a notable resort in the first half of the century (see Warwick Wroth, *London Pleasure Gardens*, 1896, pp. 247–57).

22. Lady Bath was Anna Maria Gumley (ca 1694–1758), m. (1714) William Pulteney, cr. (1742) E. of Bath.

23. George Cholmondeley (1703–70), 3d E. of Cholmondeley; HW's brother-in-law. Nothing further is known about his misadventures with his new room.

24. *Joe Miller's Jests; or the Wit's Vademecum,* a compilation by John Mottley (1692–1750) was first published in 1739, and had gone through eight editions by 1745. Joe Miller, the comedian (1684–1738), had no connection with it (DNB, *sub* Mottley and Miller).

25. Brig.-Gen. John Mordaunt (1697–1780), K.B., 1749; Gen., 1770 (DNB).

26. In Queen Anne's time a Tory coffee-house; it became a club during this period, with Jacobite leanings (see John Timbs, *Clubs and Club Life in London,* 1908, p. 69; HW to Mann 6 Feb. 1780).

To Montagu, Thursday 3 July 1746

Arlington Street, July 3d, 1746.

My dear George,

I WISH extremely to accept your invitation, but I can't bring my-self to it. If I have the pleasure of meeting Lord North[1] oftener at your house next winter, I do not know but another summer I may have courage enough to make him a visit; but I have no notion of going to anybody's house, and have the servants look on the arms of the chaise to find out one's name, and learn one's face from the Sara-cen's head.[2] You did not tell me how long you stayed at Wroxton,[3] and so I direct this thither; I have wrote one to Windsor since you left it.

The new earls have kissed hands and keep their own titles: dirty little Brook has taken no second title, to save three hundred pound, so if ever he gets a little Brookling, it must be called Lord Grevil, and can never be called up to the House of Lords.[4] The world reckon Earl Clinton obliged for his new honour to Lord Granville,[5] though they made the Duke of Newcastle go in to ask it.

Yesterday Mr Hussey's friends declared his marriage with her Grace of Manchester;[6] and said he was gone down to Englefield Green to take possession: I own that circumstance makes it a little suspicious, for by what I saw of the palace there, and what one has heard of him, there is not room for even the material part of him.

I can tell you another wedding, more certain, and fifty times more extraordinary—It is Lord Coke with Lady Mary Campbell,[7] the

1. Francis North (1704–90), 7th Bn North; cr. (1752) E. of Guilford.
2. The Walpole crest.
3. Wroxton Abbey, Oxon, seat of the North family.
4. The £300 were presumably fees. It is not clear why Lord Brooke's son could not be called to the House of Lords dur-ing his father's life if it were desired to do so. A special creation would be re-quired in any event for the (infrequent) step of elevating the son, but in this case he could be summoned by his father's sec-ond title to the barony of Brooke. Mr. Anthony R. Wagner, Portcullis of the Col-lege of Arms, suggests that either Walpole

incorrectly supposed that the secondary peerage must have a different designation or that he was under the impression that the secondary title had to be of the rank next below the principal one—in this case a Viscounty. See, however, N&Q 1939, clxxvii. 427.
5. John Carteret (1690–1763), 2d Bn Carteret, 1695; 1st E. Granville, 1744; the statesman.
6. According to GEC, *Peerage*, this mar-riage took place in 1743. The Duchess's 'palace' at Englefield Green is 'the trinket' of *ante* 28 July 1745, n. 6.
7. Lady Mary Campbell (1727–1811), m. (1747) Edward Coke (1719–53), styled Vct

Dowager of Argyle's[8] youngest daughter. It is all agreed; and was ne-
gotiated by the Countesses of Gower[9] and Leicester.[10] I don't know
why they skipped over Lady Betty,[11] who if there were any question
of beauty, is I think, as well as her sister. They drew in the girl to
give her consent when they first proposed it to her, but now, *la belle
n'aime pas trop le Sieur Leandre;*[12] she cries her red eyes to scarlet:
he has made her four visits, and is so in love that he writes to her
every other day. 'Tis a strange match; after offering him to all the
great lumps of gold in all the alleys of the City, they fish out a woman
of quality at last with a mere twelve thousand pound. She objects his
loving none of her sex but the four queens in a pack of cards, but he
promises to abandon White's and both clubs for her sake.[13] Apropos
to White's and cards, Dick Edgcumbe is shut up with the itch; the
ungenerous world ascribe it to Mrs Day, but he denies it; owning
however that he is very well contented to have it, as nobody will venture on her. Don't you like being pleased to have the itch, as a new
way to keep one's mistress to one's self?

You will be in town to be sure for the eight-and-twentieth; London
will be as full as at a coronation. The whole form is settled for the
trials,[14] and they are actually building scaffolds in Westminster Hall.

I have not seen poor Miss Townshend yet; she is in town and better, but most unhappy.

Adieu! dear George; yours ever,

H.W.

Coke, from whom she was immediately
estranged and in 1749 legally separated.
As Lady Mary Coke she was a prominent
(and eccentric) figure in English and Continental society. HW corresponded with
her and dedicated *The Castle of Otranto*
to her.

8. Jane Warburton (ca 1683–1767), m.
(1717) John Campbell, 2d D. of Argyll;
about her see *Lady Louisa Stuart, Selections from Her Manuscripts*, ed. Hon.
James Home, Edinburgh, 1899, p. 2 et seq.

9. Lady Mary Tufton (1701–85), m. (1)
(1718) Anthony Grey, E. of Harold; m. (2)
(1736) John Leveson-Gower, 2d Bn Gower,
cr. (1746) E. Gower.

10. Lady Margaret Tufton (1700–75),
m. (1718) Thomas Coke, cr. (1728) Bn

Lovel, (1744) E. of Leicester; Countess
Gower's sister and Lord Coke's mother.

11. Lady Elizabeth Campbell (ca 1722–
99), m. (1749) Hon. James Stuart-Mackenzie (*Scots Peerage*, 1904–10, i. 377).

12. If a quotation, not found.

13. There were two clubs at White's
(see *post* 6 Nov. 1756, n. 1). A somewhat
different account of this courtship is given
in *Lady Louisa Stuart, Selections from
Her Manuscripts*, ed. Hon. James Home,
Edinburgh, 1899, pp. 63–5 ('Some Account
of John Duke of Argyll and his Family,'
written in 1827). See also Coke, *Journals* i.
p. cxxiii (letter of the Duchess of Argyll
on the same subject).

14. Of the rebel lords.

To Montagu, Saturday 2 August 1746

Arlington Street, Aug. 2, 1746.

Dear George,

YOU have lost nothing by missing yesterday at the trials,[1] but a little additional contempt for the High Steward;[2] and even that is recoverable, as his long paltry speech is to be printed, for which and for thanks for it Lord Lincoln[3] moved the House of Lords. Somebody said to Sir Charles Windham,[4] 'Oh! you don't think Lord Hardwick's speech good, because you have read Lord Cowper's'[5]—'No,' replied he, 'but I do think it tolerable, because I heard Serjeant Skinner's.'[6] Poor brave old Balmerino[7] retracted his plea, asked pardon, and desired the lords to intercede for mercy. As he returned to the Tower, he stopped the coach at Charing Cross to buy honey-blobs, as the Scotch call gooseberries. He says he is extremely afraid Lord Kilmarnock[8] will not behave well. The Duke says publicly at his levee that the latter proposed the murdering the English prisoners.[9] His Highness was to have given Peggy Banks[10] a ball last night, but was persuaded to defer it, as it would have rather looked like an insult on the prisoners, the very day their sentence was passed. George Selwyn says he had begged Sir William Saunderson[11] to get him the Lord

1. See HW to Mann 1 Aug. 1746, for a full account of the trial of the rebel lords.

2. Lord Hardwicke.

3. Henry Fiennes-Clinton (later Pelham-Clinton) (1720–94), 9th E. of Lincoln; 2d D. of Newcastle-under-Lyne, 1768. There were three or more editions of Hardwicke's speech; see BM Cat. 'Several incorrectnesses have been altered in the printed copy' (Gray's Corr. i. 233–4).

4. Sir Charles Wyndham (1710–63), 4th Bt; 2d E. of Egremont, 1750.

5. William Cowper (ca 1665–1723), cr. (1706) Bn Cowper, (1718) E. Cowper; Lord Chancellor 1707–10, 1714–18; High Steward at the trial of the rebel lords in 1716. His two speeches on that occasion were printed at the time, and reprinted in 1746 with Lord Hardwicke's.

6. Matthew Skinner (1689–1749), Chief Justice of Chester, 1738; led for the crown against Lord Balmerino (DNB).

7. Arthur Elphinstone (1688–1746), 6th Bn Balmerino.

8. William Boyd (1704–46), 4th E. of Kilmarnock.

9. The rebel chiefs at the battle of Culloden supposedly ordered that no quarter be given the English. This story, which persisted into the DNB, is said to be based on a forgery; see Athenaeum 11 March 1899, no. 3724, p. 309.

10. Margaret (d. 1793), dau. of John Banks of Lincolnshire, m. (1757) Hon. Henry Grenville (Collins, Peerage, 1812, ii. 419; GM 1793, lxiii pt i. 581, q.v.). HW has added to his MS copy of The Beauties (now at Chewton Priory): 'The Duke of Montagu, who was in love with Miss Peggy Banks, not finding her name in this poem, added these two lines to it:

'Now, Ladies all, return me thanks,
Or else I'll sing of Peggy Banks.'

11. Sir William Saunderson (1692–1754), 2d Bt of Combe, Kent; Yeoman Usher of the Black Rod.

High Steward's wand after it was broke,[12] as a curiosity, but that he behaved so like an attorney the first day, and so like a pettifogger the second, that he would not take it to light his fire with: I don't believe my Lady Hardwick[13] is so high-minded.

Your cousin Sandwich[14] is certainly going on embassy to Holland: I don't know whether it is to qualify him by new dignity for the head of the Admiralty, or whether (which is more agreeable to present policy) to satisfy him instead of it. I know when Lord Malton[15] who was a young earl, asked for the Garter, to stop his pretensions they—made him a Marquis. When Lord Brook who is likely to have ten sons, though he has none yet, asked to have his barony settled on his daughters, they refused him with an earldom: and they professed making Pitt Paymaster, in order to silence the avidity of his faction.

Dear George, I am afraid I shall not be in your neighbourhood, as I promised myself; Sir Charles Williams has let his house.[16] I wish you would one day whisk over and look at Hurley House;[17] the enclosed advertisement[18] makes it sound pretty, though I am afraid too large for me. Do look at it impartially; don't be struck at first sight with any *brave old windows;* but be so good to inquire the rent, and if I can have it for a year, and with any furniture.

I have not had time to copy out the verses,[19] but you shall have them soon. Adieu with my compliments to your sisters.

Yours ever,

H. W.

12. At the dissolution of his commission after the conclusion of the trial. 'Then the White Staff being delivered to the Lord High Steward by the Gentleman Usher of the Black Rod, upon his knee, his Grace stood up uncovered; and, holding the Staff in both his hands, broke it in two, and declared the Commission to be dissolved' (*The Whole Proceedings in the House of Peers upon the Indictments against William Earl of Kilmarnock, George Earl of Cromertie, and Arthur Lord Balmerino; for High Treason*, 1746, p. 39).

13. Margaret Cocks (d. 1761), m. (1) John Lygon; m. (2) (1719) Philip Yorke, cr. (1733) Bn Hardwicke, (1754) E. of Hardwicke. HW is consistently caustic about the Yorkes, the political enemies of his father, as he himself cautions his readers (*Mem. Geo. II* iii. 161).

14. John Montagu (1718–92), 4th E. of Sandwich; politician.

15. Thomas Watson-Wentworth (ca 1690–1750), cr. (1728) Bn Malton, (1733) E. of Malton, and (1746) M. of Rockingham.

16. Sir Charles 'lived at "The White House" (subsequently "old Windsor Lodge" and now "The Grange"), Old Windsor' (T. Eustace Harwood, *Windsor Old and New*, 1929, p. 316).

17. 'Hurley House . . . stands at the south end of the village' of Hurley, Berks, perhaps 10 miles from Windsor (*Vict. Co. Hist. Berks* iii. 152).

18. Missing.

19. Probably 'The Beauties, An Epistle to Mr Eckardt the Painter,' written in July, and 'handed about till it got into print, very incorrectly' ('Short Notes'; *Horace Walpole's Fugitive Verses*, ed. W. S. Lewis, New York, 1931, pp. 23–33).

To Montagu, Tuesday 5 August 1746

Arlington Street, Aug. 5, 1746.

Dear George,

THOUGH I can't this week accept your invitation, I can prove to you that I am most desirous of passing my time with you, and therefore *en attendant* Hurley House, if you can find me out any clean little house in Windsor, ready furnished, that is not absolutely in the middle of the town, but near you, I shall be glad to take it for three or four months.[1] I have been about Sir Robert Rich's,[2] but they will only *sell* it.

I am as far from guessing why they send Sandwich in embassy, as you are: and when I recollect of what various materials our late ambassadors have been composed, Lord Stair,[3] Lord Granville, and Lord Chesterfield, I can only say, *ex quovis ligno fit Mercurius.*[4]

Murray[5] has certainly been discovering, and warrants are out, but I don't yet know who are to be their prize. I begin to think that the ministry really had no intelligence till now: I before thought they had, but durst not use it. Apropos to *not daring,* I went t'other night to look at my poor favourite Chelsea,[6] for the little mad Newcastle[7] is gone to be dipped in the sea;[8] in one of the rooms is a bed for her

1. Gray writing to Wharton from Stoke says: 'Mr W. I have seen a good deal, and shall do a good deal more, I suppose, for he is looking for a house somewhere about Windsor during the summer' (*Gray's Corr.* i. 236).

2. Sir Robert Rich (1685–1768), 4th Bt; field marshal, 1757.

3. John Dalrymple (1673–1747), 2d E. of Stair; Ambassador to Paris 1715–20. Lord Granville went to The Hague on a special mission in 1742, and Chesterfield was Ambassador there 1728–32. HW's apparent derogation of their diplomatic abilities seems quite unjustified, and was no doubt inspired by the fact that all three were determined opponents, and contributed largely to the downfall, of Sir Robert Walpole.

4. 'Ex quovis ligno non fit Mercurius'— you cannot make (i.e. carve) a Mercury out of every block of wood; attributed to Pythagoras by Apuleius, *Apologia,* c. 43, and Iamblichus, *De Vita Pythagorica,* c. 34; see N&Q 1927, clii. 410–11.

5. John Murray (1715–77), of Broughton; 7th Bt, 1770; Prince Charles's secretary during the rebellion; had turned King's evidence (i.e. 'discovering').

6. The house in Chelsea which Sir Robert Walpole owned from 1722 to his death and which at the date of this letter was occupied by the Duke of Newcastle. It is today part of Chelsea Hospital (*London Past & Present* i. 379; *The Survey of London,* vol. ii, Parish of Chelsea pt i, ed. Walter H. Godfrey, 1909, pp. 3–4).

7. Lady Henrietta Godolphin (d. 1776), m. (1717) Thomas Pelham-Holles, 1st D. of Newcastle. It does not appear that she was actually mad.

8. See John Anderson, *Practical Essay on the Good and Bad Effects of Sea-water and Sea-bathing,* 1795, p. 41: 'In *nervous* and *hypochondriacal* disorders, in which the mind is feeble, irritable, and unstable, the sea-bath, amusements, exercise, and the air of Thanet, have happy effects.'

Duke, and a press-bed for his footman, for he never dares lie alone, and till he was married had always a servant set up with him.

Lady Cromartie[9] presented her petition to the King last Sunday; he was very civil to her, but would not at all give her any hopes; she swooned away as soon as he was gone. Lord Cornwallis[10] told me that her Lord weeps every time anything of his fate is mentioned to him. Old Balmerino[11] keeps up his spirits to the same pitch of gaiety. In the cell at Westminster he showed Lord Kilmarnock how he must lay his head; bid him not winch, lest the stroke should cut his skull or his shoulders, and advised him to bite his lips. As they were to return, he begged they might have another bottle together, as they should never meet any more, till—and then pointed to his neck. At getting into the coach, he said to the gaoler, 'Take care, or you will break my shins with this damned axe.' I must tell you a bon mot of George Selwyn's at the trial; he saw Bethel's[12] sharp visage looking wistfully at the rebel lords; he said, 'What a shame it is to turn her face to the prisoners till they are condemned.' If you have a mind for a true foreign idea; one of the foreign ministers said at the trial to another, 'Vraiment cela est auguste'—'Oui,' replied t'other, 'cela est auguste, cela est vrai;—mais cela n'est pas royale!'

I am assured that the old Countess of Errol[13] made her son Lord Kilmarnock go into the Rebellion on pain of disinheriting him. I don't know whether I told you that the man at the tennis court protests he has known him dine with the man that sells pamphlets at Story's Gate,[14] and says he, 'He would often have been glad if I would have taken him home to dinner.' He was certainly so poor that in one of his wife's[15] intercepted letters, she tells him she has plagued their

9. Isabel Gordon (ca 1705–69), m. (1724) George Mackenzie (ca 1703–66), 3d E. of Cromarty. Her efforts to save him from execution were successful, thanks to her pregnancy, and to the intercession of the Prince of Wales (see HW to Mann 12 Aug. 1746).

10. Charles Cornwallis (1700–62), 5th Bn Cornwallis; cr. (1753) E. Cornwallis; Constable of the Tower.

11. '[Balmerino] shows an intrepidity that some ascribe to real courage and some to brandy' (Gray's Corr. i. 234–5).

12. Unidentified. Mrs Elizabeth Montagu mentions the 'woe-begone Mrs Bethell' in 1756 (Letters, ed. Matthew Mon-

tagu, 1809–13, iv. 13). The edge of the executioner's axe was turned to the condemned after sentence of death had been pronounced.

13. Lady Mary Hay (d. 1758), Countess of Erroll suo jure, 1718; m. (1722) Alexander Falconer. She was not Lord Kilmarnock's mother, but his wife's aunt; his son James succeeded to her title and estates.

14. Neither man has been identified. Story's Gate is in Birdcage Walk, St James's Park.

15. Lady Anne Livingston (1709–47), m. (1724) William Boyd, 4th E. of Kilmarnock.

steward for a fortnight for money, and can get but three shillings. Can one help pitying such distress? I am vastly softened too about Old Balmerino's relapse, for his pardon[16] was only granted him to engage his brother's vote at the election of Scotch peers.

My Lord Chancellor has had a thousand pound in present for his High Stewardship, and has got the reversion of Clerk of the Crown (twelve hundred a year) for his second son[17]—what a long time it will be, before his posterity are drove into rebellion for want, like Lord Kilmarnock!

The Duke gave his ball last night to Peggy Banks at Vauxhall; it was to pique my Lady Rochford,[18] in return for the Prince of Hesse.[19] I saw the company get into their barges at Whitehall Stairs, as I was going myself, and just then passed by two City Companies in their great barges, who had been a swan-hopping;[20] they laid by and played, *God save our noble King;*[21] and all together it was a mighty pretty show. When they came to Vauxhall there were assembled above five-and-twenty hundred people, besides crowds without; they huzzaed, and surrounded him so, that he was forced to retreat into the ballroom. He was very near being drowned t'other night going from Ranelagh to Vauxhall by a politeness of Lord Cathcart's,[22] who step-

16. For his part in the '15. The pardon was granted in 1733 at the intercession, according to DNB, of his father, the 4th Baron, and it was doubtless to engage the father's vote in the election of 1734 that it was granted, for Balmerino's brother James Elphinstone (1675–1746), 5th Bn Balmerino, did not succeed to the title until the father's death in 1736, and therefore was not eligible to vote for representative peers at the time of the pardon.

17. Hon. Charles Yorke (1722–70), Attorney-General 1762–3, 1765–6; Lord Chancellor 1770 (for only three days).

18. Lucy Young (ca 1723–73), m. (1740) William Henry Nassau de Zulestein, 4th E. of Rochford. 'Rather a remarkable person; a lady of free manners, who said and did whatever she pleased; but as her husband took no exceptions and she was clever and entertaining, she kept her place in general society' (Lady Louisa Stuart, *Notes on Jesse's Selwyn,* ed. W. S. Lewis, New York, 1928, p. 10). Casanova, in England ca 1763, records that 'this lady's gallantries were innumerable, and furnished a fresh topic of conversation

every day' (*Memoirs,* tr. Arthur Machen, 1922, ix. 172); see HW to Mann 17 May 1749.

19. A conquest which cost her the Duke's affection; see HW to Mann 17 May 1749. Furthermore, when Boswell visited Hesse-Cassel in 1764, the French minister there told him that 'Il y avait une dame d'honneur anglaise qui a contribué beaucoup de faire la séparation entre son Altesse et une Princesse [his wife] qu'il adorait' (James Boswell, *Private Papers,* ed. Scott and Pottle, Mt Vernon, N.Y., 1928–34, iii. 144). The 'dame d'honneur' was doubtless Lady Rochford.

20. A corruption of swan-upping: notching the beaks of the young swans to establish their ownership (OED).

21. 'God Save the King,' the beginnings of which are obscure, came into popularity following the early success of the rebels in Sept. 1745, when it was 'sung at both Playhouses' (GM Oct. 1745, xv. 552; Sir George Grove, *Dictionary of Music*).

22. Charles Schaw Cathcart (1721–76), 9th Bn Cathcart; the Duke's aide-de-camp at Fontenoy.

ping on the side of the boat to lend his arm, overset it and both fell into the water up to their chins.

I have not yet got Sir Charles's ode;[23] when I have; you shall see it—here are my own lines.[24] Goodnight.

Yours ever,

H.W.

To Montagu, ca Friday 8 August 1746

Undated; reasons for placing the letter here were given by Mrs Toynbee in N&Q 1899, 9th ser. iv. 243–4; she concludes that it was written while HW was in the neighbourhood of Windsor house-hunting at this time.

> [Eton, ca August 8, 1746].
> The Christopher[1]—Lord! how great I
> used to think anybody just landed
> at the Christopher! but here are no
> boys for me to send for!

HERE am I, like Noah just returned into his old world again, with all sorts of queer feels about me—By the way the clock strikes the old cracked sound—I recollect so much, and remember so little, and want to play about, and am so afraid of my playfellows, and am ready to *shirk*[2] Ashton,[3] and can't help *making fun* of myself, and envy a *dame*[4] over the way that has just locked in her boarders, and is going to sit down in a little hot parlour to a very bad supper, so comfortably! and I could be so *jolly* a dog if I did not *fat*, which by the way is the first time the word was ever applicable to me. In short I should be *out* of all *bounds* if I was to tell you half I feel, how

23. This was Sir Charles Hanbury Williams's 'Ode on the marriage of the Duchess of Manchester to Edward Hussey, Esq., afterwards Lord Beaulieu,' as appears from *post* 16 August 1746 *ad fin.* It appears in Williams, *Works*, 1822, i. 90. For an extended account of the ode and the personal violence offered to Williams by Hussey and the Irish as a result of it, see Earl of Ilchester, *Life of Sir Charles Hanbury-Williams*, 1929, pp. 97–102.

24. See *ante* 2 Aug. 1746, n. 19; the copy has not been preserved.

1. A famous Eton inn which existed from the middle of the 16th to the middle of the 19th century; see *Vict. Co. Hist. Bucks* iii. 263–4; any history of Eton *passim;* for a drawing of 1828, Sir Henry C. Maxwell-Lyte, *History of Eton College*, 1911, p. 295.

2. 'At Eton: to avoid meeting (a master, a sixth-form boy) when out of bounds' (OED, first illustration 1821).

3. Thomas Ashton became a fellow of Eton 10 Dec. 1745.

4. A boardinghouse keeper; see John S. Farmer, *Public School Word-Book*, 1900.

young again I am one minute and how old the next—but do come
and feel with me when you will tomorrow—for tonight I have so bad
a pen, that you will think I deserve to be *flogged*. Adieu! If I don't
compose myself a little more before Sunday morning when Ashton
is to preach, I shall certainly *be in a bill*[5] for *laughing at church;* but
how to help it, to see him in the pulpit, when the last time I saw him
here, was standing up *funking*[6] over against a *conduct*[7] to be cate-
chized![8]

Goodnight. Yours etc.,

HOR. WALPOLE

To Montagu, Monday 11 August 1746

Arlington Street, Aug. 11, 1746.

Dear George,

I HAVE seen Mr Jordan[1] and taken his house[2] at forty guineas a
year, but I am to pay taxes. Shall I now accept your offer of being
at the trouble of giving orders for the airing it? I have desired the
landlord will order the key to be delivered to you, and Ashton will
assist you. Furniture I find I have in abundance,[3] which I shall send
down immediately, but shall not be able to be at Windsor at the
quivering dame's[4] before tomorrow se'nnight, as the rebel lords are
not to be executed till next Monday: I shall stay till that is over,
though I don't believe I shall see it. Lord Cromartie is reprieved for
a pardon: if wives and children become an argument for saving rebels, they will cease to be a reason against their going into rebellion.
Lady Caroline Fitzroy's[4a] execution[5] is certainly tonight; I dare say

---

5. To be reported to the Headmaster
for punishment (Farmer, op. cit., n. 4).

6. 'To flinch or shrink through fear'
(OED, as Oxford slang, 1743).

7. 'Still used as the name of the chap-
lains at Eton College' (OED; otherwise obsolete in this sense).

8. 'It was the practice on a certain number of Sundays in the year for the first six
collegers in the fifth form to stand up and
say their catechism at some period of the
service' (information from Mr R. A. Austen-Leigh and Mr Leonard Whibley).

1. Not identified.

2. Within the precincts of the castle
('Short Notes'). It was possibly one of the

Canons' houses, now No. 4, the Cloisters,
where a chimney-piece bears the motto
'Homo homini lupus' (Plautus, *Asinaria*,
II. iv. 88), which Montagu later suggested
to Mann when the latter was seeking a
motto (HW to Mann 22 April 1755; information kindly furnished through Mr
O. F. Morshead by Dr A. V. Baillie,
K.C.V.O., Dean of Windsor).

3. Which HW had inherited from Sir
Robert.

4. Possibly a reference to a particular
dame in Montagu's and HW's time at
Eton.

4a. Crossed out in MS and supplied by
another hand.

5. Her marriage.

she will follow Lord Balmerino's advice to Lord Kilmarnock and not winch.[6]

Lord Sandwich has made Mr Keith[7] his secretary—I don't believe the founder of your race, the great Quu of Habiculeo,[8] would have chosen his secretary from California.[9]

I would willingly return the civilities and pasties you laid upon me at Windsor[10]—do command me—in what can I serve you? Shall I get you an earldom? Don't think it will be any trouble; there is nothing easier or cheaper—Lord Hobart[11] and Lord Fitzwilliam[12] are both to be earls tomorrow, the former of Buckingham, the latter by his already title.—I suppose Lord Malton will be a duke—he has had no new peerage this fortnight. Adieu! My compliments to the virtuous ladies, Arabella and Hounsibella[13] Quus.

Yours ever,

H. W.

PS. Here is an order for the key.[14]

To Montagu, Saturday 16 August 1746

Arlington Street, Aug. 16, 1746.

Dear George,

I SHALL be with you on Tuesday night, and since you are so good as to be my Rowland White,[1] must beg my apartment at the quivering dame's may be aired for me. My caravan sets out with all

6. See *ante* 5 Aug. 1746.

7. Robert Keith (d. 1774), Ambassador at Vienna 1748–58; St Petersburg, 1758–62.

8. Probably Charles Montagu (1661–1715), cr. (1700) Bn Halifax, (1714) E. of Halifax; statesman and financial expert; Montagu's great-uncle. 'Quu' is the same as 'Cu' (*ante* 22 May 1746), slang for Montagu. 'Habiculeo' in varying forms is similarly used throughout the correspondence for Halifax, and was no doubt inspired by the Swiftian nomenclature used in the *Gentleman's Magazine* and elsewhere during this period to identify the speakers in Parliamentary debates, whose names could not be printed without running afoul of the law.

9. The allusion, if there is one, is unexplained.

10. HW's visit was no doubt recent, when house-hunting.

11. John Hobart (ca 1695–1756), cr. (1728) Bn Hobart; (1746) E. of Buckinghamshire; brother of Lady Suffolk, who had been the King's mistress.

12. William Fitzwilliam (1720–56), 3d E. Fitzwilliam (Irish); cr. (1746) E. Fitzwilliam (G.B.).

13. I.e., Henrietta.

14. To the new house; the order is missing.

———

1. A steward and correspondent of the Sidney family; HW would have read his letters in Arthur Collins, *Sidney Papers* (*ante* 22 May 1746, n. 6).

my household stuff on Monday, but I have heard nothing of your sister's hamper, nor do I know how to send the bantams by it, but will leave them here till I am more settled under the shade of my own mulberry tree.

I have been this morning at the Tower, and passed under the new heads at Temple Bar,[2] where people make a trade of letting spying-glasses at a halfpenny a look. Old Lovat[3] arrived last night; I saw Murray, Lord Derwenwater,[4] Lord Traquair,[5] Lord Cromartie and his son,[6] and the Lord Provost[7] at their respective windows. The other two wretched lords are in dismal towers; and they have stopped up one of old Balmerino's windows, because he talked to the populace, and now he has only one, which looks directly upon all the scaffolding. They brought in the dead warrant at his dinner, his wife fainted;[8] he said, 'Lieutenant, with your damned warrant you have spoiled my Lady's stomach.' He has wrote a sensible letter to the Duke to beg his intercession, and the Duke has given it to the King; but gave a much colder answer to Duke Hamilton,[9] who went to beg it for Lord Kilmarnock; he told him the affair was in the King's hands, and that he had nothing to do with it. Lord Kilmarnock who has hitherto kept up his spirits, grows extremely terrified.

2. Nine officers of the Manchester regiment formed for Prince Charles were hanged, drawn, and quartered 30 July on Kennington Common. The heads of two, Francis Townley, commander of the regiment, and George Fletcher, were exposed on Temple Bar (GM 1746, xvi. 383, 437) where they remained until they fell, once giving occasion to an epigram of Goldsmith's (Boswell, *Johnson* ii. 238). Cunningham (ii. 50, n. 3) quotes a newspaper of 1 April 1772: 'Yesterday one of the rebels' heads on Temple Bar fell down,—there is only one head now remaining' (*London Chronicle* 31 March–2 April 1772).

3. Simon Fraser (ca 1667–1747), beheaded after a long career of crime and intrigue. 'Friday 15. Lord Lovat arrived at the Tower in an open landau drawn with six horses, guarded by a party of Ligonier's horse, and accompanied in the landau by an officer' (GM 1746, xvi. 438).

4. Charles Radcliffe (1693–1746), titular E. of Derwentwater; beheaded 8 Dec., having escaped from Newgate in 1716 while

under sentence of death (DNB, *sub* Radcliffe, James).

5. Charles Stewart (d. 1764), 5th E. of Traquair; discharged in 1748; 'a keen Jacobite' (Bruce Seton and Jean Arnot, *Prisoners of the '45*, 1928–9, iii. 376–9; *Scots Peerage*, 1904–10, viii. 407).

6. John Mackenzie (1727–89), styled Lord McLeod, was pardoned in 1748 for his part in the rebellion. He entered the service of the King of Sweden, who made him Count Cromarty, returned to England 1777, and became (1783) a Maj. Gen. His estates were restored in 1784.

7. Archibald Stewart (d. 1780), Lord Provost of Edinburgh; tried at Edinburgh Oct. 1747 for neglect of duty and misbehaviour, and acquitted. He was later a merchant in London (*Grenville Papers*, ed. William James Smith, 1852–3, i. 71–2; GM 1780, l. 51).

8. Margaret Chalmers (ca 1709–65), m. Arthur Elphinstone, 6th Bn Balmerino.

9. James Hamilton (1724–58), 6th D. of Hamilton.

It will be difficult to make you believe to what heights of affectation or extravagance my Lady Townshend[9a] carries her passion for my Lord Kilmarnock, whom she never saw but at the bar of his trial, and was smit with his falling shoulders. She has been under his window, sends messages to him, has got his dog and his snuff-box, has taken lodgings out of town for tomorrow and Monday night, and then goes to Greenwich, forswears conversing with the bloody English, and has taken a French master. She insisted on Lord Hervey's[10] promising her he would not sleep a whole night for my Lord Kilmarnock, and in return, says she, 'Never trust me more if I am not as yellow as a jonquil for him.'[11] She said gravely t'other day, 'Since I saw my Lord Kilmarnock, I really think no more of Sir Harry Nisbett,[12] than if there was no such man in the world.' But of all her flights, yesterday was the strongest. George Selwyn dined with her, and not thinking her affliction so entirely serious as she pretends, talked rather jokingly of the execution. She burst out into a flood of tears and rage, told him she now believed all his father and mother had said of him,[12a] and with a thousand other reproaches flung upstairs. George coolly took Mrs Dorcas her woman,[13] and made her sit down to finish the bottle. 'And pray, Sir,' said Dorcas, 'do you think my Lady will be prevailed upon to let me go see the execution? I have a friend that has promised to take care of me, and I can lie in the Tower the night before'—My Lady has quarrelled with Sir Charles Windham for calling the two lords *malefactors*—The idea seems to be general, for 'tis said Lord Cromartie is to be *transported*—which diverts me for the dignity of the peerage. The ministry really gave it as a reason against their casting lots for pardon, that it was below their dignity. I did not know but that might proceed from Balmerino's not being an earl, and therefore now their hand is in, would have them make him one.

9a. Crossed out in the MS and supplied by another hand.

10. George William Hervey (1721–75), 2d Bn Hervey, 1743; 2d E. of Bristol, 1751.

11. 'I imagine her ladyship [Lady Townshend] is as yellow as a jonquil' (Sir William Maynard to Selwyn 22 Aug. 1746; Jesse, *Selwyn* i. 106–7).

12. Sir Harry Nisbet (d. 11 Oct. 1746), 4th Bt. 'A distinguished officer and remarkably handsome, but fell at an early age' (Alexander Carlyle, *Autobiography*, 1860, p. 30).

12a. 'To be intimate with George Selwyn's own family was not the way to hear much good of him' (Lady Louisa Stuart, *Notes on Jesse's Selwyn*, ed. W. S. Lewis, New York, 1928, p. 4). His father was Col. John Selwyn (d. 1751); for his mother, see *post* i. 104, n. 8.

13. See *Letters to Henry Fox Lord Holland*, ed. Earl of Ilchester, 1915, p. 262 (Selwyn to Holland 24 July 1766), where there is a reference to 'Dorcas's niece, who succeeded her aunt in the office of *femme de chambre*' to Lady Townshend.

You will see in the papers the second great victory at Placentia.[14] There are papers pasted up in several parts of the town threatening your cousin Sandwich's head if he makes a dishonourable peace.[15]

I will bring you down Sir Charles Williams's new ode on the Manchester.[16] Adieu!

Yours ever,
H.W.

To MONTAGU, Monday 3 November 1746

Arlington Street, Nov. 3, 1746.

Dear George,

DON'T imagine I have already broke through all my wholesome resolutions and country schemes, and that I am given up body and soul to London for the winter: I shall be with you by the end of the week, but just now I am under the maidenhead-palpitation of an author; my epilogue[1] will, I believe be spoke tomorrow night, and I flatter myself I shall have no faults to answer for but what are in it, for I have kept secret whose it is.[2] It is now gone to be licensed, but as the Lord Chamberlain is mentioned,[3] though rather to his honour, it is possible it may be refused, as they are apt to think at the office, that the Duke of Grafton can't be mentioned but in ridicule.

Don't expect news, for I know no more than a newspaper; Ashton

14. After an unsuccessful campaign, the French and Spanish forces under Maillebois managed to retreat across the Po (31 July O.S.), though hard pressed by the Austrians (Spenser Wilkinson, *The Defence of Piedmont 1742–1748*, 1927, pp. 257–8). Announcement of the victory appeared in *London Gazette* 15 Aug. 1746.

15. Sandwich, as plenipotentiary at Breda, was engaged in negotiations which concluded with the Peace of Aix-la-Chapelle in 1748.

16. See *ante* 5 Aug. 1746, n. 23.

1. *Epilogue to Tamerlane*, 'Spoken by Mrs Pritchard, in the Character of the Comic Muse, November 4, 1746' at Drury Lane. Nicholas Rowe's 'Tamerlane is always acted on the 4th and 5th of November, the anniversaries of King William's birth and landing' (HW's notes, *Works* i. 25, 26).

2. It 'succeeded to flatter me' (HW to Mann 12 Nov. 1746). Dodsley's edition of it appeared 5 Nov., and he reprinted it in his *Collection*, 1748, ii. 327. It was reprinted in *The Foundling Hospital for Wit*, 1747, p. 21, in HW's *Fugitive Pieces*, 1758, p. 36, and in *Works* i. 25. Nothing is known of the circumstances of HW's writing the piece, but it was, presumably, inspired by Dodsley, a friend of Mrs Pritchard and of Rich the manager of Drury Lane.

3. 'For ah! my sons, what freedom for the stage,
When bigotry with sense shall battle wage?
When monkish laureats only wear the bays,
Inquisitors lord chamberlains of plays?' (*Works* i. 26.)

would have wrote if there were anything to tell you. Is it news that my Lord Rochford[4] is an oaf? He has got a set of plate buttons for his birthday clothes with the Duke's head in every one—Sure my good Lady[5] carries her art too far to make him so great a dupe!

How do all the comets? Has Miss Harriot found out any more ways at solitaire? Has Cloe[6] left off evening prayer on account of the damp evenings? How do Miss Rice's cold and coachman? Is Miss Granville better? Has Mrs Masham[7] made a brave hand of this bad season, and lived upon carcasses like any vampire? Adieu! I am just going to see Mrs Muscovy[8] and will be sure not to laugh if my old Lady[9] should talk of Mr Draper's[10] white skin and tittle his bosom like Queen Bess.[11]

Yours ever,

H.W.

To Montagu, Thursday 2 July 1747

Arlington Street, July 2d, 1747.

Dear George,

THOUGH we have no great reason to triumph, as we have certainly been defeated, yet the French have as certainly bought their victory[1] dear: indeed what would be very dear to us, is not so much to them.[2] However their least loss is twelve thousand men;[3] as

---

4. William Henry Nassau de Zulestein (1717–81), 4th E. of Rochford.
5. Lady Rochford (see *ante* 5 Aug. 1746, n. 18).
6. Unidentified.
7. Henrietta Winnington (d. 1761), m. (1736) Hon. Samuel Masham, 2d Bn Masham, 1758. She was a sister of HW's friend Thomas Winnington; HW believed her responsible for his death (see HW to Mann 25 April 1746).
8. Hon. Mrs George Boscawen (*post* 28 Aug. 1752). The nickname has not been explained.
9. Possibly Viscountess Falmouth (ibid.).
10. Possibly William Draper (*post* 14 Oct. 1760).
11. In his *Memoirs* (Bannatyne Club edn, 1827, p. 120), Sir James Melville tells of seeing Sidney made Earl of Leicester. As he knelt before Queen Elizabeth 'sche culd not refrain from putting hir hand in

his nek to kittle him smylingly.' Both 'tittle' and 'kittle' = tickle (OED).

---

1. Saxe defeated an allied force under the Duke of Cumberland at Laffeldt, 21 June O.S.; see Fortescue, *British Army* ii. 159–63.
2. Modern estimates place the population of England and Wales in 1750 at about 6,250,000; see Gonner, 'Population of England in the Eighteenth Century' in Royal Statistical Society, *Journal* 1913, lxxvi. 261–303; Grosvenor T. Griffith, *Population Problems of the Age of Malthus*, Cambridge, 1926, pp. 1–20. The population of 18th-century France, by contemporary estimates, was 23–4 million (Henri Sée, *Economic and Social Conditions in France during the 18th Century*, tr. Edwin H. Zeydel, New York, 1927, p. 8).
3. 'Not less than ten thousand' (Fortescue, *British Army* ii. 163).

our least loss is five thousand.[4] The truth of the whole is, that the Duke was determined to fight at all events, which the French who determined not to fight but at great odds, took advantage of: his Royal Highness's valour has shown extremely, but at the expense of his judgment. Harry Conway, whom Nature always designed for a hero of a romance, and who is *déplacé* in ordinary life, did wonders, but was overpowered, and flung down, where one French hussar held him by the hair, while another was going to stab him: at that instant an English sergeant with a soldier came up, and killed the latter, but was instantly killed himself; the soldier attacked the other, and Mr Conway escaped; but was afterwards taken prisoner: is since released on parole,[5] and may come home to console his fair widow,[6] whose brother Harry Campbell[7] is certainly killed, to the great concern of all widows who want consolation. The French have lost the Prince of Monaco,[8] the Comte de Baviere,[9] natural brother to the last emperor,[10] and many officers of great rank. The French king[10a] saw the whole through a spying-glass from a Hampstead Hill,[11] environed with twenty thousand men.[12] Our Guards did shamefully, and many officers.[13] The King had a line from Huske[14] in Zealand on the Friday night to tell him we were defeated; of his son not a word: judge of his anxiety till three o'clock on Saturday! Lord Sandwich had a letter

4. The allied loss was about six thousand (ibid. 162).

5. See Stephen Poyntz to HW 1 July 1747.

6. Caroline Campbell (1721–1803), m. (1) (1739) Charles Bruce, 3d E. of Ailesbury (d. 1747); m. (2) (Dec. 1747) Hon. Henry Seymour Conway.

7. Capt. Henry Campbell, 2d surviving son of John Campbell of Mamore, 4th D. of Argyll 1761 (Scots Peerage, 1904–10, i. 384); Lt (Capt.) in Coldstream Guards; killed at Lauffeldt, 2 July 1747.

8. Honoré-Camille-Léonor Goyon-de-Matignon de Grimaldi [Honoré III] (1720–95); his horse was shot under him, but he escaped (Nouv. Biog. Gén., incorrect on his date of death; du Deffand ii. 71n).

9. Emanuel Franz Josef, Marquis de Villacerf, called Comte de Bavière, natural son of Maximilian Emanuel, Elector of Bavaria; Lt-Gen. in the French service; d. 2 July 1747 (La Chesnaye-Desbois and Badier, Dictionnaire de la Noblesse, 1863–76, ii. 593; Wilhelm Karl, Prinz von Isen-

burg, Stammtafeln, Berlin, 1936, i. table 28).

10. Charles Albert (1697–1745), Elector of Bavaria; Emperor (1742), as Charles VII (Allgemeine Deutsche Biographie, Leipzig, 1875–1912, xv. 219).

10a. Louis XV (1710–74).

11. That is, a hill which stood in relation to the battle as Hampstead Hill stands in relation to London.

12. 'The King of France went up the hill
    With twenty thousand men;
    The King of France came down the hill,
    And ne'er went up again.'

(Old Tarleton's Song, from a tract entitled Pigges Corantoe, or Newes from the North, 1642; see Burton Stevenson, Home Book of Quotations, New York, 1937, p. 719.)

13. No similar disparagement of the conduct of the troops has been found.

14. Lt-Gen. John Huske (1692–1761), Gen. 1756 (DNB).

in his pocket all the while, and kept it there, which said the Duke was well.

We flourish at sea, have taken great part of the Domingo fleet,[15] and I suppose shall have more lords.[16] The *Countess*[17] touched twelve thousand[18] for Sir Jacob Bouverie's[19] coronet.

I know nothing of my own election,[20] but suppose it is over: as little of Rigby's, and conclude it lost.[21] For franks,[22] I suppose they don't begin till the whole is complete. My compliments to your brother and sisters.

I am, dear George,

Yours most sincerely,

Hor. Walpole

To Montagu, Thursday 1 October 1747

Arlington Street, Oct. 1, 1747.

Dear George,

I WISH I could have answered your invitation from the Tigress's[1] with my person, but it was impossible; I wish your farmer would answer invitations with the persons of more hens and fewer cocks, for I am raising a breed, and not recruits. The time before he sent two to one, and he has done so again.

15. On 20 June a British squadron of six ships put to flight four French and captured forty-eight of the convoy (GM 1747, xvii. 334; William Laird Clowes, *The Royal Navy*, 1897–1903, iii. 283).

16. After the battle off Cape Finisterre on 3 May (ibid. 125–6), Anson was created Lord Anson, Baron of Sotherton. No honours seem to have followed this engagement.

17. Of Yarmouth.

18. As a bribe; see HW to Mann 26 June 1747. Sir John Shelley told Lord Egmont that the King (in 1741) gave Lady Yarmouth 'the making of some Lords' to satisfy her demands for £30,000. Mr Fox (cr. E. of Ilchester) and Mr Bromley (cr. Bn Montfort) were bidden by Sir Robert Walpole to 'wait on the Countess, and with her they settled the sum; but how much they paid, he did not know. . . . Sir John added that it cost this Lord

Romney's father 5000l only to be made a Lord' [in 1716] (Historical Manuscripts Commission, *Diary of the First Earl of Egmont* iii (1923). 259–60).

19. Sir Jacob Bouverie (1694–1761), 2d Bt; cr. (29 June 1747) Vct Folkestone.

20. HW's return for Callington is dated 3 July (Great Britain, House of Commons, *Members of Parliament*, pt ii [1878]. 98). This borough had belonged to the Rolle family, and came under Walpole control through Margaret Rolle, Countess of Orford, q.v. (Lewis B. Namier, *Structure of Politics at the Accession of George III*, 1929, ii. 375).

21. Rigby was returned for Sudbury.

22. Franking privileges of M.P.'s ordinarily extended forty days before and after each session (William Lewins, *Her Majesty's Mails*, 1865, p. 98).

———

1. Mrs Henry Talbot.

I had a letter from Mr Conway,[2] who is piteously going into prison again; our great secretary[3] has let the time slip for executing the cartel, and the French have reclaimed their prisoners. The Duke is coming back—I fear his candles are gone to bed to Admiral Vernon's![4] He has been ill;[5] there are whisperings, as if his head had been more disordered than his body. Marshal Saxe sent him Cardinal Polignac's *Anti-Lucretius*[6] to send to Lord Chesterfield[7]—if he won't let him be a general, at least 'tis hard to reduce him to a courier.

When I saw you at *Kyk in de Pot*,[8] I forgot to tell you that seven more volumes of the Journals[9] are delivering: there's employment for Moreland.[10] I go back to Kyk in de Pot tomorrow: did you dislike it so much, that you could not bring yourself to persuade your brother to try it with you for a day or two? I shall be there till the birthday,[11] if you will come.

George Selwyn says people send to Lord Pembroke to know how the bridge rested.[12] You know George never thinks but *à la tête tranchée:* he came to town t'other day to have a tooth drawn, and told the man that he would drop his handkerchief for[13] the signal.

My compliments to your family; I am

Yours ever,

H.W.

2. The letter is missing.
3. Newcastle.
4. Admiral Edward Vernon (1684–1757), who, after a period of great popularity following his capture of Porto Bello in 1739, fell into disfavour and was cashiered in 1746 for writing two pamphlets attacking the Admiralty. HW means that Cumberland is now as unpopular as Vernon.
5. The remainder of this sentence has been scored through but is legible.
6. Melchior de Polignac (1661–1742), Cardinal, diplomatist and author. The *Anti-Lucretius,* a Latin poem in two volumes, published 1745, was an attack upon the naturalistic ideas borrowed from Lucretius by Bayle (*Nouv. Biog. Gén.*).
7. In a letter to Sir Everard Fawkener, 25 Aug. 1747, Chesterfield encloses a note to the Duke of Cumberland: 'The packet which His Royal Highness had received from the French Army directed to me, contained nothing but the Anti-Lucretius

of Cardinal de Polignac, and a civil letter to me from Abbé de la Ville, who transmitted it' (Earl of Chesterfield, *Letters,* ed. Bonamy Dobrée, 1932, iii. 990–1).
8. Kyk in de Pot was an outlying fortress at Bergen-op-Zoom, the siege of which by the French was arousing general excitement (see GM, *passim*). HW refers to Strawberry Hill, which he had leased in May 1747 (HW to Mann 5 June 1747), but which he did not yet call by that name. The date of Montagu's visit is not known.
9. Not identified.
10. A sort of agent of Montagu's, until he joined the army.
11. The King's birthday was 30 Oct.
12. Henry Herbert (ca 1689–1750), 9th E. of Pembroke; a zealous amateur architect; promoted the construction of Westminster Bridge, completed in 1750. One of its piers had settled 16 inches, necessitating considerable repairs (DNB; GM 1747, xvii. 445).
13. HW here repeats 'for.'

View of Twickenham from Strawberry Hill.

Muntz delin.

VIEW OF RADNOR HOUSE AND TWICKENHAM FROM STRAWBERRY HILL, BY MÜNTZ

To Montagu, Monday ca 5 October 1747

Dated by the references to Lord Granville and Conway.

Twickenham, Monday [ca Oct. 5, 1747].

YOU are desired to have business to hinder you from going to Northampton, and you are desired to have none to hinder you from coming to Twickenham. The autumn is in great beauty, my Lord Radnor's[1] baby houses[2] lay eggs every day, and promise new swarms, Mrs Chandler[3] treads, but don't lay, and the neighbouring dowagers order their visiting coaches before sunset[4]—can you resist such a landscape? Only send me a line, that I may be sure to be ready for you, for I go to London now and then to buy coals.

I believe there cannot be a word of truth in Lord Granville's going to Berlin;[5] by the clumsiness of the thought, I should take it for ministerial wit—and so, and so.

The Twickenham Alabouches[6] say that Legge is to marry the eldest Pelhamine infanta.[7] He loves a minister's daughter[8]—I shall not wonder if he intends it, but can the parents?[9] Mr Conway mentioned

1. John Robartes (1686?–1757), 4th E. of Radnor. His house (see *post* ca 6 June 1756) was across the road from SH on the north.

2. His toy houses in the garden. 'A View of Twickenham,' 1756, by HW's 'resident painter,' J. H. Müntz, engraved by J. Green, shows the house with several exotic outbuildings, a Chinese pagoda among them; see also Müntz's drawing of 1758 illustrated here, and, especially for the interior decoration, *Burlington Magazine*, Nov. 1937, lxxi. 168.

3. Probably wife of the 'Mr Chandler of Teddington' from whom HW bought 'a piece of land next the nursery' in 1749 (*SH Accounts* 2).

4. That is, to get home from where they had been dining, through fear of the dark and possible robberies.

5. 'Yesterday the Right Hon. the Earl of Granville waited on his Majesty at Court; who at the same time appointed him Ambassador Extraordinary to the Court of Berlin, on a commission of the greatest importance' (*St James's Evening Post* 26–9 Sept. 1747). The story seems to have been groundless.

6. À la bouche, i.e. gossips.

7. Frances Pelham (1728–1804), eld. dau. of Henry Pelham, and for many years a prominent figure in London society. She would have married Lord March (later Duke of Queensberry), but her father forbade the match. Her passion for gambling dissipated a fortune of £70,000. Many stories are told of her ungovernable temper and tearful card-playing (see Lady Louisa Stuart, *Notes on Jesse's Selwyn*, ed. W. S. Lewis, New York, 1928, pp. 24–27; Elizabeth, Duchess of Northumberland, *Diaries of a Duchess*, ed. James Greig, 1926, pp. 44, 54; Wraxall, *Memoirs* iv. 358; Joseph Farington, *Diary*, ed. James Greig, 1922–28, i. 92; Lady Mary Coke, *Journals, passim*).

8. Legge, during Sir Robert Walpole's lifetime, had wished to marry Lady Mary Walpole (see HW to Mann 26 Jan. 1748). He did not succeed in marrying an heiress until 29 Aug. 1750 when he married the Hon. Mary Stawel (cr. (1760) Baroness Stawel), the only daughter and heiress of Edward, 4th Bn Stawel.

9. For her mother, see *post* i. 128, n. 26.

nothing to me but of the prisoners of the last battle; and I hope it ext<ends> no farther,[9] but I vow I don't see why it shoul<d> not. Adieu!

Yours etc.,

H.W.

To Montagu, Wednesday 18 May 1748

Not in Kimbolton MSS. Printed in Letters . . . Walpole to . . . Montagu *(Works vi), 1818, p. 40, from which text it has been edited here. Words and names marked with an asterisk are blank in the text, and have been supplied from the key at the end of the volume.*

[London][1] May 18, 1748.

HERE I am with the poor Chutehed,[2] who has put on a shoe but today for the first time. He sits at the receipt of custom,[3] and one passes most part of the day here; the other part I have the misfortune to pass *en* Pigwiggin.[4] The ceremony of dining[5] is not over yet: I cannot say that either the Prince or the Princess look the comelier for what has happened. The town says, my lady Anson*[6] has no chance for looking different from what she did before she was married: and they have a story of a gentleman going to the Chancellor* to assure him, that if he gave his daughter to the Admiral, he would be obliged hereafter to pronounce a sentence of dissolution of the marriage. The Chancellor* replied, that his daughter had been taught to think of the union of the soul, not of the body: the gentleman then made the same confidence to the Chancelloress*, and received much

9. Apparently a reference to the lapsed cartel of the last letter.

---

1. Presumably, from Chute's house; see second sentence below.

2. 'Chutched' in the printed original. John Chute (see *post* 11 Aug. 1748, n. 12). He was inseparable from Francis Whithed (see *post* 23 June 1750, n. 19).

3. See Matthew ix. 9, 'And as Jesus passed forth from thence, he saw a man, named Matthew, sitting at the receipt of custom . . .'

4. Horatio Walpole (1723–1809), 2d Bn Walpole of Wolterton, 1757; cr. (1806) E. of Orford, n.c. 'The name "Pigwiggin" oc-

curs as that of a fairy knight in Drayton's *Nymphidia*' (Toynbee). He had just married (12 May) Lady Rachel Cavendish (1727–1805), dau. of the 3d D. of Devonshire (the 'Princess' of the text).

5. Family dinners to celebrate the wedding; see *post* 29 March 1766.

6. Hon. Elizabeth Yorke (1725–60), dau. of Lord Chancellor Hardwicke; m. (25 April 1748) Admiral George Anson (1697–1762), cr. (1747) Bn Anson. Lord Anson's alleged impotence is frequently referred to by HW, who is rebuked by DNB for his 'indelicacy' on the theme. The Ansons had no children.

such an answer: that her daughter had been bred to submit herself to the will of God. I don't at all give you all this for true; but there is an ugly circumstance in his voyages of his not having the curiosity to see a beautiful captive, that he took on board a Spanish ship.[7] There is no record of Scipio's having been in Doctor's Commons.[8] I have been reading these voyages, and find them very silly and contradictory. He sets out with telling you that he had no soldiers sent with him but old invalids without legs or arms; and then in the middle of the book there is a whole chapter[9] to tell you, what they would have done if they had set out two months sooner; and that was no less than conquering Peru and Mexico with this disabled army. At the end there is an account[10] of the neglect he received from the viceroy of Canton, till he and forty of his sailors put out a great fire in that city, which the Chinese and five hundred firemen could not do, which he says proceeded from their awkwardness; a new character of the Chinese! He was then admitted to an audience, and found two hundred men at the gate of the city, and ten thousand in the square before the palace, all new dressed for the purpose. This is about as true as his predecessor Gulliver [pissing] out the fire at Lilliput. The King* is still windbound;[11] the fashionable bon mot is, that the Duke of Newcastle* has tied a stone about his neck and sent him to sea. The City grows furious about the peace; there is one or two very uncouth Hanover articles, besides a persuasion of a pension to the Pretender, which is so very ignominious that I don't know how to persuade myself it is true.[12] The Duke of Argyll*[13] has made them give him three

7. Richard Walter, the editor of Anson's *Voyage Round the World*, 1748, speaking of Anson's kindness to captives, tells how he allowed a Spanish lady and her two beautiful daughters to retain their apartments on a captured vessel (pp. 178–9); 'all this was done without his ever having seen the women' (p. 205).

8. See *post* 5 July 1749, n. 21.

9. Bk II, ch. xiv. HW's copy (MS Cat. H. 1. 6 moved to c. 4) was sold SH i. 158 to 'Alg. Holt White, Esq.'

10. Ibid., ch. xx. 381–3.

11. At Harwich, *en route* to Hanover, May 15–19 (GM 1748, xviii. 235).

12. Article 18 of the Peace of Aix-la-Chapelle, of which only the preliminaries had been ratified, concerns some unspecified money claims of the Elector of Hanover on the Spanish crown. It is attacked in *The Pr–t–st of the M––ch––ts of G–––t B––––n*, published about this time, and is no doubt the 'uncouth Hanoverian article' to which HW refers.

The treaty guarantees the Hanoverian succession, and does not mention the Pretender at all. The *Protest of the Merchants* objects that it did not, like the Treaty of Utrecht, contain 'a solemn . . . renunciation of the *Pretender* to the Crown of these realms, without a SUBSIDY' (p. 18), and some such notion may have been in HW's mind, doubtless derived from this pamphlet. HW's copy is now WSL.

13. Archibald Campbell (1682–1761), cr. (1706) E. of Ilay; 3d D. of Argyll 1743; political manager of Scotland for Sir Robert Walpole and others.

places for life of a thousand and twelve hundred a year for three of his court, to compensate for their making a man president of the session[14] against his inclination. The Princess of Wales has got a confirmed jaundice, but they reckon her much better. Sir Harry Calthorpe*[15] is gone mad: he walked down Pall Mall t'other day with his red ribbon tied about his hair; said he was going to the King, and would not submit to be blooded till they told him the King commanded it.

I went yesterday to see Marshal Wade's[16] house, which is selling by auction: it is worse contrived on the inside than is conceivable, all to humour the beauty of the front. My Lord Chesterfield said, that to be sure he could not live in it, but intended to take the house over against it to look at it. It is literally true, that all the direction he gave my Lord Burlington[17] was to have a place for a large cartoon of Rubens that he had bought in Flanders; but my Lord found it necessary to have so many correspondent doors, that there was no room at last for the picture; and the Marshal was forced to sell the picture to my father: it is now at Houghton.[18]

As Windsor is so charming, and particularly as you have got so agreeable a new neighbor at Frogmore,[19] to be sure you cannot wish to have the prohibition taken off of your coming to Strawberry Hill. However, as I am an admirable Christian, and as I think you seem to repent of your errors, I will give you leave to be so happy as to come to me when you like, though I would advise it to be after you have been at Roel,[20] which you would not be able to bear after my paradise. I have told you a vast deal of something or other, which you

14. Robert Dundas of Arniston (1685–1753).

15. Sir Henry Calthorpe (ca 1717–88), K.B., 1744; senior Knight of that Order at his death; M.P. Hindon 1741–7; see GM 1788, lviii pt i. 371.

16. Field Marshal George Wade (1673–1748). The house, built in 1723, was in Cork St (*London Past & Present*). There is a plate of it in Colin Campbell, *Vitruvius Britannicus*, 1717–71, iii. 10.

17. Richard Boyle (1694–1753), 3d E. of Burlington; architect and patron of the arts.

18. Meleager and Atalanta; it was ten and a half feet high by almost twenty-one feet wide, and was hung in the gallery at Houghton (*Ædes Walpolianæ, Works* ii. 268–9). It was sold 1779 to Catherine of Russia for £300 (MS note in a copy of the *Ædes*, 1747, p. 71, now WSL).

19. Hon. Edward Walpole; see T. Eustace Harwood, *Windsor Old and New*, 1929, pp. 278–9.

20. An estate of Montagu's in Gloucestershire. 'Rowell or Roell' is a hamlet contiguous to Rawling, which is 5 miles SE of Winchcombe; 'Christopher Montacute, esq., [sic; Montagu's uncle] was lord of it at the beginning of this century, and Mr Montague is the present lord of the manor' (Samuel Rudder, *New History of Gloucestershire*, Cirencester, 1779, pp. 484–5).

will scarce be able to read; for now Mr Chute has the gout, he keeps himself very low and lives upon very thin ink. My compliments to all your people. Yours ever,

Hor. Walpole

To Montagu, Thursday 26 May 1748

Arlington Street, May 26, 1748.

GOOD-BYE to you! I am going to my Roel too. I was there yesterday to dine, and it looked so delightful, think what you will, that I shall go there tomorrow to settle, and shall leave this odious town to the whores and the Regency, and the dowagers; to my Lady Townshend, who is not going to Windsor,[1] to old Cobham[2] who is not going out of the world yet, and to the Duchess of Richmond,[3] who does not go out with her twenty-fifth pregnancy: I shall leave too more disagreeable Ranelagh, which is so crowded, that going there t'other night in a string of coaches, we had a stop of six-and-thirty minutes. Princess Emily,[4] finding no marriage articles for her settled at the congress,[5] has at last determined to be old and ugly, and out of danger, and accordingly has ventured to Ranelagh, to the great improvement of the pleasures of the place. The Prince has given a silver cup to be rowed for,[6] which carried everybody upon the Thames, and

1. The significance of Lady Townshend's not going to Windsor is not known.

2. Either Sir Richard Temple (1675–1749), 4th Bt; cr. (1714) Bn Cobham, (1718) Vct Cobham; field marshal, patron of literature, and opponent of Sir Robert Walpole; or his wife Anne Halsey (d. 1760), the 'Cobham' of Gray's 'Long Story.'

3. Lady Sarah Cadogan (1706–51), m. (1719) Charles Lennox, 2d D. of Richmond, by whom she had twelve children.

4. Amelia Sophia Eleanora (1711–86), 2d dau. of George II; DNB, following GM, gives her birth-date as 1710; 10 June 1711 is probably correct (Burke, Peerage). She was the intended wife of Frederick the Great. After her father's death, she lived in Cavendish Square and at Gunnersbury, maintaining a circle whose daily routine of card-playing and gossip was chronicled by Lady Mary Coke until she quarrelled with the Princess in 1780 (see Coke, Jour-

nals). About 1761, HW became a favourite of hers. In later life she was blind and deaf. Always rather apart from the court of George III, she excited some public animosity by leaving most of her moderate fortune to German relatives (see DNB, sub George II; GM 1786, lvi pt ii. 1000; Lord Hervey, Memoirs of the Reign of King George II, passim; Wraxall, Memoirs v. 386–8; 'Lord Holland's Memoir,' in Life and Letters of Lady Sarah Lennox, ed. Countess of Ilchester, 1901–2, i. 11–12).

5. Of Aix-la-Chapelle.

6. 'Last Tuesday being Prince George's birthday [24 May O.S.], in the evening a silver cup of 25 guineas value, given by his Royal Highness the Prince of Wales, was rowed for by seven pair of oars, from Whitehall to Putney-Bridge, and won by one Masterman, who plies at Paul's-Wharf, and Meads of Whitehall-Stairs. Their Royal Highnesses the Prince and

afterwards there was a great ball at Carleton House. There have two good events happened at that court: the town was alarmed t'other morning by the firing of guns, which proved to be only from a large merchantman come into the river. The City construed them into the King's return and the Peace broke; but Chancellor Bootle[7] and the Bishop of Oxford,[8] who loves a labour next to promoting the cause of it, concluded the Princess was brought to bed, and went to Court upon it. Bootle finding her dressed, said, 'I have always heard, Madam, that the women *in your country* have very easy labours, but I could not have believed it was so well as I see.' The other story is of Prince Edward: the King before he went away, sent Stainberg[9] to examine the Prince's children in their learning. The Baron told Prince Edward, that he should tell the King what great proficiency His Highness had made in his Latin, but that he wished he would be a little more perfect in his German grammar, and that it would be of signal use to him. The child squinted at him, and said, 'German grammar! Why any dull child can learn that.'—There I have told you Royalties enough!

My Pigwiggin dinners are all over, for which I truly say grace. I have had difficulties to keep my countenance at the wonderful clumsiness and uncouth nicknames, that the Duke[10] has for all his offspring: Mrs Hopeful, Mrs Tiddle, Guts and Gundy, Puss, Cat and Toe, sound so strange in the middle of a most formal banquet! The day the Peace was signed, his Grace could find nobody to communicate joy with him; he drove home, bawled out of the chariot to Lady Rachel, 'Cat, Cat!' She ran down staring over the balustrade; he

Princess of Wales, the Princes etc. were in their barge on the Thames to see the same. His Royal Highness ordered five guineas to be given to the oars that lost' (*London Evening Post* 24–6 May 1748).

7. Sir Thomas Bootle (d. 1753), Kt, 1745; Chancellor to the Prince of Wales; Attorney-General for Durham; M.P. Liverpool 1724–34; Midhurst 1734–53 (GM 1753, xxiii. 590; Cunningham ii. 249).

8. Thomas Secker (1693–1768), Bp of Bristol, 1734; Oxford, 1737; Abp of Canterbury, 1758. 'A favourable specimen of the orthodox eighteenth-century prelate . . . Horace Walpole is particularly bitter against Secker, bringing outrageous charges against him' (J. H. Overton, in

DNB). Secker was a friend and recipient of the favours of Lord Hardwicke (*Mem. Geo. II* i. 66, 362; iii. 107), a sufficient basis for HW's animosity.

9. Probably Baron Steinberg, one of George II's Hanoverian ministers, who is mentioned in several political correspondences of the period (see Earl of Chesterfield, *Letters*, ed. Bonamy Dobrée, 1932, ii. 569). He was resident minister in England 1738–49 (Basil Williams, *The Whig Supremacy in England*, Oxford, 1939, pp. 13–4).

10. William Cavendish (1698–1755), 3d D. of Devonshire; Pigwiggin's father-in-law.

cried, 'Cat, Cat, the Peace is made, and you must be very glad, for I am very glad.'

I send you the only new pamphlet[11] that is worth reading, and this more the matter than the manner. My compliments to all your tribe. Adieu!

Yours ever,

H. W.

PS. The divine Ashton has got an ague which he says prevents his coming amongst us.

To Montagu, Thursday 14 July 1748

Mistley,[1] July 14th, 1748.

I CAME hither yesterday, having stayed but three days in London, which is a desert, but in those three days and from all those nobodies, I heard the history of Lord Coke[2] three thousand different ways. I expect next winter to hear of no Whigs and Jacobites, no courtiers and patriots, but of the Cokes and the Campbells—I do assure you the violence is incredible with which this affair is talked over—as the Irish mobs used to cry Butleraboo, and Crumaboo,[3] you will see the women in the assemblies will be holloaing, Campbellaboo!—But with the leave of their violence, I think the whole affair of sending Harry Ballenden[4] first to bully Coke, and then to murder him, is a very shocking story,[5] and so bad, that I will not believe Lady Mary's family could go so far as to let her into the secret of an inten-

---

11. Not identified.

---

1. Rigby's seat in Essex.

2. His duel with Bellenden; see below.

3. The war-cries of the Earls of Ormonde and Kildare, respectively; 'Aboo' is from an Irish word meaning 'cause of' (James N. Brewer, *Beauties of Ireland*, 1825–6, ii. 92–3).

4. Hon. Henry Bellenden (d. 1761), Kt, 1749; Usher of the Black Rod, 1747; Lt-Col. 3d Dragoon Guards. His sister Mary married Lady Mary Coke's brother, the 4th Duke of Argyll (*Scots Peerage*, 1904–10, ii. 73–4).

5. Beside the unidentified memorandum at Chatsworth (n. 12 below), the only accounts of this affair in print seem to be those given by Lady Betty Mackenzie and Lady Mary Coke herself in her *Journals* i. pp. cxxv–cxxviii and in Charles W. James, *Chief Justice Coke, His Family and Descendants at Holkham*, 1929, pp. 241–2. In their narratives, naturally, the only shocking circumstance is Coke's behaviour: the quarrel grew out of a heavy drinking bout with Bellenden when Bellenden, a close friend as well as connection by marriage, 'began to talk of his [Coke's] ill-treatment' of Lady Mary. Following a series of scenes with Lady Mary and her relations, Coke went to Lady Gower to explain that their ill-treatment of him had forced him to challenge Bellenden, but that Bellenden had refused to fight. On Bellenden's hearing this he challenged Coke.

tion to pistol her husband.[6] I heard the relation in an admirable way at first from my Lady Suffolk,[7] who is one of the ringleaders of the Campbellaboos, and indeed a woeful story she made of it for poor Coke, interlarding it every minute with very villainous epithets bestowed on his Lordship by Noll Bluff,[8] and when she had run over the string of rascal, scoundrel, etc. she would stop, and say, 'Lady Dorothy,[9] do I tell the story right, for you know I am very deaf and perhaps did not hear it exactly.'—I have compiled all that is allowed on both sides,[10] and it is very certain for Coke's honour that his refusing to fight, was till he could settle the affair of his debts.[11] But two or three wicked circumstances on t'other side, never to be got over, are Ballenden's stepping close up to him after Coke had fired his last pistol and saying, 'You little dog now I will be the death of you,' and firing, but the pistol missed[12]—and what confirms the intention of these words, is, its having come out, that the Duke of Argyle knew that Coke, on having been told that his Grace complained of his usage of Lady Mary, replied very well, 'Does he talk! Why, it is impossible I should use my wife worse than he did his.'[13] When Harry Ballenden left Coke on the road from Sunning,[13a] the day before the

6. HW apparently exaggerates the Campbells' instigation of the duel, which took place 28 June 1748 in Marylebone Fields in a mist and without casualty. It is clear, however, that Coke (and therefore his supporters) believed that the Campbells had plotted to murder him, for Lady Mary writes to her uncle, the Duke of Argyll, that Coke had accused her 'of endeavouring to get him murdered, and told me (before his father and their clergyman) that to his knowledge Mr Bellenden came to tell me of the duel the night before' (James, op. cit. 244–5).

7. Henrietta Hobart (ca 1681–1767), m. (1) (1706) Charles Howard, 9th E. of Suffolk; m. (2) (1735) Hon. George Berkeley; mistress of George II. She seems to have been a principal confidante of Lady Mary's at this time (ibid. 242–6).

8. Bellenden. The truculent Captain Bluffe of Congreve's Old Bachelor refers to himself as 'Nol Bluffe' (II. ii).

9. Lady Dorothy Hobart (d. 1798), m. (1752) Sir Charles Hotham-Thompson, 8th Bt, 1771; Lady Suffolk's niece; see A. M. W. Stirling, The Hothams, 1918, ii. passim.

10. This account, if it was set down in writing, has not been discovered.

11. This is allowed in the Campbell accounts (Coke, Journals i. p. lxxvii).

12. There is nothing of this in the Campbell accounts, and a memorandum of the affair among the Chatsworth papers (in an unidentified hand, dated 28 June 1748) states that after the first ineffectual round, 'Lord Coke then discharged another, or was going to discharge another, when Bellenden snapped his second pistol which missed fire. The seconds then interposed, and prevented further mischief' (Charles W. James, Chief Justice Coke, His Family and Descendants at Holkham, 1929, p. 241).

13. Anne Whitfield (d. 1723), m. (1713) Archibald Campbell, E. of Ilay, 3d D. of Argyll. Vicary Gibbs states (GEC) that Argyll 'appears to have been very profligate,' and that he left his English estates to a mistress.

13a. Probably Sunninghill, Berks, where Coke sometimes took the waters (Coke, loc. cit.).

duel, he crossed over to the Duke,[14] which his Grace flatly denied, but Lord Gower[15] proved it to his face. I have no doubt but a man who would dispatch his wife,[16] would have no scruple at the assassination of a person that should reproach him with it.

I don't like your not meeting me at the Tyger's; I think I shall scarce go if you don't, unless the Duchess of Queensberry[17] drives me from Strawberry Hill, as is very probable, for t'other night we met her coming from making me a visit; she had been upstairs and wrote a card[18] that began—'She has been to see Mr W.' I have another distress; my brother Ned's eldest girl[19] is come to Mrs Scott,[20] the painter's wife at next door:[21] the child is in a consumption, and seeing her so ill lodged, I could not help offering her my house, for I can't be angry when I see people unhappy: I found afterwards that my brother had intended to borrow it while I am here—I can conceive forgiveness; I can conceive using people ill—but how does one feel to use anybody very ill without any provocation, and then ask favours of them?—Well, he must think of that—I shall be glad if I can save the poor girl's life.

My compliments to all your house—I have not got the fish,[22] for t'other brother has sent me word they must not be disturbed—stuff —he will borrow my house next.

Yours ever,

H. W.

14. That is, to the Duke's house, Sudbrooke, near Petersham in Surrey, which was between Sunninghill and London.

15. Lady Leicester's brother-in-law.

16. There seems to be no confirmation of this sinister statement. HW's bias towards Coke is doubtless due to personal affection and also to political prejudice, since his father Lord Leicester was a steady supporter of Sir Robert's, while the 2d Duke of Argyll was usually an opponent. HW's friendship with Lady Mary did not arise till later.

17. Lady Catherine Hyde (ca 1701–77), m. (1720) Charles Douglas, 3d D. of Queensberry; an eccentric, friend of Swift, Prior, and Pope. She lived across the Thames from SH. Her beauty at an advanced age inspired one of HW's best epi-

grams (Works iv. 403). See DNB, sub her husband, and V. M. Biddulph, Kitty, Duchess of Queensberry, 1935.

18. Missing.

19. Laura Walpole, afterwards Mrs Keppel.

20. Mrs Samuel Scott, d. 1781 (Anecdotes, Works iii. 445). See Appendix 3 for a humorous letter from Sir Edward Walpole to her. For Samuel Scott see post ca 20 Nov. 1759.

21. According to Richard S. Cobbett, Memorials of Twickenham, 1872, pp. 13–14, the Scotts lived in the Manor House, which stood 'opposite the church,' some distance from SH.

22. Possibly goldfish, which were much in vogue at this time.

I had almost forgot to tell you a pleasant bit; I had been to visit the Vere Beauclercs[23] at Hanworth,[24] and had pried about for a portrait of the black grandmother,[25] but to no purpose. As to old Chambers's[26] black leg, I did not expect to find him stepping it forth like the King of Clubs. I went another evening with Mrs Leneve;[27] Lady Vere then carried us into all the lodging rooms; over one private bedchamber chimney, what did I view but the most deplorable sooty gentlewoman that ever was beheld. I immediately guessed this was the black housemaid, flattered, for it was not absolutely negro. I asked, Mrs Leneve hemmed and coughed and was ready to die—Lady Vere answered, it was her grandmother's picture, *a Portuguese* that her grandfather had married at Fort St George[28]—a very bad likeness.—Adieu! Rigby sends you a great many compliments—we call his black nothing but the Portuguese.

23. Lord Vere Beauclerk (1699–1781), cr. (1750) Bn Vere of Hanworth; m. (1736) Mary Chambers (d. 1783), the elder sister of Anne, Countess Temple, HW's friend. She figures in Swift's correspondence with her aunt, Lady Betty Germaine; see also Henrietta, Countess of Suffolk, *Letters*, ed. John Wilson Croker, 1824, i. 316.

24. Middlesex; the house is briefly mentioned in *Country Seats* 36; it was burned down 1797; see Daniel Lysons, *Historical Account of . . . Middlesex*, 1793–1800, v. 93–6.

25. See below, n. 28.

26. Presumably Thomas Chamber of Hanworth (d. 1738) (ibid. 101). Professor Pottle suggests that 'black leg' is an early use of 'blackleg,' whose first appearance in OED is 1771. The conjecture is strengthened by n. 28.

27. Isabella (ca 1693–1759), eld. dau. and coheir of Oliver Leneve of Great Witchingham, Norfolk. After she and her sisters were deprived of the family estates through the double dealing of a solicitor and a tedious trial in chancery she became a governess-companion in the Walpole family. On the marriage of Lady Mary Walpole she became a member of HW's household; see *Norfolk Archaeology* 1849, Norwich, ii. 393–5, table opp. p. 368; HW to Mann 13 Dec. 1759.

28. Thomas Chamber, who went out to India in 1640, was H.E.I.C. agent at Madras (Fort St George) 1659–62, when he was dismissed for private trading and other misconduct by which he acquired a large fortune. Knighted 1666, he bought Hanworth 1670 and died 1692 (Sir William Foster, *English Factories in India, 1661–64*, Oxford, 1923, pp. 385–6). 12 Jan. 1659 he is reported a bachelor, but on 8 March the latest news among the English settlements was 'Mr Chambers his espousing of Capt. Bowyer's widow' (Henry D. Love, *Vestiges of Old Madras*, 1913, i. 174). She 'was probably the relict of John Boyer, master of the *Expedition*' who committed suicide 1655. The will of Chamber's predecessor at Madras 'mentions a debt to "Anne Boyer, widow," and leaves Chamber (besides 100 pagodas for a ring) a hogshead of sack for the wedding' (Foster, *English Factories . . . 1655–60*, Oxford, 1921, p. 254 n). She died 1726, and is buried at Hanworth as 'Dama Anna' Chamber (Daniel Lysons, *Historical Account of . . . Middlesex*, 1793–1800, v. 101). In view of the absence of adverse contemporary comment on the match, and her previous marriage to an Englishman, Lady Vere's 'Portuguese' seems more plausible than HW's 'black housemaid,' though the latter imputation was apparently a familiar scandal.

To Montagu, Monday 25 July 1748

Mistley, July 25, 1748.

Dear George,

I HAVE wished you with me extremely; you would have liked what I have seen. I have been to make a visit of two or three days to Nugent,[1] and was carried to see the last remains of the glory of the old Aubrey de Veres, Earls of Oxford. They were once masters of almost this entire county, but quite reduced even before the extinction of their house; the last Earl's son[2] died at a miserable cottage that I was shown at a distance, and I think another of the sisters, besides Lady Mary Vere,[3] was forced to live upon her beauty. Henningham Castle,[4] where Harry the Seventh was so sumptuously banqueted and imposed that villainous fine for his entertainment,[5] is now shrunk to one vast ruinous tower, that stands on a spacious mount raised on a high hill with a large fosse; it commands a fine prospect, and belongs to Mr Ashurst[6] a rich citizen,[7] who has built a trumpery new house[8] close to it. In the parish church is a fine square monument of black marble of one of the Earls,[9] and there are three more tombs of the family at Earl's Colne some miles from the castle.[10] I

1. Robert Nugent (ca 1702–88), cr. (1767) Vct Clare, (1776) E. Nugent, to whom Goldsmith addressed 'The Haunch of Venison.' GEC erroneously gives his birth date as ca 1720.

2. Charles de Vere, d. in infancy, son of Aubrey de Vere (1626–1703), 20th E. of Oxford. GEC suggests that he was sent to the cottage to be nursed.

3. The last Earl had three surviving daughters: Lady Diana (d. 1742), m. (1694) Charles Beauclerk, 1st D. of St Albans; Lady Mary (ca 1681–1725), unm.; Lady Henrietta (ca 1682–1730), unm. (GEC).

4. Hedingham Castle, Essex, is illustrated and described in *Royal Commission on Historical Monuments . . . Essex*, 1916–23, i. 51–7 and frontispiece. The tower still stands.

5. Francis Bacon reports the story of Henry VII visiting John de Vere, 13th Earl of Oxford, in 1498, and imposing upon him a fine of 15000 marks for exceeding the legal number of liveried retainers (*Historie of the Raigne of King Henry the Seventh*, 1622, p. 211). The story is questioned in DNB.

6. Thomas Ashurst (d. 1765); see Thomas Wright, *History . . . of Essex*, 1836, i. 519; GM 1765, xxxv. 247.

7. That is, a resident of the City, 'a man of trade, not a gentleman' (Johnson). Ashurst's father was Lord Mayor in 1693, and his grandfather Henry Ashurst (d. 1680), merchant and philanthropist, established the family fortune in trade and bought Hedingham; he was, however, a man of family and his eldest son a baronet.

8. It still (1939) stands, a handsome brick house, by no means deserving of HW's scorn (information from Mr R. W. Ketton-Cremer).

9. John de Vere (d. 1540), 15th E. of Oxford. The tomb is described and illustrated in *Royal Commission on Historical Monuments . . . Essex*, 1916–23, i. 50.

10. The Priory founded by them at Earl's Colne was the family burial-place of the Veres. The few remaining monuments, which in HW's day were in the parish church, are now in a building near it (ibid. iii. 88, plates after pp. 86 and 90; see COLE ii. 175, n. 11).

could see but little of them as it was very late, except that one of the
Countesses[11] has a headdress exactly like the description of Mount
Parnassus,[12] with two tops. I suppose you have heard much of Gosfield,[13] Nugent's seat; it is extremely in fashion, but did not answer to
me, though there are fine things about it, but being situated in a
country that is quite blocked up with hills upon hills, and even too
much wood, it has not an inch of prospect. The park is to be sixteen
hundred acres, and is bounded with a wood of five miles round, and
the lake, which is very beautiful is of seventy acres, directly in a line
with the house, at the bottom of a fine lawn, and broke with very
pretty groves, that fall down a slope into it. The house is vast, built
round a very old court, that has never been fine, the old windows
and gateway left, and the old gallery, which is a bad narrow room,
and hung with all the late patriots,[14] but so ill done, that they look
like caricatures done to expose them since they have so much dis-
graced all the virtues they pretended to. The rest of the house is all
modernized, but in patches, and in the bad taste that came between
the charming venerable Gothic, and pure architecture.[15] There is a
great deal and plenty of good furniture, but no one room very fine;
no tolerable pictures. Her dressing room is very pretty and furnished
with white damask, china, japan, loads of easy chairs, bad pictures,
and some pretty enamels. But what charmed me more than all I had
seen, is the library chimney, which has existed from the foundation
of the house: over it, is an alto-relievo in wood, far from being ill
done, of the Battle of Bosworth Field.[16] It is all white, except the helmets and trappings which are gilt, and the shields which are prop-

11. *Post* 11 Aug. 1748, n. 5.
12. 'Mons ibi verticibus petit arduus
    astra duobus,
  nomine Parnassus'
    (Ovid, *Met.* i. 316–17).
13. Two miles SW of Halstead, Essex;
see Thomas Wright, *History . . . of Essex*,
1839, ii. 1–2; *Beauties of England* v.
350–4; *Royal Commission on Historical
Monuments . . . Essex*, 1916–23, i. 104 (illustrations).
14. A group in independent opposition
to Sir Robert Walpole, including Cobham,
Lyttelton, Grenville, and Pitt (see
W. E. H. Lecky, *History of England in the
Eighteenth Century*, New York, 1878–90, i.
410).

15. When HW writes in this vein, he
usually refers to the 'barbarous composition' under James I, which terminated
when Inigo Jones 'stepped into the true
and perfect Grecian' (Cole i. 191). Gosfield was built 'about the middle of the
16th century,' and most of the exterior
changes were 18th century; but some of
the rooms may have been of the period
HW particularly disliked; see *Royal Commission on Historical Monuments . . . Essex*, 1916–23, i. 104.
16. Later at Stowe; its origin is doubt-
ful; see *Essex Review* 1903, Colchester,
xii. 30–5; Essex Archaeological Society,
Transactions 1909, Colchester, n.s., x. 6–7.

erly blazoned with the arms of all the chiefs engaged: you would adore it. We passed our time very agreeably. Both Nugent and his wife[17] are very good-humoured, and easy in their house to a degree. There was nobody else, but the Marquis of Tweedale,[18] who indeed did not enliven us, his new Marchioness, who is infinitely good-humoured, and good company and sung a thousand French songs mighty prettily, a sister of Nugent's,[19] who does not figure, and a Mrs Elliot,[20] (sister to Mrs Nugent) who crossed over and figured in with Nugent; I mean she has turned Catholic as he has Protestant. She has built herself a very pretty small house in the park, and is only a daily visitor. Nugent was extremely communicative of his own labours, repeated us an ode of ten thousand stanzas to abuse Messieurs de la Galerie,[21] and read me a whole tragedy, which has really a great many pretty things in it, not indeed equal to his glorious Ode on religion and liberty,[22] but with many of those absurdities which are so blended with his parts. One thing indeed he communicated to me for which I abominated him, and that was a private lodge, a pimp, and a whole scheme of conveniencies. I agree extremely that the woman[23] is shocking[23a] and a great fool, but when she has given him above an hundred thousand pound, from her son,[24] I cannot away with his infidelity to her, and was very far from admiring him for it. We were overturned

17. Anna Craggs (ca 1697–1756), m. (1) John Newsham; m. (2) John Knight (from whom she inherited Gosfield); m. (3) (1736) Robert Nugent.

18. John Hay (ca 1695–1762), 4th M. of Tweeddale; m. (April or May 1748) Lady Frances Carteret (d. 1788). HW may have disliked him because he had been in opposition to Sir Robert.

19. Margaret Nugent (ca 1724–94) (Claud Nugent, *Memoir of Robert, Earl Nugent*, 1898, pp. 6, 13; GM 1794, lxiv pt ii. 1063; Thomas Wright, *History . . . of Essex*, 1836, ii. 12).

20. Elizabeth Craggs (ca 1695–1765), 2d dau. of James Craggs the elder; m. (1718) Edward Eliot of Port Eliot (d. 1722). Not to be confused, as in previous editions, with Harriet Craggs (ca 1714–69), natural dau. of James Craggs the younger; m. (1) (1726) Richard Eliot of Port Eliot (d. 1748); m. (2) (1749) Hon. James Hamilton (d. 1755); see Joseph J. Howard, *Miscellanea Genealogica et Heraldica* 1876, ii. 46.

21. The 'patriots,' n. 14 above. Neither ode nor tragedy appears to have been printed.

22. *An Ode to Mr Pulteney*, 1739; for reprintings see DNB, especially Dodsley's *Collection*, 1748, ii. 203. Its theme is 'the poet's passage from the creed of Roman Catholicism to a purer faith' (W. P. Courtney in DNB). The opening lines, and the last half of the seventh stanza, became, according to Courtney, almost proverbial in the 18th century; the latter was quoted by Gibbon in his character of Brutus. The tone of the *Ode* is similar to HW's 'Epistle to Ashton.' HW later questioned Nugent's authorship of the poem (*Mem. Geo. II* i. 46).

23. Mrs Nugent.

23a. That is, shockingly ugly.

24. According to DNB, she had an only son by her first husband, John Newsham. Probably his death, as James Newsham Craggs, is reported GM 1769, xxxix. 608, at Lisle in Flanders. Nugent, in a letter to George Grenville 20 Oct. 1764, says that if 'Mr Newsham' outlives him he will

coming back, but thank you, we were not at all hurt, and have been today to see a large house and a pretty park, belonging to a Mr Williams;[25] it is to be sold.

You have seen in the papers that Dr Bloxholme[26] is dead: he cut his throat. They say he never has been easy, since he so passively let Dr Thompson[27] murder Winnington. He always was nervous and vapoured, and so good-natured that he left off his practice, from not being able to bear seeing so many melancholy objects. I remember him with as much wit as ever I knew; there was a pretty correspondence of Latin odes that passed between him and Hedges.[28]

You will be diverted to hear that the Duchess of Newcastle was received at Calais by Lochiel's[29] regiment under arms, who did duty upon her himself while she stayed. The Duke of Grafton is going to

---

have a half interest in Nugent's property at St Mawes (*Grenville Papers*, ed. William J. Smith, 1852–3, ii. 452).

25. No doubt Felix Hall, Kelvedon, Essex. A seat of the Abdy family, it went with Charlotte, dau. of Sir Anthony Abdy, 3d Bt, to 'John Williams, Esq., second son of Sir John Williams, Knt., of Tendering Hall [Tendring Hall, Suffolk], who rebuilt Felix Hall, and made it an elegant country seat' (Thomas Wright, *History . . . of Essex*, 1836, i. 262; illustration). It was not sold until 1761, since an Act of Parliament was required. It was burned down 21 Jan. 1940; see also Philip Morant, *History . . . of Essex*, 1768, ii. 153 (information from Mr C. H. Collins Baker). For John Williams (ca 1716–79), see Venn, *Alumni Cantab*.

26. Noel Broxholme (1689?–1748), physician.

27. Thomas Thompson (d. 1763), 'a man who had, by large promises and free censures of the common practice of physick, forced himself up into sudden reputation' ('Life of Pope,' in Johnson, *Lives of the Poets*, ed. George B. Hill, 1905, iii. 189). Highly popular in the '40s, he treated Pope, Fielding, and the Prince of Wales; Fielding praised him in *Amelia*, while Paul Whitehead, a fellow-satellite in Dodington's circle, glorified him in an *Epistle*, 1755. 'Dr Thompson was a peculiar sloven, and, in the practice of a physician, an utter and declared enemy to muffins, which he always forbade his patients' (Edward Thompson, *Poems and Life of*

Paul Whitehead, 1777, p. lii; see pp. xli–liii, 109–36). He later 'sunk into contempt and obscurity' (Sir John Hawkins, *Life of Johnson*, 1787, p. 301; see pp. 299–301). For his 'murder' of Thomas Winnington, see HW to Mann 25 April 1746. See also Wilbur L. Cross, *History of Henry Fielding*, New Haven, 1918, *passim*; Musgrave, *Obituary*; Pope, *Works*, ed. Elwin and Courthope, 1871–89, viii. 519–21; BM, *Satiric Prints* iii pt i. 626.

28. John Hedges (ca 1689–1737), 3d son of Sir William Hedges (1632–1701); Envoy to Turin 1726–7; M.P. Michael 1722–7; Bosinney 1727–34; Fowey 1734–7; Treasurer to the Prince of Wales 1728–37; author of Latin verses (see Lord Hervey, *Memoirs*, ed. Romney Sedgwick, 1931, pp. 309, 867; Venn, *Alumni Cantab.*; GM 1836, clix pt i. 376; D. B. Horn, *British Diplomatic Representatives, 1689–1789*, 1932, p. 123). The Latin odes do not appear to have been published. He is the same person HW inadvertently identifies as 'Charles Hedges' in *Mem. Geo. II* i. 77 n, and in a MS note in his copy of Nichols's *Select Collection of Poetry* (about which copy see note to HW to West 28 Sept. 1739). Charles Hedges (d. 1756) was a brother of John.

29. Donald Cameron of Lochiel (1695?–1748), chief of the clan Cameron; fled to France after the '45, and commanded the regiment of Albany in the French service (DNB); died 6 Sept. 1748 (GM 1748, xviii. 476).

Scarborough; don't you love that endless backstairs policy?—and at his time of life! This fit of ill health is arrived on the Prince's going to shoot for a fortnight at Thetford, and his Grace is afraid of not being civil enough to him—or too civil.[30]

Since I wrote my letter I have been fishing in Rapin for any particulars relating to the Veres, and have already found that Robert de Vere the great Duke of Ireland[31] and favourite of Richard the Second is buried at Earl's Colne and probably under one of the tombs I saw there;[32] I long to be certain that the lady with the strange coiffure is Lancerona the joiner's daughter that he married after divorcing a princess of the blood for her:[33] I have found too that King Stephen's Queen[34] died at Henningham, a castle belonging to Alberic de Vere:[35] in short I am just now Vere-mad, and extremely mortified to have Lancerona and Lady Vere Beauclerc's *Portuguese* grandmother blended with this brave old blood. Adieu! I go to town the day after tomorrow, and immediately from thence to Strawberry Hill.

Yours ever.

To Montagu, Thursday 11 August 1748

Strawberry Hill, Aug. 11th, 1748.

I AM arrived at great knowledge in the annals of the house of Vere, but though I have twisted and twined their genealogy and my own a thousand ways, I cannot discover, as I wished to do, that I am descended from them anyhow but from one of their Christian names;

30. Euston Hall, the Duke of Grafton's seat, was only four miles from Thetford. Therefore the Duke of Grafton, a staunch King's man, betook himself to Scarborough, then, as now, a health resort (see Smollett's account of the Bramble family and Scarborough in *Humphry Clinker*).

31. Robert de Vere (1362–92), 9th E. of Oxford; cr. (1386) D. of Ireland. The account of his re-burial in 1395 (he died at Louvain) is in Paul de Rapin-Thoyras (1661–1725), *Histoire d'Angleterre*, La Haye, 2d edn, 1727, iii. 309. HW had the first edition of 1724 (MS Cat. G.3.20), sold SH iv. 54. In HW's fuller account of Robert de Vere, *post* 11 Aug. 1748, there are certain details not to be found in the French (1727) edition of Rapin, which are, however, included in footnotes to the

English translation; see *post* 11 Aug. 1748, n. 6.

32. One of the remaining tombs at Earl's Colne is thought to be his (*ante*, n. 9).

33. Robert de Vere m. (1378) Philippa de Couci (1367–1411/12), granddaughter of Edward III. He divorced her in 1387 to marry one Lancerona, whose identity is not clear and whose name is variously spelled. Most of the chroniclers agree that she was a Bohemian of low birth, who came to England with Richard II's queen, Anne of Bohemia. The divorce was annulled in 1389.

34. Matilda of Boulogne (1103?–52), m. (before 1125) Stephen.

35. Aubrey de Vere (d. 1194), cr. (ca 1142) E. of Oxford.

the name of *Horace* having travelled from them into Norfolk by the marriage of a daughter[1] of Horace Lord Vere of Tilbury[2] with a Sir Roger Townshend,[3] whose family baptized some of us with it.[4] But I have made a really curious discovery; the lady with the strange head-dress at Earl's Colne, which I mentioned to you, is certainly Lance-rona, *the Portuguese*,[5] for I have found in Rapin,[6] from one of the old chronicles, that Anne of Bohemia,[7] to whom she had been maid of honour introduced the fashion of *piked horns* or high heads, which is the very attire on this tomb, and ascertains it to belong to Robert de Vere the great Earl of Oxford, made Duke of Ireland by Richard the Second, who after the banishment of this minister and his death at Louvain occasioned by a boar at a great hunting match, caused the body to be brought over, would have the coffin opened once more to see his favourite, and attended it himself in high procession to its interment at Earl's Colne. I don't know whether the *Craftsman* some years ago, would not have found out that we were descended from this Vere, at least from his name and ministry: my comfort is, that Lancerona was Earl Robert's *second* wife![8] But in this search, I have crossed upon another descent, which I am taking great pains to verify, (I don't mean a pun) and that is a probability of my being descended from Chaucer, whose daughter, the Lady Alice,[9] before her espousals with Thomas Montacute Earl of Salisbury, and afterwards with William de la Pole the great Duke of Suffolk (another famous favourite!) was married to a Sir John Philips, who I hope to find was of Picton Castle,[10] and had children by her;[11] but I have not yet

1. Hon. Mary Vere (d. 1669), m. (1) (ca 1628) Sir Roger Townshend; m. (2) (1638) Mildmay Fane, 2d E. of Westmorland.

2. Horace Vere (1565–1635), cr. (1625) Bn Vere of Tilbury; grandson of 6th E. of Oxford.

3. Sir Roger Townshend (ca 1596–1637), 1st Bt (1617), of Raynham.

4. As Norfolk neighbours and god-parents.

5. See *ante* 25 July 1748, n. 33. GEC suggests that the effigy represents the Duke of Ireland's first wife, Philippa de Couci.

6. The discussion of piked horns, as well as the fact that Robert de Vere was killed by a boar, are not in the French edition of Rapin, 1727, but are in the English translation (first published 1725–

31), Paul de Rapin-Thoyras, *History of England*, edn 1757, iv. 88 n.

7. Anne of Bohemia (1366–94), m. (1382) Richard II.

8. As Maria Skerret was Sir Robert's second wife (HW's stepmother, whom he did not love).

9. Alice Chaucer (d. 1475), dau. of the poet's son Thomas, m. (1) Sir John Philip, K.B. (d. 1418); m. (2) Thomas de Montacute (d. 1428), 4th E. of Salisbury; m. (3) William de la Pole (d. 1450), 1st D. of Suffolk.

10. Near Haverfordwest, Pembrokeshire; seat of the Philippses, HW's kin (n. 13 below).

11. HW was disappointed, for they had no children.

brought these matters to a consistency; Mr Chute[12] is persuaded I shall, for he says anybody with two or three hundred years of pedigree, may find themselves descended from whom they please; and thank my stars and my good cousin the present Sir J. Philipps,[13] I have sufficient pedigree to work upon, for he drew us up one,[14] by which *Ego et rex meus*[15] are derived hand in hand from Cadwallader,[16] and the English Baronetage[17] says from the Emperor Maximus[18] (by the Philippses, who are Welsh, *s'entend*). These Veres have thrown me into a deal of this old study; t'other night I was reading to Mrs Leneve and Mrs Pigot,[19] who has been here a few days, the description in Hall's Chronicle[20] of the meeting of Harry the Eighth and Francis the First, which is so delightfully painted in your Windsor.[21] We came to a paragraph which I must transcribe, for though it means nothing in the world, it is so ridiculously worded in the old English that it made us laugh for three days:

And thẽ wer the twoo kynges serued with a banket, & after mirthe, had communicacion in the banket tyme, and there shewed the one the other their pleasure.

12. John Chute (1701–76), HW's intimate friend and correspondent.

13. Sir John Philipps (ca 1701–64), 6th Bt, of Picton Castle. HW was related to the Philipps family through his maternal grandmother, Elizabeth Shorter, daughter of Sir Erasmus Philipps, 3d Bt.

14. Now WSL. It is written on a strip of heavy linen, 19" x 87" and is titled, 'A Genealogical Table of all the Kings and Princes of Wales from Cadwalader last King of Britain to Llewelyn last Prince of Wales of the British Blood with the Descent of his present Majesty King George, as also of the Right Honourable Robert Lord Walpole, from Cadwalader.' It is inscribed 'To the Right Honourable Robert Lord Walpole this Draught is humbly dedicated by, My Lord, your Lordship's most obedient humble servant and kinsman John Philipps.' The royal line is indicated by red circles, and is paralleled by the Philipps line. The last generation in each line is the children of George I and Sir Robert Walpole. See Gray to HW 25 Feb. 1735. The last date in the pedigree is 1723.

15. See Shakespeare, *Henry VIII*, III. ii. 313–16.

16. Cadwaladr (d. 664?), semi-mythical King of Britain.

17. By Thomas Wotton (d. 1766), 1741, i. 458. HW's copy (MS Cat. E.4.35–9) was sold SH ii. 56.

18. Magnus Maximus, Roman general in Britain, claimed the imperial throne and ruled in the West from 383 until his defeat and murder by Theodosius in 388.

19. Mrs (Isabella) Leneve's sister Henrietta married Edward Leneve; their daughter Elizabeth (d. before 1759), m. (before 1748) Hugh Pigott (later Admiral). See *Norfolk Archaeology* 1849, Norwich, ii. table opp. p. 368.

20. Edward Hall, *The union of the two noble and illustre famelies of Lancastre and Yorke*, 1548, bk viii, fol. lxxvi, *verso* (ed. Charles Whibley, 1904, as *Henry VIII*, i. 199). HW's copy (MS Cat. E.3.12) was sold SH ii. 60.

21. 'The Field of the Cloth of Gold,' a large painting by an unknown hand; see *Archaeologia* 1775, iii. 185; 1863, xxxix. 28; COLE i. 299, n. 8. Now (1939) at Hampton Court.

Would not one swear that old Hal had showed all that is showed at the Tower?[22]

I am now in the act of expecting the house of Pritchard,[23] Dame Clive[24] and Mrs Metheglin[25] to dinner, but I promise you the Clive and I will not show one another our pleasure in the banket time or afterwards. In the evening we go to a play at Kingston where the places are twopence a head.[26] Our great company at Richmond and Twickenham[27] has been torn to pieces by civil dissensions, but they continue acting: Mr Lee,[28] the ape of Garrick, not liking his part refused to play it, and had the confidence to go into the pit as spectator. The actress[29] whose benefit was in agitation made her complaints to the audience, who obliged him to mount the stage; but since that he is retired from the company: I am sorry he was such a coxcomb, for he was our best.[29a]

22. 'King Harry's cod-piece' (HW to Mann 10 Dec. 1741). This object was apparently part of a statue of Henry VIII, one of a series of English kings in the Horse Armoury which have now disappeared. Other contemporary references are as cryptic as HW's: 'Near the entrance of the hall is the figure of Henry VIII . . . standing in his royal robes, with a sceptre in his hand. . . . If you press a spot on the floor with your feet, you will see something surprising with regard to this figure; but I will not say more, and leave you to guess what it is' (César de Saussure, *Foreign View of England* [16 Dec. 1725], ed. Mme van Muyden, 1902, pp. 87–8). 'At the door is placed King Henry VIII a-foot, with a pincushion on his sleeve, wherein the ladies commonly stick a pin, in return of which they are shown another, though somewhat of larger dimensions' (*Narrative of the Journey of an Irish Gentleman through England in the Year 1752*, ed. Henry Huth, 1869, p. 115). 'In his right hand he bears a sword, but whether of cruelty or mercy, will hardly, I think, admit a doubt' (*Historical Description of the Tower of London*, 1760, p. 59). HW further reports, in his notes to Maty's *Memoirs . . . of Lord Chesterfield*, at the end of Philobiblon Society, *Miscellanies* 1867–8, xi. 51, that 'it was very indecent; young women used to stick a pin into a certain part as a good omen for getting husbands.' Finally George Selwyn in jest wrote

to Archbishop Secker in the guise of a pious young nobleman who had been shocked on visiting the Tower with his sisters; and Secker 'ordered some decent alterations to be made' (loc. cit.; HW to Hertford 20 April 1764).

23. Below, n. 52.

24. Catherine Raftor (1711–85), m. (1732) George Clive; the actress, later HW's tenant at Little Strawberry Hill.

25. Not identified.

26. Apparently a band of strolling players, since the performance was in a barn (see postscript), and the admission price was very low.

27. The Richmond company was at this time giving occasional performances at Twickenham, a practice discontinued in 1753. For the history of the Richmond theatre, see Sybil Rosenfeld, *Strolling Players and Drama in the Provinces 1660–1765*, Cambridge, 1939, pp. 274–305; E. Beresford Chancellor, *History . . . of Richmond*, Richmond, 1894, pp. 121–43. In N&Q clxxiii, 23 Oct.–6 Nov. 1937, is a list of the plays given, the players, and benefits, abstracted by Emmett L. Avery from advertisements in the *Daily Advertiser*, 1746–53.

28. John Lee (d. 1781).

29. Not identified.

29a. According to Emmett L. Avery, N&Q 1937, clxxiii. 292, he had a benefit at Richmond, 7 Sept. 1748.

You say why won't I go to Lady Mary's?[30] I say why won't you go to
the Talbots'? Mary is busied about many things, is dancing the hays[31]
between three houses; but I will go with you for a day or two to the
Talbots if you like it, and you shall come hither to fetch me. I have
been to see Mr Hamilton's[32] near Cobham, where he has really made
a fine place out of a most cursed hill. Esher[33] I have seen again twice
and prefer it to all villas, even to Southcote's;[34] Kent[35] is Kentissime
there. I have been laughing too at Claremont House,[36] the gardens
are improved since I saw them: do you know that the pineapples are
literally sent to Hanover by couriers? I am serious. Since the Duke
of N.[37] went, and upon the news of the Duke of Somerset's[38] illness,
he has transmitted his commands through the King, and by him
through the Bedford to the University of Cambridge to forbid their
electing anybody—but the most ridiculous person they could elect—
his Grace of Newcastle.[39] The Prince hearing this, has wrote to them
that having heard of his Majesty's commands, he should by no means

30. Lady Maria (Mary) Walpole (ca
1725–1801), m. (1746) Col. Charles Churchill; HW's half-sister. See COLE i. 165; Daniel Lysons, *Environs of London*, 2d edn
1810, i pt ii. 567. Her house in 1755 was
at Chalfont, Bucks (HW to Bentley 5 July
1755), and it was probably the same at this
time.

31. 'To perform winding or sinuous
movements; to go through varied evolu-
tions like those of a dance' (OED).

32. Hon. Charles Hamilton (1704–86),
9th son of the 6th E. of Abercorn; see
Scots Peerage, 1904–10, i. 61. His seat,
Painshill, a famous show-place, was one of
the earliest examples of natural landscape
gardening on a large scale; see COLE i. 44;
Owen Manning, *History . . . of Surrey*,
1804–14, ii. 768–9; [Thomas Whately] *Observations on Modern Gardening*, 3d edn
1771, pp. 184–94; Count Frederick Kielmansegge, *Diary of a Journey to England,
1761–2*, 1902, pp. 55–7; [Arthur Young]
*Six Weeks Tour through the Southern
Counties of England*, 2d edn 1769, pp.
223–8.

33. Esher Place, Surrey; seat of Henry
Pelham; celebrated by Pope and Thom-
son; see *Vict. Co. Hist. Surrey* iii. 448, 450;
'Modern Gardening,' *Works* ii. 539.

34. Woburn Farm, Chertsey; seat of
Philip Southcote (d. 1758); see COLE ii.

275, n. 15; [Thomas Whately] *Observations on Modern Gardening*, 3d edn 1771,
pp. 177–82; Owen Manning, *History . . .
of Surrey*, 1804–14, ii. 259, 768; *London
and its Environs Described*, 1761, plate
opp. vi. 361.

35. William Kent (1684–1748), artist and
architect. 'He leaped the fence, and saw
that all nature was a garden' ('Modern
Gardening,' *Works* ii. 536). HW devotes
much attention to Kent there and in
Anecdotes, Works iii. 488–92.

36. Claremont Park, Surrey, built by
Vanbrugh, and purchased by the Duke of
Newcastle in 1714. Kent 'improved' the
gardens ('Modern Gardening,' *Works* ii.
538–9). After Newcastle's death, Lord
Clive built a new house and again re-
modelled the grounds; see *Vict. Co. Hist.
Surrey* iii. 447–8; *London and its Environs
Described*, 1761, ii. 138–40, engraving opp.
p. 139.

37. Newcastle was in Hanover with the
King; see HW to Mann 7 June and 14
July 1748.

38. Charles Seymour (1662–2 Dec. 1748),
6th D. of Somerset; Chancellor of Cambridge 1689–1748.

39. He had been elected High Steward
of the University in 1737 and apparently
assumed that he would become Chancellor
on Somerset's death, but in 1747 the

oppose them. This is sensible: but how do the two secretaries[40] answer such a violent act of authority? Nolkejumskoi[41] has let down his dignity and his discipline, and invites[42] continually all officers that are members of Parliament. Doddington's[43] sentence of expulsion is sealed; Lyttelton[44] is to have his place, (the second time he has tripped up his heels;) Lord Barrington[45] is to go into the Treasury and Dick Edgcumbe into the Admiralty.[46] Rigby is gone from hence to Sir William Stanhope's[47] for the Aylesbury races, where the Grenvilles and their Peggy Banks design to appear and avow their triumph.[48] Gray has been here a few days[49] and is transported with your story of Madame Bentley's[50] diving and her white man, and in short with all your stories.—Room for cuckolds, here comes my company—

Aug. 12th.

I had not time to finish my letter last night, for we did not return from the dismal play which was in a barn at Kingston till twelve o'clock at night. Our dinner passed off very well; the Clive was very good company. You know how much she admires Ashton's[51] preach-

Prince of Wales indicated that he would be willing to succeed Somerset. The anxieties of Newcastle, Bedford, and the others engaged to elect Newcastle are set forth at length in Denys A. Winstanley, *University of Cambridge in the Eighteenth Century*, Cambridge, 1922, pp. 38–48. 'This contest for the Chancellorship is a striking instance of the close connection between parliamentary politics and the internal affairs of the university' (ibid. 48).

40. Newcastle and Bedford, the Secretaries of State. 'Answer' = 'answer for.'

41. The Duke of Cumberland.

42. To his levees, presumably to influence their votes.

43. George Bubb-Dodington (1691–1762), cr. (1761) Bn Melcombe. He was at this time Treasurer of the Navy, a post he resigned in March, 1749, on resuming his allegiance to the Prince of Wales.

44. Sir George Lyttelton (1709–1773), 5th Bt, 1751; cr. (1756) Bn Lyttelton; Lord of the Treasury 1744–54; the 'good Lord Lyttelton.' He had in 1734 supplanted Dodington in the favour of the Prince of Wales (see Lord Hervey, *Memoirs*, ed. Romney Sedgwick, 1931, pp. 385–8); this is no doubt the first tripping-up to which HW refers.

45. William Wildman Barrington-Shute (1717–93), 2d Vct Barrington; Lord of the Admiralty 1746–54; continuously in office, holding a succession of important and lucrative posts, until he was pensioned off in 1778 at £2000 a year.

46. None of these changes occurred.

47. Hon. Sir William Stanhope (1702–72), K.B., 1725; 2d son of 3d E. of Chesterfield; M.P. Lostwithiel Jan.–July, 1727. Buckinghamshire 1727–41, 1747–68. His seat, Eythorpe, was 3 miles west of Aylesbury (see George Lipscomb, *History . . . of Buckinghamshire*, 1847, i. 480–3). See 'Short Notes' for HW's speech in his name. He had recently bought Pope's home at Twickenham and so was HW's neighbour.

48. In March, 1748, the Grenvilles got through a bill moving the summer assizes from Aylesbury to Buckingham, where their interest centered; see 'Short Notes'; GM 1748, xviii. 99–104.

49. The dates of this visit are not known.

50. This seems to be the wife of HW's friend and correspondent; see *post* 19 Oct. 1760, n. 2.

51. She heard him at Eton where, through HW's influence, he became a Fel-

ing; she says she is always vastly good for two or three days after his sermons, but by the time that Thursday comes, all their effect is worn out. I never saw more proper decent behaviour than Mrs Pritchard's,[52] and I assure you even Mr Treasurer Pritchard[53] was far better than I expected. Adieu!

Yours ever,

Chaucerides

To Montagu, Saturday 3 September 1748

Strawberry Hill, Saturday night, Sept. 3d, 1748.

ALL my sins to Mrs Talbot you are to expiate; I am here quite alone, and want nothing but your fetching, to go to her. I have been in town for a day just to see Lord Bury,[1] who is come over with the Duke; they return next Thursday. The Duke is fatter, and it is now not denied that he has entirely lost the sight of one eye: this did not surprise me so much as a bon mot of his. Gumley,[2] who you know is grown Methodist, came to tell him that as he was on duty, a tree in Hyde Park near the powder magazine[3] had been set on fire; the Duke replied, *he hoped it was not by the new light*. This nonsensical *new light*[4] is extremely in fashion, and I shall not be surprised if we see a revival of all the folly and cant of the last age.[5] Whitfield[6] preaches

low in 1745. In 1770 Ashton published his *Sermons on Several Occasions*. Two of them, pp. 389, 410, were preached at Eton in 1747.

52. Mrs Hannah Pritchard (1711–68), née Vaughan; the actress.

53. Treasurer of Drury Lane Theatre; d. 1763 (GM 1763, xxxiii. 46); probably Mrs Pritchard's husband; see Miss E. G. Withycombe in N&Q 1939, clxxvii. 319.

1. George Keppel (1724–72), styled Vct Bury; 3d E. of Albemarle, 1754; favourite aide-de-camp of the Duke of Cumberland. He and the Duke had come over from Hanover to arrange about the reductions in the British forces (DNB). HW was also doubtless anxious for news of Conway.

2. Col. Samuel Gumley (d. 1763), Major in the 1st Foot Guards; brother of the Countess of Bath. He had been converted to Methodism only a few months before.

His wife or mother, probably the latter, gave Charles Wesley a house in Marylebone (*London Magazine* 1762, xxxiii. 335; *Miscellanea Genealogica et Heraldica* 1908, ed. W. Bruce Bannerman, 4th ser. ii. 11; John Wesley, *Journals*, ed. Nehemiah Curnock, 1910–16, iii. 356, viii. 158).

3. Still standing on the north side of the Serpentine, at the west end of Ladies Mile (1939). A print of it is the frontispiece to James P. Malcolm, *Anecdotes of . . . London during the 18th Century*, 2d edn, 1810, ii.

4. A slogan of Methodism.

5. Perhaps a reference to the high-church controversies of Queen Anne's time, or to 17th century Puritanism.

6. George Whitefield (1714–70), Methodist leader; for his account of his sermons at Lady Huntingdon's at this time, see Luke Tyerman, *Life of Whitefield*, New York, 1877, ii. 193–5.

continually at my Lady Huntingdon's[7] at Chelsea;[7a] my Lord Chesterfield,[8] my Lord Bath, my Lady Townshend, my Lady Thanet and others have been to hear him; what will you lay that next winter he is not run after instead of Garrick?[9]

I am just come from the play at Richmond, where I found the Duchess of Argyle and Lady Betty Campbell and their court; we had a new actress, a Miss Clough;[10] an extreme fine tall figure and very handsome; she spoke very justly and with spirit. Garrick is to produce her next winter, and a Miss Charlotte Ramsay,[11] a poetess, and deplorable actress. Garrick, Barry[12] and some more of the players were there to see these new comedians; it is to be their seminary. Since I came home I have been disturbed with a strange foolish woman[13] that lives at the great corner house yonder; she is an attorney's wife, and much given to her bottle; by the time she has finished that and daylight she grows afraid of thieves and makes her servants fire minute guns out of the garret windows. I remember persuading Mrs Kerwood that there was a great smell of thieves, and this drunken dame seems literally to smell it. The divine Ashton, who I suppose you will have seen when you receive this, will give you an account of the astonishment we were in last night at hearing guns; I began to think that the Duke had brought some of his defeats from Flanders.

I am going to tell you a long story, but you will please to remember that I don't intend to tell it well; therefore if you happen to dis-

---

7. Lady Selina Shirley (1707–91), m. (1728) Theophilus Hastings (1696–1746), 9th E. of Huntingdon; prominent Methodist.

7a. Donnington Park, which she had inherited from her husband. Her many chapels were not founded until much later (see [A. C. H. Seymour] *The Life and Times of Selina Countess of Huntingdon*, 1844, i. 87–94). Lady Huntingdon appointed Whitefield her chaplain when he left London 1 Sept.

8. Chesterfield was much impressed by Whitefield's preaching (ibid. 194; *Papers of the Earl of Marchmont*, ed. Sir George Henry Rose, 1831, ii. 377).

9. David Garrick (1717–79).

10. She does not appear in Drury Lane casts 1748–9 (Sybil Rosenfeld, *Strolling Players . . .*, Cambridge, 1939, p. 295 n).

11. Charlotte Ramsay (1720–1804), m. (?6 Oct. 1747) Alexander Lennox; author of *The Female Quixote* and other works. This seems to be the sole reference to her as an actress (Miriam R. Small, *Charlotte Ramsay Lennox*, New Haven, 1935, p. 7). Miss Ramsay's *Poems on Several Occasions* had appeared in 1747.

12. Spranger Barry (1719–77).

13. The Twickenham Rate Books throw no light on the house or its owner. However, it might be the one which appears in 'A Plan of Twickenham . . . from an actual Survey by Samuel Lewis, 1784,' as the house belonging to 'Mr Briscoe' (it was great only in contrast to SH at this time). Stafford Briscoe (d. 1789) was, however, a goldsmith, with premises in Cheapside (*London Directory* 1745, 1752; GM 1789, lix pt ii. 1150).

cover beauties in the relation, where I never intended them, don't conclude as you did in your last that I know they are there. If I had not a great command of my pen, and could not force it to write whatever nonsense I had heard last, you would be enough to pervert all one's letters, and put one upon keeping up one's character; but as I write merely to satisfy you, I shall take no care but not to write well; I hate letters that are called good letters.

You must know then, but did you know a young fellow that was called Handsome Tracy?[14] He was walking in the Park with some of his acquaintance, and overtook three girls; one was very pretty; they followed them, but the girls ran away, and the company grew tired of pursuing them, all but Tracy,—(There are now three more guns gone off successively—she must be very drunk) He followed to White-hall Gate, where he gave a porter a crown to dog them; the porter hunted them, he the porter. The girls ran all round Westminster and back to the Haymarket, where the porter came up with them; he told the pretty one she must go with him, and kept her talking till Tracy arrived, quite out of breath, and exceedingly in love. He insisted on knowing where she lived, which she refused to tell him, and after much disputing, went to the house of one of her companions and Tracy with them. He there made her discover her family, a butter woman in Craven Street, and engaged her to meet him next morning in the Park; but before night he wrote her four love letters, and in the last offered two hundred a year to her, and a hundred a year to *la Signora Madre*. Griselda made a confidence to a stay-maker's wife, who told her that the swain was certainly in love enough to marry her, if she could determine to be virtuous and refuse his offers—'Aye,' says she, 'but if I should, and should lose him by it!' However the measures of the cabinet council were decided for virtue, and when she met Tracy the next morning in the Park, she was convoyed by her sister and brother-in-law, and stuck close to the letter of her reputation. She would do nothing, she would go nowhere. At last as an

14. Robert Tracy (n. 16 *post*). Little is known of this man-about-town; see N&Q 1896, 8th ser. x. 195. He is mentioned as 'Beau' Tracy in John Taylor, *Records of my Life*, 1822, i. 411–12, as an early lover of Mrs Abington the actress (from Mr R. W. Ketton-Cremer). He is possibly the 'Tracey . . . since dead' identified by a writer in GM 1777, xlvii. 339, with the character of Beau Leicart in William Dodd's novel, *The Sisters*, 1754. The character in the novel possesses no particular individuality; he is, however, described as exceedingly handsome. Another amorous misadventure of his is related in *Town and Country Magazine* 1770, ii. 515–7, where he is also called 'Beau' Tracy, and described as affluent and charming.

instance of prodigious compliance, she told him that if he would accept such a dinner as a butterwoman's daughter could give him, he should be welcome. Away they walked to Craven Street, the mother borrowed some silver to buy a leg of mutton and they kept the eager lover drinking till twelve at night, when a chosen committee waited on the faithful pair to the minister of Mayfair. The Doctor[15] was in bed, and swore he would not get up to marry the King, but that he had a brother over the way who perhaps would, and who did.[16] The mother borrowed a pair of sheets, and they consummated at her house, and the next day they went to their own palace. In two or three days the scene grew gloomy, and the husband coming home one night swore he could bear it no longer—'Bear! bear what?'—'Why to be teased by all my acquaintance for marrying a butterwoman's daughter. I am determined to go to France and will leave you a handsome allowance'—'Leave me! Why you don't fancy you shall leave me! I will go with you'—'What you love me then!'—'No matter whether I love you or not, but you shan't go without me'—and they are gone!—If you know anybody that proposes marrying and travelling, I think they can't do it in a more compendious method.

I agree with you most absolutely in your opinion about Gray; he is the worst company in the world—from a melancholy turn, from living reclusely, and from a little too much dignity, he never converses easily—all his words are measured, and chosen, and formed into sentences; his writings are admirable; he himself is not agreeable.[17]

There are still two months to London; if you could discover your

15. HW presumably refers to Dr Alexander Keith (d. 1758), who conducted at Mayfair Chapel an extensive business in marriages without banns or license from about 1730 until 1743 when he collided with the ecclesiastical authorities and was confined to the Fleet. From the Fleet he supervised the activities of a series of deputies, one of whom performed the ceremony (next note). Lord Hardwicke's Marriage Act of 1754 ended clandestine marriages; see DNB sub Keith and John S. Burn, *History of the Fleet Marriages*, 2d edn 1834.

16. The marriage is recorded in Harleian Society, *Register of . . . St George's Chapel, Mayfair*, ed. George J. Armytage, 1889, p. 327: 'Aug. 4, Robert Tracy of St Martin's in the Fields, Bachelor, and Susannah Owens, of St Margaret's, Westminster, Spinster.' It was performed by the Rev. Peter Symson (ca 1708–?1780), who had been one of the marrying parsons within the Rules of the Fleet from 1731 (?); he describes himself as a Cambridge man, and says that a series of wretched curacies had driven him to marrying for a living (John S. Burn, *History of the Fleet Marriages*, 1834, pp. 54–5. He appears to be the Peter Simpson in Venn, *Alumni Cantab.*, who was admitted sizar at Trinity Hall in 1729, ordained 1735, and died 1780.

17. See Boswell, *Life*, ed. Hill and Powell, Oxford, 1934, ii. 516–17, for a note by Mr Whibley on Gray's 'dullness.'

own mind for any three or four days of that space, I will either go
with you to the Tygers, or be glad to see you here, but I positively
will ask you neither one nor t'other any more. I have raised seven-
and-twenty bantams from the patriarchs you sent me. Adieu!

Yours ever,

H. W.

To Montagu, Sunday 25 September 1748

Strawberry Hill, Sept. 25, 1748.

I SHALL write you a very short letter, for I don't know what business we have to be corresponding when we might be together. I
really wish to see you, for you know I am convinced of what you say
to me. It is few people I ask to come hither, and if possible still fewer
that I wish to see here.[1] The disinterestedness of your friendship for
me has always appeared, and is the only sort that for the future I will
ever accept, and consequently I never expect any more friends—as to
trying to make any by obligations, I have had such woeful success,[2]
that for fear of thinking still worse than I do of the world, I will
never try more. But you are abominable to reproach me with not letting you go to Houghton; have not I offered a thousand times to
carry you there? I mean since it was my brother's; I did not expect to
prevail with you before, for you are so unaccountable, that you not
only will never do a dirty thing, but you won't even venture the appearance of it.[3] I have often applied to you in my own mind a very
pretty passage that I remember in a letter of Chillingworth;[4] *you*

1. HW preserved this attitude throughout his life.

2. Mr R. W. Ketton-Cremer suggests
that this is a reference to Gray. HW frequently criticized Gray to Montagu and
had done so in the preceding letter.

3. See the quotation from Chillingworth, below. Apparently Montagu would
not go to Houghton when Sir Robert was
in power for fear of being suspected of
place-hunting.

4. William   Chillingworth   (1602–44),
theologian. The passage occurs in a letter
from Chillingworth to Gilbert Sheldon, 21
Sept. 1635. Discussing his rejection of an
offer from Sir Thomas Coventry, Lord

Keeper, he says, 'I would never do anything for preferment, which I would not
do but for preferment' (William Chillingworth, *Works*, ed. Thomas Birch, 1836,
p. xv). HW kept a Commonplace Book,
signed and dated 1750, though the hand is
of a later date, devoted to notes and comments on Bayle (in the possession of Sir
Wathen Waller, Bt, 1939). He quotes Chillingworth's remark: 'I would never do anything for preferment that I would not do
but for preferment,' with a reference to
vol. 4, p. 320. This reference is to the article on Chillingworth in Pierre Bayle,
*General Dictionary Historical and Critical
. . . A New . . . Translation . . . with*

would not do that for preferment, that you would not do but *for preferment.* You oblige me much in what you say about my nephews,[5] and make me happy in the character you have heard of Lord Malpas;[6] I am extremely inclined to believe he deserves it. I am as sorry to hear what a companion[7] Lord Walpole[7a] has got: there has been a good deal of noise about him, but I had laughed at it, having traced the worst reports to his gracious mother,[8] who is now sacrificing the character of her son to her aversion for her husband: if we lived under the Jewish dispensation, how I should tremble at my brother's leaving no children by her, and its coming to my turn to raise him up issue![9]

Since I gave you the account of the Duchess of Ireland's *piked horns* among the tombs of the Veres, I have found a long account in Bayle of the friar, who as I remembered to have read somewhere, preached so vehemently against that fashion: it was called *hennin,* and the monk's name was Thomas Conecte:[10] he was afterwards burnt at Rome for censuring the lives of the clergy. As our histories say that Anne of Bohemia introduced the fashion here, it is probable that the French learnt it from us, and were either long before they caught it, or long in retaining the mode, for the Duke of Ireland died in 1389, and Conecte was burnt in 1434. There were indeed several years between his preaching down hennins, and his death, but probably not near five-and-forty years, and half that term was a long duration for so outrageous a fashion.[11] But I have found a still more enter-

several thousand lives never before published, ed. Bernard, Birch, Lockman et al., 10 vols, 1734–61. HW's copy was sold SH iii. 194.

5. Lords Malpas and Walpole.

6. George Cholmondeley (1724–64), styled Vct Malpas, the son of HW's sister Mary (ca 1706–1732), who m. (1723) George, 3d E. of Cholmondeley. When Malpas died HW wrote Mann 18 March 1764: 'a worthy amiable man, whom I have loved from his childhood.'

7. Unidentified.

7a. George Walpole (1730–91), styled Vct Walpole; 3d E. of Orford, 1751.

8. Margaret Rolle (1709–81), m. (1) (1724) Robert Walpole, 2d E. of Orford; m. (2) (1751) Hon. Sewallis Shirley; Baroness Clinton suo jure, 1760. The reports have not been identified.

9. That is, presumably, if Lord Walpole died.

10. Thomas Conecte (d. 1434), preacher and reformer. In his Bayle Commonplace Book (n. 4 above) HW notes on vol. 4, p. 426: 'Thomas Conecte was the friar who preached against high heads. It was called hennin, and was like *horns*, in Charles 6th's time. He gave indulgences to children for mobbing them. There never was more nonsense than in Bayle note E on this subject. Conecte was burnt at Rome, for censuring the dissoluteness of the clergy.'

11. 'Hennin' is a general term for the towering headdresses which flourished throughout the 15th century. The 'piked horns,' otherwise 'horned coiffes,' which HW saw on the tomb at Earl's Colne (ante 25 July and 11 Aug. 1748) are be-

taining fashion in another place in Bayle, which was, the women wearing looking-glasses upon their bellies:[12] I don't conceive for what use, unless it was in the days of the huge codpieces. Adieu! Don't write any more but come.

Yours ever,

H. W.

To Montagu, Thursday 20 October 1748

Strawberry Hill, Oct. 20, 1748.

YOU are very formal to send me a ceremonious letter of thanks; you see I am less punctilious, for having nothing to tell you, I did not answer your letter. I have been in the empty town for a day; Mrs Muscovy and I cannot devise where you have planted jasmine; I am all plantation, and sprout away like any chaste nymph in the *Metamorphosis*.[1]

They say the old monarch at Hanover has got a new mistress—I fear he ought to have got something else new first. Now I talk of getting, Mr Fox[2] has got the ten thousand pound prize; and the Violette, as it is said, Coventry[3] for a husband. It is certain that at the fine masquerade, he was following her, as she was under the Countess's[4]

---

lieved to have originated in Flanders; they were popular in England in the time of Henry V. See James Robinson Planché, *Cyclopaedia of Costume*, 1879, ii. 125–8, where it is also suggested that the 'hennin' Conecte preached against were not the horned but the conical type of head-dress.

12. Probably only hanging from or attached to their girdles. HW makes substantially the same suggestion about the purpose of the mirrors in *Anecdotes, Works* iii. 29, for which he was taken to task by Dalrymple; see HW to Dalrymple 20 May 1762. HW read of the custom, which he noted in his Bayle Commonplace Book (n. 4 above) in the article on John Des Caurres in *General Dictionary* (ibid.) iv. 228.

---

1. HW's enthusiasm for planting was never higher than during these few months. See *SH Accounts* 36–8 and the references there to HW's letters: 29 Aug.

and 6 Oct. 1748 to Conway; 24 Oct., 26 Dec. 1748, 4 March and 3 May 1749 to Mann; *post* 28 Sept. 1749 to Montagu.

2. Henry Fox (1705–74), cr. (1763) Bn Holland. 'Tuesday the following numbers were drawn prizes at Guildhall, viz. No. 35,904, £10,000 . . . We are well assured, that the above prize of £10,000 is the property of the Right Hon. Henry Fox, Esq., Secretary at War' (*St James's Evening Post* 18–20 Oct. 1748). This was the annual government lottery, called the Joint-Stock Lottery Annuity, since the tickets constituted an investment in the funds as well as a chance for one of 8,750 prizes, of which three were £10,000; see Cecil L'Estrange Ewen, *Lotteries and Sweepstakes*, 1932, pp. 151–2.

3. There were several unmarried Coventrys at this time; possibly Henry Coventry.

4. Probably the Countess of Burlington, patroness of the Violette (*ante* 5 June 1746, n. 23).

arm, who pulling off her glove, moved her wedding ring up and down her finger, with a motion that does not just express matrimony,[5] but it seems was to signify that no other terms would be accepted. It is the year of contraband marriages, though I do not find Fanny Murray's[6] is certain. I liked her spirit in an instance I heard t'other night; she was complaining of want of money; Sir Richard Atkins[7] immediately gave her a twenty pound note; she said, 'Damn your twenty pound, what does that signify!'—clapped it between two pieces of bread and butter and eat it.—Adieu! Nothing should make me leave off so shortly, but that my gardener[8] waits for me, and you must allow that he is to be preferred to all the world.

Yours ever,

H. W.

To Montagu, Thursday 18 May 1749

Arlington Street, May 18, 1749.

Dear George,

WHATEVER you hear of the Richmond fireworks,[1] that is short of the prettiest entertainment in the world, don't believe it; I really never passed a more agreeable evening: everything succeeded, all the wheels played in time, Frederick[2] was fortunate and all the

5. This clause is omitted in previous editions; 'but' is rendered 'which' in Toynbee.

6. Fanny Murray (ca 1729–1778), m. (1757) David Ross; the celebrated courtesan; see Horace Bleackley, *Ladies Fair and Frail*, 1909, pp. 3, 26; Boswell knew her after her marriage, and mentions her in his journal in 1769 (*Private Papers*, ed. Geoffrey Scott and F. A. Pottle, 1928–34, Mt Vernon, N. Y., viii. 98–9) and in 1772, when he found it 'curious to see the celebrated Fanny Murray, as decent a lady at her own table as any body' (ibid. ix. 86).

7. Sir Richard Atkins (ca 1728–56), 6th Bt, of Clapham; kept Fanny Murray intermittently, and was often reported to be on the point of marrying her; Bleackley, op. cit. n. 6, pp. 18–20.

8. See *post* i. 198, n. 7.

1. Given by the Duke of Richmond 15

May, in honour of the Duke of Modena (see HW to Mann 17 May 1749). They were 'played off' in Privy Garden and on the Thames. According to the account in *St James's Evening Post* 16–18 May 1749 (also GM 1749, xix. 234), 400 'persons of distinction' saw 200 water mines, 200 air balloons, 200 fire-trees, 5000 water rockets, 5000 sky rockets, 100 fire showers, 20 suns, and 100 stars, concluded with 'a grand illumination, which lasted till two o'clock.' See illustration.

2. Charles Frederick (1709–85), K.B., 1761; M.P. New Shoreham 1741–54; Queenborough 1754–84; Clerk of the Deliveries, 1746; Surveyor-General of the Ordnance, 1750; staged the great display of fireworks two weeks before this to celebrate the Peace (HW to Mann 3 May 1749). He was also a skilled antiquarian (see COLE ii. 238–9).

Fireworks and Illuminations at the Duke of Richmond's, Whitehall, 1749

THE DUKE OF RICHMOND'S FIREWORKS TO
CELEBRATE THE PEACE, 1749

world in good humour. Then for royalty, Mr Anstis[3] himself would have been glutted; there were all the Fitzes[4] upon earth, the whole court of St Germains,[5] the Duke,[6] the Duke of Modena[7] and the two Anamaboes.[8] The King and Princess Emily bestowed themselves upon the mob on the river, and as soon as they were gone, the *Duke*[9] hoisted the music into the garden, and himself with my Lady Lincoln, Mrs Pitt,[10] Peggy Banks and Lord Holderness[11] entertained the good subjects with singing *God Save the King* to them over the rails of the terrace. The Duke of Modena supped there, and the Duke was asked, but he answered, it was impossible! In short, he could not adjust his dignity to a mortal banquet. There was another admirable scene; Lady Burlington brought the Violette, and the Richmonds[11a] had asked Garrick, who stood ogling and sighing the whole time, while my Lady kept a most fierce lookout.[12] Sabbatini, one of the Duke of Modena's court,[13] was asking me, who all the people were; and who is that? 'C'est Miladi Hartington,[14] la belle fille du Duc de Devonshire'—'Et qui est cette autre dame avec?' It was a distressing

3. John Anstis (1669–1745), Garter King-at-Arms, was succeeded by his son John (1708–54).

4. Descendants of Charles II.

5. Jacobites; the Duke of Richmond was Charles II's grandson.

6. Of Cumberland.

7. Francis III (Francesco d'Este) (1698–1780); see *Enciclopedia Italiana,* Roma, 1929–39, xv. 858.

8. According to the account in GM 1749, xix. 89–90, a 'Moorish king' entrusted his son and another youth to an English captain, to be educated in England; the captain sold them into slavery, and shortly after died, whereupon his officers revealed his treachery. The government ransomed the unhappy Africans and put them under the care of Lord Halifax, First Commissioner of Trade. They were presented to the King, and occasionally appeared at the theatre. At the tragedy of *Oroonoko,* whose situation was somewhat like their own, they were overcome with emotion, 'a circumstance which affected the audience yet more than the play, and doubled the tears which were shed.' Later in 1749 they were baptized (ibid. 522). The government's solicitude was not wholly disinterested, for, as the *St James's Evening Post* (10–12 Jan. 1749) pointed out, it 'no doubt

will contribute greatly to the credit and trade of this kingdom in those parts.' Anamabo is on the Gold Coast.

9. 'The Duke,' without clear reference to someone else, always meant the Duke of Cumberland in the mid-18th century.

10. Penelope Atkins (d. 1795), m. (1746) George Pitt, cr. (1776) Bn Rivers; see HW to Mann 17 May 1749.

11. Robert Darcy (1718–78), 4th E. of Holdernesse.

11a. Charles Lennox (1701–50), 2d D. of Richmond.

12. Garrick and the Violette were married 22 June 1749, at which time Lord and Lady Burlington were reputed to have settled £6,000 on her (DNB).

13. 'His Secretary of State' (HW to Mann 17 May 1749). 'Evidently Giuliano Sabbatini, Bishop of Modena, who was employed by the Duke and by the Pope Benedict XIV in various diplomatic negotiations. He was born at Fano in 1685 and died at Rome in 1767. He left five volumes of sermons, panegyrics, homilies and Latin and Italian poems' (G. Catalani in N&Q 1939, clxxvii. 337).

14. Lady Charlotte Elizabeth Boyle (1731–54), m. (1748) William Cavendish, styled M. of Hartington; 4th D. of Devonshire, 1755.

question.[15] After a little hesitation I replied, 'Mais c'est Mademoiselle Violette'—'Et comment Mademoiselle Violette! J'ai connu une Mademoiselle Violette par example'—I begged him to look at Miss Bishop.[16]

In the middle of all these principalities and powers was the Duchess of Queensberry in her old forlorn trim, a white apron and white hood, and would make the Duke[16a] swallow all her undress.[17] T'other day she drove to Lady Sophia Thomas[18] post at Parson's Green, and told her that she was come to tell her something of importance—'What is it?' 'Why, take a couple of beefsteaks, clap them together as if they were for a dumpling, and eat them with pepper and salt; it is the best thing you ever tasted; I could not help coming to tell you this'—and away she drove back to town.—Don't a course of folly for forty yea<rs> make one very sick?

The weather is so hot, and the roads so dusty, that I can't get to Strawberry, but I shall begin negotiating with you now about your coming. You must not expect to find it in beauty; the turf is as brown as Lady Bell Finch,[19] and there is no more shade than on Peggy Banks's forehead. I hope to get my bill[20] finished in ten days, I have scrambled it through the Lords; but altogether with the many diffi-

15. Probably because HW thought it would be incomprehensible to an Italian for a dancer to be in the best society; see Mann to HW 12 Nov. 1763, in which, discussing the expected arrival of the Garricks, he writes, 'I will get another box for Mrs Garrick in the theatre . . . [she] who will be called *the Violetta,* must too well remember the customs of her own country, however Lady Burlington and others may have spoilt her, to expect that these stately dames will associate with her.'

16. Doubtless one of the five beautiful daughters of Sir Cecil Bishopp, Bt; see HW to Strafford 7 June 1760.

16a. Charles Douglas (1698–1778), 3d D. of Queensberry.

17. The eccentricity of her dress was notorious. Her biographer suggests that she affected simple costumes to enhance her great beauty, for at other times she was splendid enough to dazzle such contemporaries as Mrs Delany; see Violet Biddulph, *Kitty Duchess of Queensberry,* 1935, pp. 117–26.

18. Lady Sophia Keppel (1711–73), dau. of 1st E. of Albemarle, m. Gen. John Thomas, 2d son of Sir Edmund Thomas, 2d Bt, of Glenvoe, Glamorgan (Collins, *Peerage,* 1812, iii. 733).

19. Lady Isabella Finch (d. 1771), 4th dau. of 6th E. of Winchelsea; first Lady of the Bedchamber to Princess Amelia (Collins, *Peerage,* 1812, iii. 401). The swarthiness of the Finch family was notorious, and 'the sable Finches' is a frequent expression with HW.

20. 'An Act for Sale of Divers Lands and Tenements in Twickenham in the County of Middlesex, devised by the Will of Paul Mansfield, deceased, pursuant to an Agreement for that Purpose, and for the Benefit of his Grandchildren.' In 1747 HW rented SH from Mrs Chenevix who had a long lease. When he decided to buy the property, an Act of Parliament was necessary, since it was owned by three minors; see 'Short Notes'; *Des. of SH, Works* ii. 399; *SH Accounts* 183–9 (giving the text of the Act). It was passed by both Houses, and received the Royal assent 13 June 1749 (House of Lords, *Journals* xxvii. 367b). HW's copy of the Act is now WSL.

culties and plagues, I am a good deal out of humour; my purchases hitch, and new proprietors[21] start out of the ground, like the crop of soldiers in the *Metamorphosis*.[22] I expect but an unpleasant summer; my indolence and inattention are not made to wade through leases and deeds. Mrs Chenevix brought me one yesterday to sign and her sister Bertrand, the toy-woman of Bath,[23] for a witness. I showed them my cabinet of enamels,[24] instead of treating them with white wine; the Bertrand said, 'Sir, I hope you don't trust all sorts of *ladies* with this cabinet'!—What an entertaining assumption of dignity! I must tell you an anecdote that I found t'other day in an old French author, which is as great a drawback on *beaux sentiments* and romantic ideas. Pasquier in his *Recherches de la France* is giving an account of the Queen of Scots' execution; he says, the night before, knowing her body must be stripped for her shroud, she would have her feet washed, because she used ointment to one of them which was sore.[25] I believe I have told you that in a very old trial of her,[26] which I bought from Lord Oxford's collection, it is said that she was a large lame woman. Take sentiments out of their pantoufles, and reduce them to the infirmities of mortality, what a falling off there is![27] I could not help laughing in myself t'other day as I went through Holborn in a very hot day, at the dignity of human nature; all those foul old-clothes women panting without handkerchiefs,[28] and mopping

21. Other people claiming interests in the land.

22. Ovid, *Met.* iii. 104.

23. Her husband died in 1755 (GM 1755, xxv. 429: 'Mr Bertraid [*sic*], who kept the great toyshop at Bath'). Pope mentions the shop (*Works*, ed. Elwin and Courthope, 1871–86, iv. 461), and John Wood, *Description of Bath*, edn 1769, p. 438, mentions a toy shop 'neighbouring' the pump house. Lady Mary Wortley Montagu's reference to 'Deard,' a Bath toy-woman (see Gray to HW, 11 June 1736, n.) aids the theory that Mrs Chenevix's maiden name was Deard, not Roussel (ibid.; *ante* 17 June 1746).

24. The cabinet of rosewood and ivory was designed by HW (see HW to Mann 19 July 1743 and illustration). It stood, ultimately, in the Tribune and was sold SH xv. 66 to 'Richards' for £126. It subsequently passed into the Redfern, Harry Guilder, Donaldson, and Murray collections, and is now in the Victoria and Albert Museum, No. W. 52–1925. See *Des. of*

SH, Works ii. 471, and a paper by Edward King in *Burlington Magazine* Feb. 1926, xlviii. 98–103, where, opp. p. 103, are several views of the cabinet and its details.

25. 'Elle avoit un mal de pieds ordinaire pour lequel on y appliquoit des unguents. Sachant qu'après son decez il la faudroit despoüiller, pour n'oublier rien de sa bienséance, elle se les fit laver le matin.' Étienne Pasquier (1529–1615), *Œuvres*, Amsterdam, 1723, i. 580–1 (*Recherches de la France*, Bk VI, ch. xv). HW's copy, MS Cat. F.2.5, was in folio, Paris, 1665; sold SH ii. 165.

26. Not found.

27. This sentence states the view of history which HW maintained throughout his life. It is perhaps an echo of the opening sentence in Gray to HW 10 Jan. 1738.

28. Not pocket-handkerchiefs, but kerchiefs or fichus worn around the neck and over the bust; see OED and Max von Boehn, *Modes and Manners*, Philadelphia, [1932–6] iv. 188.

themselves all the way down within their loose jumps. Rigby gave me as strong a picture of nature; he and Peter Bathurst[29] t'other night carried a servant of the latter's who had attempted to shoot him, before Fielding,[30] who to all his other vocations has, by the grace of Mr Lyttelton, added that of Middlesex justice. He sent them word he was at supper, that they must come next morning. They did not understand that freedom and ran up, where they found him banqueting with a blind man,[31] three Irishmen, and a whore,[32] on some cold mutton and a bone of ham, both in one dish, and the cursedest dirty cloth! He never stirred nor asked them to sit. Rigby, who had seen him so often come to beg a guinea of Sir Charles Williams, and Bathurst at whose father's he had lived for victuals,[33] understood that dignity as little, and pulled themselves chairs, on which he civilized. Millar[34] the bookseller has done very generously by him; finding *Tom Jones,* for which he had given him six hundred pounds sell so greatly, he has since given him another hundred.[34a] Now I talk to you of authors, Lord Cobham's West[35] has published his translation of Pindar: the poetry is very stiff, but prefixed to it there is a very entertaining account of the Olympic games; and that preceded by a most affected inscription to Pitt and Lyttelton.[36] The latter has declared

29. See n. 33 below. Probably Peter Bathurst (ca 1724–1801); Maj.-Gen., 1781, Lt-Gen., 1793, Gen., 1798; M.P. Eye 1784–90, 1792–5 (Collins, *Peerage,* 1812, v. 88; Foster, *Alumni Oxon.*).

30. Henry Fielding (1707–54), the novelist; at Lyttelton's recommendation, the Duke of Bedford had appointed him a Justice of the Peace in 1748; see Wilbur L. Cross, *History of Henry Fielding,* New Haven, 1918, ii. 95–8.

31. His brother John (1721–80), Kt, 1761; the well-known magistrate; see Ronald Leslie-Melville, *Life and Work of Sir John Fielding,* 1934.

32. His wife Mary Daniel (1712–1802), who had been his housekeeper, and whom he married in 1747 after the death of his first wife; see Cross, op. cit. ii. 227–8.

33. 'This racy anecdote, which Scott thought most "humiliating," should not be taken literally; large allowance must be made for a twofold distortion, first by Rigby the political parasite, who resented Fielding's coolness, and then by Walpole, whose malicious phrasing and aristocratic sense of superiority to the vulgar herd supplied the seasoning. Walpole is the only authority for the tradition that Fielding sponged upon Sir Charles Hanbury Williams, or that he dined too often with Earl Bathurst' (ibid. ii. 228). Fielding's supposed host was not Earl (then Baron) Bathurst, who had no son named Peter, but probably his brother Peter (ca 1688–1768), of Clarendon Park, Wilts (Collins, *Peerage,* 1812, v. 87–8), for whose son Peter see n. 29 above.

34. Andrew Millar (1707–68).

34a. *Tom Jones* had been published in Feb. 1749. Cross, op. cit. ii. 119–20, quotes HW's account of the extra £100 only as a rumour.

35. Gilbert West (1703–56); Lord Cobham was his uncle.

36. 'To / The Right Honourable / William Pitt, Esq. / Paymaster General of his Majesty's Forces, / One of his Majesty's most Honourable Privy Council, / And to the Honourable / George Lyttelton, Esq. / One of the Lords Commissioners of the Treasury, / This Volume / Is inscribed

his future match with Miss Rich;[37] George Grenville[38] has been married these two days to Miss Windham. Your friend Lord North is I suppose you know on the brink with the Countess of Rockingham;[39] and I think your cousin Rice[40] (but don't say that from my observation) is much inclined to double the family alliance with her sister Furnese.[41] It went on very currently for two or three days, but last night at Vauxhall his minionette[42] face seemed to be sent to languish with Lord Robert Bertie's.[43]

Was not you sorry for poor Cucumber?[44] I do assure you, I was; it was shocking to be hurried away so suddenly and in so much torment!

You have heard I suppose of Lord Harry Beauclerc's[45] resignation, on his not being able to obtain a respite till November, though the lowest officer in his regiment has got much longer leave in order to

by the Author, / Who is desirous that the Friendship, / With which they have for many Years honoured him, / And the sincere Affection and high Esteem, / Which he hath conceived for them, / From a long and intimate knowledge of their Worth and Virtue, / May be known wherever the Publication of the ensuing Pieces / Shall make known the Name of Gilbert West.'

37. Elizabeth Rich (ca 1716–95), m. (1749), as his 2d wife, Sir George Lyttelton, Bt, 1751. Her friend, Lady Hervey, writes that 'she has five thousand pounds at present, and will have as much more at her father's death: she has a good complexion, fine hair, and good teeth; has very good sense' (Lady Hervey, Letters, ed. 1821, pp. 162). The marriage was, however, unsuccessful; for disparaging accounts of her see Ananda V. Rao, A Minor Augustan, Calcutta, 1934, pp. 188, 271–3; Hester Lynch Piozzi, Autobiography, ed. A. Hayward, Boston, 1861, p. 231.

38. Hon. George Grenville (1712–70), First Lord of the Treasury 1763–5; m. Elizabeth (d. 1769), dau. of Sir William Wyndham.

39. Katherine Furnese (d. 1766), m. (1) (1736) Lewis Watson, 2d E. of Rockingham; m. (2) (1751) Francis North, 7th Bn North; cr. (1752) E. of Guilford.

40. George Rice (1724–79), Montagu's first cousin once removed; M.P. Carmar-

thenshire 1754–79; Treasurer of the Chamber, 1770; one of Newcastle's political managers for Wales; 'a very good man' (Delany, Correspondence v. 455; Lewis B. Namier, Structure of Politics at the Accession of George III, 1929, ii. 315; Collins, Peerage, 1812, vii. 508; GM 1779, xlix. 423; Foster, Alumni Oxon.).

41. Selina Furnese (d. 1757), m. (1755) Sir Edward Dering, 6th Bt, 1762.

42. 'Small and pretty' (OED, where this passage is quoted as the sole use of the word).

43. Lord Robert Bertie (1721–82), 5th son of 1st D. of Ancaster; Gen., 1777; Lord of the Bedchamber; M.P. Whitchurch 1751–4; Boston 1754–82; see Collins, Peerage, 1812, ii. 22; GM 1782, lii. 151. Apparently both he and Rice were rejected suitors.

44. Hon. Jane Conway, died suddenly 'yesterday' (St James's Evening Post 4–6 May 1749) after 'eating lemonade' (HW to Mann 17 May 1749).

45. Lord Henry Beauclerk (1701–61), 4th son of 1st D. of St Albans; M.P. Plymouth 1740–41; Thetford 1741–61; Col. 59th Foot 1743–5; 31st Foot 1745–9. His resignation from his regiment was noted without comment in the St James's Evening Post 6–9 May 1749 and in GM 1749 xix. 237. It is not known for what purpose he wanted leave.

take the benefit of the act of insolvency,[46] and avoid paying his creditors. It is incredible how Nolkejumskoi has persecuted this poor man for these four years, since he could not be persuaded to alter his vote at a court martial for the acquittal of a man, whom the Duke would have had condemned. Lord Ossulston[47] too has resigned his commission.

I must tell you a good story of Charles Townshend;[48] you know his political propensity and importance; his brother George[49] was at supper at the King's Arms[50] with some more young men; the conversation somehow or other rambled into politics, and it was started, that the national debt was a benefit: 'I am sure it is not,' said Mr Townshend; 'I can't tell why, but my brother Charles can, and I will send to him for arguments.' Charles was at supper at another tavern, but so much the dupe of this message that he literally called for ink and paper, wrote four long sides of arguments, and sent word that when his company broke up, he would come and give them more, which he did at one o'clock in the morning. I don't think you will laugh much less at what happened to me; I wanted a print out of a book which I did not care to buy at Osborne's[51] shop; the next day he sent me the print, and begged that when I had anything to publish, I would employ him.[52]—I will now only tell you and finish this long letter, how I shocked Mr Mekensie[53] inadvertently at Vauxhall; we had supped

46. By the Act of 21 Geo. II c. 31 (1748), 'An Act for Relief of Insolvent Debtors,' prisoners for debt could, by making an assignment of all their property for the benefit of their creditors, and by complying with certain formalities, be discharged, subject to some limitations on amount, etc. The same privilege extended to 'debtors beyond sea on 1 Jan. 1747.' These acts were passed periodically—the predecessor of this one appears to have been in 1743—and served to mitigate the rigour of the debtor's lot. At the Surrey quarter-sessions in July 1748, 460 prisoners and fugitives were discharged (GM 1748, xviii. 330).

47. Charles Bennet (1716–67), styled Vct Ossulston; 3d E. of Tankerville, 1753; he had been Lt-Col. of the 1st Foot Guards.

48. Hon. Charles Townshend (1725–67), Chancellor of the Exchequer 1766–7.

49. George Townshend (1724–1807), 4th Vct Townshend, 1764; cr. (1787) M. Town-

shend; soldier and politician. At this time he was 'a very particular young man, . . . with much oddness, some humour, no knowledge, great fickleness, greater want of judgment, and with still more disposition to ridicule' (Mem. Geo. II i. 39).

50. At least nine London establishments of this name existed during the 18th century; see N&Q 1921, 12th Ser. ix. 286.

51. Thomas Osborne (d. 1767), at Gray's Inn Gateway, Johnson's employer whom he thrashed (DNB).

52. Osborne's letter is missing. Possibly the humour lies in Osborne's assumption that HW was a professional writer.

53. Hon. James Stuart-Mackenzie (ca 1719–1800), brother of the Earl of Bute; at Eton with HW; M.P. 1742–80; Minister at Turin 1758–61; Keeper of the Privy Seal of Scotland 1763–5, 1766–1800; versed in mathematical sciences. See the encomiums on his character by his one-time secretary Louis Dutens, in Memoirs of a

there a great party, and coming out, Mrs More[54] who waits at the gate, said 'Gentlemen and ladies, will you walk in and hear the *surprising alteration of voice';* I forgetting Mekensie's connections and that he was formerly of the band,[55] replied, 'No, I have seen patriots enough.'

Goodnight—I intend this letter shall last you till you come to Strawberry Hill; one might have rolled it out into half a dozen. My best compliments to your sisters.

Yours ever,

H. W.

To Montagu, Wednesday 5 July 1749

Mistley, Wednesday, July 5th, 1749.

Dear George,

I HAVE this minute received your letter, and it makes me very unhappy. You will think me a brute for not having immediately told you how glad I should be to see you and your sisters; but I trust that you will have seen Mrs Boscawen, by whom I sent you a message[1] to invite you to Strawberry Hill, when we should be returned from Roel and Mistley. I own my message had rather a cross air, but as you have retrieved all your crimes with me by your letter, I have nothing to do, but to make myself as well with you, as you are with me. Indeed I am extremely unlucky, but I flatter myself that Mrs Montagu's[2] will not drop their kind intention, as it is not in my power to receive it now: they will give me infinite pleasure by a visit; I stay here till Monday se'nnight; will that be too late to see you before your journey to Roel? You must all promise at least to be engaged to me at my return. If the least impediment happens afterwards, I shall conclude my brother has got you from me; you know jealousy is the mark of our family.[3]

Traveller, now in Retirement, 1806, i. 160–1, 164–6, iv. 227–9; see also Sir Robert Douglas, *Peerage of Scotland,* ed. John P. Wood, 1813, i. 286; *Mem. Geo. III* i. 126; Richard A. Austen-Leigh, *Eton College Register 1698–1752,* 1927, p. 224; D. B. Horn, *British Diplomatic Representatives 1689–1789,* 1932, p. 125.

54. Not further identified.
55. The patriots.

1. The message, if written, is missing.
2. So in MS; HW means 'the Misses Montagu.'
3. See HW to Edward Walpole May 1745.

Mr Rigby makes you a thousand compliments, and wishes you would ever think his Roel[4] worth your seeing. You can't imagine how he has improved it! You have always heard me extravagant in the praises of the situation. He has demolished all his paternal intrenchments of walls and square gardens, opened lawns, swelled out a bow window, erected a portico, planted groves, stifled ponds, and flounced himself with flowering shrubs, and Kent-fences.[5] You may imagine that I have a little hand in all this. Since I came hither I have projected a colonnade to join his mansion to the offices, have been the death of a tree that intercepted the view of a bridge, for which too I have drawn a new white rail, and shall be an absolute travelling Jupiter at Baucis and Philemon's, for I have persuaded him[6] to transform a cottage into a church, by exalting a spire upon the end of it, as Talbot has done.[7] By the way I have dined at the Vineyard[8]—I dare not trust you with what I think—but I was a little disappointed! Tomorrow we go to see the ruins of the Abbey of St Osyth;[9] it is the seat of the Rochfords, but I never chose to go while they were there.

You will probably hear from Mr L.[10] (if in any pause of love he rests)[11] that I am going to be first minister to the Prince: in short I have occasioned great speculation, and diverted myself with the important mysteries that have been alembicked out of a trifle. In short he had seen my *Ædes Walpolianæ*[12] at Sir Luke Schaub's,[13] and sent

4. Mistley.
5. Sunken fences, which Kent was the first to employ extensively ('Modern Gardening,' *Works* ii. 535–6).
6. Rigby.
7. HW's collection of 'Drawings and Designs by Richard Bentley' (now WSL), contains, f. 40, a 'design of a fictitious steeple for Nich. Hardinge Esq. at Kingston,' which shows a Bentley-Gothic spire superimposed upon a roof.
8. No house of this name has been discovered in Essex. Possibly HW is referring to an earlier trip to Chute's house, the Vyne, in Hampshire.
9. There was a nunnery at St Osyth's, 10 miles SE of Colchester, in Saxon times; it was followed by a community of Austin Canons. Most of the ruins HW saw were of the early 16th century, though some are older. The Earl of Rochford, who had probably set out for Turin where he was Minister 1749–55, lived in a house built

by his father; see Essex Archaeological Society, *Transactions* 1873, Colchester, v. 1–52; D. B. Horn, *British Diplomatic Representatives 1689–1789*, 1932, p. 124. HW thought him a 'man of no abilities' (*Mem. Geo. III* iii. 168); and his wife was notorious; but neither of these facts would be a reason for HW's disinclination to visit them.
10. Lyttelton; he was to be married 10 Aug.
11. If a quotation, not found.
12. *Ædes Walpolianæ: or a Description of the Collection of Pictures at Houghton Hall in Norfolk,* 1747; see 'Short Notes.'
13. Sir Luke Schaub (d. 1758), Kt, 1720; Minister to Paris 1720–4, and held other diplomatic posts. He had a fine collection of pictures, for which the Prince of Wales offered him £20,000, leaving him the enjoyment for his life (HW to Mann 10 Feb. 1758; DNB says £12,000). He lived in Bond St.

by him to desire one. I sent him one, bound quite in coronation robes, and went last Sunday to thank him for the honour. There were all the new Knights of the Garter.[14] After the Prince had whispered through every curl of Lord Granville's periwig, I dare say about as errant trifles as to me, he turned to me, and said such a crowd of civil things that I did not know what to answer: commended the style and the quotations, said I had sent him back to his Livy,[15] in short that there were but two things he disliked, one that I had not given it him of my own accord, and the other that I had abused his friend Andrea del Sarto;[16] and that he insisted when I came to town again, I should come and see two very fine ones that he has lately bought of that master. This drew on a very long conversation on painting, every word of which I suppose will be reported at the other court as a plan of opposition for the winter. Prince George[17] was not there; when he went to receive the ribbon, the Prince carried him to the closet door, where the Duke of Dorset[18] received and carried him. Ayscough[19] or Nugent or some of the geniuses had taught him a speech, the child began it; the monarch bounced and cried 'No, No'; when the poor boy had a little recovered a fright, which to be sure flattered Majesty, as nobody has felt a grain of it so long, he began again, but the same tremendous sounds were repeated, and the oration stillborn. How could one exert such a silly surly triumph over a poor pretty child?

I believe that soon I shall have a pleasanter tale to tell you; 'tis said my Lady Anson not content with the profusion of absurdities she utters, by the way one of her last sayings and extremely in the style of

14. Prince George, the Markgraf of Brandenburg-Ansbach, the Dukes of Bedford and Leeds, and the Earls of Albemarle and Granville, were all nominated Knights of the Garter 22 June (William A. Shaw, *The Knights of England*, 1906, i. 44; HW to Mann 25 June 1749).
15. In *Ædes Walpolianæ*, *Works* ii. 269–70, 274–5, HW quotes at length from Livy, apropos of certain historical pictures in the Houghton collection.
16. 'You will perhaps see more paid for a picture of Andrea del Sarto, whose colouring was a mixture of mist and tawdry, whose drawing hard and forced, than for the most graceful air of a Madonna that ever flowed from the pencil of Guido'—ibid. 226.

17. George III.
18. Lionel Cranfield Sackville (1688–1765), 7th E. of Dorset; cr. (1720) D. of Dorset. At this time he was Lord President of the Council.
19. Rev. Dr Francis Ayscough (ca 1702–63), preceptor to Prince George until the Prince of Wales's death; Dean of Bristol, 1761; Sir George Lyttelton's brother-in-law. 'An insolent man, unwelcome to the clergy on suspicions of heterodoxy, and of no fair reputation for integrity' (*Mem. Geo. II* i. 79); but see a sympathetic account of how his career was obstructed by powerful enemies, in *Memoirs of a Royal Chaplain*, ed. Albert Hartshorne, 1905, pp. 282, 284; Foster, *Alumni Oxon.*; *Gray's Corr.* ii. 721.

Mr Lyttelton's making love, was, as she sat down to play at brag at the corner of a square table, Lady Fitzwalter said she was sorry she had not better room, 'Oh Madam,' said my Lady Anson, 'I can sit like a nightingale with my breast against a thorn';[20] in short that not content with so much wit, she proposes to entertain the town to the tune of Doctor's Commons.[21] She does not mince her disappointments; here is an epigram that has been made on the subject.

> As Anson his *Voyage* to my Lady was reading,
> And recounting his dangers,—thank God! she's not breeding!
> He came to the passage, where like the old Roman
> He stoutly withstood the temptation of woman.[22]
> The Baroness smil'd—when continuing he said,
> 'Think what terror must then fill the poor lover's head'—
> 'Alack,' quoth my Lady, 'he had nothing to fear,
> Were that Scipio[23] as harmless as you are, my dear![24]

It is given to Doddington and Nugent;[25] the latter's wife, who chose a little more substantially than my Lady Anson, and who does not yield to her for absurdities, though in a different style, said t'other

20. Common expression in the 16th century; see Shakespeare, *Sonnets to Sundry Notes of Music*, vi. 8; *Pass. Pil.*, xx. 8.

21. Doctor's Commons, in St Paul's churchyard, housed the ecclesiastical courts (see *London Past & Present*). Lady Anson could presumably have had her marriage annulled if it had never been consummated; but she did not. 'If you hear of any reports of a disagreement between Lord Anson and his Lady you may contradict them—*there never has been any;* she is a little coxcombical, and affects to be learned, which may sometimes put him out of countenance; but Lord Anson is a most generous, good-natured, amiable man, and he deserved a wife of more dignity' (Mrs Delany to Mrs Dewes, 20 Nov. 1749; Delany, *Correspondence* ii. 524).

22. The construction which HW (*ante* 18 May 1748 n. 7) and the epigrammatist here put on the passage in question seems unwarranted. It had nothing to do with 'temptation,' and was written only to illustrate Anson's deference towards some Spanish ladies he captured (George Anson, *Voyage Round the World*, 1748, pp. 178–9).

23. 'It is recorded of him that he refused to see a beautiful Spanish princess who had fallen into his hands after the taking of Carthago Nova, and not only restored her to her parents but added presents for the person to whom she was betrothed' (Sir Paul Harvey, *Oxford Companion to English Literature*, Oxford, 1932). See *Ædes Walpolianæ, Works* ii. 274–6, where HW quotes the story at length from Livy, and adds some verses on the subject, presumably his own.

24. The rest of the letter is omitted in previous editions.

25. It is also included in *Works of . . . Sir Charles Hanbury Williams . . . With Notes by Horace Walpole, Earl of Orford*, 1822, ii. 271. HW's note on Lady Anson repeats the nightingale and thorn story. It seems not improbable that HW himself is the author. Both the strained interpretation of the Spanish captives incident, and the comparison with Scipio, neither of which is particularly obvious, were made *ante* 18 May 1748, and in a packet of MS copies of his epigrams, etc., among the papers HW left Miss Berry (now wsl) is a fair copy of this one, written ca 1757.

day on somebody's wondering how Mr Lyttelton could marry again after losing so agreeable a wife;[26] 'Well now, I can figure myself in his situation. When one loses a husband one loves, I don't know, there is such a void, such a space that wants to be filled up'—Adieu! This last page is not for your sisters.

Yours ever,

H. W.

To Montagu, Thursday 20 July 1749

Strawberry Hill, July 20, 1749.

I AM returned to my Strawberry, and find it in such beauty, that I shall be impatient till I see you and your sisters here. They must excuse me if I don't marry for their reception, for it is said the Draxes[1] have impeached[2] fifteen more damsels, and till all the juries of matrons have finished their inquest, one shall not care to make one's choice—I was going to say, *throw one's handkerchief*,[3] but at present that term would be a little equivocal.

As I came to town, I was extremely entertained with some excursions I made out of the road in search of antiquities. At Layer-Marney[4] is a noble old remnant of the palace of the Lords Marney, with three very good tombs in the church well preserved.[5] At Messing[6] I

26. Lucy Fortescue (ca 1718–47), m. (1742) George Lyttelton; his well-known 'Monody' on her death has been frequently reprinted (see DNB).

1. Possibly the five daughters of Henry Drax of Ellerton Abbey; see Burke, *Landed Gentry*, 1836, i. 350; 16 Nov. 1754, n. 5.

2. That is, questioned the virtue of.

3. It was believed at the time that the Sultan indicated a choice by throwing his handkerchief to a member of his harem. Thus in a MS Book of Materials, dated 1759, now in the Folger Library, HW writes of a Lady Winchilsea whose husband was ambassador at Constantinople, 'She desired to see the seraglio, did, and the Sultan flung his handkerchief to her. The Duchess of Montrose has the very

handkerchief' (p. 146); and see Lady Mary Wortley Montagu, *Letters and Works*, ed. Lord Wharncliffe, 3d edn 1861, i. 345, ii. 75. 'Throw a handkerchief' also means to make a choice by association with children's games; see OED *sub* handkerchief. The gossip to which the text here refers has not been ascertained.

4. Seven miles SW of Colchester.

5. The palace was built by Sir Henry Marney (1457–1523), K.G.; cr. (1523) Bn Marney; Lord Privy Seal. The tombs are probably his, his son's (d. 1525), and his ancestor's, Sir William Marney, d. ca 1360. Both the house and monuments are illustrated and described in *Royal Commission on Historical Monuments . . . Essex*, 1916–23, iii. 154–61.

6. Three and a half miles SE of Coggeshall, Essex.

saw an extreme fine window of painted glass in the church;[7] it is the
duties prescribed in the Gospel of visiting the sick and prisoners etc.
I mistook and called it the seven deadly sins. There is a very old tomb
of Sir Robert Messing that built the church. The *Hall-Place*[8] is a frag-
ment of an old house belonging to Lord Grimston;[9] Lady Luckyn his
mother,[10] of fourscore and six, lives in it with an old son and daughter. The servant who showed it, told us much history of another
brother,[11] that had been parson there: this history was entirely composed of the anecdotes of the doctor's drinking, who as the man told
us, had been *a blood!* There are some Scotch arms taken from the
rebels in the '15, and many old coats of arms on glass, bought from
Newhall,[12] which now belongs to Olmius:[13] Mr Conyers[14] bought a
window there for only a hundred pound, on which was painted
Harry the Eighth and one of his Queens at full length:[15] he has put it
up at Copt Hall,[16] a seat which he has bought that belonged to Lord

7. The window, of early 17th-century make, is still there (ibid. 180). The legendary founder of the church is generally labelled Sir William de Messing; on his tomb was a wooden effigy, which was destroyed sometime during the 19th century (Philip Morant, *History . . . of Essex,* 1768, ii. 178; Thomas Wright, *History . . . of Essex,* 1836, i. 387; *Archaeologia,* 1909, lxi pt ii. 489).

8. Also known as Baynard's; torn down before 1836 (Thomas Wright, *History . . . of Essex,* 1836, i. 384).

9. William Grimston (formerly Luckyn) (ca 1683–1756), cr. (1719) Vct Grimston.

10. Mary Sherrington (1663–ca 24 Nov. 1749), m. (1681) Sir William Luckyn, 3d Bt. The 'old son and daughter' would be among her fifteen children whose names are given in Collins, *Peerage,* 1812, viii. 220.

11. Charles Luckyn (ca 1694–1745), Rector of Pebmarsh and Vicar of Messing (Philip Morant, *History . . . of Essex,* 1768, ii. 177, 179; Foster, *Alumni Oxon).* HW twice refers to this visit to Messing to Lady Ossory 18 July 1780, 11 Oct. 1788. Then the house servant had become the landlady of an inn, telling *mots* of 'Mr Charles Luckyn . . . who . . . had been the George Selwyn of half a dozen cottages.'

12. New Hall, Boreham, Essex, was built by Henry VIII ca 1520, rebuilt by the Earl of Sussex in 1573, and mostly torn down in 1737; it is now a nunnery; see Essex Archaeological Society, *Transactions,* Colchester, 1909, x. 6; 1911, xi. 73–6; *Royal Commission on Historical Monuments . . . Essex,* 1916–23, ii. 22, 24–6.

13. John Olmius (1711–62), cr. (1762) Bn Waltham.

14. John Conyers (ca 1718–75), M.P. Reading 1747–54; Essex 1772–5 (Venn, *Alumni Cantab.).* Both the window and Copt Hall were purchased by his father Edward Conyers, d. 1742 (Thomas Wright, *History . . . of Essex,* 1836, ii. 460–1).

15. Until recently the east window in St Margaret's, Westminster, to which Conyers sold it in 1758 for £400. The royal figures on it were probably originally intended for Prince Arthur (1486–1502) and Catherine of Aragon; see Rev. Mackenzie E. C. Walcott, *Westminster,* 1849, pp. 102–5, for its curious history, and *Royal Commission on Historical Monuments . . . London,* 1924–30, ii. plate no. 153, and p. 102. The buying of fragments of churches was not uncommon at that time; HW himself later bought some tiles from Gloucester Cathedral (HW to Bentley Sept. 1753).

16. Copt, or Copped, Hall, 2 miles SW of Epping, Essex; the old manor-house

North and Grey.[17] You see I persevere in my heraldry: t'other day
the parson of Rigby's parish[18] dined with us—he has conceived as high
an opinion of my skill in genealogies as if I could say the first chapter
of St Matthew by heart; R. drank my health to him, and that I might
come to be Garter King-at-Arms; the poor man replied with great
zeal, *I wish he may with all my heart!* Certainly I am born to preferment; I gave an old beggar woman a penny once, who prayed that I
might live to be Lord Mayor of London! What pleased me most in
my travels was Dr Sayer's[19] parsonage at Witham, which with Southcote's help, whose old Roman Catholic father[20] lives just by him, he
has made one of the most charming villas in England. There are
sweet meadows falling down a hill, and rising again on t'other side of
the prettiest little winding stream you ever saw.

You did not at all surprise me with the relation of the keeper's brutality to your family, or of his master's to the Dowager's handmaid:[21]
his savage temper increases every day: George Boscawen[22] is in a
scrape with him by a court-martial, of which he is one; it was appointed on a poor young soldier who to see his friends had counter-
feited a furlough of leave, only for a day. They ordered him two hundred lashes, but Nolkejumskoi who loves blood like a leech, insisted
that it was not enough, has made them sit three times, though everyone adheres to the first sentence, and swears they shall sit these six
months, till they increase the punishment.[23] The fair Mrs Pitt has

was replaced by John Conyers, 1753–7,
from designs by John Wyatt; see *Essex Review*, 1922, Colchester, xxxi. 212–17; Philip
Morant, *History . . . of Essex*, 1768, i
pt ii. 48–9.

17. William North (1673–1734), 6th Bn
North and 2d Bn Grey. Though Edward
Conyers purchased the adjoining manor of
Epping from his estate, Copt Hall had
been sold to the Earl of Middlesex ca
1635, and Edward Conyers bought it from
Sir Thomas Webster (see references in n.
15 above).

18. David Mustard (ca 1684–1775), Rector of Mistley (Philip Morant, *History . . .
of Essex*, 1768, i. 463; GM 1775, xlv. 407).

19. George Sayer, D.D. (ca 1696–1761),
vicar of Witham, Essex, 1722–61; he also
held other preferment (see Foster, *Alumni
Oxon;* Venn, *Alumni Cantab.*). He bought
the manor of Witham Magna in 1735 (Es-

sex Archaeological Society, *Transactions*
1893, Colchester, n.s. iv. 85, 112).

20. Sir Edward Southcote, Kt, died be-
tween 1751 and 1758; see Owen Manning,
History . . . of Surrey, 1804–14, ii. 259–60.
See *ante* 11 Aug. 1748 for HW's admira-
tion of Philip Southcote's house, Woburn
Farm.

21. Unexplained in the absence of
Montagu's letter. The Master is evidently
the Duke of Cumberland.

22. Hon. George Boscawen (1712–75),
3d son of 1st Vct Falmouth; Lt-Gen., 1760;
M.P. Penryn 1743–61; Truro 1761–74; m.
Anne Trevor, Montagu's first cousin; see
Collins, *Peerage*, 1812, vi. 69.

23. Sentences of 800 or 1000 lashes were
not at all uncommon at this time; see
quotations from the general orders in
Archibald N. Campbell-Maclachlan, *William Augustus Duke of Cumberland*,

been mobbed in the Park and with difficulty rescued by some gentle-men, only because this bashaw is in love with her. You heard I sup-pose of his other amour with the Savoyard girl: he sent her to Wind-sor, and offered her a hundred pound, which she refused because he was a heretic; he sent her back on foot. Enclosed is a new print on this subject, which I think has more humour than I almost ever saw in one of that sort.[24]

Should not I condole with you upon the death of the head of the Cues?[25] If you have not heard of his will, I will tell you. The settled estate of £8000 a year is to go between the two daughters,[26] out of which is a jointure of £3000 a year to the Duchess Dowager,[27] and to that he has added 1000 more out of the unsettled estate, which is 9000. He gives together with his blessing £4000 per annum rent charge to the Duchess of Manchester in present, provided she will con-test nothing with her sister, who is to have all the rest, and the rever-sion of the whole after Lady Cardigan and her children; but in case she disputes, Lady Hinchinbrook[28] and hers, are in the entail next to the Cardigans, who are to take the Montagu name and livery. I don't know what Mr Hussy will think of the blessing, but they say his Duchess will be inclined to mind it; she always wanted to be well with her father, but hated her mother. There are two codicils, one in favour of his servants, and the other of his dogs, cats and creatures, which was a little unnecessary, for Lady Cardigan has exactly his turn for saving everything's life.[29] As he was making the codicil, one of the

1876, pp. 231–2, 356–8. For a defense of the Duke of Cumberland, who, though a strict disciplinarian, appears to have been no more savage than the military practice of the time demanded, see Hon. Sir Evan Charteris, K.C., *William Augustus Duke of Cumberland, His Early Life and Times*, 1913, pp. 210–14 and *passim*.

24. 'The Savoyard girl has made some noise and some pictures; she is a poor mean-dressed wench, but pretty enough if she was dressed out, not at all like the picture in the print where the Duke kneels' (John Byrom to his wife, 3 Aug. 1749, in his *Private Journal and Literary Remains*, ed. Richard Parkinson, ii pt ii. 1857, p. 504 [Chetham Society, I. xliv]). She was a singer, and according to one version of the story was rescued by her

brother from the Duke's clutches. The prints on the subject (the enclosure is missing) are described, and the story told, in BM *Satiric Prints* iii pt i. 750–3.

25. John Montagu (1689–6 July 1749), 2d D. of Montagu.

26. The Duchess of Manchester and the Countess of Cardigan.

27. Lady Mary Churchill (1689–1751), 4th dau. of 1st D. of Marlborough; m. (1705) John Montagu, 2d D. of Montagu.

28. Elizabeth Popham (d. 1761), m. (1) (1707) Edward Richard Montagu, Vct Hinchingbrooke; m. (2) (1728) Francis Sey-mour; the Duke of Montagu's niece.

29. 'The Duke of Montagu has an hos-pital for old cows and horses; none of his tenants near Broughton dare kill a broken-winded horse: they must bring them all

cats jumped on his knee; 'What,' says he, 'have you a mind to be a witness too! You can't, for you are a party concerned.'[30] The Duchess was on the point of losing ten thousand pound by a fit of Marlbro' humour. It was in old Fairfax's[31] hands, when he died, she sent for it to his nephew;[32] who owned the trust, but said he was advised that he could not give it up without a release from the Duke: she said no, it was her own money, and she would have it in her own way; the Duke would do it for a word speaking, but she would have it in her own way. She sent to the South Sea Company as it is in their bonds, to order Mr F. to deliver it: they had nothing to do with it. In the interim the Duke died. Had the Manchester been a legatee,[33] she had lost it, but it will not be worth the Cardigan's while to dispute it, for she has at least ninety more, and never would lend the Duke a shilling in all his purchases.

Lord Stafford is going to send his poor wife[34] with one maid and one horse to a farmhouse in Shropshire forever![35] The Mirepoix[36] are come, but I have not yet seen them. A thousand compliments to your sisters.

Yours ever,

H. W.

to the *reservoir*.—The Duke keeps a lap-dog, the ugliest creature he could meet with: he is always fond of the most hideous, and says he was at first kind to them, because nobody else would be' (Joseph Spence, *Anecdotes*, 1820, p. 328).

30. And as such incompetent, at that time, as an attesting witness (Helliard v. Jennings, 1 Ld. Raym. 505, 91 *English Reports* 1237 [1699]). Under present law, the witness may be a beneficiary named in the will, but the bequest to him is automatically forfeited; see 1 Vict. 26 (1837), s. 15, Great Britain, *Statutes*, rev. edn, 1875, viii. 33.

31. Probably Brian Fairfax (1676–9 Jan. 1749), antiquary.

32. Probably his first cousin once removed and his heir, Robert Fairfax (1707–93), 7th Bn Fairfax, 1782; about him see Lewis B. Namier, *Structure of Politics at the Accession of George III*, 1929, ii. 498–508.

33. HW apparently means that if the Duchess of Manchester had been *residuary*

legatee, she would contest her mother's claim; but that Lady Cardigan would not.

34. Henrietta Cantillon (d. 1761), m. (1) (1743) William Matthias Stafford-Howard (1719–51), 3d E. of Stafford; m. (2) (1759) Robert Maxwell, 2d Bn Farnham, cr. (1760) Vct, and (1763) E. of Farnham.

35. The reason is unknown.

36. Charles-Pierre-Gaston-François de Lévis de Lomagne (1699–1757), Marquis de Mirepoix; Duc de Mirepoix, 1751; ambassador to England 1749–55; Maréchal de France, 1757 (*Larouse du xxe siècle* [1928–33], iv. 897; Anatole, Marquis de Granges de Surgères, *Répertoire . . . de la Gazette de France*, 1902–6). He m. (1739), as her 2d husband, Anne-Marguerite-Gabrielle de Beauvau-Craon (1707–91); see DU DEFFAND. He arrived 9 July, had a great levee at his house in Grosvenor Square 17 July, and had audience with the King 20 July, accompanied by 150 domestic servants in scarlet and silver liveries (*St James's Evening Post*, 15–18 July, 18–20 July 1749).

To Montagu, Saturday 26 August 1749

Strawberry Hill, Aug. 26, 1749.

Dear George,

I FLATTER myself that you are quite recovered of your disorder, and that your sisters will not look with an evil eye on Strawberry Hill.[1]

Mr Chute and I are returned from our expedition, miraculously well, considering all our distresses. If you love good roads, conveniencies, good inns, plenty of postilions and horses, be so kind to yourself as never to go into Sussex. We thought ourselves in the northest part of England;[2] the whole country has a Saxon air, and the inhabitants are as savage, as if King George the Second was the first monarch of the East Angles. Coaches grow there no more than balm and spices; we were forced to drop our post-chaise, in which we were thrice overturned,[3] and hire a machine that resembled nothing so much as Harlequin's calash,[4] which was occasionally[5] a chaise or a baker's cart. We journeyed over Alpine mountains, drenched in clouds, and thought of Harlequin again, when he was driving the chariot of the sun through the morning clouds, and was so glad to hear the *aqua vitæ* man crying a dram.[6] At last we got to Arundel Castle, which was visibly built for defence in an impracticable country. It is now only a heap of ruins, with a new indifferent apartment clapped up for the Norfolks,[6a] when they reside there for a week or a fortnight. Their priest[7] showed us about. There are the walls of a round tower,

1. Montagu had been at SH 17 Aug.; see HW to Mann 17 Aug. 1749.

2. HW was never there.

3. The badness of Sussex roads was notorious; in 1722 Defoe saw, not far from Lewes 'an ancient lady, and a lady of very good quality, I assure you, drawn to church in her coach with six oxen; nor was it done in frolic or humour, but mere necessity, the way being so stiff and deep, that no horses could go in it' (*Tour through . . . Great Britain*, edn 1927, i. 129).

4. 'A kind of light carriage with low wheels, having a removable folding hood or top' (OED).

5. That is, it was either, as occasion offered, as was Harlequin's equipage when he required a 'transformation,' an important element in 18th-century pantomime; see next note.

6. Possibly a reference to a pantomime

HW and Montagu had seen. In the revival of pantomime in England in the 18th century, the stock figures of the *commedia dell' arte*—Harlequin, Pierrot, Columbine, etc., were employed, though the entertainment itself wandered far from its source, becoming more and more elaborate and spectacular. At this time the comical element predominated, and topical allusions had helped to bring about the passage of the Licensing Act in 1737; see M. Willson Disher, *Clowns and Pantomimes*, Boston, 1925, pp. 225 et seq.; Cyril W. Beaumont, *History of Harlequin*, 1926, pp. 88–93.

6a. See n. 11 below.

7. Rev. Charles Cordell (1720–86) was chaplain at Arundel 1748–55; see Catholic Record Society, *Miscellanea*, Leeds, xxvii (1927). 56.

where a garrison held out against Cromwell; he planted a battery on the top of the church, and reduced them.[8] There is a gloomy gateway and dungeons, in one of which I conclude is kept the old woman who in the time of the late rebellion offered to show Lord R. Sutton[9] where arms were hid at Worksop.[10] The Duchess[11] complimented him into dining before his search, and in the meantime the woman was spirited away, and adieu the arms! There are fine monuments of the old Fitzalans Earls of Arundel in the church.[12] Mr Chute whom I have created *Strawberry King-at-Arms* has had brave sport *à la chasse aux armes*.

We were charmed with the magnificence of the park at Petworth, which is Percy to the backbone;[13] but the house and garden did not please our antiquarian spirit. The house is entirely new-fronted in the style of the Tuilleries, and furnished exactly like Hampton Court.[14] There is one room gloriously flounced all round whole-length pictures with much the finest carving of Gibbins[15] that ever my eyes

8. Arundel was besieged in Dec. 1643 and Jan. 1644, by a Parliamentary army under Sir William Waller; see Mark Tierney, *History . . . of Arundel*, 1834, i. 58–78. As part of the siege operations, two small cannon ('sacres') and some musketeers were stationed in the church steeple, and did considerable damage (ibid. 63). The ruinous condition of the castle was largely a result of this siege (ibid. 79).

9. Lord Robert Manners Sutton (ca 1722–72), 2d son of 3d D. of Rutland; took the name of Sutton on inheriting the estate of his maternal grandfather, Lord Lexington; M.P. Notts 1747–62; see Collins, *Peerage*, 1812, i. 487–8.

10. Worksop, Notts, then a seat of the Duke of Norfolk; like other Catholics, he was suspected of Jacobite leanings. Hidden stores of arms were imagined in every Tory attic during the excitement of the '45. The deposition of one Margaret Brownhill in State Papers Domestic, 1745, Bundle 75, no. 4 (printed in Robert White, *The Dukery Records*, Worksop, 1904, p. 331), in so far as it is trustworthy, supports part of HW's story. She declares that while being shown Worksop by a servant friend in 1736, a secret room under the roof was revealed to her. In this room was a secret doorway leading to another room, which 'they looked into, but it being dark they could not see anything in it, but the said Elizabeth Walkden [the ser-

vant] said they could not go into it it was so full of arms.'

11. Mary Blount (ca 1702–73), m. (1727) Edward Howard (1686–1777), 9th D. of Norfolk.

12. Formerly part of the chapel of the College of the Holy Trinity; now called the Fitzalan Chapel. The monuments, which are described in Mark Tierney, *History . . . of Arundel*, 1834, ii. 618–29, were damaged during alterations in 1782.

13. Jocelyn de Louvaine married (ca 1150) Agnes de Perci, and took her name; his sister Adeliza, widow of Henry I, gave him Petworth on that occasion; see Edward Barrington de Fonblanque, *Annals of the House of Percy*, 1887, i. 32. The daughter of the last Percy Earl of Northumberland married the Duke of Somerset, whose son left Petworth to his nephew the Earl of Egremont, through whom it descended to Lord Leconfield.

14. 'The Duke [of Somerset] pulled down the ancient edifice, and on the site of it erected the present structure, which is considered as one of the finest in England' (*Modern Universal British Traveller*, 1779, p. 45). 'Pulled down' should apparently read 'remodelled.'

15. Grinling Gibbons (1648–1720), the wood-carver. This room HW called 'the most superb monument of his skill' (*Anecdotes, Works* iii. 343). It was left unfin-

beheld. There are birds absolutely feathered, and two antique vases with bas-relieves as perfect and beautiful as if they were carved by a Grecian master. There is a noble Claud Lorrain,[16] a very curious picture of the haughty Ann Stanhope,[17] the Protector's wife, pretty but not giving one an idea of her character, and many old portraits,[18] but the housekeeper was at London, and we did not learn half. The chapel[19] is grand and proper. At the inn we entertained ourselves with the landlord, whom my Lord Hervey[20] had cabineted[21] when he went to woo one of the Lady Seymours.[22]

Our greatest pleasure was seeing Cowdry,[23] which is repairing; Lord Montacute[24] will at last live in it. We thought of old Margaret of Clarence,[25] who lived there; one of her accusations was built on the bulls found there: it was the palace of her great-uncle, the Mar-

ished by Gibbons, and completed by Jonathan Ritson in 1827–46 (DNB, sub Ritson). For photographs of the details mentioned by HW, see H. Avray Tipping, *Grinling Gibbons and the Woodwork of His Age*, 1914, pp. 185–94.

16. Claude Lorrain (Claude Gellée) (1600–82); the painting has been engraved by Woollett; see Gustav Frederick Waagen, *Treasures of Art in Great Britain*, 1854, iii. 33.

17. Anne Stanhope (ca 1497–1587), m. (1) (ca 1537) Edward Seymour (ca 1500–52), E. of Hertford, cr. (1547) D. of Somerset, the Protector; m. (2) Francis Newdigate. Her pride led her into disputes over precedence with her sister-in-law Catherine Parr which are said to have contributed to her husband's downfall (DNB). HW had a portrait of her by Sir Antonio More, sold SH xx. 30 to the Hon. Rev. Heneage Finch for 8 gns. It was engraved by Nugent after Sylvester Harding and appears in *Biographical Mirrour*, 1795, i. 3, apparently the only portrait of her to be engraved.

18. There is a list of them in James Dallaway, *Parochial Topography of . . . Western . . . Sussex*, ed. Cartwright, 1815–32, ii pt i. 318–23.

19. Part of the old house; left untouched during the rebuilding mentioned above (ibid. 316–7).

20. The Earl of Bristol to his grandson Lord Hervey, 10 Nov. 1750, about a Miss Archer: 'Your long-continued celibacy hath given me no small uneasiness; but there

now being a young woman sprung up in our Lincolnshire neighbourhood, whose mother hath . . . twenty thousand pounds a year, and can give her an immense fortune out of it . . . and who is turned of twenty and . . . is very agreeable and the sweetest tempered young woman of the age,' Bristol offers to 'make such proposals on your behalf as you shall send me, hoping you will not let this lady slip through your fingers as you did the sister[s] Seymour, three such heiresses not happening in three centuries' (*Letter-Books of John Hervey, First Earl of Bristol* [ed. Sydenham H. A. Hervey], Wells, 1894, iii. 410–11).

21. That is, closeted himself with.

22. Lady Frances Seymour (1728–60), m. (1750) John Manners, styled M. of Granby (GM 1760 xxx. 47). Lady Charlotte Seymour (1730–1805), m. (1750) Heneage Finch, styled Lord Guernsey; 3d E. of Aylesford, 1757.

23. Cowdray, near Midhurst, Sussex; built ca 1535–45, burned 1793; see Mrs Charles Roundell, *Cowdray*, 1884; *Country Seats* 76; COLE ii. 8, 128.

24. Antony Browne (1686–1767), 6th Vct Montagu.

25. Lady Margaret (1473–1541), dau. of George Plantagenet, D. of Clarence, m. (ca 1491) Sir Richard Pole; cr. (1513) Countess of Salisbury. The treason charge by which Henry VIII did away with her was based partly on her possession of certain papal bulls, found not at Cowdray, where she never lived, but at Warblington. She

quis Montacute.[26] I was charmed with the front, and the court and the fountain, but the room called Holbein's,[27] except the curiosity of it, is wretchedly painted, and infinitely inferior to those delightful histories of Harry the Eighth in the private apartment at Windsor.[28] I was much more pleased with a whole-length picture of Sir Antony Brown[29] in the very dress in which he wedded Anne of Cleves by proxy. He is in blue and white, only his right leg is entirely white, which was certainly robed for the act of putting into bed to her:[30] but when the King came to marry her, he only put his leg into bed to kick her out of it.

I have set up my staff and finished my pilgrimages for this year. Sussex is a great damper of curiosity. Adieu! My compliments to your sister.

Yours ever,

H. Walpole

was, however, imprisoned at Cowdray in 1538 by its then owner, the Earl of Southampton, before being taken to the Tower.

26. John Neville (ca 1431–71), cr. (1464) E. of Northumberland, (1470) M. of Montagu; brother of Warwick the Kingmaker. Cowdray was owned throughout the 15th century by a branch of the de Bohun family (Mrs. Charles Roundell, Cowdray, 1884, pp. 1–4; Dudley G. C. Elwes, History of the Castles, Mansions and Manors of Western Sussex, 1876, p. 77).

27. The dining-room, containing frescoes of the military triumphs of Henry VIII, by an unknown hand. HW revisited Cowdray in 1774 and reasserts his belief that Hans Holbein (ca 1497–1543) did not paint this room, 'but he might design it,' together with some of the figures and ornaments (Country Seats 76). The frescoes are described in detail in Archaeologia 1775, iii. 239–72, and attributed to Theodore Bernardi (ibid. 270). The Society of Antiquaries also published drawings of them by Grimm. See Anecdotes, Works iii. 83.

28. HW probably refers to four historical paintings now at Hampton Court, once attributed to Holbein, representing Henry VIII's Embarkation at Dover in 1520, The Field of the Cloth of Gold, The Battle of Spurs, and Henry VIII and his family; see Anecdotes, ed. Wornum, i. 58–9; Cole ii. 277, n. 9; HW to Mason 10 July 1775.

29. Sir Anthony Browne (d. 1548), Master of the Horse to Henry VIII. DNB also states that 'in 1540 [sic; Anne started for England Oct. 1539] Browne went to the court of John of Cleves to act as proxy at the marriage of Henry VIII with Anne of Cleves.' But no indication has been found elsewhere that there was any proxy marriage between Henry and Anne. Frequent references to Browne in the State Papers show that he must have been in England during the entire autumn of 1539 when Anne was preparing for and making her journey to England, for a careful account of which see Agnes Strickland, Lives of the Queens of England, 1851–2, iii. 35–43. Furthermore, he was one of the gentlemen appointed to receive her in England (Calendar of State Papers Foreign and Domestic, 1539 Part II, p. 201). The source of HW's misinformation has not been discovered.

30. This method of 'consummating' a proxy marriage was employed for the match between the Princess Mary and Louis XII of France: 'The bride undressed and went to bed in the presence of many witnesses. The Marquis of Rothelin, in his doublet, with a pair of red hose, but with one leg naked, went into bed, and touched the Princess with his naked leg. The marriage was then declared consummated' (Calendar of State Papers Foreign and Domestic, 1509–14, p. 861).

From MONTAGU, ca Monday 25 September 1749

In the possession of Sir Wathen A. Waller, Bt, Woodcote, Warwick. Answered by HW 28 Sept. 1749.

Memoranda by HW: The Comet
Millions of ancestors
Stoke Pogeis.

The last two notes were used by HW in his reply *post* 28 Sept. 'The Comet' is probably a nickname; see *ante* 3 Nov. 1746, 'How do all the comets?' Apparently, there was no comet visible in 1749.

Windsor, Sept. [ca 25], 1749.

Dear Horry,

THE person[1] I intended to employ in copying the picture of Prince Edward[2] has left Windsor. I went one day to examine it, and do not believe that it was drawn from any painting of him, for the other three, Henry VI, and V, and Edward IV[3] are not in the least like any of the pictures or coins that remain of them.

The Dean[4] showed me one day the registers of the Order, and they were very well worth seeing. The Sovereign of the Order in every reign is painted very prettily at the beginning on vellum, and all the leaves are illuminated with flowers and devices.

A servant that comes to Queen Katharine in *Henry VIII* delivers his message standing, and treating her as Princess of Wales, at which she is much offended and orders him out of her sight because he did not kneel,[5] so that it was an ancient custom to kneel when they spoke to queens. You remember we talked about the courtiers who knelt when Queen Elizabeth looked at them.

I went lately to Bisham Abbey[6] in hopes of seeing the tombs of the old Earls of Salisbury, but when I opened the chapel doors, there was, to my great disappointment, nothing but dried herbs and yellow

1. Not identified.
2. Edward (1453–71), Prince of Wales; son of Henry VI.
3. Montagu apparently refers to four panels in the south aisle of the choir of St George's Chapel, painted about 1490 with portraits of Prince Edward, Edward IV, Edward V, and Henry VII; see William H. St John Hope, *Windsor Castle,* 1913, ii. 414.
4. Peniston Booth (1681–1765), Dean of Windsor and Register of the Garter (DNB).

5. Shakespeare, *Henry VIII,* IV. ii. 100–8.
6. Four miles NW of Maidenhead, Berks; founded in 1337 by William de Montacute, first Earl of Salisbury; several of that family were buried there, as well as Warwick the Kingmaker and his son. The monastic buildings were, however, largely replaced ca 1560 by the present house, and the tombs have disappeared; see *Vict. Co. Hist. Berks* iii. 139–45.

cucumbers bursting for seed. Lord Cholmley[7] is making alterations
there, though he only hires the house of Sir Philip Hobby.[8] In the
parish church there are very fine monuments of the Hobbys, and the
painting and gilding is better preserved than any monuments that I
ever saw that were put up so long ago as Queen Elizabeth's time.
There is a Lady Hobby, wife to Sir Philip Hobby, Knight of the Garter, in a black robe and fardingale and white laced veil, and her sister, a peeress, in robes.[9] The hands and face are very well executed,
and all the veins painted, and they look almost alive, and there is a
very pretty monument of Lady Hunsdon,[10] her daughter, that is in
the print of Vertue's,[11] where the Queen is represented making her
entry into Lord Hunsdon's her husband's house.

I conclude you have enjoyed this fine weather at your pretty villa,
and I hope you have had your health well. Indeed I need not doubt
it, for you are always well. Nay, I will own, who often complain, that
I have been better for a long continuance than I ever was.

My sisters present their best compliments to you.

I am ever much yours,

G. Montagu

To Montagu, Thursday 28 September 1749

Strawberry Hill, Sept. 28, 1749.

I AM much obliged to you, my dear Sir, and agree with your opinion about that painting of Prince Edward that it can't be original,
and authentic, and consequently not worth copying. Lord Chomley
is indeed an original! but who are the wise people that build for

---

7. Cholmondeley; some 18th-century alterations, perhaps his, are mentioned ibid.

8. Sir Philip Hoby (ca 1716–66), 5th Bt,
Dean of Ardfert.

9. Montagu apparently confuses the figures on the monument. The Lady Hoby
to whom the monument in Bisham church
was erected was Elizabeth Cook (1528–
1609), m. (1) Sir Thomas Hoby (1530–66;
Sir Philip Hoby's half-brother); m. (2)
(1574) John Russell, styled Lord Russell.
'Her sister, a peeress' should be her daughter Anne Russell (d. 1639), m. (1600) Henry
Somerset, 5th E. of Worcester, cr. (1643)
1st M. of Worcester; see DNB, sub Hoby;

Vict. Co. Hist. Berks iii. 150–1; GEC sub
Bedford.

10. Probably the monument to Mar-
garet (d. 1605), dau. of Henry Carey, 1st
Bn Hunsdon; m. Sir Edward Hoby, son of
Lady (Elizabeth) Hoby (n. 9) (ibid. 151).

11. 'Procession of Queen Elizabeth to
Hunsdon-house,' engraved by George Ver-
tue (1684–1756) in 1742 from a painting at
Knole; see DNB, sub Henry Carey, Bn Huns-
don; 'Life of Vertue,' Works iv. 124–5, 147.
The Lady Hunsdon of the print is Anne
Morgan (d. 1607), m. (1545) Henry Carey,
Bn Hunsdon, mother of the lady whose
monument Montagu mistook for hers.

him?[1] Sir Philip Hobby seems to be the only person likely to be benefited by this new extravagance. I have just seen a collection of tombs like those you describe; the house of Russel, robed in alabaster and painted; there are seven monuments in all; one is immense, flaunting in marble, cherubim'd and seraphim'd, crusted with bas reliefs and titles, for the first Duke of Bedford and his Duchess.[2] All these are in a chapel of the church at Cheyneys,[3] the seat of the first Earls. There are but piteous fragments of the house remaining, now a farm, built round three sides of a court. It is dropping down, in several places without a roof, but in half the windows are beautiful arms in painted glass. As these are so totally neglected, I propose making a push and begging them of the Duke of Bedford: they would be magnificent for Strawberry Castle.[4] Did I tell you that I have found a text in Deuteronomy,[5] to authorize my future battlements? *When thou buildest a new house, then shalt thou make a battlement for thy roof, that thou bring not blood upon thy house, if any man fall from thence.* I saw Cheyneys at a visit I have been making to Harry Conway at Latimers.[6] This house which they have hired is large and bad, old but of a bad age;[7] finely situated on a hill in a beech wood, with a river at the bottom, and a range of hills and woods on the opposite side belonging to the Bedford. They are fond of it; the view is melancholy. In the church at Cheyneys, Mr Conway put on an old helmet we found there; you can't imagine how it suited him, how antique and handsome he looked, you would have taken him for Rinaldo.[8] Now I have dipped you so deep in heraldry and genealogies, I shall beg you to step into the church of Stoke, I know it is not asking you

1. The sarcasm of 'wise' is not altogether clear. Perhaps HW is reflecting on the sagacity of the people who lent Lord Cholmondeley money to build with; cf. his efforts to pay for his 'new room' *ante* 24 June 1746.

2. William Russell (1616–1700), 5th E. of Bedford, cr. (1694) 1st D. of Bedford; m. (1637) Lady Anne Carr (1615–84).

3. Chenies, Bucks, 4 miles east of Amersham; for a list of the monuments in the Bedford chapel of the church there, see *Vict. Co. Hist. Bucks* iii. 202; *Royal Commission on Historical Monuments . . . Buckinghamshire,* 1912–13, i. 88–90.

4. It does not appear that HW ever acquired this glass. One wing of the old house at Chenies, as well as some of the glass, is still in existence (ibid. 90, 92).

5. xxii. 8. This is the earliest known reference to HW's intention of Gothicising SH.

6. Near Chesham, Bucks; the house was entirely rebuilt in the 19th century (*Vict. Co. Hist. Bucks* iii. 204).

7. Probably Elizabethan or Jacobean which HW disliked; see *ante* 25 July 1748, n. 15. In George Lipscomb, *History . . . of Buckinghamshire,* 1847, iii. 268–9, is a plate of Latimer's showing a large Elizabethan house; but it is not clear whether the illustration is of the original building or the 19th-century alterations.

8. A chivalric character in *Orlando Furioso, Jerusalem Delivered,* etc.

to do a disagreeable thing to call there; I want an account of the
tomb of the first Earl of Huntingdon,[9] an ancestor of mine[10] who lies
there. I asked Gray[11] but he could tell me little about it. You know
how out of humour Gray has been about our diverting ourselves with
pedigrees, which is at least as wise as making a serious point of haranguing against the study; I believe neither Mr Chute nor I ever contracted a moment's vanity from any of our discoveries, or ever preferred them to anything but brag and whisk. Well, Gray has set himself to compute, and has found out that there must go a million of
ancestors in twenty generations to everybody's composition[12]—

I dig and plant till it is dark; all my works are revived and proceeding. When will you come and assist? You know I have an absolute promise, and shall now every day expect you. My compliments to
your sisters.

I am, dear George, yours most faithfully,

H. W.

To Montagu, Tuesday 15 May 1750

Arlington Street, May 15, 1750.

THE High Bailiff,[1] after commending himself and his own impartiality[2] for an hour this morning, not unlike your cousin,
Pelham,[3] has declared Lord Trentham;[4] the mob declare they will

9. George Hastings (1488–1544), 3d Bn
Hastings; cr. (1529) E. of Huntingdon.
Though he appears to have been buried
at Stoke Poges (GEC), no account of his
tomb has been discovered.

10. HW's descent from the Earl of
Huntingdon, via the Philippses and several female lines, is set forth in 'A Pedigree of Walpole to explain the Portraits
and Coats of Arms at Strawberry Hill,'
1776; the history of this 'Pedigree' is given
in COLE ii. 47, n. 5.

11. Gray's mother lived at Stoke Poges,
and he often visited there.

12. Gray computed this on a fly-leaf of
vol. i of his copy of *Peerage of England*,
1714 (now WSL). The total given by Gray
for 20 generations (including the individual as one generation) is 1,048,577. The
true total is 1,048,575. Two and a half
lines have been cut from the MS here.

1. Peter Leigh, High Bailiff of Westminster (*Cobbett's Parliamentary History
of England*, 1806–20, xiv. 891); not further
identified.

2. He had in fact favoured the Tory
candidate; see Nicholas Tindal, *Continuation of Mr Rapin's History of England*, ix
(1759). 423–4.

3. Henry Pelham. Montagu's paternal
grandmother, Elizabeth Pelham, was his
great-aunt.

4. Granville Leveson-Gower (1721–1803),
styled Vct Trentham, 2d E. Gower, 1754;
cr. (1786) M. of Stafford. On becoming a
Lord of the Admiralty, he had to stand
for re-election at Westminster, where he
had won his seat after a spirited contest in
1747. He was supported strongly by the
Duke of Bedford, who owned much Westminster property, but was unpopular with
the mob. Vast sums were spent on the elec-

pull his house down, to show their impartiality. The Princess has luckily produced another boy,[5] so Sir George Vandeput[6] may be recompensed with being godfather. I stand tomorrow—not for member, but godfather to my sister's girl[7] with Mrs Selwyn[8] and old Dunch;[9] were ever three such dowagers? When shall three such meet again— If the babe has not a most sentimentally yellow complexion after such sureties, I will burn my books and never answer for another skin.

You have heard I suppose that Nugent must answer a little more seriously for my Lady Lymington's[10] child. Why, she was as ugly, as Mrs Nugent, had had more children, and <w>as not young. The pleasure of wronging a woman who had <b>ought his back so dear, could be the only temptation.[11]

Lady Caroline P.[12] takes care that if she should die at an apothecary's, nobody may doubt who is the father.

tion and the subsequent scrutiny. Trentham was finally seated by a small majority; see HW to Mann 1750–1 *passim; Mem. Geo. II* i. 13–17; Joseph Grego, *History of Parliamentary Elections,* 1892, pp. 106–23; BM *Satiric Prints* iii pt i. 754–5.

5. Prince Frederick William (13 May 1750–65).

6. Sir George Vandeput (ca 1717–84), 2d Bt, of Twickenham; unsuccessful candidate in the Westminster election. He was supported by the Prince of Wales and the Tories.

7. Probably Mary Churchill, m. (1777) Charles Sloane Cadogan, 3d Bn Cadogan, cr. (1800) E. Cadogan, from whom she was divorced in 1796; Mme du Deffand speaks of her in 1771 as twenty years old (*Correspondance complète de Madame du Deffand,* ed. Sainte-Aulaire, 1866, i. 344).

8. Mary Farrington (ca 1691–1777), m. Col. John Selwyn; George Selwyn's mother; Bedchamber woman to Queen Caroline. Though Lord Hervey (*Memoirs,* ed. Romney Sedgwick, 1931, ii. 605) calls her 'a simple cunning woman,' she appears from other accounts to have been a person of considerable wit and beauty; see S. Parnell Kerr, *George Selwyn and the Wits,* 1909, pp. 15–19; Lady Louisa Stuart, *Notes on Jesse's Selwyn,* ed. W. S. Lewis, New York, 1928, pp. 3–4.

9. Elizabeth Godfrey (ca 1672–1761),

dau. of Arabella Churchill, James II's mistress; m. Edmund Dunch of Little Wittenham, Berks (Collins, *Peerage,* 1812, i. 366; GM 1761, xxxi. 539).

10. Probably Catherine Conduitt (ca 1722–50), m. (1740) John Wallop (1718–49), styled Viscount Lymington, by whom she had five children. She died 15 April 1750, and Miss Withycombe suggests (N&Q 1939, clxxvii. 427) that the scandal may have concerned her condition at death. The reference may be to Lady Bridget Bennet (1696–1738), m. (1716) John Wallop, cr. (1720) Vct Lymington, (1743) E. of Portsmouth. She had ten children (Collins, *Peerage,* 1812, iv. 326–7). Nugent, who came to London about 1729 after an equally discreditable affair with his cousin (see Claud Nugent, *Memoir of Robert, Earl Nugent,* 1898, pp. 6–9), was Bridget's junior by six years and Catherine's senior by twenty (see *ante* 25 July 1748, n. 1). Bridget, according to GEC, was 'very beautiful and lovely,' while, according to HW, Mrs Nugent was 'shocking' (see *ante* 25 July 1748, n. 17, 23a).

11. This and the following sentence are omitted in Toynbee.

12. Lady Caroline Petersham was having an affair with Harry Vane (HW to Mann 2 April 1750). She gave birth, 26 Oct. 1750, to a daughter (Collins, *Peerage,* 1812, iv. 289).

Adieu! I have told you all I know, and as much is scandal, very possibly more than is true. I go to Strawberry on Saturday, and so shall not know even scandal.

Yours ever,

H. W.

To Montagu, Saturday 23 June 1750

Arlington Street, June 23d, 1750.

AS I am not Vannecked,[1] I have been in no hurry to thank you for your congratulation, and to assure you that I never knew what solid happiness was till I was married. Your Trevors and Rices[2] dined with me last week at Strawberry Hill, and would have had me answer you upon the matrimonial tone, but I thought I should imitate cheerfulness in that style as ill as if I really were married. I have had another of your friends with me there some time, whom I adore, Mr Bentley;[3] he has more sense, judgment and wit, more taste and more misfortunes than sure ever met in any man. I have heard that Dr Bentley[4] regretting his wanting taste for all such learning as his, which is the very want of taste, used to sigh and say, 'Tully had his Marcus!'[5] If the sons resembled as much as the fathers did, at least in vanity, I would be the modest agreeable Marcus. Mr Bentley tells me that you press him much to visit you at Hawkhurst;[6] I advise him, and assure him he will make his fortune under you there, that you are agent from the Board of Trade[7] to the smugglers, and wallow in contraband wine, tea and silk handkerchiefs. I found an old newspaper t'other day with a list of outlawed smugglers; there were John Price alias Miss Marjoram, Bob Plunder, Bricklayer Tom, and Robin

---

1. GM 1750, xx. 284, announced the marriage, on 26 May, of 'Horatio Walpole Esq; brother to Lord Orford—to the eldest daughter of Joshua vanNeck, Esq; merchant.' Montagu had no doubt read a similar account in a newspaper; the marriage was actually that of Thomas Walpole, HW's first cousin and later correspondent.

2. Montagu's cousins.

3. Richard Bentley (1708–82), HW's close friend and correspondent until a quarrel in 1761.

4. Richard Bentley (1662–1742), the great classical scholar; father of the above.

5. 'Ciceronem filium quae res consulem fecit, nisi pater?' (Seneca, *De Benef.* iv. 30). 'Nam virtutes omnes aberant; stupor et vitia aderant' (Seneca, *Philosophi Opera*, ed. Iustus Lipsius, Antwerp, 1652, p. 321 n).

6. Montagu was no doubt visiting at Tongs in that parish, an estate his cousin the Earl of Halifax had acquired through his wife (Edward Hasted, *History . . . of Kent*, Canterbury, 1797–1801, vii. 149).

7. Of which Halifax was President.

Cursemother, all of Hawkhurst in Kent:[8] when Miss Harriot[9] is thoroughly hardened at Buxton,[10] as I hear she is by lying in a public room with the whole Wells, from drinking waters I conclude she will come to sip nothing but run brandy.

As jolly and abominable a life as she may have been leading, I defy all her enormities to equal a party of pleasure that I had t'other night. I shall relate it to you to show you the manners of the age, which are always as entertaining to a person fifty miles off, as to one born an hundred and fifty years after the time. I had a card[11] from Lady Caroline Petersham[12] to go with her to Vauxhall. I went accordingly to her house at half an hour after seven, and found her and little Ashe,[13] or the pollard[14] Ashe, as they call her; they had just finished their last layer of red, and looked as handsome as crimson could make them. On the cabinet stood a pair of Dresden candlesticks, a

8. Probably members of the notorious Hawkhurst gang, who among other exploits in Oct. 1747 robbed the customhouse at Poole, and tortured to death two witnesses who intended to testify against them; see Lord Teignmouth and Charles G. Harper, *The Smugglers*, 1923, i. 50–112.

9. Montagu's sister.

10. The waters at Buxton were supposed to be particularly adapted to the relief of rheumatic disorders, and, to a lesser degree, of 'pulmonary affections'; see George Saville Carey, *The Balnea*, 2d edn 1799, p. 184; [John Feltham] *A Guide to all the Watering and Sea-bathing Places*, 'new edn,' n.d. pp. 163–4. The nature of Harriet Montagu's ailment is not clear; her death in 1755 (*post* 7 Oct. 1755) seems to have resulted from tuberculosis, and it is not unlikely that she was already afflicted with it in 1750.

11. Missing.

12. It was common usage in the 18th century for the daughter of a duke or marquess marrying a courtesy peer of lower rank than her own to add his title to her Christian name. Thus Lady Caroline Fitzroy on marrying Viscount Petersham became not Lady Petersham, but Lady Caroline Petersham; Lady Mary Campbell was known invariably as Lady Mary Coke; and Lady Caroline Cavendish is referred to as Lady Caroline Duncannon. The custom is occasionally followed

today; see Ellen Countess of Desart and Constance Hoster, *Style and Title*, 1924, p. 23.

13. Elizabeth Ashe; Wraxall has a story of an intrigue between Rodney and the Princess Amelia, of which 'a living evidence existed' (Wraxall, *Memoirs* i. 224). Mrs Piozzi's comment on this was: 'Meaning, I suppose, the famous Miss Ashe, who, after many adventures, married Captain Falkner of the Royal Navy. She was a pretty creature, but particularly small in her person. *Little* Miss Ashe was the name she went by, yet I should think Rodney scarce old enough to have been her father. Her *mother* people spoke of with more certainty' (Hester Lynch Piozzi, *Autobiography*, ed. A. Hayward, Boston, 1861, i. 227). Rodney (b. 1719) was too young to be her father. Burke, *Landed Gentry*, 1875, ii. Supp. p. 32, calls her father J. Ashe. *Town and Country Magazine* 1770, ii. 517, calls her the daughter of a Commissioner of Customs and a minor official's wife. She married (1) (1751) Edward Wortley Montagu, scapegrace son of Lady Mary, but was soon after deserted by him (*post* 9 Jan. 1752, n. 31); (2) (1761) Robert Faulknor (d. 1769), Lt R.N., 1741; Capt., 1757 (John Charnock, *Biographia Navalis*, 1794–8, vi. 228–31; Burke, loc. cit.). Mason, writing to Gray 10 Sept. 1755, reports her pregnant by a Count Bryll (*Gray's Corr.* i. 438). She is said to have been for several years the mistress of Count Haszlang, the

present from the virgin hands of Sir John Bland;[15] the branches of each formed a little bower over a cock and hen treading, yes literally! We issued into the Mall to assemble our company, which was all the town if we could get it, for just so many had been summoned, except Harry Vane,[16] whom we met by *chance*. We mustered the Duke of Kingston[17] whom Lady Caroline says she has been trying for these seven years, but alas! his beauty is at the fall of the leaf, Lord March,[18] Mr Whithed,[19] a pretty Miss Beauclerc[20] and a very foolish Miss Sparre.[21] These two damsels were trusted by their mothers for the first time of their lives to the matronly conduct of Lady Caroline. As we sailed up the Mall with all our colours flying, Lord Petersham with his nose and legs twisted to every point of crossness,[22] strode by us on the outside, and repassed again on the return. At the end of the Mall, she called to him, he would not answer; she gave a familiar spring, and between laugh and confusion ran up to him, 'My Lord, my Lord, why you don't see us!' We advanced at a little distance, not a little awkward in expectation how all this would end, for my Lord never stirred his hat or took the least notice of anybody; she said, 'Do you go with us, or are you going anywhere else'—'I don't go with you,

unpopular Bavarian Minister, which ended her intimate friendship with Lady Caroline Petersham; see *Town and Country Magazine* 1770, ii. 518–20. 'Poor Ashe! She married Captain Falconer after all her exploits, and lived very happily and died aged 84' (MS note by Mrs Piozzi, to *post* 9 Jan. 1752).

14. Probably because she was conspicuously short. 'Miss Ashe is a sort of middle species between a woman and a fairy, and by her rarity worthy to be added even to so large a collection of amours [as Edward Wortley Montagu's]' (Mrs Elizabeth Montagu to her husband, 1751, in Emily J. Climenson, *Elizabeth Montagu, the Queen of the Blue-Stockings . . . 1720–61*, 1906, i. 287).

15. Sir John Bland (ca 1722–55), 6th Bt, of Kippax Park, York; see *post* 20 Sept. 1755.

16. Henry Vane (ca 1705–58), 3d Bn Barnard, 1753; cr. (1754) E. of Darlington; Lady Caroline's lover (*ante* 15 May 1750, n. 12).

17. Evelyn Pierrepont (1711–73), 2d D. of Kingston-upon-Hull.

18. William Douglas (1725–1810), 3d E.

of March and Ruglen; 4th D. of Queensberry, 1778; known later as 'Old Q' and as a famous roué.

19. Francis Whithed (1719–51), friend of HW's, and protégé of John Chute's; see HW to Mann Sept. 1741, 10 March 1742, etc.

20. Perhaps Caroline (d. 1769), m. (1756) Sir William Draper, K.B., but her mother, Lady William Beauclerk, d. 1745.

21. Amelia Wilhelmina Melesina Sparre (1733–78), dau. of Baron Sparre, one of Charles XII's generals, by Elizabeth Deritt (d. 1766), Countess Gyllenborg, an Englishwoman who, as the step-daughter of Count Gyllenborg, Prime Minister of Sweden, was given his title. After Baron Sparre's death, the Countess and her daughter had settled in Yorkshire (see GM 1781, li. 628–9). Since triple Christian names were, in England, quite rare, it seems more than a coincidence that one of the fashionable town ladies in *The Vicar of Wakefield* (1766) was named Miss Carolina Wilhelmina Amelia Skeggs.

22. From the peculiarity of his gait he was nicknamed 'Peter Shambles' (DNB).

I am going somewhere else,' and away he stalked as sulky as a ghost that nobody will speak to first. We got into the best order we could and marched to our barge, with a boat of French horns attending and little Ashe singing. We paraded some time up the river and at last debarked at Vauxhall. There if we had so pleased we might have had the vivacity of our party increased by a quarrel, for a Mrs Loyd,[23] who is supposed to be married to Lord Haddington, seeing the two girls following Lady C. and Miss Ashe said aloud, 'Poor girls, I am sorry to see them in such bad company.' Miss Sparre who desired nothing so much as the fun of seeing a duel, a thing which, though she is fifteen, she has never been so lucky to see, took due pains to make Lord March resent this, but he, who is very lively and agreeable, laughed her out of this charming frolic with a great deal of humour. Here we picked up Lord Granby,[24] arrived very drunk from Jenny's Whim[25] where, instead of going to old Strafford's catacombs[26] to make honourable love, he had dined with Lady Fitzroy,[27] and left her and eight other women and four other men playing at brag. He would fain have made over his honourable love upon any terms to poor Miss Beauclerc, who is very modest, and did not know at all what to do with his whispers or his hands. He then addressed himself to the Sparre, who was very well disposed to receive both, but the tide of champagne turned, he hiccupped at the reflection of his marriage, of which he is wondrous sick, and only proposed to the girl to shut themselves up and rail at the world for three weeks. If all the adventures don't conclude as you expect at the beginning of a paragraph, you must not wonder, for I am not making a history, but relating one

23. Mary Holt (d. 1785), m. (1) Gresham Lloyd; m. (2) (5 Sept. 1750) Thomas Hamilton (ca 1720–94), 7th E. of Haddington.

24. John Manners (1721–70), styled M. of Granby; Commander-in-chief 1766–70; m. (3 Sept. 1750) Lady Frances Seymour. There is much disagreement about the date of the marriage, but see John H. Chapman, *Register Book of Marriages . . . St George's, Hanover Square*, 1886, i. 44 (Harleian Soc., *Publications*, vol. xi).

25. A tavern and tea-house in Chelsea; see *London Past & Present*; [Henry Angelo], *Angelo's Pic Nic; or, Table Talk*, 1834, p. 106.

26. See *ante* 13 July 1745.

27. Elizabeth (d. 1788), dau. of Col. William Cosby, Gov. of New York; m. (1) (1734) Lord Augustus Fitzroy (1716–1741), 3d son of the 2d D. of Grafton, by whom she was mother of the 3d D. of Grafton; m. (2) James Jeffreys, Commissioner of Customs. After the death of his uncle the Earl of Euston in 1747, her son was heir-apparent to the Dukedom of Grafton; it was probably for this reason that she was known as Lady Fitzroy, though her proper style was Lady Augustus Fitzroy (Collins, *Peerage*, 1812, i. 218; GM 1788, lxiv pt ii. 1131). A parallel case is that of Lady John Sackville, whose son was heir-apparent and in 1769 succeeded to the Dukedom of Dorset; she is referred to as 'Lady Sackville' in 1764; see Coke, *Journals* i. 17. n. 1.

strictly as it happened, and I think with full entertainment enough to content you. At last we assembled in our booth, Lady Caroline in the front with the vizor of her hat erect, and looking gloriously jolly and handsome. She had fetched my brother Orford from the next box where he was enjoying himself with his Norsa[28] and his *petite partie*,[29] to help us mince chickens: we minced seven chickens into a china dish, which Lady C. stewed over a lamp with three pats of butter and a flagon of water, stirring, and rattling and laughing, and we every minute expecting to have the dish fly about our ears. She had brought Betty the fruit girl[30] with hampers of strawberries and cherries from Rogers's,[31] and made her wait upon us, and then made her sup by us at a little table. The conversation was no less lively than the

28. Hannah Norsa (d. 1785), dau. of a Jewish tavern-keeper (HW to Mann 1 Aug. 1746), or merchant (William Cooke, *Memoirs of Samuel Foote*, 1805, iii. 82–3), succeeded Lavinia Fenton as Polly in *The Beggar's Opera*. Lord Orford, then Lord Walpole, promised to marry her after his father's death, and borrowed £3,000 from her which was never repaid, so that upon his death she lived on the charity and in the house of Rich the manager until her death (Cooke, loc. cit.), Rich died 1761, and Miss Norsa not until 1785, according to British Museum, *Catalogue of Engraved British Portraits*, ed. O'Donoghue and Hake, 1908–25. A more likely story does not mention the £3,000, and says that the promise to marry was to be fulfilled after the death of Lady Orford, who outlived her husband (Francis G. Waldron, *Shakespearean Miscellany*, 1802, 'The English Stage,' pp. 44–5). A Norfolk neighbour describes her in 1749 as 'a very agreeable woman, and nobody ever behaved better in her station, she have everybody's good word, and bear great sway at Houghton, she is everything but lady, she came here in a landau and six horses, and one Mr Paxton a young clergyman with her' (*Memoirs of a Royal Chaplain*, ed. Albert Hartshorne, 1905, p. 244). There is a portrait of her in Waldron, loc. cit., from 'a scarce engraving in the collection of Sir William Musgrave, Bt,' from an original by Lens (*Engraved British Portraits*, above).

29. Not explained.

30. 'Aug. 30 [1797]. Aged 67, at her house, facing St James's Street, at the top of Park Place, [died] Mrs Elizabeth Neale, better known by the name of Betty. She had kept, for very many years, a house in St James's Street, as a fruit-shop, from which she had retired about 14 years. She had the first pre-eminence in her occupation, and might be justly called the Queen of Apple-women. Her knowledge of families and characters, of the last and present age, was wonderful. She was a woman of pleasing manners and conversation, and abounding with anecdote and entertainment. Her company was ever sought for by the highest of our men of rank and fortune. She was born in the same street in which she ever lived, and used to say she never slept out of it but twice, on a visit to a friend in the country, and at a Windsor installation' (GM 1797, lxvii pt ii. 891). She appears in Mason's 'Heroic Epistle' l. 116, where HW in his copy (now Harvard) notes: 'Elizabeth Munro was a celebrated fruit-woman in St James's Street, who took great liberties with the Court in her conversation—her shop was consequently much frequented by the opposition' (*Satirical Poems . . . by William Mason with Notes by Horace Walpole*, ed. Paget Toynbee, Oxford, 1926, pp. 66–7). She is also mentioned in Jesse, *Selwyn* i. 230.

31. *A Complete Guide to all Persons who have any Trade or Concern with the City of London, and Parts Adjacent*, printed for J. Osborn, 1740, p. 146, lists a William Rogers, grocer, in Leadenhall Street.

whole transaction—There is a Mr Obrien[32] arrived from Ireland who would get the Duchess of Manchester from Mr Hussey, if she were still at liberty. I took up the biggest hautboy[33] in the dish, and said to Lady Car., 'Madam, Miss Ashe desires you will eat this Obrien-strawberry'; she replied immediately, 'I won't, you Hussey!'—You may imagine the laugh this reply occasioned—after the tempest was a little calmed, the Pollard said, 'Now how anybody would spoil this story that was to repeat it, and say, I won't you jade!'—In short the whole air of our party was sufficient as you will easily imagine to take up the whole attention of the garden, so much so, that from eleven o'clock till half an hour after one, we had the whole concourse round our booth; at last they came into the little gardens of each booth on the sides of ours,[34] till Harry Vane took up a bumper and drank their healths, and was proceeding to treat them with still greater freedom. It was three o'clock before we got home—I think I have told you the chief passages. Lord Granby's temper had been a little ruffled the night before, the Prince had invited him and Dick Lyttelton[35] to Kew, where he won eleven hundred pound of the latter and eight of the former, then cut, and told them he would play with them no longer, for he saw they played so idly, that they were capable of *losing more than they would like!*

Adieu! I expect in return for this long tale, that you tell me some of your frolics with Robin Cursemother, and some of Miss Marjoram's bon mots.

Yours ever,

H. W.

PS. Dr Middleton[36] called on me yesterday; he is come to town to consult his physician[36a] for a jaundice and swelled legs, symptoms which the doctor tells him and which he believes can be easily cured: I think him visibly broke and near his end.[37] He lately advised me to

32. Not identified.

33. Species of strawberry, of taller growth than the common strawberry (OED).

34. Booths for supper-parties were arranged in semi-circular rows on two sides of the gardens; a bird's-eye view in Warwick Wroth, *London Pleasure Gardens*, 1896, p. 301, taken from Stow's *Survey of London* (1754), makes the plan clear.

35. Richard Lyttelton (d. 1770), K.B., 1753; Lt-Gen., 1759; M.P. Brackley 1747–

54; Poole 1754–61; Master of the Jewel Office 1756–62; Commander-in-chief of Minorca 1762–6; Gov. of Guernsey, 1766 (Collins, *Peerage*, 1812, viii. 350).

36. Conyers Middleton (1683–28 July 1750), divine; HW's correspondent.

36a. Probably Dr William Heberden (1710–1801); see next note.

37. Warburton to Hurd, 11 July 1750: 'I hear Dr Middleton has been lately at London (I suppose to consult Dr Heber-

marry, on the sense of his own happiness, but if anybody had advised him to the contrary at his time of life,[38] I believe he would not have broke so fast.

To Montagu, Monday 10 September 1750

Strawberry Hill, Sept. 10, 1750.

YOU must not pretend to be concerned at having missed me here, when I had repeatedly begged you to let me know what day you would call; and even after you had learnt that I was to come the next day, you paraded by my house with all your matrimonial streamers[1] flying, without even saluting the future castle. To punish this slight, I shall accept your offer of a visit on the return of your progress; I shall be here, and Mrs Leneve will not.

I feel for the poor Handasyde![2] If I wanted examples to deter one from making all the world happy, from obliging, from being always in good humour and spirits, she should be my memento. You find long wise faces every day that tell you riches can't make one happy— no, can't they? What pleasantry is that poor woman fallen from! and

den about his health), and is returned in an extreme bad condition. The scribblers against him will say they have killed him. But, by what Mr Yorke told me, his brick-layer will dispute the honour of his death with them' (*Letters from a Late Eminent Prelate* [ed. Richard Hurd], 2d edn 1809, p. 54) (Wright).

38. Dr Middleton had recently married his third wife. 'Bishop Gooch making him a matrimonial visit, told Mrs Middleton, before the Doctor appeared, that "he was glad she did not dislike the *Ancients* so much as her husband did." She replied, "that she hoped his Lordship did not reckon Dr. Middleton among the Ancients yet." The Bishop answered, "You, Madam, are the best judge of that!" '—John Nichols, *Literary Anecdotes*, 1812–15, v. 422 (Wright).

1. Montagu's sister Arabella was married to Nathaniel Wettenhall 9 Aug. (GM 1750, xx. 380). HW may refer to the knots of ribbon which were distributed at weddings and worn on the hat (see Henri

Misson de Valbourg, *Mémoires et Observations*, La Haye, 1698, p. 317; C. J. S. Thompson, *Love, Marriage and Romance in Old London*, 1936, p. 40); or, as Mr R. W. Ketton-Cremer suggests, this may be a nautical figure, and HW may have had an echo in his mind of *Samson Agonistes*, ll. 714–18, the entrance of Delilah:
'Like a stately ship
Of Tarsus, bound for the isles
Of Javan or Gadire,
With all her bavery on, and tackle trim,
Sails filled, and streamers waving.'

2. Doubtless Susannah Bunbury (1700–64), dau. of Sir Henry Bunbury, 3d Bt, m. Col. William Handasyd, later Brig. Gen. (d. 1745) (George Ormerod, *History of the County . . . of Chester*, 1882, ii. 396; Coke, *Journals* i. 16; GM 1745, xv. 164). Her misfortune has not been discovered. She was principal legatee under her husband's will (P.C.C. Seymour 169), but may have been in reduced circumstances, as is suggested by the text since she was House-keeper at Windsor ca 1756–64 (*Court and City Register*).

what a joyous feel must Vanneck[3] have expired in, who could call and think the two Schutzes[4] his friends, and leave five hundred pound apiece to their friendship—nay, riches made him so happy, that in the overflowing of his satisfaction, he has bequeathed an hundred pounds apiece to eighteen fellows, whom he calls *his good friends that favoured him with their company on Fridays*—He took it mighty kind that Capt. *James de Normandie*[5] and twenty such names that come out of the Minories,[6] would constrain themselves to live upon him once a week!

I should have liked to visit the castles and groves of your old Welsh ancestors[7] with you; by the draughts I have seen, I have always imagined that Wales preserved the greatest remains of ancient days, and have often wished to visit Picton Castle; the seat of my Philipps-progenitors.[8]

Make my best compliments to your sisters, and with their leave make haste to this side of the world; you will be extremely welcome hither as soon and for as long as you like; I can promise you nothing very agreeable, but that I will try to get our favourite Mr Bentley to meet you. Adieu!

Yours very sincerely,

Hor. Walpole

To Montagu, Thursday 30 May 1751

Arlington Street, May 30, 1751.

MRS BOSCAWEN says, I ought to write to you—I don't think so: you desired I would, if I had anything new to tell you; I have not. Lady Caroline and Miss Ashe had quarrelled about reputa-

---

3. Gerard Vanneck (d. 1750), merchant. An abstract of his will is given in GM 1750, xx. 393–4. He left dozens of legacies, ranging from £50 to £10,000, totalling £106,000.

4. Sons of Baron von Schutz, Hanoverian Ambassador to England 1689–1710; came to England with George I in 1714. Augustus Schutz (1690–1757) was Gentleman of the Bedchamber to George I, Keeper of the Privy Purse and Master of the Robes to George II, friend and confidant of Queen Caroline. Col. Armand

Johann Schutz (d. 1773) was an officer in the Guards, and sometime Warden of the Stannaries; see Falconer Madan, *The Madan Family*, Oxford, 1933, pp. 66–8, 258.

5. Not identified.

6. Street between Aldgate and the Tower; the section was inhabited largely by Huguenots.

7. Montagu's mother's family, the Trevors, were of Trevallyn, Flintshire.

8. See *ante* 11 Aug. 1748, n. 13.

tions,[1] before you went out of town; you knew the Pelhams were to be kings by Act of Parliament,[2] as they are already by majorities in Parliament, if the King dies before the boy is eighteen, and I suppose you would not give a straw to know all the circumstances of a Mr Paul's[3] killing a Mr Dalton,[4] though the town who talks of anything, talks of nothing else. *Your friend* Lord Sandwich, in the intervals of politics and cricket, has been concerting a subscription masquerade with Lord Coventry[5a] which has miscarried; the *fausse couche* is to be another jubilee. Mrs French and her Jeffery[5] are parted again —Lady Orford and Shirley[6] married; they say she was much frightened; it could not be for fear of what other brides dread happening, but for fear it should not happen.

1. When Miss Ashe went to France with Edward Wortley Montagu. The quarrel was mended later this year; see HW to Mann 22 Nov. 1751; Earl of Chesterfield, *Letters*, ed. Bonamy Dobrée, 1932, v. 1798.

2. Following the death of Frederick Prince of Wales in March, 1751, a Regency Bill was passed which provided that, in the event of the king's death before the future George III was 18, his mother the Dowager Princess should be regent. Little power was given her, however, and the real authority would have been in the hands of a council composed mostly of cabinet members; see *Mem. Geo. II* i. ch. v.

3. Horace Paul, later St Paul (1729–1812), a law student of Gray's Inn at the time of the duel, about which see next note. After a coroner's verdict of 'willful murder,' he fled to Paris and was outlawed. In 1756 he entered the Austrian service and in 1759 was made a Colonel of Cavalry and created a Count of the Empire. Pardoned 1765 through the offices of his friend Lord Stormont, he returned to England and was Secretary of the Embassy at Paris under Stormont 1772–6. After 1787 he was of Ewart, Northumberland; about him see George Grey Butler, *Colonel St Paul of Ewart, Soldier and Diplomat*, 1911; M. H. Dodds in Northumberland County History Committee, *History of Northumberland*, 1893–, xiv. 182–9; N&Q 1939, clxxvii. 249; DU DEFFAND.

4. William Dalton (ca 1726–51), of the Inner Temple. The duel was occasioned by a trifling dispute over a snuffbox be-

longing to Dalton's fiancée, a Miss Green, which she, apparently in jest, gave to St Paul. Dalton took offense, with fatal results to himself. The details were in dispute, and the complicity of Miss Green hotly debated. See N&Q 1923, 12th ser. xii. 47; GM 1751, xxi. 234; Lady Luxborough, *Letters . . . to William Shenstone*, 1775, p. 273; *Series of Letters between Mrs Elizabeth Carter and Miss Catherine Talbot*, 1809, ii. 34; *Universal Magazine*, 1751, viii. 237; *Vindication of an Innocent Lady*, 1751, from which it appears (pp. 18–19) that Miss Green died of grief and shame following an abusive letter in *The Inspector*, 30 May 1751.

5. Jeffrey French (d. 1754), m. Katherine, dau. of Hon. Richard Lloyd, Chief Justice of Jamaica (John Burke, *Genealogical . . . History of the Commoners*, 1833–8, iv. 91). He was a son of Arthur French of Tyrone, and was 'of the Middle Temple and Jamaica' (Sir [John] Bernard Burke, *Landed Gentry of Ireland*, 1904, p. 203); M.P. Milborne Port 1741–7, and lost a contest for it in 1747 (see *Mem. Geo. II* ii. 124); M.P. Tavistock 1754. For their earlier separation, see HW to Mann 6 Jan. 1743. She d. 1791 (see HW to Mary Berry 22 Jan. 1791).

5a. George William Coventry (1722–1809), 6th E. of Coventry.

6. Hon. Sewallis Shirley (1709–65), 14th son of 1st E. Ferrers; m. (25 May, at Mayfair Chapel) Margaret Rolle, Countess of Orford, whose first husband, HW's eldest brother, had died 31 March 1751; Comptroller of the Household to Queen Char-

My evening yesterday was employed—how wisely do you think? in what grave occupation? In bawding for the Duchess of Portland,[7] to procure her a scarlet spider[7a] from Admiral Boscawen.[8] I had just seen her collection,[9] which is indeed magnificent, chiefly composed of the spoils of her father's and the Arundel collections. The gems of all sorts are glorious. I was diverted with two relics of St Charles the Martyr; one, the pearl, you see in his pictures, taken out of his ear after his foolish head was off; the other, the cup out of which he took his last sacrament.[10] They should be given to that nursery of nonsense and bigotry, Oxford, where in the Bodleian Library they have stuck up two portraits to show the resemblance of Jesus Christ and Charles Christ.[11]

I condole with your journey, am glad Miss Montagu is in better health, and am

Yours sincerely,

Hor. Walpole

lotte; M.P. Brackley 1742–54; Callington 1754–61, where he succeeded HW; the interest in that borough apparently reverted to Lady Orford on her husband's death (see *ante* 2 July 1747, n. 20; Collins, *Peerage*, 1812, iv. 99).

7. Lady Margaret Cavendish Harley (1715–85), m. (1734) William Bentinck, 2d D. of Portland.

7a. If HW was successful, it is probably among the numerous 'exotic insects' listed in the *Catalogue of the Portland Museum*, 1786.

8. Admiral Hon. Edward Boscawen (1711–61).

9. For HW's account of her collection see *The Duchess of Portland's Museum*, ed. W. S. Lewis, the Grolier Club, New York, 1936. Her father was Robert Harley (1661–1724), 1st E. of Oxford. He bought many of the coins and medals sold in 1696 from the collection of the 2d Earl of Arundel (*ante* 20 May 1736, n. 16). HW's catalogue of the sale of Lord Oxford's coins, 18–23 March 1742, is now WSL and shows HW as the purchaser of several of them.

10. Both are now (1938) at Welbeck. The pearl is accompanied by a paper in the hand of Queen Mary, 'This pearle was taken out of ye King my grandfather's ear

after he was beheaded & given ye Princesse Royall' (information from Mr Francis Needham). King William gave it to the Earl of Portland (*Duchess of Portland's Museum, ante* n. 9, p. 10). It is visible in a copy by Lely of a lost Van Dyck, engraved by Faber and Vertue; see Rev. James Granger, *Biographical History of England*, 2d edn 1775, ii. 88. The chalice is illustrated and described in E. Alfred Jones, *Catalogue of Plate . . . of Welbeck Abbey*, 1935, p. 70, pl. xxi.

11. In George Agar Ellis (Lord Dover) *Historical Inquiries Respecting the Character of . . . Clarendon*, 1827, p. 177 n, they are described as 'exactly similar in every respect, and with an account of the sufferings of each at the bottom of his respective likeness. These pictures . . . were hung as *pendants* to one another in the Bodleian Library.' They were presented to the University in 1722 by a Mrs Mary Prince, who painted them herself on paper mounted on copper. They still hang at the Selden end of the Old Reading Room (information from Mr R. H. Hill). See Rev. William D. Macray, *Annals of the Bodleian Library, Oxford*, 2d edn, Oxford, 1890, p. 201; *Bodleian Quarterly Record* iii (Oxford, 1923). 4.

To Montagu, Thursday 13 June 1751

Arlington Street, June 13, 1751.

YOU have told me that it is charity to write you news into Kent; but what if my news should shock you! Won't it rather be an act of cruelty to tell you that your *relation* Sandwich is immediately to be removed, and that the Duke of Bedford and all the Gowers will resign to attend him[1]—not quite all the Gowers, for the Earl himself has been informed that he ought to resent Lord Sandwich's giving away his daughter to Col. Waldegrave[2]—He does resent it and keeps the Privy Seal and plays on at brag with Lady Catherine Pelham to the great satisfaction of the Staffordshire Jacobites, who desire, at least expect, no better diversion than a division in that house;[3] won't they be diverted? Lord Trentham does resign. Lord Hartington is to be Master of the Horse and called up to the Peers.[4] The Devonshire desired the Duke of Rutland's[4a] interest in Derbyshire for Lord Frederic;[5] this Duke replied, 'My Lord, I have always endeavoured to show my attachment to your Grace from regard and affinity; nor you nor yours have ever supported any request of mine; you will excuse me if I oppose you now tooth and nail.'—Pho! This will end in Lord Granby's having the Blues.[6] Lord Granville is to be President: if he should resent any former resignations and insist on victims, will

1. The Pelhams, jealous of their power, engineered the dismissal of Sandwich from the Admiralty. The Duke of Bedford, with whom he was allied, promptly resigned the Secretaryship of State; the Pelhams replaced them with Anson and Holdernesse, members of their own faction; see *Mem. Geo. II* i. 161–2, 187–99.

2. Col. John Waldegrave (1718–84), 3d E. Waldegrave, 1763; m. (7 May 1751) Lady Elizabeth Leveson-Gower (d. 1784). 'The Bedfords had transacted a marriage between one of the Duchess's sisters and Colonel Waldegrave, against the consent of her father, Lord Gower; and Lord Sandwich had been so imprudent as to let the ceremony be performed at his apartments at the Admiralty' (*Mem. Geo. II* i. 188).

3. The Leveson-Gowers, Staffordshire magnates, had turned Whig in 1742 and allied themselves with the Duke of Bedford; see Josiah C. Wedgwood, *Staffordshire Parliamentary History*, ii pt i. p. xiv (William Salt Archaeological Society, *Collections*, 1920). Jacobitism was still an active force in Staffordshire life and politics, more so than in most counties (see ibid. pp. xxxii–xxxv; Boswell, *Johnson* iii. 326).

4. William Cavendish (1720–64), styled M. of Hartington; cr. Bn Cavendish; 4th D. of Devonshire, 1755.

4a. John Manners (1696–1779), 3d D. of Rutland.

5. Lord Frederick Cavendish (1729–1803), field marshal, 1796; elected to the seat for Derbyshire vacated by his brother's elevation to the Lords.

6. The Royal Horse Guards, of which he was made Colonel in 1758 (GM 1758, xxviii. 245). Presumably this would be a bribe to his father, the Duke of Rutland.

Lord Harrington[7] assure the menaced that they shall not be sacrificed?

I hear your friend Lord North is wedded;[8] somebody said, 'It is very hot weather to marry so fat a bride'; G. Selwyn replied, 'Oh! she was kept in ice for three days before.'

The first volume of Spenser[9] is published with prints designed by Kent; but the most execrable performance you ever beheld—the graving not worse than the drawing: awkward knights, scrambling Unas, hills tumbling down themselves, no variety of prospect, and three or four perpetual spruce firs. Our charming Mr Bentley is doing Gray as much more honour as he deserves than Spenser. He is drawing vignettes for his Odes; what a valuable MS I shall have![10] Warburton[11] publishes his edition of Pope next week, with the famous piece of prose on Lord Hervey,[12] which he formerly suppressed at my uncle's desire,[13] who had got an abbey from Cardinal Fleury[14] for one Southcote,[15] a friend of Pope's: my Lord Hervey[16] pretended not to thank him. I am told the edition has waited, because Warburton

7. William Stanhope (ca 1683–1756), E. of Harrington, began a train of resignations in 1746, which was followed by Granville's and Bath's 48-hour ministry, 'thereby incurring the lasting resentment of George II' (Toynbee).

8. To the Dowager Countess of Rockingham, 13 June.

9. *The Faerie Queen by Edmund Spenser . . . with a new life of the Author* [by Thomas Birch], 1751, 3 vols. The edition contained thirty-two drawings by Kent. HW's copy, sold SH i. 101, is now WSL.

10. *Designs by Mr. R. Bentley for Six Poems by Mr. T. Gray.* These were published 1753. The original drawings, which were sold SH vii. 54, are now WSL.

11. William Warburton (1698–1779), Bp of Gloucester. HW's copy, MS Cat. K.3.17, sold SH iii. 165.

12. The 'Letter to a Noble Lord,' viii. 253–80, written, and, according to Warburton, printed in 1733; first published in this edition. No copy of the 1733 edition appears to be extant (Reginald H. Griffith, *Alexander Pope, A Bibliography*, Austin, Texas, 1922–7, i pt ii. 533).

13. Horatio Walpole (1678–1757), cr. (1756) Bn Walpole of Wolterton.

14. André-Hercule de Fleury (1653–1743), cardinal and diplomatist.

15. Thomas Southcote, O.S.B., living 1737, of Abingdon, who Pope believed had been instrumental in saving his life when a young man by calling Dr Radcliffe's attention to his ill health (see John Kirk, *Biographies of English Catholics*, 1909). 'It was about twenty years after this, that Mr Pope heard of an abbey's being like to be vacant in the most delightful part of France, near Avignon: . . . Mr Pope . . . sent a letter the next morning, to Sir Robert Walpole (with whom he had then some degree of friendship) and begged him to write a letter to Cardinal Fleury. . . . The affair met with some delay (on account of our court having just then settled a pension on Father Courayer) but succeeded at last' (Rev. Joseph Spence, *Anecdotes*, 1820, pp. 7–8; Pope, *Works*, ed. Elwin and Courthope, 1871–89, iii. 459, v. 26). Father Courayer came to England in 1728, and probably got his pension not long after (see DNB), which would make this incident fall within the period of old Horace Walpole's embassy to Paris, 1723–30. Since he was intimate with Fleury, the affair would actually have been settled by him, though the application was to Sir Robert; see John Nichols, *Literary Anecdotes*, 1812–15, v. 650. Courthope, op. cit. v. 263, thinks that, in the suppression of

has cancelled above a hundred sheets, (in which he had inserted notes) since the publication of the *Canons of Criticism*.[17] The new history of Christina[18] is a most wretched piece of trumpery, stuffed with foolish letters and confutations of Mademoiselle de Montpensier[19] and Madame de Motteville.[20]

Adieu! My compliments to Miss Montagu!

Yours ever,

H. Walpole

To Montagu, Monday 22 July 1751

Daventry, July 22d, 1751.

YOU will wonder in what part of the county of Twicks[1] lies this Daventry—it happens to be in Northamptonshire. My letter will scarce set out till I get to London, but I choose to give it its present date, lest you should admire that Mr Usher of the Exchequer, the Lord Treasurer of Pen, Ink and Paper,[2] should write with such coarse materials. I am on my way from Ragley,[3] and if ever the waters

the *Letter to the Noble Lord*, 'More probably the poet was moved by considerations of prudence.'

16. Hon. John Hervey (1696–1743), cr. (1733) Bn Hervey of Ickworth.

17. Thomas Edwards (1699–1757), critic of Warburton; published in 1747, upon the appearance of Warburton's edition of Shakespeare, a *Supplement*, the third edition of which in 1748 was called *Canons of Criticism*, and ran to seven editions. A hundred sheets would be 1600 pages; the possibility of such a wholesale revision is discussed in Reginald H. Griffith, *Alexander Pope, A Bibliography*, Austin, Texas, 1922–7, i pt ii. 524.

18. Johann Arckenholtz (1695–1777), *Mémoires concernant Christine, reine de Suède, pour servir d'éclaircissement à l'histoire de son règne . . .*, Amsterdam and Leipzig, 1751–60, 4 vols. 'Of primary importance . . . but . . . the author is a rampant Swede and Protestant, entirely devoid of impartiality' (Francis W. Bain, *Christina, Queen of Sweden*, 1890, p. vii). HW's copy (MS Cat. F.3.23) was sold SH ii. 54.

19. Anne-Marie-Louise de Bourbon d'Orléans (1627–93), Duchesse (known as Mademoiselle) de Montpensier, dau. of Gaston d'Orléans, niece of Louis XIII; her *Mémoires* were published 1729; HW's copy (MS Cat. F.7.41) was sold SH ii. 143.

20. Françoise Bertaut (ca 1621–89), m. (1639) —— Langlois de Motteville; her *Mémoires pour servir à l'histoire d'Anne d'Autriche*, 1723, are generally critical of Christina, as are Mlle de Montpensier's.

———

1. Twickenham[shire].

2. 'The duty of my office [Usher of the Exchequer] is to shut the gates of the exchequer, and to furnish paper, pens, ink, wax, sand, tape, pen-knives, scissors, parchment, and a great variety of other articles to the exchequer, treasury, and their officers . . .' ('Account of my Conduct relative to the Places I hold under Government,' *Works* ii. 368).

3. Near Alcester, Warwickshire, the seat of HW's cousin, Lord Hertford. The rebuilding of which HW speaks later in this letter seems to have been extensive; fur-

subside, and my ark rests upon dry land again, I think of stepping over to Tonghes:[4] but your own journey has filled my post-chaise's head with such terrible ideas of your roads, that I think I shall let it have done raining for a month or six weeks, which it has not done for as much time past, before I begin to grease my wheels again, and lay in a provision of French books and tea and blunderbusses for my journey.

Before I tell you a word of Ragley, you must hear how busy I have been upon Grammont. You know I have long had a purpose of a new edition with notes and cuts of the principal beauties and heroes, if I could meet with their portraits.[5] I have made out all the people, at all remarkable, except *Milord Janet,* whom I cannot divine, unless he be *Thanet.*[6] Well, but what will entertain you, is, that I have discovered the *philosophe Whitnell*—and what do you think his real name was?—only *Whetenhall!* Pray do you call cousins?[7] Look in Collins's Baronets, and under the article *Bedingfield* you will find that he was 'an ingenious gentleman,' and la Blanche Whitnell, 'though one of the greatest beauties of the age, an excellent wife.'[8] I am per-

---

ther changes were made by Wyatt early in the 19th century (*Beauties of England* xv pt ii. Warwickshire, pp. 269–70); for a print of the old house, see Mervyn Macartney, *English Houses and Gardens of the 17th and 18th Centuries,* 1908, pl. xlvi, or Marjorie Hope Nicolson, *Conway Letters,* New Haven, 1930, opp. 112.

4. Tongs, Hawkhurst, Kent; see *ante* 23 June 1750, n. 6.

5. HW published at SH in 1772 an edition of Anthony Hamilton's *Memoires du Comte de Grammont;* see COLE i. 293, n. 3. It was annotated, and 'l'éditeur aurait voulu ajouter les portraits des principaux personnages, mais arrêté par des difficultés insurmontables, il s'est borné à ne donner que ceux de Mademoiselle d'Hamilton, de l'auteur le Comte Antoine d'Hamilton, et de son Héros le Comte de Grammont' (HW's Avis de l'Éditeur). In his own copy, sold SH iv. 144 (now WSL), HW has added eight prints: the Duke of Ormonde, St-Évremond, Mrs Mary Kirke, Philip, 2d E. of Chesterfield, Marion Delorme, James II, Prince Rupert, Mary Duchess of Buckingham.

6. HW's conjecture was followed by later editors, and 'Milord Janet,' mentioned in

ch. iv of the *Mémoires,* identified with Nicholas Tufton (1631–79), 3d E. of Thanet, or some member of his family. See, however, Cyril H. Hartmann's edition (1930, p. 341), where it is said that the manuscript has 'Jaret,' meaning Lord Gerard, cr. (1679) E. of Macclesfield. HW's only edition seems to have been one of 1728 (MS Cat. H.6.4, sold SH iii. 30); this edition does not appear in BM, Yale, or Bibliothèque Nationale catalogues.

7. Montagu's brother-in-law Nathaniel Wettenhall was connected distantly, if at all, with the Thomas Whetenhall of the following note; see, however, *post* 22 Sept. 1755, n. 2.

8. Thomas Whetenhall (the name is variously spelled) of Hextall Court, East Peckham, Kent, m. Elizabeth (d. 1689), dau. of Sir Henry Bedingfield, Bt; see *Memoirs of the Comte de Gramont,* ed. Cyril H. Hartmann, 1930, p. 369; *Baronetage of England,* ed. Thomas Wotton, 1741 (often ascribed to Arthur Collins (?1690–1760), on whose two-volume work of 1720 it was based), iii pt i. 216: 'a very accomplished gentleman; she had the reputation of being one of the most perfect beauties of the age, and yet an excellent wife.'

suaded the Bedinfields crowded in these characters to take off the
ridicule in Grammont: they have succeeded to a miracle. Madame de
Mirepoix told me t'other day that she had known a daughter of the
Countess de Grammont,[9] an abbess in Lorrain,[10] who to the ambassadress's great scandal, was ten times more vain of the blood of Hamilton, than of an equal quantity of that of Grammont. She had told
her much of her sister my Lady Stafford,[11] whom I remember to have
seen when I was quite a child. She used to live at Twickenham when
Mary Wortley[12] and the Duke of Wharton[13] lived there too; she had
more wit than both of them: what would I give to have had Strawberry Hill twenty years ago?—I think anything but twenty years. Lady
Stafford used to say to her sister,[14] 'Well, child, I am come without
my wit today'; that is, she had not taken her opium, which she was
forced to do if she had any appointment to be in particular spirits.
This rage of Grammont carried me a little while ago to old Marlbro's
at Wimbledon,[15] where I had heard there was a picture of Lady Denham;[16] it is a charming one. The house you know stands in a hole, or
as the whimsical old creature said, seems to be making a curtsey. She
had directed my Lord Pembroke[16a] not to make her go up any steps, 'I
won't go up steps,' and so he dug a saucer to put it in, and levelled

9. Elizabeth Hamilton (1641–1708), m.
(1663) Philibert, Comte de Gramont
(1621–1707), the hero of the *Memoirs*; see
Ruth Clark, *Anthony Hamilton*, 1921,
passim.

10. Marie-Élisabeth de Gramont (1677–
1735), Abbesse de Poussay, 1695 (ibid.
166–8).

11. Claude-Charlotte de Gramont (ca
1659–1739), m. (1694) Henry Stafford-
Howard, 1st E. of Stafford (ibid.).

12. Lady Mary Pierrepont (1689–1762),
m. (1712) Edward Wortley Montagu; the
letter-writer. She and Lady Stafford were
close friends.

13. Philip Wharton (1698–1731), 2d M.
of Wharton; cr. (1718) D. of Wharton.
Seven years later HW wrote in 'The Parish Register of Twickenham,'

'Twit'nam, where frolic Wharton revel'd,
Where Montague with locks dishevel'd
(Conflict of dirt and warmth divine)
Invok'd—and scandaliz'd the Nine; . . .'

(*Works* iv. 382.)

14. The abbess.

15. There is an account of this visit in

Country Seats 13–15. The Duchess of
Marlborough had the Earl of Burlington
design her one house on this estate; she
did not like the location and tore it down.
The house HW visited, which she had left
to her grandson, Hon. John Spencer, was
burnt down in 1785 (see Owen Manning,
History . . . of Surrey, 1804–14, iii. 271–2,
where it is said that Burlington designed
this house, too).

16. Margaret Brooke (ca 1646–67), m.
(1665) Sir John Denham; became the mistress of the Duke of York. The *Memoirs*
(ch. viii) give the story that she was poisoned by Denham, but a remarkable number of others were accused by popular suspicion, though an autopsy revealed no
trace of poison (Denham, *Poetical Works*,
ed. Theodore H. Banks, New Haven, 1928,
p. 24). The portrait, by Lely, is now at Althorp (*Country Seats* 14).

16a. Henry Herbert (1693–1757), 9th E.
of Pembroke, 'the architect earl' of whom
HW said, 'No man had a purer taste in
building' (*Anecdotes of Painting*, *Works*
iii. 486).

the first floor with the ground. There is a bust of Admiral Vernon, erected I suppose by Jack Spencer, with as many lies upon it as if it was a tombstone, and a very curious old picture upstairs, that I take to be Louis Sforza the Moor, with his nephew Galeazzo:[17] there are other good pictures in the house, but perhaps you have seen them. As I have formerly seen Oxford and Blenheim,[18] I did not stop till I came to Stratford upon Avon, the wretchedest old town I ever saw, which I intended for Shakespeare's sake to find smug and pretty and *antique,* not *old.* His tomb, and his wife's and John à Combe's[19] are in an agreeable church, with several other monuments, as one of the Earl of Totness,[20] and another of Sir Edward Walker[21] the memoirs writer, our Tigress's ancestor. There are quantities of her Cloptons[22] too: but the bountiful corporation have exceedingly bepainted Shakespeare,[23] and the principal personages—Lady Caroline Petersham is not more vermilion. I was much struck with Ragley; the situation is magnificent; the house far beyond anything I have seen of that bad age, for it was begun, as I found by an old letter in the library from Lord Ranelagh[24] to Earl Conway,[25] in the year 1680. By the way I have had and am to have the rummaging of three chests of pedigrees, and letters to that Secretary Conway, which I have interceded for and saved from the flames.[26] The prospect is as fine as one desti-

17. Ludovico Maria Sforza (1451–1508), Duke of Milan 1494–1500; called 'il Moro.' His nephew was Giovanni Galeazzo Maria Sforza (1468–94), Duke of Milan 1476–94 (*Nouv. Biog. Gén.*). The portraits form one part of a triptych, attributed by HW to Dürer, now at Althorp (*Country Seats* 14–15).

18. *Ante* 20 May 1736.

19. John Combe (d. 1614) was a well-to-do inhabitant of Stratford; a doggerel epitaph, condemning him as an usurer, was once attributed to Shakespeare; see Sir Sidney Lee, *Life of William Shakespeare,* edn 1931, pp. 470–4. HW probably read about him in Nicholas Rowe's edition of Shakespeare, 1714, i. p. xxxvi; the version of the epigram there given has the name John-a-Combe, as in the text. His tomb is described and pictured in J. Harvey Bloom, *Shakespeare's Church,* 1902, pp. 185–6.

20. George Carew (1555–1629), cr. (1605) Bn Carew, (1626) E. of Totnes; statesman. For his tomb see ibid. 158–62; William

Dugdale, *Antiquities of Warwickshire,* 1656, p. 519.

21. Sir Edward Walker (1612–77), Kt; Garter King-at-arms, 1660; wrote several papers on the civil war, published in 1705 as *Historical Discourses;* his daughter married a Clopton, the family of Mrs Henry Talbot, 'our tigress.' For the tomb, see Bloom, op. cit. 152.

22. See Bloom, op. cit. *passim.*

23. The corporation in fact attempted to repaint Shakespeare's monument in its original colours; the work was done in 1748 with the proceeds of a special performance of *Othello.* The result was too much for the 18th century, and the bust was whitewashed in 1790 at the special behest of Edmond Malone; see Robert B. Wheler, *History . . . of Stratford-upon-Avon,* 1806, pp. 71–5.

24. Richard Jones (ca 1641–1712), 3d Vct Ranelagh, cr. (1674) E. of Ranelagh.

25. Edward Conway (ca 1623–83), 3d Vct, cr. (1679) E. Conway.

26. HW expected to publish some of

tute of a navigated river can be, and totally hitherto unimproved. So
is the house, which is but just covered in, after so many years. They
have begun to inhabit the naked walls of the attic story: the great one
is unfloored, and unceiled. The hall is magnificent, 60 by 40, and 38
high: I am going to pump Mr Bentley for designs.[27] The other apartments are very lofty, and in quantity, though I had suspected that
this Leviathan hall must have devoured half the other chambers. The
Hertfords[27a] carried me to dine at Lord Archer's,[28] an odious place—I
pried after Cronk's false cabinet into the buttery.[29] On my return I
saw Warwick; a pretty old town, small and thinly inhabited, in the
form of a cross. The castle is enchanting; the view pleased me more
than I can express; the River Avon tumbles down a cascade at the
foot of it. It is well laid out by one Brown[30] who has set up, on a few
ideas of Kent and Mr Southcote. One sees what the prevalence of
taste does; little Brook who would have chuckled to have been born
in an age of clipped hedges and cockle shell avenues, has submitted
to let his garden and park be natural. Where he has attempted Gothic
in the castle, he has failed woefully; and has indulged himself in a
new apartment that is most paltry.[31] The chapel is very pretty, and
smugged up with tiny pews, that look like *étuis* for the dapper Earl
and his diminutive Countess.[31a] I shall tell you nothing of the glorious

the Conway papers (*post* 20 Aug. 1758),
but never did. The third Marquess of
Hertford left them to John Wilson Croker, who left them to the nation; they are
now in the British Museum and the Public Record Office. A selection was edited
by Marjorie Hope Nicolson, as *Conway
Letters*, New Haven, 1930, q.v., pp. ix,
xxii–xxiii.

27. Apparently for 'improvements' to
the rooms. There are none in the book
HW kept of Bentley's designs (now WSL).

27a. Lady Isabella Fitzroy (1726–82), m.
(1741) Francis Seymour Conway, 2d Bn
Conway, cr. (1750) E., (1793) M. of Hertford.

28. Thomas Archer (1695–1768), cr.
(1747) Bn Archer. His seat, Umberslade,
near Henley in Arden, Warwickshire, is
described in Thomas Sharp, *Epitome of
the County of Warwick*, 1835, p. 167, as
'built about 150 years since . . . of a square
form, with two wings slightly projecting
from the main building, and the principal

or western front has a good portico of the
Doric order.'

29. Not explained.

30. Lancelot Brown (1715–83), called
'Capability' Brown, 'had been kitchen
gardener to Lord Cobham at Stowe, and
became the best imitator of Kent, and the
most fashionable designer of grounds and
gardens. At last he applied to architecture, and with no bad success' (HW's note
in William Mason, *Satirical Poems . . .
with notes by Horace Walpole,* ed. Paget
Toynbee, Oxford, 1926, p. 41). HW's opinion of him rose until he became 'Lady
Nature's second husband' (HW to Lady
Ossory 8 Feb. 1783).

31. Gray visited Warwick in Sept. 1754
and laughs at this room (*Gray Corr.* i.
409).

31a. Elizabeth Hamilton (ca 1720–1800),
m. (1) (1742) Francis Greville, 8th Bn
Brooke, cr. (1746) E. Brooke, (1759) E. of
Warwick; m. (2) Gen. Robert Clerk.

chapel of the Beauchamps in St Mary's Church, for you know it in Dugdale, nor how ill the fierce bears and ragged staves, are succeeded by puppets and corals.[32] As I came back another road, I saw Lord Pomfret's by Towcester, where there [are] a few good pictures, and many mashed statues; there is an excessive fine Cicero,[33] which has no fault—but the head being modern. I saw a pretty lodge just built by the Duke of Grafton in Whittleberry Forest;[34] the design is Kent's, but as was his manner too heavy. I run through the gardens at Stowe,[35] which I have seen before and had only time to be charmed with the variety of scenes. I do like that Albano[36] glut of buildings, let them be ever so much condemned. Adieu!

Yours etc.

H. W.

To Montagu, Tuesday 8 October 1751

Arlington Street, Oct. 8, 1751.

SO you have totally forgot that I sent you the pedigree of the Crouches,[1] as long ago as the middle of last August, and that you promised to come to Strawberry Hill in October! I shall be there sometime in next week, but as my motions neither depend on resolutions nor almanacs, let me know beforehand, when you intend me a

32. For a description of the Beauchamp chapel, see Sir William Dugdale (1605–86), *Antiquities of Warwickshire*, 1656, pp. 354–60. The bear and ragged staff formed the badge of that family; see ibid. 327–8. 'Puppets and corals' may be the paltriness of recent innovations. See N&Q 1940, clxxviii. 15, 67.

33. On his previous visit to Easton Neston in 1736, HW did not notice the modernity of Cicero's head; see *ante* 20 May 1736. The statue was included in Lady Pomfret's gift to Oxford (ibid. n. 16); Mrs Elizabeth Montagu, visiting Oxford in 1762, noticed 'a noble statue of Cicero,' in that collection (*Mrs Montagu "Queen of the Blues,"* ed. Reginald Blunt, 1923, i. 24). There is a plate of it in Richard Chandler, *Marmora Oxoniensa*, Oxford, 1763, pl. xxiv; see Adolf Michaelis, *Ancient Marbles in Great Britain*, Cambridge, 1882, p. 553.

34. In Northamptonshire; the Duke was Ranger of it.

35. Bucks, the seat of Earl Temple; the date of the earlier visit is not known. See *post* 24 Sept. 1762, n. 7, for a list of the buildings, and *post* 7 July 1770. Descriptions and prints of Stowe are in many surveys of English country seats.

36. Francesco Albani or Albano (1578–1660), Italian painter; excelled in landscapes and buildings; see *Nouv. Biog. Gén.*

1. The pedigree is missing. Montagu's paternal great-great-grandmother was Margaret (d. 1653), youngest dau. of John Crouch of Corn[er?]bury, Herts; m. (1620, the third for both parties) Sir Henry Montagu, cr. (1620) Vct Mandeville; cr. (1626) E. of Manchester; see Robert Clutterbuck, *History . . . of the County of Hertford*, 1815–27, iii. 429–30; Collins, *Peerage*, 1812, ii. 57.

visit, for though keeping an appointment is not just the thing you ever do, I suppose you know you dislike being disappointed yourself as much, as if you were the most punctual person in the world to engagements.

I came yesterday from Woburn[2] where I have been a week. The house is in building and three sides of the quadrangle finished, but as it is rather a patchwork, and upon the dimensions of the old abbey, it will be neither stately nor venerable. The park is very fine, the woods glorious, and the plantations of evergreens sumptuous—but upon the whole, it is what I rather admire than like—I fear that is what I am a little apt to do at the finest places in the world, where there is not a navigable river. You would be charmed as I was with an old gallery, that is not yet destroyed—it is a bad room, powdered with little gold stars, and covered with millions of old portraits. There are all the successions of Earls and Countesses of Bedford, and all their progenies—one Countess[3] is a whole-length dancing in the drollest dress you ever saw; and another picture of the same woman leaning on her hand, I believe by Cornelius Johnson,[4] is as fine a head as ever I saw. There are many of Queen Elizabeth's worthies, the Leicesters, Essexes, and Philip Sidneys, and a very curious portrait of the last Courtney Earl of Devonshire who died at Padua; have not I read somewhere that he was in love with Queen Elizabeth, and Queen Mary with him?[5] He is quite in the style of the former's lovers, red-bearded and not comely. There is Essex's friend the Earl of

2. Woburn Abbey, Beds; seat of the Duke of Bedford; see John D. Parry, *History . . . of Woburn and Its Abbey*, 1831. HW gives a fuller account of the house and the pictures in *Country Seats* 17–20.

3. Hon. Lucy Harington (1581–1627), m. (1594) Edward Russell, 3d E. of Bedford (Stepney parish registers). The whole-length is No. 75 in George Scharf, *Descriptive and Historical Catalogue of the Collection of Pictures at Woburn Abbey*, 1877; there is a similar one at Welbeck. According to O'Donoghue and Hake, *Catalogue of Engraved British Portraits*, 1908–25, vi. 34, it is by Marcus Gheeraerts (1561–1635). The portrait is to be found in Walpole Soc., iii (Oxford, 1914), pl. ix.

4. Cornelis Janssen van Ceulen (1593–ca 1662), 'generally, but inaccurately, called Johnson' (*Anecdotes, Works* iii. 149). The painting is described in *Country Seats* 40,

where it is anonymous, but following Vertue, whom he began to read in Sept. 1759 ('Short Notes'), HW assigned it to Gerard van Honthorst (1590–1656) in his *Anecdotes*, 1762, ii. 111 (see *Works* iii. 239). See *Vertue Notebooks*, pub. Walpole Soc., vol. xx (Oxford, 1932), p. 40; Scharf, op. cit., No. 74; O'Donoghue and Hake, op. cit., i. 154.

5. Edward Courtenay (1526–56), 11th E. of Devon or Devonshire. He was Edward IV's great-grandson, and a match between him and Mary was projected, which her union with Philip prevented. A plan was then made to marry him to Elizabeth, and Wyatt's rebellion (1554) was so to culminate. On its failure he was imprisoned and when released went to Italy where he died. The picture is No. 10 in Scharf, op. cit.

Southampton,[6] his son the Lord Treasurer,[7] and Madame l'Empoisonneuse,[8] that married Carr Earl of Somerset—she is pretty. Have not you seen a copy Vertue has made of Philip and Mary?[8a] That is in this gallery too,[9] but more curious than good. They showed me two heads, who according to the tradition of the family were the originals of Castalio and Polidore[10]—they were sons to the second Earl of Bedford,[11] and the eldest, if not both died before their father. The eldest has vipers in his hand, and in the distant landscape appears in a maze,[12] with these words, *Fata viam invenient:* the other has a woman behind him sitting near the sea with strange monsters surrounding her:[13] I don't pretend to decipher this, nor to describe half the entertaining morsels I found in this purgatory of antiquities—but I can't omit, as you know I am Grammont-mad, that I found there *le vieux Roussel, qui était le plus fier danseur d'Angleterre.*[14] The portrait is young, but has all the promise of his latter character. I am going to send them a head of a Countess of Cumberland;[15] sister to Cas-

6. Henry Wriothesley (1573–1624), 3d E. of Southampton, by Michiel van Miereveld (1567–1641) (ibid. No. 64).

7. Thomas Wriothesley (1607–67), 4th E. of Southampton; Lord Treasurer 1660–7. By Lely (ibid. No. 143).

8. Lady Frances Howard (1589–1632), m. (1) (1606) Robert Devereux, 3d E. of Essex; divorced him and m. (2) (1613) Robert Carr (ca 1587–1645), cr. (1613) E. of Somerset, James I's favourite, with whom she was convicted of poisoning Sir Thomas Overbury (both were pardoned); see Edward A. Parry, *The Overbury Mystery,* 1925. HW had a copy of the Woburn portrait made by Lady Lucan and hung it in the Breakfast Room (*Des. of SH, Works* ii. 426; not in SH Sale Cat.). It is No. 118 in Scharf, op. cit., which asserts that it is not the Countess of Somerset but her mother Frances Knevit, Countess of Suffolk.

8a. Philip II (1527–98) of Spain, and Mary (Tudor) (1516–58) of England.

9. By Lukas de Heere (1534–84); ibid. No. 12. HW had Vertue's copy in the Holbein chamber at SH, and ascribes the original to Antonio More (*Des. of SH, Works* ii. 457; sold SH xx. 38).

10. Heroes of *The Orphan,* 1680, tragedy by Thomas Otway (1652–85).

11. Francis Russell (1527–85), 2d E. of Bedford. The portraits, Nos. 30 and 31 in Scharf, op. cit., are of his eldest son Ed-

ward, Lord Russell (d. 1572), and his third son Lord Francis Russell (d. 1585, one day before his father). As HW intimates in *Country Seats* 20, there is nothing in their known history to suggest the story of *The Orphan;* but see [Thomas Pennant], *Journey from Chester to London,* 1782, pp. 369–70, for an attempt to construe the allegorical background in accordance with it.

12. HW refers to a full-length figure in the background of Edward, Lord Russell's portrait as another representation of Lord Russell (Scharf, loc. cit.).

13. 'The Italian style of allegory so prevalent in this period' (ibid. 21).

14. Hon. John Russell (1620–81). 'Ce Russel était un des fiers danseurs d'Angleterre; je veux dire, pour les contredanses; il en avait un recueil de deux ou trois cents en tablature, qu'il dansait . . . quelquefois jusqu'à extinction' (*Memoires de Grammont,* SH 1772, p. 126). He was the 3d son of the 4th E. of Bedford. The portrait, No. 103 in Scharf, op. cit., is by John Hayls; see *Anecdotes, Works* iii. 302.

15. Lady Margaret Russell (1560–1616), m. (1577) George Clifford, 3d E. of Cumberland. A bust portrait of her by an unknown artist is No. 32 in Scharf, op. cit.; but nothing has been found at Woburn to connect it with HW (information from Miss Gladys Scott Thomson).

talio and Polidore, and mother of a famous Countess of Dorset,[16] who afterwards married the mad Earl of Pembroke of Charles the First's time. She was an authoress,[17] and immensely rich: after the Restoration, Sir Joseph Williamson,[18] the Secretary of State, wrote to her, to choose a courtier at Appleby: she sent him this answer; 'I have been bullied by an usurper, I have been ill-treated by a court, but I won't be dictated to by a subject; your man shall not stand: Anne Dorset, Pembroke and Montgomery.'[19]

Adieu! if you love news an hundred years old, I think you can't have a better correspondent—For anything that passes now, I shall not think it worth knowing these fifty years.

Yours ever,

H. WALPOLE

To Montagu, Thursday 9 January 1752

The St James's Evening Post

Thursday, January 9th, 1752.

MONDAY being Twelfth Day, his Majesty according to annual custom offered myrrh, frankincense and a small bit of gold;[1] and at night in commemoration of the three *Kings* or *Wise* men, the King and royal family played at hazard for the benefit of a prince of

16. Lady Anne Clifford (1590–1676), m. (1) (1609) Richard Sackville, 3d E. of Dorset; m. (2) (1630) Philip Herbert, 4th E. of Pembroke (ca 1584–1650); Baroness Clifford, *suo jure*.

17. In *Royal & Noble Authors, Works* i. 485–6, HW attributes to her 'Memoirs of her husband Richard Earl of Dorset' (never printed), and 'Sundry memorials of herself and her progenitors.' According to George C. Williamson, *Lady Anne Clifford, Countess of Dorset, Pembroke and Montgomery*, Kendal, 1922, p. 286, the former work has not been discovered; but she did leave numerous diaries, family records, etc. (ibid. 357–67 and *passim*).

18. Sir Joseph Williamson (1633–1701), Kt.

19. This is the first known notice of this famous letter. HW repeated it to Bentley 5 Aug. 1752, and it was first printed in a paper, by HW, in *The World* 5 April 1753 (*Works* i. 168). Although it is more famous than any other event in the Countess's busy life, the letter has been frequently suspected (e.g. Hartley Coleridge, *Lives of Northern Worthies*, edn 1852, ii. 80–1; DNB), and a fairly conclusive case against its authenticity is made by Williamson, op. cit. n. 17, pp. 285–302. He points out (1) no other reference to the original has been found; (2) the phrasing is unlike that of the Countess's other correspondence; the first known use of 'bully' as a verb is 1723; she usually signed letters 'Ann Pembroke' only; (3) Sir Joseph Williamson was himself a candidate for Appleby in 1668, and carried on an extensive correspondence with Lady Pembroke in which, though refusing support, she was unfailingly polite. How or from whom HW got his information is not known.

1. George II's parsimony was notorious.

the blood.[2] There were above eleven thousand pounds upon the table; his most sacred Majesty won three guineas, and his R. H. the Duke three thousand four hundred pounds.

On Saturday last was landed at the Custom House a large box of truffles, being a present to the Earl of Lincoln[3] from Theobald Taaffe Esq.[4] who is shortly expected home from his travels in foreign parts.

Tomorrow the new-born son[5] of the Earl of Egremont is to be baptized, when his Majesty and the Earl of Granville (if he is able to stand)[6] and the Duchess Dowager of Somerset[7] are to be sponsors.

We are assured that on Tuesday last the surprising strong woman[8] was exhibited at the Countess of Holderness's[9] before a polite assembly of persons of the first quality: and sometime this week the two dwarfs[10] will play at brag at Madam Holman's.[11] N.B. The strong man[12] who was to have performed at Mrs Nugent's is indisposed.

2. The Twelfth-Night gaming was customarily for the benefit of the groom-porter (N&Q 1939, clxxvii. 445); cf. HW to Bentley 9 Jan. 1755.

3. See HW to Mann 22 Nov. 1751, where HW reports Taaffe as carrying similar dainties for Lincoln's uncle the Duke of Newcastle.

4. Theobald Taaffe, adventurer; about him see *Letters to and from Madame du Deffand and Julie de Lespinasse*, ed. Warren H. Smith, New Haven, 1938, pp. xiii–xiv. He had become notorious through an affair in which he and the younger Edward Wortley Montagu were involved in Paris. They were accused by one Abraham Payba (see n. 30 below) of cheating him at cards, and of robbing him when he refused to pay them. Though the legal proceedings ultimately resulted in their favour, it seems clear that their conduct was, to say the least, shady; see HW to Mann 22 Nov. 1751; John Nichols, *Literary Anecdotes*, 1812–15, iv. 629–35; DNB, *sub* Montagu. Taaffe's later history has not been discovered.

5. George O'Brien Wyndham (18 Dec. 1751–1837), 3d E. of Egremont, 1763; baptized 9 Jan. at St Margaret's, Westminster.

6. 'He was so drunk' (Mrs Piozzi).

7. There were two dowager Duchesses of Somerset at this time, Lady Charlotte Finch (d. 1773), m. (1726) Charles Sey-

mour, 6th D. of Somerset (d. 1748); and Frances Thynne (ca 1699–1754), m. (ca 1713) Algernon Seymour, 7th D. of Somerset (d. 1750). The latter, as Lady Hertford, was a correspondent of Lady Pomfret.

8. Advertisements appeared in *The Daily Advertiser* during 1752–3, of 'the Genoese Female Samson,' 'the true strong-woman,' etc., who exhibited in various parts of London and 'before the chief nobility of England.' Among other feats of strength, 'she puts her head on one chair and her feet on another, and bears six large men from her stomach to her instep; a large block of marble, of between two and three thousand weight, shall be put on her body, which she will permit to lie on her some time, after which she will throw it off at about six feet distance, without using her hands.'

9. Marie Doublet (ca 1720–1801), m. (1743) Robert Darcy, 4th E. of Holdernesse.

10. Probably the same mentioned in GM Dec. 1751, xxi. 571: 'Uncommon natural curiosities shewn this month in London,' where are listed two dwarfs, one from Glamorganshire and one from Norfolk, an acrobatic negro, a rhinoceros 'or true unicorn,' and a crocodile (n. 36 below). The two dwarfs appear in advertisements in *The Daily Advertiser* of this

There is lately arrived at the Lord Carpenter's[13] a curious male chimpanzee[14] which has had the honour of being shown before the ugliest princes in Europe, who all expressed their approbation; and we hear that he intends to offer to offer himself a candidate to represent the city of Westminster at the next general election. Note, he wears breeches, and there is a gentlewoman to attend the ladies.

Last night the Hon. and Rev. Mr James Brudenel[15] was admitted a Doctor of Opium in the ancient University of White's, being received *ad eundem* by his Grace the Rev. Father in Chess[16] the Duke of Devonshire President, and the rest of the Senior Fellows.[17] At the same time the Lord Robert Bertie and Col. Barrington[18] were rejected on account of some deficiency of formality in their testimonials.

time, where the Norfolk dwarf is called 'Mr John Coan,' and the Welsh one 'Hopkin Hopkins.'

11. The inclusiveness of her assemblies furnished HW an occasional subject for jest for several years. Mrs Harris writes of them to her son, 25 Oct. 1764: 'We were last night at a very genteel assembly at Mrs Holman's; most of the foreign ministers, Lady Harrington and her daughter, and most of the fine world, were there. Probably you may say, who is Mrs Holman? 'Tis one of my new acquaintances, whom I picked up at Lady Pocock's; she has two daughters; they have a good house in Park Place, and are people of *this world*' (*Series of Letters of the First Earl of Malmesbury*, ed. the [third] Earl of Malmesbury, 1870, i. 118). She may have been the wife of either James (GM 1771, xli. 239), or Philip Holman (GM 1790, lx pt i. 85), or '—— Holdman, Esq.' who died in Park Place, 1774 (GM 1774, xliv. 391).

12. Not identified. The allusion may be salacious, referring to the sexual prowess which HW thought enabled poor Irishmen like Nugent and Hussey to marry rich widows like Mrs Nugent and the Duchess of Manchester.

13. George Carpenter (1723–62), 3d Bn Carpenter; cr. (1761) E. of Tyrconnel. As there is no engraved portrait of him, it cannot be confirmed that the point of this passage is his extreme ugliness.

14. No record of a performing chimpanzee has been found at this time, but advertisements appear in *The Daily Ad-*

vertiser of learned dogs and dancing bears. Dr R. W. Chapman points out that this is an interesting anticipation of T. L. Peacock's *Melincourt*, 1817.

15. Hon. James Brudenell (1725–1811), cr. (1780) Bn Brudenell; 5th E. of Cardigan, 1790.

16. Along with the heavy gambling for which White's was notorious, chess seems to have been popular at this time; see HW to Mann 22 Nov. 1751, and several bets on the outcome of matches, recorded in the Betting Book in [William B. Boulton] *History of White's*, 1892, ii pt i. 24, 32.

17. Some time before this, the waiting-list at White's had become so long that a junior group was formed known as the 'Young Club'; several years often elapsed before elevation to the 'Old Club.' Though under the same roof, they maintained separate rooms and administration; ibid. i. 67–70. The dates given in the list of members (ibid. ii pt ii) seem to refer only to admission to the Young Club. James Brudenell appears in 1752 (p. 12); Col. Barrington (*post* n. 18) not at all. The rejection of Lord Robert Bertie, on the other hand, must have been at the Old Club, for he is listed as having joined White's in 1744 (p. 8), and in 1751 'Gilly' Williams wrote to Selwyn, 'I have desired Lord R. Bertie to propose me at White's' (Jesse, *Selwyn*, 1882, i. 140).

18. Hon. John Barrington (d. 1764), 3d son of 1st Vct Barrington; Lt-Col., 1746; Capt. in Coldstream Guards, 1748; Col., 1756; A.D.C. to the King 1757–8; Col. 40th

Letters from Grosvenor Street mention a dreadful apparition[19] which has appeared for several nights at the house of the Countess Temple,[20] which has occasioned several of her Ladyship's domestics to leave her service, except the coachman, who has drove her sons and nephews for several years and is not afraid of spectres.[21] The coroner's inquest have brought in their verdict lunacy.

Last week the Lord Downe[22] received at the Treasury the sum of an hundred kisses from the Auditor of the Exchequer,[23] being the reward for shooting at an highwayman.

On Tuesday the operation of shaving[24] was happily performed on the upper lip of her Grace the Duchess of Newcastle, by a celebrated artist from Paris, sent over on purpose by the Earl of Albemarle.[25] The performance lasted but one minute and three seconds, to the great joy of that noble family; and in consideration of his great care and expedition his Grace has settled four hundred pounds a year upon him for life. We hear that he is to have the honour of shaving the heads of the Lady Catherine Pelham,[26] the Duchess of Queensberry and several other persons of quality.

By authority, on Sunday next will be opened the Romish chapel at Norfolk House;[27] no persons will be admitted but such as are known well-wishers to the present happy establishment.

Foot, and in command in its later stages of a successful expedition against Guadeloupe 1758–9; Col. 8th Foot and Maj. Gen., 1759 (*Army Lists; Lodge, Irish Peerage*, 1789, v. 204; *Mem. Geo. II* iii. 169–70).

19. Not explained.

20. Hester Temple (ca 1690–1752), m. (1710) Richard Grenville; Viscountess Cobham, *suo jure*, 1749; cr. (1749) Countess Temple. Not to be confused with her sister-in-law, Gray's Lady Cobham.

21. Her eldest son Richard Grenville (later Grenville-Temple) (1711–79), 1st E. Temple, 1752, and Sir George Lyttelton, her nephew, were both ungainly and angular; the former was known as 'Squire Gawky,' while the latter is no doubt the 'respectable Hottentot' of Chesterfield's *Letters.* See also *post* 28 Aug. 1752, 'legs . . . as long as a Grenville's.'

22. Henry Pleydell Dawnay (1727–60), 3d Vct Downe, a popular member of White's; no exploit of his explaining this paragraph has come to light.

23. The Earl of Lincoln.

24. See also *post* 28 Oct. 1756.

25. William Anne van Keppel (1702–54), 2d E. of Albemarle, Ambassador at Paris 1749–54.

26. Lady Catherine Manners (ca 1701–80), m. (1726) Henry Pelham, First Lord of the Treasury. Other references to her by HW imply that she was rather eccentric, while the Duchess of Queensberry was undoubtedly so. The allusion, then, may be to the common 18th-century practice of shaving the heads of lunatics; see, e.g., Hogarth's *Rake's Progress*, pl. 8, and the figures of Raving and Melancholy Madness by Caius Gabriel Cibber, originally over the entrance to Bedlam, now in the Guildhall Museum (Karl Baedeker, *London and its Environs*, 1930, p. 280), illustrated in *London and Its Environs Described*, 1761, i. 298.

27. The Duke of Norfolk was a Roman Catholic and had been tried for high treason after the '15. HW is charging the government with Jacobitism.

Mass will begin exactly when the English liturgy is finished.

At the Theatre Royal in the House of Lords, *The Royal Slave*, with *Lethe*.[28]

At the theatre in St Stephen's Chapel, *The Fool in Fashion*.[29]

The Jews are desired to meet on the 20th inst. at the sign of Fort L'Évêque in Pharaoh-Street,[30] to commemorate the noble struggle made by one of their brethren in support of his property.

Deserted—Miss Ashe.[31]

Lost, an Opposition.[32]

To be let, an ambassador's masquerade, the gentleman going abroad.[33]

To be sold, the whole nation.

To be covered by any Earl going one-and-twenty, the two Miss Gunnings.[34]

Lately published, The Analogy of Political and Private Quarrels, or the Art of Healing Family Differences by Widening Them; on these words, Do evil that good may ensue. A Sermon preached before the Right Hon. Henry Pelham and the rest of the Society for propagating Christian Charity, by Wm Leveson,[35] Chaplain to her R. H.

28. *The Royal Slave* is a tragi-comedy by William Cartwright (1611–43). *Lethe, or Esop among the Shades* is a farce by Garrick, written 1740, revived and revised in 1749 (see [John Genest], *Some Account of the English Stage,* Bath, 1832, iv. 264–5). HW refers to the complete control of Parliament and Crown by the Pelhams at this time, resulting in unparalleled political apathy; see *Mem. Geo. II* i. 228, 239–40.

29. The subtitle of Colley Cibber's *Love's Last Shift;* it is not clear whether this is directed at Pelham, or at the Commons generally.

30. Another allusion to the Montagu-Taaffe affair (*ante,* n. 4) in which the complainant was Abraham Payba, alias James Roberts, a Jew who was making the grand tour in company with a Miss Rose (John Nichols, *Literary Anecdotes,* 1812–15, iv. 631). Fort L'Évêque is the Paris prison in which HW thought one of the sharpers was imprisoned; apparently, however, only Montagu was jailed, and in the Châtelet (ibid. 632); see HW to Mann 22 Nov. 1751, where HW also reports that they had been 'pharaoh-bankers to Madame de Mirepoix.'

31. By Edward Wortley Montagu, whom she had married at Mayfair Chapel 21 July 1751 (Harleian Society, *Register of . . . St George's Chapel, Mayfair,* ed. George J. Armytage, 1889, p. 195).

32. See n. 28 above.

33. Not explained.

34. The famous sisters had by this time been the toast of London for a year. Mary Gunning (1732–60), m. (5 March 1752) George William Coventry, 6th E. of Coventry. Elizabeth Gunning (1733–90), m. (1) (14 Feb. 1752) James Hamilton, 6th D. of Hamilton; m. (2) (1759) Col. John Campbell, 5th D. of Argyll, 1770. About them see Horace Bleackley, *Story of a Beautiful Duchess,* 1908. This passage is omitted in previous editions.

35. Hon. William Leveson-Gower (d. 1756), brother of 1st E. Gower; M.P. Staffordshire 1720–56 (Collins, *Peerage,* 1812, ii. 447–8). Princess Amelia had wished to have him made her Treasurer and Auditor. Leveson-Gower, who was of the Bedford faction, applied to Henry Pelham for the posts. Pelham, wishing to detach him from the Bedfords, refused unless he would ask the endorsement of his brother

the Princess Amelia; and now printed at the desire of several of the family.

For capital weaknesses, the Duke of Newcastle's true spirit of crocodiles.[36]

Given gratis, at the Turn-Style, the corner of Lincoln's Inn Fields[37] Anodyne Stars and Garters.[38]

To Montagu, Tuesday 12 May 1752

Arlington Street, May 12, 1752.

YOU deserve no charity, for you never write but to ask it. When you are tired of yourself and the country, you think over all London, and consider who will be proper to send you an account of it. Take notice, I won't be your gazetteer, nor is my time come for being a dowager, a maker of news, a day labourer in scandal: if you care for nobody, but for what they can tell you, look you, you must provide yourself elsewhere—The town is empty, nothing in it but flabby mackerel, and wooden gooseberry tarts, and a hazy east wind— My sister is gone to Paris, I go to Strawberry Hill in three days for the summer, if summer there will ever be any. If you want news, you must send to Ireland, where there is almost a civil war, between the Lord Lieutenant[1] and Primate[2] on one side (observe I don't tell you what *side* that is) and the Speaker[3] on the other, who carries questions by wholesale in the House of Commons against the Castle—and the *teterrima belli causa* is not the common one.[4] Reams of scandalous verses and ballads are come over, too bad to send you if I had

Lord Gower, an ally of Pelham's. This Leveson-Gower refused to do (see *Mem. Geo. II* i. 226).

36. Doubtless crocodile tears, with a reference to one of the 'natural curiosities shewn this month in London' (n. 10 above), 'a crocodile alive, taken on the banks of the Nile in Egypt, a creature never seen before alive in England.'

37. The location of Newcastle House.

38. Compare a worm-medicine advertisement in *Penny London Post or Morning Advertiser* 16–18 Jan. 1751, 'At M. Burchett's, at the Anodyne Necklace in Long-Acre next Drury Lane . . . the famous Little Purging Sugar Plums.' Johnson refers to 'the Anodyne Necklace, for the ease and

safety of poor toothing infants,' in his essay on advertising in *The Idler*, 1761, i. 226, No. 40.

1. Duke of Dorset.

2. Dr George Stone (ca 1708–64), Abp of Armagh.

3. Henry Boyle (ca 1686–1764), cr. (1756) E. of Shannon.

4. 'Nam fuit ante Helenam cunnus tæterrima belli causa . . .'

(Horace, *Serm.* I. iii. 107–8). The cause of the Irish quarrel was an attempt on the part of Stone and the Duke of Dorset's son Lord George Sackville to break Boyle's power; see *Mem. Geo. II* i. 278–83.

them, but I really have not—what is more provoking for the Duke of
Dorset, an address is come over directly to the King, (not as usual
through the channel of the Lord Lieutenant) to assure him of their
great loyalty and apprehensions of being misrepresented. This is
all I know, and you see, most imperfectly.

I was t'other night to see what is now grown the fashion, Mother
Midnight's Oratory[5]—it appeared the lowest buffoonery[6] in the world
even to me who am used to my uncle Horace. There is a bad oration
to ridicule, what it is too like, Orator Henley:[7] all the rest is per-
verted music. There is a man who plays so nimbly on the kettle
drum, that he has reduced that noisy instrument to be an object of
sight, for if you don't see the tricks with his hands, it is no better than
ordinary. Another plays on a violin and trumpet together; another
mimics a bagpipe with a German flute, and makes it full as disagreeable. There is an admired dulcimer, a favourite saltbox, and a really
curious Jew's harp. Two or three men intend to persuade you that
they play on a broomstick, which is drolly brought in, carefully
shrouded in a case, so as to be mistaken for a bassoon or base viol,
but they succeed in nothing but the action. The last fellow imitates
farting and[8] curtseying to a French horn.[8a] There are twenty medley
overtures, and a man who speaks a prologue and epilogue, in which
he counterfeits all the actors and singers upon earth; in short, I have
long been convinced that what I used to imagine the most difficult
thing in the world, mimicry, is the easiest; for one has seen for these
two or three years, at Foote's[9] and the other theatres, that when they

5. 'The town has been lately entertained
with a kind of farcical performance called
The Old Woman's Oratory, conducted by
Mrs Mary Midnight and her family; intended as a banter on Henley's Oratory,
and a puff to the Old Woman's Magazine'
(GM 1752, xxii. 43). A kind of vaudeville,
it was written and produced by Christopher Smart to advertise *The Midwife or
Old Woman's Magazine*, which he and
John Newbery published 1751–3 (Alexander Chalmers, 'Life of Smart' in *Works of
English Poets*, 1810, xvi. 7–8).

6. 'So it was low buffoonery, but it pretended to nothing better, and was wondrous droll, and what the wags call *fun-
ney*' (Mrs Piozzi).

7. Rev. John Henley (1692–1756), eccentric preacher.

8. Omitted without indication in previous editions.

8a. Advertisements of 'The Old Woman's
Oratory, to be conducted by Mrs Mary
Midnight, and her Family' appear in *The
Daily Advertiser* throughout 1752. It was
performed at the New Theatre, Haymarket, when HW saw it. Among other fea-
tures advertised were 'the Declamatory
Piece on the Jew's-Harp, by a Casuist,'
'the Oration on the Salt-Box by a Ration-
alist,' 'a solo on the French Horn by Mrs
Midnight's daughter.'

9. Samuel Foote (1720–77), dramatist,
manager, and actor, had been giving at his
summer seasons at the Haymarket bur-
lesques of well-known actors.

lost one mimic, they called odd man, and another came and succeeded just as well.

Adieu! I have told you much more than I intended, and much more than I could conceive I had to say, except how does Miss Montagu!

Yours ever,

H. W.

PS. Did you hear Capt. Hotham's[10] bon mot on Sir Th. Robinson's[11] making an assembly from the top of his house to the bottom? He said, he wondered so many people would go to Sir Thomas's, as he treated them all *de haut en bas!*

To Montagu, Saturday 6 June 1752

Strawberry Hill, June 6, 1752.

I HAVE just been in London for two or three days to fetch an adventure, and am returned to my Hill and my castle. I can't say I lost my labour, as you shall hear. Last Sunday night, being as wet a night as you shall see in a summer's day, about half an hour after twelve, I was just come home from White's, and undressing to step into bed: I heard Harry,[1] who you know lies forwards, roar out, 'Stop thief!' and run downstairs—I ran after him—don't be frightened, I have not lost one enamel, nor bronze; nor have been shot through the head again.[2] A gentlewoman[3] who lives at Gov. Pitt's,[4] next door but one to me, and where Mr Bentley used to live, was going to bed too, and heard people breaking into Mr Freeman's[5] house,

---

10. Sir Charles Hotham-Thompson (1729–94), 8th Bt, of Scarborough, 1771; see Anna M. W. Stirling, *The Hothams,* 1918, ii. *passim.*

11. Sir Thomas Robinson (ca 1702–77), Bt, 1731, of Rokeby, Yorkshire.

1. Henry Jones; see HW to Grosvenor Bedford 9 Sept. 1762, where, on account of his retirement, HW sets forth the qualifications and duties of a successor, who will be 'steward and butler.'

2. As he nearly was in 1749 by Maclean, the highwayman; see 'Short Notes.'

3. Not identified.

4. George Morton Pitt (d. 1756), Governor of Fort St George 1730–5; M.P. Old

Sarum 1722–4; Pontefract 1741–54; see Col. Henry Yule, *Diary of William Hedges,* 1887–9, iii. pp. xci, clxi (Hakluyt Soc. 1st ser. No. lxxviii).

5. No doubt Sambrooke Freeman (1720–82), of Fawley Court, Bucks; D.C.L. Oxon, 1773; M.P. Pontefract 1754–61; Bridport 1768–74; see Foster, *Alumni Oxon;* John S. Burn, *History of Henley-on-Thames,* 1861, p. 254; George Lipscomb, *History . . . of the County of Buckingham,* 1847, iii. 563; *Passages from the Diaries of Mrs Philip Lybbe Powys,* ed. Emily J. Climenson, 1899, pp. 145–9, 185–7. He was living in Arlington St in 1754 (*Court and City Register* for 1755, p. 59).

who like some acquaintance of mine in Albemarle Street,[6] goes out of town, locks up his doors, and leaves the community to watch his furniture. N.B. It was broken open but two years ago, and I and all the chairmen vow they shall steal his house away another time before we will trouble our heads about it. Well, madam called out 'Watch'; two men who were sentinels ran away, and Harry's voice after them. Down came I, and with a posse of chairmen and watchmen found the third fellow in the area of Mr Freeman's house. Mayhap you have seen all this in the papers, little thinking who commanded the detachment. Harry fetched a blunderbuss to invite the thief up; one of the chairmen who was drunk, cried, 'Give me the blunderbuss, I'll shoot him!' But as the general's[7] head was a little cooler, he prevented military execution, and took the prisoner without bloodshed, intending to make his triumphal entry into the metropolis of Twickenham with his captive tied to the wheels of his post-chaise.—I find my style rises so much with the recollection of my victory, that I don't know how to descend to tell you that the enemy was a carpenter and had a leather apron on. The next step was to share my glory with my friends; I dispatched a courier to White's for George Selwyn, who you know loves nothing upon earth so well as a criminal except the execution of him. It happened very luckily that the drawer who received my message has very lately been robbed himself, and had the wound fresh in his memory. He stalked up into the club-room, stopped short, and with a hollow trembling voice, said, 'Mr Selwyn! —Mr Walpole's compliments to you, and he has got a housebreaker for you!' A squadron immediately came to reinforce me, and having summoned Moreland with the keys of the fortress, we marched into the house to search for more of the gang. Col. Seabright[8] with his sword drawn went first, and then I, exactly the figure of Robinson Crusoe, with a candle and lanthorn in my hand, a carbine upon my shoulder, my hair wet and about my ears, and in a linen nightgown and slippers. We found the kitchen shutters forced, but not finished, and in the area a tremendous bag of tools, a hammer large enough for the hand of Jael, and six chisels! all which *opima spolia,* as there

6. HW's chief acquaintance in Albemarle St at this time seems to have been Lord Waldegrave.

7. HW himself.

8. Lt-Col. John Sebright (1725–94), 6th

Bt, 1761, of Besford Court, Worcs; Gen., 1782; member of White's, 1744; see G. F. R. Barker and Alan H. Stenning, *Record of Old Westminsters,* 1928.

was no temple of Jupiter Capitolinus in the neighbourhood, I was reduced to offer on the altar of Sir Thomas Clarges.[9]

I am now as I told you returned to my plough with as much humility and pride as any of my great predecessors; we lead quite a rural life, have had a sheep-shearing, a haymaking, a syllabub under the cow,[10] and a fishing—of three goldfish out of Po Yang,[11] for a present to Madam Clive: they breed with me excessively and are grown to the size of small perch. Everything grows, if tempests would let it; but I have had two of my largest trees broke today with the wind, and another last week. I am much obliged to you for the flower you offer me, but by the description, it is an Austrian rose, and I have several now in bloom. Mr Bentley is with me, finishing the drawings for Gray's *Odes;* there are some mandarin-cats fishing for goldfish which will delight you:[12] *au reste,* he is just where he was: he has heard something about a journey to Haughton[13] to the Great Cu of Haticuleo, but it don't seem[13a] fixed; unless he hears farther. Did he tell you the Rices and your Aunt Cosby[14] had dined here from Hampton Court? The minionette beauty[15] looks mighty well in his grandmother's jointure.

The memoirs of last year[16] are quite finished, but I shall add some pages of notes, that will not want anecdotes. Discontents of the na-

9. Sir Thomas Clarges (1688–1759), 2d Bt, of Aston, Herts (GM 1759, xxix. 94). He must have been a Justice of the Peace, no lists of whom have been published.

10. 'A drink or dish made of milk (freq. as drawn from the cow) or cream, curdled by the admixture of wine, cider, or other acid, and often sweetened and flavoured' (OED).

11. HW's Chinese name for his goldfish pond; see HW to Bentley 19 Dec. 1753. HW got the name from du Halde, *Description . . . de l'empire de la Chine,* 4 vols, Paris, 1735. It occurs at i. 146; Po Yang is a great lake (in northern Kiangsi province) celebrated for its many fish. HW's copy of du Halde was sold SH ii. 176 and is now WSL.

12. In the frontispiece to the *Ode on the Death of a Favourite Cat.* See illustration.

13. Horton, near Northampton, seat of the Earl of Halifax. The 18th-century house, which is illustrated in *Vict. Co.*

Hist. Northants iv. 260, was pulled down in 1936 (ibid. 259); see *post* ca 20 June 1757, n. 3; Appendix 4; *Country Seats* 52–3.

13a. HW wrote 'seemed.'

14. Grace Montagu (ca 1687–1767), m. Brig.-Gen. William Cosby, onetime governor of New York and New Jersey (Collins, *Peerage,* 1768, v. 3; Musgrave, *Obituary*).

15. George Rice; see *ante* 18 May 1749, n. 42. 'His grandmother's jointure' presumably refers to a legacy. His maternal grandmother, Lucy Montagu Trevor, died 1720. His paternal grandmother was Katherine, daughter of Philip Hoby, of Neath Abbey, Glamorgan, married Griffith Rice of Newton (Collins, *Peerage,* 1812, vii. 507). The date of her death is not known.

16. *Memoirs of the Reign of George II.* 'About this time [1751] I began to write my *Memoirs.* At first, I only intended to write the history of one year' ('Short Notes'). HW did add the notes.

THE MANDARIN CATS

ture of those about Windsor Park, are spreading about Richmond.[17] Lord Brook who has taken the late Duchess of Rutland's at Petersham,[18] asked for a key; the answer was, (mind it, for it was tolerably mortifying to an Earl) 'that the Princess had already refused one to my Lord Chancellor.'[19] By the way you know that reverend head of the law is frequently shut up here with my Lady Montrath,[20] who is as rich and as tipsy as Cacofogo in the comedy.[21] What a jumble of avarice and lewdness, dignity and claret!

You will be pleased with a story of Lord Bury, that is come from Scotland: he is quartered at Inverness: the magistrates invited him to an entertainment with fireworks which they intended to give on the morrow for the Duke's birthday.[22] He thanked him, assured them he

17. The Duke of Cumberland 'had incredibly disgusted the neighbourhood of Windsor by excluding them from most of the benefits of the park there' (*Mem. Geo. II* i. 402). New Park, Richmond, had been improved by Sir Robert Walpole; he and his predecessors allowed passage through it. Princess Amelia succeeded to the Rangership on the death of HW's brother, the second Earl of Orford, and closed the park; her right to do so was established by a lawsuit in 1754. In 1758 she was forced by another suit to open a footpath, and 'in a passion entirely abandoned the park' (ibid. 221). The 1758 case is reported as Rex v. Martha Gray, in 96 English Reports 1191, 2 Keny. 307; and 97 English Reports 424, 1 Burr. 510; see E. Beresford Chancellor, *History . . . of Richmond . . .*, Richmond, 1894, pp. 218–21, for a survey of the entire controversy.

18. Hon. Lucy Sherard (ca 1685–1751), m. (1713) John Manners, 2d D. of Rutland. The house is probably Rutland Lodge, mentioned in Chancellor, op. cit. 350.

19. Lord Hardwicke was at this time only a Baron, and a recent creation at that.

20. Lady Diana Newport (d. 1766), m. (1721) Algernon Coote, 6th E. of Mountrath. She lived at Twickenham Park (HW to Lady Suffolk 17 July 1766). HW repeats the story in detail in his marginalia to the second Earl of Hardwicke's *Walpoliana*, 1781, p. 16 (now the Sir Hugh Walpole Collection, the King's School, Canterbury, whose authorities have kindly

supplied a photostat of the passage). 'There was a mad and most wealthy widow, a Countess of Montrath, who resided at Twickenham-park, who had no child but one son, who succeeded to his father's title, and to whom from his infancy she had taken the most rooted aversion. Chancellor Hardwicke, in his youth very handsome and amorous, was supposed to have had an early intrigue with her, though latterly she had more devotion to Bacchus than to love. With that almost lunatic did the grave Chancellor keep up such a connection, that to the end of his life he very frequently passed his Saturdays and Sundays at her villa, where she scarce saw anybody else, so insatiate was his avarice, and hope of a large legacy to the prejudice of her only son, whom though she survived Lord Hardwicke, she totally disinherited of everything in her power. On that unsuitable connection were written these lines in an account of Twickenham:

'Here solemn Yorke steals down, and picking
Each Sabbath day his temperate chicken,
To mad Montrath's luxurious arms
Lets out his magisterial charms,
And while the maudlin Peeress fills,
Insinuates new codicils.'

It seems not unlikely that HW himself wrote these verses.

21. *Rule a Wife and have a Wife,* by John Fletcher (1579–1625).

22. 15 April.

would represent their zeal to his R. Highness; but did not doubt but it would be more agreeable to him, if they postponed it to the day following, the anniversary of the battle of Culloden. They stared, said they could not promise on their own authority, but would go and consult their body. They returned, told him it was unprecedented, and could not be complied with. Lord Bury replied, he was sorry they had not given him a negative at once for he had mentioned it to his soldiers, who would not bear a disappointment, and was afraid it would provoke them to some outrage upon the town. This did: they celebrated Culloden.

Adieu! my compliments to Miss Montagu.

Yours ever,

H. W.

To Montagu, Thursday ca July 1752

Placed in MSS between letters of 6 June and 30 July 1752. HW refers to this application's coming to nothing *post* 14 Dec. 1752.

Twickenham, Thursday [ca July 1752].

Dear George,

SINCE you give me leave to speak the truth, I must own it is not quite agreeable to me to undertake the commission you give me, nor do I say this to assume any merit in having obeyed you, but to prepare you against my solicitation miscarrying, for I cannot flatter myself with having so much interest with Mr Fox[1] as you think. However I have wrote to him as pressingly as I could, and wish most heartily it may have any effect. Your brother I imagine will call upon him again, and Mr Fox will naturally tell him whether he can do it or not at my request.

I should have been very glad of your company if it had been convenient. You would have found me a most absolute country gentleman: I am in the garden planting as long as it is light, and shall not have finished to be in London before the middle of next week.

My compliments to your sisters and to the Colonel, and what so

1. Secretary-at-war 1746–54; Montagu had no doubt asked HW to solicit him on behalf of his brother Charles in the army. HW's letter to Fox is missing.

poor a man as Hamlet is, may do to express his love and friending to him, God willing, shall not lack.[2] Adieu!

Yours ever,

H. W.

To Montagu, Thursday 30 July 1752

Strawberry Hill, July 30, 1752.

YOU have often threatened me with a messenger from the Secretary's office to seize my papers;[1] who would ever have taken you for a prophet? If Goody Compton[2] your colleague had taken upon her to foretell, there was enough of the witch and prophetess in her person and mysteriousness to have made a superstitious person believe she might be a cousin of Nostradamus,[3] and heiress of some of his visions; but how came you by second sight? Which of the Cues matched in the Highlands?[4] In short, not to keep you in suspense, for I believe you are so far inspired as to be ignorant how your prophecy was to be accomplished, as we were sitting at dinner t'other day, word was brought that one of the King's messengers was at the door—every drop of ink in my pen ran cold—Algernon Sydney danced before my eyes, and methought I heard my Lord Chief Justice Lee[5] in a voice as dreadful as Jefferies' mumble out *Scribere est agere*[6]—How comfort-

2. 'What so poor a man as Hamlet is May do, to express his love and friending . . .' (*Hamlet* I. v. 185–6). HW seldom quotes exactly.

---

1. The *Memoirs* which Montagu knew HW was writing, and whose tone was freely critical of the government.

2. George Compton (1692–1758), 6th E. of Northampton, 1754; Montagu's colleague as M.P. for Northampton. George Montagu was elected for Northampton 1744–7 and 1747–54 (*Members of Parliament*, 1878, pt ii. 89, 102). Aside from the reference here to his 'colleague' Compton, and the first sentence of *post* 28 Aug. 1752, no other information about Montagu's probably silent membership has been found. George Montagu's membership has been unwarrantably denied in Collins,

Peerage, 1768, v. 3, which states that Charles Montagu 'served for the town of Northampton in the parliaments elected in 1747 and 1754 [*sic*], although the list has the name of his brother George.'

3. Nostradamus (1503–66), a Provençal astrologer, whose prophecies had an extensive vogue (*Nouv. Biog. Gén.*).

4. That is, married in the Highlands where 'second sight' was allegedly common.

5. Sir William Lee (1688–1754), Chief Justice of King's Bench, 1737.

6. At the trial for treason of Algernon Sidney (1622–83), the republican, the most important evidence against him was an unpublished answer to Sir Robert Filmer's *Patriarcha*. In *The Arraignment, Tryal & Condemnation of Algernon Sidney, Esq.*, 1684, p. 56, 'scribere est agere' is part of Chief Justice Jeffreys' charge to the jury.

able it was to find, that Mr Amyand[7] who was at table, had ordered this appanage of his dignity to attend him here for his orders!—However I have buried the Memoires under an oak in my garden, where they are to be found a thousand years hence, and taken perhaps for a Runic history in rhyme. I have part of another valuable MS to dispose, which I shall beg leave to commit to your care, and desire it may be concealed behind the wainscot in Mr Bentley's Gothic house whenever you build it. As the great person is living to whom it belonged, it would be highly dangerous to make it public; as soon as she is in disgrace, I don't know whether it will not be a good way of making court to her successor to communicate it to the world as I propose doing under the following title,

The Treasury of Art and Nature
or a Collection of inestimable Receipts,
stolen out of the Cabinet of Madame de Pompadour,
and now first published for the Use
of his fair Countrywomen,
By a true born Englishman
and Philomystic.[8]

To beautify the skin.

Take a hogshead of large orient pearl, and dissolve them in an elixir of rubies, and boil down the whole syrup to about six quarts. Then take the underfeathers of a phœnix's wing, and brush your complexion gently over night and morning for about sixteen years. Then take a pound of pink diamonds, and beat them to powder in the thinnest old china cup you can get, a white one will do best; and then with the little finger of a new-born child, cut off fresh every morning, rub the powder upon your cheeks, nipples, palms of your hands and tips of your ears, and it will not fail of giving a bloom and lustre of youth equal if not superior to anything in nature.[9]

7. Claudius Amyand (1718–74), son of Claudius Amyand, a Huguenot, surgeon to George II; M.P. Tregony 1747–54; Sandwich 1754–6; Undersecretary of State 1750–5; Commissioner of Customs 1756–63; Receiver-General 1765–74 (Rev. William Betham, *Baronetage of England*, 1801–5, iii. 314–15; *Miscellanea Genealogica et Heraldica* 1884, ed. Joseph J. Howard, n.s. iv. 181).

8. The passage from this point to the final paragraph of the letter has been omitted in previous editions.

9. Compare this with a serious recipe in *The Ladies Companion*, pp. 21–2, n.d. but published by 'A. Baldwin at the Oxford-Arms' and therefore between 1698–1711 (see Henry R. Plomer, *Dictionary of Printers and Booksellers . . . 1668–1725*, Oxford, 1922): 'Take what quantity of

To make lips red.

Take a sharp knife and separate the upper skin a quarter of an inch deep, and fling it away. Then take a strong transparent gum and cover your lips while they are bleeding, as thick as the flesh that you amputated. You must be careful not to eat or use your mouth for ten or twelve days, or longer if the gum should not have settled to a proper consistency.

To make a fine head of hair.

Take your own head and clean it thoroughly from any remains of hair. Then dig as large a hole as you can conveniently in the skull and water it well for a month with bear's grease and puppy water; you may add now and then a handful of bean flowers; then when you have agreed for a head of hair to your mind, take it up by the roots with as large a ball of flesh around them as possible, always observing the exposition[9a] it grew in upon the former skull. Then cover your head for a whole winter with a thick coat of human dung, carefully strained from all urine, for fear of the shoots coming up red.—[10]

It is impossible that Miss Montagu should ever have occasion for any of these recipes, or I should beg that she would make no scruple of trying them. They have all had wonderful success, though practiced only imperfectly from faulty and erroneous copies. Mrs Bethel had only a small vial of the first given her at Paris, and it had such effect, that my sister, though she made all the interest imaginable, could not get any of the French to think her[11] confounded ugly. The younger Lady Suffolk[12] only spread a small quantity made into oint-

pearls you please, dissolve them in the juice of lemons, or in distilled vinegar, lay them in a close vessel well-stopped, in horse dung till they send forth a clear oil which swims at the top, which gather for use: this is an incomparable beautifier, and very safe, but it is exceeding dear, for one ounce of it will be well worth eight pound.'

9a. A play on its obsolete meaning: 'Situation with respect to the quarter of the heavens; "aspect" ' (OED, sb. 2).

10. Compare *The Ladies Companion*, n. 9 above, pp. 67, 69: 'Take bears-grease, mix it with the ashes of a mouse, and anoint the bald place with it, but when the hair begins to grow, use it no longer, for it would make them grow white . . . or . . . take the distilled water of man's dung, it is reported to be very effectual.'

11. Mrs Bethel.

12. Sarah Inwen (1714–76), m. (1) (1735) Henry Howard, 10th E. of Suffolk; m. (2) (10 Oct. 1752) Lucius Charles Cary, 7th Vct Falkland (ca 1707–85). 'Have you heard of the generosity of our new cousin Falkland? She was in love with him at nineteen years of age, her father not approving of the match, it broke off, she married the Earl of Suffolk, and he Lady Villiers: Lord Suffolk has been dead some years, Lady Falkland this year; Lord Falk-

ment on a bank bill of 70,000 pound, and it has made her first love Lord Falkland marry her: Sir Th. Robinson who intended to outlive his Barbadoes ironmongress,[13] is dying for love of the same Countess. Three spoonfuls taken inwardly by Charlotte Howe[14] and three bottles of burgundy taken in the same way by young Fettiplace, a lad of seven thousand a year, has wrought a match between them. Lady   [15] had begun to try the lip salve with great success, but as eating was only prohibited, she thought champagne did not come under the description, and washed off the preparation before it had time to operate thoroughly. The only person, on whom any of the nostrums has failed, was Lord Granby, who had too barren a soil,[16] and had neglected it too long to receive any benefit from the hair dung. *Nota bene,* the hair dung is equally efficacious in any part of the body; her Grace of Norfolk is under a regimen of it.

Apropos to one of the persons I mentioned, Miss Howe was going under Mr Coventry's window t'other day reading a note, George Selwyn called out, 'Yours till death Gregory[17] Fettiplace!' So the pretty Miss Bishop[18] instead of being my niece is to be Mrs Bob Brudenel! What foolish birds are turtles when they have scarce a hole to roost in! Adieu!

Yours till death,

GREGORY WHITEWASH

land is worth nothing as to fortune; she has £2500 a year, £60,000 in money, £20,000 of it she has settled on *his children*—she has none of her own. I hope they will be happy, if he *is grateful* I think they must; she is very good-natured, and well principled' (Delany, *Correspondence* iii. 173).

13. Sarah Booth, m. (1) Samuel Salmon; m. (2) (between 1742–7, when he was Gov. of Barbadoes) Sir Thomas Robinson, Bt, of Rokeby. 'An ironmonger's widow, who gave him 10,000*l*. to be a lady, but would not follow him to England' (HW's notes to Maty's *Memoirs . . . of . . . Chesterfield*, at end of Philobiblon Society, *Miscellanies* 1867–8, xi. 71; GEC, *Baronetage;* Emily J. Climenson, *Elizabeth Montagu,* 1906, ii. 276).

14. Hon. Charlotte Howe (d. 1787), 2d dau. of 2d Vct Howe; m. (12 Aug. 1752) Robert Fettiplace, of Swinbrooke, Oxon, High Sheriff of Oxfordshire 1758 (Lodge,

Irish Peerage, 1789, v. 86; GM 1787, lvii pt i. 548; William N. Clarke, *Parochial Topography of the Hundred of Wanting,* Oxford, 1824, opp. 68).

15. The name has been obliterated, apparently by HW.

16. He was quite bald.

17. Apparently a nickname; cf. 'Gilly' Williams to Selwyn Aug. 1752, unpublished (now WSL); 'Gregory Fettyplace has likewise brought his wife.'

18. Anne Bishopp (ca 1728–1803), dau. of Sir Cecil Bishopp, Bt, of Parham, Sussex; m. (not until 1759) Hon. Robert Brudenell; Bedchamber-woman to Queen Charlotte (GM 1759, xxix. 45; 1803, lxxiii pt ii. 993; Collins, *Peerage,* 1812, iii. 498). HW's only marriageable nephew was Lord Orford. Though nothing more is said of a connection between him and Miss Bishopp, she may have been the reason for his spurning the great fortune, Miss Nicoll (see HW to Mann 30 May 1751).

To Montagu, Friday 28 August 1752

Strawberry Hill, Aug. 28, 1752.

WILL you never have done jigging at Northampton with that old harlotry Major Compton?[1] Peggy Trevor[2] told me, she had sent you a mandate to go thither. Shall I tell you, how I found Peggy, that is, not Peggy but her sister Muscovy?[3] I went, found a bandage upon the knocker, an odd woman and child in the hall, and a black boy at the door—Lord, thinks I, this can't be Mrs Boscawen's—however, Pompey[4] let me up; above, were fires blazing, and a good old gentlewoman, whose occupation easily spoke itself to be midwifery: 'Dear madam, I fancy I should not have come up!' 'Lass-a-day, Sir, no, I believe not, but I'll step and ask.' Immediately out came old Falmouth,[5] looking like an ancient fairy who has just been muttering a malediction over a newborn prince, and told me forsooth, that Madam Muscovy was but just brought to bed, which Peggy Trevor soon came and confirmed—I told them, I would write you my adventure. I have not thanked you for your travels, and the violent curiosity you have given me to see Welbeck.[6] Mr Chute and I have been a progress too, but it was in a land you know full well, the county of Kent. I will only tell you that we broke our necks twenty times to your health,[7] and had a distant glimpse of Hawkhurst from that Sierra Morena, Silver Hill.[8] I have since been with Mr Conway at

1. See *ante* 30 July 1752, n. 2.
2. Margaret Trevor (1711–69), Montagu's double first cousin. Despite the variations in style, she is probably the 'Miss Trevor' and 'Mrs Trevor' who is frequently mentioned *post*. The references to Mrs Trevor of Bath (*post* 5 Oct.–22 Oct. 1766) are, however, to her sister, Grace (b. 1706). They had other unmarried sisters who may occasionally be meant: Mary (1708–80), Ruth (1712–64), Arabella (1714–89). But the references are not, as in Mrs Toynbee's edition, to their mother Lucy Montagu Trevor; she died 1720. See John Comber, *Sussex Genealogies, Lewes Centre*, Cambridge, 1933, pp. 292–3; Musgrave, *Obituary; post* Appendix 7.
3. Hon. Mrs George Boscawen. The child was William, born the date of this letter, died 1811; barrister and translator of Horace (DNB; GM 1811, lxxxi pt i. 470, 500–1).

4. 'The usual designation' of negro slave boys; see Charlotte M. Yonge, *History of Christian Names*, 1863, i. 323.
5. Charlotte Godfrey (ca 1679–1754), m. (1700) Hugh Boscawen, cr. (1720) Vct Falmouth.
6. Welbeck Abbey, Notts, then the seat of the Earl of Oxford, now of the Duke of Portland; see A. S. Turberville, *History of Welbeck Abbey and Its Owners*, 1938–9. HW visited it in 1756 (see HW to Bentley Aug. 1756).
7. To do justice to Montagu's association with the county; he frequently visited at Hawkhurst.
8. 'Silver Hill is in Sussex about 2 miles north of Robertsbridge where the London-Battle-Hastings road starts to descend to the Rother Valley' (see G. D. Johnston in N&Q 1939, clxxvii. 337).

Park Place, where I saw the individual Mr Cooper,[9] a banker and lord of the manor of Henley, who had those two extraordinary forfeitures from the executions of the Misses Blandy[10] and Jefferies,[11] two fields from the former, and a malthouse from the latter. I had scarce credited the story, and was pleased to hear it confirmed by the very person; though it was not quite so remarkable as it was reported, for both forfeitures were in the same manor.[12] Mr Conway has brought Lady Ailesbury from Minorca, but originally from Africa, *a jeribo:*[13] to be sure you know what that is; if you don't, I will tell you, and then I believe you will scarce know any better. It is a composition of a squirrel, a hare, a rat and a monkey, which altogether looks very like a bird. In short, it is about the size of the first, with much such a head, except that the tip of the nose seems shaved off, and the remains are like a human hare-lip: the ears and its timidity are like a real hare. It has two short little feet before like a rat, but which it never uses for walking, I believe never but to hold its food. The tail is naked like a monkey's with a tuft of hair at the end, striped black and white in rings. The two hind legs, are as long as a Grenville's, with feet more like a bird than any other animal, and upon these it hops so immensely fast and upright, that at a distance you would take it for a large thrush. It lies in cotton, is brisk at

9. Gislingham Cooper (ca 1688–1768), banker in the Strand, 'worth upwards of £200,000' (*Annual Register* for 1768, xi. 77; John S. Burn, *History of Henley-on-Thames*, 1861, p. 253).

10. Mary Blandy, of Henley, poisoned her father, and was hanged 6 April 1752. Her protestations of innocence aroused considerable public feeling in her favour (DNB); see also GM 1752, xxii. 108–17 and *Trial of Mary Blandy*, ed. William Roughead, 1914.

11. Elizabeth Jeffreys, hanged 28 March 1752, for the murder of her uncle at Walthamstow. Both she and Mary Blandy were heiresses of their victims, and both were abetted by ineligible lovers. Miss Jeffreys received little sympathy, though it appeared that her uncle had seduced her; see GM 1752, xxii. 121–4; Thomas B. Howell, *Complete Collection of State Trials*, 1816–26, xviii. 1194–1202. The land of felons escheated to the lord of the manor, or to the crown. Of feudal origin, the forfeiture was practically abolished in 1870 (Sir James Fitzjames Stephen, *History of the Criminal Law of England*, 1883, i. 487–8).

12. In *Country Seats* 50, describing Cooper's house, HW says he 'had forfeitures from both, as happening to be Lord of two manors which belonged to those women.' So *Annual Register* for 1768, xi. 77, says that one forfeiture was in Henley, the other in Walthamstow, Cooper being lord of both manors. But John S. Burn, *History of Henley-on-Thames*, 1861, p. 255, agrees with the text here that both properties were in Henley; he identifies them, however, with two houses in the Market Place, and not with HW's 'fields and malthouse.'

13. 'It is a Jerboa, smallest of the Opossum tribe, among which Kangaroo is largest' (Mrs Piozzi). OED follows HW's definition closely and quotes from this passage.

night, eats wheat and never drinks; it would, but drinking is fatal to them. Such is a jeribo!

Have you heard the particulars of the Speaker's[14] quarrel with a young officer,[15] who went to him, on his landlord refusing to give his servant the second best bed in the inn. He is a young man of eighteen hundred a year and passionately fond of the army. The Speaker produced the Mutiny Bill[16] to him; 'Oh Sir,' said the lad, 'but there is another Act of Parliament[17] which perhaps you don't know of!' *The Person of Dignity*, as the newspapers[18] call him, then was so ingenious as to harangue on the dangers of a standing army—the boy broke out, 'Don't tell me, of your privileges, what would have become of you and your privileges in the year '45, if it had not been for the army? and pray why do you fancy I would betray my country?—I have as much to lose as you have!'—In short this abominable young Hector treated the Speaker's *oracular decisions* with a familiarity, that quite shocks *me* to think of![19]

The Poemata Grayo-Bentleiana, or Gray's Odes better illustrated than ever odes were by a Bentley, are in great forwardness, and I trust will appear this winter[20]—I shall tell you one little anecdote about the authors, and conclude. Gray is in love to distraction with a figure of Melancholy which Mr Bentley has drawn for one of the odes,[21] and told him he must have something of his pencil: Mr Bentley desired him to choose a subject:—he chose *Theodore and Honoria*[22]—don't mention this, for we are shocked—it is loving *Melancholy*,

14. Arthur Onslow (1691–1768), Speaker of the House of Commons 1728–61.

15. Unidentified.

16. The annual Mutiny Act provided that soldiers on the march should be quartered at inns, and that the landlord should furnish them with beer and victuals; the rate at this time was 1s. a day for officers, and 4d. for men. The landlord could avoid the duty of supplying food by furnishing gratis candles, vinegar, salt, firing etc. There was nothing in the act to support the young officer's demand for the second-best bed, and quartering was restricted to the limits set in the act; see Stanley M. Pargellis, *Lord Loudoun in North America*, New Haven, 1933, p. 188.

17. Possibly the Act of Succession; see the young officer's next remarks.

18. There is an account of the affair in *Daily Advertiser* 19 Aug. 1752. It agrees in substance with HW's.

19. In the affair of the Aylesbury assizes (*ante* 11 Aug. 1748, n. 48), HW had a tiff with Onslow about a matter of procedure, in which he referred to the Speaker's 'oracular decision. . . . The Speaker was in a great rage, and complained to the House. I said I begged his pardon' ('Short Notes').

20. They were published 29 March 1753 (Ralph Straus, *Robert Dodsley*, 1910, p. 348). HW's copy, MS Cat. L.1.12, sold SH iii. 193, is now WSL.

21. It is the tail-piece to the *Hymn to Adversity*.

22. One of Dryden's *Fables*, imitated from Boccaccio—a gruesome tale of a sable

till it is not strong enough, and he grows to dram with *Horror!* Good night; my compliments to Miss Montagu: did you receive my recipes![23]

Yours ever,

H. W.

To Montagu, Thursday 14 December 1752

White's, Dec. 14, 1752, N.S.

I SHALL be much obliged for the passion-flower, notwithstanding it comes out of a garden of Eden, from which Eve my sister-in-law long ago gathered passion-fruit.[1] I thank you too for the offer of your Roman Correspondences,[2] but you know I have done with virtu, and deal only with the Goths and Vandals.

You ask a very improper person why my Lord Harcourt[3] resigned —my Lord Coventry says, it is the present great arcanum of government, and you know I am quite out of the circle of secrets. The town says, that it was on finding Stone[4] is a Jacobite; and it says too, that the Whigs are very uneasy. My Lord Egremont says, the Whigs can't be in danger, for then my Lord Hartington would not be gone a-hunting! Everybody is as impatient as you can be, to know the real cause, but I don't find that either Lord or Bishop[5] are disposed to let the world into the true secret. It is pretty certain that one Mr Cresset[6] has abused both of them without ceremony, and that the Solic-

knight who through eternity pursues and kills with his dogs a woman who had spurned him. For a study of melancholy in Gray and his predecessors, see Amy Louise Reed, *The Background of Gray's Elegy,* New York, 1924.

23. In *ante* 30 July 1752.

1. 'Eve my sister-in-law' presumably refers to Margaret Rolle, Lady Orford; the 'garden of Eden,' to the scene of one of her affairs.

2. Not explained.

3. Simon Harcourt (1714–77), 2d Vct Harcourt; cr. (1749) E. Harcourt; resigned as governor of the Prince of Wales.

4. Andrew Stone (1703–73), politician (DNB); sub-governor of the Prince; he was cleared of the charges of Jacobitism made

against him (see *Mem. Geo. II* i. 289–90, 298–332); but HW later accuses him of implanting Tory principles in the Pelhams, and in the Prince of Wales (see *Mem. Geo. III* iv. 91–2). The whole affair, and HW's part in the apparently baseless charges against Stone and Mansfield, are elucidated in the introduction to *Letters from George III to Lord Bute, 1756–66,* ed. Romney Sedgwick, 1939.

5. Thomas Hayter (1702–62), Bp of Norwich, 1749; of London, 1761; preceptor to the Prince of Wales; resigned with Harcourt. See HW to Mann 11 Dec. 1752; *Mem. Geo. II* i. 283–4, 289–92.

6. James Cresset (d. 1775), secretary of the Princess of Wales, and, at this time, 'her principal adviser: a cautious man, uncommonly skilful in the politics of the back-

itor-General[7] told the Bishop in plain terms that my Lord Harcourt was a cipher and was put in to be a cipher: an employment that, considering it is a sinecure, seems to hang unusually heavy upon their hands. They have so lately quarrelled with poor Lord Holderness for playing at blindman's-buff at Tunbridge,[8] that it will be difficult to give him another place only because he is fit to play at blindman's-buff; and yet it is much believed that he will be the governor,[9] and your cousin[10] his successor.

I am as improper to tell you why the Governor of Nova Scotia[11] is to be at the head of the Independents.[12] I have long thought him one of the greatest dependents, and I assure you I have seen nothing since his return to make me change my opinion—he is too busy in the Bedchamber, to remember me!

Mr F.[13] said nothing about your brother: if the offer was ill designed from one quarter, I think you may make the refusal of it have its weight in another.[14]

It would be odd to conclude a letter from White's without a bon mot of George Selwyn's: he came in here t'other night and saw James Jefferies[15] playing at piquet with Sir Everard Falkener[16]—'Oh!' says he, 'now he is robbing the mail!' Good night, when do you come back?

Yours ever,

H. W.

stairs, trusted by Lady Yarmouth, Munchausen, and all the German faction; giving hints and intelligence both at St James's and at Leicester House. Yet it must be acknowledged that he acted no dishonest part, that every article of his information was perfectly innocent, and that the good understanding between the king and his daughter-in-law had been chiefly owing to his good offices' (James Earl Waldegrave, *Memoirs*, 1821, pp. 29-30). 'I dined at the Bed-chamber woman's table, where was Mr Cresset, who behaved very courteously to me, and is a very knowing man' (George Bubb Dodington, Baron Melcombe, *Diary*, ed. Henry Wyndham, Salisbury, 1784, p. 152; GM 1775, xlv. 207).

7. William Murray (1705-93), cr. (1756) Bn Mansfield, (1776) E. of Mansfield; Chief Justice of King's Bench, 1756.

8. The only other account of this incident seems to be Lord Holdernesse's rela-

tion of it to HW; see HW to Mann 11 Dec. 1752.

9. Lord Waldegrave took the post.

10. Lord Halifax. Holdernesse remained Secretary of State.

11. Hon. Edward Cornwallis (1713-76), Lt-Gen., 1760; M.P. Eye 1743-9; Gov. Nova Scotia 1749-52; M.P. Westminster 1753-62; Gov. Gibraltar 1762-76; Groom of the Bedchamber, 1747 (Collins, *Peerage*, 1812, ii. 553-4).

12. Not explained.

13. Fox; see *ante* ca July 1752.

14. That is, with someone hostile to Fox.

15. James Jeffreys (d. ?1786), Commissioner of Customs, 1766; m. (her 2d husband) Lady Augustus Fitzroy (Collins, *Peerage*, 1812, i. 218; Musgrave, *Obituary*; GM 1786, lvi pt ii. 908).

16. Sir Everard Fawkener (1684-1758), Kt, 1735; merchant, and friend of Voltaire; joint Postmaster-General 1745-58.

To MONTAGU, Tuesday 22 May 1753

Strawberry Hill, May 22d, 1753.

YOU may very possibly be set out for Greatworth, but what house Greatworth[1] is, or whose, or how you came to have it, is all a profound secret to us: your transitions are so Pindaric, that without notes we don't understand them, especially as neither Mr Bentley nor I have seen any of the letters which I suppose you have written to your family, in the intervals of your journeyings from Sir Jonathan Cope's[2] to Roel, and from Roel to Greatworth. Mr Bentley was just ready to send you down a packet of Gothic, and brick and mortar, and arched windows and taper columns to be erected at Roel[3]—no such matter, you have met with some brave chambers belonging to Sir Jonathan Somebody in Northamptonshire, and are unloading your camels and caravans, and pitching your tents among your own tribe. I can't be quite sorry, for I shall certainly visit you at Great-worth, and it might have been some years before the curtain had drawn up at Roel. We emerge very fast out of shavings, and hammer-ings and pastings:[4] the painted glass is full-blown in every window,[5]

1. Near Brackley, Northants; see *Country Seats* 51, for a brief account of it on a visit in 1763: 'Greatworth, near Brackley, Northamptonshire; a house hired by Mr George Montagu. I have been there twice before. He has some good portraits of his family, and two small landscapes, a morn-ing, and an evening, which I gave him, done by Müntz, and the best of his works.' Built at the beginning of the 18th century by Charles Howe (1661–1742), Greatworth was sold in 1751 to William Higginson, from whom Montagu no doubt rented it. It was burned in 1793 (George Baker, *History . . . of the County of Northampton*, 1822–41, i. 509).

2. Sir Jonathan Cope (ca 1690–1765), 1st Bt (1714), of Bruern Abbey, Oxon. He also had a house at Orton Longueville, Hunts. Bruern Abbey was almost directly in Mon-tagu's way to Roel in Gloucestershire. Bruern Abbey burned down around 1800 (*Beauties of England* xii pt ii. 505). In *post* 16 Nov. 1754, Cope is called 'our old friend,' but is never mentioned again, and no particular connection between him and HW and Montagu, many years his juniors, appears.

3. These do not appear in HW's col-lection of Bentley's drawings and they were perhaps never made.

4. The first really extensive additions to SH were made at this time, when the following rooms were either built or re-modelled (the numbers in each case refer to *Des. of SH, Works* ii): ground floor, the Little Parlour (418), Yellow Bedchamber, later the Beauty Room (418), Hall (401), and Staircase (420, 439); principal floor, the Red Bedchamber (436), Armoury (440), Green Closet (427), and (?) Star Chamber (453); see 'Genesis of SH' 91; *SH Accounts* 4–5 and notes; HW to Mann 12 June 1753.

5. HW had begun collecting Flemish painted glass as early as 1750 (HW to Mann 18 Oct. 1750); it was brought him by 'one Asciotti,' whose first importation had been purchased by HW's rival Goth, Richard Bateman (see *Anecdotes, Works* iii. 159; *SH Accounts* 62–3). HW also had many pieces of old English glass (ibid.), and wrote to Mann 12 June 1753 that 'the castle, when finished, will have two-and-thirty windows enriched with painted glass.'

and the gorgeous Saints that were brought out for one day on the festival of Saint George Montagu,[6] are fixed forever in the tabernacles they are to inhabit. The castle is not the only beauty, the garden is at the height of all its sweets, and today we had a glimpse of the sun as he passed by, though I am convinced the summer is over; for these two last years, we have been forced to compound for five hot days in the pound.

News there is none to tell you; we have had two days in the House of Commons that had something of the air of Parliament; there has been a Marriage Bill, invented by my Lord Bath, and cooked up by the Chancellor,[7] which was warmly opposed by the Duke of Bedford in the Lords, and with us by Fox[8] and Nugent; the latter made an admirable speech last week against it, and Charles Townshend another very good one yesterday, when we sat till near ten o'clock, but were beat, we minority, by 165 to 84.

I know of nothing else but elopements; I have lost my man Henry,[9] who is run away for debt, and my Lord Bath his only son,[10] who is run away from thirty thousand pounds a year, which in all probability would have come to him in six months. There had been some

6. Probably on the occasion of a visit to SH by Montagu, which may possibly have been made on St George's Day, 23 April. 'The gorgeous saints' were probably the 'rich saints in painted glass' in the windows in the hall; see HW to Mann 12 June 1753.

7. It provided that 'with the exception of Jewish and Quaker marriages, no marriage should be valid in England which was not celebrated by a priest in orders, and according to the Anglican liturgy, that the ceremony could not be performed unless the banns had been published for three successive Sundays in the parish church, or unless a license had been procured. . . . All marriages which did not conform to these provisions were null, and all who celebrated them were liable to transportation' (W. E. H. Lecky, *History of England in the Eighteenth Century*, 2d edn, New York, 1892–3, ii. 118). For a summary of the conditions which led to the passage of this salutary Act, see ibid. 115–18. HW gives its parliamentary history, and the speeches and arguments against it, in *Mem. Geo. II* i. 336–53.

Lecky (op. cit. 125 n.) remarks that 'it is curious to observe what nonsense Horace Walpole talked about this Bill'—its sponsorship by Hardwicke, however, would account for HW's exaggerations. See also Philip C. Yorke, *Life . . . of . . . Hardwicke*, Cambridge, 1913, ii. 58–76, 120–4.

8. He had married, clandestinely, a daughter of the Duke of Richmond.

9. Possibly Henry Jones (Harry), but if so he returned.

10. William Pulteney (ca 1731–63), styled Vct Pulteney. At Westminster School 1740–7, he chafed under parental restrictions until the outbreak chronicled here, but was later reconciled to his father, who raised a regiment for him in 1759, and survived him. See the comments in next note; A. M. W. Stirling, *The Hothams*, 1918, ii. 5–70 *passim*, where some of his letters are printed; Dr Thomas Newton's *Life* (by himself), 1816, pp. 122–4; Lewis B. Namier, *Structure of Politics at the Accession of Geo. III*, 1929, ii. 325–8 (interesting light on his regiment, the Royal Volunteers); *Mem. Geo. II* ii. 78 ('had vivacity, and did not want parts').

great fracas about his marriage; the stories are various on the why; some say, his father told Miss Nichols[11] that his son was a very worthless young man; others, that the Earl could not bring himself to make tolerable settlements, and a third party say, that the Countess has blown up a quarrel in order to have her son left in her power and at her mercy. Whatever the cause was, this ingenious young man, who you know has made my Lady Townshend his everlasting enemy by repeating her histories of Miss Chudleigh[11a] to that *Miss,* of all counsellors in the world picked out my Lady Townshend to consult on his domestic grievances. She, with all the good nature and charity imaginable, immediately advised him to be disinherited. He took her advice, left two dutiful letters for his parents to notify his disobedience, and went off last Friday night to France. The Earl is so angry, that he could almost bring himself to give Mr Newport[12] and twenty other people their estates again. Good night—here's the Goth Mr Bentley wants to say a word to you—

Yours ever

H. W.

11. Frances Catherine Gunter Nicoll (ca 1733–1805), m. (1755) William Legge, 2d E. of Dartmouth. Her match with Lord Pulteney had been settled almost a year before: 'Lord Pulteney is certainly going to be married to Miss Gunter Nicholls; . . . Lady Carlisle observed, the lady must have as much humility as money to bear such an address' (Rigby to the Duke of Bedford, 13 Aug. 1752, *Correspondence of John Fourth Duke of Bedford,* 1842–6, ii. 112). Mrs Delany writes, 6 July 1754, 'Lord Dartmouth is certainly to be married to Miss Nichols, with above an hundred thousand pounds. She is pretty, and they say has been well brought up and is good humoured; but . . . I cannot have a high opinion of this young lady's understanding if she had any inclination for Lord Pulteney' (Delany, *Correspondence* iii. 283).

11a. Elizabeth Chudleigh (ca 1720–88), m. (1) (privately, 1744) Hon. Augustus John Hervey, 3d E. of Bristol, 1775; m. (2) (illegally, 1769) Evelyn Pierrepont, 2d D. of Kingston.

12. John Newport (ca 1720–83), natural son of the 3d E. of Bradford. The allusion is explained by the following obituary (GM 1742, xii. 602–3): '[Died] Nov. 1. Mrs Smyth of Chelsea, to whom the late E. of

Bradford left an estate of about 7 or 8000 *l. per ann.* since raised to 12,000, which she has left to her son by the said Earl (who changed his name by Act of Parliament from Smyth to Newport) for his life and in reversion to the Earl of Bath. . . . It is further said, that Mr Newport is a lunatic, under the care of Dr Munro, that the Earl of Bath and the Hon. Mr Herbert are Trustees, that by an act passed last session lunatics cannot marry.' Abstracts of the wills of the Earl of Bradford and of Mrs Anne Smyth, printed in *Marriage, Baptismal, and Burial Registers of the . . . Abbey . . . Westminster,* ed. Joseph L. Chester, 1876, pp. 343, 361, do not name the Earl of Bath, except as an executor of Mrs Smyth's; but there was a trust fund for the benefit of the son, of which Lord Bath apparently acquired the reversion from Mrs Smyth. Chesterfield, discussing Bath's will, speaks of 'the Bradford estate, which he smuggled,' as worth £15,000 a year (Earl of Chesterfield, *Letters,* ed. Bonamy Dobrée, 1932, vi. 2603). See Chester, op. cit. 436; L. B. Namier, *Structure of Politics at the Accession of George III,* 1929, ii. 320, n. 3; N&Q 1858, 2d ser. v. 379; GM 1783, liii. 452 (death of 'William' Newport).

Dear Sir,

I wrote you a supernumerary letter, on Saturday, but as I find you have shifted your quarters, since I heard from you, imagine it may not have reached you yet. If you want to know what made me so assiduous, it was to tell you Sir Danvers Osborn[13] has kissed hands for New York, that's all. I am

Sincerely yours

R. Bentley

PS. I wish you would write a line to him mentioning me; that's more.

To Montagu, Monday 11 June 1753

Strawberry Hill, June 11th, 1753.

YOU will think me very fickle, and that I have but slight regard to the castle (I am building) of my ancestors, when you hear that I have been these last eight days in London amid dust and stinks, instead of syringa, roses, battlements and niches; but you perhaps recollect that I have another Gothic passion, which is for squabbles in the Wittenagemot. I can't say that the contests have run so high in either House, as they have sometimes done in former days; but this age has found out a new method of parliamentary altercations. The Commons abuse the Barons, and the Barons return it. In short Mr Fox attacked the Chancellor violently on the Marriage Bill, and when it was sent back to the Lords, the Chancellor made the most outrageous invective on Fox that ever was heard. But what offends still more (I don't mean offends Fox more) was the Chancellor's describing the chief persons who had opposed his bill in the Commons, and giving reasons why he *excused* them. As the Speaker was in the number of the *Excused,* the two maces are ready to come to blows.

---

13. Sir Danvers Osborn (1715–53), 3d Bt, of Chicksands Priory, Beds; m. (1740) Lady Mary Montagu, George Montagu's first cousin. Sir Danvers' brother-in-law Lord Halifax, then President of the Board of Trade, appointed him Governor of New York in the hope that business would curb his excessive grief over her recent death; but on 12 Oct. 1753, having landed on 7 Oct., and taken office on the 10th, he hanged himself; see William Smith, *History of the Late Province of New-York* ii. 151–7 (in New York Hist. Soc., *Collections,* New York, 1829, vol. v); John R. Brodhead and E. B. O'Callaghan, *Documents Relative to . . . New-York,* Albany, N. Y., 1853–87, vi. 802–5. He thus achieved the shortest term of any colonial governor (Leonard W. Labaree, *Royal Government in America,* New Haven, 1930, p. 126).

The town says that Mr Fox is to be dismissed, but I can scarce think it will go so far.[1]

My Lord Cornwallis is made an earl; Lord Bristol's sisters[2] have the rank of earls' daughters; Damer[3] is Lord Milton in Ireland; and the new Lord Barnard is I hear to be Earl of Darlington.[4]

Poor Lady Caroline Brand[5] is dead of a rheumatic fever, and her husband as miserable a man as ever he was a cheerful one: I grieve much for her, and pity him, they were infinitely happy and lived in the most perfect friendship I ever saw.

You may be assured that I will pay you a visit sometime this summer, though not yet, as I cannot leave my workmen, especially as we have a painter who paints the paper on the staircase under Mr Bentley's direction.[6] The armoury[7] bespeaks the ancient chivalry of the lords of the castle, and I have filled Mr Bentley's Gothic lanthorn

1. This exchange of abuse between the Houses is reported at greater length in *Mem. Geo. II* i. 340–53. Nothing came of it.

2. Daughters of John Lord Hervey, who pre-deceased his father, the Earl of Bristol, so that they had only the rank of Baron's daughters. Lepell (1723–80), m. (1743) Constantine Phipps, cr. (1767) Bn Mulgrave. Mary (1725–1815), m. (1747) George Fitzgerald, of Turlough, Co. Mayo. See *Journals of the Hon. William Hervey* [ed. Sydenham H. A. Hervey], Bury St Edmunds, 1906, p. xxxviii. Emily (1735–1814) and Caroline (1736–1819) were unmarried, and lived together; ibid. pp. xxxix–xl; 'she [Emily] seemed to have been pretty, Lady Caroline still prettier' (see Lady Louisa Stuart, *Notes on Jesse's Selwyn*, ed. W. S. Lewis, New York, 1928, p. 41). Lady Sarah Bunbury writes of them in 1766, 'They go on just in the same queer style, Lady Emily leads her puddling, retired life, and poor Lady Car. gets abused because she goes to the play constantly' (*Life and Letters of Lady Sarah Lennox*, ed. Countess of Ilchester, 1901–2, i. 203; ibid. i. 153, 195). According to Mrs Piozzi, Lady Emily (qu. Lady Caroline?) was the 'lady of quality' who, Johnson said, was a 'wonderful mimic' and made him 'laugh immoderately' (Boswell, *Johnson* ii. 154, 492).

3. Joseph Damer (1718–98), cr. (1753) Bn Milton (Irish); (1762) Bn Milton (English); (1792) E. of Dorchester.

4. Not so created until April 1754.

5. Lady Caroline Pierrepont (d. 9 June 1753), 4th dau. of 1st D. of Kingston; m. (1749) Thomas Brand, of the Hoo, Kimpton, Herts (Collins, *Peerage*, 1768, ii. 83). He, who d. 1770, was a correspondent of HW's. 'They lived at the Hoo, Hertfordshire—our family at Offley visited them in summer, but it was too long for a mere dinner visit we said' (Mrs Piozzi). The distance, cross-country, is perhaps six miles; by passable 18th-century roads, it was more probably twelve; see John Cary, *New Itinerary*, 1798, p. 298; idem, *English Atlas*, 1793.

6. 'This hall is united with the staircase, and both are hung with gothic paper, painted by one Tudor, from the screen of Prince Arthur's tomb in the cathedral of Worcester' (*Des. of SH, Works* ii. 401). Nothing more is known of Tudor; see *SH Accounts* 64. From a passage in HW to Bentley 20 Nov. 1754, about Gothic paper (quoted in *SH Accounts* 67), it would appear that, after Bentley himself had undertaken to do the work, HW had had to get a man from Bromwich, the paper-maker (ibid. 66). The paper was 'painted in perspective to represent Gothic fretwork' (HW to Mann 12 June 1753).

7. At the head of the stairs; for a list of the miscellany of weapons it contained, see *Des. of SH, Works* ii. 440.

with painted glass, which casts the most venerable gloom on the stairs
that was ever seen since the days of Abelard.[8] The lanthorn itself in
which I have stuck a coat of the Veres is supposed to have come from
Castle Henningham.[9] Lord and Lady Vere were here t'other day, and
called cousins with it, and would very readily have invited it to Hanworth, but her *Portuguese* blood has so *blackened* the true stream,[10]
that I can't bring myself to offer so fair a gift to their chapel.

I shall only tell you a bon mot of Keith's the marriage-broker and
conclude. 'G–d damn the bishops!' said he (I beg Miss Montagu's
pardon), 'so they will hinder my marrying! Well, let 'em! but I'll be
revenged: I'll buy two or three acres of ground, and by God I'll
under-bury 'em all.'

Adieu!

Yours ever
H. W.

Dear Sir,

It is about ten days since I sent you a design for your mantelpiece,
which if you approved of, you were desired to return forthwith in
order to its being put in execution. I want to know whether you
don't like it, or have not got it.

For God's sake if it is possible to come at some answer from Sir
Danvers, do, for it is horrible to float upon suspense; my best compliments to Miss Montagu. I am, dear Sir,

Yours sincerely,
R. Bentley

To Montagu, Tuesday 17 July 1753

Strawberry Hill, July 17, 1753.

Dear Sir,

YOU are so kind, that I am peevish with myself for not being able
to fix a positive day for being with you: as near as I can guess it
will be some of the very first days of the next month: I am engaged to

8. The hall was called the Paraclete,
after the oratory founded by Abelard; see
HW to Mann 27 April 1753.

9. HW means that the 'coat of the
Veres' was supposed to convey the im-
pression that the lantern had come from
Hedingham. The lantern, which is now

WSL, was, as is indicated in the previous
sentence, designed by Bentley: 'the door
of it has an old pane with the arms of
Vere Earl of Oxford' (*Des. of SH, Works*
ii. 401).

10. See *ante* 14 and 25 July 1748.

go with Lady Ailesbury and Mr Conway to Stowe the 28 of this month,[1] if some little business which I have here, does not prevent me, and from thence I propose to meet Mr Chute at Greatworth. If this should at all interfere with your schemes, tell me so; especially I must beg that you will not so far depend on me, as to stay one minute from doing anything else you like, because it is quite impossible for me to be sure that I can execute just at the time I propose such agreeable projects. Meeting Mrs Trevor will be a principal part of my pleasure; but the summer shall certainly not pass without my seeing you.

You will I am sure be concerned to hear that your favourite Miss Brown,[2] the pretty Catholic who lived with Madame d'Acunha,[3] is dead at Paris, by the ignorance of the physician—if one could make you laugh immediately, it would be by a charming mob-story of the two eldest Mesdames[4] of France being with child by their royal father —what Unigenitus's[5] the offspring would be!

Tom Hervey[6] who always obliges the town with a quarrel in a dead season, has published a delightful letter to Sir William Bunbury,[7] full of madness and wit. He had given the Doctor[8] a precedent for a

1. The visit to Greatworth preceded that to Stowe; see HW to Chute, written from Stowe, 4 Aug. 1753.

2. Hon. Catherine Browne, 2d dau. of Valentine Browne, 3d (titular) Vct Kenmare; enrolled in the Blue Nuns' School at Paris, 1737; went from there to the Abbey of Panthémont in 1742, and died at Paris in 1753; see Catholic Record Society, Miscellanea, vol. viii, Diary of the Blue Nuns, 1910, pp. 101, 110, 330; Mrs Toynbee's note in N&Q 1899, 9th ser. iv. 323, suggesting this identification from a list of Blue Nuns' pupils in The Jerningham Letters, ed. Egerton Castle, 1896, ii. 399.

3. 'Probably the wife of Don Louis d'Acunha, the Portuguese Ambassador at Paris, mentioned by d'Argenson (see Mémoires, ed. 1857, iii. 133)' (Toynbee). D'Acunha was ambassador ca 1738–ca 1750 (see Almanach royal). If the identification is correct, Miss Browne must have become Montagu's favourite while on a visit to London; Montagu's only known trip to France was in 1739, when she was in the convent school.

4. Marie-Adélaide (1732–1800), and Victoire-Louise-Marie-Thérèse (1733–99); see DU DEFFAND.

5. Unigenitus Dei Filius, a bull issued by Pope Clement XI, 1713, condemning the Jansenist heresy, is doubtless the inspiration of this joke.

6. Hon. Thomas Hervey (1699–1775), eccentric pamphleteer (DNB).

7. Rev. Sir William Bunbury (ca 1710–64), 5th Bt of Bunbury, Cheshire, and Barton Hall, Suffolk; he was a nephew and heir of Sir Thomas Hanmer, with whose wife Hervey had eloped. It appears from Mr Hervey's Letter to the Rev. Sir William Bunbury, Bart, that Hervey accused Bunbury of mistreating or defrauding Hervey's and Lady Hanmer's child, and that Bunbury, who was Rector of Mildenhall, declined a challenge and had Hervey bound to keep the peace. HW's copy is now WSL.

8. Sir William was not D.D. until 1755; see Foster, Alumni Oxon.

clergyman's fighting a duel, and I furnished him with another story of the same kind that diverted him extremely, A Dr Suckling[9] who married a niece of my father, quarreled with a country squire, who said, 'Doctor, your gown is your protection.' 'Is it so?' replied the parson, 'but by God it shall not be yours'; pulled it off and thrashed him—I was going to say *damnably,* but at least, divinely. Do but think, my Lord Coke and Tom Hervey are both bound to the peace,[10] and are always going to fight together; how comfortable for their sureties!

My Lord Pomfret is dead: George Selwyn says, 'That my Lord Ashburnham[11] is not more glad to get into the parks, than Lord Lempster[12] is to get out of them'—you know he was forced to live in a privileged place.

Jack Hill[13] is dead too, and has dropped about a hundred legacies;[14] a thousand pound to the Dowager of Rockingham;[15] as much, with all his plate and china to her sister Bel.[16] I don't find that my Uncle[17] has got so much as a case of knives and forks: he always paid great court, but Mary Magdalen my aunt[18] undid all by scolding the man, and her spouse durst not take his part.

9. Rev. Dr Maurice Suckling (ca 1675–1730), Rector of Barsham, Suffolk, and Prebend of Westminster; m. Anne, dau. of Sir Charles Turner and Sir Robert Walpole's sister Mary. Dr Suckling's daughter Catherine was Nelson's mother; see Rev. Alfred Suckling, *History . . . of Suffolk,* 1846–8, i. 40, 43 and GEC. The story is repeated by Pinkerton in *Walpoliana,* i. 1–2.
10. Lord Coke by his estranged wife, Lady Mary (Coke, *Journals* i. p. lxviii).
11. John Ashburnham (1724–1812), 2d E. of Ashburnham; succeeded Lord Pomfret (who d. 8 July) as Ranger of Hyde and St James's Parks.
12. George Fermor (1722–85), styled Lord Lempster; 2d E. of Pomfret on his father's death. He was in 1752 convicted of manslaughter for killing a man in a duel (GM 1752, xxii. 90, 190); though the punishment for this was not necessarily severe, he could scarcely escape it by living in the parks, and it is more likely that his 'deep debts' (HW to Mann 21 July 1753) had made him liable to arrest. In that case, it is probable that he would be immune while in the parks because they were considered 'within the verge of the royal palace,' where no arrest could be made. On succeeding to a peerage his immunity would become complete; see Sir William Blackstone, *Commentaries,* IV. xiv. 192, III. xix. 288–90; Norman Maclaren Trenholme, *Right of Sanctuary in England,* U. of Missouri Studies I. 5, 1903, p. 98.
13. John Hill (d. 1753), of Thornton, near Malton, Yorkshire; Commissioner of Customs 1723–47; M.P. Higham Ferrers 1747–53; Gov. of Scarborough Castle; F.R.S. (*Court and City Register* for 1749, p. 34; Joseph Haydn, *Book of Dignities,* ed. Ockerby, 1890, p. 275; GM 1753, xxiii. 344).
14. Actually about 12 or 15; see his will, P.C.C. Pinfold 42.
15. Lady Mary Finch (d. 1761), m. (1716) Thomas Watson-Wentworth, cr. (1728) Bn Malton, (1733) E. of Malton, (1746) M. of Rockingham.
16. Lady Isabella Finch, 'as a trifling acknowledgment of her friendship' (ibid.).
17. Old Horace.
18. Marie-Madeleine Lombard (d. 1783),

Lady Anne Powlett's[19] daughter is eloped with a country clergyman: the Duchess of Argyle harangues against the marriage bill's not
taking place immediately and is persuaded that all the girls will go
off before next Lady Day.[20]

Before I finish, I must describe to you the manner in which I overtook Monsieur le Duc de Mirepoix t'other day, who lives at Lord
Dunkeron's[21] house at Turnham Green. It was seven o'clock in the
evening of one of the hottest and most dusty days of this summer. He
was walking slowly in the *beau milieu* of Brentford Town, without
any company, but with a brown lapdog with long ears, two pointers,
two pages, three footmen and a *vis-à-vis* following him. By the best accounts I can get, he must have been to survey the ground of the battle
of Brentford,[22] which I hear he has much studied, and harangues
upon.

Adieu! I enclose a *World* to you, which by a story I shall tell you, I
find is called mine. I met Mrs Clive two nights ago, and told her I
had been in the meadows,[23] but would walk there no more, for there
was all the world—'Well,' says she, 'and don't you like the *World;* I
hear it was very clever last Thursday.'[24]—all I know is, that you will
meet some of your acquaintance[25] there. Good night, with my compliments to Miss Montagu!

Yours ever

H. W.

m. (1720) Horatio Walpole, cr. (1756) Bn
Walpole of Wolterton. Peter le Neve says
her father was a staymaker, but she had
£50,000 (*Norfolk Archaeology*, Norwich,
1849, ii. 374).

19. Lady Annabella Bennet (d. 1769),
dau. of 1st E. of Tankerville, m. William
Powlett, grandson of 1st D. of Bolton. Her
dau. Annabella (d. 1761), m. Rev. Richard
Smyth of Itchen and Crux Easton, Hants,
Rector of Myddle, Salop (see Burke, *Peerage, sub* Winchester). He may be the Richard Smyth in Foster, *Alumni Oxon,* who
matriculated at Pembroke 1744, aet. 18.

20. The Marriage Act (26 Geo. II. c. 33)
was to go into effect then (25 March 1754).

21. James Petty (ca 1708–50), styled Vct

Dunkeron; son of Henry Petty, 1st E. of
Shelburne, d. 1751.

22. Brentford 'was the scene of a Danish
defeat (1016) and of a Royalist victory
(1642)' (J. G. Bartholomew, *Survey Gazetteer*, 1904).

23. No doubt Twickenham meadows,
adjacent to SH. They were much improved at about this time by Richard
Owen Cambridge; see his *Works,* ed.
George O. Cambridge, 1803, p. xxxviii,
and pl. xv.

24. No. 28 of *The World*, 12 July 1753,
was by HW, on the subject of old women
making the best lovers; see *Works* i. 169.

25. Helen, Queen Elizabeth, Diane de
Poitiers, and Ninon Lenclos.

To Montagu, Thursday 16 August 1753

Strawberry Hill, Aug. 16, 1753.

DON'T you suspect that I have not only forgot the pleasure I had at Greatworth and Wroxton,[1] but the commissions you gave me too? It looks a little ungrateful not to have vented a word of thanks, but I stayed to write till I could send you the things, and when I had them, I stayed to send them by Mr Chute, who tells you by tonight's post when he will bring them. The butter-plate is not exactly what you ordered, but I flatter myself you will like it as well: there are a few seeds; more shall follow at the end of the autumn. Besides Tom Hervey's Letter, I have sent you maps of Oxfordshire and Northamptonshire, having felt the want of them when I was with you. I found the road to Stowe above twelve miles, very bad, and it took me up two hours and [a] half: but the formidable idea I conceived of the breakfast and way of life there by no means answered; you was a prophet; it was very agreeable.

I am ashamed to tell you that I laughed half an hour yesterday at the sudden death of your new friend Sir Harry Danvers,[2] *after a morning's airing,* the news call it; I suspect it was after a negus.

I found my garden brown and bare, but these rains have recovered the greenth. You may get your pond ready as soon as you please, the goldfish swarm; Mr Bentley carried a dozen to town t'other day in a decanter; you would be entertained with our fishing; instead of nets and rods and lines and worms, we use nothing but a pail, and a basin and a tea-strainer, which I persuade my neighbours is the Chinese method.

Adieu! my best compliments to Miss Montagu.

Yours ever

H. W.

PS.

Since writing my letter, I have received your twin dispatches. I am extremely sensible of the honour my Lord Guildford does me, and

1. Lord Guildford's. See HW to Chute 4 Aug. 1753, for an account of this visit.
2. Sir Henry Danvers (1731–53), 4th Bt, of Culworth, Northants. HW had been greatly impressed by his drinking, at breakfast-time, a 'very large jug indeed' of negus, 'a mixture of wine (esp. port or sherry) and hot water, sweetened with sugar and flavoured' (OED); see HW to Chute 4 Aug. 1753.

beg you to transmit my gratitude to him: if he is ever at Wroxton when I visit Greatworth, I shall certainly wait upon him and think myself happy in seeing that charming place again. As soon as I go to town, I shall send for Moreland, and harbour your wardrobe with great pleasure. I find I must beg your pardon for laughing in the former part of my letter about your baronet's death, but *his wine and water a little warm* had left such a ridiculous impression upon me that even his death could not efface it. Good night.

Mr Miller[3] told me at Stowe that the chimney-piece (I think from Steane[4]) was he believed at Banbury, but he did not know exactly. If it lies in your way to inquire, on so vague a direction, will you? Mr Chute may bring me a sketch of it.[5]

To Montagu, Thursday 6 December 1753

Arlington Street, Dec. 6, 1753.

I HAVE at last found a moment to answer your letter, a possession of which I think I have not been master these ten days. You must know that I have an uncle dead, a sort of event that could not possibly have been disagreeable to me, let his name have been what it would,[1] and to make it still less unpleasant, here am I, one of the heirs-at-law to a man worth £30,000. One of the heirs you must construe, one of five—in short, my uncle Erasmus is dead,[2] and I think at last we may depend on his having made no will. If a will should appear, we are but where we were; if it does not, it is not uncomfortable to have a little sum of money drop out of the clouds, to which

3. Sanderson Miller (1717–80), of Radway Grange, Warwickshire, amateur architect. One of the earliest Gothicisers, he altered a number of houses (e.g., his own, Belhus, Wroxton), attempted church restorations (Kilkenny Cathedral, chapel at Hartlebury), and was a leading designer of 'ruined castles' (at Hagley, Wimpole, Edgehill). His Palladian work at Hagley and the Warwick County Hall is more successful; see *An Eighteenth-Century Correspondence,* ed. Lillian Dickins and Mary Stanton, New York, 1910, consisting of letters to Miller, from which much of his work has been identified. He was especially intimate with the Grenville-Lyttelton-Pitt coterie; during the period of his greatest architectural activity (1745–60), his services were in demand all over England, though he often accepted commissions and carried out alterations to buildings which he had never seen.

4. Near Brackley, Northants; HW had visited the chapel and the 'remains of the mansion-house, but quite in ruins' (HW to Chute 4 Aug. 1753).

5. He was an amateur artist.

———

1. E.g., his uncle Horace's.

2. Erasmus Shorter, HW's mother's brother. The other heirs besides Edward Walpole were Lord Hertford, H. S. Conway, and Anne S. Conway, whose mother was Charlotte Shorter.

one has as much right as anybody, for which one has no obligation, and paid no flattery. This death and the circumstances have made extreme noise,[3] but they are of an extent impossible to tell you within the compass of any letter, and I will not raise your curiosity, when I cannot satisfy it, but by a narration which I must reserve till I see you. The only event I know besides within this atmosphere is the death of Lord Burlington, who I have just heard has left everything in his power to his relict. I tell you nothing of Jew-Bills and Jew-Motions,[4] for I dare to say you have long been as weary of the words as I am. The only point that keeps up any attention, is expectation of a mail from Ireland, from whence we have heard by a side wind, that the Court have lost a question by six; you may imagine one wants to know more of this.[5]

The opera is indifferent;[6] the first man[6a] has a finer voice than Monticelli,[7] but knows not what to do with it; ancient Visconti[8] does so much with hers that it is intolerable. There is a new play of Glover's,[9] in which Boadicia the heroine[10] rants as much as Visconti screams; but happily you hear no more of her after the third act, till in the last scene somebody brings a card with her compliments and she is very sorry she can't wait upon you, but she is dead. Then there is a scene

3. According to a note by Miss Berry to HW to Bentley 19 Dec. 1753 (*Works* v. 282), Shorter's Swiss servant 'was not without suspicion of having hastened his master's death.'

4. In 1752 an Act had been passed to permit the naturalization of Jews in England (which was already permitted for those who settled in the colonies). Now, on the eve of a general election, a considerable public clamour was raised, and the Act repealed, the government giving it up for fear of losing the election; see W. E. H. Lecky, *England in the Eighteenth Century*, 2d edn, New York, 1892, i. 327–31; *Mem. Geo. II* i. 357–67.

5. This was a continuation of the struggle between the Castle and Archbishop Stone on one side, and the adherents of Boyle on the other (*ante* 12 May 1752, n. 4). The question lost by 'six' votes was probably the 'money-bill,' defeated by five votes; see *Mem. Geo. II* i. 367–8; *Correspondence of John, Fourth Duke of Bedford*, ed. Lord John Russell, 1842–6, ii. 142–4.

6. 'In 1753 and 1754, serious operas, after languishing in poverty and disgrace from the departure of Monticelli, in 1746, were again attempted under the management of Signor Vaneschi.' The performances 'were all received with great indifference, as performed by Serafini, the first man, with little voice, though a good actor; Visconti, first woman, but now *passée*' (Charles Burney, *General History of Music*, 1776–89, iv. 463).

6a. Serafini.

7. Angelo Maria Monticelli (ca 1710–64), tenor, in England 1741–6; see Sir George Grove, *Dictionary of Music*.

8. Came to England 1741; 'had a shrill flexible voice, and pleased more in rapid songs than in those that required high colouring and pathos' (Burney, op. cit. iv. 447).

9. Richard Glover (1712–85), merchant and poet; his *Boadicea* was performed at Drury Lane nine nights; there are several printed editions.

10. Played by Mrs Pritchard.

between *Lord Sussex*[11] and *Lord Cathcart,* two captives, which is most incredibly absurd; but yet the parts are so well acted, the dresses so fine, and two or three scenes pleasing enough, that it is worth seeing.

There are new young Lords, fresh and fresh:[12] two of them are much in vogue: Lord Huntingdon[13] and Lord Stormont:[14] I supped with them t'other night at Lady Caroline Petersham's: the latter is most cried up; but he is more reserved, seems sly,[14a] and to have sense; but I should not think extreme: yet it is unfair to judge on a silenter man at first: the other is very lively and very agreeable. This is the state of the town you inquire after; and which you do inquire after, as one does after Mr Somebody that one used to see at Mr Such an one's formerly: do you never intend to know more of us! Or do you intend to leave me to wither upon the hands of the town like Charles Stanhope[15] and Mrs Dunch? My cotemporaries seem to be all retiring to their proprieties—if I must too, positively I will go no farther than Strawberry Hill!—you are very good to lament *our* goldfish: their whole history consists in their being stolen *à deux reprises,*[16] the very week after I came to town.

Mr B.[17] is where he was, and well, and now and then makes me as happy as I can be, having lost him, with a charming drawing. We don't talk of his abode, for the Hecate his wife endeavours to discover it. Adieu! my best compliments to Miss Montagu; I am

Most truly yours

H. W.

11. George Augustus Yelverton (1727–58), 2d E. of Sussex. He and Lord Cathcart were in 1748–9 sent to Paris as hostages for the performance of the Treaty of Aix-la-Chapelle. The captives in *Boadicea* are two Romans, Flaminius and Aenobarbus; of the several scenes between them, it is hard to say which HW considered absurd.

12. Possibly an echo of a street cry. Such repetition was a common style of intensification and popular with HW.

13. Francis Hastings (1729–89), 10th E. of Huntingdon.

14. David Murray (1727–96), 7th Vct Stormont; succeeded his uncle as 2d E. of Mansfield, 1793. 'Sir Joshua Reynolds (when he lived in Newport Street) painted

them in one picture—two tall whole lengths; and the wags said it looked like the sign *Salutation* at a tavern near Temple Bar. I remember writing an epigram upon it myself' (Mrs Piozzi).

14a. Perhaps HW meant to write 'shy.'

15. Charles Stanhope (1673–1760), of Elvaston, politician; as Secretary of the Treasury, involved in the South Sea scandal. For a picture of him as an elderly bore, see Sir Charles Hanbury Williams's 'Isabella, or The Morning' (*Works*, 1822, i. 72).

16. The thief was a heron (HW to Bentley 19 Dec. 1753).

17. Bentley, who had gone to Jersey to escape his creditors; see *post* 26 July 1755; HW to Bentley 13 April 1755.

To Montagu, Tuesday 19 March 1754

Arlington Street, March 19, 1754.

YOU *will* live in the country; and then you are amazed that people use you ill. Don't mistake me; I don't mean, that you deserve to be ill-treated for living in the country; at least, only by those who love you and miss you; but if you inhabited the town a little, you would not quite so much expect uprightness, nor be so surprised at ingratitude and neglect. I am far from disposed to justify the great Cû;[1] but when you had declined being *his* servant, do you wonder that he will not serve *your* friends? I will tell you what, if the news of today holds at all, which is what no one piece of news of this last fortnight has done, you may be worse used by your cousin as soon as you please, for he is one of the first upon the list for Secretary of State in the room of the Duke of Newcastle.[2] Now are you again such a rusticated animal as to suppose, that the Duke is dismissed for inability, on the death of his brother.[3] So far from it, it is already certainly known that it was he who supported Mr Pelham; and the impediments and rubs thrown in the way of absolute power long ago, were the effects of the latter's timidity and irresolution. The Duke, freed from that clog, has declared himself sole minister, and the K. has kissed his hand upon it. Mr Fox, who was the only man in England that objected to this plan, is to be sent to a prison which is building on the coast of Sussex after the model of Fort l'Évêque, under the direction of Mr Taaffe.[4]

Harry Legge is to be Chancellor of the Exchequer; but the declared favour rests on Lord Duplin.[5] Sir George Lyttelton to be Treasurer of the Navy.[6] The Parliament is to be dissolved on the fourth of

1. Halifax; his ill-treatment of Montagu is not further explained. Cf. *post* 29 June 1754.

2. This did not happen; Sir Thomas Robinson took the post.

3. Henry Pelham died 6 March.

4. See HW to Mann 22 Nov. 1751 for another allusion to a connection between Taaffe and Newcastle. Fox was offered a Secretaryship of State and the leadership of the House of Commons in the new government, but withdrew on a dispute with Newcastle about the control of the secret service fund; see Earl of Ilchester, *Henry*

Fox, First Lord Holland, 1920, i. 198–212; *Mem. Geo. II* i. 378–89.

5. Thomas Hay (1710–87), styled Vct Dupplin; 9th E. of Kinnoull, 1758; held several offices; one of Newcastle's chief advisers on questions of party management; see Lewis B. Namier, *Structure of Politics at the Accession of George III*, 1929; *England in the Age of the American Revolution*, 1930, *passim*.

6. George Grenville became Treasurer of the Navy; Lyttelton, Cofferer of the Household.

next month, till when I suppose none of the changes will take place. These are the politics of the day; but as they are a little fluctuating, notwithstanding the headiness of the new first minister, I will not answer that they will hold true to Greatworth; nothing lasts now but the bad weather.

I went two days ago with Lady Ailesbury, and Mr Conway and Miss Anne[7] to hear the rehearsal of Mrs Clive's new farce,[8] which is very droll, with very pretty music.[9] The first singer[10] was not perfect, and being to begin *O my country,* he forgot his recitative, and made the broadest stop in the middle of the last word that ever was made; except now and then by my Lady Townshend. Good night!

Yours ever

H. W.

From Montagu, ca April 1754

G.D. 15/8, No. 719.

Dated by the references to the weather and building at SH. The month seems clearly April. Either 1753 or 1754 would fit the building, but GM records an exceptionally 'uniform' April in 1753 (xxiii. 158), and an 'excessively retarded' spring in April 1754 (xxiv. 152).

[ca April 1754].

WHEN you have a moment let me know how you do for this cold weather pierces even my fat sides, and I am afraid must pinch yours that are not near so well fenced, and I shall be truly glad to hear you are well. However I am much alone and the country ugly I am more comfortable here than amidst all the amusements of London. The backwardness of the spring suits my schemes well for your Strawberry will be in beauty when it will be convenient to me to pay my visit to you towards the end of May; and your workmen will have made a great progress.[1]

7. Hon. Anne Seymour Conway (d. 1774), m. (1755) John Harris (*post* 7 Jan. 1755, n. 4); HW's cousin (Collins, *Peerage*, 1812, ii. 563).

8. Probably *The London Apprentice*, 'a new operetta,' performed at Drury Lane on 23 March, Mrs Clive's benefit night, along with *Love's Last Shift* ([John Genest],

Some Account of the English Stage, Bath, 1832, iv. 387).

9. Rest of letter omitted in previous editions.

10. Not identified.

———

1. See HW to Bentley 18 May 1754.

I hope you had your grate[2] safe; you have my old clothes in pawn and you may pay yourself.[3] Adieu, believe me,

Always very truly yours,

G. MONTAGU

To MONTAGU, Tuesday 21 May 1754

Arlington Street, May 21, 1754.

I DID not intend to write to you till after Thursday, when all your Boscawens, Rices, and Trevors are to dine at Strawberry Hill, but an event has happened, of which I can't delay giving you the instant pleasurable notice—now will you, according to your custom be guessing—and according to your custom, guessing wrong; but lest you should from my spirits make any undutiful or disloyal conjectures for me, know, that the great Cû of the Vine[1] is dead, and that John the first was yesterday proclaimed undoubted monarch—nay, champion Dimmock[2] himself shall cut the throat of any Tracy, Atkins or Harrison[3] who shall dare to gainsay the legality of his title. In short, there is no more will, than was left by the late Erasmus Shorter of particular memory.

I consulted Madam Rice, and she advised my directing to you at Mrs Whettenhal's, to whom I beg as many compliments as if she wrote herself *la Blanche Whitnell*.[4] As many to your sister Harriot and to your brother who I hear is with you.

I am sure though both you and I had reason to be peevish with the poor Tigress,[5] that you grieve with me for her death. I do most sincerely, and for her Bessy;[6] the man Tyger will be so sorry, that I am sure he will marry again to comfort himself.[7]

2. Probably the 'old grate of Henry VIII' which Bentley bought for him (HW to Bentley 18 May 1754).

3. The old clothes were presumably left behind by Montagu after a visit.

---

1. Anthony (b. 1691), John Chute's elder brother (Chaloner W. Chute, *A History of the Vyne*, 1888, p. 83).

2. John Dymoke (d. 1784), champion of England, as lord of the manor of Scrivelsby, Lincs; see DNB, *sub* Sir John Dymoke; *post* 24 Sept. 1761, n. 25.

3. Relatives of Chute's who HW had

feared might get the estates; see HW to Chute 21 May 1754.

4. See *ante* 22 July 1751, n. 8.

5. Mrs Henry Talbot, d. 15 May (GM 1754, xxiv. 243); the reason for the peevishness is not known.

6. Ely, or Elizabeth, Talbot, Henry Talbot's daughter by his first wife, Elizabeth Lloyd; m. Capt. Thomas Cornwall, R.N. (Collins, *Peerage*, 1812, v. 233; John Burke, *History of the Commoners*, 1833-8, iv. 91).

7. Apparently he did not (Collins, loc. cit.).

I am so tired with letters I have written on this event, that I can scarce hold the pen.[8] How we shall wish for you on Thursday—*and shan't you be proud to cock your tail[9] at the Vine?* Adieu!

Yours ever

H. W.

To Montagu, Saturday 8 June 1754

Strawberry Hill, Saturday June 8, 1754.

BY my computation you are about returned to Greatworth; I was so afraid of my letter's missing you on the road, that I deferred till now telling you how much pleasure I shall have in seeing you and the Colonel at Strawberry. I have long been mortified that for these three years you have seen it only in winter: It is now at the height of its greenth, blueth, gloomth, honeysuckle-and-syringahood. I have no engagement till Wednesday se'nnight, when I am obliged to be in town on law business.[1] You will have this tomorrow night; if I receive a letter, which I beg you will direct to London, on Tuesday or Wednesday, I will meet you here whatever day you will be so good as to appoint. Thank the Colonel a thousand times; I can't write a word more, for I am getting into the chaise to whisk to the Vine for two days, but shall be in town on Tuesday night. Adieu!

Yours ever

H. W.

To Montagu, Saturday 29 June 1754

Strawberry Hill, June 29, 1754.

I SHALL take care to send your letter, the first time I write to Mr Bentley: It is above a fortnight since I heard from him. I am much disappointed at not having seen you yet; I love you should execute your intentions, while you intend them, because you are a little apt

8. See the long letter to Chute on this date, in which HW says he will write to Gray, Bentley, and Montagu. The letters to Gray and Bentley are missing.

9. Doubtless one of Montagu's expressions to signify being at home.

1. Possibly connected with the settlement of Erasmus Shorter's estate.

to alter your mind, and as I have set mine on your seeing Strawberry Hill this summer, while it is in its beauty, you will really mortify me by changing your purpose.

It is in vain that you ask for news: I was in town two days ago, but heard nothing; indeed there were not people enough either to cause or make news. Lady Caroline Petersham had scraped together a few foreigners, after her christening;[1] but I cannot say that the party was much livelier, than if it had met at Madame Montandre's.[2] You must let me know a little beforehand when you have fixed your time for coming, because as I am towards flying about, on my summer expeditions,[3] I should be unhappy not to be here, just when you would like it. Adieu!

Yours ever
H. W.

PS. I supped at White's t'other night with the great Cû, and he was by far more gracious, both on your topic and my own, than ever I knew him.

To Montagu, Thursday 29 August 1754

Strawberry Hill, Aug. 29, 1754.

YOU may be sure that I shall always be glad to see you whenever you like to come hither, but I can't help being sorry that you are determined not to like the place, nor to let the Colonel like it; a conclusion I may very justly make, when I think for these four years you have contrived to visit it only when there is not a leaf upon the trees. Villas are generally designed for summer, you are the single person who think[s] they look best in winter. You have still a more unlucky thought, which is to visit the Vine in October. When I saw

1. Her second son, Henry Fitzroy Stanhope (d. 1828), was baptised 26 June 1754 (Burke, *Peerage, sub* Harrington; Collins, *Peerage*, 1812, iv. 289).
2. Mary Anne (ca 1683–1772), dau. of Ezekiel, Baron von Spanheim, onetime Prussian ambassador to England; m. (1710) François de la Rochefoucauld, Marquis de Montandre, a religious refugee who d. 1739 a field marshal (David C. A. Agnew, *Protestant Exiles from France*, 1871–4, ii. 122–5). For another slighting reference to her circle, see *Harcourt Papers*, ed. Edward W. Harcourt, Oxford, n.d., viii. 15–16 (Lady Cecilia West to Lord Nuneham). Musgrave cites death notices about a Marchioness de Montandre who d. 1774 aged 92, but Joseph L. Chester, *Marriage, Baptismal, and Burial Registers of . . . Westminster*, 1876, p. 415, confirms Agnew's dates for her.
3. Only a trip to Park Place, and possibly one to Hagley, are mentioned in extant letters; HW to Conway 6 Aug. 1754.

it in the middle of summer, it was excessively damp; you will find it
a little difficult to persuade me to accompany you thither on stilts,
and I believe Mr Chute will not be quite happy that you prefer that
season; but for this I can't answer at present, for he is at Mr Morris's[1]
in Cornwall. I shall expect you and the Colonel here at the time you
appoint; I engage for no farther, unless it is a very fine season indeed.
I beg my compliments to Miss Montague, and am

Yours ever

Hor. Walpole

From Montagu, Tuesday 15 October 1754

G.D. 15/8, No. 731.

The final digit of the date of this letter would appear to be either a 7 or a 9
but HW's notes and reply definitely locate it in 1754.

Memoranda by HW: Barrets—no fault. Lord Dacre hangd

Lord Petre's cracks. to see for, not
to see a prosp.
GM.—Incense. massbooks. lights. sermon.
clubs. diamonds.
Lord Druml.
View of Vine
Solomon and Hester
Mr Beckf. Princess Em.
Mrs Burgess—how if her list. die.
Leeds etc.

All but the last two lines of these notes have been cancelled by HW. Through
'clubs. diamonds' they are for HW to Bentley 3 Nov. 1754, q.v. 'Lord Druml.' is
Lord Drumlanrig, whose suicide is mentioned in HW to Conway 24 Oct. 1754.
'Solomon and Hester' was Lady Townshend's nickname for Pitt and his intended wife Lady Hester Grenville (*post* 16 Nov. 1754). The remaining notes do
not seem to have been used. 'Mr Beckf.' is no doubt William Beckford, 'Princess
Em.' Princess Amelia. Mrs Burgess has not been identified.

Greatworth, Tuesday Oct. 15, 1754.

THE Colonel was obliged to go this morning to Horton to wor-
ship my cousin.[1] You cannot imagine how fretted I am that I
have been constrained to defer my waiting on you till this time of the

---

1. Humphrey Morice (1723–85), politi-   1. Halifax.
cian; of Werrington, Devonshire (DNB); he
also had considerable estates in Cornwall.

year which is on many accounts as inconvenient to me as can be, and perhaps will be found not the most commodious to travel about the cross-roads of Great Britain; for you are to know we are engaged to end at Waldershare² and leave Miss³ alone for three weeks but as she is perfectly well we are easy about her. Monday next we begin our progress to your honour first, and hoping old horses will convey me to Strawberry Hill the second day; if the weather continues as fine as at this present writing 'tis preferable to the summer; we propose great pleasure and satisfaction and⁴ seeing you and yours and the Chute, to whom my compliments; my sister desires you will accept of hers; I am most truly and faithfully yours.

G. MONTAGU

To MONTAGU, Thursday 17 October 1754

Month and year ascertained by *ante* 15 Oct. 1754, to which this is clearly a reply.

Strawberry Hill, Thursday [Oct.] 17th [1754].

I ONLY write you a line to tell you, that as you mention Miss Montagu's being well and alone, if she could like to accompany the Colonel and you to Strawberry Hill and the Vine, the seneschals of those castles will be very proud to see her. I am sorry to be forced to say anything civil in a letter to you; you deserve nothing but ill usage for disappointing us so often,¹ but we stay till we have got you into our power, and then—why then, I am afraid we shall still be what I have been so long

Ever yours
H. W.

To MONTAGU, Saturday 16 November 1754

Arlington Street, Nov. 16, 1754.

YOU are over good to me, my dear Sir, in giving yourself the trouble of telling me you was content with Strawberry Hill. I will not however tell you that I am content with your being there

2. Near Dover; a seat of the Earl of Guilford.
3. Henrietta Montagu.
4. Montagu has written 'and.'

1. Montagu's much postponed visit finally took place, apparently on the date set in *ante* 15 Oct. 1754; see HW to Conway 24 Oct. 1754; HW to Bentley 3 Nov. 1754.

till you have seen it in all its greenth and blueth. Alas! I am sorry I can't insist upon as much with the Colonel![1]

Mr Chute I believe was so pleased with the tenebræ in his own chapel, that he has fairly buried himself in it: I have not even had so much as a burial-card from him since.[2]

The town is as full as I believe you thought the room was at your ball at Waldeshare. I hear of nothing but the parts and merit of Lord North.[3] Nothing has happened yet; but sure so many *English* people can't be assembled long, without committing something extraordinary!

I have seen and conversed with our old friend Cope; I find him grown very old; I fear he finds me so too; at least as old as I ever intend to be. I find him very grave too, which I believe he does not find me.

Solomon and Hesther, as my Lady Townshend calls Mr Pitt and Lady Hesther Grenville,[4] espouse one another today. I know nothing more but a new fashion which my Lady Hervey has brought from Paris. It is a tin funnel covered with green ribband, and holds water, which the ladies wear to keep their bouquets fresh—I fear Lady Caroline and some others will catch frequent colds and sore throats with overturning this reservoir.

Apropos there is a match certainly in agitation, which has very little of either Solomon or Hesther in it—you will be sorry when I tell you that Lord Walgrave[5] certainly dis-Solomons himself with the Drax.[6] Adieu! my dear sir, I congratulate Miss Montagu on her good health and am ever yours

H. W.

To Montagu, Tuesday 7 January 1755

Arlington Street, Jan. 7, 1755.

I IMAGINED by your letter that the Colonel was in town, and was shocked at not having been to wait on him: upon inquiry I find he is not; and now, can conceive how he came to tell you that the

1. Miss E. G. Withycombe suggests that he might be on active service in the summer.

2. Since HW's and Montagu's visit there, when they 'had most Catholic enjoyment of the Chapel' (HW to Bentley 3 Nov. 1754).

3. Frederick North (1732–92), styled

Lord North; 2d E. of Guilford, 1790; First Lord of the Treasury in 1770.

4. Lady Hester Grenville (1720–1803), cr. (1761) Baroness Chatham s.j.; m. (1754) William Pitt, cr. (1766) E. of Chatham.

5. James Waldegrave (1715–63), 2d E. Waldegrave.

6. 'Harriet Drax whom Lord Waldegrave

town has been entertained with a paper of mine:[1] I send it you, to show you, that this is one of the many fabulous histories[2] which have been spread in such quantities, and without foundation.

I shall take care of your letter to Mr Bentley. Mr Chute is at the Vine,[3] or I know he would, as I do, beg his compliments to Miss Montagu. You don't wish me joy on the approaching nuptials of Mr Harris[4] and our Miss Anne. He is so amorous, that whenever he sits by her (and he can't stand by her) my Lady Townshend by a very happy expression says, *he is always setting his dress.* Have you heard of a Countess Chamfelt,[5] a Bohemian, rich and hideous, who is arrived here, and is under the protection of Lady Caroline Petersham? She has a great facility at languages, and has already learnt, *damn you* and *kiss me*—I beg her pardon, I believe she never uses the former, but upon miscarriage of the latter: in short, as Doddington says, she has had the honour of performing at most courts in Europe. Adieu!

Yours ever

H. W.

To Montagu, Tuesday 13 May 1755

Arlington Street, May 13th, 1755.

IT is very satisfactory to me to hear that Miss Montagu was pleased with the day[1] she passed at Strawberry Hill; but does not it silently reproach you, who will never see it but in winter? Does not she assure you that there are leaves and flowers and verdure? And why will you not believe that with those additions it might look pretty, and

deserted for Maria Walpole' (Mrs Piozzi, note to *post* 16 May 1759). She m. (1765), as his 3d wife, Sir William Hanham, 4th Bt, of Wimborne, Dorset, and d. 1786. According to *Town and Country Magazine* 1769, i. 14, when Lord Waldegrave married Maria Walpole, an illegitimate, instead of 'Miss D---,' George II said that 'he had prevented him marrying a W----, and now he had wedded a B------.'

1. Probably *The World* of 19 Dec. 1754 (No. 103), on politeness (*Works* i. 174).
2. That is, the rumour that HW was entertaining the town.

3. See HW to Bentley 9 Jan. 1775.
4. John Harris (d. 1767), of Hayne, Devonshire; Master of the Household ca 1747–67; M.P. Ashburton 1741–67; m. (10 March 1755) as his 2d wife, Anne Seymour Conway, HW's cousin; after his death she was housekeeper at Somerset House, and d. 1774 (Collins, *Peerage*, 1812, ii. 563; Burke, *Landed Gentry*).
5. Not further identified.

1. Not determined.

might make you some small amends for a day or two purloined from Greatworth? I wish you would visit it when in its beauty and while it is mine! You will not, I flatter myself, like it so well, when it belongs to the *Intendant* of Twickenham, when a cockleshell walk is made cross the lawn, and everything without doors is made regular, and everything within *riant* and modern; for this must be its fate![2] Whether its next master is already on board the Brest fleet,[3] I don't pretend to say; but I scarce think it worth my while to dispose of it by my will, as I have some apprehension of living to see it granted away *de par le roy*. My Lady Hervey dined there yesterday with the Rochfords; I told her, that as she is just going to France, I was unwilling to let her see it, for if she should like it, she would desire Mademoiselle,[4] with whom she lives, to beg it for her. Adieu!

Yours ever

H. Walpole

To Montagu, Thursday 17 July 1755

Strawberry Hill, July 17th, 1755.

HAVING done with building and planting, I have taken to farming; the first fruits of my proficience in that science I offer to you, and have taken the liberty to send you a couple of cheeses.[1] If you will give yourself the trouble to inquire at Brackley for the coach which set out this morning, you will receive a box and a roll of paper.[2] The latter does not contain a cheese, only a receipt for making them. We have taken so little of the French fleet,[3] that I fear none of it will come to my share, or I would have sent you part of the spoils. I have nothing more to send you but a new ballad which my Lord

2. That is, after the forthcoming conquest of England by France.

3. Heralded by frontier clashes in America the year before, war between France and England was now obviously impending, though no formal declarations had been made; the French fleet fitting out at Brest was designed for Canada; see W. E. H. Lecky, *History of England in the Eighteenth Century*, 2d edn, New York, 1892–3, ii. 351–5.

4. Presumably one of the king's daughters; Lady Hervey was a great Francophil.

1. The 'mystery' of the following letter.

2. Probably the picture mentioned ibid.

3. Admiral Boscawen was sent to intercept the French fleet mentioned in the last letter; it escaped him in a fog, except for two ships, captured by Capt. Richard Howe; see William L. Clowes, *The Royal Navy*, 1897–1903, iii. 141.

Bath has made on this place: you remember the old burden of it,[4]
and the last lines allude to Billy Bristow's[5] having fallen in love
with it.

1.

> Some talk of Gunnersbury,[6]
> For Sion[7] some declare;
> And some say that with Chiswick House
> No villa can compare:
> But all the beaux of Middlesex,
> Who know the country well,
> Say that Strawb'ry Hill, that Strawberry
> Does bear away the bell.

2.

> Though Surry boast its Oatlands,[8]
> And Claremont kept so gim,[9]
> And though they talk of Southcote's,
> It's but a dainty whim;
> For ask the gallant Bristow,
> Who does in taste excell,
> If Strawb'ry Hill, if Strawberry
> Don't bear away the bell.[10]

I am a little pleased to send you this, to show you that in summer
we are a little pretty, though you will never look at us but in our
ugliness. My best compliments to Miss Montagu; and my service to

4. HW to Bentley 17 July 1755 says the
stanzas were 'to the old tune . . . of
Rowe's ballad on Dodington's Mrs Strawbridge'; in *Des. of SH, Works* ii. 513, HW
says 'to the tune of a former song written
by George Bubb Doddington . . . The song
was written in praise of Mrs Strawbridge,
a lady with whom Mr Doddington was in
love.' HW subsequently wrote three supplementary verses (ibid.).

5. William Bristow (d. 1758), 'brother
of the Countess of Buckingham, friend of
Lord Bath, and a great pretender to taste'
(*Des. of SH, Works* ii. 514). Son of Robert
Bristow, M.P., a London merchant; Commissioner of the Revenue in Ireland (*GM*
1758, xxviii. 146).

6. Ealing, Middlesex; built 1663 by John
Webbe; seat of Henry Furnese, purchased
by Princess Amelia, 1761; the grounds

covered 95 acres; see Daniel Lysons, *Environs of London*, 1792–6, ii. 226. Drawings of the house are in Colin Campbell,
Vitruvius Britannicus, 1715–71, i. 17, 18.

7. Sion or Syon House, Isleworth, Middlesex; originally a monastery; rebuilt in
the 17th century, and again ca 1761 by
Robert Adam; seat of the Earl (now Duke)
of Northumberland; see H. Avray Tipping, *The English Home*, Period VI, vol.
i (1926). 139–64; *Beauties of England* x pt
iv. 361–73.

8. Oatlands, near Weybridge, Surrey,
seat of the Earl of Lincoln, and later of the
Duke of York; burned 1794 (Edward W.
Brayley, *Topographical History of Surrey*,
1850, ii. 386–7).

9. Spruce, smart (obs.—OED).

10. A parody appears in H. Howard,
The Choice Spirits Museum, A Collection

whatever Baronet breakfasts with you on negus[11]—have you heard
that poor Lady Browne is so unfortunate as to have lost her last
daughter?[12] And that Mrs Barret[13] is so lucky as to have lost her
mother-in-law,[14] and is Baroness Dacre of the South? I met the great
Cû t'other day, and he asked me if I ever heard from you; that he
never did; I told him that I did not neither; did not I say true?

Yours ever

H. W.

To MONTAGU, Saturday 26 July 1755

Strawberry Hill, July 26, 1755.

WHO would not turn farmer, when their very first essay turns to
so good account? Seriously I am quite pleased with the success of my mystery, and infinitely obliged to you for the kind things
you say about my picture.[1] You must thank Mrs Whetenhall too for
her prepossession about my cheeses; I fear a real manufacture of milk
at Strawberry Hill would not have answered quite so well as our old
commodities of paint and copper-plates.

I am happy for the recovery of Miss Montagu and the tranquillity
you must feel after so terrible a season of apprehensions. Make my
compliments to her, and if you can be honest on so tender a topic,
tell her that she will always be in danger while you shut her up in
Northamptonshire; and that with her delicate constitution, she ought

of *Songs*, 1765, pp. 12–14, 'The Hills of
London' (HW notes in his copy, now WSL,
'To the Tune of Strawberry'). Stanza 4
reads:
'Since W-----e sung of Strawberry Hill,
   And other Hills around,
There's not a Hill among them all,
   That does his praise resound.
Ah, peace be to his flummery,
   I wish him vastly well,
But Ludgate Hill, but Ludgate Hill,
   Shall ever bear the bell.'
11. See *ante* 16 Aug. 1753, n. 2.
12. She had had two (Rev. William
Betham, *Baronetage of England*, 1801–5,
iii. 219).
13. Anna Maria Pratt (d. 1806), m. (1739)

Thomas Barrett-Lennard, 17th Bn Dacre
of the South on his mother's death.
14. Anne Lennard (1684–1755), Baroness Dacre *suo jure*, 1741; m. (1) (1716)
Richard Barrett; m. (2) (1718) Henry
Roper, 8th Bn Teynham; m. (3) (1725)
Hon. Robert Moore.

1. It is not clear what this was; perhaps
the 'roll of paper' sent as a receipt for
making cheese (*ante* 17 July 1755) was a
picture and perhaps the box contained
copper-plates. Cf. HW to Mason 15 March
1782, where HW elaborately refers to
Mason's *Archaeological Epistle* as a cheese,
for purposes of mystification.

to live nearer friends and help; that I know no spot so healthy or convenient for both as the county of Twicks.

Charles Townshend is to be married next month; as the lady had a very *bad* husband before,[2] she has chosen prudently, and has settled herself in a family of the best sort of people in the world, who will think of nothing but making her happy. I don't know even whether the bridegroom won't be afraid of getting her any more children, lest it should prejudice those she has already![3] They are a wonderful set of people for good-natured considerations!

You know to be sure that Mr Humberston[4] is dead, and your neighbouring Brackley likely to return under the dominion of its old masters.[5] Lady Dysart[6] is dead too, and Mrs Cavendish[7] *in-cun-sole-able*.[8]

2. Lady Caroline Campbell (1717–94), m. (1) (1742) Francis Scott (1721–50), styled E. of Dalkeith; m. (2) (1755) Rt Hon. Charles Townshend; cr. (1767) Baroness Greenwich. Lady Louisa Stuart considered Lord Dalkeith 'essentially good, amiable, and worthy' (*Selections from her Manuscripts*, ed. Hon. James A. Home, Edinburgh, 1899, p. 31; and Lady Hervey, *Letters*, 1821, p. 176, agrees with HW to Mann 2 April 1750 that 'they were extremely happy' (HW's 'bad' is not serious). Lady Mary Wortley Montagu, *Letters and Works*, ed. Lord Wharncliffe, 3d edn 1861, ii. 292, said of the match with Townshend, 'No man ever was in love with a woman of forty, since the Deluge.'

3. She had six children by Lord Dalkeith, and two sons by Townshend.

4. Thomas (or James) Humberston (d. 27 June 1755), of Lower Layton, Essex (GM 1755, xxv. 333); of Humberston, Lincs (*Lists of Members of Parliament*); M.P. Brackley 1754-5.

5. The 'old masters' of Brackley were the Egertons, Dukes of Bridgewater; the third Duke, who was under the political leadership of his uncle the Duke of Bedford, usually filled at least one seat with connections of his. After a contest in 1754 Humberston and Marshe Dickenson, the latter a member of the Bedford party, were returned; Henry Vernon, also a Bedford adherent, was defeated. From the Bedford MSS it appears that when Humberston first announced his candidacy for Brackley, no one had heard of him, and

it was thought that he was 'only a phantom conjured up to create an expense.' But he secured 18 of the 33 members of the Corporation, who were apparently in a rebellious mood, for they not only spurned Bedford's attempts to outbid Humberston but told him, when he visited the town with Vernon and Dickenson, that unless he would be content with the latter's election they would 'throw both his candidates out' (Bedford MSS, xxix. f. 49, 53, 85, 103, 116; xxx. f. 30, 32, 40; information from Miss Scott Thomson and Prof. L. B. Namier).

6. Hon. Grace Carteret (1713–55), m. (1729), Lionel Tollemache, 4th E. of Dysart.

7. Elizabeth (d. 1779), dau. of Lord James Cavendish, 3d son of 1st D. of Devonshire; m. (1732) Richard, eld. son of Edward Chandler, Bp of Durham; he changed his name to Cavendish, 1752 (Collins, *Peerage*, 1812, i. 354; GM 1793, lxiii pt ii. 1000). She can be identified by a statement in HW to Bentley 5 July 1755, 'Latimers belongs to Mrs Cavendish'; see *Vict. Co. Hist. Bucks* iii. 209.

8. The second half of the sentence has been omitted in previous editions. Mrs Cavendish's interest in her own sex is affirmed in an unpublished letter (now WSL) from 'Gilly' Williams to George Selwyn 16 Oct. 1755, 'I have no intrigue, or curiosity to find out anyone who has one. Mrs Cavendish, by the heat of the waters, and the natural richness of her constitution seems more wickedly inclined than any

Mr Chute is at the Vine. Your poor Cliquetis[9] is still a banished man. I have a scheme for bringing him back, but can get Mrs Tisiphone[10] into no kind of terms; and without tying her up from running him into new debts, it is in vain to recover him.

I believe the declaration of war has been stopped at the Custom House, for one hears nothing of it.[11] You see I am very paragraphical, and in reality have nothing to say; so good night!

Yours ever
H. W.

To Montagu, Saturday 20 September 1755

Year determined by the contents.

Arlington Street, Sept 20th [1755].

My dear Sir

I HAVE been roving about Hampshire with Mr Chute,[1] and did not receive your very kind note till yesterday, or I should certainly not have deferred a moment to thank you for it, and to express my great concern for Miss Montagu's bad health. You do me justice when you reckon on my feeling most sincerely for you—but let me ask why you will not bring her to town? She might not only have more variety of assistance, but it would be some relief to you: it must be dreadful, with your tenderness and feeling to have nobody to share and divert your uneasiness!

I did not, till on the road the day before yesterday, hear the catastrophe of poor Sir John Bland,[2] with the execrable villainy, or what our ancestors, would have called, the *humours* of Taaffe.[3] I am ex-

young fellow here, and if Lady Betty Spencer is not sent away, I believe she will by force go in unto her and know her.'

9. A nickname for Bentley, probably derived from the French *cliqueter:* 'faire un bruit sec en se choquant,' the noun form of which is *cliquetis;* see HW to Chute 21 May 1754, 'our poor cliquetée.'

10. His wife (*post* 19 Oct. 1760, n. 2).

11. War was not declared until May 1756; see HW to Mann 16 May 1756.

———

1. See HW to Bentley 18 Sept. 1755.

2. He committed suicide ca 3 Sept. Having '*flirted* away his whole fortune at hazard' (HW to Bentley 23 Feb. 1755), he had gone to France, and there became involved in further gambling difficulties; see next note.

3. Taaffe's villainy is explained by the following, from a contemporary copy (now WSL) of a letter from Charles Selwyn, the English banker in Paris, to Henry Fox:

'Paris, Sept. 6, 1755.

'. . . You'll hear the unfortunate death of Sir John Bland in his way to England;

tremely sorry for Bland! He was good-natured and generous and well-bred; but never was such infatuation; I can call it by no term but *flirting* away his fortune and his life; he seemed to have no passion for play, while he did it, nor sensibility when it ruined him; but I fear he had both! What judgments the good people in the City (I mean *good* in their own style, *monied*) will construe upon White's, when two of the most remarkable members have dispatched themselves in nine months![4]

I shall be most sincerely glad to receive another letter to tell me that Miss Montagu mends: you have both my most hearty wishes!

Yours ever

H. W.

From MONTAGU, Monday 22 September 1755

G.D. 15/8, No. 720.

In reply to *ante* 20 Sept. 1755.

Greatworth [Sept.] 22 [1755].

MY sister desires me to tell you she is vastly obliged to you for your concern for her and begs you will receive her best thanks. I think she now is a little better; her fever is abated, and she is

the subject of it was some money he lost at play with Mr Taaffe, for which he gave bills of exchange payable at two and three months date—which contrary to his intentions and knowledge were sent to London and protested for non-acceptance, and in virtue of that protest under pretence that the bills were for money he took up of an *écuyer* who buys horses for the King and to whom they were designedly made payable. Mons. D'Argenson gave a *lettre de cachet* to have him put in prison. Under these circumstances, the Exempt being in his lodgings in order to execute his orders, we were sent for, and engaged to advance him £500 to save him from the affront, and prevent his killing himself on the spot, which he infallibly would have done. But his resentment was so great, as we had taken from him the power of procuring himself any satisfaction by engaging his honour that he would not see the person who had done him this injury till he had paid us this money, that he could

not get over it, and we are persuaded must have occasioned what followed at Clermont, where he died. We immediately sent away a lawyer, who by the *tournure* he gave the affair, got him buried in the church yard which was a point extremely nice and very difficult to be compassed, considering the manner of his death was known to every body in the town. We have done all this out of regard to the distress he was in here, his banker Sir John Lambert being just then dead. We hope his family will consider the nature of the service and not let us suffer by it. If you could any way contribute to it, we should be vastly obliged to you.'

One Robinson tried unsuccessfully to sue Bland's estate in the King's Bench for gambling debts incurred by him in France; see 96 English Reports 129, 1 Black W. 234.

4. Henry Bromley (b. 1705), cr. (1741) Bn Montfort; killed himself 1 Jan. 1755; see HW to Bentley 9 Jan. 1755.

freer from pain. As to coming to London it is absolutely impossible; for she cannot walk from her bed to her chair, and to travel more than ten miles a day she could not be able to bear. If she recovers strength enough even to undergo a journey she is advised to try Bristol waters.

The Colonel is at Guilford and intends waiting on you at dinner now he hears you are returned.

My sister has prevented him from coming here; it would disorder and affect her too much.

We expect Miss Trevor in a few days and I believe Miss Rice too.

My sister Wetenhall was with us five weeks and was obliged to return home about a lawsuit; and they have recovered a little estate that belonged to Bishop Wetenhall[1] a kinsman of the Blanche Witnell's.[2]

The North[3] raves of your commandery[4] and thinks it the completest thing he ever saw.

If it pleases God my sister recovers enough to go to Bristol and thence to Hankalow,[5] I shall come for some months to London, and I shall be happy to see you and yours well and flourishing. I have been myself very poorly. You must expect to see a little lean body somewhat turned of forty; my sister's being better has made me happy and gayer and I begin to revive. I am ever most truly yours,

G. M.

To Montagu, Tuesday 7 October 1755

Arlington Street, Oct. 7, 1755.

My dear Sir

NOBODY living feels more for you than I do: nobody knows better either the goodness and tenderness of your heart, or the real value of the person you have lost.[1] I cannot flatter myself that any-

1. Edward Wetenhall (1636–1713), Bp of Cork and Ross, 1679; of Kilmore and Ardagh, 1699 (DNB).
2. See *ante* 22 July 1751.
3. Lord North.
4. The word is not clear in MS. A commandery was an estate of one of the orders of knights; the term was also applied to non-military conventual priories (see

OED); here, of course, Montagu refers to SH. The date of Lord North's visit is not known.
5. Hankelow, near Nantwich, Cheshire; seat of Nathaniel Wettenhall.

1. His sister Harriet; see HW to Bentley 19 Oct. 1755.

thing I could say would comfort you under an affliction so well-founded; but I should have set out and endeavoured to share your concern, if Mrs Trevor had not told me that you was going into Cheshire. I will only say, that if you think change of place can contribute at all to divert your melancholy, you know where you would be most welcome; and whenever you will come to Strawberry Hill, you will at least, if you do not find a comforter, find a most sincere friend, that pities your distress, and would do anything upon earth to alleviate your misfortune. If you can listen yet to any advice, let me recommend to you, to give up all thoughts of Greatworth; you will never be able to support life there any more: let me look out for some little box for you in my neighbourhood: you can live nowhere, where you will be more beloved: and you will there always have it in your power to enjoy company or solitude as you like. I have long wished to get you so far back into the world; and now it is become absolutely necessary for your health and peace. I will say no more, lest too long a letter should be either troublesome, or make you think it necessary to answer; but don't, till you find it more agreeable to vent your grief this way than in any other.

I am my good sir with hearty concern and affection

Yours most sincerely

HOR. WALPOLE

From MONTAGU, Wednesday 15 October 1755

G.D. 15/8, No. 721.

In reply to *ante* 7 Oct. 1755.

Hankelow, Oct. 15 [1755].

I AM most extremely obliged to you, my dear Sir, for your kind and obliging letter, and do assure you would rather have gone to your friendly house and assistance than any other place in the world had it been convenient to me, and return you many thanks for an offer so cordially made and that I know I may depend upon. I am but very indifferent in my health, but as I ride out every day when I am able I hope to receive benefit; I intend when I think I shall bear it [to] come to town to a lodging and have the Colonel with me for some months, for my own house will be not fit for me to live in and never can be more agreeable to me. But I cannot conveniently leave it as I have a lease and my goods and family settled there, but shall be absent from it as much as possible.

Miss Trevor has showed us all the kindness and assistance imaginable and acted all that could be from her good sense and the best of hearts. Excuse me from writing any more and assure yourself my dear Sir I am unalterably yours

G. MONTAGU

To MONTAGU, Saturday 8 November 1755

Strawberry Hill, Nov. 8, 1755.

My dear Sir

YOU oblige me extremely by giving me this commission,[1] and though I am exceedingly unlike Solomon in everything else, I will at least resemble him, in recommending you to the Hiram from whom I obtained my cedars of Libanus.[1a] He is by men called Christopher Gray,[1b] nurseryman at Fulham. I mention cedars first, because they are the most beautiful of the evergreen race, and because they are the dearest; half a guinea apiece in baskets. The arbutus are scarce and a crown apiece, but they are very beautiful. The lignum vitæ I would not recommend to you; they stink abominably if you touch them and never make a handsome tree: the Chinese arbor vitæ is very beautiful. I have a small nursery myself, scarce bigger than *one of those pleasant gardens* which Solomon describes,[2] and which if his *fair one* meant the *church,* I suppose must have meant the *churchyard.* Well, out of this little *parsley-bed*[3] of mine, I can furnish you

1. In a missing letter.
1a. Latin form of Lebanon.
1b. Payments to him are noted in *SH Accounts* 4. He was grandson of Christopher Gray (ca 1666–1742), who founded the Fulham nursery before 1740, when he published a catalogue. Ca 1764 he was succeeded by William Burchell, and the nurseries continued through the 19th century; see W. Roberts in N&Q 1939, clxxvii. 302; George W. Johnson, *History of English Gardening,* 1829, p. 202; Charles J. Fèret, *Fulham Old and New,* 1900, i. 291, ii. 70–1, iii. 214; James Britten and George S. Boulger, *Biographical Index of Deceased British and Irish Botanists,* edn 1931, p. 128.

2. In the *Song of Songs* iv. 16, vi. 11.
3. Parsley beds are one of the traditional sources of newborn children; see William G. Smith, *Oxford Dictionary of English Proverbs,* Oxford, 1935, p. 353. Mrs Toynbee suggests as HW's source a couplet from Gay's 'Receipt for Stewing Veal' (*Poetical Works,* ed. G. C. Faber, 1926, p. 213):

'Some sprigs[1] of that bed
Where children are bred.

[1] Parsley' (Gay's note).

with a few plants, particularly three Chinese *arbor vitæs;* a dozen of
the New England or Lord Weymouth's pine,[4] which is that beautiful
tree we have so much admired at the Duke of Argyle's for its clean
straight stem, the lightness of its hairy green, and for being feathered
quite to the ground: they should stand in a moist soil, and care must
be taken every year to clear away all plants and trees round them,
that they may have free air and room to expand themselves. Besides
these I shall send you, twelve stone or Italian pines; twelve pinasters,
twelve black spruce firs; two Carolina cherries; thirty evergreen cyti-
sus, a pretty shrub that grows very fast, and may be cut down as you
please; fifty Spanish brooms; and six acacias, the genteelest tree of all,
but you must take care to plant them in a first row, and where they
will be well sheltered, for the least wind tears and breaks them to
pieces. All these are ready, whenever you will give me directions how
and when to send them. They are exceedingly small, as I have but
lately taken to propagate myself; but then they will travel more
safely, will be more sure of living, and will grow faster than larger.
Other sorts of evergreens that you must have, are silver and Scotch
firs; Virginia cedars, which should stand forwards and have nothing
touch them; and above all cypresses, which I think are my chief passion: there is nothing so picturesque when they stand two or three in
a clump upon a little hillock or rising above low shrubs, and particularly near buildings. There is another bit of picture of which I am
fond, and that is, a larch or a spruce fir planted behind a weeping willow, and shooting upwards as the willow depends.[5] I think for courts
about a house or winter gardens, almond trees mixed with evergreens, particularly with Scotch firs have a pretty effect, before anything else comes out; whereas almond trees, being generally planted
among other trees, and being in bloom before other trees have leaves,

4. 'Pinus strobus, otherwise known as
the White Pine, introduced into England
about 1705, and largely planted at Longleat by Thomas Thynne (ca 1640–1714),
first Viscount Weymouth, President of the
Board of Trade and Foreign Plantations,
1702–7' (Toynbee; see also N&Q 1898, 9th
ser. ii. 389, 498).
5. 'The introduction of foreign trees
and plants, which we owe principally to
Archibald duke of Argyle, contributed essentially to the richness of colouring so
peculiar to our modern landscape. The
mixture of various greens, the contrast of
forms between our forest-trees and the
northern and West-Indian firs and pines,
are improvements more recent than Kent,
or but little known to him. The weeping-
willow and every florid shrub, each tree
of delicate or bold leaf, are new tints in
the composition of our gardens. . . . The
Weymouth pine has long been naturalized
here; the patriarch plant still exists at
Longleat. The light and graceful acacia
was known as early' (*Essay on Modern
Gardening* (written 1770), *Works* ii. 537).

have no ground to show the beauty of their blossoms. Gray at Fulham sells cypresses in pots at half a crown apiece; you turn them out of the pot with all their mould and they never fail. I think this is all you mean; if you have any more garden questions or commissions, you know you command my little knowledge.

I am grieved that you have still any complaints left: dissipation in my opinion will be the best receipt, and I don't speak merely for my own sake, when I tell you how much I wish to have you keep your resolution of coming to town before Christmas. I am still more pleased with the promise you make to Strawberry, which you have never seen in its green coat since it cut its teeth.[6] I am here all alone, and shall stay till Tuesday, the day after the Birthday.[7] On Thursday begins our warfare, and if we may believe signs and tokens, our winter will be warlike; I mean at home; I have not much faith in the invasion: her Royal Highness, and his Royal Highness, whose nicknames are Pitt and Fox, are likely to come to an open rupture.[8] His Grace of Newcastle, who, I think has gone under every nickname, waits I believe to see to which he shall cling.

There have been two *Worlds* by my Lord Chesterfield[9] lately very pretty: the rest very indifferent.

I beg my best compliments to Mrs Whetenhall, and am with great wishes for your health and tranquillity

Yours most sincerely

H. W.

To Montagu, Tuesday 25 November 1755

Arlington Street, Nov. 25, 1755.

I HAVE been so hurried since I came to town,[1] and so inclosed in the House of Commons,[2] that I have not been able to write a line sooner. I now write to notify that your plants will set out according

6. Montagu's last visit when SH was in 'greenth' seems to have been in 1751 (see *ante* 8 June 1754). Presumably SH 'cut its teeth' with the completion of the remodeling in 1753.

7. The King's.
8. See *post* 25 Nov. 1755.
9. No. 146, 16 Oct. 1755, on country

captivity, and No. 148, 30 Oct., on good breeding (Earl of Chesterfield, *Miscellaneous Works*, 1777, i pt ii. 199, 203).

1. HW came to town between the 9th and the 13th (HW to Bentley 16 Nov. 1755).
2. By debates on the Address, the trea-

to your direction next Monday, and are ordered to be left at Nampt-wich.[3]

I differ with the doctors about planting evergreens in spring:[4] if it happens to be wet weather, it may be better, than exposing them to a first winter; but the cold dry winds that generally prevail in spring, are ten times more pernicious. In my own opinion the end of September is the best season, for then they shoot before the hard weather comes. But the plants I send you are so very small, that they are equally secure in any season, and would bear removing in the middle of summer. A handful of dung will clothe them for the whole winter.

There is a most dreadful account of an earthquake in Lisbon, but several people will not believe it. There have been lately such earth-quakes and water-quakes, and rocks rent and other strange phenomena that one would think the world exceedingly out of repair.[5] I am not prophet enough to believe that such convulsions relate solely to the struggles between Mr Pitt and Mr Fox, or even portend any between the Georges and James's.[6] You have already heard, I suppose, that Pitt, Legge, and George Grenville are dismissed;[7] and that Sir George Lyttelton is Chancellor of the Exchequer. My Lord Temple says, that Sir George said he would quit his place when they did, and that he has kept his word! The world expects your cousin to resign, but I believe all efforts are used to retain him. *Joan, the fair maid of Saxe-Gotha,*[8] did not speak to Mr Fox[9] or Sir George when they kissed her hand last Sunday. No more places are vacated or filled up yet.

It is an age since I have heard from Mr Bentley; the war or the

ties, Fox's circular letter, and the number of seamen (*Mem. Geo. II* ii. 47–76).

3. Nantwich, Cheshire, the nearest town to Hankelow, for which the trees were apparently designed.

4. John Dicks, in his *New Gardener's Dictionary,* 1771, *sub* fir, pine, cedar, etc., recommends that they be planted in the spring.

5. The great Lisbon earthquake, which almost entirely destroyed the city, occurred 1 Nov. The news reached England via Paris, and was reported in the *London Evening Post* 22–5 Nov. 1755. For a week or so there had been accounts from nearer places of the effects of the same earth-

quake, which was felt all over Europe; ibid. 13–15 Nov. 1755 et seq.

6. The Jacobites.

7. Pitt broke with the government on the question of Hanoverian subsidies and protection; Legge and Grenville followed him into opposition; see *Mem. Geo. II* ii. 33–47.

8. The Princess of Wales (Joan, The Fair Maid of Kent, was widow of the Black Prince).

9. He became Secretary of State in place of Sir Thomas Robinson, who was given the Great Wardrobe and a pension (ibid. ii. 43–4).

weather have interrupted all communication. Adieu! Let me know at your leisure when one is likely to see you.

Yours ever

H. W.

To MONTAGU, Saturday 20 December 1755

Arlington Street, Dec. 20th, 1755.

I AM very much pleased that you are content with what are to be trees a thousand years hence; though they were the best my Libanus[1] afforded, I was afraid you would think I had sent you a bundle of picktooths, instead of pines and firs; may you live to chat under their shade! I am still more pleased to hear that you are to be happy in some good fortune to the Colonel;[2] he deserves it, but alas! what a claim is that! Whatever makes him happy, makes you so and consequently me.

A regular opposition, composed of immense abilities has entertained us for this month. George Grenville, Legge, a Dr Hay,[3] a Mr Elliot[4] have shone; Charles Townshend has lightened, Pitt has rode in the whirlwind and directed the storm[5] with abilities beyond the common reach of the genie of a tempest. As soon as that storm has a little spent its fury, the dew of preferments begins to fall and fatten the land. Moses and Aaron[6] differ indeed a little in which shall dispense the manna, and both struggle for their separate tribes. Earl Gower is Privy Seal, the Lords Darlington and Duplin joint Paymasters; Lord Gage,[7] Paymaster of the Pensions, Mr Obrien[8] in the Treasury; that old rag of a dishclout ministry, Harry Furnese,[8a] is to be the other Lord. Lord Bateman[9] and Dick Edgcumbe are the new

1. See *ante* 8 Nov. 1755, n. 1a; by extension HW probably means 'nursery of cedars.'

2. Charles Montagu, who had been Lt-Col. of the 11th Foot, was promoted to a colonelcy and given command of a new regiment, the 61st Foot (*Army Lists;* GM 1755, xxv. 572).

3. Dr George Hay (1715–78), D.C.L., 1742; Kt, 1773; lawyer and politician.

4. Sir Gilbert Elliot (1722–77), 3d Bt of Minto, 1766; statesman, philosopher, and poet.

5. 'Rides in the whirlwind, and directs the storm' (Addison, *The Campaign*, l. 292; Pope, *Dunciad* iii. 264).

6. Newcastle and Fox; see HW to Mann 21 Dec. 1755, where, to a full list of promotions and preferments, HW has added the affiliation, whether with Newcastle or Fox, of each man.

7. William Hall Gage (1718–91), 2d Vct Gage.

8. Percy Wyndham (later Wyndham-O'Brien) (ca 1713–74), cr. (1756) E. of Thomond.

8a. Henry Furnese (d. 1756); M.P. Dover 1720–34, Morpeth 1738–41, New Romney 1741–56 (GM 1756, xxvi. 451).

9. John Bateman (1721–1802), 2d Vct Bateman.

Admirals; Rigby, Soame Jennings,[10] and Talbot,[11] the Welsh judge, to your amazement and mine (for it seems as odd as if my Lord Chancellor were to turn Groom of the Chambers to my Lady Fitzroy) Lords of Trade. The Duke of Leeds,[12] Cofferer; Lord Sandwich[13] scrambles into Chief Justice in Eyre; Ellis[14] and Lord Sandys, (*autre* dishclout) divide the half of the Treasury of Ireland; George Selwyn, Paymaster of the Board of Works; Arundel is to have a pension in Ireland, and Lord Hilsborough[15] succeeds him as Treasurer of the Chambers, though I thought he was as fond of his white staff, as my Lord Hobart[16] will be, who is to have it.—There if you love new politics!—You understand, to make these vacancies, that Charles Townshend and John Pitt[17] are added to the dismissed and dead.

My Lord Townshend[18] is dying; the young Lord Pembroke[19] marries the charming Lady Betty Spenser. The French are thought to have *passed eldest* as to England, and to intend *to take in*[20] Hanover. I know an old potentate who had rather have the gout in his stomach, than in that little toe. Adieu! I have sent your letter;[21] make my compliments and come to town.

Yours ever

H. W.

10. Soame Jenyns (1704–87), politician and author.

11. Hon. John Talbot (d. 1756), 3d son of 1st Bn Talbot; M.P. Brecon 1734–54; Ilchester 1754–6; Justice for counties of Chester, Flint, Denbigh, and Montgomery, 1740; Lord of Trade 1755–6 (Collins, *Peerage*, 1812, v. 235–6).

12. Thomas Osborne (1713–89), 4th D. of Leeds.

13. Lord Sandys became Chief Justice in Eyre; Sandwich, Joint Vice-Treasurer of Ireland.

14. Welbore Ellis (1713–1802), cr. (1794) Bn Mendip; politician.

15. Wills Hill (1718–93), 2d Vct Hillsborough; cr. (1751) E. of Hillsborough; cr. (1789) M. of Downshire; Comptroller of the Household 1754–5.

16. John Hobart (1723–93), styled Lord Hobart; 2d E. of Buckinghamshire, 1756; Comptroller of the Household 1755–6.

17. John Pitt (d. 1787), of Encombe, Dorset; M.P. Wareham 1734–51, 1761–8; Dorchester 1751–61; Commissioner of Trade 1745–55; Lord of the Admiralty,

1756 (John Hutchins, *History . . . of Dorset*, 3d edn 1861–73, iv. 91).

18. Charles Townshend (1700–64), 3d Vct Townshend.

19. Henry Herbert (1734–94), 10th E. of Pembroke; m. (1756) Lady Elizabeth Spencer (1737–1831).

20. Terms probably used at this time in the game of loo, and, at other times, in brag, gleek, etc. 'To pass eldest' is a 'loophrase' (HW to Lady Ossory 18 Jan. 1792); 'He who is eldest hand hath the privilege of passing by the benefit thereof [being on the left of the dealer he is the first to play], that is, he hath the advantage of hearing what every one will say, and, at last, may play, or not play, according as he finds his game good or bad' (Richard Seymour, *Compleat Gamester*, 6th edn 1739, p. 210). 'To take in' is to discard part of one's hand and take new cards in its place; apparently not permitted in 1739, it is described in *Hoyle's Games Improved*, New York, 1829, pp. 154, 170.

21. Probably a letter to be franked by HW; many such are mentioned later.

To Montagu, Tuesday 30 December 1755

Arlington Street, Dec. 30, 1755.

AS I know how much you are my friend and take part in my joy, I can't help communicating to you an incident that has given me much pleasure. You know how much I love Mr Mann[1]—well, I won't enter into that, nor into a detail of many hardships[2] that he has suffered lately, which made me still more eager to serve him. As some regiments have been just given away, I cast my eyes about to see if I could not help him to clothing. Among the rest there was one new colonel, whom I could not assume enough to call my friend, but who is much connected with one that is so. As the time pressed, I did not stay to go round about, but addressed myself directly to the person himself.—But I was disappointed—the disaster was that he had left his quarters and was come to town. Though I immediately gave it up in my own mind, knew how incessantly he would be pressed from much more powerful quarters, and concluded he would be engaged, I wrote again—that letter was as useless as the first—and from what reason do you think?—Why, this person, in spite of all solicitations, nay, previous to any, had already thought of Mr Mann, had recollected it would oblige me and my friend in the country, and had actually given his clothing to Mr Mann, before he received either of my letters.[3] Judge how agreeably I have been surprised, and how much the manner has added to my obligation! You will be still more pleased, when you hear the character of this officer, which I tell you willingly, because I know you country gentlemen are apt to contract prejudices and to fancy that no virtues grow out of your own shire. Yet by this one sample you will find them connected with several circumstances that are apt to nip their growth. He is of as good a family as any in England, yet in this whole transaction he has treated me with as much humility as if I was of as good a family, and as if I had obliged him, not he me. In the next place, I have no power to oblige him: then though he is young and in the army, he is as good, as temperate, as meek, as if he was a curate on preferment; and yet with all these meek virtues, nobody has distinguished themselves by more personal bravery—and what is still more to his praise, though he has so

1. Galfridus Mann (d. Dec. 1756; see *post* 23 Dec. 1756), Horace Mann's brother; an army clothier.

2. He was at this time very ill, probably of tuberculosis (see HW to Mann 25 Jan. 1756, and succeeding letters to Mann).

3. Both are missing.

greatly established his courage, he is as regular in his duty, and submits as patiently to all the tedious exiles and fatigues of it, as if he had no merit at all—but I will say no more, lest you imagine that the present warmth of my gratitude makes me exaggerate—no, you will not, when you know that all I have said, relates to your own brother Colonel Charles Montagu. I did not think he could have added still to my satisfaction, but he has, by giving me hopes of seeing you in town next week—till then adieu!

Yours as entirely as is consistent with
my devotedness to your brother

Hor. Walpole

PS. I must not forget to thank you much for your pork.

To Montagu, Tuesday 20 April 1756

Arlington Street, April 20, 1756.

YOUR steward called on me just as I was going to keep my New-market[1] at Strawberry Hill; he promised to leave me the direction to the statuary;[2] but as I have not heard from him, I wish you would send it me.

The cold and the wet have driven me back to London, empty London! where we are more afraid of the deluge than the invasion. The French are said to be sailed for Minorca,[3] which I hold to be a good omen of their not coming hither, for if they took England, Port Mahon I should think would scarcely hold out.

Pray don't die, like a country body, because it is the fashion for gentlefolks to die in London; it is the *bon ton* now to die; one can't show one's face without being a death's head: Mrs Bethel and I are come strangely into fashion; but true critics in mode object to our having underjaws, and maintain that we are not dead *comme il faut*.

1. Newmarket races opened 19 April, the day after Easter; HW alludes to his annual Easter houseparty (see below, n. 26).

2. James Lovell (*post* 28 Aug. 1756). His shop was near Cavendish Square (GM 1760, xxx. 201). Mrs K. A. Esdaile has kindly supplied the following list of his works:

Monument to Benjamin Lord Mildmay (d.

1759), Chelmsford. 'Very fine ornate work.'
Wolfe monument, Westerham.
Mantelpiece in the state bedchamber at Stowe.
Two marble chimney-pieces in the state dining-room, Stowe.
Montagu monument, Horton.

3. They besieged Port Mahon, which fell 29 June.

The young Lady Exeter[4] died almost suddenly, and has handsomely confirmed her father's will, by leaving her money to her Lord only for his life, and then to Thomas Townshend.[5] Sir William Lowther[6] has made a charming will, and been as generous at his death, as he was in his short life; he has left thirteen legacies of £5000 each to friends, of which you know by sight Reynolds,[7] Mrs Brudenel's son,[8] and young Turner.[9] He has given £1700 a year, that is, I suppose, £1700 to old Mrs Lowther[10]—what an odd circumstance! A woman passing an hundred years to receive a legacy from a man of 27! After her it goes to Lord George Cavendish.[11] £600 per year he gives to another Mrs Lowther,[12] to be divided afterwards between Lord Frederick and Lord John.[13] Lord Charles,[14] his uncle, is residuary legatee. But what do you think of young Sir James Lowther,[15] who, not of

4. Letitia Townshend (ca 1726–56), m. (1748 or 1749) Brownlow Cecil (1725–93), 9th E. of Exeter. She left £70,000 (*Grenville Papers,* ed. William J. Smith, 1852–3, i. 157).

5. Hon. Thomas Townshend (1701–80), politician and scholar (DNB); he was a nephew of Hon. Horatio Townshend (d. 1751), whose only surviving child was Lady Exeter.

6. Sir William Lowther (b. 1727), 3d Bt, of Marske, Yorkshire; d. 15 April 1756 (GM 1756, xxvi. 206), not 1753, as in GEC, *Baronetage.* His will is P.C.C. Glazier 110 from which the names and amounts of legacies in this letter are derived.

7. Francis Reynolds (d. 1773), of Strangeways, Lancs; father of 2d and 3d Barons Ducie; Whig M.P. Lancaster 1745–73 (Collins, *Peerage,* 1812, vii. 412–13; W. D. Pink and Alfred B. Beavan, *Parliamentary Representation of Lancashire,* 1889, p. 125).

8. George Bridges Brudenell (1725–1801), of Ayston, Rutland; M.P. Rutland 1754–61, 1768–90; Stamford 1761–8; Equerry to George II; Clerk of the Green Cloth, 1765; 'a great friend of Lord Lincoln,' and a follower of Newcastle (Lewis B. Namier, *Structure of Politics at the Accession of George III,* 1929, ii. 533); son of Hon. James Brudenell, and Susan, dau. of Bartholomew Burton, M.P. (Venn, *Alumni Cantab.;* Collins, *Peerage,* 1812, iii. 497).

9. Charles Turner (ca 1726–83), 1st Bt (1782), of Kirkleatham, Yorkshire; as M.P. for York (1768–83), a devoted adherent of

Rockingham. Though a great sportsman, he denounced the Game Laws, and was considered 'one of the most eccentric men who ever sat in Parliament' (Wraxall, *Memoirs* ii. 267; *Letters of Laurence Sterne,* ed. Lewis P. Curtis, Oxford, 1935, p. 382 n).

10. Hannah, 5th dau. of Alderman Robert Lowther; maid of honour to Queens Mary and Anne; d. 1757, aged 106 (GM 1757, xxvii. 46), or 103 (Collins, *Peerage,* 1812, v. 702). Her legacy was £5000, and not an annuity. Though HW is substantially correct in his list of legatees, his figures, as is often the case, are incorrect.

11. Lord George Cavendish (d. 1794), 2d son of 3d D. of Devonshire; M.P. Weymouth 1751–4; Derby 1754–94; Comptroller of the Household, 1761 (Collins, *Peerage,* 1812, i. 358).

12. Probably his aunt, Katherine Lowther, who got a legacy of £6000, not an annuity.

13. Lord John Cavendish (1732–96), politician (DNB). Lords George, Frederick, and John Cavendish were first cousins of Sir William Lowther. His will gave them interests in land of unascertainable value.

14. Lord Charles Cavendish (ca 1693–1783), 3d son of 2d D. of Devonshire; M.P. Heytesbury 1725–7; Westminster 1727–34; Derby 1734–41; F.R.S., trustee of the British Museum (Collins, *Peerage,* 1812, i. 355–6; GM 1783, liii. 366, 'a most amiable character, and an excellent philosopher').

15. Sir James Lowther (1736–1802), 5th

age, becomes master of one or two and forty thousand pounds a year. England will become a Heptarchy, the property of six or seven people! The Duke of Bedford is fallen to be not above the fourth rich man in the island.

Poor Lord Digby[16] is likely to escape happily at last, after being cut for the stone, and bearing the preparation and execution with such heroism, that waking with the noise of the surgeons, he asked if that was to be the day? 'Yes.' 'How soon will they be ready?' 'Not for some time'—'Then let me sleep till they are.' He was cut by a new instrument of Hawkins,[17] which reduced an age of torture to but one minute.

The Duke has appeared in form on the causeway[18] in Hyde Park with my Lady Coventry; it is the new office, where all lovers now are entered. How happy she must be with Billy[19] and Bully![20] I hope she will not mistake, and call the former by the nickname of the latter! At a great supper t'other night at Lord Hertford's, if she was not the best humoured creature in the world, I should have made her angry; she said in a very vulgar accent, if she drank any more, she should be *muckibus*[21]—'Lord!' said Lady Mary Coke, 'what is that?'—'Oh! it is Irish for *sentimental*.'

There is a new Morocco ambassador,[22] who declares for Lady Caroline Petersham, preferably to Lady Coventry: Lady Caroline Fox[23] says he is the best bred of all the foreign ministers, and at one dinner said more obliging things than Mirepoix did during his whole embassy. He is so fashionable that George Selwyn says he is sure my Lady Winchelsea[24] will ogle him instead of Haslang.[25]

Bt, of Lowther; cr. (1784) E. of Lonsdale; see HW to Mann 18 April 1756.

16. Edward Digby (1730–57), 6th Bn Digby.

17. Caesar Hawkins (1711–86), Bt, 1778; surgeon; inventor of the cutting gorget.

18. Not located.

19. The Duke of Cumberland.

20. Lord Bolingbroke. HW refers frequently to 'her passion for the young Lord Bolingbroke' (HW to Bentley 2 March 1754 and *post* 6 Nov. 1756, 19 April 1760).

21. OED (giving this passage as the sole use): '[a humorous formation from muck *sb*.1, with the ending of a Latin ablative plural] Intoxicated, tipsy, fuddled.' Mr Whibley asks, 'Had Lady Coventry ever heard of a Latin ablative?'

22. Not identified.

23. Lady Georgiana Caroline Lennox (1723–74), m. (1744) Henry Fox, cr. (1763) Bn Holland; cr. (1762) Baroness Holland. Mrs George Grenville, writing to her husband 20 April 1756, confirms the ambassador's charm, but adds that 'he does not speak a word in any known language' (*Grenville Papers*, ed. William J. Smith, 1852–3, i. 157–8).

24. Mary Palmer (d. 1757), m. (1738) Daniel Finch, 7th E. of Winchilsea.

25. Joseph Xaver (ca 1700–83), Freiherr (later Graf) von Haszlang, Bavarian minister to England 1741–83 (*Genealogisch*

I shall send you the fruits of my last party to Strawberry; Dick Edgcumbe, George Selwyn and Williams[26] were with me; we composed a coat of arms for the two clubs at White's, which is actually engraving, from a very pretty painting of Edgcumbe,[27] whom Mr Chute, as Strawberry-King-at-arms has appointed our chief Herald painter. Here is the blazon:

Vert (for card-table) between three parolis proper, on a chevron sable (for hazard table) two rouleaus in saltire between two dice, proper. In a canton, sable, a white ball (for election) argent.

Supporters. An old knave of *clubs,* on the dexter; a young knave, on the sinister side, both accoutred, proper.

Crest. Issuing out of an earl's coronet (Lord Darlington's) an arm, shaking a dice box, all proper.

Motto, (alluding to the crest) *Cog*it amor nummi.[27a]

The arms encircled, by a claret bottle ticket,[27b] by way of order.

By the time I hope to see you at Strawberry Hill, there will be a second volume of the Horatiana ready for the press;[28] or a full and true account of the bloody civil wars of the house of Walpole, being a narrative of the unhappy differences between Horatio and Horace Walpoles—in short, the old wretch, who aspires to be one of the Heptarchy,[29] and who I think will live as long as old Mrs Lowther, has

[later *Neue Genealogische*] *Historische Nachrichten,* Leipzig, 1740 p. 645, 1741 p. 771, 1750 pp. 593–4, 1751 p. 81; Ernst von Destouches, *Geschichte des Königlich Bayerischen Haus-Ritter-Ordens,* Bamberg, 1890, p. 81; GM 1783, liii pt i. 454, 540). About him see HW to Mann 5 June 1780, BM, *Satiric Prints* No. 4467, iv. 690, and an extremely unflattering account in *Town and Country Magazine* 1770, ii. 513, which charges him with pawning the candlesticks from the embassy chapel (p. 519).

26. George James 'Gilly' Williams (ca 1719–1805), 4th son of William Peere Williams, barrister, and brother of Sir Hutchins Williams, Bt; had a place in the Excise Office, and in 1774 became Receiver-General, worth £2500 a year. With George Selwyn and the Hon. Richard Edgcumbe he formed HW's 'out-of-town party' at SH at Christmas and Easter, an association commemorated by Reynolds's conversation-piece of the three (*post* 30 Dec. 1761). Williams is best known for his letters to Selwyn, which contain the most penetrat-

ing comments on HW made by any of his English contemporaries (see COLE i. p. xxiv).

27. Bought by Arthur's Club at SH sale (SH xxii. 12); reproduced in [W. B. Boulton], *History of White's,* 1892, i. 78. It was engraved by Charles Grignion the elder, and some impressions (such as those on pink or red paper) were perhaps made at SH; one at Eton is in green ink.

27a. A parody of 'crescit amor nummi' (Juv. xiv. 139). *Cog* is a pun: cog, 'To practise certain tricks in throwing dice' (OED).

27b. A metal tag attached to the bottle by a chain.

28. The 'first volume' no doubt concerned the match between Miss Nicoll and Lord Orford, the second the squabble over the mutual entail of the Orford estates. HW probably did not intend to print the documents; see his correspondence with his uncle Horace, Lord Walpole. The MSS of these accounts are now WSL.

29. See *ante* 30 Dec. 1755.

accomplished such a scene of abominable avarice and dirt, that I, notwithstanding my desire to veil the miscarriages of my race, have been obliged to drag him and all his doings into light—but I won't anticipate—adieu!

Yours ever

H. W.

To Montagu, Tuesday 4 May 1756

Arlington Street
May 4th, as they call it, but
the weather and the almanac
of my feeling affirm it is
December—

I WILL answer your questions as well as I can, though I must do it shortly, for I write in a sort of hurry.

Osborn could not find Lord Cuts,[1] but I have discovered another in an auction for which I shall bid for you. Mr Müntz[2] has been at Strawberry these three weeks, tight at work, so your picture is little advanced; but as soon as he returns, it shall be finished. I have chosen the marbles for your tomb;[3] but you told me you had agreed on the price, which your steward now says I was to settle. Mr Bentley still waits the conclusion of the session, before he can come amongst us again: everything has passed with great secrecy: one would think the devil was afraid of being tried for his life, for he has not even directed Madam Bentley to the Old Baily.[4] Mr Mann[5] does not mend, but how should he in such weather!

We wait with impatience for news from Minorca. Here is a Prince of Nassau Welbourg,[6] who wants to marry Princess Caroline of Orange: he is well-looking enough, but a little too tame to cope with

1. That is, a print of John Cutts (1661–1707), cr. (1690) Bn Cutts; soldier; m. (1) (1690) Elizabeth Trevor, née Clark, Montagu's grandmother.

2. Johann Heinrich Müntz (1727–98), Swiss painter employed by HW through 1759 (Ulrich Thieme and Felix Becker, *Allgemeines Lexikon der bildenden Künstler*, Leipzig, 1907—; HW to Bentley 3 Nov. 1754). The picture is doubtless the same mentioned *post* 12 and ca 13 July 1756.

3. Of Henrietta Montagu.

4. Apparently some legal process for the relief of Bentley's debts had been undertaken; but its nature is not clear.

5. Galfridus Mann.

6. Karl Christian (1735–88), Prince of Nassau-Weilburg; m. (1760) Wilhelmina Carolina (1743–87), Princess of Orange, granddaughter of George II (Wilhelm Karl Prinz von Isenburg, *Stammtafeln*, Berlin, 1935–7, table 113).

such blood. He is established at the Duke of Richmond's[7] with a large train for two months. He was last night at a great ball at my Lady Townshend's, whose Audrey[8] will certainly get Lord George Lenox.[9] George Selwyn t'other night, seeing Lady Euston with Lady Caroline Petersham, said, 'There's my Lady Eus*ton*[10] and my Lady us'd *to't.*'

Adieu!

Yours ever
H. W.

I inclose a print of the arms.

I forgot another bon mot of G. Selwyn's; somebody said, they should not dislike Mrs Deering;[11] 'Ah!' said he, 'if you was to see *la petite* Guildford!'[12]

To Montagu, Wednesday 19 May 1756

Address: To George Montagu Esq. at Greatworth near Brackley, Northamptonshire. Free Hor. Walpole. *Postmark:* 20 MA.

Arlington Street, May 19, 1756.

NOTHING will be more agreeable to me than to see you at Strawberry Hill; the weather does not seem to be of my mind, and will not invite you—I believe the French have taken the sun.

7. Charles Lennox (1735–1806), 3d D. of Richmond, Duc d'Aubigny; intimate friend and correspondent of HW's; m. Lady Mary Bruce, dau. of Lady Ailesbury by her first husband.

8. Hon. Audrey Townshend (d. 1781); in 1750 Lord March (later third Duke of Richmond) describes her in an amusing letter to Henry Fox as 'a great coquette'; he had a youthful passion for her (Earl of March, *A Duke and his Friends*, 1911, ii. 707–11). She did not marry Lord George, but eloped with Capt. Robert Orme (Burke, *Peerage*), who had been Braddock's aide-de-camp in America (see Stanley Pargellis, *Military Affairs in North America, 1748–1765*, New York, 1936, p. 98 n). Mrs Delany details the elopement of 'that vile Miss T. who has run away with Mr O., and poor Mrs O. *run mad,* and gone into the bedlam' (Delany, *Correspondence* iii. 452). Rev. Edmund Pyle adds that they had gone to Flanders, that she had given him £14,000, was with child, and 'besides all her other infamy . . . deeply in debt to all sorts of trades-people' (*Memoirs of*

a Royal Chaplain, 1729–1763, ed. Albert Hartshorne, 1905, p. 272). No doubt this affair was responsible for the apparent termination, at about this time, of his military career. In 1769 she appears again at an election of a Master of Ceremonies at Bath, where 'Mrs Hillman, our acquaintance, and Mrs Orme (Lady Townshend's daughter) had a fight, and Mrs Hillman was knocked down' (*Series of Letters of the First Earl of Malmesbury,* ed. [3d] Earl of Malmesbury, 1870, i. 179).

9. Lord George Henry Lennox (1737–1805), 2d son of 2d D. of Richmond; Gen., 1793 (DNB); M.P. Chichester 1761–7, Sussex 1767–90.

10. Hon. Anne Liddell (ca 1738–1804), m. (1) (1756) Augustus Henry Fitzroy, styled E. of Euston, 3d D. of Grafton, 1757; divorced 1769; m. (2) (1769) John Fitzpatrick, 2d E. of Upper Ossory; she was HW's friend and correspondent.

11. Unidentified.

12. Apparently Lady Guilford was even larger than Mrs Deering.

Among other captures I hear their King has taken another English mistress, a Mrs Pope,[1] who took her degrees in gallantry some years ago. She went to Versailles with the famous Mrs Quon;[2] the King took notice of them; he was told *that* they were not so rigid as *all* other English women are—mind, I don't give you any part of this history for authentic; you know we can have no news *now* from France but what we run.[2a] I have rambled so, that I forgot what I intended to say; if ever we can have spring, it must be soon; I propose to expect you any day you please after Sunday se'nnight the thirtieth. Let me know your resolution—and pray tell me in what magazine is the Strawberry-ballad![3] I should have proposed an earlier day to you, but next week the Prince of Nassau is to breakfast at Strawberry Hill, and I know your aversion to clashing with grandeurs.

As I have already told you one mob story of a king, I will tell you another; *they say,* that the night the Hanover troops were voted, *he*[4] sent, that is, *a King* sent for his German cook, and said, 'Get me a very good supper; get me all de rarities; I don't mind expense.'

I tremble lest his Hanoverians should be encamped at Hounslow; Strawberry would become an inn, all the Misses would breakfast there, to go and see the camp!

My Lord Denbigh[5] is going to marry a fortune, I forget her name: my Lord Gower asked him how long the honeymoon would last? He replied, 'Don't tell me of the honeymoon; it is harvest moon with me.' Adieu!

Yours ever

H. W.

1. Unidentified. The other English mistress HW refers to was no doubt Mary Louise Murphy (ca 1749–1815), who was of Irish parentage; see Maurice, Comte Fleury, *Louis XV intime et les petites maîtresses,* 4th edn 1909, pp. 111–20, 127–9, 165, 205; HW to Bentley 18 May 1754.

2. Deodata Roach (ca 1731–1759), m. (ca 1743) Richard Quane; she earned her fame playing Desdemona at a special performance at Drury Lane in 1751 ([John Genest], *Some Account of the English Stage,* Bath, 1832, iv. 325; HW to Mann 13 March 1751; Horace Bleackley, in N&Q 1916, cxxxiii. 272–3). 'Mrs Quon and her

sister Miss La Roche were famous demireps of the day—and wonderfully handsome' (Mrs Piozzi). In Pierre Manuel, *La Police de Paris dévoilée* [1791?], ii. 216, there is a reference, as of about this date, to 'la Dame Quane, anglaise, maîtresse du Duc d'Olonne.'

2a. That is, smuggle.

3. The Earl of Bath's verses (*ante* 17 July 1755) appeared in GM 1756, xxvi. 192.

4. George II.

5. Basil Feilding (1719–1800), 6th E. of Denbigh, m. (1) (1757) Mary Cotton (d. 1782) 'a fortune of £30,000' (GEC).

From MONTAGU, Wednesday 26 May 1756

G.D. 15/8, No. 722.

In reply to *ante* 19 May 1756; June 1 fell on Tuesday in 1756.

Greatworth, May 26 [1756].

I THINK of being with you at Strawberry Hill at dinner on Tuesday next the first of June as I am sure I shall not be offended with a garden full of white roses; they are all withered since the orange[1] has been there. I hope to see, however, the place in beauty and the flowering shrubs out for you are a month forwarder than I am here northwards, nor can I conveniently defer my journey longer, seeing I am to go soon to Cheshire.

You know I conclude young Rice is to be married to Lord Talbot's daughter.[2]

The Colonel's regiment is just ordered to Bristol which alarms me something as I am [?afraid][3] they may send him the Lord knows where. I have only time to add I am most truly yours,

G. M.

To MONTAGU, Sunday ca 6 June 1756

Hitherto printed among letters of 1757; the reference to Lord Radnor (n. 1 below) definitely locates it in June 1756.

Address: To Mr Montagu.

[Strawberry Hill] Sunday evening [ca June 6, 1756].

I LEAVE Mr Müntz in commission to do the honours of Strawberry to you: if he succeeds well, will you be troubled with him in your chaise to London on Wednesday? He will tell you the *history* of Queen Mab[1] being attacked—not in her virtue, but in her very pal-

1. So in MS.
2. Cecil (1735–93), dau. and heir of William Talbot, 1st E. Talbot; m. (1756) George Rice; Baroness Dinevor in her own right, 1782.
3. Montagu omitted a word on turning the page after 'am.'

1. The Earl of Radnor, whose estate was called 'Mabland' by HW and Bentley from its profusion of statues (HW to Bentley 18 May 1754; *ante* ca 5 Oct. 1747, n. 1). The attack is reported in GM 1756, xxxvi. 309: June 3—'About one o'clock in the afternoon the Earl of Radnor was audaciously attacked in his own house by a villain, who demanded immediate relief, or his lordship was a dead man.'

ace—if all this does not fill up the evening, and you should have no engagement to your aunt Crossby,[2] or to your grandmother,[3] you know how welcome you will be at Clivden.[4] Adieu!

From MONTAGU, ca Monday 21 June 1756

G.D. 15/8, No. 768.

Among letters of 1761 in Kimbolton MSS, but, from references to the Byng episode and the statuary, clearly written at the time of Montagu's visit to London in 1756. The assigned month and day are conjectural; HW was at Arlington Street 14 June (HW to Mann); the first news about Byng and the Gibraltar officers had been received 3 June (*Mem. Geo. II* ii. 214).

Address: To the Honourable Mr Walpole.

[London, ca June 21, 1756].

TO be sure you will think me the greatest brute in the world, after having made an inn of your house and been so agreeably entertained there with your company, to run away without saying a word; but I must tell you it was really a mistake that has caused me a good deal of trouble, for I thought you was not to go till tomorrow and therefore came this morning to Arlington Street to your levee and found only a drab of a maid with her hair about her ears and Mr Myntz, who I carried with me to help abuse the statuary, who has not struck a stroke since you was there. I am horribly fretted at him. London is outrageous about our admirals, Colonel Cornwallis and Co.[1] I must run away as fast as I can lest I am taken prisoner by the

2. Mrs Cosby.

3. That is, to hunting among HW's prints for one of Elizabeth Clark (ca 1655–93), m. (1) (1671) William Morley of Glynde, Sussex (d. 1679); m. (2) (1679) John Trevor (ca 1652–86) of Plas Teg, Flint; m. (3) (1690) John Cutts, 1st Bn Cutts. Montagu's mother was a child of her second marriage (John Comber, *Sussex Genealogies, Lewes Centre,* Cambridge, 1933, pp. 194, 291).

4. The cottage, Little Strawberry Hill, on the edge of HW's property towards Teddington, occupied by Mrs Clive (see HW to Bentley 3 Nov. 1754).

1. Admiral Hon. John Byng (1704–57) was sent with the Mediterranean fleet to the relief of Minorca. At Gibraltar he was refused reinforcements by the officers of the garrison, who themselves feared a siege; Col. Edward Cornwallis, in command of the 24th Foot stationed there, was one of those whose timidity aroused such resentment at home (HW to Chute 8 June 1756; *Army Lists*). Byng, after an indecisive meeting with the French fleet off Port Mahon 20 May, withdrew and was recalled to be court-martialled; HW was active in trying, unsuccessfully, to save him from execution; see *Mem. Geo. II* ii. 209 et seq.

French; perhaps I may walk without chains or a lighted taper a fortnight longer.—Adieu! I wish you your health and am most truly yours,

G. M.

To MONTAGU, Monday 12 July 1756

Strawberry Hill, July 12, 1756.

WHEN I have told you that Mr Müntz has finished the drapery of your picture and the copy of it, and asked you whither and how they must be sent, I think I have done all the business of my letter; except telling you, that if you think of conveying them through Moreland, he is gone a-soldiering. All the world is going the same road, except Mr Müntz, who had rather be knocked of the head for fame, than paint for it. He goes tomorrow to Kingston to see the great drum pass by to Cobham, as women go to take a last look of their captains. The Duke of Marlbro and his grandfather's triumphal car[1] are to close the procession—what would his granddame, if she were alive, say to this pageant? If the war lasts, I think well enough of him to believe he will earn a sprig, but I have no notion of trying on a crown of laurel, before I had acquired it. The French are said to be embarked at Dunkirk—lest I should seem to know more than any minister, I will not pretend to guess whither they are bound. I have been but one night in town, and my head sung ballads about Admiral Byng, all night, as one is apt to dream of the masquerade minuet: the streets swarm so with lampoons, that I begin to fancy myself a minister's son again.

I am going tomorrow to Park Place; and the first week in August into Yorkshire. If I hear that you are at Greatworth, that is if you will disclose your motions to me for the first fortnight of that month; I will try if I cannot make it in my road either going or coming. I know nothing of roads, but Lord Strafford[2] is to send me a route, and I should be glad to ask you how you do for one night—but don't ex-

---

1. *London Evening Post* 10–13 July 1756 reports that a large train of artillery left the Tower 'yesterday,' to encamp at Byfleet, near Cobham, Surrey. 'The drum-major rode in a kind of triumphal car drawn by six grey horses. . . . The Duke of Marlborough, Master-General of the Ordnance, was at the Tower to see the procession.'

2. William Wentworth (1722–91), 2d E. of Strafford; HW's friend and correspondent. HW visited him at Wentworth Castle, Yorkshire, in August (HW to Bentley Aug. 1756).

pect me, don't be disappointed about me, and of all things don't let so uncertain a scheme derange the least thing in the world that you have to do.

There are going to be as many camps and little armies, as when England was an Heptarchy. Adieu!

Yours faithfully
H. W.

From Montagu, ca Tuesday 13 July 1756

G.D. 15/8, No. 813.
Written the day HW's letter of 12 July was received; i.e. 13–15 July.

[Greatworth, ca July 13, 1756].

MR BENTLEY and Mr Muntz said they would come to Great-worth when you was to make your tour to Yorkshire which will give me great pleasure. Now I should be glad to know about what time that will be that I may not be from home and that I may regulate some little jaunts that I have so as to be ready to receive them and send my equipage to Buckingham to pick them up and convey them here.

I think it an age since I have heard from you and you have had many a comfortable wet evening to put pen to paper to tell me how you do and how the world goes on.

Lady Pomfret[1] had a sort of a box made up for her and her girls[2] near the Vice-chancellor[3] in the theatre.[4] She was violently clapped as she came in, appeared sulky and ill-dressed and her attendants fright-ful. A parson played on the kettledrum at the oratorio.[5] Parson

1. Hon. Henrietta Louisa Jeffreys (d. 1761), m. (1720) Thomas Fermor, 2d Bn Leominster; cr. (1721) E. of Pomfret; her literary and intellectual pretensions are frequently ridiculed by HW. The occasion was her presentation to Oxford of the Pomfret marbles (*ante* 20 May 1736, n. 16); the ceremonies, which began 6 July and lasted 3 days, are reported in *London Evening Post* 10–13 July 1756; for HW's account see HW to Mann 24 July 1756.

2. According to *London Evening Post* 10–13 July 1756, she was accompanied by her daughter, Lady Louisa Fermor (1731–1809),

m. (1767) William, son of Sir William Clayton, Bt (John Debrett, *Peerage*, 1822, i. 248–9), and by her granddaughter, Lady Sophia Carteret (1745–71), m. (1765) William Petty, 2d E. of Shelburne, 1761; cr. (1784) M. of Lansdowne.

3. George Huddesford (ca 1699–1776), D.D., Vice-Chancellor 1753–6; President of Trinity 1731–76 (Foster, *Alumni Oxon*).

4. The Sheldonian.

5. Händel's *Judas Maccabeus, Joshua,* and *Messiah* were performed on successive evenings.

Fletcher[6]—you may remember at Eton—had a beam from one of the windows fall on his head but he was brute enough to set with a vast beaver on which preserved his brains. There were above three thousand people there.[6a]

The Colonel is at Plymouth; I hope poor Mr Mann's[7] better by the Bristol waters.

I am thank God much better in my health than I expected. I hope you have had no gout;[8] I most truly wish you your health and everything you can wish and am most sincerely yours

G. M.

My compliments to all the friends of Strawberry.

Thus much I had wrote when I received your letter. You make me happy in telling me I have a chance of seeing you. I go to my sister's the 29 of this month and stay only a week there and shall be three days going and coming and therefore shall be returned home and settled before you can come into this part of the country and shall be ready to receive you. I was in hopes of having Mr Bentley and Mr Muntz with me during your absence but as I was uncertain what day you would be here and engaged to go with Mr Blencow[9] to Cheshire and he not able to go till his hay was in, I cannot have that pleasure till I return; then if they please to give you the meeting I shall be most glad.[9a]

Be so good as to give Mr Muntz five guineas for me if you think that will be enough.

I should be glad Harry would carry or send to town the pictures carefully boxed up to Mr Richard Brown[10] a tobacconist in King Street near Golden Square and give him orders to send them to me here; 'tis old Richard that you remember.

Adieu; I wish you a good journey and much diversion.

6. William Fletcher (1715–79), admitted to King's as a scholar from Eton, 1732; fellow of King's, 1736; rector of Dunton, Essex, and Leire, Leics (Venn, *Alumni Cantab.*).

6a. Not more than one thousand could have been accommodated in the Sheldonian.

7. Galfridus Mann.

8. HW reports his first attack to Bentley 16 Nov. 1755, and had doubtless told Montagu about it.

9. Probably John Blencowe (ca 1720–77), who lived at Marston St Lawrence, two miles from Greatworth (Foster, *Alumni Oxon*).

9a. This idiom is in OED *sub* 'meeting' *sb*. 1b.

10. He apparently had been in Montagu's family at some time; not further identified. Montagu frequently in later letters has 'old Richard' execute commissions for him.

To Montagu, Saturday 28 August 1756

Arlington St, Aug. 28, 1756.

AS you was so kind as to interest yourself about the issue of my journey, I can tell you that I did get to Strawberry on Wednesday night, but it was half an hour past ten first—besides floods the whole way, I had twenty accidents with my chaise, and once saw one of the postilions with the wheel upon his body; he came off with making his nose bleed. My castle, like a little ark, is surrounded with many waters, and yesterday morning I saw the Blues wade halfway up their horses through Teddington lane.

There is nothing new, but what the pamphlet shops produce; however it is pleasant, to have a new print or ballad every day—I never had an aversion to living in a Fronde. The enclosed cards[1] are the freshest treason; the portraits by George Townshend[2] are droll—the other is a dull obscure thing as can be. The *Worlds* are by Lord Chesterfield on Decorum,[3] and by a friend of yours and mine[4] who sent it before he went to Jersey; but this is a secret: they neglected it till now, though so preferable to hundreds they have published—I suppose Mr Moore[5] finds what everybody else has found long, that he is aground.[6]

I saw Lovel today; he is very far advanced, and executes to perfection; you will be quite satisfied; I am not discontent with my own design, now I see how well it succeeds. It will certainly be finished by Michaelmas, at which time I told him he might depend on his money, and he seemed fully satisfied. My compliments to your brother, and adieu!

Yours ever

H. W.

1. Missing.
2. 'July 26th . . . a new series of . . . [satiric print] now first appeared, invented by George Townshend; they were caricatures on cards' (*Mem. Geo. II* ii. 228).
3. No. 189, 12 Aug. 1756.
4. Bentley. It is no doubt No. 190 (19 Aug.), which is on cruelty to animals. According to a MS list of Bentley's works by HW in the Waldegrave collection at Chewton Priory, Bentley published a letter in the *London Chronicle* 8 Sept. 1760, signed R.R., on the cruelty of killing dogs during a rabies panic (in *London Chron-icle* 6–9 Sept. 1760, viii. 243; it is signed not R.R. but 'Farmer Truth'). In 1758 was published Bentley's *Reflections on the Different Ideas of the French and English in Regard to Cruelty*, with a dedication by HW ('Short Notes').
5. Edward Moore (1712–57), dramatist; editor of *The World*.
6. *The World* ceased publication 30 Dec. 1756. The last number was 'A World Extraordinary' by HW. It reached Moore on that day and was printed after No. 209, nominally the last number.

From MONTAGU, Thursday 7 October 1756

G.D. 15/8, No. 724.

Answered *post* 14 Oct. 1756.

Greatworth, Thursday [Oct. 7, 1756].

I AM much obliged to you my dear Sir for your notice¹ of my lady['s]² chariot; pray let Peter³ examine it and see what order it is
in and how long it has been made. More than ten pounds I would
not certainly give; perhaps in the country which abounds so with
coach keepers it may fetch more; at London they are mere waste paper.

Should there be any family pictures of the House of Pelham to be
sold, as their price too is now much fallen, I should be glad to have
you purchase me an ancestor or two.⁴

I am vastly sorry for the poor Chute⁵ and pray tell him so when
you see him. Surely if you are at your castle when I come to town I
will make you a visit in my way to London; but it is at present uncertain when I shall move towards town, as I have at present my health
better than for many months last past.

There is a report in the papers that Charles's regiment is going on
a secret expedition,⁶ which, as he has received orders to embark for
Ireland, and expects the ship every moment for that purpose to convey them there, I hope has no foundation. Be so good as to inquire
concerning it, and let me know what can be known in this time of
ignorance and uncertainty.

There is a most inflaming letter from a German officer to his
brother published in the last *Oxford Journal*,⁷ that the good people
of the neighbouring counties believe genuine.

1. Missing.
2. From the references here and in the next letter to 'Pelhams,' 'dowager,' etc., it seems likely that the sale under discussion was of the effects of Frances Pelham (d. 27 June 1756), sister of the D. of Newcastle, m. (1717) Christopher Wandesford, 2d Vct Castlecomer (d. 1719). The sale does not appear in Frits Lugt, *Répertoire des catalogues de ventes*, La Haye, 1938—.
3. Probably HW's coachman.
4. Montagu's paternal grandmother was Elizabeth, dau. of Sir John Pelham, 3d Bt.
5. Who had the gout (HW to Mann 19 Sept. 1756).

6. *General Evening Post* 30 Sept.—2 Oct. 1756, p. 1: 'We hear that the first battalion of each of the three regiments of Foot Guards, have received orders to hold themselves in readiness to march on the shortest notice to Portsmouth, where they will be joined by Napier's and Lambton's regiments at Portsmouth, and by Anstruther and Montagu's, now at Plymouth, with a large train of battering cannon, mortars, bombs, etc., and embark on some important expedition.' The report seems to have been groundless.
7. In William Jackson's *Oxford Journal*, Saturday 2 Oct. 1756; it was entitled 'E-g-

Pray my compliments to Mr Bentley and Mr Muntz.

I wish you would let a poor body hear a little what you are doing.

Adieu; yours most truly,

G. Montagu

To Montagu, Thursday 14 October 1756

Strawberry Hill, Oct. 14, 1756.

I SHALL certainly not bid for the chariot for you; do you estimate an old Dowager's new machine but at ten pound? You could scarce have valued herself at less! It is appraised here at fifty. There are no family pictures but such as you might buy at any perpe[tu]al sale, that is, there are three portraits without names. If you had offered ten pounds for a set of *Pelhams,* perhaps I should not have thought you had underprized them.

You bid me give you some account of myself; I can in very few words: I am quite alone; in the morning I view a new pond¹ I am making for goldfish, and stick in a few shrubs or trees wherever I can find a space, which is very rare: in the evening I scribble a little;² all this mixed with reading, that is, I can't say I read much, but I pick up a good deal of reading. The only thing I have done that can compose a paragraph, and which I think you are Whig enough to forgive me, is, that on each side of my bed I have hung the *Magna Charta,* and the warrant for King Charles's execution,³ on which I have written *Major Charta,* as I believe without the latter the former by this

l-d's *Warning; or the Copy of a Letter from a H***** Officer in E——d, to his Brother in H——r.'* An introductory note declares that it had been picked up on the road near Canterbury, and faithfully translated. The body of the 'letter' compares England (without naming it) unfavourably with Hanover; says that in England there are higher taxes, more poverty, stricter laws, and less liberty than in Hanover; that England is full of whores; that the English army is blasphemous, idle and dissolute; and that there will soon be so many Germans in the English army that they can easily conquer England.

1. This is doubtless 'the lower pond' for

which HW paid £25 on 28 May 1758 (*SH Accounts* 7). The location of this pond and of Po-Yang is not clear. Toynbee states that 'the lower pond' is the one shown on Plan IV in *SH Accounts,* but in the absence of a plan of SH at this time it cannot be said to be so with certainty.

2. On his *Memoirs of George II.*

3. Probably the print by Vertue made in 1750 for distribution to members of the Society of Antiquaries (John Nichols, *Literary Anecdotes,* 1812–15, vi. 153), and reproduced by the society in *Vetusta Monumenta,* 1789, ii. pl. 6. The two prints were sold to the Earl of Buckinghamshire SH xxi. 22.

time would be of very little importance. You will ask where Mr Bentley is; confined with five sick Infantas,[3a] who live in spite of the epidemic distemper[4] and as if they were Infantas, and in bed himself with a fever and the same sore throat, though he sends me word he mends.

The King of Prussia has sent us over a victory;[5] which is very kind, as we are not likely to get any of our own—not even by the secret expedition which you apprehend, and which I believe still less than I did the invasion—perhaps indeed there may be another port on the coast of France, which we hope to discover as we did one in the last war.[6] By degrees and somehow or other I believe we shall be fully acquainted with France. I saw the German letter you mention, think it very mischievous and very well written for the purpose.

You talk of being better than you have been for many months; pray, which months were they, and what was the matter with you? Don't send me your fancies; I shall neither pity nor comfort you. You are perfectly well, and always was, ever since I knew you, which is now—I won't say how long; but within this century. Thank God you have good health, and don't call it names.

John[7] and I are just going to Garrick's with a grove of cypresses in our hands, like the Kentish men at the conquest.[8] He has built a temple to his master Shakespear,[9] and I am going to adorn the outside, since his modesty would not let me decorate it within, as I proposed, with these mottoes;

3a. Applied 'fancifully' to young ladies (OED, which gives as a reference HW to Mann 31 Jan. 1750).

4. Not in Theophilus Thompson, *Annals of Influenza . . . in Great Britain from 1510 to 1837*, Sydenham Society, 1852.

5. Frederick the Great defeated the Austrians under Marshal Brown at Lobositz in Bohemia 1 Oct. 1756.

6. See HW to Conway 16 June 1758: 'Well! in half a dozen more wars we shall know something of the coast of France. Last war we discovered a fine bay near Port l'Orient.' The same expression is used in *Mem. Geo. II* iii. 125.

7. Presumably John Cowie, 'my old gardener,' to whom HW left an annuity of £20. He died 1795 (HW to Mary Berry 24 Nov. 1795, 1 Dec. 1795).

8. 'Everyone knows the legend . . . about the Kentish men coming with boughs in their hands and extorting from William a confirmation of their rights' (Edward A. Freeman, *History of the Norman Conquest*, Oxford, 1869–79, iii. 539 n). HW probably read this version of the Birnam Wood story in Paul de Rapin-Thoyras, *Histoire d'Angleterre*, Amsterdam, 1724. HW's copy (MS Cat. G.3.20) sold SH iv. 54. The reference may be found also in a later edition, La Haye, 1727, ii. 11.

9. It stands between the house and the river at Garrick's villa at Hampton.

Quod spiro et placeo, si placeo, tuum est.[10]

That I spirit have and nature,
That sense breathes in ev'ry feature,
That I please, if please I do,
Shakespear, all I owe to you.

Adieu!

Yours ever

H. W.

To Montagu, Thursday 28 October 1756

Arlington Street, Oct. 28, 1756.

CAN you recommend one a first minister,[1] ho? We want one so much, that we do not insist upon his having a character from his last place: there will be good vails.—But I forget; one ought to condole with you; the Duke of Newcastle is your cousin;[2] and as I know by experience how much one loves one's relations, I sympathize with you! But alas! all first ministers are mortal; and as St Jonathan Swift said, crowned heads and cane heads, good heads and no heads at all, may all come to disgrace.[3] My father who had no capacity, and the Duke of Newcastle who has so much, have equally experienced the mutability of this world! Well-a-day! Well-a-day! His Grace is gone! He has bid adieu to courts, retires to a hermitage, and will let his beard grow as long—as his Duchess's.

And so you are surprised! And the next question you will ask, will be, who succeeds? Truly that used to be a question the easiest in the world to be resolved upon change of ministries. It is now the most unanswerable. I can only tell you that all the atoms are dancing, and as atoms always do, I suppose, will range themselves into the most durable system imaginable.

Beyond the past hour I know not a syllable; a good deal of the pre-

---

10. Horace, *Carm.* IV. iii. 24.

1. The Duke of Newcastle tendered his resignation 26 Oct. (see HW to Mann 4 Nov. 1756).

2. See *ante* 7 Oct. 1756.

3. Not found in Swift. Cf. Gray to HW ca 12 Nov. 1737: 'Crowned heads, and heads moutonnées, scald heads and lousy heads, quack heads and cane heads must all come together to the grave.'

ceding hours—a volume would not contain it—and yet you will believe that I shall try whether a volume will contain it.[4] There is some notion that the Duke of Bedford and your cousin Halifax[5] are to be the Secretaries of State—as Witwoud says, they will sputter at one another like roasted apples.[6]

The Duchess of Hamilton has brought her beauty to London at the only instant when it will not make a crowd—I believe we should scarce stare at the King of Prussia, so much are we engrossed by this ministerial ferment.

I have been this morning to see your monument; it is not put together, but the parts are admirably executed—there is a helmet that would tempt one to enlist. The inscription suits wonderfully, but I have overruled the gold letters, which not only are not lasting, but would not do at all, as they are to be cut in statuary marble. I have given him the arms, which certainly should be in colours, but a shield for your sister's, would be barbarous tautology.[7] You see how arbitrary I am, as you gave me leave to be. Adieu!

Yours ever

H. W.

From MONTAGU, Wednesday 3 November 1756

G.D. 15/8, No. 725.

Greatworth, Wednesday Nov. 3, 1756.

Dear Sir:

I THANK you much for your chat and much for your instructions to Lovel and approve of what you have ordered and am very glad you approve of what he has executed.

When all things are settled and the passengers jumbled together in their stage-coach[1] I shall be obliged to you to tell me how they are placed and who drives—not that I am likely to send a parcel by them

---

4. That is, HW's *Memoirs*.

5. Pitt and Holdernesse became Secretaries of State.

6. 'And so fell a sputt'ring at one another like two roasting apples' (Congreve, *Way of the World*, IV. viii).

7. I.e., in addition to the shield and arms at the top of the monument, which

is illustrated opposite. In *Vict. Co. Hist. Northants* iv. 262 the monument is incorrectly described as having been erected by the Earl of Halifax to his brother Edward and sister Henrietta.

---

1. The new ministry.

MONTAGU'S MONUMENT TO HIS FAMILY, DESIGNED BY
WALPOLE, IN THE CHURCH AT HORTON

but shall be glad some of my friends—I am not anxious for my kin—would be able to give a lift to those I love and value, and then I shall wish the equipage a good journey.

I propose much pleasure and reading[2] when I see you but I fancy that will not be till after Christmas, as I am going to pass some time in Cheshire at Hankelow. If I come early to town I shall be apt to get out of it too early and this place is not bearable till the leaves and sun are come out.

I have lately been passing a few days with my sister Ann Jekyll[3] at Dallington near Northampton. She lives à la Maintenon doing good and praying daily, now she has left her court life. Her place is pretty and the country about her sandy, though within a mile of Northampton, which you will never believe, nor that I went there in a little more than four hours—the individual road you plunged through not long ago. The Thanet[4] is hunting here near Stean with a Mr Douglass.[5] He don't mingle with our squires so that I hear a thousand stories of bad horsemanship and the penury of his stables.

I take it [in] my head my Waldershare's sons[6] will figure among the new established; I wish I could see Strawberry Hill come to the Exchequer wood.[6a]

How does poor Mr Man do? And the poor Cliquetis and his fondling hospital?

The Colonel is not yet embarked for Ireland. My Lord Mayor[7] and his brethren speak good English; I wish their representation[8] was translated for the use of the courts of Germany and Count Isenberg.[9]

2. The first letter is not clear in MS. Miss E. G. Withycombe makes the excellent suggestion that Montagu is referring to HW's Memoirs.

3. Lady Anne Montagu (ca 1715–66), dau. of 1st E. of Halifax (n.c.), m. (1750) Joseph Jekyll (ca 1714–52), of Dallington, Northants (George Baker, History . . . of the County of Northampton, 1822–41, i. 132). She was Montagu's first cousin.

4. Presumably Sackville Tufton (1733–86), 8th E. of Thanet.

5. Unidentified.

6. Waldershare was a seat of the Earl of Guilford in Kent (see ante 15 Oct. 1754). Montagu means his friend Lord North, and possibly the Earl of Thanet, who had estates near Waldershare. Neither got a place at this time.

6a. Since HW already had a lucrative post at the Exchequer, Montagu may mean the chancellorship itself.

7. Slingsby Bethell (d. 1758), Lord Mayor, 1756; M.P. London 1747–58; see GM 1758, xxviii. 556.

8. In instructions to its M.P.'s (GM 1756, xxvi. 543), the City of London censured the conduct of the war, especially the introduction into England of German mercenaries.

9. Christian Ludwig, Graf zu Ysenburg-Birstein (1710–91), Lt-Gen. in Hesse-Cassel; in command of the Hessian troops then in England (see Allgemeine Deutsche Biographie, Leipzig, 1875–1912, xliv. 609).

When you have a leisure moment bestow it on me, your most humble and faithful servant,

G. M.

My brother presents his compliments to you.

To MONTAGU, Saturday 6 November 1756

Arlington Street, Nov. 6, 1756.

AFTER an interministerium of seventeen days, Mr Pitt has this morning accepted the government, as Secretary of State; the Duke of Newcastle and Mr Fox being both excluded. The Duke of Devonshire is to be at the head of the Treasury; the Chancellor retires, the Seals to be in commission. Remnants of both administrations must be preserved, as Mr Pitt has not wherewithal to fill a quarter of their employments—did you ever expect to see a time when he would not have cousins enough? It will take some days to adjust all that is to follow. You see that unless Mr Pitt joins with either Fox or Newcastle, his ministry cannot last six months; I would bet that the *lightness* of the latter emerged first. George Selwyn hearing some people at Arthur's[1] t'other night lamenting the distracted state of this country, joined in the discourse with the whites of his eyes, and his prim mouth, and fetching a sigh; said, 'Yes, to be sure it is terrible! There is the Duke of Newcastle's faction, and there is Fox's faction, and there is Leicester House![2] Between two factions and one fuction,[3] we are torn to pieces!'

Thank you for your Exchequer-ward wishes for me; but I am apt

---

1. From about this time until ca 1765, HW invariably refers to White's as Arthur's, from Robert Arthur (d. 1761), in whose premises and under whose direction White's flourished. This interchangeable usage in HW and other contemporary writers has occasioned some belief that Arthur's and White's in HW's time were separate clubs, as they later were. See [William B. Boulton], *History of White's*, 1892, i. 121–2, for the evidence of their identity. In 1755 its numbers had so increased that White's had to move to larger quarters, and Boulton, *Amusements of Old London*, 1901, ii. 205, suggests that 'it is probable that the present Arthur's Club,

established early this [19th] century, takes its name from a coffee-house continued at the old premises under the style of "Arthur's".' For a clear example of HW's application of 'Arthur's' to White's, see HW to Ducarel 12 Jan. 1758, sending him, 'a little print . . . the arms of the two clubs at Arthur's'; this is the same as the 'arms for the two clubs at White's,' designed at SH (*ante* 20 April 1756).

2. Where the Prince of Wales and his mother lived. HW probably refers to the scandal of the Princess of Wales and Bute.

3. Printed 'faction' in previous editions.

to think that I have enough from thence already[4]—don't think my horns and hoofs are growing, when I profess indifference to my interest—Disinterestedness is no merit in me; it happens to be my passion. It certainly is not impossible that your two young lords[5] may appear in the new system. Mr Williams is just come from his niece Lady North's,[6] and commends her husband exceedingly. He tells me that the plump Countess[7] is in terrors, lest Lord Coventry should get a divorce from his wife,[8] and Lord Bolinbroke should marry her—'tis a well-imagined panic!

Mr Mann,[9] I trust, does not grow worse; I wish I could think he mended. Mr B. is sitting in his chimney-corner literally, with five girls; I expect him to meet me tomorrow at Strawberry.

As no provision is made for the great Cû in this new arrangement, is it impossible but he may pout a little? My best compliments to your brothers and sister. Adieu! Will this find you at Greatworth?

Yours ever

H. W.

To Montagu, Thursday 25 November 1756

Arlington Street, Nov. 25, 1756.

YOU must tell me what or whose the verses are, that you demand; I know of none. I could send you reams of *Tests, Con-tests*,[1] and such stupid papers, and bushels of more stupid cards. I know of nothing good; nor of any news, but that the committee of creations is not closed yet: Mr Obrien was yesterday created Irish Earl of Thomond.

Mr Pitt is to be wrapped up in flannel, and brought to town tomorrow to see King George the Second; and I believe, to dissolve the

---

4. As Usher of the Exchequer.

5. Montagu's 'Waldershare sons' (*ante* 3 Nov. 1756).

6. Anne Speke (ca 1740–97), m. (1756) Frederick North, styled Lord North; 2d E. of Guilford, 1790. Her mother was Gilly Williams's sister.

7. The Countess of Guilford, Lord Bolingbroke's aunt.

8. Maria Gunning; for Coventry's ill-treatment of her, see HW to Mann 28 Oct. 1752.

9. Galfridus Mann.

1. The *Test* was a virulent weekly paper supporting Fox, apparently written by Arthur Murphy and Philip Francis (*Mem. Geo. II* ii. 276; Earl of Ilchester, *Henry Fox, First Lord Holland*, 1920, ii. 33–5). The *Contest*, equally violent, was the work of Owen Ruffhead (1723–61) (DNB).

new ministry, rather than to cement it: Mr Fox has commenced hostilities, and has stolen the borough of Stockbridge from under Dr
Hay, one of the new Admiralty:[2] this enrages extremely: the new
ministers, who have neither members nor boroughs enough, will
probably recur to their only resource, popularity.

I am exceedingly obliged to the Colonel, but is that new? To whom
am I so much obliged? I shall not trouble him with any commissions;
the little money I have, I am learning to save: the times[3] give one a
hint, that one may have occasion for it.

I beg my best compliments to Mr and Mrs Wetenhall and Mr John
Montagu.[4] Don't you wish me joy of my Lord Hertford's having the
Garter?[5] It makes me very happy. Adieu!

Yours ever

H. W.

TO MONTAGU, Thursday 23 December 1756

Dec. 23, 1756.

YOU who have always cultivated rather than stifled tender sensations, will know how to feel for me, who have at last lost my
dear friend Mr Mann![1] Not unexpectedly, certainly; but I never
could find that one grew indifferent to what pains, as one does to
what pleases one! With all my consciousness of having been more
obliged to your brother than I could possibly deserve, I think I
should have trespassed on his kindness and have asked him to continue his favour to Mr Mann's son[2] and brother,[3] if I had not known

2. Fox had leased Stockbridge from
Lord Henley, and refused to support the
re-election of Dr Hay, who got a seat at
Calne (Earl of Ilchester, op. cit. ii. 13–14).

3. A poor harvest had created a scarcity
of grain; there was great distress among
the poor, and some rioting; see GM 1756,
xxvi. 486, 534, 544, 557, 575–7, 591. For
HW's income, see DU DEFFAND ii. 359 n.

4. George Montagu's youngest brother
but one. Practically nothing is known
about him except Sir Walter Scott's statement (Quarterly Review 1818, xix. 131)
that he 'was a midshipman at the age of
sixty, and found his chief occupation in
carrying about his brother's snuff-box.' Sir
Walter's MS (now WSL) has 'sixty and

four'; whether the discrepancy is inten-
tional or significant cannot be said. John
is not mentioned in George Montagu's
will, and may have pre-deceased him. He
may have attended Eton (see R. A. Austen-
Leigh, Eton College Register 1698–1752,
1927).

5. He was invested 18 Nov. 1756.

───

1. Galfridus Mann (d. 20 Dec.).

2. Horace Mann (d. 1814), succeeded his
uncle, HW's friend, as 2d Bt in 1786.

3. Galfridus Mann had two brothers
who were army clothiers: Edward Louisa
(d. 1775), and James (d. 1764); see HW's
correspondence with Mann; ante 30 Dec.
1755.

that he was good beyond doubt: it is just necessary for me as trans-
ferring my friendship to the family, to tell you that if the contrary
should be insinuated, they do continue the business.

Had I anything to tell you, it would be unpardonable in me to
communicate my grief to you, and neglect your entertainment, but
Mr Pitt's gout has *laid up* the nation: we adjourn tomorrow for the
holidays, and have not had a single division. Mr Pitt, Mr Fox, France
and the King of Prussia will not leave us idle much longer.

Adieu! I am most unaffectedly grieved,

and most unfeignedly yours

H. W.

To Montagu, Thursday 12 May 1757

Wrongly placed in Kimbolton MSS among letters of 1756; full reasons for re-
assigning it are given by Mrs Toynbee in N&Q 1897, 8th ser. xii. 291.

May 12th [1757].

DON'T imagine I write to you for anything but form; there is
nothing like news, except the Prussian victories,[1] which you see
in the papers; by next courier we expect he will send us at least a leg
or an arm of the Empress-Queen.

Our domestic politics are far from settled. The King is gone to
Kensington, and when any ministry can be formed, it is to be sent
after him. The Parliament draggles on, till any two of the factions
can unite.[2]

I have not got my tickets[3] yet, but will certainly reserve what you
want. Adieu!

Yours ever

H. W.

1. Minor engagements of Frederick's campaign in Bohemia; reported in *London Chronicle* 7–10 and 10–12 May 1757.
2. Pitt and Temple were dismissed 5 April; a coalition ministry under Pitt and Newcastle did not take office until 29 June; see following letters, and *Mem. Geo. II* iii. 1–35.
3. Lottery tickets (see *post* 27 May 1757), probably for the government lottery of 1757; see C. L'Estrange Ewen, *Lotteries and Sweepstakes*, 1932, p. 155.

To Montagu, Thursday 19 May 1757

Address: To George Montagu Esq. at Greatworth near Brackley, Northamptonshire, Free Hor. Walpole.
Postmark: 19 MA.

May 19th [1757].

IT is on the stroke of eleven and I have but time to tell you that the King of Prussia has gained the greatest victory that ever was,[1] except the Archangel Michael's—King Frederick has only demolished the dragoness.[2] He attacked her army in a strong camp on the sixth, suffered in the beginning of the action much, but took it with all the tents baggage etc. etc. 250 pieces of cannon, 6000 prisoners, and they say, Prague since.[3] The Austrians have not stopped yet; if you see any man scamper by your house, you may venture to lay hold on him, though he should be a Pandour.[4] Marshal Schwerin[5] was killed. Good night.

Yours ever

H. W.

To Montagu, Friday 27 May 1757

May 27, 1757.

I HAVE ticketed you with numbers 58321, 58322, 58323, 58324, 58325, 58326.[1] I think you bespoke six. I do not send them by the post, unless you order it; but I have writ your name on each, lest in case of accident my executors should put them into my auction for

1. The battle of Prague, against an Austrian army under Prince Charles of Lorraine and Marshal Browne; see *Cambridge Modern History*, ed. A. W. Ward, Cambridge, 1902–11, vi. 257–9. The news had just been received in London; see the *London Gazette Extraordinary* 20 May 1757.

2. Maria Theresa (1717–80), Empress, Queen of Hungary.

3. The later siege of Prague was unsuccessful.

4. 'The name borne by a local force organized in 1741 by Baron Trenck on his own estates in Croatia . . . subsequently enrolled as a regiment in the Austrian army, where, under Trenck, their rapacity and brutality caused them to be dreaded over Germany, and made *Pandour* a synonym in Western Europe with "brutal Croatian soldier" ' (OED).

5. Kurt Christoph, Graf von Schwerin (1684–1757), Prussian Field-Marshal (*Allgemeine Deutsche Biographie*, Leipzig, 1875–1912).

1. Lottery tickets.

which you are so impatient, and then you would have to buy them over again.

I am glad you like Xo Ho;[2] I think everybody does, which is strange, considering it has no merit but truth. Mrs Clive cried out like you, 'Lord! You will be sent to the Tower!'[3] 'Well,' said I coolly, 'my father was there before me.'[4]

Lord Abercorn's picture[5] is extremely like; he seems by the Vandyke habit to be got back into his own times; but nothing is finished yet, except the head.

You will be diverted with a health which my Lady Irwin[6] gave at supper with the Prince t'other night—' 'tis a health you will all like,' she said. "Well! what is it?'—'The three *Ps*.'—The boy coloured up to the eyes.[7] After keeping them in suspense some time, she named, *P*itt, *P*eace, and *P*lenty. The *P*ss. has given Hume,[8] the author of *Douglas*, an hundred a year. Prince and Princess Edward[9] continue to amuse themselves and Ranelagh every night.

I wish your brother and all heirs to estates joy, for old Schutz is dead, and cannot wriggle himself into any more wills.[10]

2. *A Letter from Xo Ho, a Chinese Philosopher at London, to his Friend Lien Chi at Peking.* 'May 12th . . . I wrote in less than an hour and a half the *Letter from Xo Ho;* it was published on the 17th, and immediately passed through five editions' ('Short Notes'). It was reprinted with notes in *Works* i. 205–9, and was an inspiration of Goldsmith's *Citizen of the World* (see W. S. Lewis in *Times Literary Supplement* 1928, xxvii. 617). HW's copy with his notes is now WSL.

3. HW, in the character of Xo Ho, satirizes the monarchy and government.

4. Sir Robert Walpole, on a trumped-up charge of 'breach of trust and notorious corruption,' was impeached as Secretary at War, and was committed to the Tower from January to July 1712 (George M. Trevelyan, *England under Queen Anne*, 1930–4, iii. 199).

5. James Hamilton (1712–89), 8th E. of Abercorn, a friend of Montagu's for whom this picture was being painted by Eccardt (see *post* ca 20 June 1757); from the allusion to 'the Vandyke habit' and 'his own times,' he seems to have shared Montagu's affection for the 17th century. Bent-

ley, Gray, and HW were also painted by Eccardt in Van Dyck dress.

6. Lady Anne Howard (ca 1696–1764), m. (1) (1717) Rich Ingram, 5th Vct Irvine; m. (2) (1737) Col. William Douglas.

7. Unexplained; but compare the famous indecent toast, 'the Beggar's Benison' in Boswell, *Private Papers*, ed. Geoffrey Scott and Frederick A. Pottle, Mt Vernon, N. Y., 1929–33, xiv. 206–7.

8. John Home (1722–1808), dramatist. He had just become Bute's private secretary, and tutor to the Prince of Wales.

9. According to HW to Mann 30 Jan. 1757, Frances Hanbury-Williams (d. 1759), dau. of Sir Charles Hanbury Williams, m. (1754) William Anne Holles Capel, 4th E. of Essex: 'Sir Charles's daughter, Lady Essex, has engaged the attentions of Prince Edward.' 'A charming creature with wit equal to her beauty' (Mrs Piozzi, note to *post* 26 July 1759).

10. HW mentions (*ante* 10 Sept. 1750) one legacy to Augustus Schutz, who also inherited the manor of Shotover in Oxfordshire from a relative of his wife's (Falconer Madan, *The Madan Family*, Oxford, 1933, p. 67).

The ministry is not yet hatched; the King of Prussia is conquering the world; Mr Chute has some murmurs of the gout; and I am

Yours ever

H. W.

From Montagu, ca Sunday 29 May 1757

G.D. 15/8, No. 726.

In reply to *ante* 27 May 1756; answered by HW *post* 2 June.

[Greatworth, ca May 29, 1757].

I WILL venture the tickets by the post if you will be so good as to send them.

I am delighted to hear Eckardt has taken off the Earl so well; if it is speakingly like it is not like his Lordship.[1]

I conclude the Epistle was printed at the Theatrum Walpolianum[2] for I have never seen it advertised.[3]

Charles writes me word my cousin has recommended him to the Lord Lieutenant[4] and his Grace's secretary[5] and that his regiment is to be ordered to Dublin which is esteemed a great favour.

Mr Denton[6] who lately died in this neighbourhood has left his family estate to Sir James Chamberlain's son.[7] Some years ago the young

1. For Lord Abercorn's taciturnity, see *post* 29 March 1766, and his obituary in GM 1789, lix pt ii. 961, which describes his 'Castilian pomp,' and gives several anecdotes of his laconic rudeness.

2. This is the first mention of the SH Press, which, according to HW, was not erected till 25 June 1757 (*Journal of the Printing Office* 3). HW did not publish the *Letter to Xo Ho* himself (see *post* 2 June 1757, n. 6).

3. See next letter.

4. The Duke of Bedford.

5. Rigby. Charles Montagu's regiment, the 61st Foot, had probably been on duty elsewhere in Ireland.

6. George Chamberlayne (later Denton), of Hillesden, Bucks; son of George Chamberlayne of Wardington, Oxon; adopted by his uncle Sir Alexander Denton (n. 10 below); M.P. Buckingham 1728–47; d. at Bath 14 May (GM 1757, xxvii. 241; George

Lipscomb, *History . . . of the County of Buckingham*, 1847, iii. 18).

7. Thomas Chamberlayne, son of Sir James Chamberlayne (d. 1767), 4th Bt. There is considerable confusion about him in the Baronetages. He was a Cornet in the Royal Horse Guards 1754–7, when he was promoted to a Lieutenancy; his last appearance in the *Army List* is in Nov. 1763 (*List* for 1764). He must have predeceased his father; his uncle succeeded to the baronetcy. The will of George Chamberlayne Denton (P.C.C. Herring 187) reads in part: 'My manor of Wardington . . . to my cousin Thomas Chamberlayne now a Cornet in H.M. Horse Guards Blue son of my cousin Sir James Chamberlayne Baronet of Dunstow Oxfordshire. . . . This not out of disaffection to my only daughter and child Elizabeth Coke . . . but because said estates have long been enjoyed by the family of

man told his father Miss Denton[8] had consented to run away with him. Sir James took horse and acquainted Mr Denton with the young folks' project, upon which he immediately married her to Lord Leicester's nephew Mr Roberts.[9] Now in return he has left the family estate to Sir James his nearest relation, for Denton changed his name of Chamberlain for an old judge's[10] estate. We here approve of this much in the country.

I wish you joy of the rain we have lately had which I presume has been of great service to your lawn and flowering shrubs.

I am sorry to hear the poor Chute is not yet free from the gout. Pray my compliments to Mr Bentley.

Adieu; believe me most truly yours,

G. M.

To MONTAGU, Thursday 2 June 1757

Arlington Street, June 2d, 1757.

THE ministry is to be settled today; there are different accounts, how: some say, that the Duke of Newcastle is to take orders and to have the reversion of the bishopric of Winchester;[a] that Mr Pitt is to have a regiment and to go serve in Germany with the Duke; that Mr Fox is to have Sir William Irby's[1] place and be Chamberlain to the Princess;[2] that my Lord Bute[2a] is to be divorced and marry Princess

Chamberlayne and I wish them so to continue, and my daughter after my death will be entitled to the estate of my uncle the Hon. Alexander Denton.'

8. Elizabeth Denton (ca 1732–1810), m. Wenman Roberts Coke (next note; GM 1810, lxxx pt ii. 667).

9. Wenman Roberts (d. 1776), of Longford, Derbyshire; son of Philip Roberts and Anne Coke, sister of Thomas Coke (1697–1759), cr. (1728) Bn Lovel, (1744) E. of Leicester; took the name of Coke, 1750; succeeded to the Holkham estates, 1774; by his second wife, Elizabeth Denton, father of Thomas William Coke the agriculturist; M.P. Harwich 1753–61; Oakhampton 1761–8; Derby 1772–4; Norfolk 1774–6; see A. M. W. Stirling, *Coke of Norfolk and his Friends*, edn 1912, pp. 44–6 et seq.

10. Sir Alexander Denton (1679–1740),

M.P. Buckingham 1708–10, 1715–22; Justice of Common Pleas 1722–40; see Edward Foss, *Judges of England*, 1848–64, viii. 119–20; George Lipscomb, *History . . . of the County of Buckingham*, 1847, iii. 18, for an account of his hospitality at Hillesden; Historical Manuscripts Commission, *Diary of the First Earl of Egmont*, 1920–3, ii. 348–9, which gives an extraordinary reason for his failure to become Chief Justice of King's Bench.

a. A rich see, the incumbent of which, Benjamin Hoadly, was almost eighty-one.

1. Sir William Irby (1707–75), 2d Bt; cr. (1761) Bn Boston; Lord Chamberlain to the Princess of Wales.

2. With whom he was not on good terms.

2a. John Stuart (1713–92), 3d E. of Bute; First Lord of the Treasury 1762–3.

Emily; and that my Lord Darlington is to be first minister. Others say, that the Duke of Newcastle is to be sole minister, having broken with Mr Pitt, that Sir Thomas Robinson[3] is to be again Secretary of State, Sir George Lee[4] Chancellor of the Exchequer, and Mr Fox Paymaster, but with no place in the cabinet, nor any power. I believe the Duke himself has said this; but as I think the former establishment would be the less ridiculous of the two, I intend to believe that.

I send you your tickets and a curious new print.[5] The blue ribband in the corner and the line that explains it, but leaves it still in the dark, makes much noise. I choose to think it my Lord Lincoln, for having a tenderness for royalties, I will not suppose, as most do, that it points higher. The rest are certainly admirable: the times are very entertaining; one cannot complain that no wit is stirring, as one used to do. I never thought I should feel glad for the death of poor Mr Pelham; but really it has opened such scenes of amusement, that I begin to bear it better than I did!

I rejoice to hear that your brother is accommodated, though not by my means. The Duke of Bedford might have reflected that what I asked was a very trifle, or that I should never have asked it; nay, that if I could have asked a favour of consequence, I should not have applied to himself, but to those who govern him; to the Duchess, or to those who govern him *through* her.

I certainly am glad of rain, but could wish it was boiled a little over the sun first: Mr Bentley calls this *the hard summer,* and says he is forced to buy his fine weather at Newcastle. Adieu!

Yours ever

H. W.

PS. Pray acknowledge the receipt of your tickets. I don't know how you came not to see the advertisements of *Xo Ho,* which have been in continually;[6] four editions were published in twelve days.

3. Sir Thomas Robinson (1695–1770), K.B.; cr. (1761) Bn Grantham.
4. Sir George Lee (ca 1700–58), Kt, 1752; lawyer and politician (DNB). Obituary notices give his age at death as 64, but Foster and Venn confirm the birth date in DNB.
5. *The Treaty or Shabear's Administration,* called by HW *The Turnstile,* represented the Duke of Newcastle on a turnstile, with a group of supplicant politi-

cians kneeling before him, and a figure wearing the blue ribbon standing behind him, to whom, in the accompanying verses, the line 'See the blue-ribbon'd, silly proud son of a w---e' is applied. Though this seems clearly to have been meant for Lord Lincoln, many thought it was directed at the Prince of Wales; see a long discussion of this print in HW to Mann 1 June 1757; BM *Satiric Prints* iii pt ii. 1149–51.
6. The only advertisements in *London*

From Montagu, ca Friday 10 June 1757

G.D. 15/8, No. 727.

Undated: written between *ante* 2 June 1757 and *post* 18 June 1757.

Memoranda by HW:

Duke of Newcastle —— Duke of Devon		Chancellor
Lord Anson ———— Lord Winchelsea		Pope
Lord Gower ———— Duke of Dorset		
Lord Temple ——— Lord Gower		
Mr Fox ————— Potter and Duplin		
Lord Duplin ——— Lord Halifax		
Lord G. Sackville —— Lord Barrington		
Legge ————— Chancellor of Exchequer		
Lord Holderness ——		
G. Grenville		
—Townshend		
Mr Mackensy ——— Dr Lee		

These notes were probably used for HW to Mann 20 June 1757, in an account of the new government.

[Greatworth, ca June 10, 1757].

THAT your executor may not lose by me no more than mine by you,[1] which is not likely I trust to be the case yet these thirty years, I have enclosed a receipt[2] for the six tickets and thank you for your trouble and much for the print which has made me a great deal of mirth as I think it is very humorous and I am not very nice and punctilious about the great vulgar.

My newspaper[3] has made amends for not advertising *Xo Ho* by giving me a large extract from it and it reads very well in that manner.

My compliments to Mr Bentley I presume to send *à la glace* and to yourself my warmest wishes for better weather[4]

Evening Post were 17–19 May, 'This day was published *A Letter from Xo Ho . . .* printed for Josiah Graham, the corner of Craven Street in the Strand'; 28–31 May, 'This day was published price 6d. the fourth edition of *A Letter . . .*'; and 25–28 June, 'this day was published, price 6d. the fifth edition of *A Letter . . .*' The *London Chronicle* did not advertise the work; see *post* ca 10 June 1757; no other newspapers have been seen.

1. See *ante* 27 May 1757.
2. Missing.
3. Probably *London Chronicle*, which carried no advertisements for the *Letter to Xo Ho*, but published a considerable extract from it in the issue of 31 May–2 June.
4. About a third of the page has been cut off, but probably only the signature is lacking.

TO MONTAGU, Saturday 18 June 1757

Year determined by the political references.

[Arlington Street] June 18th [1757].

THE two drawings[1] of the Vine and Strawberry which you desired are done and packed up in a box; tell me how I must send them.

The confusion about the ministry is not yet settled; at least it was not at noon today; but for fear that confusion should ever finish, all the three factions[2] are likely to come into place together.

Poor Mr Chute has had another bad fit; he took the air yesterday for the first time.

I came to town but last night and return to my château this evening, knowing nothing but that we are on the crisis of battles and ministries. Adieu!

Yours ever

H. W.

PS. I just hear that your cousin Halifax has resigned on Pitt's not letting him be Secretary of State for the West Indies.[3]

From MONTAGU, ca Monday 20 June 1757

G.D. 15/8, No. 723.

Undated; a reply to *ante* 18 June 1757.

Memoranda by HW:

Honeysuckles

Idogatry

Bentley's Horace

The third item is from Bentley's 'Sonnet.' *To the Printingpress at Strawberry hill,*

1. These were probably by Bentley. Müntz had done nothing all summer but 'paste two chimney-boards' (HW to Chute 26 July 1757). The drawings have not been found.

2. Newcastle's, Pitt's, Fox's.

3. Almost from the time of his appointment to the Presidency of the Board of Trade in 1748, Halifax had been agitating for increased power, and for the creation of a new Secretaryship of State. The Secretary for the Southern Province (the office Pitt had taken in the coalition ministry then forming) had charge of most colonial affairs, and the Board of Trade could act only through him. Newcastle promised Halifax his Secretaryship; Pitt, who wished to keep control of American affairs in his own hands, and who had no particular liking for Halifax, flatly refused. Halifax resigned, but was placated in September by admission to the cabinet; see Arthur H. Basye, *The Lords Commissioners of Trade and Plantations, . . . 1748–1782,* New Haven, 1925, pp. 65–103.

not seen by HW until 19 Aug. (see *post* 8 Sept. 1757). These memoranda are probably for a missing letter.

[?Roel, ca June 20, 1757].

I HAVE nothing to say but to tell you I am much obliged to you for sending me Strawberry Hill to Dunsinane.[1] I marvel at my cousin's resignation; three thousand a year[2] when one is building a fine house[3] goes a good way towards paying the workmen's bills.

I have wrote to Mrs Morland to send me the box down by the first carrier and hope on Saturday to ornament my chamber with two of the prettiest places in England. I wish Eckardt may have finished Lord Abercorn's picture to come at the same time; I have got the Bishop of Durham[4] by Gossette[5] and very like; every year you find I am scratching up some thing or other for Roel and meet with very generous obliging friends—I grieve much for the poor Mr Chute who has had such terrible returns of the gout.

My brother desires his compliments to you.

I am very much yours,

G. Montagu

To Montagu, Saturday 16 July 1757

Address: To George Montagu Esq. at Greatworth near Brackley, Northamptonshire. Free Hor. Walpole.

Strawberry Hill, July 16, 1757.

YOU do me justice in believing that I enjoy your satisfaction; I do heartily; and particularly on this point: you know how often I have wished this reconciliation; indeed you have taken the hand-

1. The drawings.
2. Halifax computed his income from the Board of Trade at £2300 a year (Arthur H. Basye, *The Lords Commissioners of Trade and Plantations, . . . 1748–1782*, New Haven, 1925, pp. 13, 196). HW states that the loss of salary led him to reconsider his resignation (*Mem. Geo. II* iii. 34).
3. Possibly the 'elegant villa, a few miles distant from the capital . . . furnished in the most sumptuous taste' he built for his mistress, Miss Faulkner (*Town and Country Magazine*, May 1769, i. 227); Cole describes it as a 'most elegant house not far

from the gate of Bushy Park near Hampton Court' (*post* Appendix 4). Montagu may, however, refer to Horton, which Lord Halifax partially rebuilt; see *Country Seats* 52; [Thomas Pennant], *Journey from Chester to London*, 1782, p. 324: 'The house is in a very unfinished state; part modern, part ancient and embattled.'
4. Hon. Dr Richard Trevor (1707–71), Bp of St David's, 1744; of Durham, 1752 (DNB); Montagu's first cousin once removed; see table 3, Appendix 7.
5. Isaac Gosset (1713–99), wax modeller.

somest manner of doing it; and it has been accepted handsomely. I
always had a good opinion of your cousin,¹ and I am not apt to throw
about my esteem lightly. He has ever behaved with sense, and dignity, and this country has more obligations to him than to most men
living.

The weather has been so hot, and we are so unused to it, that nobody knew how to behave themselves. Even Mr Bentley has done
shivering.

Elzevirianum opens today;² you shall taste its first fruits. I find
people have a notion that it is very mysterious³—they don't know how
I should abhor to profane Strawberry with politics! Adieu!

Yours ever

H. W.

To Montagu, Thursday 4 August 1757

Address: To George Montagu Esq. at Greatworth near Brackley, Northamptonshire. Free Hor. Walpole. *Postmark:* 4 AV.

Strawberry Hill, Aug. 4, 1757.

I SHALL tomorrow deliver to your agentess Mrs Moreland—some-
thing¹—to send you.

The Duke² is beaten by the French; he and his family are safe; I
know no more particulars—if I did, I should say as I have just said to
Mr Chute,³ I am too busy about *something,* to have time to write
them. Adieu!

1. Halifax. The subject of Montagu's
quarrel with him is lost with the missing
letters.
2. The Officina Arbuteana, the SH
Press. *Journal of the Printing Office* 3
states: 'July 16th. Began to print. The first
work was an edition of two new Odes by
Mr Gray; one, on the power and progress
of Poetry; the other, on the destruction of
the Welsh Bards by Edward Ist.' HW to
Chute 12 July 1757 announces that the
opening is to be on Monday 18 July, and
that the leading London booksellers are
'summoned to meet here on Sunday night.'

3. That is, they assumed that HW was
going to use it to print political pamphlets. He never did so.

1. Gray's *Odes.*
2. 'The Duke of Cumberland in the affair at Hastenbeck' (HW). On 26 July; as
a result the Duke, opposed by a far superior French force, had to give up the
campaign; a full account of the battle is
in Hon. Sir Evan Charteris, *William Augustus Duke of Cumberland and the Seven
Years' War,* 1925, pp. 274–82.
3. Presumably in a missing letter.

To Montagu, Thursday 25 August 1757

Strawberry Hill, Aug. 25th, 1757.

I DID not know that you expected the pleasure of seeing the Colonel so soon: it is plain that *I* did *not* solicit leave of absence for him.[1] Make him my many compliments. I should have been happy to have seen you and Mr John, but must not regret it as you was so agreeably prevented. You are very particular I can tell you in liking Gray's *Odes*—but you must remember that the age likes Akinside,[2] and did like Thomson![3] Can the same people like both? Milton was forced to wait till the world had done admiring Quarles.[4] Cambridge[5] told me t'other night that my Lord Chesterfield had heard Stanley[6] read them as his own, but that must have been a mistake of my Lord's deafness. Cambridge said, 'Perhaps they are Stanley's, and not caring to own them, he gave them to Gray.' I think this would hurt Gray's dignity ten times more than his poetry not succeeding. My humble share as his printer has been more favourably received. We proceed soberly.[7] I must give you some account of *les amusements des eaux de Straberri*. T'other day[8] my Lady Rochford, Lady Townshend, Miss Bland[9] and the new Knight of the Garter[10] dined here, and were carried into the printing-office, and were to see the man[11] print. There were some lines ready placed, which he took off; I gave them to my Lady Townshend; here they are;

> The Press speaks;
> From me wits and poets their glory obtain;
> Without me their wit and their verses were vain.

1. See *ante* 2 June 1757; apparently HW had asked a favour of the Duke of Bedford for Charles Montagu, and had been rebuffed.

2. Mark Akenside (1721–70), poet and physician; wrote *Pleasures of the Imagination*.

3. James Thomson (1700–48), author of *The Seasons* etc.

4. Francis Quarles (1592–1644).

5. Richard Owen Cambridge (1717–1802), author of *The Scribleriad*. He was HW's contemporary at Eton and neighbour at Twickenham.

6. Hans Stanley (ca 1720–80), politician.

7. With Hentzner's *Account of England*, translated by Bentley and with 'an advertisement' by HW (*Journal of the Printing Office* 3).

8. 19 August (ibid. 4).

9. Probably one of the daughters of Sir John Bland, 5th Bt, of Kippax, two of whom, Elizabeth and Anne, survived their brothers Sir John and Sir Hungerford, 6th and 7th Baronets, who both d. by 1756 (GEC, *Baronetage*). Anne d. 1786, aet. 68 (GM 1786, lvi pt i. 181).

10. Lord Waldegrave (*Journal of the Printing Office* 4).

11. William Robinson, HW's printer until March 1759; see *Journal of the Printing Office, passim*.

Stop, Townshend, and let me but *print*[11a] what you say;
You, the fame I on others bestow, will repay.[12]

They then asked, as I foresaw, to see the man compose; I gave him four lines out of *The Fair Penitent,* which he set, but while he went to place them in the press, I made them look at something else; without their observing, and in an instant he whipped away what he had just set, and to their great surprise when they expected to see *Were ye, ye Fair,*[13] he presented to my Lady Rochford the following lines;

The Press speaks;
In vain from your properest name you have flown,
And exchanged lovely Cupid's for Hymen's dull throne;
By my art shall your beauties be constantly sung,
And in spite of yourself you shall ever be Young.[14]

You may imagine, whatever the poetry was, that the gallantry of it succeeded.

Poor Mr Bentley has been at the extremity with a fever and inflammation in his bowels; but is so well recovered that Mr Müntz is gone to fetch him hither today.

I don't guess what sight[14a] I have to come in Hampshire, unless it is Abbotstone.[15] I am pretty sure I have none to come at the Vine, where I have done advising, as I see Mr Chute will never execute anything. The very altar-piece[16] that I sent for to Italy is not placed yet. But when he could refrain from making the little Gothic columbarium[17] for his family which I proposed and Mr Bentley had drawn so divinely, it is not probable he should do anything else.

Adieu! Yours ever

H. Walpole

11a. Printed as 'paint' in all editions before Mrs Toynbee's; see Allen T. Hazen, *Bibliography of the SH Press,* New Haven, 1942.

12. See ibid. 4, 27. One of the rarest of SH detached pieces; no. 2 of the detached pieces in Hazen, op. cit.

13. At the end of Act II of Nicholas Rowe's *The Fair Penitent.* These lines were apparently not printed; no copy has been found.

14. Lady Rochford's maiden name. See *Journal of the Printing Office* 4, 27. Also extremely rare; no. 3 of the detached pieces in Hazen, op. cit.

14a. See OED *sb*¹ 11b.

15. A seat of the Duke of Bolton's, near Alresford; see *Vict. Co. Hist. Hants* iv. 192–3.

16. A copy of 'a small picture' by Santo di Tito (1526–1603). See HW to Mann 16 July 1755, and Mann to HW 16 Aug. 1755 and 21 Feb. 1756, with which last Mann enclosed the bill of lading for the picture.

17. The designs are in *Drawings and Designs by Richard Bentley, only son of Dr. Bentley, Master of Trinity-College, Cambridge,* a scrap-book for which HW had the above title-page printed (now WSL). In the same book are two 'Designs [not executed] for the ante-chapel at the Vine in Hampshire' (HW). See illustration. One of them is dated by HW on the back, 1750.

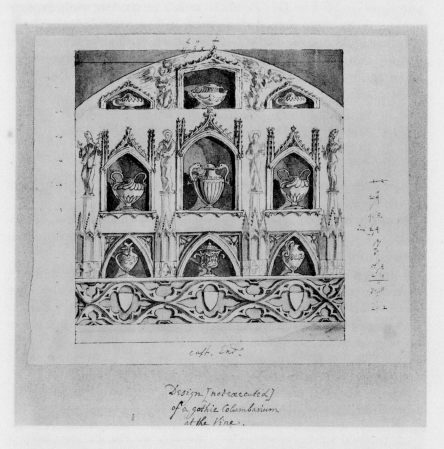

Design [not executed]
of a gothic columbarium
at the Vine.

BENTLEY'S DESIGN FOR A COLUMBARIUM AT THE VYNE

To Montagu, Thursday 8 September 1757

Strawberry Hill, Sept. 8th, 1757.

HOW I laughed at your picture of the shrine of *Notre Dame de Straberri,* and of the vows hung up there! I little thought that when I converted my castle into a printing-office, the next transformation would be into an hospital for the *filles repenties* from Mrs Naylor's[1] and Lady Fitzroy's. You will treat the enclosed,[2] I trust, with a little more respect, not for the sake of the hero but of the poet. The poet, poor soul, has had a relapse, but is again recovering.

As I know no earthly history, you must accept the sonnet as if it was written into my letter, and therefore supposing this the end of the third page, I bid you good night.

Yours ever

H. W.

To Montagu, Tuesday 18 October 1757

Address: To George Montagu Esq. at Mr Wetenhall's at Hankelow, Cheshire. Free Hor. Walpole. *Postmark:* 18 OC.

Arlington Street, Oct. 18, 1757.

YOU never begged news at a worse time, for though I could tell you much, I have neither time nor inclination. This sounds brusque, but I will explain it. With regard to the expedition, I am so far easy about Mr C.[1] that he will appear with great honour, but it is not pleasant to hear him complicated with others in the meantime. He cannot speak till forced. In short there are twenty delicacies not

---

1. Carlotta or Charlotte, dau. of Joseph Alston of Edwardstone, Suffolk; m. (ca 1740) Francis Hare-Naylor, of Hurstmonceaux, Sussex, her sister's stepson; see Augustus J. C. Hare, *Memorials of a Quiet Life,* 9th edn 1873, i. 78–9; Burke, *Landed Gentry,* sub Hare. See HW to Mann 2 April 1750, for a low estimate of her assemblies and morals.

2. Missing; it was Bentley's 'Sonnet' *To the Printingpress at Strawberry hill,* printed 19 Aug. as a surprise for HW, who is 'the

hero' of the text. The illness of Bentley, 'the poet,' is mentioned *ante* 25 Aug. 1757; see *Journal of the Printing Office* 4–5.

---

1. Gen. Conway, who had just returned from an ill-planned and fruitless expedition against Rochefort. He and his colleague in command, Sir John Mordaunt, were blamed by Pitt and the King for its failure, but were cleared; see HW–Conway Corr.

for a letter. The big event is, the Duke's resignation.[2] He is not so patient as Mr C. under unmerited reproach, and has thrown up everything, Captain-General, regiment and all. You and I wish for a Fronde, but I don't expect one. At worst it will produce *Mémoires de la Fronde*.[3] I rejoice that all your family is well and beg my compliments to them. For this time you must excuse a very short letter; I am only in town for this evening to meet Mr C., and snatch a moment that you might not think me neglectful of you, which I certainly never will be. Adieu!

Yours ever

H. W.

To Montagu, Thursday 4 May 1758

Arlington Street, May 4th, 1758.

YOU are the first person I believe that ever thought of a Swiss[1] transcribing Welsh, unless, like some commentator on the Scriptures, you have discovered great affinity between those languages, and that both are dialects of the Phœnician. I have desired your brother to call here today, to help us in adjusting the inscriptions. I can find no Lady Cutts in your pedigree,[2] and till I do, cannot accommodate her with a coronet.[2a]

My book[3] is marvelously in fashion, to my great astonishment. I did not expect that so much truth and such notions of liberty[4] would have made their fortune in this our day. I am preparing an edition for publication,[5] and then I must expect to be a little less civilly treated. My Lord Chesterfield tells everybody that he subscribes to

2. He infuriated the King by signing the Convention of Kloster-Zeven, which ended Hanoverian participation in the war.
3. That is HW's own *Memoirs*.

1. Müntz.
2. Probably a pedigree in Welsh of Montagu's mother's family, the Trevors of Flintshire; Lady Cutts was his grandmother.
2a. It was customary in making pedigrees to place a coronet of their rank be-side the name of peers and peeresses in their own right.
3. *A Catalogue of the Royal and Noble Authors of England*.
4. HW wrote his biographies with a strong Whig bias.
5. The first edition, of 300 copies, was completed at SH 15 April. HW then sold the copy 'for two years to Dodsley and Graham for £200 for Mr B[entley].' A second (revised) edition of 2000 copies appeared 5 Dec. (*Journal of the Printing Office* 7, 31; 'Short Notes').

all my opinions; but this mortifies me about as much as the rest flatter me; I cannot, because it is my own case, forget how many foolish books he has diverted himself with commending. The most extraordinary thing I have heard about mine is, that it being talked of at Lord Arran's[6] table, Dr King,[7] the Dr King of Oxford, said of the passage on my father;[8] 'It is very modest, very genteel, and *very true.*' I asked my Lady Cardigan if she would forgive my making free with her grandmother;[9] she replied very sensibly, 'I am sure she would not have hindered anybody from writing against me; why should I be angry at any writing against her?'[10]

The history I promised you of Dr Brown[11] is this. Sir Charles Williams had written an answer to his first silly volume of the *Estimate,* chiefly before he came over, but finished while he was confined at Kensington.[12] Brown had lately lodged in the same house, not mad now, though he has been so formerly. The landlady[13] told Sir Charles and offered to make affidavit, that Dr Brown was the most profane curser and swearer that ever came into her house. Before I proceed in my history, I will tell you another anecdote of this great reformer. One of his antipathies is the opera—yet the only time I ever saw him was in last *Passion-week* singing the *Romish Stabat Mater with* the *Mingotti*[14] behind a harpsichord at a great concert at my Lady Carlisle's.[15]—Well—in a great apprehension of Sir Charles divulging the

6. Charles Butler (1671–1758), cr. (1693) E. of Arran; Chancellor of Oxford 1715–58.

7. Dr William King (1685–1763), Principal of St Mary Hall; a strong Jacobite.

8. 'Sir Robert Walpole, Earl of Orford, is only mentioned in this place in his quality of author: it is not proper nor necessary for me to touch his character here—sixteen unfortunate and inglorious years since his removal have already written his elogium!' (*Royal and Noble Authors, Works* i. 447).

9. The Duchess of Marlborough; HW wrote a satiric criticism of her *Apology for her Conduct,* 1742 (*Royal and Noble Authors, Works* i. 489–91).

10. But it appears that she was angry. See *post* 23 July 1763, n. 14.

11. Dr John Brown (1715–66), author; his *Estimate of the Manners and Principles of the Times,* 2 vols, 1757–8, was highly successful.

12. Sir Charles Hanbury Williams had been confined for insanity for some months since his return from St Petersburg. At the time of this letter he seemed to have recovered, but later in the year relapsed; see Earl of Ilchester and Mrs Langford-Brooke, *Life of Sir Charles Hanbury-Williams,* 1929, pp. 421–8. His reply to the *Estimate,* though praised by some of his friends, was not published.

13. A 'Mrs Clark, at Pitt's Buildings, near Campden House' (ibid. 423).

14. Regina Mingotti (1728–1807), *née* Valentini; opera singer (Sir George Grove, *Dictionary of Music*).

15. Hon. Isabella Byron (1721–95), m. (1) (1743) Henry Howard, 4th E. of Carlisle; m. (2) (1759) Sir William Musgrave, 6th Bt. HW repeats this anecdote in COLE ii. 187 n. 5; which see for passages against the opera from Brown's *Estimate.*

story of his swearing, Brown went to Dodsley[16] in a most scurrilous
and hectoring manner, threatening Dodsley if he should publish anything personal against him, abusing Sir Charles for a coward and
most abandoned man, and bidding Dodsley tell the latter, that he had
a cousin in the army, who would call Sir Charles to account for any
reflections on him, Brown. Stay; this Christian message from a divine, who by the way has a chapter in his book against duelling,[17] is
not all. Dodsley refused to carry any such message unless in writing.
The Doctor, enough in his senses to know the consequences of that,[18]
refused; and at last a short verbal message more decently worded was
agreed on. To this Sir Charles made Dodsley write down this answer;
'that he could not but be surprised at Brown's message, after that he,
Sir Charles, had at Ranby's[19] desire sent Brown a written assurance
that he intended to say nothing personal of him—nay, nor should yet,
unless Brown's impertinence made it necessary.' This proper reply
Dodsley sent: Brown wrote back that he should send an answer to Sir
Charles himself; but bid Dodsley take notice that printing the works
of a supposed lunatic might be imputed to the printer himself, and
which he the Doctor should *chastise*. Dodsley, after notifying this
new and unprovoked insolence to Mr Fox and Garrick, the one
friend of Sir Charles, the other of Brown,[20] returned a very proper,
decent yet firm answer, with assurances of *repaying chastisement* of
any sort. Is it credible? This audacious man sent only a card back,
saying, '*Footman's language I never return, J. Brown.*' You know
how decent, humble, inoffensive a creature Dodsley is, how little apt
to forget or disguise his having been a footman! But there is no ex-
aggerating this behaviour by reflections! On the same card he tells
Dodsley that he cannot now accept but returns his present of the two
last volumes of his collection of poems,[21] and assures him that they
are not soiled by the reading—He wrote in the first volumes himself
—nothing else is worth his reading. But the best picture of him is his
own second volume, which beats all the Scaligers and Scioppius's[22]

16. Robert Dodsley (1703–64), poet,
dramatist, and leading bookseller; began
life as a footman.

17. Vol. ii, p. 153.

18. He could have been bound to keep
the peace.

19. John Ranby (1703–73), surgeon. He
attended Sir Robert Walpole in his last
illness.

20. Garrick had produced Brown's trage-
dies *Barbarossa* and *Athelstane* and had
acted in them.

21. Vols. 5 and 6 of Dodsley's *Collection
of Poems by Various Hands*, 1748–58, were
published in this year. Brown had contributed to vol. 3.

22. Joseph Justus Scaliger (1540–1609),
and Kaspar Scioppius (1576–1649), famous

for vanity and insolent impertinence. What is delightful; in the first
volume he had deified Warburton, but the success of that trumpery
has made Warburton jealous, and occasioned a coolness—but enough
of this jackanapes!

Your brother has been here, and as he is to go tomorrow, and the
pedigree is not quite finished and as you will be impatient, and as it
is impossible for us to transcribe Welsh which we cannot read, without your assistance, who don't understand it neither, we have determined that the Colonel should carry the pedigree to you; you will
examine it, and bring it with you to Strawberry, where it can be finished under your own eye, better than it is possible to do without.
Adieu! I have not writ so long a letter this age and am quite weary.

Yours ever

H. W.

To Montagu, Thursday 6 July 1758

Address: To George Montagu Esq. at Greatworth near Brackley, Northamptonshire. Free Hor. Walpole. *Postmark:* 6 IY.

Strawberry Hill, July 6th, 1758.

YOU may believe I was thoroughly disappointed in not seeing
you here as I expected. I grieve for the reason, and wish you had
told me that your brother was quite recovered. Must I give you over
for the summer? Sure you are in my debt.

That regiments are going to Germany is certain; which, except the
Blues, I know not. Of all secrets, I am not in any Irish ones. I hope
for your sake, your Colonel is not of the number—but how can you
talk in the manner you do of Prince Ferdinand?[1] Don't you know,
that next to Mr Pitt and Mr Delaval,[2] he is the most fashionable man

scholars and polemists; Scaliger was hu-
miliated by Scioppius's ad hominem attacks on his descent, of which he was very
vain (*New International Encyclopædia*, 2d
edn, New York, 1914–16).

1. Prince Ferdinand of Brunswick (1721–
92), 'Herzog von Braunschweig-Lüneburg,'
son of Ferdinand Albert II of Brunswick-
Wolfenbüttel, defeated the French 23 June

at Crefeld. He had taken command of the
Hanoverian armies when they resumed
the field after George II's refusal to ratify
the Convention of Kloster Zeven (*Allgemeine Deutsche Biographie*, Leipzig, 1875–
1912, vi. 682–90).

2. Francis Blake Delaval (ca 1727–71),
K.B., 1761; M.P. Andover 1754–68; brother
of John Hussey Delaval, 1st Bn Delaval;
one of the volunteers who had accompa-

in England? Have not the Tower guns and all the parsons in London been ordered to pray for him? You have lived in Northamptonshire till you are ignorant that Hanover is in Middlesex,[3] as the Bishop's palace at Chelsea is in the diocese of Winchester.[4] In hopes that you will grow better acquainted with *your own country,* I remain your affect.

HORATIUS VALPOLHAUSEN

To MONTAGU, Sunday 20 August 1758

Strawberry Hill, Aug. 20, 1758.

AFTER some silence, one might take the opportunities of Cherburg and Louisbourg,[1] to revive a little correspondence with popular topics: but I think you are no violent politician, and I am full as little so; I will therefore tell you of what I of course care more, and I am willing to presume you do too, that is myself. I have been journeying much since I heard from you: first to the Vine, where I was greatly pleased with the alterations;[2] the garden is quite beautified and the house dignified. We went over to the Grange,[3] that sweet house of my Lord Keeper's that you saw too. The pictures are very good, and I was particularly pleased with the procession, which you was told was by Rubens, but is certainly Vandyke's sketch for

nied the expedition against St Malo; 'so ridiculous a character, that it has put a stop to the mode [of volunteering] which was spreading' (HW to Mann 31 May 1758); William Cole, in a glowing account of him in John Nichols, *Literary Illustrations,* 1817–58, viii. 574, declares that he 'acquired his ribband in the noblest way; it was given him on his return from the coast of France where he had served as a volunteer and conducted himself bravely.' He was one of the Duke of York's set, and an exponent of aristocratic amateur theatricals; see Lodge, *Peerage of Ireland,* 1789, vii. 232–3; GEC; GM 1771, xli. 378; Foster, *Alumni Oxon; Whitehall Evening Post* 6–8 Aug. 1771; William Cooke, *Memoirs of Samuel Foote,* 1805, ii. 65–79 (several anecdotes).

3. Alluding to the King's preoccupation with Hanoverian affairs.

4. Winchester House, next to the manor house in Chelsea, was purchased in 1663,

and by an act of Parliament of that year constituted a part of the diocese of Winchester (Thomas Faulkner, *Historical . . . Description of Chelsea,* 1810, p. 327). It was pulled down in 1828.

1. Both had been recently captured; see HW to Mann 12 Aug. 1758.

2. Exactly what these were is not clear. Mr Charles L. Chute of the Vyne writes that perhaps a Tudor wall which ran across the SE front was removed at this time.

3. Near Alresford, Hants; designed by Inigo Jones (see *Anecdotes, Works* iii. 276), whose square brick structure forms 'the nucleus of the present house' (*Vict. Co. Hist. Hants* iii. 394). At the time of HW's visit, it was the seat of Sir Robert Henley (ca 1708–72), Kt; cr. (1760) Bn Henley, (1764) E. of Northington; Lord Keeper 1757; Lord Chancellor 1761.

part of that great work that he was to have executed in the Banqueting House.[4] You did not tell me of a very fine Holbein,[5] a woman, who was evidently some princess of the white rose.

I am just now returned from Ragley, which has had a great deal done to it since I was there last.[6] Browne has improved both the ground and the water, though not quite to perfection. This is the case of the house, where there are no striking faults, but it wants a few Chute—or Bentley—touches. I have recommended some dignifying of the salon with Seymours and Fitzroys, Henry the Eighths and Charles the Seconds. They will correspond well to the proudest situation imaginable. I have already dragged some ancestors out of the dust there and written their names on their portraits; besides which I have found and brought up to have repaired an incomparable picture of Van Helmont[7] by Sir Peter Lely—But now for recoveries—think what I have in part recovered! Only the state papers, private letters etc. etc. of the two Lords Conway, Secretaries of State.[8] How you will rejoice and how you will grieve!—They seem to have laid up every scrap of paper they ever had from the middle of Queen Elizabeth's reign to the middle of Charles II's. By the accounts of the family there were whole rooms full, all which, during the absence of the last[8a] and the minority of the present lord, were by the ignorance of a steward consigned to the oven and to the uses of the house. What remained, except one box that was kept till almost rotten in a cupboard, were thrown loose into the lumber-room, where spread on the pavements, they supported old marbles and screens and boxes. From thence I have dragged all I could, and have literally, taking altogether, brought away a chest near five feet long, three wide and two

4. HW's identification is correct; see Lionel Cust, *Anthony Van Dyck*, 1900, pp. 141, 286; in 1900 the work was at Belvoir.

5. Possibly an unnamed portrait 'head with hands, by Holbein' which Waagen saw at Lord Ashburton's town house (Gustav Frederick Waagen, *Treasures of Art in Great Britain*, 1854, ii. 112). The Grange had passed from the Henley family to the Drummonds, and in 1816 to Alexander Baring, cr. (1835) Bn Ashburton (*Vict. Co. Hist. Hants* iii. 395).

6. Apparently the visit described *ante* 22 July 1751.

7. Francis Mercurius van Helmont (1614–98), physician and philosopher; lived

at Ragley as physician to Anne Finch, Viscountess Conway (Marjorie Hope Nicolson, *Conway Letters*, New Haven, 1930, pp. 310–77, 456–7). The Lely portrait is now in the National Gallery; see ibid., where it is reproduced p. 308. HW had Müntz copy the picture and hung it in the Great North Bedchamber (*Des. of SH, Works* ii. 497). It was sold SH xx. 95 for 6 gns to Luxmoore.

8. Edward Conway (ca 1564–1631), 1st Vct Conway; Secretary of State 1623–8. The Secretary of State 1681–3 was the 3d Vct.

8a. Francis Seymour Conway (1679–1732), cr. (1703) Bn Conway.

deep, brimful. Half are bills, another part rotten, another gnawed by rats, yet I have already found enough to repay my trouble and curiosity, not enough to satisfy it. I will only tell you of three letters of the great Strafford,[9] and three long ones of news of Mr Garrard Master of the Charterhouse,[10] all six written on paper edged with green, like modern French paper. There are handwritings of everybody, all their seals perfect, and the ribbands with which they tied their letters: The original proclamation of Charles I signed by the Privy Council, a letter to King James from his son-in-law of Bohemia[11] with his seal, and many, very many letters of negotiation from the Earl of Bristol[12] in Spain, Sir Dudley Carleton,[13] Lord Chichester[14] and Sir Thomas Roe[15]—what say you?—will not here be food for the press?[16]

I have picked up a little painted glass too, and have got a promise of some old statues,[17] lately dug up, which formerly adorned the cathedral of Litchfield—you see, I continue to labour in my vocation —of which I can give you a comical instance; I remembered a rose in painted glass in a little village going to Ragley, which I remarked passing by five years ago, told Mr Conway on which hand it would be and found it in the very spot. I saw a very good and perfect tomb at Aulcester[18] of Sir Fulke Grevile's[19] father and mother, and a wretched old house with a very handsome gateway of stone, at Colton,[20] belonging to Sir Robert Throckmorton.[21] There is nothing else tolerable

9. Sir Thomas Wentworth (1593–1641), cr. (1628) Vct Wentworth, (1640) E. of Strafford.

10. George Garrard, b. ca 1580; Master of the Charterhouse 1637–50, when he retired from age (Foster, *Alumni Oxon;* [Robert Smythe] *Historical Account of Charter-House,* 1808, p. 236). Many of his letters to Strafford are in *The Earl of Strafford's Letters and Dispatches,* ed. William Knowle, 1739.

11. Frederick V (1596–1632), King of Bohemia and Elector Palatine; m. James I's dau. Elizabeth.

12. John Digby (1586–1653), cr. (1618) Bn Digby, (1622) E. of Bristol; ambassador.

13. Sir Dudley Carleton (1574–1632), Kt; cr. (1626) Bn Carlton, and (1628) Vct Dorchester; ambassador and Secretary of State.

14. Arthur Chichester (1563–1625), cr. (1613) Bn Chichester; Lord Deputy in Ireland and ambassador to the Palatinate.

15. Sir Thomas Roe (?1581–1644), explorer and ambassador.

16. HW did not print any of these; see *ante* 22 July 1751, n. 26.

17. HW apparently failed to get these, for they do not appear in SH Sale Cat.

18. Alcester.

19. Sir Fulke Greville (d. 1606), Kt; father of 1st Bn Brooke; the tomb of his father Sir Fulke Greville (d. 1559), and of his mother Elizabeth Willoughby (d. 1560), is illustrated in William Dugdale, *Antiquities of Warwickshire,* 1656, p. 573; see also pp. 570–1.

20. Coughton, near Alcester, Warw. Dugdale (ibid. 561) speaks of a 'castle-like gatehouse of free-stone' built by Sir George Throckmorton (d. 1553) 'intending (as it should seem) to have made the rest of his house suitable thereto.'

21. Sir Robert Throckmorton (1702–91), 4th Bt, of Coughton.

but 22 coats of the matches of the family in painted glass.[22] You cannot imagine how astonished a Mr Seward[23] a learned clergyman was, who came to Ragley while I was there. Strolling about the house he saw me first sitting on the pavement of the lumber room, with Louis,[24] all over cobwebs, and dirt and mortar, then found me in his own room on a ladder writing on a picture,[25] and half an hour afterwards lying on the grass in the court with the dogs and the children in my slippers and without my hat. He had had some doubt whether I was the painter or the factotum of the family but you would have died at his surprise when he saw me walk into dinner dressed and sit by my Lady Hertford. Lord Lyttelton was there and the conversation turned on literature—Finding me not quite ignorant, added to the parson's wonder, but he could not contain himself any longer, when after dinner he saw me go to romps and jumping with the two boys[26]—He broke out to my Lady Hertford, and begged to know who and what sort of man I really was, for he had never met with anything of the kind. Adieu!

Yours ever

H. W.

To Montagu, Tuesday 3 October 1758

Address: To George Montagu Esq. at Greatworth near Brackley, Northamptonshire. Free Hor. Walpole. *Postmark:* 3 OC RG.

Arlington Street, Oct. 3d, 1758.

HAVING had no news to send you, but the massacre at St Cas,[1] not agreeable enough for a letter, I stayed till I had something

22. Dugdale (loc. cit.) illustrates all twenty-two, together with seven other coats (not all from the same window).

23. Rev. Thomas Seward (1708–90), Canon of Lichfield; father of Anna Seward the poetess (DNB). 'He was a genteel, well-bred, dignified clergyman, had travelled with Lord Charles Fitzroy [1718–39] . . . who died when abroad, and he had lived much in the great world' (Boswell, *Johnson* ii. 467). As Lady Hertford was Lord Charles's sister, Seward's presence at Ragley is explained.

24. HW's Swiss servant, d. 1767 (*post* 13 Jan. 1767).

25. An habitual practice of HW's.

26. Hon. (after 1793 Lord) Henry Seymour-Conway (1746–1830), of Norris Castle, Isle of Wight; M.P. Coventry 1766–74; Midhurst 1774–80; Downton 1780–84; Orford 1784–94. Hon. (after 1793 Lord) Robert Seymour-Conway (1748–1831), of Taliaris, Carmarthenshire; M.P. Orford 1771–84, 1794–1807; Wootton Bassett 1784–90; Carmarthen 1807–20 (Collins, *Peerage*, 1812, ii. 564–5; Richard A. Austen-Leigh, *Eton College Register 1753–90*, 1921). Both dropped the name Conway in later life.

1. St-Cast, Brittany; on 11 Sept., 750

to send you, and behold a book! I have delivered to portly old Richard,[2] your ancient nurse, the new produce of the Strawberry-press.[3]

You know that the wife of Bath[4] is gone to maunder at St Peter,
and before he could hobble to the gate, my Lady Burlington,[5] cursing
and blaspheming, overtook t'other Countess, and both together made
such an uproar, that the cock flew up into the tree of life for safety,
and St Peter himself turned the key and hid himself; and as nobody
could get into t'other world, half the guards[6] are come back again,
and appeared in the park today, but such dismal ghostly figures, that
my Lady Townshend was really frightened, and is again[7] likely to
turn Methodist.

Do you design or do you not, to look at Strawberry as you come to
town? If you do, I will send a card to my neighbour Mrs Holman to
meet you any day five weeks that you please—or I can amuse you
without cards—such fat bits of your *dear Dad* old Jammy,[8] as I have
found among the Conway papers, such morsels of all sorts!—but come
and see—adieu!

Yours ever

H. W.

men of the Guards were killed or wounded
in a rearguard action defending an embarkation, chiefly owing to the carelessness
of Gen. Bligh the commander; see HW to
Mann 22 Sept. 1758; Fortescue, *British
Army* ii. 350–1.

2. Richard Brown the tobacconist; *ante*
ca 13 July 1756.

3. *An Account of Russia, as it was in
the year 1710,* by Charles Whitworth
(1675–1725), cr. (1721) Bn Whitworth; HW
wrote the Advertisement. See *Journal of
the Printing Office* 7; 'Short Notes.'

4. The Countess of Bath d. 14 Sept.

5. Messenger Monsey to Mrs Elizabeth
Montagu, 23 Sept. 1758: 'Lady Burlington
is dead. Mrs G[arrick] gets nothing, but
rid of her, and that's a great deal, I think.
She gives the Duke of D[evonshire] £3000
per annum . . . not a farthing to any one
servant, she had some lived with her 20
or 25 years' (Emily J. Climenson, *Elizabeth Montagu the Queen of the Blue-
stockings,* 1906, ii. 145). For her 'cursing
and blaspheming' see HW to Conway 19
Sept. 1758.

6. Above n. 1.

7. See *ante* 3 Sept. 1748.

8. James I. The Duke of Buckingham
addressed him in his letters as 'Dear Dad
and Gossip,' while in the letters which the
King wrote to Buckingham and Prince
Charles in Spain, he signs himself, 'Your
dear Dad, James R.,' and on one occasion
calls himself 'your old Dad' (14 June 1623).
See HW to Dalrymple 13 Feb. 1762: 'The
letters of the Duke of Buckingham are
truly valuable. . . . I have three of James
among the Conway papers, a proper coun-
terpart.' The allusive manner in which
HW describes James suggests that both
he and Montagu were already familiar
with the extraordinary tone of the James
I–Buckingham correspondence. But at
this time none of their letters had been
published, with the exception of some extracts in *Complete History of England* [ed.
White Kennett] 1706–19, ii. 697. The bulk
of them were in the Harleian collection
in the British Museum (No. 6987), and
were not open to inspection; see HW to
Dalrymple 23 Feb. 1764. HW, however,
seems to have been familiar with them in
1742; see HW to Mann 8 March 1742. The
letters in the Conway papers probably
found their way there from Edward Con-

To Montagu, Tuesday 24 October 1758

Arlington Street, Oct. 24, 1758.

I AM a little sorry that my preface,[1] like the show-cloth to a sight, entertained you more than the *Bears*[2] that it invited you in to see. I don't mean that I am not glad to have written anything that meets your approbation; but if Lord Whitworth's work is not better than my preface, I fear he has much less merit than I thought he had.

Your complaint of your eyes makes me feel for you: mine have been very weak again, and I am taking the bark, which did them so much service last year. I don't know how to give up the employment of them, I mean, reading—for as to writing, I am absolutely winding up my bottom,[2a] for twenty reasons. The first and perhaps the best, I have writ enough—the next; by what I have writ, the world thinks I am not a fool, which was just what I wished them to think, having always lived in terror of that oracular saying, Ἡρώων παῖδες λῶβοῖ,[3] which Mr Bentley translated with so much more parts than the vain and malicious *Hero* could have done that set him the task, I mean his father, 'The sons of heroes are loobies.' My last reason is, I find my little stock of reputation very troublesome, both to maintain, and to undergo the consequences—it has dipped me in *erudite* correspond-ences[4]—I receive letters every week that compliment my learning—now as there is nothing I hold so cheap as a learned man, except an unlearned one, this title is insupportable to me; if I have not a care, I shall be called learned, till somebody abuses me, for *not* being learned, as they, not I, fancied I was. In short, I propose to have noth-ing more to do with the world, but divert myself in it as an obscure passenger—pleasure, virtu, politics, and literature, I have tried them all, and have had enough of them—content and tranquillity with now

way, first Viscount Conway, Secretary of State at the time of the Spanish Marriage fiasco; they seem not to have been printed. A selection of the Harleian letters was published by the 2d Earl of Hardwicke in his *Miscellaneous State Papers*, 1778, i. 399–472.

1. The Advertisement to Lord Whit-worth's *Account of Russia*, reprinted in *Works* i. 223–7.

2. Cf. *Macbeth* III. iv. 100, 'the rugged Russian bear'; and perhaps HW is play-ing on bears as (1) uncouth, unlettered persons (OED *sb.*1 I.2), (2) exhibits at 18th-century shows and fairs.

2a. Literally, to coil a skein of thread (OED: 'bottom' *sb.* 15; 'wind,' *v.*1 22 c. *b*).

3. Dr R. W. Chapman believes that the last word in this epigram should be spelt λῶβαι, and that it is not classical Greek but by Dr Bentley himself.

4. With Dr Ducarel, Sir David Dalrym-ple, Dr Birch, Hume, and the Rev. Henry Zouch.

and then a little of three of them,[5] that I may not grow morose, shall satisfy the rest of a life that is to have much idleness and I hope a little goodness—for politics—a long adieu![6] With some of the Cardinal de Retz's[7] experience, though with none of his genius, I see the folly of taking a violent part without any view (I don't mean to commend a violent part *with* a view, that is still worse). I leave the state to be scrambled for by Mazarine,[8] at once cowardly and enterprising, ostentatious, jealous and false; by Louvois,[9] rash and dark; by Colbert,[10] the affector of national interest, with designs, not much better; and I leave the Abbé de la Rigbière[11] to sell the weak Duke of Orleans,[12] to whoever has money to buy him, or would buy him to get money—at least these are my present reflections[13]—if I should change them tomorrow, remember, I am not only a human creature, but that I am I, that is, one of the weakest of human creatures; and so sensible of my fickleness, that I am sometimes inclined to keep a diary of my mind, as people do of the weather—Today, you see it is temperate—tomorrow, it may again blow, politics and be stormy—for while I have so much quicksilver left, I fear my Passionometer will be susceptible of sudden changes. What do years give one? Experience. Experience, what? Reflections. Reflections, what?—nothing that ever I could find —nor can I well agree with Waller that

> The soul's dark cottage batter'd and decay'd
> Lets in new light through chinks that Time has made—[14]

chinks I am afraid there are, but instead of new light, I find nothing but darkness visible,[14a] that serves only to discover sights of woe! I

---

5. HW kept his resolution about literature until he began, 1 Jan. 1760, to write the most ambitious of all his scholarly works, *Anecdotes of Painting in England* ('Short Notes').

6. HW wrote in *Mem. Geo. II* that he had 'abandoned the theatre of affairs' 'at the end of 1758' (iii. 160), in a passage 'Finished Oct. 27, 1759' (ibid. 163).

7. Jean-François-Paul de Gondi (1614–79), Cardinal de Retz, had, like HW, 'a propensity to faction' (ibid. 159). He took a leading part in the disturbances of the Fronde, was exiled, and on his return withdrew from politics and court life; see his *Mémoires*, 1717.

8. Newcastle.

9. Fox.

10. Pitt.

11. Rigby. Louis Barbier (d. 1670), known as the Abbé de la Rivière, Bp of Langres 1656, completely dominated Gaston, Duc d'Orléans (1608–60), brother of Louis XIII; see Ludovic Lalanne, *Dictionnaire historique de la France*, 1872.

12. Duke of Bedford.

13. Compare *Mem. Geo. II* iii. 158–63, where HW, as here, renounces politics and discusses briefly the leaders of the state.

14. Edmund Waller (1606–87), 'On the foregoing Divine Poems,' *Works*, ed. Elijah Fenton, 1729, p. 317. HW's copy (now wsl) bears his youthful inscription and the date 1729.

14a. *Paradise Lost* i. 63.

look back through my chinks—I find errors, follies, faults—forwards, old age and death; pleasures fleeting from me, no virtues succeeding to their place—*il faut avouer,* I want all my quicksilver to make such a background receive any other objects![15]

I am glad Mr Frederick Montagu thinks so well of me as to be sure I shall be glad to see him without an invitation. For you, I had already perceived that you would not come to Strawberry this year—adieu!

Remember, nobody is to see this letter, but yourself and the clerks of the post office.[16]

Yours ever

H. W.

To Montagu, Sunday 26 November 1758

Address: To George Montagu Esq. at Greatworth near Brackley, Northamptonshire. Free Hor. Walpole.

Arlington Street, Nov. 26, 1758.

HOW can you make me formal excuses for sending me a few covers to frank? Have you so little right to any act of friendship from me, that you should apologize for making me do what is scarce any act at all?—however, your man has not called for the covers, though they have been ready this fortnight.

I shall be very glad to see your brother in town, but I cannot quite take him in full of payment. I trust you will stay the longer for coming the later.

There is not a syllable of news. The Parliament is met, but empty, and totally oppositionless. Your great Cu moved in the Lords,[1] but did not shine much. The great Cu of all Cues[2] is out of order; not in danger, but certainly breaking.

15. HW's mood may have been caused by his reflections on Galfridus Mann's death in HW to Mann 24 Oct. 1758.
16. The common 18th-century practice of opening letters at the postoffice was not illegal if done under a warrant from one of the Secretaries of State; and it is still permissible, even in peacetime; see *English Historical Review* 1918, xxxiii. 320–7.

HW's references to surveillance of his correspondence are innumerable; but it is not definitely known that his mail was ever opened or copied in England. Cf. DU DEFFAND.
1. Probably the Address, on 24 Nov. (GM 1758, xxviii. 553); the debates have not been preserved.
2. The King.

My eyes are performing such a strict quarantine, that you must excuse my brevity. Adieu!

Yours faithfully

H. W.

To Montagu, Tuesday 26 December 1758

Arlington Street, Dec. 26, 1758.

IT is so little extraordinary to find you doing what is friendly and obliging, that one don't take half notice enough of it. Can't you let Mr Conway go to Sluys[1] without taking notice of it? How would you be hurt, if he continued to be oppressed? What is it to you whether I am glad or sorry? Can't you enjoy yourself whether I am happy or not?—I suppose if I was to have a misfortune, you would immediately be concerned at it! How troublesome it is to have you sincere and good-natured!—Do, be a little more like the rest of the world.

I have been at Strawberry these three days and don't know a tittle—the last thing I heard before I went, was, that Colonel Yorke[2] is going to be married to one or both of the Miss Crasteyns, nieces of the rich grocer that died three years ago.[3] They have £260,000 apiece. A Marchioness Grey[4] or a grocer, nothing comes amiss to the digestion of that family. If the rest of the trunk was filled with money, I believe they would really marry Carafattatonadaht—what was the lump of deformity called in the Persian Tales, that was sent to the Cady in a

1. Conway had been sent to Hellevoet-sluis to settle a cartel about prisoners; see HW to Conway 19 Jan. 1759. He was in disfavour with Pitt and the King on account of the Rochfort expedition of the year before, from which arose the 'oppression' HW speaks of.

2. Col. the Hon. Joseph Yorke (1724–92), K.B. 1761; cr. (1788) Bn Dover; ambassador to the Hague.

3. 'Deaths . . . Dec. 7, Abraham Crasteyn, Esq., an eminent Hamburg merchant, worth 400,000 l. He has left 100,000 l. to his relict, with all his plate jewels, etc. and . . . 200,000 l. to his brother Francis' (GM 1754, xxiv. 579). 'I remember when the famous peddling Crastein died some 10 years ago immensely rich, and raised from the dunghill, and who gave his wife, an apothecary's daughter at Bath, and a very clever woman, £100,000 leaving the rest to his sister, a deformed crooked woman in Holland, where Sir Joseph Y. was our Ambassador (for Crastein was a Dutchman), it was, by way of joke, in most of the public papers, that he was paying his addresses to that lady' (William Cole, *Blecheley Diary*, ed. Francis G. Stokes, 1931, pp. 37–8). The Crasteyn heiresses have not been identified.

4. Jemima Campbell (1722–97), Marchioness Grey *suo jure*; m. (1740) Philip Yorke, 2d E. of Hardwicke, 1764.

coffer?[5]—and as to marrying both the girls, it would cost my Lord Hardwicke but a new Marriage Bill; I suppose it is all one to his conscience whether he prohibits matrimony or licenses bigamy.

Poor Sir Charles Williams is relapsed, and strictly confined. As you come so late, I trust you will stay with us the longer. Adieu!

Yours ever

H. W.

To Montagu, Thursday 26 April 1759

Don't read this letter even to your parson.[1]

Arlington Street, April 26, 1759.

YOUR brother, your Wetenhalls, and the ancient Baron[2] and Baroness Dacre of the South, are to dine with me at Strawberry Hill next Sunday. Divers have been the negotiations about it; your sister you know is often impeded by a purge or a prayer; and I on the other hand who never rise in a morning, have two balls[3] on my hands this week to keep me in bed the next day till dinner time—well! it is charming to be so young! The follies of the town are so much more agreeable than the wisdom of my brethren the authors, that I think for the future I shall never write beyond a card, nor print beyond Mrs Clive's benefit tickets.

Our great match[4] approaches: I dine at Lord Waldegrave's presently, and suppose I shall then hear the day. I have quite reconciled my Lady Townshend to the match (saving her abusing us all) by desiring her to choose my wedding clothes—but I am to pay the additional price of being ridiculous, to which I submit: she has chosen

5. *The Thousand and One Days: Persian Tales,* translated from the French of François Pétis de la Croix by Ambrose Philips. The tale for the fifty-second day (4th edn 1726, pp. 306–24) tells how a wicked Cadi of Bagdad was tricked into marrying a monstrosity named Cayfacattaddahri, who was brought to him in a chest.

1. Rev. Charles Everard (later Booth) (ca 1726–92), M.A. Brasenose; Rector of Greatworth, 1752; of Middleton Cheney,

Northants, which he held with Greatworth, 1764 (George Baker, *History . . . of the County of Northampton,* 1822–46, i. 510). He seems to have been Montagu's chief confidant at Greatworth (see *post* 25 May 1763).

2. Thomas Barrett-Lennard (1717–86), 17th Bn Dacre of the South; antiquary.

3. At Bedford House and at the Conollys'; both described below.

4. Between Lord Waldegrave and HW's niece, Maria Walpole.

me a white ground with purple and green flowers. I represented, that however young my spirits may be, my bloom is rather past; but the moment I declared against juvenile colours, I found it was determined I should have nothing else—so be it! I have not tried the same methods of reconciling the Bedfords to the match:[5] as they counterfeit deeper civility, I shall not come off with them by letting them dress me up like Garrick or a shepherd. T'other night I had an uncomfortable situation with the Duchess: we had played late at loo at Lady Jane Scot's;[6] I came downstairs with their two Graces of Bedford and Grafton: there was no chair for me; I said I would walk till I met one: 'Oh!' said the Duchess of Grafton, 'the Duchess of Bedford will set you down.' There were we charmingly awkward and complimenting. However, she was forced to press it, and I to accept it—in a minute she spied a hackney chair—'Oh! there is a chair—but I beg your pardon, it looks as if I wanted to get rid of you, but indeed I don't—only I am afraid the Duke will want his supper'—you may imagine how much I was afraid of making him wait. The ball at Bedford House on Monday was very numerous and magnificent: the two princes[7] were there, deep hazard and the Dutch deputies,[8] who are a proverb for their dullness: they have brought with them a young Dutchman,[9] who is the richest man of Amsterdam—I am amazed Mr Yorke has not married him!—But the delightful part of the night was the appearance of the Duke of Newcastle, who is veering round again, as it is time to betray Mr Pitt. The Duchess was at the very upper end of the gallery, and though some of the Pelham court were there too, yet they showed so little cordiality to this revival of connection, that Newcastle had nobody to attend him but Sir Edward Montagu,[10] who kept pushing him all up the gallery. From thence he went into the hazard-room, and wriggled, and shuffled, and lisped and winked and spied, till he got behind the Duke of Cumberland, the Duke of Bedford and Rigby; the first of whom did not deign to take notice of him—but he must come to it. You would have died to

5. Aside from the general interest in the marriage of a K.G. to the beautiful illegitimate Maria Walpole, the Bedfords were concerned and connected through the marriage of the Duchess's sister to the bridegroom's brother.

6. Lady Jane Scott (1723–79), dau. of 2d D. of Buccleuch (Scots Peerage, 1904–10, ii. 241; Coke, Journals, passim).

7. The Prince of Wales and Prince Edward.

8. In England to settle a dispute about English seizures of Dutch ships loaded with contraband; see Mem. Geo. II iii. 139–40; Grenville Papers, ed. William J. Smith, 1852–3, i. 296–302.

9. Not identified.

10. Sir Edward Hussey-Montagu.

see Newcastle's pitiful and distressed figure—nobody went near him, he tried to flatter people that were too busy to mind him—in short he was quite disconcerted—his treachery used to be so sheathed in folly that he was never out of countenance—but it is plain he grows old. To finish his confusion and anxiety, George Selwyn, Brand and I went and stood near him, and in half whispers that he might hear, said, 'Lord, how he is broke! How old he looks!' Then I said, 'This room feels very cold; I believe there never is any fire in it.' Presently afterwards, I said, 'Well, I'll not stay here; this room has been washed today.' In short, I believe we made him take a double dose of Gascoign's powder[11] when he went home. Next night, Brand and I communicated this interview to Lord Temple, who was in agonies, and yesterday his chariot was seen in forty different parts of the town. I take for granted that Fox will not resist these overtures—and then we shall see the Paymastership, the Secretaryship of Ireland and all Calcraft's[12] regiments once more afloat!

May 1st

I did not finish this letter last week, for the picture[12a] could not set out till next Thursday. Your kin brought Lord Mandeville[13] with them to Strawberry; he was very civil and good-humoured, and I trust I was so too. My nuptialities dined there yesterday. The wedding is fixed for the fifteenth. The town, who saw Maria set out in the Earl's coach, concluded it was yesterday. He notified his marriage to the monarch last Saturday, and it was received civilly.

Mrs Thornhill[14] is dead, and I am impatient to hear the fate of

11. Not identified.
12. John Calcraft (1726–72), politician; became, through his friendship with Fox, agent for many regiments, and acquired an immense fortune. HW's meaning in this passage is obscure, but it is clear that he expected the upshot of the maneuvers he had set in train to be the loss of their places by Fox (Paymaster), Rigby (Secretary in Ireland), and Calcraft (regimental agent), the chief placeholders in the Bedford-Fox faction which was otherwise in eclipse. How their removal was to come about is not clear. The 'interview' HW communicated to Temple must have been Newcastle's with Cumberland, Bedford, and Rigby; it is the only incident mentioned of any possible political signifi-

cance. This might conceivably agonize Lord Temple as indicating a combination of Newcastle with the Bedford-Fox group to oust the dominant Pitt-Temple-Grenville faction in the coalition government, and such a proposal might be the overtures Fox could not resist. Finally, HW's thought may have been that as a result of such plotting the alarmed Pitt-Temple group would have Fox and Rigby dismissed.
12a. See next letter.
13. George Montagu (1737–88), styled Vct Mandeville; 4th D. of Manchester 1762.
14. 'Daughter of the late Sir Robert Thornhill' (Lloyd's Evening Post 2–4 May 1759, iv. 429).

Miss Mildmay.[15] The Princes Ferdinand and Henry[16] have been skir-
mishing, have been beaten and have beat, but with no decision.

The ball at Mr Conolly's[17] was by no means delightful—the house
is small, it was hot, and composed of young Irish. I was retiring when
they went to supper, but was fetched back to sup with Prince Edward
and the Duchess of Richmond,[18] who is his present passion. He had
chattered as much love to her as would serve ten balls: the conversation turned on the *Guardian*[19]—most unfortunately the Prince asked
her, if she should like *Mr Clackit*—'No indeed, sir,' said the Duchess.
Lord Tavistock[20] burst into a loud laugh, and I am afraid none of the
company quite kept their countenance—Adieu! This letter is gossiping enough for any Mr Clackit, but I know you love these details—

Yours ever

H. W.

To MONTAGU, Wednesday 16 May 1759

Arlington Street, May 16, 1759.

I PACKED up a long letter[1] to you in the case with the Earl of
Manchester,[2] which I suppose did not arrive at Greatworth before
you left it. Don't send for it, for there are private histories in it, that
should not travel post, and which will be full as new to you a month
hence.

Well! Maria was married yesterday. Don't we manage well? The

15. Probably Mr Chute's 'good and
amiable friend Miss Mildmay,' whose
death is noted *post* 4 June 1763.

16. Friedrich Heinrich Ludwig (1726–
1802), Prince of Prussia, brother of Frederick the Great (*Allgemeine Deutsche Biographie*, Leipzig, 1875–1912, xi. 561).

17. Right Hon. Thomas Conolly (1738–
1803), of Castletown, Ireland; landowner
and politician.

18. Lady Mary Bruce (1740–96), dau. of
Lady Ailesbury; m. (1757) Charles Lennox,
3d D. of Richmond. 'Prince Edward is
grown very fickle. Lady Millbank is already forgot, and given place to the
Duchess of Richmond, who he pursues
with great earnestness, but meets with so
little encouragement from her Grace that

I fancy he will soon grow weary' (Lady
Mary Coke to Lady Dalkeith 8 April 1758,
Coke, *Journals* i. p. lxxxiii, n; see also GM
1740, x. 203).

19. 'The *Guardian* was a favourite aft-
erpiece, and Clackit one of the characters'
(Mrs Piozzi). It was by Garrick; Clackit is
a silly, garrulous young man whom the
heroine spurns.

20. Francis Russell (1739–67), styled M.
of Tavistock; pre-deceased his father the
4th D. of Bedford.

1. The previous letter.

2. A portrait, probably of Sir Henry
Montagu (ca 1563–1642), cr. (1620) Vct
Mandeville and (1626) E. of Manchester;
Montagu's great-great-grandfather.

original day was not once put off, lawyers and milliners were all ready canonically. It was as sensible a wedding as ever was: there was neither form, nor indecency, both which generally meet on such occasions. They were married at my brother's in Pall Mall, just before dinner, by Mr Keppel;[3] the company, my brother, his son, Mrs Keppel and Charlotte, Lady Elizabeth Keppel,[4] Lady Betty Waldegrave and I. We dined there; the Earl and new Countess got into their post-chaise at eight o'clock, and went to Navestock[5] alone, where they stay till Saturday night: on Sunday she is to be presented—and to make my Lady Coventry distracted;[6] who t'other day told Lady Anne Conolly[7] how she had dreaded Lady Louisa's[8] arrival—'But,' said she, 'now I have seen her, I am easy.'

Maria was in a white and silver night gown with a hat very much pulled over her face; what one could see of it was handsomer than ever; a cold maiden blush gave her the sweetest delicacy in the world. I had like to have demolished the solemnity of the ceremony by laughing—when Mr Keppel read the words, *Bless thy servant and thy handmaid,* it struck me how ridiculous it would have been, had Miss Drax been the *handmaid* as she once was to have been.[9] Did I ever tell you what happened at my Lord Hertford's wedding? You remember that my father's style was not purity itself. As the bride was so young and so exceedingly bashful, and as my Lord Hertford is a little of the prude himself, great means were used to keep Sir Robert within bounds. He yawned and behaved decently. When the dessert was removed, the bishop,[10] who married them, said, 'Sir Robert, what health shall we drink?'—It was just after Vernon's conquest of Porto Bello—'I don't know,' replied my father;—'why, drink the admiral in the straits of Boccacieca!'[11]

We have had a sort of debate in the House of Commons on the bill for fixing the augmentation of the salaries of the judges: Charles

3. Hon. Frederick Keppel (1729–77), Canon of Windsor; Bp of Exeter, 1762; Dean of Windsor, 1765; m. Laura Walpole.

4. Lady Elizabeth Keppel (1739–68), m. (1764) Francis Russell, styled M. of Tavistock.

5. Near Chipping Ongar, Essex.

6. With her beauty.

7. Lady Anne Wentworth (ca 1712–97), dau. of 1st E. of Strafford, n.c.; m. (1733) William Conolly of Castletown, Kildare (GM 1797, lxvii pt. i. 253).

8. Lady Louisa Augusta Lennox (1743–1821), m. (1758) the Right Hon. Thomas Conolly of Castletown, Kildare, son of the above (Collins, *Peerage,* 1812, i. 209; Burke, *Landed Gentry*).

9. See *ante* 16 Nov. 1754, n. 5.

10. Not identified.

11. Boca Chica, the narrow entrance to the harbor of Cartagena, which Vernon was then (1741) besieging (William Laird Clowes, *The Royal Navy,* 1897–1903, iii. 69).

Townshend says, the book of *Judges* was saved by the book of *Numbers*.[12]

Lord Weymouth[13] is to be married on Tuesday, or as he said himself, to be *turned off;*[14] George Selwyn told him he wondered that he had not been *turned off*[15] before, for he still sits up drinking all night and gaming.

Well, are you ready to be invaded? for it seems invasions *from* France are coming into fashion again. A descent on Ireland at least is expected.[16] There has been a great quarrel between Mr Pitt and Lord Anson,[17] on the negligence of the latter—I suppose they will be reconciled by agreeing to hang some admiral, who will come too late to save Ireland, after it is impossible to save it.

Dr Young has published a new book,[18] on purpose as he says himself to have an opportunity of telling a story that he has known these forty years—Mr Addison sent for the young Lord Warwick,[19] as he was dying, to show him in what peace a Christian could die—unluckily he died of brandy—nothing makes a Christian die in peace like being maudlin![20]—but don't say this in Gath,[21] where you are! Adieu!

Yours ever

H. W.

PS. I forgot and must tell you two good stories of the little Prince Frederick.[22] He was describing to Lady Charlotte Edwin[23] the eu-

12. HW repeats this in *Mem. Geo. II* iii. 182–3; the opposition was rather captious, and significant only as indicating the underlying disharmony of the coalition government. The additional salary was passed by a vote of 169 to 39.

13. Thomas Thynne (1734–96), 3d Vct Weymouth; cr. (1789) M. of Bath; m. Lady Elizabeth Cavendish Bentinck, and, despite his aversion for the match, had fifteen children (Collins, *Peerage*, 1812, ii. 510–11).

14. Hanged.

15. Dismissed (of a servant) (OED).

16. The French were making 'immense preparations' (*Mem. Geo. II* iii. 184–6). See letters at this time between the Duke of Bedford (the Lord Lieutenant) and Archbishop Stone, relative to the defense of Ireland, in *Correspondence of John, Fourth Duke of Bedford,* ed. Lord John Russell, 1842–6, ii. 373–82.

17. Nothing more has been discovered about this.

18 'The book was *Conjectures on Original Composition,* and a very beautiful little work it is' (Mrs Piozzi).

19. Edward Henry Rich (1698–1721), 7th E. of Warwick; Addison's stepson.

20. The well-known story of Addison's last words is on pp. 100–2 of Dr Edward Young's *Conjectures.* He got it from Tickell, who is supposed to have made an earlier poetical allusion to it; see DNB, *sub* Addison. HW's version has no better authority, and is perhaps grounded on a 'report current in Johnson's time' that Addison's life 'was shortened by overdrinking'; this William J. Courthope, *Addison,* 1884, p. 151, rejects as unfounded.

21. Montagu was probably at his sister's.

22. Aged nine.

23. Lady Charlotte Hamilton (ca 1704–77), dau. of the 4th D. of Hamilton; m.

nuchs of the opera, but not easily finding proper words he said, 'I can't tell you, but I'll show you how they make them,' and began to unbutton. T'other day as he was with the Prince of Wales, Kitty Fisher[24] passed by, and the child named her—the Prince, to try him, asked, who that was?—'Why, a Miss'—'A Miss,' said the P. of W., 'why are not all girls, Misses?'—'Oh; but a particular sort of Miss—a Miss that sells oranges'—'Is there any harm in selling oranges?'—'Oh! but they are not such oranges as you buy—I believe they are a sort that my brother Edward buys'—apropos to this latter sort, I am going to dine at my Lord Hertford's with Lord Bute.[25]

To Montagu, Saturday 2 June 1759

[Strawberry Hill] June 2d, 1759.

STRAWBERRY HILL is grown a perfect Paphos, it is the land of beauties. On Wednesday the Duchesses of Hamilton and Richmond, and Lady Ailesbury dined there, the two latter stayed all night. There never was so pretty a sight as to see them all three sitting in the shell;[1] a thousand years hence, when I begin to grow old, if that can ever be, I shall talk of that event and tell young people how much handsomer the women of my time were than they will be then; I shall say, 'Women alter now. I remember Lady Ailesbury looking handsomer than her daughter the pretty Duchess of Richmond, as they were sitting on the shell on my terrace with the Duchess of Hamilton, one of the famous Gunnings'—Yesterday the t'other, more famous, Gunning dined there—she has made a friendship with my charming niece,[2] to disguise her jealousy of the new Countess's beauty. There were they two, their lords, Lord Buckingham and Charlotte[2a]—you will think that I do not choose men for my parties so well as women—I don't include Lord Waldegrave in this bad election.

(1736) Charles Edwin of Dunraven, Glamorgan (*Scots Peerage*, 1904–10, iv. 391). Musgrave, *Obituary*, citing several periodicals, gives the date of her death as 4 Dec. 1776, and her age at death as 64.

24. Catherine Maria Fisher (ca 1738–1767), m. John Norris; noted courtesan; see Horace Bleackley, *Ladies Fair and Frail*, 1909, ch. ii.

25. Apparently an early reference to Bute's supposed liaison with the Princess of Wales.

1. The shell bench, designed by Bentley, in the garden at SH; illustrated in *Des. of SH*, *Works* ii. 508. It was sold SH xxiv. 93 to the Earl of Derby, but it is not now at Knowsley and the present whereabouts is not known.

2. Maria, the new Countess Waldegrave.

2a. Walpole.

Loo is mounted to its zenith; the parties last till one and two in the morning: We played at Lady Hertford's last week, the last night of her lying-in, till deep into Sunday morning,[3] after she and her lord were retired. It is now adjourned to Mrs Fitzroy's,[4] whose child the town calls *Pam*-ela.[5] I proposed that instead of receiving cards for assemblies, one should send in a morning to Dr Hunter's,[6] the man-midwife, to know where there is loo that evening.

I find poor Charles Montagu[7] is dead—is it true, as the papers say, that his son comes into Parliament?

The invasion is not half so much in fashion as loo; and the King's demanding the assistance of the militia, does not add much dignity to it. The great Pam of Parliament,[8] who made the motion, entered into a wonderful definition of the several sorts of fear; *from fear that comes from pusillanimity,* up to *fear from magnanimity.*[9] It put me in mind of that wise Pythian my Lady Londonderry,[10] who when her sister Lady Donegal[11] was dying, pronounced, that if it was a *fever from a fever* she would live, but if it was a *fever from death* she would die.

Mr Mason[12] has published another drama, called *Caractacus;* there are some incantations poetical enough, and odes so Greek as to have very little meaning. But the whole is laboured, uninteresting, and no more resembling the manners of Britons than of Japanese.[13] It is in-

3. Which was illegal; see Casanova, *Memoirs,* tr. Arthur Machen, 1922, ix. 164–5: 'This lady [Lady Harrington] lived in the precincts of the Court, and received company every Sunday. It was allowable to play in her house, as the park is under the jurisdiction of the Crown. In any other place there is no playing cards or singing on Sundays. The town abounds in spies, and if they have reason to suppose that there is any gaming or music going on, they watch for their opportunity, slip into the house, and arrest all the bad Christians. . . . But to make up for this severity, the Englishman may go in perfect liberty to the tavern or the brothel, and sanctify the Sabbath as he pleases.'

4. Anne Warren (d. 1807), m. (1758) Charles Fitzroy, cr. (1780) Bn Southampton. The child was 'Anne Caroline, born May 9th, 1759, and died an infant' (Collins, *Peerage,* 1812, vii. 540).

5. In loo 'Pam is the knave of clubs, and ranks above every other card in the

pack' (*Hoyle's Games Improved,* New York, 1829, p. 152).

6. Dr William Hunter (1718–83), the anatomist.

7. Charles Montagu, of Papplewick, Notts; see DNB, *sub* Frederick Montagu, his son, who succeeded him as M.P. for Northampton.

8. Pitt.

9. Mentioned by HW in *Mem. Geo. II* iii. 184.

10. Lady Frances Ridgeway (ca 1702–72), m. (1) (1717) Thomas Pitt, cr. (1719) Bn, and (1726) E. of Londonderry; m. (2) (1732) Robert Graham.

11. Lady Lucy Ridgeway (d. 1732), m. (1716) Arthur Chichester, 4th E. of Donegall.

12. Rev. William Mason (1725–97), poet, and biographer of Gray; later a correspondent of HW's.

13. This judgment was radically altered by HW when he became intimate with Mason.

troduced by a piping elegy;[14] for Mason, in imitation of Gray, *will cry and roar all night*[15] without the least provocation.

Adieu! I shall be glad to hear that your Strawberry tide is fixed.

Yours ever

H. W.

To Montagu, Saturday 23 June 1759

Address: To George Montagu Esq. at Greatworth near Brackley, Northamptonshire. Free Hor. Walpole. *Postmark:* 23 IV.

Strawberry Hill, June 23d, 1759.

AS you bid me fix a day about six weeks from the date of your last, it will suit me extremely to see you here the first of August. I don't mean to treat you with a rowing for a badge,[1] but it will fall in very commodely between my parties.

You tell me nothing of the old house you was to see near Blenheim;[2] I have some suspicion that Greatworth is coming into play again.[3] I made your speeches to Mr Chute, and to Mr Muntz and to myself; your snuff-box is bespoke, your pictures not done, the print of Lady Waldegrave[4] not begun.

News there are none, unless you have a mind for a panic about the invasion. I was in town yesterday, and saw a thousand people from Kensington[5] with faces as loyally long as if it was the last accession of this family that they were ever to see. The French are coming with fifty thousand men, and we shall meet them with fifty addresses. Pray, if you know how, frighten your neighbours and give them courage at the same time.

My Lady Coventry and my niece Waldegrave have been mobbed

14. To Richard Hurd (1720–1808), Bp of Lichfield, 1774; Worcester, 1781.

15. Apparently a phrase of Montagu's; see *post* 9 Aug. 1759, 25 Oct. 1760.

———

1. 'An orange-colour livery with a badge representing liberty' given in 1716 by Thomas Doggett the comedian, to be rowed for annually by six Thames watermen on 1 Aug., the anniversary of the accession of George I; see DNB, *sub* Doggett. 'Doggett's Coat and Badge' is still rowed for under the supervision of the Fishmongers' Company, but on 31 July.

2. See *post* 29 July 1759.

3. I.e., that Montagu would stay there.

4. James McArdell made in 1762 a print of Lady Waldegrave from the first (1759) Reynolds portrait of her (Algernon Graves and William V. Cronin, *History of the Works of Sir Joshua Reynolds*, 1899–1901, iii. 1013).

5. Where the King was.

in the Park—I am sorry the people of England take all their liberty out in insulting pretty women![6]

You will be diverted with what happened to Mr Meynell[7] lately. He was engaged to dine at a formal old lady's, but stayed so late hunting that he had not time to dress, and went as he was, though with forty apologies. The matron, very affected, and meaning to say something very civil, cried, 'Oh! sir, I assure you I can see the gentleman through a pair of buckskin breeches as well as if he was in silk or satin.'

I am sure I can't tell you anything better, so good night!

Yours ever

H. W.

PS. I hope you have as gorgeous weather as we have—it is even hot enough for Mr Bentley. I live upon the water.

To MONTAGU, Thursday 19 July 1759

Address: To George Montagu Esq. at Greatworth near Brackley, Northamptonshire. Free Hor. Walpole. *Postmark:* 19 IY.

Strawberry Hill, July 19th,[1] 1759.

WELL, I begin to expect you; you must not forget the first of August. If we do but look as well as we do at present, you will

---

6. There appears to have been an outburst of this form of mob rudeness in June 1759; see GM 1759, xxix. 291. A guard was provided, and Lady Coventry, having been mobbed one Sunday, on the next (24 June) 'pretended to be frightened directly, desired the assistance of the officer on guard, who ordered the twelve sergeants to march a-breast before her, and the sergeant and twelve behind her, and in this pomp did the idiot walk all the evening with more mob about her than ever, as you may imagine; her sensible husband supporting her on one side and Lord Pembroke on the other. This is at present the talk of the whole town' (Hon. J. West to Lord Nuneham, 26 June 1759, Harcourt MS, quoted by Cunningham, iii. 233). There is a slightly different version in *The Grenville Papers*, ed. William J. Smith, 1852–3, i. 309.

7. Hugo Meynell (1735–1808), of Bradley, Derby, and Quorndon, Leics; M.P. Lichfield 1762–8; Lymington 1769–74; Stafford 1774–80. 'This gentleman has . . . been long esteemed the first fox-hunter in the kingdom' (John Nichols, *History . . . of the County of Leicester*, 1795–1815, iii pt i. 101). He was called the 'father of foxhunting' by the Duke of Beaufort (Robert Black, *The Jockey Club and its Founders*, 1891, pp. 13, 105), and was Master of the Quorn (ibid. 121; see also Josiah C. Wedgwood, *Staffordshire Parliamentary History*, ii. 284, in William Salt Arch. Soc. [later called the Staffordshire Record Society], *Collections*, 1922; A. L. Reade, *Johnsonian Gleanings* vi (1933). 165–6).

1. Incorrectly dated 17 July in Toynbee.

own Strawberry is still in its bloom. With English verdure, we have had an Italian summer, and

> Whatever sweets Sabæan springs disclose,
> Our Indian jasmine and the Persian rose.[2]

I am forced to talk of Strawberry lest I should weary you with what everybody wearies me, the French and the militia. They—I mean the latter only, not the former, passed just by us yesterday, and though it was my own *clan*,[2a] I had not the curiosity to go and see them. The crowds in Hyde Park when the King reviewed them, were inimaginable. My Lord Orford their colonel, I hear, looked gloriously martial and genteel, and I believe it; his person and air have a noble wildness[3] in them: the regimentals too are very becoming, scarlet faced with black, buff waistcoats and gold buttons.[4] How knights of shires, who have never shot anything but woodcocks, like this warfare, I don't know: but the towns through which they pass adore them: everywhere they are treated and regaled. The Prince of Wales followed them to Kingston, and gave fifty guineas amongst the private men.

I expect some anecdote from you of the coronation at Oxford: I hear my Lord Westmorland's[5] own retinue was all be-James'd with true-blue ribbands;[6] and that because Sir William Calvert[7] who was a

2. 'What sweets soe'er Sabæan springs
   disclose,
   Our Indian jasmine, or the Syrian
   rose.'
   (Dryden, *Aureng-Zebe* IV. ll. 102–3.)
2a. That is, the Norfolk militia; for a list of its officers see R. Hindry Mason, *History of Norfolk*, 1884, pp. 451–2.
3. He became mad in 1773.
4. 'Nothing could make a better appearance than the two Norfolk battalions. Lord Orford, with the port of Mars himself, and really the genteelest figure under arms I ever saw, was the theme of every tongue. The King was extremely pleased, and the public' (William Pitt to his wife, 17 July 1759, *Correspondence of William Pitt, Earl of Chatham*, 1838–40, ii. 4–5).
5. John Fane (1685–1762), 7th E. of Westmorland, installed as Chancellor of Oxford 3 July. The ceremonies, with the attendant Commemoration, lasted from 2 to 7 July; see GM 1759, xxix. 341–2. Lord Westmoreland had been a strong Hano-

verian, but his resentment against Sir Robert Walpole, who deprived him of his regiment for going into opposition, 'led him to imbibe all the nonsensical tenets of the Jacobites' (*Mem. Geo. II* iii. 167).
6. The colour blue had long been identified with the Stuart dynasty through Scottish banners of blue bearing St Andrew's cross. It was also adopted by the Covenanters in 1639 in contradistinction to the then Royalist colour, red. Prince Charles dressed all in blue in 1745, and it is said that George I changed the colour of the Garter ribbon 'from the light blue as worn by Jacobite Princes and Knights to the "royal" (dark) blue which it has ever since retained' (John H. Jesse, *Memoirs of the Pretenders*, 1860, p. 151; cf. ibid. 134; see William J. Gordon, *Flags of the World, Past and Present*, 1915, pp. 38–41, 51; John H. Burton, *History of Scotland*, Edinburgh, 1873, vi. 248; Grant R. Francis, *Scotland's Royal Line*, 1928, p. 227). And as the use here would indicate, the Ja-

fellow of a college and happened to be Lord Mayor, attended the Duke of Newcastle at his inthronization, they dragged down the present Lord Mayor[8] to Oxford, who is only a dry-salter.

I have your Butler's posthumous works;[9] the poetry is most uncouth and incorrect, but with infinite wit—especially one piece on plagiaries[10] is equal to anything in *Hudibras*. Have you read my Lord Clarendon?[11] I am enchanted with it; 'tis very incorrect, but I think more entertaining than his *History*. It makes me quite out of humour with *other mémoires*.[12] Adieu!

Yours ever

H. W.

From Montagu, ca Tuesday 24 July 1759

G.D. 15/8, No. 728.

Written between HW's letters of 19 and 26 July.

[Greatworth, ca July 24, 1759].

I AM afraid I shall not be able to come to you at Strawberry the first of August as I intended, for my steward will not be returned from Gloucestershire by that time. However, a few days or a week I hope will not cause much inconvenience to you, and the moment I am able you may depend upon seeing me. I am as much charmed with Lord Clarendon's memoirs as you are but they have not put the noses of others out of joint. I have been forced to take up with Voltaire's *Candide*[1] in English and have yet found great amusement in it.

cobite blue was no doubt influenced by the association with true blue, meaning constant (since the 17th century, OED).

7. Sir William Calvert (ca 1704–61), Kt, 1744; Lord Mayor of London 1749–50; B.A. Fellow and M.A. of Emmanuel; made D.C.L. at the installation of the Duke of Newcastle as Chancellor of Cambridge (Venn, *Alumni Cantab.*; Foster, *Alumni Oxon*). He was M.P. London 1747–54; Old Sarum 1755–61.

8. Sir Richard Glyn (1712–73), Kt, 1752; Bt, Sept. 1759; Lord Mayor 1758–9; cr. D.C.L. of Oxford at the installation 3 July; he was a banker, and a Master Salter, 1751 (Alfred B. Beaven, *Aldermen of the City of London*, 1908, p. 142).

9. *Genuine Remains in Verse and Prose of Mr Samuel Butler*, ed. Robert Thyer, 1759, 2 vols. Montagu was one of the subscribers. HW's copy (MS Cat. K.4.32) was sold SH iii. 164.

10. A 'Satyr upon Plagiaries' i. 168.

11. *The Life of Edward Earl of Clarendon, written by himself*, 1759. HW's copy (MS Cat. A.1.9) was sold SH i. 70.

12. His own.

———

1. For the introduction into England of *Candide*, which was first published in Feb. 1759, see Appendix 6.

In my high house I have had no cause to complain of the charming sun and blue sky that we have had hot and hot[2] for such a length of time. I fancy your dusty roads will make me wish for my clays. I have been really frightfully ill for a week and thought more of going to Horton, a place I don't much love, than to Strawberry. Adieu; believe me most truly yours,

G. MONTAGU

You shall hear from me about fixing my time, though I shall not appoint a day for fear of keeping you at home.

To MONTAGU, Thursday 26 July 1759

Address: To George Montagu Esq. at Greatworth near Brackley, Northamptonshire. Free Hor. Walpole. *Postmark:* 26 IY.

Arlington Street, July 26, 1759.

I AM dying in a hot street, with my eyes full of dust, and my table full of letters to be answered[1]—yet I must write you a line. I am sorry your first of Augustness is disordered; I'll tell you why. I go to Ragley on the twelfth. There is to be a great party at loo for the Duchess of Grafton, and thence they adjourn to the Warwick races.[2] I have been engaged so long to this that I cannot put it off, and besides I am under appointments at George Selwyn's etc. afterwards.[3] If you cannot come before all this to let me have enough of your company, I should wish you to postpone it to the first of September, when I shall be at leisure for ten or twelve days, and could go with you from Strawberry to the Vine; but I could like to know certainly, for as I never make any of my visits while Strawberry is in bloom, I am a little crowded with them at the end of the season.

I came this morning in all this torrent of heat from Lord Waldegrave's at Navestock. It is a dull place though it does not want prospect backward. The garden is small consisting of two French *allées* of old limes that are comfortable, two groves that are not so, and a green canal; there is besides a paddock. The house was built by his

---

2. A street cry. Cf. *ante* 6 Dec. 1753, n. 12.

1. Perhaps one of these was Mann's letter of 30 June.

2. They were run on the 14th and 15th (*Baily's Racing Register*, 1845, i. 184).

3. HW did not pay either of these visits; see HW to Selwyn 14 Aug. 1759.

father[4] and ill-finished, but an air seigneurial in the furniture; French glasses in quantities, handsome commodes, tables, screens etc. goodish pictures in rich frames, and a deal of noblesse *à la St Germain*. James II, Charles II, the Duke of Berwick,[5] her Grace of Buckingham,[6] the Queen Dowager[7] in the dress she visited Madame Maintenon,[8] her daughter the Princess Louisa,[9] a Lady Gerard[10] that died at Joppa returning from a pilgrimage to Jerusalem, and above all *la Godfrey;*[11] and not at all ugly, though she does not show her thighs.[12] All this is a little leavened with the late King, the present King, and Queen Caroline—and I shall take care to sprinkle a little *unholy* water from our *well*.[13]

I am very sorry you have been ill: take care of yourself, there are wicked sore throats in vogue; poor Lady Essex[14] and Mrs Charles Yorke[15] died of them in an instant.

4. James Waldegrave (1684–1741), 2d Bn Waldegrave, cr. (1729) E. Waldegrave.

5. James Fitzjames (1670–1734), 1st D. of Berwick; son of James II and Arabella Churchill, and thus Lord Waldegrave's great-uncle (see n. 11 below).

6. Lady Catherine Darnley (ca 1682–1743), dau. of James II by the Countess of Dorchester; m. (1) (1699) James Annesley, 3d E. of Anglesey; m. (2) (1706) John Sheffield, M. of Normanby, cr. (1703) D. of Buckingham (his 3d wife).

7. Mary (1658–1718) of Modena, queen of James II.

8. This is probably a slip; since the exiled Queen of England was always treated with royal honours in France, she would not by French etiquette visit Mme de Maintenon, whatever the latter's real position. There is no record of such a visit in Mme de Maintenon's letters, memoirs, etc., although the Queen was interested in St Cyr, and apparently visited it frequently. The reference is to something which Montagu probably knew, doubtless from the letters of Mme de Sévigné. There is no visit of the Queen to Mme de Maintenon therein (Mme de Maintenon visits the Queen) but there is a visit of the Queen to the Dauphine, and it is probably to this visit HW refers: 'cette reine la vint voir il y a trois jours, habillée en perfection; une robe de velours noir, une belle jupe, bien coiffée . . . beaucoup de majesté' (*Lettres de Madame de Sévigné,*

ed. Monmerqué, 1862–6, viii. 413, to Mme de Grignan, 17 Jan. 1689). For Mme de Maintenon's relationship to the Queen, see her *Lettres,* ed. Marcel Langlois, 1935–9, iii. 403; A. Geffroy, *Mme de Maintenon d'après sa correspondance authentique,* 1887, ii. 250, 340. The Navestock pictures do not seem to be recorded.

9. Princess Louisa Maria Theresa (1692–1712), youngest dau. of James II.

10. Mary Webb (d. 1731), m. Charles Gerard, 6th Bn Gerard.

11. Arabella Churchill (1648–1730), m. Col. Charles Godfrey; mistress of James II (as Duke of York), by whom she had a daughter Henrietta who married Sir Henry Waldegrave, 1st Baron Waldegrave, grandparents of the second (HW's) Earl.

12. She is described in ch. 10 of Anthony Hamilton's *Mémoires de . . . Grammont* as having a very ugly face; but at the end of the chapter is an account of how a fall from a horse discovered hidden beauties to the Duke of York and the court, who witnessed the accident.

13. Possibly Walpole family pictures are meant.

14. Gray attributes her death to 'a fever during her lying-in' (*Gray's Corr.* ii. 628).

15. Catherine, dau. and heir of William Freeman, m. (1755) Hon. Charles Yorke; d. 10 July; see Philip C. Yorke, *Life . . . of . . . Hardwicke,* Cambridge, 1913, ii. 574, 590–1.

Do let me have a line and do fix a day, for instead of keeping me at home one by fixing it, you will keep me there five or six by not fixing it. Adieu!

Yours ever

H. W.

From Montagu, Sunday 29 July 1759

G.D. 15/8, No. 729.

Greatworth, July 29, 1759.

I AM extremely glad it suits your convenience to put off my coming to Strawberry [to] the first of September; it is most convenient to me as I dreaded the journey this hot weather, being weak, and am forced to be careful; I wish you much entertainment at Ragley and at Mr Selwyn's and good luck.

I need not say if you come within ten miles of me that I shall be glad to see you most surely. I expect every post to hear from the Duchess of Marlborough's[1] steward concerning Walcot House;[2] if they will not put it into thorough repair I cannot go into it; if they do I believe you will like it; the part of the world is pretty and near my kin and my Roel.

Pray my compliments to Mr Bentley and Mr Myntz. I am most sincerely yours,

G. Montagu

To Montagu, Thursday 9 August 1759

Strawberry Hill, Aug. 9th, 1759.

UNLESS your Colonel Johnson[1] is a man of no note, he is safe and well, for we have not lost one officer of any note—now will you conclude that we are beaten, and will be crying and roaring all

1. See *post* i. 392, n. 3.
2. The nearest Walcot House seems to be one in NE Northants (John Cary, *New Itinerary*, 1798, p. 670), at the other end of the county from his relatives and from Gloucestershire, where Roel was. Montagu did not take any Walcot House.

1. Lt-Col. James Johnston (d. 1795), Gen., 1793; Col. 1st Horse 1762–75; 11th Dragoons 1775–85; 2d Dragoons 1785–95; m. Lady Charlotte Montagu, George Montagu's cousin (GM 1795, lxv pt ii. 1056; Collins, *Peerage*, 1768, v. 9; *Army Lists*). He was Lt-Col. of the Royal Horse Guards at this time (see *Army Lists*, and *ante* 5 June 1746, n. 19) and later Colonel of the Scotch Greys (GM, loc. cit.). He should be distinguished from his kinsman and namesake *ante* 5 June 1746, n. 19. See p. 5 of a

night for Hanover!—Lord! where do you live? If you had any ears, as I have none left with the noise, you would have heard the racket that was made from morning till night yesterday on the news of the total victory gained by Prince Ferdinand over the French.[2] He has not left so many alive as there are at any periwig-maker's in London.[3] This is all we know, the particulars[4] are to come at their leisure, and with all the gravity due to their importance. If the King's heart were not *entirely English*,[5] I believe he would be complimented with the title of Germanicus, from the name of the country where this great event happened, for we don't at all know the precise spot, nor has the battle yet been christened—all that is certain is, that the poor Duke is neither father nor godfather.

I was sent for to town yesterday, as Mrs Leneve was at the point of death, but she has had a surprising change, and may linger on still. I found the town distracted, and at night it was beautiful beyond description. As the weather was so hot, every window was open and all the rails illuminated;[6] every street had one or two bonfires, the moon was in all its glory, the very middle of the streets crowded with officers and people of fashion talking of the news. Every squib in town got drunk, and rioted about the streets till morning. Two of our regiments are said to have suffered much, of which Napier's[7] most. Adieu! If you should be over-English with this, there is a party of fifteen hundred men stolen out of Dunkirk,[8] that some weeks hence may bring you to your senses again, provided they are properly planted and watered in Scotland.

Yours ever

H. W.

supplementary note at the end of vol. vi of Wright's 2d edn, 1846, describing the remarkably similar careers of the two Johnstons.

2. The battle of Minden, 1 Aug., at which Prince Ferdinand defeated a much larger French army; see Fortescue, *British Army* ii. 494–507.

3. Wig-making, hairdressing, and similar occupations were commonly assumed to be monopolized by Frenchmen; see R. Campbell, *The London Tradesman*, 3d edn 1757, p. 204.

4. See the *London Gazette Extraordinary* of 8 Aug., on which HW's account is based, and which consists only of a letter from Col. Yorke at the Hague, saying

that there had been a great victory; details were received three days later (*Mem. Geo. II* iii. 190–1).

5. An allusion to the phrase in Queen Anne's first speech from the throne, 'she knew her heart to be entirely English' (DNB, *sub* Anne).

6. That is, the railings in front of the houses.

7. Maj. Gen. Robert Napier (d. 1766), Lt-Gen., 1759; Col. of 12th Foot (GM 1766, xxxvi. 551; *Army Lists*); his regiment and the 20th Foot suffered most heavily (Fortescue, *British Army* ii. 504).

8. There seems to be no foundation for this story.

From MONTAGU, Tuesday 9 October 1759

G.D. 15/8, No. 730.

Answered by HW *post* 11 Oct. 1759.

Memoranda by HW: Letter from J. Bland
an apology—exactly printed
An Epistle to noble Lord.

These are all pamphlets on the case of Lord George Sackville, accused of cowardice at Minden: *An epistle to a noble Lord; A letter from Jn Bland to the friends, in which the conduct of G.S. is defended on the principles of religion; His Lordship's apology* (from a list in GM 1759, xxix. 499). HW mentions the 'paper war' centering around Lord George, to Conway 14 Oct. 1759.

There is also a rough sketch, perhaps by HW.

Greatworth, Oct. 9th [1759].

I AM full of impatience for Mr Myntz's pictures[1] and my old snuff[2] and I know no better way to get them than by putting them into the hands of your vivacity.

I am but just got well; though you think I am never ill, you would have been convinced had you seen me. The General[3] will be in town, I believe the end of this month. Poor Frederick Montagu is at the Bath drinking the waters for a fit of the gout by orders of his physician who says he must get a stout fit in his limbs to save his head and stomach where he has already had it at five and twenty. My old-fashioned sofa of ribbed velvet with carved black frame would so suit your Holbein[4] room that were Mr Holbeck[5] not to take it ill, you should see it stop at your door; but you will have it at my auction.

Lord Northampton[6] had a running footman[7] at the races[7a] in white

---

1. Possibly the 'two small landscapes, a morning, and an evening, which I gave him [Montagu], done by Müntz, and the best of his works' (*Country Seats* 51); see *post* 17 Nov. 1759.

2. A snuff-box; see *ante* 23 June and *post* 11 Oct. 1759.

3. Charles Montagu was gazetted a Major-General 15 Sept.

4. HW wrote Lord Strafford, 13 Sept. 1759, that it was 'just finished'; its chief adornments were an elaborate chimney-piece and a wooden screen designed by Bentley, and a considerable number of Holbein paintings, drawings, and copies, especially Vertue's tracings of the Holbein chalk portraits now at Windsor; see

SH Accounts 8, 102–3; *Des. of SH, Works* ii. 454–61; *Anecdotes,* ed. Wornum, i. 85–6. HW was partial to frames of black and gold.

5. Not identified. There is no tradesman named Holbeck or Beck (in case Montagu was punning on Holbein) in *Baldwin's New Complete Guide,* 1768. Mr Whibley suggests that this may have been a present to Montagu from Holbeck.

6. Charles Compton (1737–63), 7th E. of Northampton. He seems to have been addicted to such finery. 'Lord Northampton had a fine suit for the birthday, the waistcoat silver and gold, the coat gold and silver' (Mrs Montagu to Mrs Carter, 7 June 1759, in Emily J. Climenson, *Mrs Montagu*

satin and gold lace, his shoes and cap white and the apparel cost four-score pounds.

Sir George Osborn[8] a boy of 17 is major of the Bedford militia and student of Trinity College. There are but two officers in that corps that are not minors; he called here in his way to Horton and showed me his commission; I should else have taken it for a joke. I have been but once at Wroxton since I came home. Had Roger Townshend not gone back to look for the General's[9] spying-glass he left under a tree he had not been shot;[10] the General begged to send his servant.

How does Mr Chute do? And Mr Bentley? Pray my compliments to all your court.

I am always most truly yours,

G. M.

To MONTAGU, Thursday 11 October 1759

Strawberry Hill, Oct. 11, 1759.

I DON'T desire any such conviction of your being ill as seeing you ill, nor can you wonder that I wish to persuade myself that what I should be very sorry for, never happens. Poor Fred. Montagu's gout seems more serious: I am concerned that he has so much of a judge in him already.[1]

You are very good in thinking of me about the sofa, but you know the Holbein chamber is complete,[2] and old matters are not flung away

the Queen of the Blue-stockings, 1906, ii. 161).

7. When Lady Northampton 'made a most brilliant appearance at court' shortly after, Lloyd's Evening Post 22–24 Oct. 1759, v. 398, noted that 'her equipage . . . was preceded by a running footman, a fashion which has been dropped some years.'

7a. Presumably the Northampton Races which were run 25 and 26 Sept. and at which Lord Northampton raced (Baily's Racing Register, 1845, i. 186).

8. Sir George Osborn (1742–1818), 4th Bt, of Chicksand Priory, Beds; son of Sir Danvers Osborn and Montagu's first cousin Lady Mary Montagu.

9. Probably Jeffery Amherst (1717–97), K.B., 1761; cr. (1776) Bn Amherst; com-

mander-in-chief in America; took Ticonderoga.

10. He was killed at Ticonderoga 25 July (Collins, Peerage, 1812, ii. 477); HW wrote an epitaph for him, which was not used ('Short Notes').

1. Frederick Montagu was a barrister.

2. On 20 Oct. 1760 HW printed a few copies of a Catalogue of Pictures and Drawings in the Holbein-Chamber at Strawberry Hill (Journal of the Printing Office 9, 36–7). It mentions 58 pictures and drawings, but only one article of furniture, 'the chair of Johannes Arthurus, Monk of Glastonbury.' The 1784 Des. of SH mentions an additional table, seven additional chairs and a bed. Presumably, HW did not want Montagu's sofa.

upon you yourself: had not you rather have your sofa than Lord
Northampton's running footman? Two hundred years hence one
might be amused with reading of so fantastic a dress, but they are
horrid in one's own time.

Mr Bentley and I go tomorrow to Chaffont[3] for two or three days.
Mr Chute is at the Vine alone, but I believe will be in town this
week.

I don't know whether it proceeds from the menaced invasion or
the last comet,[4] but we are all dying of heat. Everybody has put out
their fires, and if it lasts, I suppose will next week make summer
clothes. The mornings are too hot for walking: last night I heard of
strawberries. I impute it to the hot weather that my head has been
turned enough to contend with the bards of the newspapers. You have
seen the French epigram on Madame Pompadour,[5] and fifty vile trans-
lations of it[6]—here is mine;

> O yes!—here are flat-bottom boats to be sold,
> And soldiers to let—rather hungry, than bold.
> Here are ministers richly deserving to swing,
> And commanders, whose recompense should be a string.
> O France, still your fate you may lay at ———'s door;
> You was saved by a Maid, are undone by a Whore.

People again believe the invasion—and I don't wonder, considering
how great a militia we have, with such boys as you mention. I own

3. Chalfont, Bucks, where Lady Mary
Churchill lived (see HW to Bentley 5 July
1755).

4. This was the comet which has since
been called Halley's. In 1705 Halley, who
had observed it in 1682, calculated it had
a period of about 76 years, and predicted
its return in 1758; it was visible in England chiefly in May, 1759, having been
first observed at Paris several months earlier (GM 1759, xxix. 521–4; DNB *sub* Halley).

5. Jeanne-Antoinette Poisson (1721–64),
Marquise de Pompadour; Louis XV's mistress.

6. The verses and a translation appeared
in GM Oct. 1759, xxix. 496, with an ex-
planation: 'The French ministers are in
such dread of popular resentment, that
they have recourse to the grossest and
most direct falsehoods, merely to conceal

for a time what cannot fail to be known
at last, so that they even caused *Te Deum*
to be sung for the defeat of the English
before Quebec, at the very time they
knew it was taken. The people, however,
know so much, and are so little disposed
to suppress their indignation, that Pasquinades are almost every morning found
pasted up in the most public parts of
Paris, among which was the following . . .

> *Bateaux plats à vendre,*
> *Soldats à louer,*
> *Ministre à pendre,*
> *Généraux à rouer*
>
> *O France! le sexe femelle,*
> *Fit toujours ton destin;*
> *Ton bonheur vint d'une pucelle,*
> *Ton malheur vient d'une catin.'*

before I begin to be afraid, I have a little curiosity to see the militia tried—I think one shall at least laugh before one cries.

Adieu! what time have you fixed for looking southwards?

Yours ever

H. W.

PS. Your pictures you may have when you please; I think you had better stay and take them with you, than risk the rubbing them by the wagon. Mr Muntz has not been lately in town, that is, Hannah[7] has drawn no bill on him lately, so he knows nothing of your snuff-box. This it is to trust to my vivacity, when it is past its bloom— Lord! I am a mere antiquarian, a mere painstaking mortal: Mr Bentley says that if all antiquarians were like me, there would be no such thing as an antiquarian, for I set down everything for posterity so circumstantially, that I leave them nothing to find out.

To Montagu, Sunday 21 October 1759

Address: To George Montagu Esq. at Greatworth near Brackley, Northamptonshire. Free Hor. Walpole. *Postmark:* 22 OC.

Strawberry Hill, Oct. 21, 1759.

YOUR pictures shall be sent as soon as any of us go to London, but I think that will not be till the Parliament meets. Can one easily leave the remains of such a year as this? It is still all gold. I have not dined or gone to bed by a fire till the day before yesterday. Instead of the glorious and ever-memorable year 1759, as the newspapers call it, I call it this ever-warm and victorious year. We have not had more conquest than fine weather: one would think we had plun-

7. A term frequently used by HW in this correspondence ca 1759–61 to denote a mistress. See Paget Toynbee's letter in *Times Literary Supplement* 1923, xxii. 12, where he quotes a number of passages in which it occurs, and suggests that its origin may be found in the supposed romance, at about this time, between the future George III and one Hannah Lightfoot, 'the fair Quaker.' The persistent connection of the young man's name with an obscure but identifiable woman suggests a basis in fact, and might have been sufficient to make her name a by-word. The first journalistic references to the affair, however, do not occur until 1770; see a review of the evidence in Charles E. Pearce, *The Amazing Duchess* [1911], i. 227–42. The story that George III contracted a secret marriage with Hannah was demolished by William J. Thoms (*Hannah Lightfoot . . .*, 1867, reprints from N&Q); cf. John Lindsey [John St Clair Muriel], *The Lovely Quaker*, 1939.

dered East and West Indies of sunshine. Our bells are worn threadbare with ringing for victories. I believe it will require ten votes of
the House of Commons before people will believe that it is the Duke
of Newcastle that has done all this and not Mr Pitt. One thing is very
fatiguing; all the world is made knights or generals. Adieu! I don't
know a word of news less than the conquest of America.

Yours ever

H. W.

PS. You shall hear from me again if we take Mexico or China before Christmas.

PPS. I had sealed my letter, but break it open again, having forgot to tell you that Mr Cowslade[1] has the pictures of Lord and Lady
Cutts, and is willing to sell them.

From Montagu, ca Thursday 25 October 1759

G.D. 15/8, No. 732.

In reply to *ante* 21 Oct. 1759; answered by HW *post* 8 Nov. 1759; month and
day conjectural only.

Memoranda by HW: sunk at Charingcross[1]

There is certainly an objection to this construction: if Pliny had meant to say
they used the cestrum *on* wax as well as *on* ivory, one should naturally think he
would have used the preposition *in* before cerâ, as he has, *in* ebore. To this I answer; in the two first manners they had not the use of the pencil: I therefore apply the use of the cestrum to both wax and ivory, as being the only tool men-

1. Since Chute acted as intermediary in
the negotiations about this picture, the Mr
Cowslade was probably John Cowslade, a
friend of Chute's and occasional correspondent of HW's (see especially HW to
Cowslade 16 Sept. [1773]). In his copy of
John Nichols's *Select Collection of Poems*,
1780–2, iii. 314, now in the Victoria and
Albert Museum, Dyce Collection, HW
notes that 'The Cowslades are gentlemen
of an ancient family in Hampshire'; they
were settled chiefly at Basingstoke, near
the Vyne (Francis J. Baigent and James E.

Millard, *History . . . of Basingstoke*, 1889,
passim). John Cowslade was a gentleman-
usher to Queen Charlotte, and may be the
Mr Cowslade of Mrs Delany's letter from
Bulstrode, 19 Dec. 1760: '. . . here is also
Mr Cowslade, who used to be very much
with the late Duchess of Somerset, a favourite on account of his having been a
distinguished play-fellow of Lord Beauchamp; a good-humoured sing-song man'
(Delany, *Correspondence* iii. 619–20).

1. See *post* 8 Nov. 1759, n. 17.

tioned by Pliny. If it was not so used—he has not given the most distant hint of what the first sort of encaustic was. Perhaps we are all disputing idly upon what Pliny did not know enough of the matter to explain.[2]

[Greatworth, ca Oct. 25, 1759].

PRAY inform yourself of Mr Chute concerning the pictures of Lord and Lady Cutts for if hers be the right I shall be delighted. What I want chiefly to know is whether Lord Cutts had two wives;[3] in that case I should fear the picture that is at Mr Couslade's of the Lady is not my grandmother's unless the Couslades are related to her, whose name was Clarke widow of Morley and then widow of Trevor. My mother[3a] used to say there was a picture of Lady Cutts her mother at Mr Earnley's[4] whose daughter Drax married; these Earnleys and Draxes were related to my grandmother. If the picture came from any of these families it has a chance of being the right. Lady Cutts lived but a little while with Lord Cutts; I cannot say how long. As he is one of your authors[5] you may I hope excuse you me for desiring you to get Mr Chute to unravel all this. The tradition in our family is he came down in a chariot and six Flanders mares and carried off our afflicted widow grandmother and poxed her. Swift you know has an epigram upon him in the character of the salamander;[6] upon this score the Duke of Marlborough whose great favourite he was gave him that name for being always in the hottest fire in all engagements.[6a]

2. Though it was not used, this is undoubtedly a note for Müntz's Encaustic, or Count Caylus's Method of Painting, 1760. It concerns a passage in Pliny's Natural History, Bk xxxv. sec. 149, 'encausto pingendi duo fuere antiquitus genera, cera et in ebore cestro.' 'Owing to Pliny's obscure wording of the . . . passage the whole subject of ancient encaustic is beset with the gravest difficulties' (K. Jex-Blake and E. Sellers, The Elder Pliny's Chapters on the History of Art, 1896, p. 172, q.v.).

3. He had. See post i. 261, n. 6.

3a. See Appendix 7.

4. Sir Edward Ernle (d. 1729), 3d Bt, of Brimslade Park, Wilts; his dau. Elizabeth (d. 1759), m. Henry Drax (d. 1755) of Ellerton Abbey, Yorkshire, and Charborough, Dorset; M.P. Wareham 1718–22, 1734–47, 1751–5; Lyme Regis 1727–34; Secretary to

Frederick, Prince of Wales (GM 1759, xxix. 293; John Burke, History of the Commoners, 1833–8, iv. 208–9).

5. See Royal and Noble Authors, Works i. 521. HW first introduced him in the 2d edition, 1759, where he says, 'I have been favoured by a near relation of his Lordship with the sight of a very scarce volume of poems of his writing' (p. 245). It is probable that the 'near relation' was Montagu.

6. 'The Description of a Salamander,' a venomous attack written 1705, containing another reference to Cutts's 'pox'; see Poems of Jonathan Swift, ed. Harold Williams, Oxford, 1937, i. 82–5.

6a. Cutts is said to have acquired his nickname after leading a gallant attack at the siege of Namur in 1695 (DNB), in which case it could not have been applied by

You see I am very frank in my anecdotes of my pseudo-grand-father; what belongs to my own flesh and blood you shall never have for your next edition.

I rejoice at the accounts of all our victories, that will, I trust, procure us peace. I conclude Lady Townshend acts the Mater Gracchorum[7] when she waits upon Mrs Wolfe.[8] The fine weather has done me as much good as it seems to have pleased you. St Évremond said a fair day in autumn and a good stomach was all an old man had to wish;[9] I wish you may live to be as old and jolly as he was. If you pick up any kind of news when you are in town be so kind as to let me have some. My aunt Cosby has been very ill and writes me word she is advised to jumble in a cock.[10]

Pray give my compliments to Mr Bentley and Mr Myntz and believe me to be most sincerely yours,

G. M.

To MONTAGU, Thursday 8 November 1759

Arlington Street, Nov. 8th, 1759.

YOUR pictures will set out on Saturday; I give you notice that you may inquire for them.

I did not intend to be here these three days, but my Lord Bath taking the trouble to send a man and horse to ask me to dinner yesterday, I did not know how to refuse; and 'besides,' as Mr Bentley said to me, 'You know he was an old friend of your father.'

The town is empty, but is coming to dress itself for Saturday.[1] My Lady Coventry showed George Selwyn her clothes; they are blue with

Marlborough, who was in England and in disgrace.

7. Her son Roger had been killed at Ticonderoga (*ante* 9 Oct. 1759, n. 10); and her son George took command at Quebec on Wolfe's death, 13 Sept. 1759.

8. Henrietta Thompson (d. 1764), m. Lt-Gen. Edward Wolfe; mother of Maj. Gen. James Wolfe, the hero of Quebec (DNB, *sub* Wolfe, James).

9. Not found in works of Charles de Marguetel de Saint-Denis de Saint-Évremond (1610–1703); possibly Montagu had it by oral tradition; see *post* 27 May 1762.

10. Mr Ketton-Cremer suggests this should read 'coach'; that she had been recommended to take 'carriage exercise.' Cf. Gray to Wharton 14 Nov. 1745, 'our hackney coach jumbled us into a sort of reconciliation' (*Gray's Corr.* i. 226).

1. The King's birthday.

spots of silver the size of a shilling and a silver trimming and cost my
Lord will know what—she asked George how he liked them—he replied, 'Why, you will be change for a guinea.'[2]

I find nothing talked of but the French bankruptcy[3]—Sir Robert
Brown I hear and am glad to hear,[3a] will be a great sufferer. They put
gravely into the article of bankrupts in the newspaper, Lewis le Petit,
of the City of Paris, peacebreaker, dealer and chapman—it would
have been still better, if they had said, Lewis Bourbon, of petty
France.[4] We don't know what is become of their Monsieur Thurot,[5]
of whom we had still a little mind to be afraid. I should think he
would do like Sir Thomas Hanmer,[6] make a faint effort, beg pardon
of the Scotch for their disappointment, and retire. Here are some very
pretty verses just arrived;

> Pourquoi le bâton à Soubise,[7]
> Puisque Chevert[8] est le vainqueur?
> C'est de la cour une méprise,
> Ou bien le but de la faveur.
> 'Je ne vois rien là qui m'étonne,'
> Répond aussitôt un railleur;
> 'C'est à l'aveugle qu'on le donne,
> Et non pas au conducteur.'

2. 'I don't comprehend the joke' (Mrs
Piozzi).

3. 'Three arrêts were published by the
court of France in October, suspending for
a year the payment of the orders upon the
general receipts of the finances, and al-
lowing five per cent. on the respective
sums as an indemnification. The second,
of the same tenour with respect to the
bills of the general farms; and the third
suspending the reimbursement of capi-
tals' (Mem. Geo. II iii. 223–4).

3a. He was noted for his avarice (see
post 25 Oct. 1760; 22 April 1763).

4. The name of two London streets, one
in Bishopsgate Ward, one in Westminster
(London Past & Present).

5. Capt. François Thurot (1727–60),
French naval commander. Of plebeian
birth, he acquired such a reputation for
seamanship (probably as a smuggler) that
he was given a small squadron and for
two years harassed English shipping. 15
Oct. 1759 he sailed from Dunkirk with six
ships and about 2200 men. At the time of

this letter he was at Gothenburg (HW to
Mann 16 Nov. 1759). After making a successful but ineffectual attack on Carrick-
fergus, 21 Feb. 1760 (see HW to Mann 28
Feb. 1760), he was killed in action when
an English squadron caught up with him,
28 Feb.; see John K. Laughton, Studies in
Naval History, 1887, pp. 324–62.

6. Presumably Sir Thomas Hanmer
(1677–1746), 4th Bt; Speaker of the House
of Commons 1713–15; Shakespearian critic.
The incident to which HW refers has not
been discovered. Mr R. W. Ketton-Cremer
suggests that this is a reference to Hanmer's impotency; Thomas Hervey's pamphlet letter to Hanmer, 1741, makes a
similar insinuation.

7. Charles de Rohan (1715–87), Prince
de Soubise; made a Marshal of France 19
Oct. 1758, after winning victories at Sun-
derhausen (23 July) and Lutzelburg (10
Oct.), the latter 'due en partie à Chevert'
(Nouv. Biog. Gén.).

8. François de Chevert (1695–1769),
French Lt-Gen., 1748 (ibid.).

Lady Meadows[9] has left 9000 in reversion after her husband[10] to Lord Sandwich's daughter.[11] Apropos to my Lady Meadows's maiden name, a name I believe you have sometimes heard, I was diverted t'other day with a story of a lady of that name, and a lord whose initial is no farther from hers than he himself is sometimes supposed to be.[12] Her postilion, a lad of sixteen, said, 'I am not such a child but I can guess something: whenever my Lord ———— comes to my lady, she orders the porter to let in nobody else, and then they call for a pen and ink, and say, they are going to write history.'[12a]—Is not this finesse so like him? Do you know, that I am persuaded now he is parted, that he will forget he is married, and propose himself in form to some women or other?

When do you come? if it is not soon, you will find a new town. I stared today at Piccadilly like a country squire: there are twenty new stone houses; at first I concluded that all the grooms that used to live there, had got estates and built palaces.[13] One young gentleman, who was getting an estate, but was so indiscreet as to step out of his way to rob a comrade, is convicted and to be transported[14]—in short, one of

9. Jemima, dau. of Charles Montagu, 5th son of 1st E. of Sandwich; m. Sir Sidney Meadows; d. 30 Oct. 1759 (Collins, *Peerage*, 1812, iii. 465; *Lloyd's Evening Post* 31 Oct.–2 Nov. 1759, v. 430).

10. Sir Sidney Meadows (ca 1699–1792), Knight Marshal of the Marshalsea court, the jurisdiction of which is explained in his obituary in GM 1792, lxii pt ii. 1060. 'Sir S. was so extravagantly fond of horsemanship, that he has been known to tire eleven horses in a day. . . . It was said of him, that he had not been on the east side of Bond-street more than twice a-year for the last 30 years, and that was in his way to receive dividends at the Bank' (ibid.).

11. Lady Mary Montagu (1748–61), dau. of 4th E. of Sandwich (Collins, *Peerage*, 1812, iii. 472).

12. Improbable as it may seem, HW must be referring to Lord Lyttelton and Elizabeth Robinson (1720–1800), m. (1742) Edward Montagu; she was a blue-stocking, and contributed to Lyttelton's *Dialogues of the Dead*, 1760; he was recently parted from his second wife (*post* 23 Dec. 1759, n. 24); and see *post* ca 15 Nov. 1759, n. 9.

12a. This sentence is printed verbatim in Sir Charles Hanbury Williams, *Works*, 1822, ii. 35, in a note to an obscene 'Ode to [the 9th] Lord Lincoln.' It is there applied to Lady W. Montagu and Lincoln, and the note is signed with HW's initial. The sentence was omitted in the 1818 edition of HW's letters to Montagu. HW did write notes to Hanbury Williams's verse (see Earl of Ilchester, *Life of Sir Charles Hanbury-Williams*, 1929, p. 137), but the misapplication of this passage remains a puzzle.

13. Piccadilly had formerly been inhabited by statuaries and livery-stable keepers (*London Past & Present* iii. 88; Arthur I. Dasent, *Piccadilly*, 1920, pp. 84–5). *London and its Environs Described*, 1760–1, v. 194, says: 'At present there are several noble houses in it. . . . The last house built in Piccadilly is the Earl of Egremont's' (between Half Moon and White Horse Streets; now [1940] Naval and Military Club, no. 94; see Dasent, op. cit. 88, 93, 102–3).

14. Probably at the sessions at the Old Bailey, 22–26 Oct. The numbers of the *London Chronicle* and *Lloyd's Evening Post* reporting the trials do not identify any of the prisoners as a waiter from Arthur's.

the waiters at Arthur's—George Selwyn says, 'What a horrid idea he will give of us to the people in Newgate!'[15]

I was still more surprised t'other day, than at seeing Piccadilly, by receiving a letter[16] from the North of Ireland from a clergyman, with violent encomiums on my catalogue of noble authors—and this, when I thought it quite forgot. It put me in mind of the Queen that *sunk* at Charingcross, and rose at Queenhithe.[17]

Mr Chute has got his commission to inquire about your Cutts's, but he thinks the lady is not your grandmother. You are very ungenerous to hoard tales from me of your ancestry: what relation have I spared? If your grandfathers were knaves, will your bottling up their bad blood, mend it? Do you only take a cup of it now and then by yourself, and then come down to your parson and boast of it as if it was pure old metheglin? I sat last night with the Mater Gracchorum —oh! 'tis a Mater Iagorum[18]—if her descendants taste any of her black blood, they surely will make as wry faces at it as the servant in Don John does, when the ghost decants a corpse.[19] Good night, I am just returning to Strawberry, to husband my two last days, and to avoid all the pomp of the Birthday—Oh! I had forgot, there is a Miss Wynne[20] coming forth that is to be handsomer than my Lady Coven-

15. 'Well! where is the joke?' (Mrs Piozzi).

16. Missing.

17. Eleanor of Castile (d. 1290), queen of Edward I. In a ballad of undetermined antiquity, 'A Warning-Piece to England Against Pride and Wickedness,' she is, without foundation, portrayed as a monster of pride and cruelty, who, when accused of her crimes, declared:

'If that upon so vile a thing,
  Her heart did ever think,
She wish'd the ground might open wide,
  And therein she might sink!
With that at Charing-cross she sunk
  Into the ground alive;
And after rose with life again,
  In London, at Queenhithe.'

George Peele seems to have based his chronicle play of *King Edward I* (1593) upon the same incidents; it depicts 'Lastly, the sinking of Queene Elinor, who sunck at Charingcross and rose againe at . . . Queenehith' (George Peele, *Works*, ed. Alexander Dyce, 2d edn 1829–39, i. p. xxvi; *idem*, ed. A. H. Bullen, 1888, i. pp. xxxiii,

77). HW uses this allusion in his letters to Gray 25 Jan. 1766 and to Lady Ossory 26 Jan. 1777.

18. Lady Townshend (*ante* ca 25 Oct. 1759); HW calls her mother of Iagos because of her vengeful and bitter disposition, which her sons had inherited (see HW to Conway 13 Sept. 1759).

19. In the final scene of Shadwell's version of the Don Juan theme, *The Libertine*, Shadwell improves upon Molière by having the ghosts of all of Don John's victims lined up in the church. Don John demands wine; at a signal from the Statue, who had invited Don John and his companions there for supper, 'Two of the ghosts go out, and bring four glasses full of blood.' The revulsion of the servant Jacomo is the last bit of comic business before Don John and his confederates are engulfed in the flames of hell (Thomas Shadwell, *Works*, 1720, ii. 175–6).

20. 'Daughter to Sir John Wynne and sister to the 2d Lord Newbrough' (Mrs Piozzi). Sir John Wynn, 2d Bt, had two daughters, 'Frances, m. to [Henry] Soame, Esq. of the county of Suffolk, who is de-

try—but I have known one threatened with such every summer for these seven years, and they are always addled by winter. Yours ever

H. W.

From Montagu, ca Thursday 15 November 1759

G.D. 15/8, No. 733.

In reply to *ante* 8 Nov. 1759; answered by HW 17 Nov. 1759.

[Greatworth, ca Nov. 15, 1759].

LARGESS, largess, thanks for your gracious and kind epistle; I will communicate a piece of good news to you concerning your young General in Ireland[1] that you will be glad to hear. He is going to be put on the staff in Ireland—a good thirty shillings a day for life and pretentions to an old regiment if his own is broke; and all this through the favour and (perhaps by your intercession) of your old friend Mr Secretary Rigby! Give me leave to return you my thanks.[2] He will not by this means come over this year and therefore I shall not come to town so soon as I intended, for he was to have taken an house to hold us all and I must be forced and on this occasion I am not sorry to stay here and save my lodging money as long as I can hold out.

I have had a letter from the Duke of Manchester[3] to tell me Lord Mandevill's picture for me is arrived. I have desired him to send it to your house, and when you have opened Pandora's box and taken a peep I beg you will have it sent to my carrier.

I am somewhat minded to hang my best room that I am to have new sashed hung white, plain blue paper, to hang all my Cu-doms[4] in. Young Montagu will send you also a book of our family[5] that you may peep in too and send with the picture. I am providing myself with playthings as they amuse children that are sick and keep their rooms.

Lord Sandwich and Lord Manchester have composed their old

---

ceased; and Dorothy, unmarried' (Lodge, *Peerage of Ireland*, 1789, vii. 103; Burke, *Peerage, sub* Newborough).

1. Charles Montagu.
2. HW's friendship with Rigby had

cooled, and he had not interceded for Charles Montagu (see next letter).
3. Robert Montagu (ca 1710–62), 3d D. of Manchester.
4. His family pictures.
5. Not identified.

family and county feuds.[6] The lord of the castle[7] has been to the lord of the nunnery[8] to a ball and concert and graciously lay there all night. I am very happy to hear Lady Meddows has provided for Lady Mary Montagu so handsomely and that her brother's sublime wife[9] has provided for herself so philosophically.

Pray frank Charles' letter;[10] he begs leave to trouble you with some for me—you know my pilfering foible and will excuse as you have done all your life, which is the very no reason why I ought not to continue doing so, but you are good—and oh! I most truly wish you your health and a disposition now and then to let me hear from you and I shall not want to go to London, when you send it me down in a letter free.

Still my Lord Cutts is the man; we must get him a wife if we can. My compliments to Mr Chute and Mr Bentley.

Believe me ever most truly yours,

G. MONTAGU

Look at the end of the 16 Satire of Dr Donne and you will find something in your way of Lord Essex and Queen Elizabeth.[11]

To MONTAGU, Saturday 17 November 1759

Arlington Street, Nov. 17th, 1759.

I REJOICE over your brother's honours, though I certainly had no hand in them. He probably received his staff from the Board of

6. Professor Namier says these were rivalry for the political leadership and patronage of the county. Manchester headed a senior branch of the family, but Sandwich was far more important politically.

7. Duke of Manchester (Kimbolton Castle, Hunts).

8. Earl of Sandwich (Hinchingbrooke, Hunts, 'stands on the site of a Benedictine nunnery,' John Gorton, *Topographical Dictionary of Great Britain*, 1833, ii. 228).

9. Mrs Elizabeth Montagu (*ante* 8 Nov. 1759, n. 12), m. Edward Montagu (1691–1775), of Allerthorpe, Yorkshire (see Emily J. Climenson, *Elizabeth Montagu the Queen of the Blue-stockings*, 1906, i. 111 *et passim*). He was the only one of Lady Meadows's brothers who was married (Collins, *Peerage*, 1812, iii. 465–6).

10. I.e. a letter to Charles Montagu.

11. In the so-called sixth 'Satire' of John Donne (there is no sixteenth), lines 115–30 concern Elizabeth and Essex; the author credits Essex with having said, among other things, that Elizabeth 'stunck.' The only appearance of this work available to Montagu was in the 1669 edition of Donne's *Poems*, p. 138 (Geoffrey Keynes, *Bibliography of Dr John Donne*, Cambridge, 2d edn 1932, p. 129). It is credited to Sir John Roe by Sir Herbert J. C. Grierson in his *Poems of John Donne*, Oxford, 1912, i. 401, ii. pp. cxxviii–cxxxv. HW quoted the couplet referred to above in the article on Essex in the third edition of *Royal and Noble Authors* 320 n. (the abortive SH edition of *Works*, 1770–87; see *Journal of the Printing Office* 13, 51, 89), and it is reprinted in *Works* i. 320 as a note to the passage about Essex and Elizabeth's appearance.

Trade.[1] If any part of the consequences could be placed to *partiality* for me, it would be the prevention of *your* coming to town, which I wished.

My Lady Cutts is indubitably your own venereal grandmother: the Trevors would once have had it,[2] but by some misunderstanding, the old Cowslade refused it. Mr Chute has twenty more corroborating circumstances, but this one is sufficient.

Fred. Montagu told me of the pedigree: I shall take care of all your commissions. Felicitate yourself on having got from me the two landscapes; that source is stopped. Not that Mr Müntz is eloped to finish the conquest of America, nor promoted by Mr Secretary's[3] zeal for my friends, nor because the ghost of Mrs Leneve has appeared to me and ordered me to drive Hannah and Ishmael[4] into the wilderness—a cause much more familiar to *me* has separated us—nothing but a tolerable quantity of ingratitude on his side, both to me and Mr Bentley. The story is rather too long for a letter; the substance was, most extreme impertinence to me, concluded by an abusive letter against Mr Bentley, who sent him from starving on seven pictures for a guinea, to £100 a year, my house, table and utmost countenance. In short, I turned his head, and was forced to turn him out of doors. You shall see the *documents,* as it is the fashion to call proof-papers.[5]   [6] I suppose, will naturally think me to blame. Poets and painters imagine *they* confer the honour when they are protected —and they set down impertinence to the article of their own virtue, when you dare to begin to think that an ode or a picture is not a patent for all manner of insolence.[7]

My Lord Temple as vain as if he was descended from the stroller Pindar, or had made up card-matches at the siege of Genoa;[8] has re-

---

1. Lord Halifax.
2. Lady Cutts's picture.
3. Rigby (*ante* ca 15 Nov. 1759).
4. Mrs Toynbee suggests that Müntz's Hannah was a servant at SH, which seems likely in the light of the context here.
5. The only one which has been found is Müntz's final letter to HW, 12 Nov. 1759, which throws no light on the particular cause of the quarrel.
6. Name cut out. 'Poets and painters' indicates the person is a poet and the association of Ode and Pindar in the following lines suggests Gray, whose odes,

The Bard and *The Progress of Poesy* are Pindaric. 'Gray' would fit the space.
7. 'Exactly so; and this was exemplified by the painter that insulted Louisa Beresford and her husband Mr Hope, 40 years after; he painted them as La Belle and Le Bête' (Mrs Piozzi).
8. Probably a slighting reference to Müntz, who had been 'a Swiss engineer in the French service' (HW to Mann 9 Sept. 1758). Genoa was besieged in 1747 by the Austrians, but was successfully defended by the Genoese, with French assistance.

signed the Privy Seal, because he has not the Garter. You cannot imagine what an absolute prince I feel myself with knowing that nobody can force me to give the Garter to Müntz.

My Lady Carlisle is going to marry a Sir William Musgrave,[9] who is but three and twenty; but in consideration of the match and of her having years to spare, she has made him a present of ten, and calls him three and thirty. I have seen the new Lady Stanhope[10]—I assure you her face will introduce no plebeian charms into the faces of the Stanhopes.[11] Adieu!

Yours ever

H. W.

From Montagu, ca Tuesday 20 November 1759

G.D. 15/8, No. 734.

In reply to *ante* 17 Nov. 1759; date otherwise conjectural.

Memoranda by HW: Dean of Exeter
Lord Luxborough
Lady Mary Coke
Lord Waldegrave

These are probably names of correspondents, although the only letter near this time to any of them that has been discovered is HW to Lady Mary Coke 27 Dec. 1759.

Greatworth [ca Nov. 20, 1759].

I HAVE long seen the Muntz was filling up his vessel of impertinence and own his airs and insolence have been insupportable to me. I know nobody but Mr Horace Walpole the younger that would have bore it so long.

9. Sir William Musgrave (1735–1800), 6th Bt, of Hayton Castle, Cumberland, compiler of the *Obituary* which bears his name. He was just 24, and Lady Carlisle, whom he m. 10 Dec., was 38. The marriage was a failure; see Lady Louisa Stuart, *Notes on Jesse's Selwyn,* ed. W. S. Lewis, New York, 1928, pp. 46–9. HW later became friendly with Musgrave and bequeathed him a copy of *Des. of SH* 1784 (now wsl).

10. Anne (1737–1811), dau. of Francis Blake Delaval, m. (1) (1759) the Hon. Sir William Stanhope, K.B.; m. (2) (1773) Capt. Charles Morris, the song-writer (N&Q 1910, 11th ser. i. 392). 'The lady . . . has been so-

berly and modestly educated in the country, and is of a very good gentleman's family. She is full young enough to have children, being but two and twenty, and my brother is not too old to beget some' (Chesterfield to Arthur Stanhope, 28 Sept. 1759, *Letters,* ed. Bonamy Dobrée, 1932, v. 2357). She was separated from her husband in 1763 (ibid. vi. 2397–8, 2544; HW to Mann 1 Sept. 1763).

11. In 1765 she sat for Reynolds, whose portrait of her was engraved by Watson (see Algernon Graves and William V. Cronin, *History of the Works of Sir Joshua Reynolds,* 1899–1901, iii. 927–8).

I must desire you will tell me what I am to give him for my two landscapes and the case they came in as also a case for Lord Manchester[1] and dressing[2] his hand; for if he leaves England he must not say I am in his debt.

I fancy Scot[3] has debauched him to set up landscape painter. I am sure you would not have been against any way he wanted to put himself in. Those who do much good and oblige so often must find as many vexations and as much ingratitude as you have done.

Lord Temple's demands[4] are like the Sybil's leaves; as Mr Pitt's popularity increases he rises his price. I am for having them all burnt.

Pray give the enclosed[5] or send it to Mr Chute; 'tis about the Lady Cutts, not her that Bishop Atterbury[6] preached so fine a funeral sermon on; we don't call kin. Our Magdalen was virtuously poxed by her husband and had but little time to repent of her matrimony. I am charming well and hope you are so too. I wish you a merry London. Believe me most truly, my dear Sir, much and ever yours,

G. Montagu

To Montagu, ca Tuesday 27 November 1759

Missing; see *post* 4 Dec. 1759. HW apparently asked Montagu to solicit through Lord North a pension for Bentley.

From Montagu, Tuesday 4 December 1759

G.D. 15/8, No. 735.

Year determined by the further reference *post* 29 Dec. 1759 to the subject of this letter.

Greatworth, Dec. 4th [1759].

I RETURNED home from Wroxton yesterday where I had been passing a week, and found your letter and one from Mr Bentley

1. The portrait mentioned *ante* 16 May 1759, n. 2.

2. Repairing.

3. Samuel Scott (1710–72), landscape painter; a neighbour of HW's at Twickenham (*Anecdotes, Works* iii. 444–5; *ante* 14 July 1748, n. 21; Col. Maurice H. Grant, *Old English Landscape Painters*, [1926?], i. 42–3).

4. Relying on the popularity of his brother-in-law Pitt, Lord Temple asked for the Garter, and on its refusal resigned his place as Lord Privy Seal. He was prevailed upon to resume the post two days later, and was given the Garter shortly afterwards (*Mem. Geo. II* iii. 228–9; *post* 14 Jan. 1760).

5. Missing.

6. Francis Atterbury (1662–1732), Bp of Rochester, 1713; in his *Sermons and Discourses*, 5th edn 1740–5, i. 203 is a sermon (no. VI) preached at the funeral of Elizabeth Pickering (ca 1679–97), m. (1697, his 2d wife) John Cutts, Bn Cutts.

concerning his pension.[1] I must deal fairly with you and tell you I know not how to solicitate Lord North upon such an affair, for though we are very good friends and relations I cannot think myself entitled to ask him such a matter, as I know also that he has a deal of jobs to get for his Banbury[2] people and therefore I should distress him or lay myself under too great obligations to him, a thing I am very averse to. I know you will be so good as to enter into my notions and be assured I am really sorry and mortified that I cannot oblige you and serve Mr Bentley. I am almost ashamed to write myself sincerely yours,

G. MONTAGU

To MONTAGU, Sunday 23 December 1759

Strawberry Hill, Dec. 23d, 1759.

HOW do you do? Are you thawed again? How have you borne the country in this bitter weather? I have not been here these three weeks till today, and was delighted to find it so pleasant, and to meet a comfortable southeast wind, the fairest of all winds, in spite of the scandal that lies on the east;[1] though it is the west that is the parent of all ugliness. The frost was succeeded by such fogs that I could not find my way out of London.

Has your brother told you of the violences in Ireland?[2] There

1. HW's and Bentley's letters are both missing; nothing more is known about the pension.
2. For which he was M.P.

———

1. As a bringer of depressing weather; HW praises the east and southeast winds for bending the trees and blowing the dust from the hedges, *post* 30 May 1763. For a hyperbolic account of the depressing effect of the east wind on English temperament and manners, see a letter of Voltaire of 1727 (Voltaire, *Œuvres complètes*, 1877–85, xxii. 21–2); see also Tobias Smollett, *Letters*, ed. Edward S. Noyes, New York, 1926, p. 61 (to Wilkes 20 April 1759).
2. Irish unrest, aroused by rumours of a projected union with England, was brought to a head by the introduction in the Irish Parliament of a bill providing that in cases of invasion and insurrection it could be summoned on shorter notice than was usually necessary. This innocuous and well-intended measure was taken to be the entering wedge for the destruction of the Irish Parliament, and serious riots resulted. The mob insulted and assaulted numerous peers and dignitaries, invaded the Houses of Parliament, and was dispersed by troops with some loss of life; see *post* 29 Dec. 1759; *Mem. Geo. II* iii. 239–41; GM 1759, xxix. 638–9 (*Annual Register* for 1759, ii. 229 gives the date of the riot as 3 Dec.). Gray to Wharton 23 Jan. 1760 gives a detailed account of the 'Irish Disturbances,' which Gray may have had from HW (*Gray's Corr.* ii. 657–9).

wanted nothing but a Massaniello[3] to overturn the government; and luckily for the government and for Rigby, he who was made for a Massaniello, happened to be first minister there. Tumults and insurrections and oppositions

Like arts and sciences have travelled west.[4]

Pray make the General collect authentic accounts of those civil wars against he returns—you know where they will find their place,[5] and that you are one of the very few that will profit of them.[6] I will grind and dispense to you all the corn you bring to my mill.

We, good-humoured souls, vote eight millions[7] with as few questions, as if the whole House of Commons was of the club at Arthur's: and we live upon distant news as if London was York or Bristol. There is nothing domestic, but that Lord George Lenox, being refused Lord Ancram's[8] consent, set out for Edingburgh with Lady Louisa Kerr, the day before yesterday; and Lord Buckingham is going to be married to our Miss Pitt of Twickenham,[9] daughter of that strange

3. Tommaso Aniello, contracted to Masaniello (ca 1622–47), a Neapolitan fisherman, led a successful popular uprising against Spanish misrule in Naples in 1647. Soon after peace had been restored by the promised removal of onerous taxes, Masaniello was assassinated by agents of the Spanish viceroy (*Nouv. Biog. Gén.; Enciclopedia Italiana*, Roma, 1929–39).

4. This has not been located. It may not be a quotation, but merely a line invented by HW, perhaps echoing Bishop Berkeley's 'Westward the course of empire takes its way.'

5. In the *Memoirs*.

6. In MS, since HW had determined to reserve publication until several years after his death.

7. This was a combined loan and lottery, at 4 per cent (GM 1759, xxix. 604). The total supplies for the year 1759–60 amounted to £15,503,565, as compared to £4,014,137 in 1749–50 ([Charles Whitworth] *Collection of the Supplies, and Ways and Means*, 1763, pp. 97, 137; figures given to the nearest pound).

8. William Henry Ker (ca 1710–75), styled E. of Ancram; 4th M. of Lothian, 1767; his eldest dau., Lady Louisa Ker (1739–1830), m. (at Dumfries, 25 Dec. 1759) Lord George Lennox, and was mother of the

4th D. of Richmond (*Scots Peerage*, 1904–10, v. 481; DU DEFFAND). 'Lord Ancram . . . desired his daughter to stay at least till she was of age, which is in less than a twelvemonth, but love got the better of duty' (*Grenville Papers*, ed. William J. Smith, 1852–3, i. 335). Lord and Lady George became HW's correspondents and intimate friends.

9. The affair fell through (HW to Conway 21 June 1760). The only Miss Pitt of Twickenham appears to have been Harriot (1745–63), dau. of George Morton Pitt (d. 1756). She m. (1762) Brownlow Bertie, 5th D. of Ancaster. Her mother, according to GEC (*sub* Ancaster) was 'Sophia, sometime wife of George Drake, dau. of —— Bugden'; she appears to have been in 1761 living in Orleans House near SH, which her second husband, Pitt, had owned before his death in 1755. She died 1762 (*London and its Environs Described*, Dodsley, 1761, vi. 212; Richard S. Cobbett, *Memorials of Twickenham*, 1872, p. 213; *London Chronicle* 3–6 July 1762, xii. 24). HW reports six months later that Miss Pitt, then aged 15, threw over Buckingham, saying, 'damn her eyes that she will marry some captain' (HW to Conway 21 June 1760). She is no doubt the Miss Pitt extolled in Count Frederick Kielman-

woman, who had a mind to be my wife, and who sent Mr Raftor[10] to know why I did not marry her—I replied, because I was not sure that the two husbands that she had at once, were both dead.[10a] Apropos to my wedding, Prince Edward asked me at the opera t'other night, when I was to marry Lady Mary Coke; I answered, as soon as I got a regiment; which you know is now the fashionable way.[11]

The kingdom of beauty is in as great disorder as the kingdom of Ireland. My Lady Pembroke looks like a ghost—poor Lady Coventry is going to be one.[12] Molly Howe[13] has not done pining for Sir Armitage; and the Duchess of Hamilton is so altered I did not know her. Indeed she is big with child,[14] and so big, that as my Lady Northumberland says, it is plain she has a camel in her belly; and my Lord Edgcumbe says, it is as true, that it did not go through the eye of a needle. That great vulgar Countess[15] has been laid up with a hurt in her leg; Lady Rebecca Poulett[16] pushed her on the birthnight against a bench: the Duchess of Grafton asked if it was true that Lady Rebecca kicked her?—'Kicked me, Madam! When did you ever hear of a Percy that took a kick?' I can tell you another anecdote of that

segge, *Diary of a Journey to England . . . 1761–1762*, 1902, p. 224, as 'a very pleasant young lady, who possesses at least £100,000, and who dances remarkably well into the bargain.'

10. James Raftor (d. 1790), brother, or half-brother of Mrs Clive (GM 1790, lx pt ii. 861). Cunningham, ii. 458, n. 1, quotes a MS letter from Whitehead to Lord Nuneham, 30 Oct. 1770: 'Raftor has left the stage; Mrs Clive has very kindly taken him to live entirely with her, and I hear he is excessively happy at it'; to which Lord Nuneham added: 'Mr. Raftor, a wretched actor, brother to Mrs Clive— hideous in person and face, and vulgarly awkward in his general appearance, but a man of some information, of much observation, and possessing an extraordinary fund of original humour. In the talent of relating a story he was unrivalled.' The last observation is confirmed by HW to Conway 9 July 1775.

10a. Nothing further has been found on the subject of her bigamy, which HW implies. When a widow she gave HW an Indian scimitar and dagger (*Des. of SH, Works* ii. 440), the extent of her recorded overtures to him.

11. This exchange of witticisms inspired HW's mock petition to Pitt for a regiment in the French service, since there was nothing left for England to conquer. He sent it to Lady Mary, explaining that his martial spirit arose only from his passion for her; see HW to Lady Mary Coke 27 Dec. 1759; to Lady Ailesbury 29 Dec. 1759; *Horace Walpole's Fugitive Verses*, ed. W. S. Lewis, New York, 1931, pp. 128–31.

12. She lived until 30 Sept. 1760.

13. Hon. Mary Howe (ca 1733–1819), 4th dau. of 2d Vct Howe; m. Gen. Sir William Augustus Pitt (Lodge, *Peerage of Ireland*, 1789, v. 86; *Annual Register* for 1819, lxi. 116. Her fiancé, Sir John Armytage (1732–58), 2d Bt, of Kirklees, York, was killed at St Cast 10 Sept. 1758 (HW to Mann 22 Sept. 1758).

14. Lady Augusta Campbell (31 March 1760–1831), m. Col. Henry Clavering (*Scots Peerage*, 1904–10, i. 387).

15. Lady Northumberland. See n. 18 below.

16. Lady Rebecca Poulett (1716–65), youngest dau. of 1st E. Poulett (Collins, *Peerage*, 1812, iv. 14).

house, that will not divert you less: Lord March making them a visit this summer at Alnwic-castle,[17] my Lord received him at the gate, and said, 'I believe, my Lord, this is the first time that ever a Douglas and a Percy met here in friendship'—think of this from a Smithson[18] to a true Douglas.[18a]

I don't trouble my head about any connection: any news into the country, I know, is welcome, though it comes out higlepigledy, just as it happens to be packed up. The cry in Ireland has been against Lord Hilsborough, supposing him to meditate an union of the two islands:[19] George Selwyn seeing him sit t'other night between my Lady Harrington and Lord Barrington,[20] said, 'Who can say that my Lord Hilsborough is not an enemy to an union?'

I will tell you one more story, and then good night. Lord Lyttelton was at Covent Garden; Beard[21] came on: the former said, 'How comes Beard here? What made him leave Drury Lane?' Mr Shelley[22] who sat next to him, replied, 'Why, don't you know he has been such a fool as to go and marry a Miss Rich?[23]—He has married Rich's daughter.' My Lord coloured, Shelley found out what he had said, and ran away.[24]

I forgot to tell you that you need be in no disturbance about Muntz's pictures; they were a present I made you. Good night

Yours ever

H. W.

17. Alnwick Castle, Northumberland, an ancient seat of the Percys, which the Duke of Northumberland rehabilitated; see George Tate, *History . . . of Alnwick*, 1866–9, i. 357–8, 372–87.

18. Sir Hugh Smithson (after 1750, Percy) (1714–86), 4th Bt, m. (1740) Lady Elizabeth Seymour (1716–76), dau. of 7th D. of Somerset, and great-granddaughter of the last Percy Earl of Northumberland; he became 2d E. of Northumberland under a special remainder, 1750; cr. (1766) D. of Northumberland. His great-great-grandfather was the first of his family to emerge from obscurity; a Yorkshireman, he became a successful London merchant, was made a Baronet in 1663; see ibid., i. 355–6.

18a. March's family name.

19. 'The union was, indeed, a favourite object with Lord Hilsborough. He had hinted such a wish a year or two before

in the Parliament of England; and being now in Ireland, let drop expressions of the same tendency'—one of the causes for the riots of n. 2 above (*Mem. Geo. II* iii. 239).

20. This pair appear in a *tête-à-tête* in *Town and Country Magazine* Jan. 1771, iii. 9, where she is called 'The Stable-yard Messalina' and he, 'The Hostiler Scribe.'

21. John Beard (ca 1716–91), actor and vocalist; he had been at Drury Lane the season before.

22. Not identified; probably one of the Sussex Shelleys.

23. Charlotte Rich (ca 1726–1818), m. (1759) John Beard (DNB, *sub* Beard). Her father, John Rich (1682?–1761), was a patentee of Covent Garden.

24. 'Comical enough. Lyttelton had undone himself by marry[ing] a Miss Rich' (Mrs Piozzi; see *ante* 18 May 1749, n. 37).

From Montagu, Saturday 29 December 1759

G.D. 15/8, No. 736.

In reply to *ante* 23 Dec. 1759.

Memorandum by HW: our ancestors christened us—it is but just we should return the compliment—
HW doubtless used this in a missing letter.

Greatworth, [Dec.] 29 [1759].

I AM much obliged to you for your very entertaining letter, and most extremely for your present of the two landscapes that I had no idea of but reckoned upon paying my hard money [for] as soon as I came to town. Charles sent me a few particulars only from Dublin of their riot. You know how much he is obliged to his honour ye Master of ye Rolls[1] for his general's staff. He said they seized Sir Thomas Pendergass[2] and dragged [him] through all the kennels[3] and about the streets. They forced the Chief Justice[4] in the House of Lords to administer an oath to the Chancellor,[5] and held his head to the Book. The two next days there were great balls and high play and the company stayed till morning;[6] this I think was very careless and indecent.

I do not believe I shall come to town till the beginning of February as I shall have a good many things to do here and shall find London enough for my use when other people have almost done with it.

There is a paraphrase of the *Magnificat* in the *Atalantis* by Lady Winchelsea.[7] How the devil did it come there? Maybe you have men-

1. Rigby, 'whom the Duke of Bedford had lately made their Master of the Rolls. The office there is no post of business: still the choice of a man so little grave was not decent' and the infuriated mob wanted to hang him. Also, he and the Duke were eager to hush up the riot (*Mem. Geo. II* iii. 242–3).

2. Sir Thomas Prendergast (d. 1760), 2d Bt, Irish Postmaster-General.

3. Gutters.

4. St George Caulfeild (d. 1778), of Donamon, son of William Caulfeild; Irish Solicitor-General, 1739; Attorney-General, 1741; Chief Justice of King's Bench and Privy Councillor, 1751 (Lodge, *Irish Peerage*, 1789, iii. 139–40).

5. John Bowes (ca 1690–1767), cr. (1758) Bn Bowes of Clonlyon; Irish Chancellor, 1757.

6. Presumably at the Castle.

7. Anne Kingsmill (1661–1720), poetess; m. (1684) Heneage Finch, 5th E. of Winchilsea, 1712. Two of her poems appear in Mrs Mary Manley's satirical novel *Secret Memoirs . . . from the New Atalantis*, 1709. Montagu probably refers to the second (ii. 160–3), which is a paraphrase, not of the Magnificat (Luke i. 46–55), but of the 148th Psalm, and is a part of Lady Winchilsea's 'A Pindarick Poem Upon the Hurricane' (*Poems of Anne Countess of Winchilsea*, ed. Myra Reynolds, Chicago, 1903, p. 252). The poem was written in

tioned it in your new edition[8] but it is an old Twickenham trick to make the most of one's work.[9] I shall stay for your auction and last words together. My cousin and I correspond, and I am to have the regulating and nomination of his pictures at Horton. Did I tell you Mr Bentley's designs are executed and put up in the great chamber at Hinchingbroke, of the life and death of your admirable Earl of Sandwich?[10] Apropos of Mr B.; you cannot tell how I have fretted about not doing what you desired me; excepting Charles and yourself, there is not another person in the world I could ask favours of, and I am sure, no one else would grant me one. Have you your Christmas set[11] this year? Adieu; believe me ever most sincerely yours,

G. Montagu

I wish you a happy new year.

To Montagu, Monday 14 January 1760

Arlington Street, Jan. 14, 1760.

HOW do you contrive to exist on your mountain in this rude season? Sure you must be become a snowball! As I was not in England in '41,[1] I had no notion of such cold. The streets are abandoned, nothing appears in them; the Thames is almost as solid.[2]

1703; Miss Reynolds gives as its source the only contemporary collection of Lady Winchilsea's poems, published in 1713 (ibid., pp. xv, 252). Montagu's question remains unanswered.

8. HW does not mention the poem in his brief notice of Lady Winchilsea in *Royal and Noble Authors*, 1759, ii. 196–7.

9. Not clear; perhaps Montagu means that it was HW's habit to exploit fully information received from his friends.

10. These are probably the designs mentioned by HW in his account of Hinchingbrooke in *Country Seats* 49–50: 'In the best eating-room fitted up by this Lord, is the pedigree of the family in the windows, done by Peckitt of York, the Admiral receiving Charles II at Dover, and another piece of the Admiral's death.' The room containing the windows, now the library, is on the south side of the house (information from Lord Sandwich). Montagu refers to Edward Montagu (1625–72),

cr. (1660) E. of Sandwich, as 'your' Earl of Sandwich because HW had copied extracts of his diary at Hinchingbrooke. These extracts, in HW's hand, are now WSL.

11. Selwyn, Williams, and Edgcumbe, the 'out-of-town party' (*ante* 20 April 1756).

---

1. *The Ladies Diary: or, The Woman's Almanack*, 1741, which gives the weather of each day, shows that this is a slip for '40 (HW was in Italy both winters). 'The great frost' commenced 25 Dec. 1739 and continued to 16 Feb. 1740, and March was 'very cold and barren' with 'scarce anything green.' See West to HW 23 Jan. 1740. Lady Hertford writes to Lady Pomfret 5 Feb. 1741 that they have had 'the finest season imaginable' (*Correspondence*, 1805, ii. 279), which is borne out by *The Ladies Diary*, 1742.

2. 'The navigation of the river Thames,

Then think what a campaign must be in such a season! Our army was under arms for fourteen hours on the twenty-third expecting the French;[3] and several of the men were frozen when they should have dismounted. What milksops the Marlboroughs and Turennes, the Blakes and the Van Trumps appear now, who whipped into winter quarters and into port, the moment their noses looked blue. Sir Cloudesly Shovel[4] said that an admiral would deserve to be broke who kept great ships out after the end of September; and to be shot if after October—There's Hawke[5] in the bay weathering *this* winter, after conquering in a storm. For my part, I scarce venture to make a campaign in the Opera House, for if I once begin to freeze, I shall be frozen through in a moment. I am amazed, with such weather, such ravages, and distress, that there is anything left in Germany, but money; for thither half the treasure of Europe goes: England,[6] France, Russia, and all the Empress can squeeze from Italy and Hungary, all is sent thither, and yet the wretched people have not subsistence! A pound of bread sells at Dresden for eleven pence.[7] We are going to send many more troops thither; and it is so much the fashion to raise regiments, that I wish there were such a neutral kind of beings in England as abbés, that one might have an excuse for not growing military mad, when one has turned the heroic corner of one's age. I

above-bridge, is entirely obstructed by the frost. The river is frozen over at Putney; and all the small craft and wherries are laid up' (*London Chronicle* 14 Jan. 1760, vii. 50). See GM 1760, xxx. 45 for an account of even severer cold on the continent.

3. *London Chronicle* 10–12 Jan. 1760, vii. 47, in a dispatch from Frankfort dated 30 Dec., reports that in the night of 21–22 Dec. 10,000 French marched out of camp, and that Prince Ferdinand prepared to meet them at the river Lahn. The French retreated to go into winter quarters. It is probably to this episode that HW refers.

4. Sir Clowdisley Shovell (1650–1707), Kt; admiral of the fleet.

5. Admiral Sir Edward Hawke (1710–81), K.B., 1749; cr. (1776) Bn Hawke; First Lord of the Admiralty 1766–71. He was in Quiberon Bay, where he had destroyed a French fleet under Conflans 20 Nov.

6. In addition to the troops maintained in Germany, by a convention signed 9 Nov.

England undertook to pay Frederick of Prussia £670,000 as a direct subsidy (GM 1759, xxix. 610).

7. 'Dresden, Dec. 15—The great scarcity of provisions here increases daily, and the price of bread is so much advanced, that a loaf of two pounds weight sells for 23d. sterling, and an ammunition loaf at the rate of 3s. 6d. and firing is not to be had at any price' (*London Chronicle* 7 Jan. 1760, vii. 25). At this time bread did not cost more than 1½d. per lb. in London, where a 'wheaten peck loaf' cost 20d. (GM 1760, xxx. 48). This was a loaf made from a peck of flour (OED *sub* peck); 'wheaten' was a superior grade; a cheaper variety was called 'household.' Both weighed 17 lb. 6 oz.; cf. *Observations and Examples to Assist Magistrates in Setting the Assize of Bread* [1759] p. 3; [John Penkethman] *Authentic Accounts of the History and Price of Wheat, Bread, Malt . . . to . . . 1745*, 1765, pp. 29–31; *London Chronicle* 28–30 April 1763, xiii. 411.

HORACE WALPOLE, BY ECCARDT, ABOUT 1755

am ashamed of being a young rake, when my seniors are covering their grey toupées with helmets and feathers, and accoutering their pot-bellies with cuirasses and martial masquerade habits. Yet rake I am, and abominably so for a person that begins to wrinkle reverendly. I have sat up twice this week till between two and three with the Duchess of Grafton at loo, who by the way has got a Pam-child[8] this morning; and on Saturday night I supped with Prince Edward at my Lady Rochford's, and we stayed till half an hour past three. My favour with that Highness continues or rather increases; he makes everybody make suppers for him to meet me, for I still hold out against going to Court. In short, if he were twenty years older, or I could make myself twenty years younger, I might carry him to Cambden-House,[9] and be as impertinent as ever my Lady Churchill[10] was— but as I dread being ridiculous, I shall give my Lord Bute no uneasiness. My Lady Maynard[11] who divides the favour of this tiny court with me, supped with us. Did you know she sings French ballads very prettily? Lord Rochford played on the guitar, and the Prince sung; there were my two nieces and Lord Waldgrave, Lord Huntingdon, and Mr Morrison,[12] the groom, and the evening was pleasant; but I had a much more agreeable supper last night at Mrs Clive's with Miss West,[13] my niece Chomley,[14] and Murphy,[15] the writing actor, who is

8. George Henry Fitzroy (1760–1844), 4th D. of Grafton, 1811.

9. Campden House, Kensington; Princess Anne lived there 1691–6 (*London Past & Present*).

10. Sarah Jennings, later Duchess of Marlborough.

11. Charlotte (ca 1731–62), one of the beautiful daughters of Sir Cecil Bishopp; m. (1751) Sir William Maynard, 4th Bt, of Walthamstow, Essex.

12. Capt. George Morrison (ca 1704–99), equerry to Prince Edward till the latter's death in 1767; Col., 1772; Maj. Gen., 1777; Gen., 1796 (*Court & City Register;* see *Army Lists*). He died 'the oldest staff-officer in the service, having been appointed quartermaster-general in 1761' (*Annual Register* for 1799, xli. [pt ii] 67). 'This Morrison, whom I remember an old general, was a tall, lank man, with a visage uncommonly rueful and ugly' (Lady Louisa Stuart, *Selections from her Manuscripts*, ed. Hon. James A. Home, Edinburgh, 1899, p. 109).

13. Hon. Henrietta Cecilia West (1727–1817), dau. of John West, 7th Bn, cr. (1761) E. Delawarr; m. (1762) Gen. James Johnston; became an intimate friend of HW's. 'She called herself the *Lump of Beauty*' (Mrs Piozzi). Some of her sprightly (but much bowdlerized) letters to Lord Harcourt are in *Harcourt Papers,* ed. Edward W. Harcourt, Oxford, n.d., viii. 11–29. See GM 1817, lxxxvii pt i. 281; *Register Book of Marriages . . . St George, Hanover Square,* ed. John H. Chapman, 1886–97, i. 111 (Harleian Soc. Publications: *Registers* xi); Collins, *Peerage,* 1812, v. 26; *ante* 5 June 1746, n. 19.

14. Mary Woffington (ca 1729–1811), sister of Peg Woffington the actress; m. (1746) Rev. Hon. Robert Cholmondeley, HW's nephew (Burke, *Peerage, sub* Cholmondeley; GM 1811, lxxxi pt i. 403). She was well acquainted with Dr Johnson and his circle; Johnson called her 'a very airy lady' (Boswell, *Johnson* iii. 318 n).

15. Arthur Murphy (1727–1805), author and actor.

very good company; and two or three more. Mrs Chomley is very lively, you know how entertaining the Clive is, and Miss West is an absolute original.

There is nothing new but a very dull pamphlet, written by Lord Bath and his chaplain Douglas,[16] called a *Letter to Two Great Men*.[17] It is a plan for the peace, and much adopted by the City; and much admired by all who are too humble to judge for themselves. I don't tell you of it for the thing itself, but for what Lord Bath said on it. The Dowager Pembroke[18] asked him if he writ it? 'Writ it!' he said; 'yes—and it was all about her'—'Don't you see,' said he, 'In every page that it mentions *you*? It talks of a good $\begin{Bmatrix} peace \\ piece \end{Bmatrix}$, and a safe piece, and an honourable piece, and a lasting piece, as you are, for so I have known you these forty years.'

I was much diverted t'other morning with another volume on birds by Edwards,[19] who has published four or five.[20] The poor man, who is grown very old and devout, begs God to take from him the love of natural philosophy; and having observed some heterodox proceedings among bantam cocks, he proposes that all schools of boys and girls should be promiscuous, lest, if separated, they should learn wayward passions.[21] But what struck me most were his dedications; the last was to God;[22] this to Lord Bute; as if he was determined to make his fortune in one world or t'other.

Pray read Fontaine's fable of the lion grown old;[23] don't it put you in mind of anything? No! Not when his shaggy majesty has borne the insults of the tiger, and the horse etc. and the ass comes last, kicks out his only remaining fang, and asks for a blue bridle?[24] Apropos, I will

---

16. Rev. John Douglas (1721–1807), Bp of Carlisle, 1787; Salisbury, 1791.

17. 'I remember it. *My Lord and Sir etc.* meaning the Duke of Newcastle and Mr Pitt' (Mrs Piozzi). Mrs Piozzi's recollection, 58 years after, of the salutation of the pamphlet is correct; in it Newcastle and Pitt were advised to mistrust the French, to destroy Dunkirk, to keep all of Canada, and to barter other conquests for concessions to Continental allies.

18. Hon. Mary Fitzwilliam (1707–69), m. (1) (1733) Henry Herbert, 9th E. of Pembroke; m. (2) (1751) Maj. North Ludlow Bernard.

19. *Gleanings of Natural History*, Part

II, 1760, by George Edwards (1694–1773), naturalist.

20. Actually six at this time. The first four were *Natural History of Birds*, 1743–51; the first part of *Gleanings of Natural History* appeared 1758; the third, 1764.

21. *Gleanings*, Part II, pp. xxi–xxii.

22. Not the last, but the fourth, in the last volume of *Natural History*. HW was a subscriber to the first six volumes. They were sold SH vii. 146 (Lond. 1136–7).

23. Jean de la Fontaine (1621–95), *Fables*, Bk III, Fable xiv, 'Le lion devenu vieux.'

24. This is an addition by HW, and refers, as is made clear below, to Lord Tem-

tell you the turn Charles Townshend gave to this fable. 'My Lord Temple,' said he, 'has quite mistaken the thing; he soars too high at first: people often miscarry by not proceeding by degrees: he went, and at once asked for my *Lord* Carlisle's Garter[25]—if he would have been contented to ask first for my *Lady* Carlisle's garter, I don't doubt but he would have obtained it.'[26] Adieu!

Yours ever

H. W.

To Montagu, Monday 28 January 1760

Arlington Street, Jan. 28th, 1760.

I SHALL almost frighten you from coming to London, for whether you have the constitution of a horse or a man, you will be equally in danger. All the horses in town are laid up with sore throats and colds, and are so hoarse you cannot hear them speak. I with all my immortality have been half killed; that violent bitter weather was too much for me; I have had a nervous fever these six or seven weeks every night, and have taken bark enough to have made a rind for Daphne:[1] nay, have even stayed at home two days; but I think my eternity begins to bud again. I am quite of Dr Garth's[2] mind, who, when anybody commended a hard frost to him, used to reply, 'Yes, Sir, 'fore Gad, very fine weather, Sir, very wholesome weather; kills trees, Sir, very good for a man, Sir.' There has been cruel havoc among the ladies; my Lady Granby[3] is dead, and the famous Polly

---

ple's importunate demands on George II for the Garter (*ante* ca 20 Nov. 1759), which were not satisfied until 31 Jan. 1760. See the exchange of letters in *Grenville Papers*, ed. William J. Smith, 1852–3, i. 333–9, in one of which Temple is constrained, apparently for face-saving purposes only, to decline acceptance because of the King's grudging attitude (to Devonshire 31 Jan.). See Wraxall, *Memoirs*, i. 89, for a story of the King's rudeness to Temple, whom he cordially hated, at the investiture.

25. Henry Howard (1694–1758), 4th E. of Carlisle; K.G., 1756. His death created a vacancy in the Order.

26. Lady Carlisle's gaiety, according to Lady Louisa Stuart, did not commence until Carlisle's death (Lady Louisa Stuart, *Notes on Jesse's Selwyn*, ed. W. S. Lewis, New York, 1928, pp. 47–9).

---

1. The nymph who, pursued by Apollo, was turned into a laurel (Ovid, *Met.* i. 548–52).

2. Sir Samuel Garth (1661–1719), Kt; physician and poet.

3. 'A lovely creature, and *so* good!' (Mrs Piozzi).

Duchess of Bolton,[4] and my Lady Besborough.[5] I have no great reason to lament the last,[6] and yet the circumstances of her death, and the horror of it to her family make one shudder. It was the same sore throat and fever that carried off four of their children a very few years ago. My Lord now fell ill of it, very ill, and the eldest daughter slightly.[7] My Lady caught it, attending her husband, and concealed it as long as she could. When at last the physician insisted on her keeping her bed, she said as she went into her room, 'Then, Lord have mercy upon me, I shall never come out of it again,' and died in three days. Lord Besborough grew outrageously impatient at not seeing her, and would have forced into her room when she had been dead about four days—they were obliged to tell him the truth—never was an answer that expressed so much horror! He said, 'And how many children have I left?'—not knowing how far his calamity might have reached. Poor Lady Coventry is near completing this black list.[7a] You have heard I suppose a horrid story of another kind, of Lord Ferrers[8] murdering his steward in the most barbarous and deliberate manner. He sent away all his servants but one, and like that heroic murderess Queen Christina,[9] carried the poor man, through a gallery and several rooms, locking them after him, and then bid the man kneel down for he was determined to kill him. The poor creature flung himself at his feet but in vain, was shot and lived twelve hours. Mad as this action was, from the consequences, there was no frenzy in his behaviour. He got drunk, and at intervals talked of it coolly: but did not attempt to escape till the colliers beset his house and were determined to take him alive or dead. He is now in the jail at Leicester, and will soon be removed to the Tower, then to Westminster Hall, and I suppose to Tower-Hill; unless as Lord Talbot prophesied in the House of Lords, 'Not being thought mad enough to be shut

4. Lavinia Fenton (ca 1708–60), m. (1751) Charles Powlett, 3d D. of Bolton, whose mistress she had been since her triumphal stage success in 1728 as Polly in *The Beggar's Opera*.

5. Lady Caroline Cavendish (1719–60), m. (1739) William Ponsonby, Vct Duncannon; 2d E. of Bessborough, 1758.

6. The reason for HW's coolness is not known; he may simply have been not well acquainted with her.

7. Lady Catherine Ponsonby (1742–89), m. (1763) Hon. Aubrey Beauclerk, 2d Bn Vere, 1781; 5th D. of St Alban's, 1787.

7a. She died 30 Sept. 1760.

8. Laurence Shirley (1720–60), 4th E. Ferrers, had quarreled with his steward John Johnson over the latter's management of the estates, and 18 Jan. murdered him as HW describes; his trial and execution are described *post* 19 April and 6 May 1760.

9. In punishment of his confessed treachery, Christina had her Grand Equerry the Marquis Monaldeschi murdered in a gallery at Fontainebleau by other members of her entourage; see F. W. Bain, *Christina, Queen of Sweden*, 1890, 282–96.

up till he had killed somebody, he will then be thought too mad to
be executed.' But that madman, Lord Talbot, was no more honoured
in his vocation, than other prophets are in their own country.

As you seem amused with my entertainments, I will tell you how
I passed yesterday. A party was made to go to the Magdalen-House.[10]
We met at Northumberland House at five, and set out in four
coaches; Prince Edward, Colonel Brudenel[11] his groom, Lady Northumberland, Lady Mary Coke, Lady Carlisle, Miss Pelham, Lady
Hertford, Lord Beauchamp,[12] Lord Huntingdon, old Bowman, and
I. This new convent is beyond Goodman's Fields, and I assure you
would content any Catholic alive. We were received by—oh! first, a
vast mob, for princes are not so common at that end of the town as at
this. Lord Hertford at the head of the Governors with their white
staves met us at the door, and led the Prince directly into the chapel,
where before the altar was an armchair for him, with a blue damask
cushion, a prie-dieu, and a footstool of black cloth with gold nails.
We sat on forms near him. There were Lord and Lady Dartmouth,[13]
in the odour of devotion, and many City ladies. The chapel is small
and low, but neat, hung with Gothic paper[14] and tablets of benefac-
tions. At the west end were inclosed the sisterhood, above an hundred and thirty, all in greyish brown stuffs, broad handkerchiefs, and
flat straw hats with a blue ribband, pulled quite over their faces. As
soon as we entered the chapel, the organ played, and the Magdalens
sung a hymn in parts; you cannot imagine how well. The chapel was
dressed with orange and myrtle, and there wanted nothing but a little incense, to drive away the devil—or to invite him. Prayers then be-

10. Goodman's Fields, in a building
previously occupied by the London In-
firmary. It 'opened the 10th day of August, 1758, when eight unhappy objects
were received' (George Reeves, *New History of London*, 1764, p. 89; see *London
and its Environs Described*, Dodsley, 1761,
iv. 224–38). A new building in St George's
Fields, erected by subscriptions (see the
list in *London Evening Post* 7–9 Jan. 1768),
was occupied in 1772 (*London Past & Present*); the institution is now (1940) located
in Streatham.

11. Lt-Col. Hon. Robert Brudenel
(1726–68), 3d son of 3d E. of Cardigan;
M.P. Great Bedwin 1756–61, 1768 (March–
May); Marlborough 1761–8; Col., 1762; 4th
Foot, 1765; first groom of the bedchamber

to Prince Edward (Collins, *Peerage*, 1812,
iii. 498; Burke, *Peerage*, *sub* Ailesbury;
Army Lists).

12. Francis Seymour-Conway (later In-
gram-Seymour-Conway) (1743–1822), styled
Vct Beauchamp; 2d M. of Hertford, 1794;
HW's kinsman and correspondent.

13. William Legge (1731–1801), 2d E. of
Dartmouth, m. Frances Catherine Gunter
Nicoll (*ante* 22 May 1753, n. 11). They
were both very pious. Cowper refers to
him in *Truth* as 'one who wears a coronet
and prays,' while Wraxall records that he
was nicknamed 'the Psalm-singer' (*Memoirs* iii. 268).

14. Wallpaper with Gothic designs, a
new mode championed by HW at SH (see
SH Accounts 39–41).

gan, psalms, and a sermon; the latter by a young clergyman, one
Dodd;[15] who contributed to the Popish idea one had imbibed, by
haranguing entirely in the French style, and very eloquently and
touchingly. He apostrophized the lost sheep, who sobbed and cried
from their souls—so did my Lady Hertford and Fanny Pelham, till I
believe the City dames took them both for Jane Shores.[16] The confessor then turned to the audience, and addressed himself to the
Royal Highness, whom he called, most illustrious Prince, beseeching
his protection. In short, it was a very pleasing performance, and I
got *the most illustrious* to desire it might be printed.[17] We had another hymn, and then were conducted to the *parloir,* where the Governors kissed the Prince's hand, and then the lady abbess or matron
brought us tea. From thence we went to the refectory, where all the
nuns, without their hats, were ranged at long tables ready for supper. A few were handsome, many who seemed to have no title to their
profession, and two or three of twelve years old: but all recovered,
and looking healthy. I was struck and pleased with the modesty of
two of them, who swooned away with the confusion of being stared
at—one of these is a niece[18] of Sir Clement Cotterel.[19] We were showed
their work, which is, making linen, and bead-work; they earn ten
pounds a week. One circumstance diverted me, but amidst all this
decorum I kept it to myself. The wands of the governors are white,
but twisted at top with black and white, which put me in mind of
Jacob's rods[20] that he placed before the cattle to make them breed.
My Lord Hertford would never have forgiven me if I had joked on
this; so I kept my countenance very demurely, nor even inquired
whether among the pensioners there were any *novices* from Mrs
Naylor's.

15. Rev. William Dodd (1729–77), the
celebrated forger; he acted as Chaplain to
the Magdalen House until 1774.

16. Jane Shore (d. 1527?), mistress of
Edward IV and of Thomas Grey, 1st M.
of Dorset; forced to do penance by Richard III, according to historical tradition
(see, however, HW's *Historic Doubts on
. . . Richard III, Works,* ii. 174). She was
familiar to the 18th century as the heroine
of a tragedy by Nicholas Rowe.

17. It was: *A Sermon on Luke XIX:10,
Preached at the Chapel of the Magdalen-
House, Jan. 27, 1760* (BM Catalogue).

18. Not further identified.

19. Sir Clement Cottrell-Dormer (1686–
1758), Kt, of Rousham, Oxon; Vice-Presi-
dent of the Society of Antiquaries; Master
of the Ceremonies, a position apparently
hereditary in his family from 1641 (Burke,
Landed Gentry; George Lipscomb, *History
. . . of the County of Buckingham,* 1847,
i. 119; R. A. Austen-Leigh, *Eton College
Register, 1698–1752,* 1927, p. 86).

20. Genesis xxx. 37–43.

The court-martial on Lord George Sackville is appointed; General *Onslow*[21] is to be *Speaker* of it. Adieu! till I see you; I am glad it will be so soon.

Yours ever

H. W.

From Montagu, Sunday 3 February 1760

G.D. 15/8, No. 737.

Greatworth, Sunday, February 3, 1760.

I AM very sorry to hear you have been so much out of order and hope your bark will prevent any return; the dreadful sore throats you mention are very common in this part of the country and in a neighbouring village every person has had it. I never have yet been ill, nay, last week went a-riding upon a real[1] horse three times for two or three hours.

Your last letter is always the best and most charming; if you would promise me to write every week I would never come to town as long as I lived. Think that I have a box full of them of above twenty years old; think what a treasure they will be a hundred years hence to a Madame Sévigné of the House of Montagu. Look you, Sir, they are my property; you may burn your own works but you shall as soon burn me as make me burn them. No; they are in a box which I will cover with yellow velvet turned up grey[2] and enclosed in a tin case for fear of fire, and bequeathed with the most solemn trust and precautions to the last Cu of ye Cudoms. None of them will relish them more than me. I come to town, I believe, on Saturday, perhaps, to dinner somewhere, I don't know, in Bond Street. I will call on you on Sunday in the morning and kiss your hand; till when farewell.

Yours most assuredly,

G. Montagu.

21. Lt-Gen. Richard Onslow, brother of Speaker Onslow; M.P. Guilford, 1727–60; died 17 March 1760, before the court-martial started (Collins, *Peerage*, 1812, v. 476).

1. So apparently in MS; perhaps as opposed to a hobby-horse.
2. Yellow and grey were the Montagu livery.

To Montagu, Thursday 27 March 1760

Address: To George Montagu Esq. at Greatworth near Brackley, Northamptonshire. Free Hor. Walpole. *Postmark:* 27 MR.

Arlington Street, March 27, 1760.

I SHOULD have thought·that you might have learnt by this time that when a tradesman promises anything on Monday or Saturday or any particular day of the week, he means any Monday or any Saturday of any week, as nurses quiet children and their own consciences by the refined salvo[1] of *tomorrow is a new day*. When Mr Smith's[2] Saturday and the frame do arrive I will pay the one and send you the other.

Lord George's[3] trial is not near being finished: by its draggling beyond the term of the old Mutiny Bill,[3a] they were forced to make out a new warrant; this lost two days, as all the depositions were forced to be read over again to and resworn by the witnesses; then there will be a contest whether Sloper[4] shall re-establish his own credit by pawning it farther. Lord Ferrers comes on the stage on the sixteenth of next month.

I breakfasted the day before yesterday at Ælia Lælia[5] Chudleigh's. There was a concert for Prince Edward's birthday, and at three a

---

1. Quibbling evasion (OED).

2. No doubt the same Mr Smith who gilded and perhaps carved the ceiling and frames in the Tribune at SH (*SH Accounts* 9). The reference is obscure in the absence of Montagu's letter.

3. Lord George Sackville's court-martial for disobedience of orders and cowardice at Minden.

3a. Courts martial and a standing army, both otherwise illegal, were authorized by the annual passage of a Mutiny Act for one year only.

4. Lt-Col. Robert Sloper (d. 1802), K.B., 1788; Col., 1772; Maj. Gen., 1777; Col. 14th Dragoons, 1778; Lt-Gen., 1782; Gen., 1796; Col. 4th Dragoons, 1797 (*Army Lists;* GM 1802, lxxii pt ii. 790). He testified that he had asked one of the A.D.C.'s who brought Sackville orders to advance, to repeat the order so that Sackville could not misunderstand it 'for you see the condition he

is in.' This damaging testimony was impugned by one of Lord George's witnesses (GM 1760, xxx. 138, 141), and from what HW says there apparently was a question whether Sloper should testify again. He did not, since he was fully corroborated by another witness (ibid. 143).

5. 'Ælia Lælia Crispis. The unknown subject of a very celebrated enigmatical inscription, preserved in Bologna, which has puzzled the heads of many learned men who have attempted to explain it. It is as follows:

Ælia Lælia Crispis,
Nec vir, nec mulier, nec androgyna;
Nec puella, nec juvenis, nec anus;
Nec meretrix, nec pudica:
Sed omnia. . . .'

(William A. Wheeler, *Explanatory and Pronouncing Dictionary of the Noted Names of Fiction,* Boston, edn 1917, p. 6).

vast cold collation, and all the town. The house[6] is not fine nor in good taste, but loaded with finery.[7] Execrable varnished pictures, chests, cabinets, commodes, tables, stands, boxes, riding on one another's backs, and loaded with terreens,[8] filigree, figures and everything upon earth. Every favour she has bestowed is registered by a bit of Dresden china. There is a glass case full of enamels, eggs, ambers, lapis lazuli, cameos, toothpick-cases and all kind of trinkets, things that she told me were her playthings; another cupboard full of the finest japan; and candlesticks and vases of rock crystal ready to be thrown down in every corner.[9] But of all curiosities are the *conveniencies* in every bedchamber: great mahogany projections, as big as her own bubbies, with the holes, brass handles and cocks etc.—I could not help saying, it was the *loosest* family I ever saw! Never was such an intimate union of love and a closestool! Adieu!

Yours ever

H. W.

From Montagu, ca Wednesday 9 April 1760

G.D. 15/8, No. 739.

Undated; the year can be ascertained by references to Miss Drury and the hamper for Bentley; Easter fell on 6 April.

Greatworth [ca April 9, 1760].

I HAVE sent a hamper of cider and good things directed for you which I desire you would send to Mr Bentley and I hope it will come safe.

I conclude you have been passing your Easter at Strawberry Hill, and I hope the air of the country has been of service to you. You

6. Kingston House, Knightsbridge; see Charles E. Pearce, *The Amazing Duchess* [1911] i. 243–51; it is illustrated in E. Beresford Chancellor, *Knightsbridge and Belgravia*, 1909, p. 183.

7. Count Frederick Kielmansegge admired it unreservedly, while reporting that 'there is hardly a place in the whole house left bare or without decoration, like a doll's house'; see his account of a concert there in his *Diary of a Journey to England . . . 1761–1762*, 1902, pp. 280–1.

8. Early spelling of tureen (this passage is the only one quoted in OED with exactly this spelling of the word).

9. Auctions of her collections occurred in Paris, 2 April 1789, in London (Christie's), 20–3 May, 10–23 June 1789, and 2 Feb. 1791 (Frits Lugt, *Répertoire des catalogues de ventes*, La Haye, 1938–).

have heard Lord Halifax is going to be married to Sir Thomas Drury's daughter[1] and that his Miss Falkener[2] is retired upon half-pay.

I most truly wish you your health and am always very sincerely
yours,

G. MONTAGU

The hamper will be in town on Saturday.

To MONTAGU, Saturday 19 April 1760

HW's memoranda for this letter are Add. MS 23218, f. 14, at the top of which
J. W. Croker has written, 'These are the memoranda from which Walpole wrote
his shocking letter to George Montague 19 April 1760. J.W.C.' ('shocking' should
perhaps be read 'striking'; the MS is not clear).

> Lord H. acts ill. would not learn of Garrick
> Duke of York would not take his seat.
> He and three brothers there. Lady Aug.
> Lady Coventry
> Glory in it. Indignation at it.*
> Lord Lincoln's gallery
> Tried by his Peers
> to prove by sense out of his senses.
> Johnson's Dr.*
> his 2 brothers. Ragged and Dangerous.
> Lord Jersey and Lord Foley. Lord Huntingdon. Lord Orford.
> 117 Peers. Duke of Richmond. Marlborough.
> old Robes Lord Temple
> Duke of Bolton Duel

All but the notes marked with an asterisk have been crossed through and are
used in this letter. The two remaining were not used; 'Johnson's Dr.' no doubt
means the daughter of Johnson whom Lord Ferrers murdered; she testified at the
trial. Beside these notes are faint pencilled memoranda by HW for six lines of
verse (heroic couplets). The first line ends with 'reign'; the second contains 'to
the world'; the third, 'to form the flow'ring'; the fourth, 'to furl.'

Arlington Street, April 19th, 1760.

WELL! this big week is over! Lord George's sentence, after all
the annunciations of how terrible it was, is ended in proclaim-
ing him unfit for the King's service—very moderate in comparison of

1. Mary Anne (1740–69), 'a fortune of
£50,000' (GEC), dau. of Sir Thomas Drury,
Bt (d. 1759), of Overstone, Northants. Her
match with Lord Halifax was broken off

after a few months (post 16 Sept. 1760),
and on 14 July 1761 she married John Hobart, 2d Earl of Buckinghamshire.

2. Mary Anne Faulkner, niece of George

what was intended and desired, and truly not very severe considering what was proved. The other trial, Lord Ferrers's, lasted three days. You have seen the pomp and awfulness of such doings, so I will not describe it to you. The judge and criminal were far inferior to those you have seen.[1] For the Lord High Steward,[2] he neither had any dignity, nor affected any—nay, he held it all so cheap, that he said at his own table t'other day, 'I will not send for Garrick and learn to act a part.' At first I thought Lord Ferrers shocked—but in general he behaved rationally and coolly; though it was a strange contradiction to see a man trying by his own sense to prove himself out of his senses. It was more shocking to see his two brothers brought to prove the lunacy in their own blood,[3] in order to save their brother's life. Both are almost as ill-looking men as the Earl; one of them is a clergyman,[4] suspended by the Bishop of London[4a] for being a Methodist; the other a wild vagabond,[5] whom they call in the country *Ragged and Dangerous*. After Lord Ferrers was condemned, he made an excuse for pleading madness, to which, he said, he was forced by his family. He is respited[6] till Monday fortnight, and will then be hanged, I believe, in the Tower—and to the mortification of the peerage, is to be anatomized,[7] conformably to the late act for murder. Many peers were absent; Lord Foley[8] and Lord Jersey attended only the first day; and Lord Huntingdon[9] and my nephew Orford (in compliment to his mother[10]) as related to the prisoner, withdrew without voting. But

Faulkner the Dublin printer, sang in London theatres, was married and deserted by one Donaldson, and was thereafter for many years Lord Halifax's mistress (see DNB, *sub* Dunk, George, Earl of Halifax; BM *Satiric Prints* iv. 586).

1. The trial of the rebel Lords (n. 14 below).

2. Sir Robert Henley, Lord Keeper, created Baron Henley especially to fill this post at the trial.

3. 'The Washingtons were certainly a very frantic race' (HW to Mann 7 May 1760; Lord Ferrers's grandmother was a Washington).

4. Rev. Hon. Walter Shirley (1725–86) (DNB). This sentence is curiously paralleled in Gray to Wharton, 22 April 1760 (*Gray's Corr.* ii. 669). HW perhaps repeated it in a missing letter to Gray.

4a. Thomas Sherlock (1678–1761), Bp of

Bangor 1728–34; of Salisbury 1734–48; of London 1748–61. There seems to be no foundation for HW's statement that he suspended Shirley.

5. Robert Shirley (1723–87), 6th E. Ferrers, 1778 (identification by Mrs Piozzi).

6. By the Act of 25 Geo. II c. 37 (1752), 'An Act for better preventing the horrid Crime of Murder,' murderers were to be hanged the next day but one after their conviction; see Alfred Marks, *Tyburn Tree* [1908] pp. 247–8, 250.

7. By the same Act (above n. 6) the bodies of all murderers were to be given to the Surgeons' Company for dissection (ibid. 246–9, 250).

8. Thomas Foley (ca 1703–66), 2d Bn Foley of Kidderminster.

9. His mother, Lady Selina Shirley, was Lord Ferrers's first cousin.

10. Her second husband, Hon. Sewallis Shirley, was Lord Ferrers's uncle.

never was a criminal more literally tried by his *peers,* for the three persons who interested themselves most in the examination, were at least as mad as he, Lord Ravensworth,[11] Lord Talbot and Lord Fortescue[12]—indeed the first was almost frantic. The seats of the peeresses were not near full; and most of the beauties absent; the Duchess of Hamilton and my niece Waldegrave, you know, lie in—but to the amazement of everybody, Lady Coventry was there[13]—and what surprised me much more, looked as well as ever. I sat next but one to her, and should not have asked if she had been ill—yet they are positive she has few weeks to live. She and Lord Bolinbroke seemed to have very different thoughts, and were acting over all the old comedy of eyes. I sat in Lord Lincoln's gallery; *you* and *I* know the convenience of it;[14] I thought it no great favour to ask, and he very obligingly sent me a ticket immediately, and ordered me to be placed in one of the best boxes. Lady Augusta[15] was in the same gallery; the Duke of York and his young brothers[16] were in the Prince of Wales's box, who was not there, no more than the Princess, Princess Emily, or the Duke. It was an agreeable humanity in my friend the Duke of York; he would not take his seat in the House, before the trial, that he might not vote in it. There are so many young peers, that the show was fine even in that respect; the Duke of Richmond was the finest figure.[17] The Duke of Marlborough[18] with the best countenance in the world, looked clumsy in his robes. He had new ones, having

11. Sir Henry Liddell (1708–84), 4th Bt; cr. (1747) Bn Ravensworth.

12. Matthew Fortescue (1719–85), 2d Bn Fortescue of Castle Hill.

13. 'Yes, pretty creature, I saw her—and Princess Augusta afterwards Duchess of Brunswick supporting her—she did not sit among the Peeresses, she was too ill' (Mrs Piozzi).

14. This gallery was apparently a perquisite of the Auditor of the Exchequer, a position in which the Earl of Lincoln had been preceded by HW's brother the Earl of Orford. HW occupied it during the trial of the rebel Lords in 1746 (HW to Mann 1 Aug. 1746); and apparently Montagu, who attended the first two days of the 1746 trials (*ante* 2 Aug. 1746), sat in it too. In *A Perspective View of Westminster Hall* published by Carington Bowles, 1747, it is shown as a balcony running along the entire east side of the hall.

15. Princess Augusta (1737–1813), dau. of Frederick Prince of Wales, m. (1764) Karl Wilhelm Ferdinand, Prince (later Duke) of Brunswick-Wolfenbüttel (Burke, *Peerage*).

16. Prince Edward was cr. D. of York 1 April 1760. His brothers were Prince William Henry (1743–1805), cr. (1764) D. of Gloucester; Prince Henry Frederick (1745–90), cr. (1766) D. of Cumberland; Prince Frederick William (*ante* 13 May 1750, n. 5). The Prince of Wales had already taken his seat in the House; see his invitation to the trial in *Correspondence of King George the Third,* ed. Sir John Fortescue, 1927–8, i. 1–2.

17. 'No no; the Duke of Ancaster' (Mrs Piozzi).

18. George Spencer (1739–1817), 4th D. of Marlborough, 1758.

given away his father's to the valet de chambre. There were others not at all so indifferent about the antiquity of theirs: Lord Huntingdon's, Lord Abergavenny's,[19] and Lord Castlehaven's[20] scarce hung on their backs; the two former, they pretend, were used at the trial of the Queen of Scots. But all these honours were a little defaced by seeing Lord Temple, as Lord Privy Seal, walk at the head of the Peerage. Who, at the last trials,[21] would have believed a prophecy, that the first three men at the next, should be, Henley the lawyer, Bishop Secker, and Dick Grenville?

The day before the trial the Duke of Bolton[22] fought a duel at Marybone with Stuart[23] who lately stood for Hampshire—the latter was wounded in the arm and the former fell down.[24]

Adieu!

Yours ever

H. W.

From Montagu, ca Friday 25 April 1760

G.D. 15/8, No. 738.

In reply to *ante* 19 April 1760.

Greatworth [ca April 25, 1760].

I AM much obliged to you for your particular account of the trial and am very glad to hear Lord George came off so well.

I had a letter from Mr Bentley to thank me for my liquors and to present Mrs Bentley's compliments to me who has not the honour to be known to me, as also his second daughter's[1] duty who has the

19. George Nevill (1727–85), 17th Bn Abergavenny; cr. (1784) E. of Abergavenny.

20. James Tuchet (1723–69), 7th E. of Castlehaven, 7th Bn Audley.

21. In 1746 and 1747.

22. Charles Powlett (ca 1718–65), 5th D. of Bolton, 1759.

23. Simeon Stuart (d. 1779), 3d Bt, of Hartley Maudit, Hants, 1761.

24. 'What the quarrel was, I do not know: but they met near Marybone, and the D: in making a pass overreached himself, fell down, and hurt his knee. The other bid him get up, but he could not.

Then he bid him ask his life, but he would not. So he let him alone, and that's all. Mr Steuart was slightly wounded' (Gray to Wharton, 22 April 1760, *Gray's Corr.* ii. 667). The duel may have been an outgrowth of the Hampshire by-election 3 Dec. 1759, required by the Duke of Bolton's elevation to the House of Lords; in it Stuart, backed by Bute, was defeated by Henry Legge (later Bilson-Legge), who split with Bute over the matter (DNB *sub* Legge; *Mem. Geo. II* iii. 237). Stuart was M.P. for Hampshire 1761–79.

———

1. Not further identified.

honour to be my god-daughter—an honour truly I was totally ignorant of, and I say God bless her and make her as good as her
mother. Do you know anything of this, for I am at a loss about it?

The frame-maker[2] has sent the frame but forgot the coronet which
I have ordered him to send down and then to wait on you with his
bill which I beg you will please to pay for me till I see you again.

I truly wish you your health.

I am yours ever,

G. MONTAGU

From MONTAGU, Monday 5 May 1760

G.D. 15/8, No. 740.

Year determined by references to Müntz's book and HW's Oxford visit.
Address: To the Honourable Mr Walpole, Arlington Street, London. Free
M.P.

[Greatworth] May 5 [1760].

DO me the favour, my good sir, as to let your man put the enclosed[1] into the penny post; it is to my landlord[2] about my
workmen here. I believe you will be pleased when you see my alterations; not that the curtain will draw up till July. Perhaps that may
be the time that you visit Lord Beauchamp at Oxford.[3] I hope you
are well and have had as much of this fine rain as we.

I have got Myntz's book.[4] My compliments I pray to Mr Chute
and Mr Bentley. I most heartily wish you your health and all possible
happiness and am always your most faithful

G. MONTAGU

2. See *ante* 27 March 1760, n. 2.

———

1. As usual, Montagu wished to save
postage from Greatworth to London; letters were carried anywhere within a ra-
dius of 10 miles from the General Post Office in Lombard St for a penny; see Herbert Joyce, *History of the Post Office,* 1893,
pp. 36–41; John G. Hendy, *History of the
Early Postmarks,* 1905, p. 55.

2. See *ante* 22 May 1753, n. 1.

3. It was; see *post* 19 July 1760.

4. *Encaustic: or Count Caylus's Method
of Painting in the Manner of the Ancients.*
By J. H. Müntz. London: Printed for the
Author; and A. Webley . . . 1760. Montagu's copy is now WSL.

George Montagu Esqr

MONTAGU'S BOOK-PLATE AND
SIGNATURE IN HIS COPY OF
MÜNTZ'S *ENCAUSTIC*

To Montagu, Tuesday 6 May 1760

Arlington Street, May 6, 1760.

THE extraordinary history of Lord Ferrers is closed: he was executed yesterday. Madness, that in other countries is a disorder, is
here a systematic character. It does not hinder people from forming
a plan of conduct, and from even dying agreeably to it. You remember how the last Ratcliffe[1] died with the utmost propriety. So did this
horrid lunatic—coolly and sensibly. His own and his wife's[2] relations
had asserted that he would tremble at last. No such thing; he shamed
heroes. He bore the solemnity of a pompous and tedious procession
of above two hours from the Tower to Tyburn with as much tranquillity as if he was only going to his own burial not to his own execution. He even talked on indifferent subjects in the passage; and if
the sheriff[3] and the chaplain[4] had not thought they had parts to act
too, and had not consequently engaged him in more particular conversation, he did not seem to think it necessary to talk on the occasion. He went in his wedding-clothes, marking the only remaining
impression on his mind. The ceremony he was in a hurry to have
over. He was stopped at the gallows by the vast crowd, but got out of
his coach as soon as he could, and was but seven minutes on the scaf-
fold, which was hung with black, and prepared by the undertaker of
his family at their expense. There was a new contrivance for sinking
the stage under him,[5] which did not play well, and he suffered a little
by the delay, but was dead in four minutes. The mob was decent, admired him, and almost pitied him—so they would Lord George, whose
execution they are so angry at missing. I suppose every highwayman
will now preserve the blue handkerchief they have about their necks
when they are married, that they may die like a lord. With all the frenzy
in his blood, he was not mad enough to be struck with his aunt Hunt-

1. Titular Earl of Derwentwater; see
ante 16 Aug. 1746, n. 4.
2. Mary (ca 1738–1807), sister of Sir William Meredith, 3d Bt; m. (1) (1752) Laurence Shirley, 4th E. Ferrers; m. (2) (1769)
Lord Frederick Campbell; see Wraxall,
Memoirs iv. 77–8.
3. Paul Vaillant (ca 1715–1802), 'an opu-
lent and respectable bookseller in the
Strand' (John Nichols, Literary Anecdotes,
1812–15, iii. 309–10; HW to Mann 7 May

1760). He wrote an Account of Earl Fer-
rer's Behaviour (n. 8 below).
4. 'Rev. Mr Humphries the chaplain of
the Tower' (An Account of the Execution
of the late Laurence Earl Ferrers . . .,
1760, p. 5); he d. 1770 (GM 1770, xl. 47,
where his name is spelled Humphreys).
5. This is supposed to have been the
first use of the modern drop; see Alfred
Marks, Tyburn Tree [1908] pp. 251–3.

ingdon's sermons[6]—the Methodists have nothing to brag of in his conversion, though Whitfield prayed for him and preached about him —even Tyburn has been above their reach. I have not heard that Lady Fanny[7] dabbled with his soul—but I believe she is prudent enough to confine her missionary zeal to subjects where the body may be her perquisite.[8]

When am I likely to see you? The delightful rain is come; we look and smell charmingly. Adieu!

Yours ever

H. W.

To MONTAGU, Friday 4 July 1760

Strawberry Hill, July 4th, late, 1760.

I AM this minute returned from Chaffont, where I have been these two days. Mr Conway, Lady Ailesbury, Lady Lyttelton, and Mrs

6. Countess of Huntingdon, the patroness of Whitefield.

7. Lady Frances Shirley (ca 1706–78), dau. of 1st E. Ferrers, and Lady Huntingdon's aunt; a reigning beauty in the 'thirties. She is the subject of the well-known verses 'When Fanny blooming fair' which are attributed (probably incorrectly) to Chesterfield. In 1749 she was converted to Methodism; she was a Twickenham neighbour of HW's, who probably underrates her religious sincerity; see [Aaron C. H. Seymour] *Life and Times of Selina, Countess of Huntingdon*, 1844, i. *passim;* Roger Coxon, *Chesterfield and his Critics*, 1925, pp. 167–73; HW to Mason 16 July 1778.

8. The bibliography of Lord Ferrers's trial and execution is extensive. The late Horace Bleackley has made one on the fly-leaves of his copy of *The Trial of Lawrence Earl Ferrers*, Dublin, 1760 (now WSL). Only those references from it are given here which do not appear in DNB under Laurence Shirley, 4th Earl Ferrers, and which seem to be of some value.
The Trial of Lawrence, Earl Ferrers, for the Murder of John Johnson . . ., Dublin, 1760; *An Account of the Execution of the Late Lawrence Earl Ferrers* . . ., Dublin, 1760; J. Coote, *Memoirs of Lord Ferrers,* 1760; *Earl Ferrers's Trial*, By Authority, 1760; *The Sheriff's Account of Earl Ferrers's Behaviour*, 1760; N&Q 1909, 10th ser. xi. 209, 335, 434, 498; Thomas B. Howell, *A Complete History of State Trials*, 1816–26, xix. 885–980; John W. Croker, *Correspondence and Diaries*, 1884, iii. 15–16; *Annual Register* for 1760, iii [pt ii]. 38–47; GM 1760, xxx. 44, 100, 151, 198, 199, 200, 230, 246, 247, 251; Andrew Knapp and William Baldwin, *The Newgate Calendar*, 1824–8, ii. 275–83; George T. Wilkinson, *The Newgate Calendar Improved* [1825?] ii. 398–411; [George H. Borrow], *Celebrated Trials* . . ., 1825, iv. 253–61; Camden Pelham, *The New Newgate Calendar,* Philadelphia, 185?, pp. 162–6; Alfred Marks, *Tyburn Tree* [1908], pp. 249–51; Félix-Sébastien Feuillet de Conches, *Causeries d'un Curieux,* 1862–8, ii. 333–40; [George Walter Thornbury], *Old and New London,* [1873–8], v. 191–3; James Caulfield, *Portraits . . . of Remarkable Persons,* 1819–20, iii. 233–46; *Series of Letters between Mrs Elizabeth Carter and Catherine Talbot,* 1809, ii. 317, 321, 326; Elizabeth Carter, *Letters . . . to Mrs Montagu,* 1817, i. 87–8; *Bygone Leicestershire,* ed. William Andrews, 1892, pp. 176–92; Collins, *Peerage,* 1812, iv. 102–3; Emily J. Climenson, *Eliza-*

Shirley[1] are there; and Lady Mary is going to add to the number again.[2] The house and grounds are still in the same dislocated condition; in short, they finish nothing but children; even Mr Bentley's Gothic stable,[3] which I call Houynhm-Castle, is not rough cast yet.

We went to see More-park,[4] but I was not much struck with it, after all the miracles I had heard that Brown had performed there. He has undulated the horizon in so many artificial molehills, that it is full as unnatural as if it was drawn with a rule and compasses. Nothing is done to the house; there are not even chairs in the great apartment. My Lord Anson is more slatternly than the Churchills, and does not even finish children.

I am going to write to Lord Beauchamp that I shall be at Oxford on the 15th where I depend upon meeting you. I design to see Blenheim, and Rousham (is not that the name of Dormer's?[4a]) and Althrop and Drayton before I return—but don't be frightened, I don't propose to drag you to all or any of these if you don't like it.

Mr Bentley has sketched a very pretty Gothic room for Lord Holderness,[5] and orders are gone to execute it directly in Yorkshire.[6] The first draught was Mason's,[7] but as he does not pretend to much skill, we were desired to correct it—I say *we*, for I chose the ornaments. Adieu!

> Yours ever
>
> HOR. WALPOLE

PS. My Lady Ailesbury has been much diverted, and so will you be too: Gray is in their neighbourhood[8]—my Lady Carlisle says *he is*

beth Montagu the Queen of the Blue-stockings, 1906, ii. 183; *Letters of Mrs. Elizabeth Montagu*, 1809–13, iv. 261–2; William Hickey, *Memoirs*, ed. Alfred Spencer, 1913–25, i. 20; Delaney, *Correspondence* iii. 588–9, 591; John Nichols, *Literary Anecdotes*, 1812–15, iii. 310; Casanova, *Memoirs*, tr. Arthur Machen, 1922, ix. 169; *Public Advertiser* 18, 19, 30 April, 3, 5, 6, 16 May 1760; Joseph Cradock, *Literary . . . Memoirs*, 1826–8, i. 8–9; *Royal Magazine* May 1760, ii. 225–32.

1. Not identified.
2. Possibly her child was Sophia Churchill (d. 1797), m. (1781) Hon. Horatio Walpole, 2d E. of Orford (n.c.), 1809.
3. Plans or drawings have not been found.

4. Moor Park, Rickmansworth, Herts, was built in the second quarter of the century from designs by Leoni; Lord Anson bought it in 1754; see description and illustrations in *Vict. Co. Hist. Herts*, ii. 377–8; *Country Seats* 24.
4a. Rousham had been Gen. James Dormer's (*post* 5 July 1763).
5. This has not been found.
6. Probably at Aston, his chief seat.
7. William Mason was Lord Holdernesse's chaplain.
8. Gray was probably visiting Mrs Henry Jennings, who lived at Grovelands, Shiplake, Oxon. He noted a visit to Park Place in his diary 7 July, but did not record the excursion mentioned here. Gray wrote Clerke 12 Aug. 1760 that he disliked his visit to Shiplake: 'For me, I am come to

extremely like me in his manner. They went a party to dine on a cold loaf,[9] and passed the day; Lady A. protests he never opened his lips but once, and then only said, 'Yes, my Lady, I believe so.'

From Montagu, Tuesday 8 July 1760

G.D. 15/8, No. 742.

In reply to *ante* 4 July 1760.

Greatworth, Tuesday 8th [July 1760].

DON'T let your vivacity now run away with my excuse in the egg, for I must tell you I had a letter from my sister last post to say she should be with me about the middle of July. I take your fifteenth for Oxford to be that very time. One of her horses is, however, not very well, and I am to hear again from her to know the exact day; if she does not come till the seventeenth or eighteenth I will most surely give you the meeting at Oxford, a place I long to see with you, and so I do Althrop. Drayton I know nothing of, nor where it is nor who it belongs to. I long to see your bold Beauchamp and much I long to see you. Now I must tell you if you do not care to come here while my sister and Mr Wetenhall are here say so and come here at your return from the north, or any other time you shall find it convenient, for I shall return from Cheshire and seeing the General the end of August.

I delight in Lady Carlile's judgment that finds a perfect resemblance between Gray's sage taciturnity and your bold intrepid impetuosity; 'tis very like a whale or a camel.[1]

I hope you are as well as I have been ever since my Sussex tour; may you always be well and happy is much the wish of your very sincere and affectionate

G. Montagu

my resting-place, and find it very necessary after living for a month in a house with three women that laughed from morning to night, and would allow nothing to the sulkiness of my disposition. Company and cards at home, parties by land and water abroad, and (what they call) *doing something*, that is, racketting about from morning to night, are occupations, I find, that wear out my spirits' (*Gray's Corr.* ii. 647, 692–3).

9. According to Emily J. Climenson, in *Elizabeth Montagu the Queen of the Bluestockings,* 1906, ii. 12, this was 'the usual expression for a picnic'; it does not seem to have been noticed by oed. 'Picnic' came into use in England in the early 19th century.

1. *Hamlet* III. ii.

To Montagu, Thursday 10 July 1760

Address: To George Montagu Esq. at Greatworth near Brackley, Northamptonshire. Free Hor. Walpole. *Postmark:* 10 IY.

Strawberry Hill, July 10th, 1760.

I SHALL be very sorry if I don't see you at Oxford on Tuesday next; but what can I say? If your Wetenhalls will break into my almanac and take my very day, can I help it? I must own I shall be glad if their coach-horse is laid up with the fashionable sore-throat and fever: can you recommend no coachman to them like Dr Wilmot,[1] who will dispatch it in three days? If I don't see you at Oxford, I don't think I shall at Greatworth till my return from the north which will be about the 20th or 22d of August. Drayton,[2] be it known, to you, is Lady Betty Germayn's, is in your own county, was the old mansion of the Mordaunts, and is crammed with whatever Sir John[3] could purloin from them and the Norfolks. Adieu!

Yours ever

H. W.

From Montagu, Friday 11 July 1760

G.D. 15/8, No. 741.

Dated by reference to HW's Oxford expedition.
Address: To the Honourable Mr Walpole at Lord Beauchamp's at Christ Church, Oxon.

Greatworth, Friday [July 11, 1760].

I HAVE this day had a letter from my sister to say she will be with me on Tuesday next, the very day I believe you will be at Christ Church. This I am much grieved at as I had promised great pleasure

1. Sir Edward Wilmot (1693–1786), Bt, 1759; physician to George II.
2. Lowick, Northants; illustrated and described in *Vict. Co. Hist. Northants* iii. 231–6; H. Avray Tipping, *English Homes*, Period IV, vol. i (1920). 249–76; HW visited it *post* 23 July 1763; see *Country Seats* 55–8.

3. Sir John Germain (ca 1650–1718), Bt, 1698; Dutch soldier and favourite of William III (DNB); m. (1) (1701) Lady Mary Mordaunt, dau. and heiress of 2d E. of Peterborough and divorced wife of 7th D. of Norfolk; m. (2) (1706) Lady Elizabeth Berkeley, and left her Drayton, which he had inherited from his first wife.

in seeing Oxford with you as also your cousin Lord Beauchamp to whom I beg you will present my compliments and say that if he will come with you to Greatworth I shall think it an honour and am sure it will be a great pleasure to me. You know how happy I shall always be to see you, which I shall not expatiate upon, only assure you I am,

Most truly yours,

G. MONTAGU

To MONTAGU, ca Tuesday 15 July 1760

[?Oxford, ca July 15, 1760].

From the statement in the next letter that 'Mr Conway, as I told you, was with me at Oxford' it appears that there is a missing letter here, since HW had not seen Montagu.

To MONTAGU, Saturday 19 July 1760

Address: To George Montagu Esq. at Greatworth near Brackley, Northamptonshire. Free Hor. Walpole. *Postmark:* 19 IY.

Strawberry Hill, Saturday, July 19, 1760.

MR CONWAY, as I told you, was with me at Oxford, and I returned with him to Park-place, and today hither. I am sorry you could not come to us, we passed four days most agreeably, and I believe saw more antique holes and corners than Tom Hearne[1] did in threescore years. You know my rage for Oxford; if King's College would not take it ill, I don't know but I should retire thither, and profess Jacobitism that I might enjoy some venerable set of chambers. Though the weather has been so sultry, I ferreted from morning to night, fatigued that strong young lad Lord Beauchamp,[2] and harassed his tutors, till they were forced to relieve one another. With all this, I found nothing worth seeing, except the colleges themselves,

1. Thomas Hearne (1678–1735), the antiquary, who lived in St Edmund Hall.
2. The Countess of Northumberland wrote in her diary '11 July, 1760. Lord Beauchamp not liked at Oxford, very proud and too fond of the superiority of his abilities in a literary way' (Elizabeth, Duchess of Northumberland, *Diaries of a Duchess*, ed. James Greig, 1926, p. 19).

painted glass, and a couple of croziers.[3] Oh! yes in an old buttery at
Christ Church I discovered two of the most glorious portraits by Holbein[4] in the world. They call them, Dutch Heads. I took them down,
washed them myself, and fetched out a thousand beauties. We went
to Blenheim[5] and saw all Vanbrugh's[6] quarries,[7] all the Acts of Parliament and gazettes on the Duke in inscriptions, and all the old flock
chairs,[8] wainscot tables, and gowns and petticoats of Queen Anne,
that old Sarah could crowd amongst blocks of marble. It looks like
the palace of an auctioneer who has been chosen King of Poland, and
furnished his apartments with obsolete trophies, rubbish that nobody bid for, and a dozen pictures that he had stolen from the in-
ventories of different families.[9] The place is as ugly as the house, and
the bridge like the beggars at the old Duchess's gate, begs for a drop
of water and is refused.[10]

We went to Ditchley,[11] which is a good house, well furnished, has
good portraits, a wretched salon, and one handsome scene behind the
house. There are portraits of the Litchfield-Hunt, in *true-blue*
frocks,[12] with ermine capes. One of the colleges has exerted this loyal

3. At St John's, 'a crozier of black and
silver, given by Laud'; and at New College, 'William of Wickham's fine crozier
of gold and enamel'; see *Country Seats*
24–5, for HW's account of this visit.

4. HW's ascription is questioned in
Tancred Borenius, *Pictures by the Old
Masters in the Library of Christ Church
Oxford*, 1916, pp. 104–5; see *Country Seats*
25.

5. See *Country Seats* 25–6 for HW's
notes on his excursion to Rousham, Ditchley, and Blenheim, 17 July 1760. HW had
with him on this tour *The New Oxford
Guide . . . To Which is added A Tour to
Blenheim, Ditchley, and Stow*, Oxford,
1759. His copy (sold SH vi. 71) is now WSL.
HW annotated the section on the three
houses, and made notes on the Colleges on
the fly-leaf, e.g.: 'Baliol—fine windows,'
'Merton-Library—Wm Reade,' 'New College—Crozier library—chapel,' 'Jesus—Dr
H. Price, Holbein,' etc.

6. Sir John Vanbrugh (1664–1726), Kt;
architect, playwright, herald.

7. The palace he had erected there.

8. Doubtless they were chairs stuffed
with flocks—tufts of cotton, wool, etc.

9. HW's comment on the pictures at
Blenheim in *The New Oxford Guide* are
uniformly favourable; of the rest he notes:
'Doors and chimnies horrid. Wretched
furniture.'

10. 'About the middle of the grand approach is a magnificent bridge, chiefly consisting of one arch, in the style of the Ri-
alto at Venice; the water above the bridge
is formed into a spacious lake' (*New Oxford Guide*, Oxford [1759], p. 90). But under the bridge there was only a 'little
stream' with which it was 'dreadfully out
of proportion' (Count Frederick Kielmansegge, *Diary of a Journey to England*, . . .
1761–1762, 1902, p. 95), until 'Capability'
Brown widened the stream by a dam; see
post 18 June 1770; Boswell, *Johnson* iii.
451.

11. Four miles NW of Woodstock; seat
of the Earls of Lichfield; designed by
James Gibbs; see *Beauties of England* xii
pt ii. 447–53; *Country Seats* 26; *Passages
from the Diaries of Mrs Philip Lybbe
Powys*, ed. Emily J. Climenson, 1899, pp.
198–9.

12. The Earl of Lichfield was a Jacobite
(DNB).

pun, and made their east window entirely of blue glass.[13] But the greatest pleasure we had was in seeing Sir Charles Cotterel's at Rousham;[14] it has reinstated Kent with me; he has nowhere shown so much taste.[15] The house is old and was bad. He has improved it, stuck as close as *he* could to Gothic, has made a delightful library[16] and the whole is comfortable—the garden is Daphne[17] in little; the sweetest little groves, streams, glades, porticos, cascades and river, imaginable; all the scenes are perfectly classic—well, if I had such a house, such a library, so pretty a place, and so pretty a wife[18]—I think I should let King George send to Herenhausen for a Master of the Ceremonies.[19]

Make many compliments to all your family for me; Lord Beauchamp was much obliged by your invitation. *I* shall certainly accept it as I return from the north; in the meantime find how Drayton and Althrop lie according to your scale. Adieu!

Yours most sincerely

Hor. Walpole

From Montagu, Sunday 20 July 1760

G.D. 15/8, No. 743.

[Greatworth] July 20, 1760.

I CAN only tell with great regret that I am to be at my sister's in Cheshire at the time you are graciously minded to come here.

You know how glad I am always to see you and I am sure you would be really charmed with my new apartment; 'tis blue and all

---

13. Not located.

14. Five miles NE of Woodstock, seat of Sir Charles Cottrell-Dormer (d. 1779), Kt. The house was built ca 1635, 'a small old indifferent house, built by a Dormer' (*Country Seats* 25). See F. E. Cottrell Dormer, *Account of Rousham, Oxfordshire*, Oxford, 1865, pp. 16–32.

15. 'The most engaging of all Kent's works' (*Modern Gardening, Works* ii. 538).

16. 'A half kind of Gothic; odd ceiling, does not seem to belong to the room; chimney with Ionic pillars' (ibid. 25); see *post* 5 July 1763, n. 5.

17. Apollo's grove near Antioch. 'The

whole is as elegant and antique as if the Emperor Julian had selected the most pleasing solitude about Daphne to enjoy a philosophic retirement' (*Modern Gardening, Works* ii. 538).

18. Jane (d. 1802), dau. of Charles Adelmare Caesar; m. (1) Sir Charles Cottrell-Dormer; m. (2) (1782) Lt-Gen. Hon. George Lane Parker (John Burke, *History of the Commoners*, 1833–8, iv. 747; Collins, *Peerage*, 1812, iv. 194–5; *Annual Register* for 1802, xliv. 512).

19. A place hereditary in the Cottrell-Dormer family, which inspired HW's joke on Clement Quoteherald in *Works* i. 141.

blue; all my best matters are got together and make a pretty decoration I will assure. Lady Ann Jekyll has been with me for a few days; the Rices come tomorrow for a few days too, and the Guilfords and the young lovers[1] dine here tomorrow. You know perhaps Miss Legge the elder[2] is going to be married to Mr Brudenel Lord Cardigan's brother, about the Prince of Wales.[3]

If you would bring Mr Chute here in the middle or the end of September or any time after that I shall be happy to see [you].[4]

If you have a moment to spare let me have an account of your seeings.

My sister and brethren desire their respects to you.

I am always most sincerely yours,

G. Montagu

To Montagu, Tuesday 12 August 1760

Strawberry Hill, Aug. 12th, 1760.

IN what part of the island you are just now, I don't know; flying about somewhere or other I suppose—well! It is charming to be so young! Here am I lying upon a couch, wrapped up in flannels, with the gout in both feet—oh yes! gout in all the forms. Six years ago I had it, and nobody would believe me—now they may have proof—my legs are as big as your cousin Guilford's—and they don't use to be quite so large. I was seized yesterday se'nnight; have had little pain in the day, but most uncomfortable nights—however I move about again a little with a stick. If either my father or mother had had it, I should not dislike it so much; I am herald enough to approve it if descended genealogically—but it is an absolute upstart in me; and what is more provoking, I had trusted to my great abstinence for keeping me from it—but thus it is; if I had had any gentleman-like virtue, as patriotism or loyalty, I might have got something by them; I had nothing but that beggarly virtue, temperance, and she had not interest enough to keep one from a fit of the gout. Another plague

1. Probably Hon. Elizabeth Louisa St John (ca 1744–1820), an orphan, and a niece of Lady Guilford's; m. (20 Aug. 1760) Sir William Bagot (1728–98), 6th Bt; cr. (1780) Bn Bagot; see post 23 Aug. 1760.
2. Anne Legge (d. 1786), m. (24 Nov.

1760) Hon. James Brudenell, cr. (1780) Bn Brudenell; 5th E. of Cardigan, 1790.
3. He was the Prince's Master of the Robes.
4. Montagu wrote 'me.'

is, that everybody that ever knew anybody that had it, are so good as to come with advice, and direct me how to manage it—that is, how to continue to have it for a great many years. I am very refractory—I say to the gout, as great personages do to the executioner, 'Friend, do your work as quick as you can.' They tell me of wine to keep it out of my stomach—but I will starve temperance itself—I will be virtuous indeed; that is, I will stick to virtue, though I find it is not its own reward.

This confinement has kept me from Yorkshire; I hope however to be at Ragley by the twentieth from whence I shall still go to Lord Strafford's, and by this delay you may possibly be at Greatworth by my return, which will be about the beginning of September. Write me a line as soon as you receive this; direct it to Arlington Street; it will be sent after me. Adieu!

Yours ever

H. W.

PS. My tower[1] erects its battlements bravely; my *Anecdotes of Painting*[2] thrive exceedingly, thanks to the gout that has pinned me to my chair; think of Ariel the Sprite in a slit shoe!

From Montagu, Saturday 23 August 1760

G.D. 15/8, No. 744.

In reply to *ante* 12 Aug. 1760.

Memoranda by HW: Nott to North 57
North to London 66
Talman designed Chatsworth

These are apparently jottings HW made in preparation for his journey (*post* 1 Sept. 1760). The figures represent miles: Nottingham to Northampton, Northampton to London. *Country Seats* 28 notes that Chatsworth 'was designed by Talman' (William Talman, fl. 1670–1700).

Hankelow, Saturday, August 23 [1760].

OH sad! Oh sad! All I can say upon this occasion is that I most heartily wish this horrid gout of yours may carry off all manner of ills for the rest of your days, and to tell you that you are not par-

1. The Round Tower; it was not entirely finished until 1771 (*SH Accounts* 106–7).

2. He finished the first volume, which he had begun 1 Jan., 14 Aug. 1760 ('Short Notes').

ticular in your complaint. Mr Wetenhall flew from Greatworth at an hour's warning to nurse it here. Lord Guilford I left laid up with it, St Anthony's,[1] a fever, and Mrs Bagot raving for the delay[2] these disorders occasioned; and I am with all my indulgence and port every hour with threatening pains in my feet that will manifest themselves in all their real terrors. I am sure when you are able to journey you will find it do you good. I shall not be able to leave this place yet as Charles is not yet come, though we expect him every day; and then you are sensible I must stay to see him some time. Therefore I am afraid I shall not be able to have the pleasure of seeing you when you return from Ragley, which would not be much out of the way, but flatter myself you may be at leisure the end of September, and a little riding about may be salutary, and I will amble by your side.

God bless you and believe me I pray you your most affectionate and ever obliged

G. MONTAGU

To MONTAGU, Monday 1 September 1760

Arlington Street, Sept. 1, 1760.

I WAS disappointed at your not being at home as I returned from my expedition; and now I fear it must be another year before I see Greatworth, as I have two or three more engagements on my books for the residue of this season. I go next week to Lord Waldegrave, and afterwards to George Selwyn, and shall return by Bath, which I have never yet seen. Will not you and the General come to Strawberry in October?

Thank you for your lamentations on my gout; it was in proportion to my size, very slender—my feet are again as small as ever they were; when I had what I called *big shoes,* I could have danced a minuet on a silver penny.

My tour[1] has been extremely agreeable. I set out with winning a good deal at loo at Ragley; the Duke of Grafton[2] was not so success-

1. Presumably St Anthony's fire, or erysipelas.
2. Presumably her wedding, which took place 20 Aug. (*ante* 20 July 1760, n. 1), was delayed by Lord Guilford's complicated ailments.

1. See *Country Seats* 26–33 for more detailed accounts of the houses HW mentions in this letter.
2. Augustus Henry Fitzroy (1735–1811), 3d D. of Grafton; First Lord of the Treasury 1766–70.

ful, and had some high words with Pam.[3] I went from thence to Offley's[4] at Whichenovre,[5] the individual manor of the flitch of bacon,[6] which has been growing *rusty* for these thirty years in his hall.[7] I don't wonder; I have no notion that one could keep in good humour with one's wife for a year and day, unless one was to live on the very spot, which is one of the sweetest scenes I ever saw. It is the brink of a high hill; the Trent wriggles through a lovely meadow at the foot; Litchfield and twenty other churches and mansions decorate the view. Mr Anson[8] has bought an estate close by, whence my Lord[9] used to cast many a wishful eye, though without the least pretensions even to a bit of lard.

I saw Litchfield cathedral, which has been rich, but my friend Lord Brook[10] and his soldiery treated poor St Chadd[11] with so little ceremony that it is in a most naked condition. In a niche at the very summit they have crowded in a statue of Charles II;[12] with a special pair of shoestrings big enough for a weathercock. As I went to Lord

3. Probably the Duchess, whose passion for gambling led, in part, to their estrangement (*post* 28 April 1761, n. 9).

4. John Offley (d. 1784), son of Crewe Offley; M.P. Bedford 1747–54; Orford 1754–68; East Retford 1768–74; Groom of the Bedchamber 1757–62; a particular friend of the Pelhams, from whom he had pensions from the secret service funds for several years (Lewis B. Namier, *Structure of Politics at the Accession of George III*, 1929, *passim*; idem, *England in the Age of the American Revolution*, 1930, p. 429; Josiah C. Wedgwood, *Staffordshire Parliamentary History*, ii. 284, in William Salt Arch. Soc., *Collections*, 1922).

5. Whichnor, Staffs; Offley sold it in 1765 to the Levett family, who still had it in 1922 (Wedgwood, loc. cit.).

6. As far back as the time of Edward III, one of the services on which the manor of Whichnor was held was that the lord of the manor should give a flitch of bacon to any man who would swear that for a year and a day he had never regretted marrying, and that he would, if free, take the same spouse again. The ceremonies and conditions are set out in great detail in the old charter in William Dugdale, *Baronage of England*, 1675–6, ii. 106–8. Apparently no record of successful claimants has been preserved. The 'Dunmow flitch,' given at Dunmow, Essex, to the *couple* who could swear uninterrupted

felicity for a year and a day, is much better known; see Robert Chambers, *The Book of Days*, Edinburgh, 1863–4, i. 748–51; Chaucer, *Wife of Bath's Tale*, 218. A Staffordshire historian, however, hints that the Essex flitch was only a gammon (Robert Plot, *Natural History of Staffordshire*, 1686, p. 444).

7. *Country Seats* 27 states that it was carved in wood and hung over the chimney in the hall.

8. Thomas Anson (ca 1695–1773), of Shugborough, Staffs; M.P. Lichfield 1747–70; see Josiah C. Wedgwood, *Staffordshire Parliamentary History*, ii. 261–2, in William Salt Arch. Soc., *Collections*, 1922, for his part in county politics.

9. Lord Anson, his brother, whose supposed marital difficulties HW frequently ridicules.

10. Robert Greville (1607–43), 2d Bn Brooke; killed while besieging Lichfield with a Parliamentary army. Although he bombarded and sacked the Cathedral, HW admired him as a patriot, and championed him against the Royalist writers (*Royal & Noble Authors, Works* i. 356–9).

11. St Ceadda (d. 672), generally known as Chad, to whom Lichfield is dedicated. For the ravages of the war on the Cathedral, see A. B. Clifton, *Cathedral Church of Lichfield*, 1898, pp. 12–20.

12. This statue was removed during 19th-century alterations (ibid. 22).

Strafford's, I passed through Sheffield, which is one of the foulest towns in England in the most charming situation. There are two and twenty thousand[13] inhabitants making knives and scissors; they remit £11,000 a week to London. One man there has discovered the art of plating copper with silver[14]—I bought a pair of candlesticks for two guineas, that are quite pretty. Lord Strafford has erected the little Gothic building which I got Mr Bentley to draw;[15] I took the idea from Chichester cross[16]—It stands on a high bank in the menagerie, between a pond and a vale, totally bowered over with oaks. I went with the Straffords[16a] to Chatsworth and stayed there four days; there was Lady Mary Coke, Lord Besborough and his daughters,[17] Lord Thomond, Mr Bonfoy,[18] the Duke, the old Duchess,[19] and two of his brothers—would you believe that nothing was ever better humoured than the ancient Grace? She stayed every evening, till it was dark, in the skittle ground,[20] keeping the score; and one night that the servants had a ball for Lady Dorothy's[21] birthday, we fetched the fiddles into the drawing-room, and the Dowager herself danced with us!

I never was more disappointed than at Chatsworth,[22] which ever

13. Arthur Young gives the population of Sheffield in 1770 as 30,000 (*Six Months Tour through the North of England*, 1770, i. 132).

14. Silver plating was invented in 1742 by Thomas Bolsover (ca 1704–88; GM 1788, lviii pt ii. 836); the first to apply it to candlesticks and similar articles was Joseph Hancock (ca 1711–91, see GM 1791, lxi pt ii. 1160). Both were unsuccessful at plating, and went into other lines ca 1760; one John Winter specialized in candlesticks, most of which, at first, were simple reproduction of Greek pillars. All three were Sheffield men; see Joseph Hunter, *Hallamshire*, edn 1869, pp. 156, 168.

15. See HW to Bentley Aug. 1756 (illustration); Arthur Young noted it in his account of Wentworth Castle (*Six Months Tour through the North of England*, 1770, i. 139–48, at 147): 'a gothic temple, over a little grot, which forms an arch, and together have a most pleasing effect; on a near view, this temple is found a light, airy, and elegant building.'

16. Illustrated in Aymer Vallance, *Old Crosses and Lychgates*, [1920] pp. 8, 136.

16a. Lady Anne Campbell (ca 1715–85), m. (1741) William Wentworth, 2d E. of Strafford.

17. Lady Catherine Ponsonby (*ante* 28 Jan. 1760, n. 5); Lady Charlotte Ponsonby (1747–1822), m. (1770) William Fitzwilliam (after 1807 Wentworth-Fitzwilliam), 4th E. Fitzwilliam; Lady Sarah Ponsonby (d. 1765) (Lodge, *Irish Peerage*, 1789, ii. 282).

18. Nicholas Bonfoy (d. 1775), of Abbott's Ripton, Hunts; Sergeant-at-Arms to the House of Commons, 1762 (*Gray's Corr.* i. 254, n. 11; *Herald and Genealogist* 1871, vi. 359).

19. Catherine Hoskins (d. 1777), m. (1718) William Cavendish, 3d D. of Devonshire.

20. Apparently played by all classes in the 18th century; see quotations in OED.

21. Lady Dorothy Cavendish (1750–94), m. (1766) William Henry Cavendish-Bentinck, 3d D. of Portland.

22. For other accounts and illustrations of Chatsworth, see *Country Seats* 28–9; *Modern Universal British Traveller* [1779], p. 108; John B. Firth, *Highways and Byways in Derbyshire*, 1905, pp. 285–311; Llewellynn F. W. Jewitt and S. C. Hall, *Stately Homes of England*, [1873] i. 322–87; H. Avray Tipping, *English Homes*, Period IV, vol. i (1920). 313–50.

since I was born, I have heard condemned[22a]—It is a glorious situation; the Vale rich in corn and verdure, vast woods hang down the hills, which are green to the top, and the immense rocks only serve to dignify the prospect. The river runs before the door, and serpentizes more than you can conceive in the next vale. The Duke is widening it, and will make it the middle of his park, but I don't approve an idea they are going to execute, of a fine bridge with statues under a noble cliff—if they will have a bridge (which by the way will crowd the scene) it should be composed of rude fragments, such as the giant of the Peak[23] would place to step upon that he might not be wetshod. The expense of the works now carrying on will amount to £40,000. A heavy quadrangle of stables is part of the plan, is very cumbrous; and standing higher than the house, is ready to overwhelm it. The principal front of the house is beautiful, and executed with the neatness of wrought plate. The inside is most sumptuous, but did not please me. The heathen gods, goddesses, Christian virtues, and allegoric gentlefolks are crowded into every room, as if Mrs Holman had been in heaven and invited everybody she saw. The great apartment is trist; painted ceilings, inlaid floors, and unpainted wainscot make every room sombre. The tapestries are fine, but not fine enough, and there are few portraits. The chapel is charming. The great *jet d'eau* I like, nor would I remove it—whatever is magnificent of the kind in the time it was done,[24] I would retain—else all gardens and houses wear a tiresome resemblance—I except that absurdity of a cascade tumbling down marble steps, which reduces the steps to be of no use at all.

I saw Haddon, an abandoned old castle of the Rutlands in a romantic situation, but which never could have composed a tolerable dwelling.[25] The Duke sent Lord John with me to Hardwicke,[26] where I was again disappointed—but I will not take relations from others—they either don't see for themselves, or can't see for me. How I had

22a. Probably HW meant to write 'commended.'

23. Of Derbyshire.

24. At the end of the 17th century.

25. Haddon Hall had not yet acquired the romantic associations of the Dorothy Vernon legend. The 19th century adopted it as a setting for medieval romance; contemporaries shared HW's low opinion; for descriptions and illustrations see *Country Seats* 29; W. Adam, *The Gem of the Peak*, 3d edn 1843, pp. 178–96; John B. Firth, *Highways and Byways in Derbyshire*, 1905, pp. 270–80; Llewellynn F. W. Jewitt and S. C. Hall, *Stately Homes of England*, [1873] i. 221–93.

26. Completed in 1599; described and illustrated ibid. 116–46; Firth, op. cit. 451–2; Fletcher Moss, *Fourth Book of Pilgrimages to Old Homes*, Didsbury, 1908, pp. 346–77; *Country Seats* 29–30.

been promised that I should be charmed with Hardwicke, and told that the Devonshires ought to have established themselves there! Never was I less charmed in my life. The house is not Gothic, but of that betweenity, that intervened when Gothic declined and Palladian was creeping in—rather, this is totally naked of either. It has vast chambers, aye, vast, such as the nobility of that time delighted in and did not know how to furnish. The great apartment is exactly what it was when the Queen of Scots was kept there.[27] Her council-chamber —the council-chamber of a poor woman who had only two secretaries, a gentleman usher, an apothecary, a confessor and three maids, is so outrageously spacious, that you would take it for King David's, who thought, contrary to all modern experience, that in the multitude of counsellors there is wisdom. At the upper end is a state,[28] with a long table covered with a sumptuous cloth, embroidered and embossed with gold,—at least what was gold—so are all the tables. Round the top of the chamber runs a monstrous frieze, ten or twelve feet deep, representing stag-hunting in miserable plastered relief. The next is her dressing-room, hung with patchwork on black velvet. Then her state bedchamber—the bed has been rich beyond description, and now hangs in costly golden tatters. The hangings, part of which they say her Majesty worked, are composed of figures as large as life sewed and embroidered on black velvet, white satin etc., and represent the virtues that were necessary for her or that she was forced to have, as Patience and Temperance etc. The fire-screens are particular; pieces of yellow velvet fringed with gold hang on a crossbar of wood, which is fixed on the top of a single stick that rises from the foot. The only furniture which has any appearance of taste, are the tables and cabinets, which are all of oak richly carved. There is a private chamber within, where she lay; her arms and style[28a] over the door. The arras hangs over all the doors. The gallery is 60 yards long, covered with bad tapestry, and wretched pictures, of Mary herself,

27. Mary Queen of Scots could scarcely have stayed at this house, because it was at most half-built at her death (Llewel-lynn F. W. Jewitt and S. C. Hall, *Stately Homes of England*, [1873] i. 145). An earlier Hardwick Hall, which stood nearby, also belonged to the Countess of Shrewsbury (*post* n. 32), whose last husband as keeper of Mary moved her from one house to another for fifteen years; but it seems clear that she was never even there, tradi-

tion to the contrary; the relics HW saw probably came from Chatsworth; see Rev. Joseph Hunter, 'On the Claim of Hardwick in Derbyshire to have been one of the Residences of Mary Queen of Scots during her Captivity in England,' *Archaeologia* 1847, xxxiii. 73–82.

28. Obsolete, probably even in HW's time, for chair of state, i.e. 'a raised chair with a canopy, etc.' (OED *sb*. 20).

28a. Her name and titles (OED *sb*. 18).

Elizabeth in a gown of sea-monsters, Lord Darnley,[29] James V and his queen,[30] curious, and a whole history of Kings of England, not worth sixpence apiece.[31] There is an original of old Bess of Hardwicke[32] herself, who built the house. Her estates were then reckoned at £60,000 a year and now let for £200,000.[33] Lord John Cavendish told me that the tradition in the family is, that it had been prophesied to her that she should never die as long as she was building, and that at last she died in a hard frost, when the labourers could not work. There is a fine bank of old oaks in the park over a lake—nothing else pleased me there. However, I was so diverted with this old beldame and her magnificence, that I made this epitaph for her;

> Four times the nuptial bed she warm'd,
> And ev'ry time so well perform'd,
> That when Death spoiled each husband's billing,
> He left the widow ev'ry shilling.[34]
> Fond was the dame, but not dejected;
> Five stately mansions she erected
> With more than royal pomp, to vary
> The prison of her captive Mary.[35]
>   When Hardwicke's tow'rs shall bow their head,
> Nor mass be more in Worksop[36] said;
> When Bolsover's[37] fair frame shall tend,
> Like Oldcotes,[38] to its mouldring end;
> When Chatsworth tastes no Candish bounties,
> Let Fame forget this costly Countess.[39]

29. Henry Stuart (1545–67), styled Lord Darnley; husband of Mary Queen of Scots.

30. James V of Scotland (1512–42), m. Mary of Guise (1515–60).

31. There are extracts from the inventory of furniture and pictures at Hardwicke in Bess of Hardwicke's will in Arthur Collins, *Historical Collections of the Noble Families of Cavendish . . . .*, 1752, pp. 15–19.

32. Elizabeth Hardwick (ca 1521–1608), m. (1) (1532) Robert Barley (d. 1533); m. (2) (1549) Sir William Cavendish (d. 1557; by him she was ancestress of the Dukes of Devonshire, etc.); m. (3) Sir William St Loe; m. (4) (1568) George Talbot, 6th E. of Shrewsbury.

33. HW got this figure from 'The Duke of Devon's steward' (*Country Seats* 30).

34. Poetic license as to her fourth hus-

band, from whom she was estranged for many years before his death.

35. Also not strictly accurate; her husband was Mary's keeper, and she disapproved so strongly that she led Mary, Elizabeth, and her husband into quarrels by her scurrilous inventions.

36. Worksop House, Notts, in the 18th century a seat of the Duke of Norfolk; burned down in 1761 (*post* 24 Oct. 1761; John B. Firth, *Highways and Byways in Nottinghamshire*, 1916, pp. 232–9).

37. Derbyshire; in Bess of Hardwicke's time a seat of her husband the Earl of Shrewsbury; it does not appear that she had any part in its construction; see H. Avray Tipping, *English Homes*, Period III, vol. i (1922). 350 (described and illustrated ibid. 348–70). But according to tradition her men were working on Bolsover

As I returned, I saw Newstead[40] and Althorpe; I like both. The former is the very abbey. The great east window of the church remains, and connects with the house; the hall entire, the refectory entire, the cloister untouched with the ancient cistern of the convent and their arms on it, a private chapel quite perfect. The park, which is still charming, has not been so much unprofaned; the present Lord[41] has lost large sums, and paid part in old oaks, five thousand pounds worth of which have been cut near the house. In recompense he has built two baby forts,[42] to pay his country in castles for the damage done to the navy,[43] and planted a handful of Scotch firs, that look like plough-boys dressed in old family liveries for a public day! In the hall is a very good collection of pictures,[44] all animals; the refectory, now the great drawing-room is full of Byrons; the vaulted roof remaining—but the windows have new dresses making for them by a Venetian tailor![45] Althorpe has several very fine pictures by the best Italian hands, and a gallery of all one's acquaintance by Vandyke and Lely.[46] I wonder you never saw it; it is but six miles from Northampton.

when the fatal frost occurred (Francis L. Bickley, *Cavendish Family*, 1911, p. 33). Bolsover was later a seat of the Dukes of Portland.

38. In the parish of Sutton Scarsdale, Derbyshire, three miles from Hardwick; built, according to tradition, to outshine a neighbour, Sir Francis Leake, who was building a great house in the vicinity. The site is now occupied by a farmhouse; fragments of the original walls remain (information from Prof. Turberville and Mr Francis Thompson).

39. HW also wrote these verses in his copy (sold SH ii. 99) of Arthur Collins, *Historical Collections of the Noble Families of Cavendish, Holles, Vere, Harley, and Ogle . . .*, 1752, p. 14 (now BM).

40. Now famous as the home of Byron; see *Country Seats* 30–1; [Washington Irving], *Abbotsford and Newstead Abbey*, Philadelphia, 1835 (*Crayon Miscellany*, no. 2); John B. Firth, *Highways and Byways in Nottinghamshire*, 1916, pp. 183–200. Wright quotes Evelyn's description of Newstead in 1654 and points out that Byron describes it in the 13th canto of *Don Juan*. HW's drawing of Newstead by Barrow is now WSL.

41. William Byron (1722–98), 5th Bn Byron, who killed William Chaworth in a duel (HW to Hertford 27 Jan. 1765), allowed Newstead to fall into a very dilapidated condition; see Firth, op. cit. 183–6; John Throsby, *Thoroton's History of Nottinghamshire*, 1797, ii. 289–90.

42. According to Augusta Z. Fraser, *Livingstone and Newstead*, 1913, p. 82, he built the forts to embellish mimic sea-fights he staged on a lake which at that time was quite large; and see [Arthur Young], *Farmer's Tour through the East of England*, 1771, i. 140–1. A print in *Modern Universal British Traveller*, [1779] opp. 542, shows one of the forts.

43. By cutting his timber.

44. Frits Lugt, *Répertoire des catalogues de ventes*, La Haye, 1938–, No. 2018, records a sale in London, March 1772, of Lord Byron's pictures.

45. In *Country Seats* 31, HW notes: 'This Lord going to make three Venetian windows in it.' Venetian windows, which were Palladian in manner, 'a kind calculated for show, and very pompous in their nature' (see Isaac Ware, *Complete Body of Architecture*, 1756, pp. 467–8), would of course have been quite incongruous at Newstead. It does not appear that they were ever installed.

46. See *Country Seats* 31–3.

Well, good night; I have writ you such a volume, that you see I am
forced to page it.[47] The Duke[48] has had a stroke of a palsy, but is quite
recovered, except in some letters which he cannot pronounce, and it
is still visible in the contraction of one side of his mouth. My compliments to your family.

Yours ever

H. W.

From Montagu, Tuesday 16 September 1760

G.D. 15/8, No. 745.

In reply to *ante* 1 Sept. 1760.

Address: To the Honourable Mr Walpole, Arlington Street, London. Free M.P.
Postmark: 17 SE Banbury.

Greatworth, Sept. 16 [1760].

Dear Sir:

I AM returned from Cheshire and am to tell you the General is not
able to wait on you at Strawberry as he returns to his Ireland in a
few days. I hope you continue well; this hot summer has almost
ripened my gout, but I am afraid I don't water it so much as you do.

Many thanks to you for your tour to Chatsworth et cetera.

The great Cu[1] was the most disconsolate and neglected of beings at
his races;[2] the young lady was there and only presented her Cu.

I am tired to death from the heat of my journey and am, however,
much yours.

G. M.

---

47. The letter is six pages long; HW
numbered pages 4, 5, and 6.
48. Of Cumberland.

———

1. Lord Halifax; his match with Mary
Anne Drury (*ante* ca 9 April 1760) had apparently been broken off during the summer. See *Town and Country Magazine*,

May 1769, i. 227, for a dramatic tale ascribing the break to the tearful interposition
of his mistress and her child.

2. No doubt the Northampton races on
10–12 Sept. (*Lloyd's Evening Post* 15–17
Sept. 1760; *Baily's Racing Register*, 1845, i.
198).

To Montagu, Thursday 2 October 1760

Strawberry Hill, Oct. 2d, 1760.

I ANNOUNCE my Lady Huntingtower to you. I hope you will approve the match a little more than I suppose my Lord Dysart[1] will, as he does not yet know, though they have been married these two hours, that at ten o'clock this morning his son[2] espoused my niece Charlotte at St James's church.[3]

The moment my Lord Dysart is dead, I will carry you to see Hamhouse;[4] it is pleasant to call cousins with a charming prospect over against one. Now you want to know the detail; there was none. It is not the style of our court to have long negotiations: we don't fatigue the town with exhibiting the betrothed for six months together in public places. *Vidit, venit, vicit;* the young Lord has liked her sometime; on Saturday se'nnight he came to my brother and made his demand: The princess[5] did not know him by sight, and did not dislike him when she did; she consented, and they were to be married this morning. My Lord Dysart is such a brute, that nobody will feel for him; he has kept his son till six and twenty and would never make the least settlement on him; 'Sure,' said the young man, 'if he will do nothing for me, I may please myself; he cannot hinder me of ten thousand pounds a year and sixty thousands that are in the funds, all entailed on me'—a reversion one does not wonder the bride did not refuse, as there is present possession too of a very handsome person, the only thing his father has ever given him. His grandfather Lord Granville has always told him to choose a gentlewoman and please himself—yet I should think the Ladies Tweedale and Cowper[6] would cackle a little.

I wish you could have come here this October for more reasons than one. The Teddingtonian history is grown woefully bad. Marc Antony,[7] though no boy, persists in losing the world two or three

1. Lionel Tollemache (1708–70), 4th E. of Dysart. Apart from his native 'brutishness' (see below), his displeasure would naturally be heightened by Charlotte Walpole's illegitimacy.
2. Lionel Tollemache (1734–99), styled Lord Huntingtower; 5th E. of Dysart, 1770.
3. Piccadilly. See HW to Mann 5 Oct. 1760 for a fuller account of the marriage.
4. Petersham; see *post* 11 June 1770, n. 3.

5. Charlotte Walpole.
6. Lady Georgiana Caroline Carteret (d. 1780), m. (1) (1734) Hon. John Spencer; m. (2) (1750) William Cowper (after 1762, Clavering-Cowper), 2d E. Cowper. She and her sister Lady Tweeddale (*ante* 25 July 1748, n. 18) were Lord Huntingtower's aunts.
7. Bentley.

times over for every gipsy, that he takes for a Cleopatra. I have laughed, been cool, scolded, represented, begged, and at last spoken very roundly—all with equal success—at present we do not meet—I must convince him of ill usage, before I can make good usage of any service to him. All I have done is forgot, because I will not be enamoured of Hannah Cleopatra too. You shall know the whole history when I see you; you may trust me for still being kind to him;[8] but that he must not as yet suspect. They are bent on going to London, that she may visit and be visited, while he puts on his red velvet and ermine, and goes about begging in robes!

Poor Mr Chute has had another very severe fit of the gout; I left him in bed, but by not hearing he is worse, trust on Saturday to find him mended. Adieu!

Yours ever

H. W.

PS. I have kept a copy of my last memorial,[9] which you, who know all the circumstances, will not think a whit too harsh.

From MONTAGU, Sunday 5 October 1760

G.D. 15/8, No. 746.

In reply to *ante* 2 Oct. 1760.

Greatworth, October 5, 1760.

THOUGH I take it kind, yet it was your duty to notify to me this brave match of your niece's, which I most truly rejoice at and congratulate you upon. I don't see but Katherine Swinford's[1] children may make a figure in the world since there is no issue by the

8. See George Hardinge to HW 17 July 1780, 'I met *your* Bentley. . . . I discovered by an accident that you are still generous to him.' 'Mr Horace Walpole . . . told me some eight years ago that their friendship was cooled on account of [Bentley's] being forward to introduce his wife at his house when people of the first fashion were there, and which he thought illjudged. Mr W. told me that his chief subsistence then was a place he had procured for him of about £100 per annum' (William Cole, writing ca 1772, in John Nichols,

Literary Illustrations, 1817–58, ix. 572–3).

9. Presumably a letter to Bentley; missing.

1. Lady Huntingtower's mother, Dorothy Clement, the mistress of Sir Edward Walpole, and so a parallel to Katharine Roet (1350–1403), who m. (1) Sir Hugh Swynford; m. (2) (1396) John of Gaunt, D. of Lancaster, whose mistress she had been for many years (for Dorothy Clement see *ante* 25 May 1745, n. 3).

rest of the family;[2] I reckon the Pigwiggen's[3] absolute issues in its most nasty sense.

I am abominably vexed with the indiscretion of Cliquetis and his weakness for his honest woman, the burthen of whose follies I know will be sent from the Fleet upon your shoulders. It would not have been in my power to prevent his journey to London though I should have endeavoured at it. He has never opened his lips to me in his life concerning his domestic happiness, and till they were married I would never know there was a Miss Falkener[4] in the world.

Young Frederick Montagu has been here for a few days. He came from Chatsworth; his intimacy are[5] with the two younger lords;[6] Lord John he extols to the peak. He tells me Gray is settled for good in London[7] and as happy as he can be.

If you write to your Lord Beauchamp ever, you may tell him when Lord Grevill Montagu[8] comes from Christ Church here if he will come with him I shall be glad to see him. We[9] have not seen each other since we learned to dance at Rheims.

I hope you are as well and as well pleased with this lovely autumn as I[10] am very sorry for poor Mr Chute.

I have now gone through all your paragraphs and tagged a grief and joy to each of them; and nothing more remains than that I remain, as long as I remain, most faithfully yours,

G. MONTAGU

To MONTAGU, Tuesday 14 October 1760

Strawberry Hill, Oct. 14, 1760.

IF you should see in the newspapers, that I have offered to raise a regiment at Twickenham, am going with the expedition,[1] and

2. The Walpole family.
3. Lord Walpole of Wolterton.
4. Since Miss Faulkner was Lord Halifax's mistress, this suggests that Mrs Bentley had been Bentley's.
5. *Sic.*
6. Lords John and Frederick Cavendish.
7. Gray took up residence in London, July 1759 (see Gray to Wharton 21 July 1759; *Gray's Corr.* ii. 624), but returned into residence at Cambridge in Nov. 1761 (Gray to Brown 22 Oct. 1761, ibid. ii. 759).
8. Lord Charles Greville Montagu (1741–84), 2d son of 3d D. of Manchester; M.P.

Hunts 1762–5; Governor of South Carolina 1765–73 (Edward McCrady, *History of South Carolina under the Royal Government 1719–1776*, 1899, passim).

9. This refers not to Lord Beauchamp, but to HW, who was at Rheims with Montagu in 1739 (HW to West 20 July 1739; Gray to Wharton 25 Aug. 1739, *Gray's Corr.* i. 116).

10. Possibly Montagu intended a full stop here and a new sentence beginning with 'I.'

———

1. A force, assembled at Portsmouth,

have actually kissed hands, don't believe it—though, I own, the two first would not be more surprising than the last. I will tell you how the latter calamity befell me, though you will laugh instead of pitying me. Last Friday morning I was very tranquilly writing my *Anecdotes of Painting:* I heard the bell at the gate ring—I called out as usual, 'Not at home'; but Harry who thought it would be treason to tell a lie when he saw red liveries, owned I was, and came running up, 'Sir, the Prince of Wales is at the door, and says he is come on purpose to make you a visit!' There was I in the utmost confusion; undressed, in my slippers, and with my hair about my ears; there was no help, *Insanum vatem aspiciet[2]*—and down I went to receive him— him was the Duke of York. Behold my breeding of the old court; at the foot of the stairs I kneeled down and kissed his hand. I beg your uncle[3] Algernon Sidney's pardon, but I could not let the second prince of the blood kiss my hand first. He was, as he always is, extremely good-humoured; and I, as I am not always, extremely respectful. He stayed two hours, nobody with him but Morrison;[3a] I showed him all my castle, the pictures of the Pretender's sons,[4] and that type of the Reformation, Harry the Eighth's *measure,* moulded into a weight to the clock he gave Anne Boleyn[5]—But observe my luck; he would have the sanctum sanctorum in the library[6] opened; about a month ago I removed the MSS[7] into another place—all this is very well; but now for the consequences: what was I to do next? I have not been in a court these ten years; consequently have never kissed hands in the next reign. Could I let a Duke of York visit me, and never go to thank him? I know, if I was a great poet, I might be so

which was supposed to be destined for the French possessions, Mauritius and Réunion. After embarking and disembarking and awaiting orders and favourable winds until late in December, it was postponed; it formed the core of a force sent against Belleisle the next spring; see Julian S. Corbett, *England in the Seven Years' War,* 1907, ii. 81–2, 136–7, 141 et seq.; *London Chronicle* Oct.–Dec. 1760, *passim.*

2. *Insanam vatem aspicies (Æn.* iii. 443).
3. Montagu's paternal grandmother, Elizabeth Pelham, was a daughter of Lady Lucy Sidney, Algernon Sidney's sister; he was therefore Montagu's great-great-uncle; see *post* Appendix 7.

3a. The Duke's equerry.
4. Prince Charles Edward and Prince Henry Benedict Maria Clement (1725–1807), Cardinal of York, 1747. The pictures were doubtless those in the Green Closet, 'The two sons of the old Pretender; painted at Rome in 1740' (*Des. of SH, Works* ii. 431). There was also a miniature of Prince Charles Edward by Bartoni, in the Tribune (sold SH xiv. 100).
5. See Cole ii. 334, n. 4.
6. Probably the glass closet in which HW kept his choicest books and manuscripts; see *Des. of SH, Works* ii. 447–51; *SH Sale Cat.* 6th day.
7. Of the *Memoirs.*

brutal, and tell the world in rhyme, that rudeness is virtue;[8] or if I was a patriot, I might, after laughing at kings and princes for twenty years, catch at the first opening of favour and beg a place. In truth, I can do neither; yet I could not be shocking; I determined to go to Leicester House, and comforted myself that it was not much less meritorious to go there for nothing, than to stay quite away. Yet I believe I must make a pilgrimage to St Liberty of Geneva,[9] before I am perfectly purified, especially as I am dipped even at St James's:[10] Lord Hertford[11] at my request begged my Lady Yarmouth to get an order for my Lady Hervey to go through the park, and the Countess said so many civil things about me and my suit, and granted it so expeditiously, that I shall be forced to visit her, even before she lives here next door to my Lady Suffolk.[12] My servants are transported; Harry expects to see me first minister like my father, and reckons upon a place in the Custom House. Louis, who drinks like a German, thinks himself qualified for a page of the backstairs—but these are not all my troubles. As I never dress in summer, I had nothing upon earth but a frock,[13] unless I went in black, like a poet, and pretended that a cousin was dead, one of the Muses. Then I was in panics lest I should call my Lord Bute, your Royal Highness. I was not indeed in much pain at the conjectures the Duke of Newcastle would make on such an apparition, even if he should suspect that a new opposition was on foot, and that I was to write some letters to the Whigs.[14]

Well! but after all, do you know that my calamity has not befallen me yet? I could not determine to bounce over head and ears into the drawing-room at once, without one soul knowing why I came thither. I went to London on Saturday night, and Lord Hertford was to carry

8. Perhaps HW had in mind Swift's lines on Pope:

'Hail! happy Pope, whose gen'rous mind,
Detesting all the statesmen kind,
Contemning courts, at courts unseen,
Refus'd the visits of a queen.'

('Libel on Dr. Delany,' *Poems of Jonathan Swift*, ed. Harold Williams, Oxford, 1937, ii. 482.)

The passage refers to an apocryphal story that Pope left his villa when he heard Queen Caroline intended visiting it (see Johnson, *Lives of the English Poets*, ed. G. B. Hill, Oxford, iii. 171).

9. Possibly a reference to Voltaire, specifically, whose house at Ferney was near Geneva, or merely to Geneva as the seat of toleration.

10. Where Lady Yarmouth lived.

11. Who was a Lord of the Bedchamber.

12. Not literally, but figuratively as a former royal mistress.

13. A coat with long skirts (OED), as opposed to a dress coat.

14. In 1747–8, HW wrote *A Letter to the Whigs, A Second Letter . . ., A Third Letter . . .* (see 'Short Notes').

me the next morning; in the meantime I wrote to Morrison,[15] explaining my gratitude to one brother, and my unacquaintance with t'other, and how afraid I was that it would be thought officious and forward if I was presented now, and begging he would advise me what to do, and all this upon my bended knee as if Schutz[16] had stood over me and dictated every syllable. The answer was by order from the Duke of York, that he smiled at my distress, wished to put me to no inconvenience, but desired that as the acquaintance had begun without restraint, it might continue without ceremony—now I was in more perplexity than ever. I could not go directly—and yet it was not fit it should be said that I thought it an *inconvenience,* to wait on the Prince of Wales. At present it is decided by a jury of court matrons, that is, courtiers, that I must write to my Lord Bute, and explain the whole, and why I desire to come now—don't fear; I will take care they shall understand how little I come for. In the meantime, you see it is my fault if I am not a favourite—but alas! I am not heavy enough to be tossed in a blanket like Doddington;[17] I should never come down again; I cannot be driven in a royal curricle to wells and waters; I can't make love now to my cotemporary Charlotte Dives;[18] I cannot quit Mufti[19] and my perroquet, for Sir William Irby[20] and the prattle of a drawing-room, nor Mrs Clive for Ælia Lælia Chudleigh;—in short, I could give up nothing but an earldom of Eglinton[21]—and yet I foresee that this phantom of the reversion of a reversion[22] will make me plagued; I shall have Lord Egmont[23] whisper me again; and every tall woman and strong man[24] that comes to town will make interest

15. The letter is missing.

16. Probably Augustus Schutz (*ante* 10 Sept. 1750, n. 4).

17. Bubb Dodington was said to have submitted to such treatment when in favour with Frederick Prince of Wales (*Mem. Geo. II* i. 438).

18. Maid of Honour to the Princess of Wales.

19. Either a dog or a cat; see *post* 12 March 1766, n. 2.

20. Vice-Chamberlain to the Princess of Wales.

21. HW in using this phrase apparently means to signify something of little value, or something not possessed, but the allusion is not clear. He may possibly have had in mind Hugh Montgomerie (1584–1612), 5th E. of Eglintoun, who having no male issue attempted in his lifetime to deed his earldom to a kinsman, or the 10th Earl (*post* 13 Nov. 1760 *bis,* n. 4), who wanted to 'dispeer himself' to sit in the Commons (*Scots Peerage,* 1904–10). The 6th E. of Eglintoun resigned his title only to have it restored (DNB *sub* Alexander Montgomerie, 6th E. of Eglintoun).

22. HW seems to mean the likelihood that court gossip will now bestow upon him a tangible mark of royal favour, like the reversion of the reversion of a place.

23. John Perceval (1711–70), 2d E. of Egmont; an industrious and ambitious politician who was always eager to be on the winning side (see DNB).

24. Performers (see *ante* 9 Jan. 1752).

with me to get the Duke of York to come and see them. Oh! dreadful, dreadful! It is plain I never was a patriot, for I don't find my virtue a bit staggered by this first glimpse of court sunshine.

Mr Conway has pressed to command the new Quixotism[25] on foot, and has been refused; I sing a very comfortable *Te Deum* for it. Kingsley,[26] Crauford[27] and Keppel[28] are the generals, and Commodore Keppel[29] the admiral. The mob are sure of being pleased; they will get a conquest or a court-martial. A very unpleasant thing has happened to the Keppels; the youngest brother,[30] who had run in debt at Gibraltar and was fetched away to be sent to Germany, gave them the slip, at the first port they touched at in Spain, surrendered himself to the Spanish governor, has changed his religion, and sent for a whore that had been taken from him at Gibraltar—*naturam expellas furcâ*[31]— there's the true blood of Charles II,[32] sacrificing everything for popery and a bunter!

Lord Bolinbroke on hearing the name of Lady Coventry[33] at Newmarket, affected to burst into tears and left the room, not to hide his crying, but his not crying.

Draper[34] has handsomely offered to go on the expedition and goes. Ned Finch[35] t'other day on the conquest of Montreal wished the King

25. The new expedition (n. 1 above).

26. William Kingsley (d. 1769), Col., 1750; Col. 20th Foot, 1756; Lt-Gen., 1760 (*Army Lists;* Musgrave, *Obituary*).

27. Col. John Craufurd (d. 1764), M.P. Berwick 1761–4; Col. of Royal Volunteers 85th Foot), 1759 (see L. B. Namier, *Structure of Politics at the Accession of George III,* 1929, ii. 326).

28. Col. Hon. William Keppel (d. 1782), 4th son of 2d E. of Albemarle; Lt-Gen., 1773; M.P. Chichester 1767–82 (Collins, *Peerage,* 1812, iii. 740).

29. Hon. Augustus Keppel (1725–86), 2d son of 2d E. of Albemarle; cr. (1782) Vct Keppel; Rear Admiral, 1762; Admiral, 1782; First Lord of the Admiralty 1782–3 (DNB).

30. His Christian name has not been found. The youngest Keppel brother in the peerages is the Rev. Frederick, obviously not the subject of HW's story. He is no doubt the Capt. Keppel mentioned in *London Chronicle* 29 June–1 July 1762, xii. 3, where, denying a report that one of the

brothers had died at the siege of Havana, it states that all *four* of them engaged there, Lord Albemarle, Commodore Keppel, Col. Keppel of the 56th Foot, and Capt. Keppel, are well. He seems not to be in the *Army List* for 1763, and no other reference to him has been found.

31. 'Naturam expelles furca,' Horace, *Epist.* I. x. 24.

32. Lady Albemarle was a granddaughter of Charles II and the Duchess of Portsmouth, through the 1st Duke of Richmond.

33. She died 30 Sept.

34. Lt-Col William Draper (1721–87), K.B., 1765; Lt-Gen., 1777. He went on this expedition as deputy quarter-master-general. It was 'handsome' of him to go because earlier in the year he had been invalided home from service in India (DNB; William A. Shaw, *Knights of England,* 1906, i. 171).

35. Hon. Edward Finch (Finch-Hatton, 1764), d. 1771; diplomatist and politician (DNB).

joy of having lost no subjects but those that perished in the *rabbits*. Fitzroy[36] asked him if he thought they crossed the great American lakes in such little boats as one goes in to Vauxhall? He replied, 'Yes, Mr Pitt said the *rabbits*'[37]—it was in the falls, the *rapids*.[38]

I like Lord John, almost as well as Fred Montagu; and I like your letter better than Lord John: the application of Miss Falkener was charming. Good night.

Yours ever

H. W.

PS. If I had been told in June that I should have the gout and kiss hands before November, I don't think I should have given much credit to the prophet.

From Montagu, Sunday 19 October 1760

G.D. 15/8, No. 747.

In reply to *ante* 14 Oct. 1760.

Greatworth, [Oct.] 19 [1760].

WHY, truly, you amaze me, not at the honours you have received, but at your fancying you shall be conjectured as *sic notus*, etc. You are just at the age when virtue rots and is fit for use and I put in for some of your parings. Hanah Bernard[2] has, I dare-

---

36. Charles Fitzroy (1737–97), cr. (1780) Bn Southampton; brother of 3d D. of Grafton (DNB).

37. This was apparently an ephemeral use of the word; it is not noted by OED or John S. Farmer and William E. Henley, *Slang and its Analogues*, 1890–1904. OED *sb*.² gives 'wooden drinking-vessel,' from which the name for the boats may have been derived.

38. The force under Amherst which took Montreal embarked at Oswego, N.Y., and proceeded down Lake Ontario and the St Lawrence; 84 men were drowned in the rapids of the latter; see Fortescue, *British Army* ii. 404–6.

1. 'Sic notus Ulixes?' (*Aen*. ii. 44).

2. Mrs Bentley. Why Montagu should refer to her as Hannah Bernard is not clear. Johanna Bernard was Bentley's *mother*, dau. of Sir John Bernard, Bt, of

Brampton, Hunts; see James H. Monk, *Life of Bentley*, 1833, i. 151. It is possible that Bentley had married a cousin with the same given name as his mother; or, of course, the identity may be purely coincidental, and Montagu may be using Hannah in the Walpolian sense of a loose woman (see *ante* 11 Oct. 1759, n. 6). Little information about Mrs Bentley has been found outside these letters. William Cole, writing ca 1772 (John Nichols, *Literary Illustrations*, 1817–58, viii. 572–3), states that Bentley 'married imprudently, and lived . . . at Teddington, near Twickenham, being much acquainted with Mr Horace Walpole, who told me some eight years ago that their friendship was cooled on account of his being forward to introduce his wife at his house when people of the first fashion were there, and which he thought illjudged. . . . His wife seems an agreeable woman.' As to the imprudence of the marsay, got a tasselled sedan and her McAnthony[3] a service of plate. I wish their ideas better success in this scheme than in any of their other romantic ones; I wish Alcibiades[4] under the tuition of such a Socrates who will only teach good doctrine and will be a counter-balance for the Highland Aristippus[5]—Lord, you have wrote out your eyes; let others see with them. A grain of good leaven would ferment a whole court—I must take a better pen and moderate my impatience or you will never be able to read the good things I can say on this subject—but I think I will stay till I hear of real effects.

I have just been on the Horton side of Northamptonshire; I went over there and am more outrageous than Goneril and Regan and could pull out his eyes. He[6] has pissed upon twenty brave old Cus worth an hundred Drurys; believe me there are ancestors mildewing and eligible in his hall worth all the Sunburys in kelder.[7]

Will you believe that one morning as I was riding out I met this poor Dido[8] near her park? Mr Isted[9] at whose house I have been, and intimate with her, said, 'Shall we finish your ride with you?' A most gracious 'Yes' made me show my horsemanship. Isted commodiously talked business and taxes with the uncle[10] and I with the Garter robes[11] on my arm made many bows and looked as like a fool as Sir Charles Cotterel.[12]

riage, several passages suggest that she had been Bentley's mistress before she became his wife; see *ante* 5 Oct. 1760 and 14 Oct. 1760; *post* 23 Dec. 1761. John Nichols, *Literary Anecdotes*, 1812–15, v. 86 n, states that 'a niece of Dr. Robert Freind was married to a son of Dr Bentley.' HW's Bentley was Dr Bentley's only son, but nothing has been discovered to confirm his marriage to Freind's unidentified niece.

3. HW called Bentley Marc Antony, *ante* 2 Oct. 1760.

4. Probably the Prince of Wales.

5. A student of Socrates who diverged from his teachings and advocated a life of pleasure obtained by self-control; here represents Lord Bute.

6. Lord Halifax.

7. Montagu has a double grievance, defined in the second paragraph below. First, Lord Halifax will not give him any family pictures; second, 'he will not get an heir to his estate' by Miss Drury. An heir would bear the courtesy title of Viscount Sunbury. Montagu is most concerned over the pictures; the mildewed ancestors are worth 'all the Sunburys in kelder.' 'Kelder' (obs., rare, from Dutch *kelder* a cellar, cf. the phrase Hans-*in-kelder*) = the womb (OED).

8. Miss Anne Drury, whom the Earl of Halifax was to have married (*ante* ca 9 April 1760).

9. Ambrose Isted (ca 1718–81), of Ecton, Northants, Trinity College, Oxford, and the Middle Temple (see Foster, *Alumni Oxon*). He was a friend and neighbour of Lord Halifax; Richard Cumberland eulogizes him in his *Memoirs*, 1807, i. 161–4.

10. Probably Sir John Tyrrell (ca 1728–66), 5th Bt, of Heron, Essex. Miss Drury's father was an only son (George Baker, *History . . . of the County of Northampton*, 1822–41, i. 57), and Sir John was the only surviving brother of her mother (Philip Morant, *History . . . of Essex*, 1768, i. 210).

11. I.e., behaving ceremoniously.

12. Master of Ceremonies at court.

Child, I never closed my eyes all night! She behaved so prettily, looked so fresh, so *délaissée,* I could have cried, which I am apt like a fool to do for those who are no friends at all to me—why he will neither get an heir to his estate and fill the county with Cudoms or give me any of my old kin—that would please me as well.

St Durham[13] told my Lord Manchester, who is just come from Auckland,[14] that he has laid out sixteen thousand pounds there, and has now an hundred men at work a day. Mr Hampden[15] will put his son into orders that nothing may be lost. I wish you would go to Kimbolton for me; there are not above three sets of company to pass the autumn there. You know you have served your time under her Grace of Devonshire.[16]

Write to me again and again; if I was to write forever I can say no more from hence than that I am always most truly yours, especially if I write by sunshine which makes me as loving as a princess at a stud.

Is the poor Chute got well? Pray my compliments when you pull off your dressed clothes from a drawing-room to go to Strawberry.

I need not sign my name.

To MONTAGU, Saturday 25 October 1760

Misdated by HW; see *post* 28 Oct. 1760.

> Arlington Street, Oct. 26 [25], 1760.
> I tell a lie, I am at Mr Chute's.

WAS ever so agreeable a man as King George the Second, to die the very day it was necessary to save me from a ridicule? I was to have kissed hands tomorrow—but you will not care a farthing about that now—so I must tell you all I know of departed majesty.

13. Dr Richard Trevor, Bp of Durham.

14. Bishop Auckland, Durham, palace of the Bishops of Durham. According to *English Episcopal Palaces, Province of York,* ed. Robert S. Rait, 1911, pp. 233–4, Bishop Trevor began the south front and built a Gothic gateway at the entrance to the park. In HW's 'Drawings and Designs by Mr Bentley' (now WSL) is a 'Gateway designed for Dr Trevor Bishop of Durham,' but the one erected was, according to William Fordyce, *History . . . of Durham,* 1857, i. 549, designed by Sir Thomas Robinson of Rokeby. It appears in the lower left-hand corner of a print of the palace, ibid. opp. p. 548, and does not resemble Bentley's plan. Fordyce also states (p. 549) that Bishop Trevor spent £8000 on improvements to the palace; the same figure is given in other topographical works.

15. Hon. Robert Hampden (until 1754, Trevor) (1706–83), 4th Bn Trevor, 1764; cr. (1776) Vct Hampden; older brother of the Bishop. Neither of his sons entered holy orders.

16. Presumably referring to HW's visit to Chatsworth (*ante* 1 Sept. 1760).

He went to bed well last night; rose at six this morning as usual, looked I suppose if all his money was in his purse, and called for his chocolate. A little after seven he went into[1] the water-closet—the German valet de chambre[1a] heard a noise, louder than royal wind, listened, heard something like a groan, ran in and found the hero of Oudenarde and Dettingen on the floor, with a gash on his right temple by falling against the corner of a bureau—he tried to speak, could not and expired. Princess Emily was called, found him dead, and wrote to the Prince. I know not a syllable more, but am come to see and hear as much as I can. I fear you *will cry and roar all night,* but one could not keep it from you. For my part, like a new courtier, I comfort myself, *considering what a gracious prince comes next.*[2] Behold my luck; I wrote to Lord Bute,[3] thrust in all the *unexpecteds, want of ambition, disinteresteds* etc. that I could amass, gilded with as much duty, affection, zeal, etc. as possible. I received a very gracious and sensible answer, and was to have been presented tomorrow, and the talk of the few people that are in town for a week. Now I shall be lost in the crowd, shall be as well there as I desire to be, have done what was right, they know I want nothing, may be civil to me very cheaply, and I can go and see the puppet show for this next month at my ease—but perhaps you will think all this a piece of art—to be sure I have timed my court as luckily as possible, and contrived to be the last man in England that had made interest with the successor—you see, virtue and philosophy always prove to know the world and their own interest—however I am not so abandoned a patriot yet as to desert my friends immediately—you shall hear now and then the events of the new reign—if I am not made Secretary of State—if I am I shall certainly take care—to let you know it.

I had really begun to think that the lawyers for once talked sense, when they said *the King never dies.* He probably got his death as he had liked to have done two years ago by viewing the troops for the expedition from the wall of Kensington garden.[4] My Lady Suffolk

---

1. The phrase 'went into' has been crossed out and 'came from' substituted, apparently by HW. This correction was probably made when the letters were returned to him, in response to the first paragraph of the next letter, which was then crossed out.

1a. Schröder (Romney Sedgwick, *Letters from George III to Lord Bute,* 1939, pp. 46, 48).

2. 'Consid'ring what a *gracious Prince* was next' (Pope, *Epilogue to the Satires,* Dialogue i. 108).

3. See HW to Bute 20 Oct. 1760, answered 22 Oct.

4. 'Yesterday morning [23 Oct.], about seven o'clock, the 3d battalion of the 1st regiment of foot-guards, consisting of 1000 men, marched from the Tower . . . for Portsmouth. . . . His Majesty saw them pass by Kensington' (*Lloyd's Evening Post* 22–24 Oct. 1760, vii. 396).

told me about a month ago that he had often told her, speaking of the dampness of Kensington, that he never would die there. For my part, my man Harry will always be a favourite—he tells me all the amusing news; he first told me of the late Prince of Wales's death, and today of the King's.

Thank you, Mr Chute is as well as can be expected—in this national affliction. Sir Robert Brown[5] has left everything to my Lady, aye, everything, I believe his very avarice.

Lord Huntingtower wrote to offer his father £8000 of Charlotte's fortune, if he would give them £1000 a year in present and settle a jointure on her. The Earl returned this truly laconic, for being so unnatural an, answer, 'Lord Huntingtower, I answer your letter as soon as I receive it: I wish you joy: I hear your wife is very accomplished. Yours, Dysart.' I believe my Lady Huntingtower must contrive to make it convenient for *me* that my Lord Dysart should die[6]—and then he will. I expect to be a very respectable personage in time, and to have my tomb set forth, like the Lady Margaret Douglas's,[7] 'that I had four earls to my nephews, though I never was one myself'—adieu! I must go govern the nation.

Yours ever

H. W.

To Montagu, Tuesday 28 October 1760

Year determined by the contents.

Arlington Street, Tuesday, Oct. 28 [1760].

THE day after I had writ to you last, I perceived that I had misdated my letter, the 26th instead of the 25th, and that instead of the water-closet I should have said coming from the water-closet. In the relation of the death of a king these are important circum-

5. Died 5 Oct. See HW to Mann 4 Oct. 1785 for his avarice; *post* 31 Oct. 1760 for hers.

6. As George II had.

7. Lady Margaret Douglas (1515–78), m. (1544) Matthew Stuart, 4th E. of Lennox; mother of Lord Darnley. Her tomb in Westminster Abbey, erected by James I, bears 'a pompous recital of her relationships to royal personages' (DNB). It was (1940) in the south aisle of Henry VII's Chapel near the monument erected by HW to Lady Walpole. The epitaph is printed in *History of the Abbey Church . . . Westminster*, R. Ackermann, 1812, ii. 167.

stances; pray correct them—Harry would call me an historian of no
veracity.[1]

The new reign dates with great propriety and decency. The civilest
letter to Princess Emily,[2] the greatest kindness to the Duke; the utmost respect to the dead body. No changes to be made but those absolutely necessary, as the household etc., and what some will think
the most unnecessary, in the representative of power. There are but
two new cabinet counsellors named, the Duke of York and Lord
Bute, so it must be one of them. The Princess does not remove to St
James's, so I don't believe it will be she. Today England kissed
hands; so did I, and it is more comfortable to kiss hands with all England, than to have all England ask why one kisses hands—well! my
virtue is safe; I had a gracious reception, and yet I am almost as impatient to return to Strawberry, as I was to leave it on the news.
There is great dignity and grace in the King's manner—I don't say
this, like my dear Madame Sévigné, because he was civil to me;[3] but
the part is well acted. If they do as well behind the scenes, as upon
the stage, it will be a very complete reign. Hollingshed[4] or Baker[5]
would think it begins well, that is, begins ill; it has rained without
intermission, and yesterday there came a cargo of bad news, all which
you know are sinister omens to a man who writes history upon the
information of the clouds. Berlin is taken by the Russians;[6] the
Hereditary Prince beaten by the French.[7] Poor Lord Downe has

1. This paragraph has been almost obliterated with ink in MS, probably by HW.
2. Doubtless in answer to the 'letter notifying the King's death . . . from Princess
Amelia,' Sir John Fortescue, Correspondence of King George the Third, 1927–8, i.
3. It is not among the Archives at Windsor (information from Mr O. F. Morshead).
3. See Roger, Comte de Bussy-Rabutin,
Histoire amoureuse des Gaules, 1754, i.
239–40, speaking of Mme de Sévigné (Marie
de Rabutin-Chantal [1626–96], m. [1644],
Henri, Marquis de Sévigné): 'Un soir que
le roi venait de la faire danser, s'étant re-
mise à la place qui était auprès de moi,
"Il faut avouer," me dit-elle, "que le roi a
des grandes qualités; je crois qu'il obscur-
cira la gloire de tous ses prédécesseurs." Je
ne pus m'empêcher de lui rire au nez,
voyant à quel propos elle lui donnait ces

louanges, et de lui répondre, "On n'en
peut pas douter, Madame, après ce qu'il
vient de faire pour vous." '
4. Raphael Holinshed (d. 1580?). HW's
copy of his Chronicles of England, Scotland, and Ireland was sold SH ii. 82.
5. Sir Richard Baker (ca 1568–1645), Kt,
wrote a Chronicle of the Kings of England
from the Time of the Romans' Government unto the Death of King James, which
was long popular (DNB); HW's copy (folio,
1643) was sold SH ii. 163.
6. The allied Austrian and Russian
troops occupied Berlin 9–13 Oct. (GM 1760,
xxx. 483).
7. Karl Wilhelm Ferdinand (1735–1806),
Prince and Duke of Brunswick-Wolfenbüttel, defeated at the battle of Kloster
Kampen, 16 Oct. 1760, in an attempt to
surprise the French (Fortescue, British
Army ii. 524–6).

three wounds;[8] he and your brother's Billy Pitt[9] are prisoners. Johny Waldegrave was shot through the hat and through the coat, and would have been shot through the body if he had any. Irish Johnson is wounded in the hand, Ned Harvey[10] somewhere, and Prince Ferdinand mortally in his reputation, for sending this wild detachment. Mr Pitt has another reign to set to rights. The Duke of Cumberland has taken Lord Sandwich's in Pallmall;[11] Lord Chesterfield has offered his house to Princess Emily[12]—and if they live at Hampton Court, as I suppose this court will, I may as well offer Strawberry for a royal nursery, for at best it will become a cake-house; 'tis such a convenient airing for the Maids of Honour! If I was not forced in conscience to own to you, that my own curiosity is exhausted, I would ask you, if you would not come and look at this new world;—but a new world only re-acted by old players is not much worth seeing; I shall return on Saturday. The Parliament is prorogued till the day it was to have met;[13] the will is not opened—what can I tell you more? Would it be news, that all is hopes and fears, and that great lords look as if they dreaded wanting bread? Would this be news? Believe me it all grows stale soon—I had not seen such a sight these three and thirty years:[14] I came eagerly to town; I laughed for three days, I am tired already. Good night!

Yours ever

H. W.

PS. I smiled to myself last night. Out of excess of attention, which costs me nothing, when I mean it should cost nobody else anything, I

8. He died 9 Dec. 1760; see HW to Mann 2 Jan. 1761.

9. Lt-Col. William Augustus Pitt (1728–1809), K.B., 1792; Gen., 1793 (DNB sub George Pitt); M.P. Wareham 1754–61; probably a friend of Charles Montagu.

10. Lt-Col. Edward Harvey (1718–78), 3d son of William Harvey of Chigwell, Essex; Maj.-Gen., 1763; Lt-Gen., 1772; Gov. of Portsmouth 1773–7; M.P. Gatton 1761–8; Harwich 1768–78 (Army Lists; Annual Register for 1778, xxi pt i. 225 [not 225*]; Philip Morant, History . . . of Essex, 1768, i. 167; G. F. Russell Barker, The Record of Old Westminsters, 1928, i. 433–4, Supplementary Volume, p. 71).

11. He took Schomberg House (post 31 Oct. 1760).

12. In Mayfair; reported in London Chronicle 30 Oct.–1 Nov. 1760, viii. 425; see post 31 Oct. 1760.

13. It would open on the same date (13 Nov.), but as a new session. At this time, a Parliament could exist for six months after the demise of the Sovereign. Until the time of William III it dissolved automatically when the King died (Josef Redlich, Procedure of the House of Commons, 1908, ii. 65–6).

14. Since George I died. HW was then at Eton and 'shed a flood of tears for that Sovereign's death, when with the other scholars at Eton College I walked in procession to the proclamation of the successor' (HW, Reminiscences, Oxford, 1924, p. 13).

went to Kensington to inquire after Princess Emily and Lady Yarmouth, nobody knew me, they asked my name—when they heard it, they did not seem ever to have heard it before, even in that house.[15] I waited half an hour in a lodge with a footman of Lady Yarmouth's: I would not have waited so long in her room a week ago—now it only diverted me. Even moralizing is entertaining, when one laughs at the same time; but I pity those who don't moralize till they cry!

From MONTAGU, ca Thursday 30 October 1760

G.D. 15/8, No. 748.

In reply to HW's letter of 25 Oct. 1760. Dated by London postmark.
Address: To the Honourable Mr Walpole, Arlington Street, London. Free.
Postmark: 31 OC.

[Greatworth, ca Oct. 30, 1760].

I CAN only thank you from this scene of tranquillity for your kind remembrance of me in this time of joy, and beg you will remember me in the day of your exaltation. I am glad to hear Mr Chute is well; pray my compliments to him. I expect to hear he is a suitor to the fair widow Brown. Do let me hear a little news as they occur in this bustle.

I am assuredly yours,

G. M.

To MONTAGU, Friday 31 October 1760

Arlington Street, Oct. 31st, 1760.

WHEN you have changed the cipher of George the II into that of George III, and have read the addresses,[1] and have shifted a few lords and grooms of the Bedchamber, you are master of the history of the new reign, which is indeed but a new lease of the old one. *The favourite*[2] took it up in a high style, but having, like my Lord Granville,[3] forgot to ensure either house of Parliament, or the mob,

15. Where Sir Robert Walpole had served George II and Queen Caroline.

1. The one Montagu was most likely to read was that of the City of London, delivered at Leicester House 30 Oct., and printed in *London Chronicle* 30 Oct.–1 Nov. 1760, viii. 425.
2. Bute.
3. In his attempt to form a ministry in 1746.

the third house of Parliament, he drove all the rest to unite. They have united, and have notified their resolution of governing as before. Not but the Duke of Newcastle,[4] cried for his old master, desponded for himself, protested he would retire, consulted everybody whose interest it was to advise him to stay, and has accepted today, thrusting the dregs of his ridiculous life into a young court, which will at least be saved from the imputation of childishness, by being governed by folly of seventy years' growth.

The young King has all the appearance of being amiable. There is great grace to temper much dignity, and extreme good-nature, which breaks out on all occasions. He has shown neither inveteracy nor malice—in short we must have gained—he cannot be so unfeeling, so avaricious, or so German as his grandfather.

Even the Household is not settled yet. The greatest difficulty is the Master of the Horse. Lord Huntingdon is so by all precedent.[5] Lord Gower I believe will be so, by that liberty of unreasonableness which the Duke of Bedford assumes, as heir of my Lord Russel.[6] Poor Lord Rochford[7] is undone: nobody is unreasonable to save him.

The Duke of Cumberland has taken Schomberg-house in Pall-mall;[8] Princess Emily is dealing for Sir Richard Lyttelton's in Cavendish Square.[9] People imagined the Duke of Devonshire had lent her Burlington House; I don't know why, unless they supposed that she was to succeed my Lady Burlington in *everything*.[10]

A week has finished my curiosity fully; I return to Strawberry tomorrow; and I fear go next week to Houghton, to make an appearance of civility to Lynn, whose favour I never asked, nor care if I have or not; but I don't know how to refuse this attention to my Lord Orford who begs it.

4. 'Poor thing!' (Mrs Piozzi).

5. He had held the post under George III when Prince of Wales. HW supposed that the Bedford group would insist on the retention of Lord Gower, George II's Master of the Horse. He, however, became Keeper of the Great Wardrobe to make way for Huntingdon (*post* 13 Nov. 1760).

6. William Russell (1639–83), styled Lord Russell; 'the patriot'; executed for complicity in the Rye House Plot, and one of HW's heroes (see COLE ii. 60).

7. He was pensioned and supplanted by Bute as Groom of the Stole; see *Mem. Geo. III* i. 10–11.

8. *London Chronicle* 28–30 Oct. 1760, viii. 419, notes that 'this day' the Duke of Cumberland 'will remove into the house he has taken in Pall Mall, lately inhabited by Lord Fitzwalter.' *London Past & Present* says that it was let to the Duke by Lord Holdernesse who acquired it on Schomberg's death.

9. She took it (GM 1760, xxx. 538).

10. The Duke of Devonshire acquired Burlington House through his marriage to Lady Burlington's daughter. If the italics imply a particular significance, it has not been discovered.

I trust you will have approved my behaviour at Court, that is, my mixing extreme politeness with extreme indifference. Our predecessors, the philosophers of ancient days, knew not how to be disinterested without brutality; I pique myself on founding a new sect. My followers are to tell kings with excess of attention that they don't want them, and to despise favour with more good breeding than others practice in suing for it. We are a thousand times a greater nation than the Grecians, why are we to imitate them? Our sense is as great, our follies greater; sure we have all the pretensions to superiority! Adieu!

Yours ever

H. W.

PS. As to the fair widow Brown, I assure you the devil never sowed £200,000 in a more fruitful soil: every guinea has taken root already. I saw her yesterday: it shall be some time before I see her again.

To Montagu, Tuesday 4 November 1760

Arlington Street, Nov. 4, 1760.

I AM not gone to Houghton you see; my Lord Orford is come to town, and I have persuaded him to stay and perform decencies.[1]

King George the II is dead richer than Sir Robert Brown, though perhaps not so rich as my Lord Hardwicke.[2] He has left fifty thousand pounds between the Duke, Emily and Mary; the Duke has given up his share. To Lady Yarmouth a cabinet with the contents; they call it eleven thousand pounds. By a German deed he gives the Duke to the value of £180,000 placed on mortgages, not immediately recoverable. He had once given him twice as much more; then revoked it, and at last excused the revocation, on the pretence of the expenses of the war; but owns that he was the best son that ever lived and had never

1. At court.
2. Contemporary accounts vary as to the details of the King's will, but are substantially in agreement with HW, except for Mrs Delany; she was at Bath, and her figures are much exaggerated (Delany, *Correspondence* iii. 609). There is also some divergence over the amount to be divided by the two Princesses and the Duke (see *Gray's Corr.* ii. 710–11; 'Lord Holland's Memoir,' *Life and Letters of Lady Sarah Lennox*, ed. Countess of Ilchester, 1901–2, i. 9–12; Emily J. Climenson, *Elizabeth Montagu the Queen of the Blue-stockings*, 1906, ii. 213–14. According to DNB, 'he died comparatively poor,' and the amount was £50,000.

offended him—a pretty strong comment on the affair of Closterseven! He gives him besides all his jewels in England—but had removed all the best to Hanover, which he makes crown jewels, and his successor residuary legatee. The Duke too has some uncounted cabinets. My Lady Suffolk has given me a particular of his jewels, which plainly amount to £150,000. It happened oddly to my Lady Suffolk. Two days before he died, she went to make a visit at Kensington, not knowing of the review;[3] she found herself hemmed in by coaches, and was close to him, whom she had not seen for so many years, and to my Lady Yarmouth; but they did not know her. It struck her, and has made her very sensible to his death.

The changes hang back. Nothing material has been altered yet. Ned Finch, the only thing my Lady Yarmouth told the new King she had to ask for, is made Surveyor of the Roads, in the room of Sir Harry Erskine, who is to have an old regiment.[4] He excuses himself from seeing company as favourite of the favourite. Arthur[5] is removed from being Clerk of the Wine-cellar, a sacrifice to morality: the Archbishop has such hopes of the young King, that he is never out of the circle. He trod upon the Duke's foot on Sunday in the haste of his zeal; the Duke said to him, 'My Lord, if your Grace is in such a hurry to make your court, that is the way.'[6] Bon mots come thicker than changes: Charles Townshend, receiving an account of the impression the King's death had made, was told Miss Chudleigh cried—'What?' said he, 'Oysters?'[7] And last night Mr Dawnay[8] asking George Selwyn if Princess Emily would have a guard? he replied, 'Now and then one, I suppose.'

An extraordinary event has happened today; George Townshend sent a challenge to Lord Albemarle, desiring him to be with a second in the fields. Lord Albemarle took Colonel Crauford and went to

3. *Ante* 25 Oct. 1760, n. 4.

4. Sir Henry Erskine (d. 1765), 5th Bt (DNB), a favourite of Bute's, was now made a Major-General and given the command of the 67th Foot (*Army Lists*), thus restoring him to the rank he had lost by his dismissal from the army (as a Colonel) for 'opposing *in Parliament* the importation of the Hanoverians and Hessians in 1756' (*London Chronicle* 13 Nov. 1760, viii. 472).

5. Robert Arthur (d. 1761), proprietor of White's Club 1736–55 (see [W. B. Boulton], *History of White's*, 1892, *passim*).

6. Gray tells the same story, and adds that the Duke pointed to the King and then to the Count de Fuentes, the Spanish ambassador (*Gray's Corr.* ii. 711).

7. Oyster-women, who generally were coarse slatterns, were familiar figures on London streets; see Andrew W. Tuer, *Old London Street Cries*, 1885, pp. 15, 90; Charles Hindley, *History of the Cries of London*, 2d edn, *passim*.

8. Probably Hon. John Dawnay (1728–80), 4th Vct Downe, 9 Dec. 1760.

Marybone. George Townshend bespoke Lord Buckingham, who loves a secret too well not to tell it; he communicated it to Stanley, who went to St James's, and acquainted Mr Caswall[9] the captain on guard. The latter took a hackney coach, drove to Marybone, and saw one pair. After waiting ten minutes, the others came: Townshend made an apology to Lord Albemarle for making him wait—'Oh!' said he, 'men of spirit don't want apologies—come, let us begin what we came for'—at that instant, out steps Caswall from his coach, and begs their pardon, as his superior officers, but told them they were his prisoners; he desired Mr Townshend and Lord Buckingham to return in their coach; he would carry back Lord Albemarle and Crauford in his. He did, and went to acquaint the King, who has commissioned some of the matrons of the army, to examine the affair and make it up. All this while, I don't know what the quarrel was—but they hated one another so much on the Duke's account,[10] that a slight word would easily make their aversions boil over.

Don't you, nor even your General come to town on this occasion? Good night!

Yours ever

H. W.

From MONTAGU, ca Sunday 9 November 1760

G.D. 15/8, No. 749.
In reply to *ante* 28 Oct. 1760; dated by the postmark.
Address: <To> the Honourable Mr Walpole, Arlington <Stre>et, London. Free. *Postmark:* 10 NO.

[Greatworth, ca Nov. 9, 1760].

THE chief business of my letter is to beg mine and Charles' pardon for troubling you with his letters and to tell you how happy yours make me, who never desire to come to town to know how things go on, while you are so good as to relate them so agreeably.

9. Capt. Timothy Caswall (d. 1802), of Sacombe Park, Herts; Lt in the Coldstream Guards, 1756; M.P. Hertford 1761–8; Brackley, 1771–90; Commissioner of Excise, 1789 (GM 1802, lxxii pt ii. 880; *Army Lists;* COLE ii. 1).

10. Townshend had caricatured the Duke, whose aide-de-camp Albemarle was. The immediate cause of the duel was Townshend's resentment over a pamphlet condemning his conduct at Quebec (see *Mem. Geo. III* i. 17–18).

Lord Charles Spencer,[1] who we here thought sure of being accepted as representative for the county of Oxford, has been rejected by the clamours of two hot parsons of colleges and two tradesmen near Reading, and Lord Abingdon[2] will support Sir James Dashwood,[3] and promised to turn out a bag fox at their next meeting. To join him the peaceable ones were forced to subscribe to support this interest. You make kings and ministers while we support the Pretender and High Church after they are gone mad and turned Methodist.

I am pleased to hear how well you are come off from your presentation, and that you remain the last of the Romans. I shall for many other reasons remain to my last yours most assuredly,

G. MONTAGU

TO MONTAGU, Thursday 13 November 1760

Arlington Street, Nov. 13th, 1760.

EVEN the honeymoon of a new reign don't produce events every day. There is nothing but the common toying of addresses and kissing hands. The chief difficulty is settled; Lord Gower yields the Mastership of the Horse to Lord Huntingdon, and removes to the Great Wardrobe, from whence Sir Thomas Robinson was to have gone into Ellis's place, but he is saved, and Sir Thomas remains as lumber, not yet disposed of.[1] The City however have a mind to be out of humour; a paper has been fixed on the Royal Exchange with these words, 'No petticoat government, no Scotch minister, no Lord George Sackville.'[2] Two hints totally unfounded, and the other scarce

1. Lord Charles Spencer (1740–1820), politician. He was returned unopposed for Oxfordshire as a result of a compromise, the terms of which are suggested in Lewis B. Namier, *Structure of Politics at the Accession of George III*, 1929, ii. 384.
2. Willoughby Bertie (1740–99), 4th E. of Abingdon.
3. Sir James Dashwood (1715–1779), 2d Bt of Kirtlington Park, Oxfordshire; M.P. Oxfordshire 1740–54, 1761–8; see William R. Williams, *Parliamentary History of the County of Oxford*, Brecknock, 1899, p. 75. He was also returned in 1761 without a contest.

1. Ellis was Joint Vice-Treasurer of Ireland, 'a place much above his pretensions'; but Newcastle would not remove him ('Lord Holland's Memoir,' *Life and Letters of Lady Sarah Lennox*, ed. Countess of Ilchester, 1901–2, i. 15). Sir Thomas Robinson was given a pension and a peerage.
2. 'So soon! I had forgotten it' (Mrs Piozzi). 'I hear that Lord George Sackville has been at court, and that the King was civil to him . . . which has, I find, already created a clamour' (Henry Jenkinson to George Grenville, Nov. 1760, *Grenville Papers*, ed. William J. Smith, 1852–3, i. 357); see also Emily J. Climenson, *Eliza-*

true. No petticoat ever governed less; it is left at Leicester-house; Lord George's breeches are as little concerned; and except Lady Susan Stuart,[3] and Sir Harry Erskine, nothing has yet been done for any Scots. For the King himself he seems all good-nature, and wishing to satisfy everybody. All his speeches are obliging. I saw him again yesterday, and was surprised to find the levee room had lost so entirely the air of the lion's den. This young man don't stand in one spot, with his eyes fixed royally on the ground, and dropping bits of German news. He walks about and speaks to everybody. I saw him afterwards on the throne, where he is graceful and genteel, sits with dignity, and reads his answers to addresses well. It was the Cambridge address, carried by the Duke of Newcastle in his Doctor's gown, and looking like the *médecin malgré lui*. He had been vehemently solicitous for attendance, for fear my Lord Westmorland, who vouchsafes himself to bring the address from Oxford, should outnumber him.[4] Lord Litchfield[5] and several other Jacobites have kissed hands; George Selwyn says they go to St James's, because now there are so many *Stuarts* there.[6]

Do you know I had the curiosity to go to the burying t'other night;[7] I had never seen a royal funeral. Nay, I walked as a rag of quality,[8] which I found would be, and so it was, the easiest way of seeing it. It is absolutely a noble sight. The Prince's Chamber[9] hung with purple and a quantity of silver lamps, the coffin under a canopy of purple velvet, and six vast chandeliers of silver on high stands had a very good effect: the ambassador from Tripoli[10] and his son were carried to see that chamber. The procession through a line of foot-guards, every seventh man bearing a torch, the horse-guards lin-

beth Montagu the Queen of the Blue-stockings, 1906, ii. 216, reporting that placards had also appeared on all the palaces demanding 'A Pittical administration.'

3. Lady Susanna Stewart (ca 1745–1805), m. (1768) Granville Leveson-Gower, 2d E. Gower, cr. (1786) M. of Stafford. She was made Lady-in-Waiting to Princess Augusta.

4. Though the Oxford address was presented by the Vice-Chancellor rather than by Lord Westmorland, the Chancellor, the attendant dignitaries seem to have outdone Cambridge by at least one bishop and a number of peers (see GM 1760, xxx. 512–13).

5. George Henry Lee (1718–72), 3d E. of Lichfield; a thoroughgoing Tory.

6. Lord Bute's family name.

7. 11 Nov.

8. I.e., as an earl's younger son.

9. Near the House of Peers.

10. Hussem Bey (*Court and City Register* for 1761, p. 108). In *London Chronicle* 18 Nov. 1760, viii. 487, is a letter purporting to be to him and his son; it calls them Mum Faz and Zing Zagg. His difficulty at assemblies because of his lack of English is noted in Count Frederick Kielmansegge, *Diary of a Journey to England . . . 1761–1762*, 1902, pp. 144–5, 236.

ing the outside, their officers with drawn sabres and crape sashes, on horseback, the drums muffled, the fifes, bells tolling and minute guns, all this was very solemn. But the charm was the entrance of the Abbey, where we were received by the Dean[11] and chapter in rich copes, the choir and almsmen all bearing torches; the whole Abbey so illuminated, that one saw it to greater advantage than by day; the tombs, long aisles, and fretted roof[12] all appearing distinctly, and with the happiest chiaroscuro. There wanted nothing but incense, and little chapels here and there with priests saying mass for the repose of the defunct—yet one could not complain of its not being Catholic enough. I had been in dread of being coupled with some boy of ten years old—but the heralds were not very accurate, and I walked with George Grenville,[13] taller and older enough to keep me in countenance. When we came to the chapel of Henry VII all solemnity and decorum ceased—no order was observed, people sat or stood where they could or would, the yeomen of the guard were crying out for help, oppressed by the immense weight of the coffin, the Bishop read sadly, and blundered in the prayers, the fine chapter, *Man that is born of a woman*,[14] was chanted not read, and the anthem,[15] besides being unmeasurably tedious, would have served as well for a nuptial. The real serious part was the figure of the Duke of Cumberland, heightened by a thousand melancholy circumstances. He had a dark brown adonis,[16] and a cloak of black cloth with a train of five yards. Attending the funeral of a father, how little reason soever he had to love him, could not be pleasant. His leg extremely bad, yet forced to stand upon it near two hours, his face bloated and distorted with his late paralytic stroke, which has affected too one of his eyes, and placed over[16a] the mouth of the vault, into which in all probability he must himself so soon descend—think how unpleasant a situation! He bore it all with a firm and unaffected countenance. This grave scene was

---

11. Zachary Pearce (1690–1774), Bp of Bangor, 1748; of Rochester, 1756; Dean of Westminster, 1756.

12. Doubtless an unconscious echo of Gray's 'long-drawn aisle and fretted vault,' a line which may have been inspired by HW's 'Verses in Memory of King Henry the Sixth'; see *Horace Walpole's Fugitive Verses*, ed. W. S. Lewis, New York, 1931, pp. 4–5.

13. It is not clear why this is inaccurate. HW would walk with 'earls' younger sons'; Grenville's mother was a Countess in her own right, created a few years after Sir Robert; so Grenville (a younger son) and HW would presumably be of nearly equal dignity; see the order of the procession in GM 1760, xxx. 539.

14. Job xiv.

15. By William Boyce (GM 1760, xxx. 621).

16. A kind of wig.

16a. 'Over' has been substituted for 'himself at' by HW.

fully contrasted by the burlesque Duke of Newcastle—he fell into a fit of crying the moment he came into the chapel and flung himself back in a stall, the Archbishop hovering over him with a smelling bottle—but in two minutes his curiosity got the better of his hypocrisy[17] and he ran about the chapel with his glass to spy who was or was not there, spying with one hand and mopping his eyes with t'other. Then returned the fear of catching cold, and the Duke of Cumberland, who was sinking with heat, felt himself weighed down, and turning round, found it was the Duke of Newcastle standing upon his train to avoid the chill of the marble. It was very theatric to look down into the vault, where the coffin lay,[18] attended by mourners with lights. Clavering,[19] the Groom of the Bedchamber, refused to sit up with the body, and was dismissed by the King's order.[19a]

I have nothing more to tell you but a trifle, a very trifle—the King of Prussia has totally defeated Marshal Daun.[20] This which would have been prodigious news a month ago, is nothing today; it only takes its turn among the questions, 'Who is to be Groom of the Bedchamber?' 'What is Sir T. Robinson to have?' I have been at Leicester Fields[21] today; the crowd was immoderate; I don't believe it will continue so. Good night.

Yours ever

H. W.

To Montagu, Thursday 13 November 1760 *bis*

It is not entirely clear whether this letter was written 13 or 20 November. Its informality and the fact that it is a postscript, without a full date, suggest that it was written in the evening of the same day as the preceding letter, during which HW had heard nothing more of the Prussian victory. The full account of the victory appears in *London Chronicle* 20–22 Nov., dated from Norwich 19 Nov., and had this letter been written on the 20th, HW would doubtless have mentioned it. The fact that the Bedchamber appointments were not printed in *London Chron-*

17. 'Not hypocrisy at all' (Mrs Piozzi).
18. HW states that George II had requested 'that the side of the late Queen's coffin, left loose on purpose, might be taken away and his body laid close to hers' (*Mem. Geo. III* i. 7). Cunningham notes (iii. 362) that when the vault was opened in 1837 the sides of the coffins were found open.
19. John Clavering (d. 1762), 'a relative

of Sir Thomas Clavering, Bt, of Axwell Park, Durham' (*Mem. Geo. III* i. 7 n).
19a. 'So he ought to be. What a whim!' (Mrs Piozzi).
20. Leopold Joseph Maria, Graf von Daun (1705–66), Austrian field marshal. He was defeated at Torgau in Saxony, 3 Nov. 1760 (Constant von Wurzbach, *Biographisches Lexikon,* Wien, 1856–90).
21. Leicester House.

icle until 25–7 Nov. is not material, since it was frequently late with such announcements (cf. the announcement of Erskine's appointment 12–14 Nov., although HW speaks of it *ante* 31 Oct.).

Arlington Street, Thursday [Nov. 13, 1760].

AS a codicil to my last letter, I send you the Bedchamber: there are to be eighteen Lords and thirteen Grooms. All the late King's remain, but your cousin Manchester, Lord Falconberg,[1] Lord Essex,[2] and Lord Hyndford,[3] replaced by the Duke of Richmond, Lord Weymouth, Lord March and Lord Eglinton;[4] the last at the earnest request of the Duke of York.[4a] Instead of Clavering, Nassau,[5] and General Campbell,[5a] who is promised something else, Lord Northampton's brother[6] and Commodore Keppel are Grooms. When it was offered to the Duke of Richmond, he said, he could not accept it, unless something was done for Colonel Keppel, for whom he had interested himself; that it would look like sacrificing Keppel to his own views: this was handsome.[7] Keppel is to be Equerry.

Princess Emily goes everywhere, as she calls it; she was on Monday at Lady Holderness's, and next Monday is to be at Bedford House; but there is only the late King's set, and the court of Bedford: so she makes the houses of other people as trist as St James's was. Good night.

Not a word of the King of Prussia: did you ever know a victory mind the wind so?

1. Thomas Belasyse (1699–1774), 4th Vct Fauconberg; cr. (1756) E. Fauconberg.

2. William Anne Holles Capel (1732–99), 4th E. of Essex. He was removed 'through the Princess' pique to him about the ground she rents of him at Kew (wherein he behaved sillily, she says dirtily)' ('Lord Holland's Memoir,' *Life and Letters of Lady Sarah Lennox*, ed. Countess of Ilchester, 1901–2, i. 16).

3. John Carmichael (1701–67), 3d E. of Hyndford, 'removed from the fear Lord Bute has of employing too many Scotch' (loc. cit.).

4. Alexander Montgomerie (1723–69), 10th E. of Eglintoun. 'Everybody was ashamed and vexed to see so worthless and silly a wretch so placed' (ibid. i. 17). From the accounts of him in DNB and in *Douglas's Peerage of Scotland*, ed. John P. Wood, 1813, i. 506–7, Lord Holland's criticism seems unjustified. But Professor Pottle says that Boswell, who had at an earlier period set Eglintoun up as a model, keeps reminding himself in his European memoranda to 'shun being Eglintoun,' 'swear not Eglint.,' 'not to be Eglint.,' etc.

4a. Boswell's unpublished notes, according to Professor Pottle, show that Eglintoun led the Duke into a life of pleasure; see also *Diary of George Ridpath*, ed. Sir James Balfour Paul, Edinburgh, 1922, p. 366 (Scottish Historical Society, III. ii).

5. No one of this name appears in the lists of bedchamber functionaries in the closing years of George II's reign. Possibly Hon. Richard Savage Nassau (1723–80), son of 3d E. of Rochford; M.P. Colchester 1747–54; Maldon 1774–80; see Collins, *Peerage*, 1812, iii. 725.

5a. *Post* 16 April 1761, n. 16.

6. Spencer Compton (1738–96), 8th E. of Northampton, 1763.

7. See *post* 11 Dec. 1760.

To Montagu, Monday 24 November 1760

Address: To George Montagu Esq. at Greatworth near Brackley, Northamptonshire. Free Hor. Walpole.
Postmark: 27 NO; IO (which probably stands for Inland Office).

Strawberry Hill, Monday Nov. 24, 1760.

UNLESS I were to send you journals, lists, catalogues, computations of the bodies, tides, swarms of people that go to Court to present addresses or to be presented, I can tell you nothing new. The day the King went to the House,[1] I was three quarters of an hour getting through Whitehall: there were subjects enough to set up half a dozen petty kings. The Pretender would be proud to reign over the footmen only—and indeed unless he acquires some of them, he will have no subjects left: all their masters flock to St James's. The palace is so thronged, that I will stay till some people are discontented. The first night the King went to the play,[2] which was civilly on a Friday, not on the opera night as he used to do, the whole audience sung *God save the King* in chorus. For the first act, the press was so great at the door, that no ladies could get to the boxes; and only the servants appeared there who kept places. At the end of the second the whole mob broke in and seated themselves. Yet all this zeal is not likely to last, though he so well deserves it. Seditious papers are again stuck up: one t'other day in Westminster Hall declared against a Saxe-Gothan princess. The Archbishop, who is never out of the drawing-room, has great hopes from the King's goodness that he shall make something of him—that is something bad of him. On the address Pitt and his zany Beckford quarreled on the latter's calling the campaign languid.[3] What is become of our *magnanimous ally*[4] and his victory I

1. 19 Nov. 'It was remarked by many old people yesterday, who were to see his Majesty go to the House, that there never was so great a crowd of people, of almost all ranks, both in the park, and in the houses, on any similar occasion. Nor ever did the people appear so unanimous in testifying their applause. His Majesty was pleased to express his satisfaction both in his countenance and behaviour, bowing from each window several times as he passed along' (*London Chronicle* 18–20 Nov. 1760, viii. 490).

2. 22 Nov. 'Yesterday his Majesty went to Drury Lane theatre, to see the tragedy of King Richard III. The house was filled before three o'clock, to the great disappointment of a prodigious number of genteel company, who came there expecting to get in at the usual hour for opening the house' (ibid. 20–22 Nov. 1760, viii. 502).

3. See *Mem. Geo. III* i. 18.

4. Frederick of Prussia. HW's emphasis of 'magnanimous' is apparently a standing joke referring to Lord Lyttelton's pompous manner of speech. See HW to Lady

know not. In eleven days no courier was arrived from him; but I have been here these two days, perfectly indifferent about his magnanimity. I am come to put my *Anecdotes of Painting* into the press. You are one of the few that I expect will be entertained with it. It has warmed Gray's coldness so much that he is violent about it[5]—in truth there is an infinite quantity of new and curious things in it; but as it is quite foreign from all popular topics, I don't suppose it will be much attended to. There is not a word of Methodism in it, it says nothing of the disturbances in Ireland, it does not propose to keep all Canada, it neither flatters the King of Prussia nor Prince Ferdinand, it does not say that the City of London are the wisest set of men in the world, it is silent about George Townshend, and does not abuse my Lord George Sackville—how should it please? I want you to help me in a little affair that regards it. I have found in a MS. that in the church of Beckley or Becksley, in Sussex, there are portraits on glass in a window of Henry III and his Queen.[6] I have looked in the map and find the first name between Bodiham and Rye, but I am not sure it is the place.[7] I will be much obliged to you if you will write directly to your Sir Whistler[8] and beg him to inform himself very exactly if there is any such thing in such a church near Bodiham. Pray state it minutely, because if there is, I will have them drawn for the frontispiece to my work.[9]

Did I tell you that the Archbishop tried to hinder *The Minor*[10] from being played at Drury Lane? For once the Duke of Devonshire was firm, and would only let him correct some passages, and even of

Mary Coke ? Nov. 1771 and to Lady Ailesbury 31 July 1762 where he uses the word in stilted passages which, he asserts, are in Lyttelton's style.

5. Gray assisted HW materially in his editing of the *Anecdotes;* see Gray to HW 2 Sept. 1760 and ca 28 Oct. 1760.

6. Henry III (1207–72), m. (1236) Eleanor of Provence (d. 1291).

7. The window HW wanted was at Beckley, now Bexhill, 5 miles SW of Hastings. Lord Ashburnham presented the window to HW in 1771, who put it in the chapel in the garden at SH (*Works* ii. 508; Cole i. 244). In 1890 it was at Hardwick House, Bury St Edmunds (N&Q 1890, 7th ser. ix. 276); it is now restored to St Peter's Church, Bexhill, through the will of G. G.

M. G. Cullum, whose grandfather bought it SH xxiv. 84 (N&Q 1938, clxxv. 421).

8. Sir Whistler Webster (ca 1690–1779), 2d Bt, of Battle Abbey, Sussex. Possibly Montagu had made his acquaintance while visiting at Lord Halifax's at Hawkhurst, nearby in Kent (*ante* 23 June 1750).

9. As he did, to vol. i.

10. A comedy by Samuel Foote, which satirised Whitefield and the Methodists. After an unsuccessful Dublin run early in the year, it opened at the Haymarket 28 June 1760, and produced a storm of pamphlets and discussion. Lady Huntingdon, the leading Methodist, applied without success to the Duke of Devonshire to have it suppressed for the winter season; see Mary M. Belden, *Dramatic Work of Samuel Foote,* New Haven, 1929, pp. 81–106.

HENRY the THIRD and ELEANOR of Provence his Queen. Brought from Bexhill Church in Sussex. The only Portraits of them extant.

HENRY THE THIRD AND HIS QUEEN

those the Duke has restored some.[11] One that the prelate effaced, was, 'You snub-nosed son of a bitch.' . . .[12] Foote says he will take out a license to preach, Sam. Cant against Tom Cant.[13]

The first volume of Voltaire's *Peter the Great*[14] is arrived. I weep over it! It is as languid as the campaign; he is grown old. He boasts of the materials communicated to him by the Czarina's order[15]—but alas! he need not be proud of them. They only serve to show how much worse he writes history with materials than without. Besides, it is evident how much that authority has cramped his genius. I had heard before, that when he sent the work to Petersburg for imperial approbation, it was returned, with orders to increase the panegyric. I wish he had acted like a very inferior author: Knyphausen[16] once hinted to me that I might have some authentic papers, if I was disposed to write the life of his master[17]—but I did not care for what would lay me under such restrictions. It is not fair to use weapons against the persons that lend them—and I do not admire his master enough to commend anything in him but his military actions. Adieu!

Yours ever

H. W.

11. The Duke's version of the story is slightly different; in a letter to Garrick, 25 Oct. 1760, the Duke writes, 'I had a long conversation with his Grace, who would have authorized me to have used his name to stop "The Minor," but I got off from it, and concluded with sending a recommendation by Mr Pelham to the author, to alter those passages that are liable to objection; his Grace would not point them out, so I think very little alteration may do' (*Private Correspondence of David Garrick*, [ed. James Boaden] 1831–2, i. 120; the editor adds that Secker's reason for refusing to make any alterations himself was that if he did Foote would publish the play as 'corrected and prepared for the press by His Grace the Archbishop of Canterbury'). 'On Saturday night [22 Nov.] the Minor was performed at Drury Lane to a crowded audience. The late clamour against many expressions in it, said to be profane, occasioned, it was observed, several alterations; among which Mr Foote, in Mrs Cole, instead of saying "regeneration is not the work of a day," said "reformation;" for, "I had been a lost sheep,"

said "lost woman;" and instead of "got me with a new birth and I became regenerate, and another creature," said to this purport, "washed me with the soap-suds and scouring sand of the Tabernacle, and I became as clean and bright as a pewter-platter"' (*London Chronicle* 22–5 Nov. 1760, viii. 507).

12. A line has been scored out in the MS, apparently by HW.

13. As Archbishop of Canterbury, Thomas Secker's signature was of course Thomas Cantuar., or further abbreviated, Cant.

14. *Histoire de l'Empire de Russie sous Pierre le Grand*, 2 vols [Geneva], 1759–63.

15. p. vi.

16. Dodo Heinrich, Baron von Knyphausen (1729–89), Prussian Ambassador to England 1758–63 (*Allgemeine Deutsche Biographie*, Leipzig, 1875–1912, xvi. 341–2; Earl of Chesterfield, *Letters*, ed. Bonamy Dobrée, 1932, v. 2294).

17. Knyphausen's thought of HW as a desirable English biographer of Frederick the Great may have been inspired by HW's *Catalogue of Royal and Noble Authors*.

From MONTAGU, ca Sunday 30 November 1760

G.D. 15/8, No. 750.
In reply to *ante* 24 Nov. 1760; date of month conjectural.

[Greatworth, ca Nov. 30, 1760].

I HAVE this very post wrote to my little baronet to Battle Abbey,[1] and as soon as I receive his answer you shall have it.

I am delighted to hear you are so well pleased with your *Anecdotes,* for I think you more difficult about your own work than Gray can be about anyone's.

I am sorry to hear of pasquinades already but really I am so surfeited with your fulsome parliamentary addresses that I stand in need of a bit of lemon to put my mouth [?in] taste. If I had an inclination to come to town I should postpone my journey till the mal-aria was passed.

I am charming well and ride about all morning for I have no books to read nor can I read long as I used to do.

I wish you your health and am always most faithfully yours,

G. MONTAGU

Be so good as to put your name to Charles's letter.

To MONTAGU, Thursday 11 December 1760

Address: To George Montagu Esq. at Greatworth near Brackley, Northamptonshire. Free Hor. Walpole. *Postmark:* 11 DE.

Arlington Street, Dec. 11th, 1760.

I THANK you for the inquiries about the painted glass, and shall be glad if I prove to be in the right.

There is not much of new to tell you; and yet there is much dissatisfaction. The Duke of Newcastle has threatened to resign on the appointment of Lord Oxford[1] and Lord Bruce[2] without his knowledge. His court rave about Tories, which you know comes with a sin-

1. Sir Whistler Webster.
———
1. Edward Harley (1726–90), 4th E. of Oxford.

2. Thomas Bruce Bruce-Brudenell (later Brudenell-Bruce) (1729–1814), 2d Bn Bruce; cr. (1776) E. of Ailesbury. He and Lord Oxford were made Lords of the Bedcham-

gular grace from them, as the Duke never preferred any—Murray,[3] Lord Gower,[4] Sir John Cotton,[5] Jack Pitt[6] etc. etc. etc. were all firm Whigs. But it is unpardonable to put an end to all faction, when it is not for factious purposes. Lord Fitzmaurice[7] made aide-de-camp to the King has disgusted the army; the Duke of Richmond whose brother[8] has no more been put over others than the Duke of Newcastle has preferred Tories, has presented a warm memorial in a warmer manner, and has resigned the Bedchamber, not his regiment —another propriety.

Propriety is so much in fashion, that Miss Chudleigh has called for the council-books of the subscription-concert, and has struck out the name of Mrs Naylor[9]—I have some thoughts of remonstrating that General Waldegrave is too *lean* to be a Groom of the Bedchamber.[10]

ber; Newcastle considered them Tories; see Lewis B. Namier, *England in the Age of the American Revolution*, 1930, pp. 153–4.

3. William Murray, Lord Mansfield, came of a Jacobite family; HW always had somewhat exaggerated suspicions of his loyalty; see *Mem. Geo. II* i. 303–32; HW to Lady Ossory 13 June 1782.

4. His family led the Staffordshire Tories (*ante* 13 June 1751, n. 3).

5. Sir John Hinde Cotton (ca 1688–1752), 3d Bt, of Madingley Hall, Cambs; M.P. Cambridge 1708–22, 1727–41; Cambridgeshire 1722–7; Marlborough 1741–52; a staunch Tory, but held a place in the Household for two years in the '40s (*Mem. Geo. II* i. 33).

6. Also a Tory; see Lewis B. Namier, *England in the Age of the American Revolution*, 1930, p. 488.

7. William Petty (1737–1805), styled Vct Fitzmaurice; 2d E. of Shelburne, 1761; cr. (1784) M. of Lansdowne; Prime Minister 1782–3. His appointment disgusted the army because he was 'put over the head of Lord George Lennox, Mr Fitzroy, and also of almost all the American officers' (i.e. those who had served in America; Gray to Mason 10 Dec. 1760, *Gray's Corr.* ii. 716). He was also promoted to a colonelcy after the battle of Kloster Kampen, while Lord George Lennox, who had served with equal distinction in that battle, was not. But, as HW suggests, Lord George 'had been put over the heads of a

hundred' ('Lord Holland's Memoir,' in *Life and Letters of Lady Sarah Lennox*, ed. Countess of Ilchester, 1901–2, i. 21). The Duke of Richmond nevertheless resigned in protest from his Lordship of the Bedchamber, which he had only acquired after composing another quarrel with the King and Bute. The several accounts of this incident agree substantially with HW's; see 'Lord Holland's Memoir,' 21–4; *Mem. Geo. III* i. 19–21; Mary Lepell, Lady Hervey, *Letters*, 1821, p. 274; *Diary of . . . George Bubb Dodington*, ed. Henry P. Wyndham, Dublin, 1784, pp. 284–5; but cf. Newcastle's justification of his action, ibid. 343–6.

8. Lord George Lennox.

9. It is probable that HW's language here is not to be taken literally, and that he alludes to a comparably stringent measure George II had twice taken. See HW to Mann 9 Nov. 1762: 'the King in Council called for the Council book, and ordered the Duke's [Duke of Devonshire] name to be struck out of it:—a proceeding almost novel, having never happened but to Lord Bath and Lord George Sackville.' Cf. *Mem. Geo. II* iii. 273.

10. Gen. Waldegrave, like HW, was excessively thin (*ante* 28 Oct. 1760). For HW to object to him as too lean would be as ridiculous as was the notorious Miss Chudleigh's objection to Mrs Naylor's morals, about which see HW to Mann 2 April 1750.

Mr Chute has sold his house[11] to Miss Speed[12] for £3000 and has taken one for a year in Berkeley Square.

This is a very brief letter; I fear this reign will soon furnish longer! When the last King could be beloved, a young man with a good heart has little chance of being so. Moreover, I have a maxim, that *the extinction of party is the origin of faction*. Good night.

Yours ever

H. W.

To Montagu, Wednesday 7 January 1761

Misdated by HW.
Address: To George Montagu Esq. at Greatworth near Brackley, Northamptonshire. Free Hor. Walpole. *Postmark:* 8 IA IO.

Arlington Street, Jan. 7th, 1760 [1761].

YOU must not wonder I have not writ to you a long time; a person of my consequence!—I am now almost ready to say *we* instead of *I*. In short, I live amidst royalty—considering the plenty, that is no great wonder. All the world lives with them and they with all the world. Princes and princesses open shops[1] in every corner of the town, and the whole town deals with them. As I have gone to one, I chose to frequent all, that I might not be particular, and seem to have views; and yet it went so much against me, that I came to town on purpose a month ago for the Duke's levee, and had engaged Brand to go with me—and then could not bring myself to it. At last, I went to him[2] and Princess Emily yesterday. It was well I had not flattered myself with being still in my bloom; I am grown so old since they saw me,[3] that neither of them knew me. When they were told, he just

---

11. HW to Chute 4 Nov. 1759 is addressed to 'Tilney Street, near Lord Chesterfield's.'

12. Henrietta Jane Speed (1728–83), m. (1761) Francesco Maria Giuseppe Giustino, Barone di La Perrière; Conte di Viry, 1766. She was a friend of Gray, and a protégée of Viscountess Cobham, from whom she inherited a fortune in 1760; see *Gray's Corr.* i. 331–2; *Harcourt Papers*, ed. Ed-

ward W. Harcourt, Oxford, n.d., viii. 1–3; du Deffand iii. 360 and *passim*.

---

1. Their levees.

2. The Duke of Cumberland.

3. Apparently HW had not seen the Duke since he called at SH (HW to Bentley 2 March 1754), nor the Princess since she called there (HW to Bentley 10 June 1755).

spoke to me, (I forgive him, he is not out of my debt even with that[4])
she was exceedingly gracious, and commended Strawberry to the
skies.[5] Tonight I was asked to their party at Norfolk House. These
parties are wonderfully select and dignified: one might sooner be a
Knight of Malta[6] than qualified for them; I don't know how the
Duchess of Devonshire, Mr Fox and I were forgiven some of our ancestors.[7] There were two tables at loo, two at whisk and a quadrille.
I was commanded to the Duke's loo; he was set down; not to make
him wait, I threw my hat upon the marble table, and broke four
pieces off a great crystal chandelier. I stick to my etiquette, and treat
them with great respect, not as I do my friend the Duke of York—but
don't let us talk any more of princes—my Lucan[8] appears tomorrow;
I must say it is a noble volume.[9] Shall I send it you, or won't you
come and fetch it?

There is nothing new of public, but the violent commotions in
Ireland, whither the Duke of Bedford still persists in going, Æolus
to quell a storm.[10]

I am in great concern for my old friend, poor Lady Harry Beauclerc;[11] her Lord dropped down dead two nights ago, as he was sitting

4. Possibly because of some undisclosed
favour HW performed for him.

5. She had apparently not done so on
the occasion of her visit there (HW to
Bentley 10 June 1755). The present en-
counter marks the beginning of HW's intimacy with her; see HW to Mann 29 May
1786.

6. Rigid evidence of noble ancestry was
required for admission to the Knights of
Malta; see Whitworth Porter, *History of
the Knights of Malta*, 1883, p. 158.

7. The Duchess of Devonshire was the
daughter of 'John Hoskins of Oxted, Surrey, Steward to the Duke of Bedford' (GEC).
Henry Fox's father, Sir Stephen Fox, was
thought to have been a footman (HW to
Mann 29 May 1744). Actually, after serving
as page to Lord Sunderland, he was put
in charge of Prince Charles's stables and
hounds in 1646 (Earl of Ilchester, *Henry
Fox, First Lord Holland*, 1920, i. 6). HW
was probably thinking of his own grandfather Shorter, who was a timber merchant
(HW to Mason 13 April 1782).

8. *M. Annæi Lucani Pharsalia cum
notis Hugonis Grotii, et Richardi Bentleii*,
Strawberry Hill, 1760; prepared for the

press by HW and Bentley (see HW to
Mason 30 Jan. 1780; *Journal of the Printing Office* 38–9). Montagu's copy, with his
autograph and book-plate, is in the Mer-
ritt Collection, Harvard College Library.

9. It is the most ambitious, typographi-
cally, of all the SH volumes.

10. The commotion arose from a dispute
over the relation between Poyning's Law,
which required approval by the English
Privy Council of Irish legislation, and
Irish money bills, which the Irish insisted
did not have to be sent over to England;
see *Mem. Geo. III* i. 23–5; William E. H.
Lecky, *History of Ireland in the Eighteenth Century*, edn 1892, ii. 60–2. The
Duke of Bedford resigned his Lord-Lieu-
tenantcy and did not return to Ireland.

11. Hon. Martha Lovelace (d. 1788), sister and heir of 6th Bn Lovelace; m. (1739)
Lord Henry Beauclerk; they had one son
and six daughters (Collins, *Peerage*, 1812,
i. 248). She got a pension of £400 a year
on the Irish establishment (*Gray's Corr.* ii.
721–2). HW wrote verses to her in 1736
on the death of her brother (see *Horace
Walpole's Fugitive Verses*, ed. W. S. Lewis,
New York, 1931, pp. 103–5).

with her and all their children. Admiral Boscawen is dead by this time[12]—Mrs Osborn[13] and I are not much afflicted. Lady Jane Coke[14] too is dead, exceedingly rich; I have not heard her will yet.

If you don't come to town soon, I give you warning, I will be a Lord of the Bedchamber or a gentleman-usher—if you will, I will be nothing but what I have been so many years, my own and

Yours ever

H. Walpole

From Montagu, Sunday 11 January 1761

G.D. 15/8, No. 751.

Greatworth, Jan. 11, 1761.

I SHALL come to town the beginning of February and propose much pleasure in seeing you and your Lucan. As to your royalties, I shall content myself with their births and marriages as Mr Baldwin sets them out in his almanac.[1]

What became of your Christmas party?[2] The General my brother does not leave Dublin till the summer. You know he has got a new old regiment and so will not be broke when the Empresses put up their swords.[3] I have been reading Mlle Montpensier's *Mémoires* with

12. He d. 10 Jan. (GM 1761, xxxi. 44).

13. Hon. Sarah Byng (1693–1775), m. (1710) John Osborn (d. 1719), son of Sir John Osborn, 2d Bt, of Chicksands, Beds. She was Admiral Byng's sister, and, like HW, active in his defence. According to HW, Admiral Boscawen strongly favoured Byng's execution (*Mem. Geo. II* ii. 286–7); his wife certainly did (Cecil Aspinall-Oglander, *Admiral's Wife*, [1940] p. 235). Mrs Osborn's letters have been twice printed (*Political and Social Letters of a Lady of the Eighteenth Century*, ed. Emily F. D. Osborn, [1890]; *Letters of Sarah Byng Osborn*, ed. John McClelland, Stanford Press, 1930).

14. Lady Jane Wharton, dau. of 1st M. of Wharton, m. (1) John Holt, of Red-grave, Suffolk (d. ca 1729); m. (2) (1733) Robert Coke of Longford, Derby (d. 1750). According to a House of Lords decision in 1845, she was *suo jure* Baroness Wharton

after 1738, but she was never so regarded in the 18th century (Burke, *Peerage, sub* Wharton, and Leicester). Her fortune went to Anna Maria Draycott, Countess of Pomfret (GEC).

1. Henry Baldwin, publisher of the *St James's Chronicle*, published in 1762 *The Yearly Chronicle for 1761* (Miss E. G. Withycombe in N&Q 1939, clxxvii. 390).

2. No other reference to HW's out-of-town party of this Christmas has been found.

3. Charles Montagu was transferred from the colonelcy of the 59th to that of the 2d (Queen's Royal) Foot (*Army Lists*). At the end of a war, the army's size was decreased by disbanding the most recently formed regiments. As a matter of fact, only regiments junior to the 70th Foot were 'broken' in 1763 (Fortescue, *British Army* iii. 10).

notes by Princess Emily.[4] 'Tis strange how much I love to read of the court of Lewis the XIV, I, who am so indifferent to my own that I have at hand; I know more of the Fronde than the Jew Bill,[5] and think the Duke of Beaufort[6] an abler man than my cousin Newcastle, the King of Clare Market.[7]

If I had Lucan here I should read it for Brutus Hampden's sake; such a suffusion has fifty years[8] and Greatworth air cast over my eyes and rendered all objects alike.

I hope this new edition will be profitable to Mr Bentley and that he may get as much money as his father used to get credit; this last is an ominous word; our friend is apt to love credit better than money. Adieu! I wish you a many happy new years and a many old friends such as your most faithful

G. MONTAGU

From MONTAGU, Saturday 17 January 1761

G.D. 15/8, No. 752.

No doubt written in 1761, when Saturday fell on the 17th of January, and Montagu was planning a visit to London, as appears from the reply *post* 22 Jan. 1761.

Greatworth, Saturday 17 [Jan. 1761].

BE so good as to let your servant carry the enclosed over the way to Mrs Morland's; it is about her looking me out a lodging for the

4. Humorously intended; Princess Emily was George III's aunt; Mlle de Montpensier was Louis XIV's.

5. An Act permitting the naturalization of Jews, passed in the parliament of 1752–3 (26 Geo. II, c. 26, 1753), was repealed in November of the same year, on account of the popular clamour against it (27 Geo. II, c. 1; *Mem. Geo. II* i. 357–8; I. S. Leadam, *Political History of England, 1702–60*, 1909, pp. 428–9).

6. François de Vendôme (1616–69), Duc de Beaufort; grandson of Henri IV; active on the side of the Parisians in the Fronde; apparently not particularly able (*Nouv. Biog. Gén.*).

7. Lincoln's Inn Fields, where stood a chapel built by the Duke of Newcastle, who was ground landlord of the Market (*London Past & Present*).

8. Montagu seems to have been somewhat uncertain about his age. The present reference is too indefinite to be at all decisive. *Post* 17 Nov. 1761 he writes, 'My fiftieth year begins charmingly'; this would make his birthdate ca Nov. 1712. But 23 Dec. 1764 he writes: 'Yesterday my brother John would, what he called it, *keep* my birthday. When I had finished my fifty-first year . . . I had a bevée of ladies and squires.' If this statement is correct, he was born ca 22 Dec. 1713. The latter date is supported by *post* 11 Jan. 1764, n. 10, where HW (who was born Oct. 1717 and was now 46), speaking of being gay, says, 'I wish we may be so at 76 and 80!'—showing unmistakably that he thought of Montagu as four years older than himself.

beginning of February, when I shall be glad to come and take a peep at you and all my good friends for a few months.

How does the terrible weather agree with you? I often think of you in it. As to myself I have not stirred out of my house or had a soul with me but once since its first beginning, by which care I believe the gout has not shifted out of my hand where it is very welcome to stay with its swelling and think myself very well off. I have not been able to get my letters for three posts from Brackley; a poor devil who is obliged to go there from hence today—and I pity him—stays for this. Adieu; believe me ever most faithfully yours

G. M.

To Montagu, Thursday 22 January 1761

Arlington Street, Jan. 22d, 1761.

I AM glad you are coming, and now the time is over, that you are coming so late, as I like to have you here in the spring. You will find no great novelty in the new reign. Lord Denbigh is made Master of the Harriers with two thousand a year; Lord Temple asked it, and Newcastle and Hardwicke gave into it for fear of Denbigh's brutality in the House of Lords[1]—does this differ from the style of George II?

The King designs to take a new motto;[2] he will not have a French one, so the Pretender may enjoy *Dieu et mon Droit* in quiet.

Princess Emily is already sick of being familiar; she has been at Northumberland House, but goes to nobody more. That party was larger but still more formal than the rest, though the Duke of York had invited himself and his commerce[3]-table. I played with Madam Emily, and we were mighty well together—so well, that two nights afterwards she commended me to Mr Conway and Mr Fox, but calling me *that Mr Walpole,* they did not guess whom she meant. For my part I thought it very well that when I played with her she did not call me *that gentleman.* I was surprised at her being so vulgar; as she went away she *thanked* my Lady Northumberland, like a parson's wife, *for all her civilities.*

1. For an example, see *Mem. Geo. III* iii. 35–6.
2. This did not happen.
3. 'A [card] game in which exchange or barter is the chief feature' (OED *sb.*[6]; see examples there, and Miss E. G. Withycombe in N&Q 1939, clxxvii. 390).

I was excessively amused on Tuesday night; there was a play at Holland House acted by children; not all children, for Lady Sarah Lenox[4] and Lady Susan Strangways[5] played the women. It was *Jane Shore;* one Price,[6] Lord Barrington's nephew, was Gloster, and acted better than three parts of the comedians. Charles Fox,[7] Hastings; a little Nichols[8] who spoke well, Belmour; Lord Ofaly,[9] Lord Ashbroke[10] and other boys did the rest—but the two girls were delightful; and acted with so much nature and simplicity, that they appeared the very things they represented. Lady Sarah was more beautiful than you can conceive, and her very awkwardness gave an air of truth to the shame of the part, and the antiquity of the time, which was kept up by her dress, taken out of Montfaucon.[11] Lady Susan was dressed from Jane Seymour,[12] and all the parts were clothed in ancient habits, and with the most minute propriety.[13] I was infinitely more struck with the last scene between the two women than ever I was when I have seen it on the stage. When Lady Sarah was in white with her hair about her ears and on the ground, no Magdalen by Correggio was half so lovely and expressive. You would have been charmed too with

4. Lady Sarah Lennox (1745–1826), 4th dau. of 2d D. of Richmond; m. (1) (1762) Sir Thomas Charles Bunbury, 6th Bt (divorced, 1776); m. (2) (1781) Hon. George Napier. George III was also impressed with her unusual beauty, and might have married her had it not been for the opposition of his family. She was divorced by her first husband in 1776, having eloped with her cousin Lord William Gordon some years before; three of her sons by her second husband—Charles, George, and William—became famous soldiers; see her *Life and Letters,* ed. Countess of Ilchester, 2 vols, 1901–2.

5. Lady Susan Fox-Strangways (1743–1827), eld. dau. of 1st E. of Ilchester; m. (1764) William O'Brien, an actor; see the *Life and Letters of Lady Sarah Lennox* (n. 4 above), her lifelong friend and correspondent.

6. Uvedale Price (1747–1829), Bt, 1828; writer on the picturesque (DNB); then at Eton, as were the other named boys in the cast.

7. Charles James Fox (1749–1806), the statesman.

8. Not identified; C. J. Fox writes to Lady Susan Fox-Strangways from Eton, 29

Nov. 1761: 'Our play of *Creusa* goes on swimmingly. . . . Nicoll can say all Ilyssus already' (Earl of Ilchester, *Henry Fox, First Lord Holland,* 1920, ii. 173–4). Richard A. Austen-Leigh, *Eton College Register, 1753–90,* 1921, p. 391, lists a John Nicoll and a George Nicholls who were in the school at this time. He was no doubt a relation of Henry Fox's friend John Luke Nicholl, for whom see Earl of Ilchester, op. cit. ii. 194 et seq.

9. George Fitzgerald (1748–65), styled Lord Offaly, later styled E. of Offaly; predeceased his father, the E. and M. of Kildare.

10. William Flower (1744–80), 2d Vct Ashbrook.

11. Bernard de Montfaucon (1655–1741), monk and scholar; his *Antiquité expliquée et représentée en figures,* 10 vols folio, 1719, marked a great advance over any previous general archaeological work (*Nouv. Biog. Gén.*). HW wished to supervise a similar work for England (HW to Bute 15 Feb. 1762).

12. Jane Seymour (1509?–37), Henry VIII's third queen. HW is probably thinking of a Holbein portrait.

13. A novelty in the 18th century.

seeing Mr Fox's little boy of six years old,[14] who is beautiful, and acted the Bishop of Ely, dressed in lawn sleeves and with a square cap; they had inserted two lines for him, which he can hardly speak plainly. Francis[15] had given them a pretty prologue.

You give me no account from Sir Whistler of the painted glass; do, press him for an answer. Adieu!

Yours ever

H. W.

From Montagu, Tuesday 3 February ca 1761

G.D. 15/8, No. 838.

The time-limits of this letter are (1) 1754, since Montagu acquired Greatworth in 1753, (2) 1762, because after that year there were not 'two ladies' of the manor of Sulgrave, but only one. It had been held by three sisters: Theodosia Hodges, d. 1757 unmarried; Anne, m. (1744) Rev. John Lord, d. 24 April 1762; Lydia, m. (1744) Rev. Launcelot Jackson, living 1764 (George Baker, *History of . . . North-ampton*, 1822–41, i. 515). 'Young Montagu' is no doubt Frederick Montagu; it seems unlikely that he would be concerned in the case before his admission to the bar (1757) or, moreover, his entrance into Parliament (June 1759); Montagu's assurance that HW would see him suggests the latter. If the assumption that Frederick Montagu was interested as an M.P. be accepted, the letter falls between 1760–2. There is another letter of 3 Feb. in 1760, making that date unlikely, and Montagu was in Dublin in 1762; the only positive objection to 1761 is that *post* 7 Feb. 1761 does not mention this letter; but it is not the sort of letter that required a reply.

Greatworth, February 3d [ca 1761].

I HAVE been solicited by two ladies[1] in my neighbourhood to desire any friends I have in Parliament to attend in their behalf if they find their cause just. It is with regard to an enclosure of Sulgrave,[2] which they oppose by a petition in the house. They are ladies of the manor, and apprehend they shall be injured. Young Montagu[3]

14. Henry Edward Fox (1755–1811), soldier (DNB).

15. Rev. Philip Francis (1708?–73), writer; at the time tutor to Charles James Fox (DNB); his prologue to *Jane Shore* seems not to have been printed.

1. See heading.

2. The home of the Washingtons, in Northamptonshire. Apparently the private bill required for the enclosure did not go through; at any rate it does not appear in the indexes of such measures in the *Commons Journals* 1752–68, and is therefore of no assistance in dating the letter.

3. Probably Frederick Montagu; see heading.

when you see him will inform you of the nature of the case, and if the weather will permit you to attend when the petition is heard, I shall be obliged to you. I shall say no more than to assure you I am always yours,

G. Montagu

To Montagu, Saturday 7 February 1761

Address: To George Montagu Esq. at Greatworth near Brackley, Northamptonshire. Free Hor. Walpole. *Postmark:* 7 FE.

Arlington Street, Feb. 7th, 1761.

I HAVE not writ to you lately, expecting your arrival. As you are not come yet, you need not come these ten days, if you please, for I go next week into Norfolk, that my subjects of Lynn may at least once in their lives see me. 'Tis a horrible affair to dine with a Mayor! I shall profane King John's cup,[1] and taste nothing but water out of it, as if it was St John Baptist's.

Prepare yourself for crowds, multitudes. In this reign all the world lives in one room. The capital is as vulgar as a county-town in the season of horse-races. There were no fewer than four of these throngs on Tuesday last, at the Duke of Cumberland's, Princess Emily's, the opera, and Lady Northumberland's—for even operas, Tuesday's operas, are crowded now. There is nothing else new. Last week was a magnificent ball at Norfolk House: the two royal Dukes and Princess Emily were there. He of York danced; the other and his sister had each their table at loo. I played at hers, and am grown a favourite—nay, have been at her private party, and was asked again last Wednesday, but took the liberty to excuse myself—and yet am again summoned for Thursday. It is trist enough: nobody sits till the game begins, and then she and the company are all on stools. At Norfolk House were two arm-chairs placed for her and the Duke of Cumber-

1. King John gave Lynn its charter, and stopped there on the flight that ended in his death. Though it is actually of a later date (Cunningham iii. 377), the Lynn tradition was that 'he gave them his most curious cup, and most venerable piece of antiquity, of silver gilt with gold on the inside, . . . in the keeping of every mayor, used on certain solemn occasions, and shewn to gentlemen as a great curiosity, in memory of their founder and great benefactor, filled with sack' (Francis Blomefield and Charles Parkin, *An Essay towards a Topographical History of Norfolk*, 1805–10, viii. 489).

land, the Duke of York being supposed a dancer, but they would not use them.[2] Lord Huntingdon arrived in a frock, pretending he was just come out of the country—unluckily he had been at Court full-dressed in the morning. No foreigners were there but the son and daughter-in-law of Monsieur de Fuentes:[3] the Duchess told the Duchess of Bedford that she had not invited the Ambassadress[4] because her rank is disputed here—you remember the Bedford took place of Madame de Mirepoix[5]—but Madame de Mora[6] danced first, the Duchess of Norfolk saying she supposed that was of no consequence.

Have you heard what immense riches old Wortley[7] has left? One million three hundred and fifty thousand pounds. It is all to center in my Lady Bute;[8] her husband is one of fortune's prodigies. They talk of a print in which her mistress[9] is reprimanding Miss Chudleigh—the latter curtsies, and replies, '*Madame, chacun à son But.*'

Have you seen a scandalous letter in print from Miss Ford[10] to

2. Doubtless out of politeness.

3. Juan Joaquín Atanasio Pignatelli de Aragón (1724–76), Conde de Fuentes; Spanish ambassador to England, and also to Turin and France; 'a dull, cold man, and wedded to all the weakness of his religion' (*Mem. Geo. III* i. 100; La Chesnaye-Desbois and Badier, *Dictionnaire de la Noblesse*, 1863–76, xv. 864–5; DU DEFFAND). His son, José Pignatelli y Gonzaga (1744–74), Marqués de Mora, was a lover of Julie de Lespinasse and a disciple of the Encyclopedists; about him see Marquis de Ségur, *Julie de Lespinasse* (translation), 1907, pp. 238–86, 331–6. He married (1756) María Ignacia del Pilar (1745–64), dau. of the Conde de Aranda; she being eleven and he twelve years old; see ibid. 241–5; Count Frederick Kielmansegge, *Diary of a Journey to England 1761–1762*, 1902, p. 223.

4. María Luisa Gonzaga (1726–73), Duquessa di Solferino; m. (1741) Conde de Fuentes (preceding note; *Enciclopedia Storico-Nobiliare Italiana*, Milano, 1928–36, v. 358; *Enciclopedia Universal Ilustrada*, Barcelona, 1905–33, xliv. 832).

5. At another ball at Norfolk House in Dec. 1749; see HW to Mann 25 Feb. 1750.

6. Above, n. 3.

7. Edward Wortley Montagu (ca 1678–1761), Lord of the Treasury, 1714; Ambassador to Turkey, 1716; M.P.; husband of

Lady Mary Wortley Montagu; his miserliness satirized by Pope (DNB, *sub* Lady M. W. Montagu; Collins, *Peerage*, 1812, iii. 460–1). HW to Mann 27 Jan. 1761, which gives a more detailed account of his will, reduces the size of his fortune to half a million; *Gray's Corr.* ii. 727 says 'better than half a million of money.'

8. His daughter Mary Wortley Montagu (1718–94), m. (1736) John Stuart, 3d E. of Bute.

9. The Princess of Wales.

10. *A Letter from Miss F--d Addressed to a Person of Distinction*, 1761. HW's copy, the 2d edn, is now WSL. Ann Ford (1737–1824), author and musician, m. (1762) Philip Thicknesse. William Whitehead, in a letter to Lord Nuneham 16 Dec. 1758, ironically proposed her as a wife for William Mason: 'She is excellent in music, loves solitude, and has unmeasurable affectations' (*Harcourt Papers*, ed. Edward W. Harcourt, Oxford, n.d., vii. 220). Her letter to Lord Jersey (also GM 1761, xxxi. 33–4) accuses him of trying to make her his mistress, abetted by her father. Her refusal, she says, forced her to earn her living by giving concerts; but instead of subscribing to them, he sent her an inedible boar's head. He replied, feebly (ibid. 79–80). A print of the affair is described in BM *Satiric Prints* iv. 2–3, and is in HW's copy of the *Letter*.

Lord Jersey? with the history of a boar's head—George Selwyn calls him Meleager.[11] Adieu! this is positively my last.

Yours ever

Hor. Walpole

From Montagu, ca Wednesday 25 February 1761

G.D. 15/8, No. 753.

Conjectural date assigned by the reference to the short visit early in March; see *post* 13 and ca 15 March 1761.

[Greatworth, ca Feb. 25, 1761].

I CONCLUDE you will expect I should signify to you that I am likely to be in London about the second of March. Truly there are fewer of my friends, to whom I have wrote, I shall be gladder to see, and therefore I write to you amongst the first; and happy I shall be to find you as well, as gay, as young as I am at this moment of time, and indeed have been all this winter.

I come to town merely to see my friends that I cannot see elsewhere; nor could I come before for many reasons. I shall make but a short stay for many of the same reasons. I come with a good will; that is enough in this torpid state of existence that you all think being buried alive; I have kept myself fat and eatable; you will find, 'tis true, no pearl in my shell, but you will find me sound and faithful and cleaving. I walk out of it merely to show you I am alive and not to be trod underfoot, and shall just take a peep at you and close again *totus teres atque rotundus.*[1]

I know no more of what is passing in the world than the veriest oyster on the bank, and make my appearance in Lent,[2] when only I may be fit for the table; you will have been cloyed with flesh-pots, and be glad to set with Daniel at his pulse.[2a] Sir, I would have you to know I never was less fit for the great world and never fitter. I never had better spirits to cope with the humours of the times and never so humoursome. I am all Almanzor;[3] I could fight, drink, swear—do any-

11. Meleager slew the Calydonian boar and gave the heart to Atalanta, thereby setting in train a series of disasters which ended in his death.

1. Horace, *Sat.* II. vii. 86.
2. Which began 4 Feb.
2a. Daniel i. 12.
3. The valiant hero of Dryden's *Conquest of Granada*, 1672.

thing. I know not what it is to be old, for I will not try my strength. I now repent me I am of no consequence; I would I were a thousand strong to take the young man[4] by the leg.

Upon the other part of the paper, which I have tore off,[5] there was some verses of Dryden's which, though better than ever anyone wrote, would not be in your way though they were in mine, and indeed luckily for you were in mine; for I had a vein of enthusiasm that might have carried me beyond bounds and got me a flogging. I am checked in my career and will not wait for the return of the moody inspiration. He has pulled me by the ear and kindly told me, 'You are writing much at your ease at your fireside,[6] while Mr Walpole may be at home tired with a long fruitless day, or ready to go and dress for a dull ceremonious assembly. He cannot care for that you say; 'tis enough he cares for what you do or are to do. Prithee have done and write your name; 'twill be enough.'

I am therefore, as I am bid, your most obedient humble servant,

G. MONTAGU

To MONTAGU, Friday 13 March 1761

Arlington Street, March 13th, 1761.

I CAN now tell you with great pleasure that your cousin[1] is certainly named Lord Lieutenant[2]—I wish *you* joy. You will not be sorry too to hear that your Lord North is much talked of for succeeding him at the Board of Trade.[3] I tell you this with great composure, though today has been a day of amazement. All the world is staring, whispering and questioning—Lord Holderness has resigned the Seals, and they are given to Lord Bute—which of the two Secretaries of State is first minister? The latter or Mr Pitt? Lord Holderness received the command but yesterday at two o'clock, till that moment thinking himself extremely well at Court—but it seems the King said

---

4. Doubtless the King.
5. The second leaf of the letter.
6. After, apparently, dining well.

---

1. Lord Halifax. 'So he was; and my Father accompanied him to Dublin to

shew him the beauties of North Wales on the road. H. L. P[iozzi].'
2. 'To the great disappointment of the E. of Hertford' ('Lord Holland's Memoir,' *Life and Letters of Lady Sarah Lennox,* ed. Countess of Ilchester, 1901–2, i. 35).
3. He did not.

he was tired of having two Secretaries, of which one would do nothing and t'other could do nothing;[4] he would have a Secretary who both could act and would.[5] Pitt had as short notice[6] of this revolution as the sufferer, and was little better pleased; he is something softened for the present by offer of Cofferer for Jemmy Grenville, which is to be ceded by the Duke of Leeds, who returns to his old post of Justice in Eyre, from which Lord Sandys is to be removed, some say to the head of the Board of Trade.[7] Newcastle who enjoys this fall of Holderness, who had deserted him for Pitt, laments over the former, but seems to have made his terms with the new favourite[8]—if the Bedfords have done so too, will it surprise you? It will me, if Pitt submits to this humiliation—if he does not, I take for granted the Duke of Bedford will have the other Seals.

The temper with which the new reign has hitherto proceeded, seems a little impeached by this sudden act, and the Earl now stands in the direct light of a minister, if a House of Commons should choose to cavil at him.

Lord Delawar[9] kissed hands today for his earldom; the other new peers are to follow on Monday.

There are horrid disturbances about the militia in Northumberland,[10] where the mob have killed an officer and three of the Yorkshire militia, who in return fired and shot twenty-one.

Adieu! I shall be impatient to hear some consequence of my first paragraph.

Yours ever

H. W.

4. Pitt had been confined with the gout (HW to Mann 3 March 1761).

5. HW's epigrammatic summary oversimplifies the factors involved in Bute's taking office, though 'Lord Holland's Memoir,' loc. cit. 36–7, in what purports to be a direct quotation of the King, says substantially the same thing. See Lewis B. Namier, England in the Age of the American Revolution, 1930, pp. 178–95, for a thorough treatment of the incident and the motives behind it.

6. 'Lord Holland's Memoir,' loc. cit., says Pitt was notified the day before. But he must have known that the change was

likely; see Earl of Ilchester, Henry Fox, First Lord Holland, 1920, ii. 127.

7. This was correct.

8. See Namier, loc. cit., for Newcastle's part in the affair.

9. John West (1693–1766), 7th Bn de la Warr, cr. (1761) E. de la Warr; for the other new peers see post 17 March 1761.

10. The riot occurred at Hexham 'on the deputy-lieutenants meeting to ballot for the militia' (the first three-year term had expired, and they were making a new enrollment). The Northumberland pitmen, who for some unexplained reason opposed the militia, attacked a body of

PS. Saturday

I forgot to tell you that Lord Hardwicke has writ some verses to Lord Lyttelton upon those the latter made on Lady Egremont.[11] If I had been told that he had put on a bag[12] and was gone off with Kitty Fisher, I should not have been more astonished!

Poor Lady Gower[13] is dead this morning of a fever in her lying-in: I believe the Bedfords are very sorry—for there is a new opera[14] this evening.

From MONTAGU, ca Sunday 15 March 1761

G.D. 15/8, No. 755.

Answered *post* 17 March 1761.
Address: To the Honourable Mr Walpole, Arlington Street, London. Free.
Postmark: 16 MR.

Greatworth, March [ca 15, 1761].

I QUITE forgot to tell you[1] that Miss Rice begged you would speak to Mrs Clive for the last and least of the side boxes for her benefit,[2] and she would take tickets and fill it; perhaps I have spoke too

Yorkshire militia who were there to keep order. An ensign and two privates of the militia were killed, and, in the mob, forty-two were killed and forty-eight wounded (GM 1761, xxxi. 137–8; *Annual Register* for 1761, iv. 82–3).

11. Alicia Maria Carpenter (d. 1794), m. (1) (1751) Charles Wyndham, 2d E. of Egremont; m. (2) (1767) Hans Moritz, Graf von Brühl, Saxon Ambassador. Lord Lyttelton's verses, Lord Hardwicke's addition, Lord Lyttelton's reply to Lord Hardwicke's addition, and an epigram on each of the three, are in *Annual Register* for 1761, iv. [pt ii] 240–3.

12. 'A bag wig instead of a tye. The ties were just going out, and I remember Lord Sandwich saying he was ashamed of his bag' (Mrs Piozzi). Sir John Cust's brother Peregrine wrote later this year that Sir John was uneasy before he was made Speaker as to what wig to wear on the election day. If he wore a bag (the current mode) it would be 'ridiculous to have him put into the chair with it. But if he wore a tye (suitable to his new dignity), as he has not been used to it it will

look presumptuous' (Lionel Cust, *Records of the Cust Family, Series III, Sir John Cust*, 1927, p. 58). Cf. the portrait of a dandy in Christopher Anstey, *New Bath Guide*, 1766, letter x. lines 59–60:

'But what with my *Nivernois'* hat can compare,
Bag-wig, and lac'd ruffles, and black solitaire.'

13. Lady Louisa Egerton (1723–61), m. (1748) Granville Leveson-Gower, 2d E. Gower; the Duchess of Bedford was his sister.

14. *Didone Abandonata*, melodrama by Metastasio, with music by Perez and Galuppi (Charles Burney, *General History of Music*, 1776–89, iv. 475; Allardyce Nicoll, *History of Late Eighteenth Century Drama*, Cambridge, 1927, p. 354).

1. Presumably in London, when Montagu made the visit mentioned *ante* ca 25 Feb. 1761.

2. *The Inconstant*, by George Farquhar, at Drury Lane 26 March (see [John Genest], *Some Account of the English Stage*, Bath, 1832, iv. 609–10).

late. Cliquetis's drawings have been shown to Worsley³ to show to the ——⁴

Mr Cumberland⁵ has been with the Bishop of Durham and Mr Hampden to make his uncle's peace and beg pardon for his conduct towards them. I am better since I came into the country but am far from well.

I most heartily wish you your health and am sincerely yours,

G. Montagu

To Montagu, Tuesday 17 March 1761

Address: To George Montagu Esq. at Greatworth near Brackley, Northamptonshire. Free Hor. Walpole. *Postmark:* 17 MR IO.

Arlington Street, March 17th, 1761.

IF my last letter raised your wonder, this will not allay it. Lord Talbot is Lord Steward! The stone which the builders refused, is become the headstone of the corner.¹ My Lady Talbot,² I suppose, would have found no charms in Cardinal Mazarin.³ As the Duke of Leeds was forced to give way to Jemmy Grenville,⁴ the Duke of Rutland has been obliged to make room for this new Earl. Lord Hunt-

3. Thomas Worseley (d. 1778), Surveyor-General of the Board of Works; M.P. Orford 1761–8; Callington 1768–74; 'a creature of Lord Bute, and a kind of riding-master to the King' (*Mem. Geo. III* i. 29, 331).

4. So in MS; probably the King is meant.

5. Richard Cumberland (1732–1811), dramatist; Bentley's nephew. Possibly he had to 'make his uncle's peace' on account of a quarrel arising out of the designs Bentley made for Bishop Auckland (*ante* 19 Oct. 1760, n. 14).

———

1. Psalms cxviii. 22. Lord Talbot had until this time been inconspicuous except for his gallantries; see *Mem. Geo. III* i. 35–7.

2. Mary de Cardonnel (ca 1719–87), m. (1748) William Talbot, 2d Bn, cr. (1761) E. Talbot.

3. This sentence is obscure: Cardinal Mazarin may be intended to represent

Bute, for, like Bute, he was at the same time the favourite of a King (Louis XIV), and on exceedingly intimate terms with the King's mother (Anne of Austria), which to the eighteenth century would have made a parallel to the alleged liaison between Bute and the Princess of Wales. Professor Namier writes that in his opinion and that of Mr Romney Sedgwick, such a liaison never existed. Lord Talbot was said to have got his Stewardship through the influence of the Princess of Wales (see the cryptic passage in HW to Mann 17 March 1761; and Count Fuentes to M. Wall, *Correspondence of William Pitt, Earl of Chatham,* 1838–40, ii. 106). Therefore, HW may mean that though the Princess of Wales was charmed with Lord Talbot, Lady Talbot would find no charms in Bute.

4. When James Grenville was made Cofferer he displaced the Duke of Leeds, who became Chief Justice in Eyre (*Mem. Geo. III* i. 34).

ingdon is Groom of the Stole, and the last Duke I have named, Master of the Horse[5]—the red liveries[6] cost Lord Huntingdon a pang. Lord Holderness has the reversion of the Cinque Ports for life, and I think may pardon his expulsion.[7]

If you propose a fashionable assembly, you must send cards to Lord Spenser,[8] Lord Grosvenor,[9] Lord Melcomb,[10] Lord Grantham,[11] Lord Boston,[12] Lord Scarsdale,[13] Lady Mountstewart,[14] the Earl of Tirconnel,[15] and Lord Wintertown.[16] The two last you will meet in Ireland. No joy ever exceeded your cousin's[17] or Doddington's. The former came last night to Lady Hilsborough's[18] to display his triumph. The latter too was there and advanced to me. I said, 'I was coming to wish you joy.' 'I concluded so,' replied he, 'and came to receive it.' He left a good card yesterday at Lady Harrington's. 'A very young Lord was to wait on Lady Harrington, to make her Ladyship the first offer of himself.'[19] I believe she will be content with the Exchequer.[20] Mrs Grey[21] has a pension of £800 a year.

Mrs Clive is at her villa for Passion Week;[22] I have writ to her for

---

5. The Duke of Rutland was first made Groom of the Stole, but demanded and got Lord Huntingdon's Mastership of the Horse, because there was too little patronage attached to the former office (ibid. 36).

6. The Master of the Horse had the unique privilege 'of making use of any horses, pages, or footmen belonging to the King's stables, so that his coaches, horses, and attendants are the King's, and have the King's arms and liveries' (*The True State of England*, 1729, p. 56).

7. He was Warden of the Cinque Ports 1769–78, a post worth £2500–3000 a year (see George, Marquess Curzon, *The Personal History of Walmer Castle and its Lords Warden*, 1927, p. 39). In addition, he had a pension of £4000 a year.

8. John Spencer (1734–83), cr. (1761) Vct, and (1765) E. Spencer.

9. Sir Richard Grosvenor (1731–1802), 7th Bt, cr. (1761) Bn, and (1784) E. Grosvenor.

10. Bubb-Dodington.

11. Sir Thomas Robinson.

12. Sir William Irby; these three were all made Barons.

13. Sir Nathaniel Curzon (1727–1804), 5th Bt, cr. Bn Scarsdale.

14. The Countess of Bute, cr. Baroness Mount Stuart to get an English peerage into the family.

15. Baron Carpenter, cr. Earl of Tyrconnel.

16. Edward-Turnour Garth (after 1744 Garth-Turnour) (1734–88), cr. (1761) Bn, and (1766) E. Winterton; he and Lord Tyrconnel were in the Irish peerage.

17. Halifax, over his Lord-Lieutenant-ship.

18. Lady Margaretta Fitzgerald (1729–66), m. (1748) Wills Hill, 2d Vct Hillsborough, cr. (1751) E. of Hillsborough.

19. Richard Cumberland, in his *Memoirs*, 1806, p. 159, recalls Dodington sending substantially the same offer to, he says, Lady Hervey—possibly a slip for Lady Harrington.

20. Viscount Barrington, with whom she was apparently having an affair (see *ante* 23 Dec. 1759), had recently been made Chancellor of the Exchequer.

21. Probably Lucy Danvers (d. 1799), m. (1748) Hon. John Grey (GM 1799, lxix pt i. 535; Collins, *Peerage*, 1812, iii. 368); she is the 'Mrs Grey' of HW to Lady Ossory 12 Feb. 1780. It is not clear, however, why she should have a pension, when her husband was alive, an M.P., and Clerk of the Green Cloth.

22. When the theatres were closed.

the box, but I don't doubt of its being gone—but, considering her alliance,[23] why does not Miss Rice bespeak the play and have the stage-box?

I shall smile if Mr Bentley and Müntz and their two Hannahs meet at St James's. So I see neither of them, I care not where they are.

Lady Hinchinbrook[24] and Lady Mansel[25] are at the points of death. Lord Hardwicke is to be Poet-Laureate, and according to modern usage, I suppose it will be made a cabinet-counsellor's place. Good night!

Yours ever

H. W.

From Montagu, ca Tuesday 17 March, 1761

G.D. 15/8, No. 754.
Answered by HW 21 March 1761.
Address: To the Honourable Mr Walpole, Arlington Street, London. Free.
Postmark: Banbury 18 MR.

[Greatworth, ca March 17, 1761].

I AM much obliged to you my dear sir for your comfortable letter;[1] it was a cordial to me; I had just been mortified with an account of the loss of my cause[2]—indeed by knavery of my antagonist who tampered with the jury. The judge directed them to find for me and declared himself much dissatisfied with my sentence. I hope, however, I shall have better success in the other kingdom.[3] I have wrote to my cousin to congratulate and to hope he will remember me which I

---

23. Miss Rice's brother married the daughter of Lord Talbot, the new Lord High Steward.

24. Died 20 March.

25. Lady Barbara Villiers (d. 11 June 1761), m. (1) (1725) Sir William Blackett, 2d Bt; m. (2) (1729) Bussy Mansell, 4th Bn Mansell.

---

1. This must refer to *ante* 13 March 1761, which tells Montagu of Lord Halifax's appointment. HW's letter of 17 March, postmarked the same day, could not get to Montagu in time for a reply to

get back to London 18 March, the date of the postmark of this letter (date postmarks were always applied at London; John G. Hendy, *History of the Early Postmarks of the British Isles*, 1905, p. 4). The speed of the post at this time was only 4–5 m.p.h. (William Lewins, *Her Majesty's Mails*, 2d edn 1865, pp. 124–5); the distance from London to Brackley was 66 miles, and from London to Banbury, 75 (John Cary, *New Itinerary*, 1798, p. 186).

2. Nothing more is known of Montagu's lawsuit.

3. Ireland.

have great reason to think he will. Do you want any usquebaugh, or a bunter?[4] I shall be ready to send you Hanah Cliquetis.

I am amazed at the revolution you have mentioned to me, but I begin already to consider myself as not a person interested in what passes in England. I will not detain you a moment longer than to assure you wherever I am, I am always most faithfully yours,

G. MONTAGU

To MONTAGU, Saturday 21 March 1761

March 21st, 1761.

OF the enclosed,[1] as you will perceive, I tore off the seal, but it has not been opened.

I grieve at the loss of your suit and for the injustice done you—but what can one expect but injury when forced to have recourse to law? Lord Abercorn asked me this evening, if it was true that you are going to Ireland? I gave a vague answer, and did not resolve him how much I knew of it. I am impatient for the reply to your compliment.

There is not a word of newer news than what I sent you last. The Speaker[2] has taken leave, and received the highest compliments, and substantial ones too—he did not overact, and it was really a handsome scene.

I go to my election on Tuesday, and if I do not tumble out of the chair[3] and break my neck, you shall hear from me at my return. I got the box for Miss Rice. Lady Hinchinbrook is dead.

Yours ever

H. W.

4. 'A cant word for a woman who picks up rags about the street; and used, by way of contempt, for any low vulgar woman' (Johnson, *Dictionary*).

1. A letter to Montagu which HW was evidently to forward. It had apparently been enclosed in a letter (missing) to HW

and in opening his own letter he had inadvertently unsealed the letter to Montagu as well.

2. Arthur Onslow; he retired on account of age; see *Mem. Geo. III* i. 39–41.

3. In which he would be carried after his election.

From MONTAGU, ca Sunday 29 March 1761

G.D. 15/8, No. 757.

By the closing sentence, the date can be set between 21 March 1761, which states that HW is going to his election, and Montagu's receipt of 25–30 March 1761.

Incomplete; probably the first two 'sides' missing.
Address: To the Honourable Mr Walpole, Arlington Street, London.
Postmark: Banbury.

[Greatworth, ca March 29, 1761].

. . . and he[1] answered and said, 'I am much pleased with the desire you express of accompanying me to Ireland; I can say nothing very positive at present, but hope I shall be able to place you in such a situation there as will be agreeable to you.'

So you may tell Lord Abercorn when you see him that I am to go to Ireland and pray tell the Chute, who used to hear my pipings, that I am now gay and lively.

Perhaps you are to pay three pence for this piece of news,[2] but I will risk your being so much out of pocket.

I hope you are well and well returned in all its senses from Lynn.

I am always yours

G. MONTAGU

To MONTAGU, Wednesday 25–Monday 30 March 1761

Houghton, March 25th, 1761.

HERE I am, at Houghton! and alone! in this spot, where (except two hours last month) I have not been in sixteen years! Think, what a crowd of reflections!—No, Gray and forty churchyards could not furnish so many. Nay, I know one must feel them with greater indifference than I possess, to have patience to put them into verse. Here I am, probably for the last time of my life, though not for the last time—every clock that strikes tells me I am an hour nearer to

1. 'Lord Halifax' (HW).
2. If HW were by any chance not elected he would have no Parliamentary frank and would have to pay postage.

yonder church—that church,[1] into which I have not yet had courage
to enter, where lies that mother on whom I doted, and who doted on
me! There are the two rival mistresses of Houghton,[2] neither of
whom ever wished to enjoy it! There too lies he who founded its
greatness, to contribute to whose fall Europe was embroiled—there
he sleeps in quiet and dignity, while his friend and his foe, rather his
false ally and real enemy, Newcastle and Bath, are exhausting the
dregs of their pitiful lives in squabbles and pamphlets!

The surprise the pictures gave me is again renewed—accustomed
for many years to see nothing but wretched daubs and varnished
copies at auctions, I look at these as enchantment. My own description[3] of them seems poor—but shall I tell you truly—the majesty of
Italian ideas almost sinks before the warm nature of Flemish colouring! Alas! Don't I grow old? My young imagination was fired with
Guido's[3a] ideas—must they be plump and prominent as Abishag[3b] to
warm me now? Does great youth feel with poetic limbs, as well as see
with poetic eyes? In one respect I am very young; I cannot satiate myself with looking—an incident contributed to make me feel this more
strongly. A party arrived, just as I did, to see the house, a man and
three women in riding-dresses, and they rode post through the apartments—I could not hurry before them fast enough—they were not so
long in *seeing* for the first time, as I could have been in one room to
examine what I knew by heart. I remember formerly being often diverted with this kind of *seers*—they come, ask what such a room is
called, in which Sir Robert lay, write it down, admire a lobster or a
cabbage in a market-piece, dispute whether the last room was green
or purple, and then hurry to the inn for fear the fish should be over-
dressed—how different my sensations! Not a picture here, but recalls
a history; not one, but I remember in Downing Street or Chelsea,
where queens and crowds admired them, though *seeing* them as little
as these travellers![3c]

1. HW is buried in its crypt.
2. Sir Robert m. (1) (1700) Catharine
Shorter (ca 1682–1737), HW's mother; m.
(2) (1738) Maria Skerret (ca 1702–38), formerly his mistress.
3. The *Ædes Walpolianæ*.
3a. HW concludes his 'Introduction' to
the *Ædes* with 'In short, in my opinion,
all the qualities of a perfect painter never
met but in Raphael, Guido, and Annibal
Caracci' (*Works* ii. 236).

3b. I Kings i. 1–4.
3c. The pictures were probably moved
to Houghton some time before Sir Robert
Walpole moved from 10 Downing Street
to his small house in Arlington Street,
July 1742 (*Survey of London*, ed. Montagu
H. Cox and Philip Norman, 1900–40, xiv.
129–30). Sir Robert occupied 10 Downing
Street in 1735, the year that Houghton
was finished (ibid.; *Ædes Walpolianæ*
1747, p. 37).

When I had drunk tea, I strolled into the garden—they told me, it was now called *the pleasure ground*—what a dissonant idea of pleasure—those groves, those *allées,* where I have passed so many charming moments, are now stripped up, or overgrown; many fond paths I could not unravel, though with a very exact clue in my memory—I met two gamekeepers, and a thousand hares! In the days when all my soul was tuned to pleasure and vivacity (and you will think perhaps it is far from being out of tune yet) I hated Houghton and its solitude[4]— yet I loved this garden; as now, with many regrets, I love Houghton —Houghton, I know not what to call it, a monument of grandeur or ruin! How I have wished this evening for Lord Bute! How I could preach to him! For myself, I do not want to be preached to—I have long considered, how every Balbec must wait for the chance of a Mr Wood.[5]

The servants wanted to lay me in the great apartment—what to make me pass my night as I have my evening! It were like proposing to Margaret Roper[6] to be a Duchess in the court that cut off her father's head, and imagining it would please her. I have chosen to sit in my father's little dressing-room, and am now by his scrutoire, where, in the height of his fortune, he used to receive the accounts of his farmers, and deceive himself—or us, with the thoughts of his economy—how wise a man at once and how weak! For what has he built Houghton? For his grandson to annihilate, or for his son to mourn over! If Lord Burleigh[7] could rise and view his representative driving the Hatfield stage,[8] he would feel as I feel now—poor little Strawberry! At least it will not be snipped to pieces by a descendant! —You will think all these fine meditations dictated by pride, not by philosophy—pray consider, through how many mediums philosophy must pass, before it is purified—

How often must it weep, how often burn![9]

4. See HW to Chute 20 Aug. 1743.

5. Robert Wood (ca 1717–71), traveller and politician; published *Ruins of Balbec,* 1757; HW's occasional correspondent.

6. Margaret (1505–44), dau. of St Thomas More; m. (ca 1525) William Roper.

7. William Cecil (1521–98), cr. (1571) Bn Burghley; statesman.

8. James Cecil (1713–80), 6th E. of Salisbury. His passion for driving stage-

coaches is perhaps noticed in Pope's *Dunciad* (iv. 588–9), and Hogarth's 'Night' (George Ravenscroft Dennis, *The House of Cecil,* 1914, pp. 233–4). See Rev. Frederic Barlow, *Complete English Peerage,* 1775, i. 301: 'His lordship, whose chief excellence consists in driving a set of horses skillfully, lives a sequestered life.' See Appendix 5 for Mrs Piozzi's account of him.

9. Not located.

My mind was extremely prepared for all this gloom, by parting with
Mr Conway yesterday morning—moral reflections on commonplaces
are the livery one likes to wear, when one has just had a real misfortune—he is going to Germany—I was glad to dress myself up in transi-
tory Houghton, in lieu of very sensible concern. Tomorrow I shall be
distracted with thoughts—at least images, of very different complexion—I go to Lynn, and am to be elected on Friday. I shall return
hither on Saturday, again alone, to expect Burleighides[10] on Sunday,
whom I left at Newmarket—I must once in my life see him on his
grandfather's throne—

Epping, Monday night, 31st.[11]

—No, I have not seen him, he loitered on the road, and I was kept at
Lynn till yesterday morning. It is plain I never knew for how many
trades I was formed, when at this time of day I can begin electioneer-
ing and succeed in my new vocation. Think of me, the subject of a
mob, who was scarce ever before in a mob! Addressing them in the
town-hall, riding at the head of two thousand people through such a
town as Lynn, dining with above two hundred of them amid bumpers, huzzas, songs and tobacco, and finishing with country dances at
a ball and six-penny whisk! I have borne it all cheerfully; nay, have
sat hours in *conversation,* the thing upon earth that I hate, have been
to hear misses play on the harpsichord, and to see an alderman's
copies of Rubens and Carlo Marat.[12] Yet to do the folks justice, they
are sensible and reasonable, and civilized; their very language is pol-
ished since I lived among them. I attribute this to their more frequent intercourse with the world and the capital, by the help of good
roads and post-chaises, which, if they have abridged the King's dominions, have at least tamed his subjects.—Well! how comfortable it
will be tomorrow, to see my perroquet, to play at loo, and not to be
obliged to talk seriously—the Heraclitus of the beginning of this letter, will be overjoyed on finishing it to sign himself

Your old friend

DEMOCRITUS.[13]

10. Lord Orford.
11. 30th, unless HW was writing after midnight.
12. Carlo Maratti (1625–1713), prolific Roman painter, much in evidence at Houghton.
13. Often contrasted, as 'the laughing philosopher,' with the melancholy Hera-clitus. HW had Bentley design a frontis-piece for his *Memoirs* in which 'the au-thor, leaning on a globe of the world, be-tween Heraclitus and Democritus, presents his book to the latter.' The drawing is now WSL.

PS. I forgot to tell you that my ancient Aunt Hammond[14] came over to Lynn to see me—not from any affection, but curiosity—the first thing she said to me, though we have not met these sixteen years, was, 'Child, you have done a thing today, that your father never did in all his life, you sat as they carried you; he always stood the whole time.' 'Madam,' said I, 'when I am placed in a chair, I conclude I am to sit in it—besides, as I cannot imitate my father in great things, I am not at all ambitious of mimicking him in little ones.'—I am sure she proposes to tell her remark to my uncle Horace's ghost, the instant they meet.

From Montagu, ca Saturday 4 April 1761

G.D. 15/8, No. 756.

Undated; in reply to *ante* 25–30 March 1761, and, from the references to Mrs Rice in both letters, written before *post* ca 6 April 1761.

[Greatworth, ca April 4, 1761].

I RECEIVED your letter from Norfolk and am glad to hear you are returned safe and well.

I foresaw how much cause for reflection you would have at Houghton, and that your nephew would depatriate.[1]

As to my affairs they seem pretty prosperous for I had a letter last night from Mrs Rice to tell me she had just heard I was to be the Black Rod[2] and I fancy she picked it up from the Talbots, who are apprised of most of my cousin's motions of that sort. This I shall be glad of as it will pay its way and be much better than appearing there as an expectant, and a great saving of mortification were I to behold many preferences given to my fellow followers.

14. Susan Walpole (1681–1763), Sir Robert's sister; m. (1707) Anthony Hamond of Wootton, Norfolk (Walter Rye, *Later History of the Family of Walpole*, Norwich, 1920, p. 18).

1. Possibly Montagu has invented a word to express Lord Orford's lack of interest in his ancestral estate.

2. In the English Parliament, the Gentleman Usher of the Black Rod is an officer of the House of Lords; he is sent to desire the attendance of the Commons on the upper house, and performs other ceremonial functions (Sir Thomas Erskine May, *A Treatise on the Law . . . and Usage of Parliament*, ed. Sir T. Lonsdale Webster, 1924, p. 196). The Irish House of Lords was apparently identically organized; see John T. Gilbert, *Account of the Parliament House, Dublin*, Dublin, 1896, pp. 29–32. The title comes 'from the black wand surmounted by a golden lion which he carries as his symbol of office' (OED *sub* Black Rod).

Pray send me word when you hear that he[3] is to go to Ireland, whether in May or October; for my preparations you shall hear from me again soon. Please to put your name to the General's letter.

I most truly wish you your health and all you can wish, and that I am by ten years older a better friend to myself than I thought I should have been.[4] I am always yours.

G. MONTAGU

From MONTAGU, ca Monday 6 April 1761

G.D. 15/8, No. 758.

Undated; answered by HW <i>post</i> 7 April 1761.</div>

Greatworth [ca April 6, 1761].

PRAY you now send me word when you hear *your*[1] friend the Lord Lieutenant of Ireland is to go to his post, that I may be preparing my embellishments. I should hope not till towards the October. I had last night a letter from Lord Guilford to tell me he had had Sir George Osborn to wait on him to inform him Lord Halifax had provided me a good employment; this with what my cousin Rice had notified to me before makes me clutch the Black Rod whose point is towards me.[2]

I am shedding my grey hairs one by one; not that I mean to appear the young creature but that I have youth coming to me with purple wings and a bag of counters to play with the rest of my days. You will hear more of my joy than you have of my complaints.

I am much obliged to you for your letter from Houghton. I don't wonder you were melancholy there with such an heir who has sense enough to make a great figure, but bad education has rendered him the little Lord O.

We have had cold weather but I am now writing with my windows up and violent zephyrs a little warmed over the fire. I passed two days

---

3. Halifax.

4. This may mean that Montagu finds himself better off than he had supposed ten years earlier he would be at this time. Professor Namier suggests that he had once turned down another offer from Halifax; see *ante* 19 March 1754.

---

1. Possibly Montagu styles him so be-

cause the dedication of HW's *Lucan*, which was written by Richard Cumberland, is to Halifax. Or perhaps Montagu is merely sarcastic, because HW is better informed about Halifax's movements than he is.

2. Cf. *Macbeth*, II. i. 33: 'Is this a dagger . . .' etc.

with Lord Guilford and Lord North at Wroxton and we talked over
divers things that one must only think of in town. Adieu; believe me
ever most faithful.

Yours,
G. Montagu

To Montagu, Tuesday 7 April 1761

Misdated 'March' by HW.
Address: To George Montagu Esq. at Greatworth near Brackley, Northamptonshire. Free Hor. Walpole.

Arlington Street, March [April] 7th, 1761.

I REJOICE, you know, in whatever rejoices you; and though I am
not certain what your situation is to be, I am glad you go, as you
like it. I am told it is Black Rod. Lady Anne Jekyll[1] said she had writ
to you on Saturday night. I asked when her brother was to go, if before August; she answered, yes, if possible. Long before October, you
may depend upon it—in the quietest times no Lord Lieutenant ever
went so late as that. Shall not you come to town first? You cannot
pack up yourself and all you will want, at Greatworth.

We are in the utmost hopes of a peace; a congress is agreed upon at
Ausbourg;[2] but yesterday's mail brought bad news. Prince Ferdinand has been obliged to raise the siege of Cassel and to retire to
Paderborn; the Hereditary Prince having been again defeated,[3] with
the loss of two generals, and to the value of five thousand men, in
prisoners and exchanged.[4] If this defers the peace, it will be grievous
news to me, now Mr Conway is gone to the army.

1. Mrs Piozzi notes on the 1818 edition's
identification of her as 'Sister of the Earl
of Halifax': 'and very kind to poor H. L.
Piozzi.'

2. Augsbourg was fixed as the place for
a peace conference; but though negotiations between France and England continued for several months, it was not held;
Pitt's demands were high, and the French,
secretly arranging the Family Compact
with Spain, were insincere; see William
Hunt, *Political History of England, 1760–
1801*, 1905, p. 23 et seq.

3. At Grünberg, in a rear-guard action,
following the combination of French reinforcements and the destitution of the
country, which had forced the allies to

raise the siege of Cassel and other towns
as well; see GM 1761, xxxi. 191. HW got
his news quickly. The *London Chronicle* reported the arrival of a courier on Wednesday, but had only sketchy information until the end of the week (7–9 and 9–11
April 1761, ix. 342, 349–50).

4. GM 1761, xxxi. 191 gives the number
of prisoners as 3,000; Fortescue, *British
Army* ii. 532, as 2,000. The two generals
HW refers to are perhaps two staff officers
who in saving the Hereditary Prince from
capture were themselves taken. One of
these was Janneret, Lieutenant-Colonel of
Malachowsky's Hussars (*London Chronicle*
9–11 April 1761, ix. 350).

The town talks of nothing but an immediate queen; yet I am certain the ministers know not of it. Her picture is come, and lists of her family given about; but the latter I do not send you, as I believe it apocryphal.⁵ Adieu!

Yours ever

H. W.

PS. Have you seen the advertisement of a new noble author? A Treatise of Horsemanship by Henry Earl of Pembroke!⁶—as George Selwyn said of Mr Greville,⁷ so far from being a writer, I thought he was scarce a courteous reader.

From Montagu, ca Thursday 9 April 1761

G.D. 15/8, No. 759.

Undated; probably answered by *post* ca 11 April 1761 (missing); see *post* ca 14 April 1761.

[Greatworth, ca April 9, 1761].

YOU say I must be rigged out creditably; I say I will be grave, decent, and not fine. I have ordered my tailor¹ to call on you to choose a pattern of lace for my clothes; as it is for the summer I think gold gauze lace on cloth of a very dark colour that is fashionable is better than a heavy *ornie²* lace.

I have a notion that as my hair is very thin and bald behind, a

5. 'His Majesty having been pleased to declare his intention of marrying her Serene Highness the Princess of Brunswick, we hear that the following are to be of the bedchamber, viz. Lady Mary Bute, Mistress of the Robes; Duchess of Richmond, Lady Northumberland, Lady Mary Cook, Lady Bolingbroke, Lady Aylesbury, Lady Waldegrave' (*London Chronicle* 1761, 4–7 April, ix. 334). The entire article is incorrect.

6. *A Method of Breaking Horses, and Teaching Soldiers to Ride, Designed for the Use of the Army.* It reached a 4th edition in 1793.

7. Fulke Greville (ca 1717–ca 1806) of Wilbury, Wilts; son of Hon. Algernon Greville, 2d son of 5th Bn Brooke; Winchester and Brasenose; M.P. Monmouth 1745–52; Envoy to Bavaria 1764–70; published 1756 *Maxims, Characters, and Reflections;* m. Frances Macartney, author of the well-known *Ode to Indifference;* their dau. Frances, a famous beauty, m. John (later Bn) Crewe. Fanny Burney describes him as, in 1748, an early patron of her father's, 'the first gentleman about town,' and an ardent athlete; she portrays him again in 1791: 'querulous from ill-luck in his perilous pursuits [gambling] . . . he . . . retired from public view, and lived a rambling, unsettled sort of life, as ill at ease with his family as with the world.' See Frances Burney, Mme d'Arblay, *Memoirs of Dr Burney,* 1832, i. 24–48, iii. 134–6, 342–5, and *passim;* D. B. Horn, *British Diplomatic Representatives 1689–1789,* 1932, pp. 42, 46; Foster, *Alumni Oxon;* Collins, *Peerage,* 1812, iv. 357–8; N&Q 1863, 3d ser. iv. 5, 97; 1869, 4th ser. iii. 459.

1. Not identified.

2. So in MS; Montagu perhaps meant *orné.*

tour,[3] such as you wear, would be of service to my deformities. I know you will say why not come to town and manage your own matters than employ me to dress up an old doll? An hundred and forty miles out of my way and I not very well into the bargain, I look over many times before I undertake, and the patching up my old body for Dublin is a matter of little moment to me. Charles told me they embroider well and cheap in Ireland. I am minded therefore to stay till I get there to bespeak my other suit but I still am in doubt when my cousin goes and for how long a time. Lord Guilford said there was a design of keeping him there for three years to settle them; well, that would be dreadful to me, but I should hope, as their parliament sets but every other year, that I might be indulged a vacation.

I am certainly appointed Black Rod; my aunt Cosby tells me my cousin did it in the prettiest manner. I have not yet had it notified from him or his secretary but am at ease about it.

You never told me how you liked my sister Ann[4] and her house; you are a great favourite there and you should cultivate her; she will let you off for a bon mot.

My cousin does not take Pandora.[5] Is it the mode to have a thorough suit of cloth, that is waistcoat and all, or a silk one?[6] I have not made anything of the sort or minded any for so many years I am as ignorant as if I came from Jamaica. If silk, I like watered tabby. What stuff! And how am I employing you? Excuse me, I pray you; I will send you some Irish poetry[7] or a crozier—anything to make amends, and to show you how truly I am

Yours,

G. Montagu

? To Montagu, ca Saturday 11 April 1761

There seems to have been a letter of HW's, now missing, in reply to *ante* ca 9 April 1761, and answered by Montagu in the following letter.

3. 'A compromise between the wig and the natural head was afforded by the "tower" or "half" wig, which was intended for those who were bald on the top of the head only. These "towers" came as far as the crown of the head and the back of the ears where the real hair joined' (Georgiana Hill, *History of English Dress*, New York, 1893, ii. 26–7). In the Falconet portrait (1768) HW seems to be wearing a plain tye wig; the style is not clear in the Reynolds (1757) or Eccardt (1755) portraits.

4. His cousin Lady Anne Jekyll.

5. His mistress Miss Faulkner.

6. Portraits, etc., of the time indicate that silk waistcoats were still fashionable.

7. HW's enthusiasm for *Ossian* and early British poetry was at its height at this time (see HW to Dalrymple 14 April 1761).

From MONTAGU, ca Tuesday 14 April 1761

G.D. 15/8, No. 760.

The dating of this letter is conjectural. From the references to Mr Chute's offer, and a mishap to HW's eye, neither of which is mentioned elsewhere, it would appear to have been preceded by a missing HW letter, which, with this one, must be fitted into the sequence of letters, mostly undated, concerning Montagu's Irish aspirations. From a consideration of the subject-matters common to all these letters—dress, Black Rod, Montagu's visit to London, the date of Halifax's departure—and making due allowance for the contents of the missing HW letter, the present assignment seems the most reasonable; it assumes that the missing HW letter was written ca 11 April in reply to *ante* ca 9 April. The only serious objection to this arrangement is that it makes Montagu's reference to the death of Sir Harry Bellenden ('the example of my brother Black Rod,' below n. 4) antedate HW's discussion *post* 16 April. But Sir Harry died 7 April (GM 1761, xxxi. 188), and Montagu may well have known of the circumstances from the missing HW letter. Also, it is barely possible that the missing letter may have been from Chute to Montagu.

[Greatworth, ca April 14, 1761].

I CAN now, my dear Sir, write myself Black Rod; I have had a most kind letter from my cousin which you shall see by and by. I thank you much for all the troublesome commissions I have given you and must tell you that I have no thoughts of coming yet to town to kiss the Vice-King's hand. I have divers cogent reasons to the contrary, I think. I am not likely to leave England without seeing you, but it seems as if I was not likely to see Ireland yet a few months. Strawberry will be grown and blown some time hence; pray tell Mr Chute I am much obliged to him for his obliging offer[1] but must beg to be excused accepting it. I am vastly sorry to hear you have a grain or knatt[2] in your eye. I have an handkerchief—a princess wrought it[3]—to wipe it with; if it does not mend I shall not close mine all night.

1. See next letter.
2. Obsolete spelling for gnat (OED); 'grain or gnat' is an allusion to *King John*, IV. i. 93.
3. '. . . When your head did but ache,
   I knit my handkercher about your brows,
   (The best I had, a princess wrought it me)'
   (*King John* IV. i. 48–9.)
In his Book of Materials, 1771 (now Folger Library), HW writes: 'Is there an incident in all Racine, Corneille, Voltaire, Addison or Otway, so natural, so pathetic, so sublime, as Prince Arthur's reminding Hubert of his having bound a handkerchief wrought by a Princess on the jailer's temples? It is that contrast between royalty and the keeper of a prison that exalts both, and augments the compassion for Arthur.'

I am to tell you I love gauze lace of all things in season and out and therefore I desire you will choose me one out of hand. There will come weddings and birthdays and coronations that will raise the price of all commodities for the importation of one. My brows shall be measured at Strawberry. Charles sends me word he will take another year's lease of his house at St Stephen's Green to do me the honours of Ireland. I know you will frank his letter for that.

I hear Lord Buckingham is to be married to the Ariadne Drury; it will whitewash my cousin who has been so blackened for gaining her young tender heart. (Halifax)

So far from following the example of my brother Black Rod,[4] I have wrote to the General to lay me in a cargo of Bristol water[5] to extinguish my fire with.

Adieu! Believe me ever and everywhere your most faithful

G. MONTAGU

[On a separate sheet is a copy by Montagu of Lord Halifax's letter to him:]

'What I had in view for you when I wrote you last was Black Rod. I wish it was better; such as it is, I wish you much joy of it and hope we shall pass many happy [hours?] in the revival of a friendship which has never been interrupted on my part, though different scenes of life have prevented the intercourse I have always wished.'

[This is followed by a paragraph which is no doubt another item of news from Montagu, since it is set off from the first by a double parenthesis:]

Lord Robert Spencer[6] who represented his brother and was chaired for him, made the gentlemen a pretty speech and returned thanks in his brother's name and acquitted himself extremely well.

4. Sir Harry Bellenden, Usher of the Black Rod in the English House of Lords; died of drink (post 16 April 1761).

5. The water of the Hot-Well near Bristol was supposed to be remedial of practically any human ailment; see [John Feltham] Guide to all the Watering and Sea-Bathing Places [1815], pp. 82–5.

6. Lord Robert Spencer (1747–1831), 3d son of 2d D. of Marlborough; M.P. Woodstock 1768–71, 1818–20; Oxford 1771–90;

Wareham 1790–9; Tavistock 1802–7, 1817–18; Lord of Trade 1772–81; Vice-Treasurer of Ireland 1782–3; Surveyor General of Woods and Forests 1806–7. He probably represented his brother Lord Charles at the Oxfordshire election 9 April, when, since his birthday was 3 May, he was not quite 14 years old (see William R. Williams, Parliamentary History of County of Oxford, Brecknock, 1899, pp. 77, 129).

To Montagu, Thursday 16 April 1761

Arlington Street, April 16, 1761.

YOU are a very mule—one offers you a handsome stall and manger in Berkeley Square[1] and you will not accept it.

I have chosen your coat, a claret-colour, to suit the complexion of the country you are going to visit—but I have fixed nothing about the lace. Barret[2] had none of gauze, but what were as broad as the Irish Channel. Your tailor found a very reputable one at another place, but I would not determine rashly; it will be two or three and twenty shillings the yard—you might have a very substantial real lace,[2a] and that would wear like your buffet,[3] for twenty. The second order of gauzes are frippery, none above twelve shillings, and those tarnished, for the species is out of fashion. You will have time to sit in judgment upon these important points, for Hamilton,[4] your Secretary, told me at the opera two nights ago, that he had taken a house near Bushy,[5] and hoped to be in my neighbourhood for four months.

I was last night at your plump Countess's,[6] who is so shrunk, that she does not seem now to be composed of above a dozen hassocks. Lord Guilford rejoiced mightily over your preferment. The Duchess of Argyle was playing there, not knowing that the great Pan[7] was just dead, to wit, her brother-in-law.[8] He was abroad in the morning, and was seized with a palpitation after dinner, and was dead before the surgeon could arrive—there's the crown of Scotland too fallen upon my Lord Bute's head![9] Poor Lord Edgcumbe is still alive and may be so for some days;[10] the physicians who no longer ago than Friday se'ennight persisted that he had no dropsy, in order to prevent

---

1. Probably the invitation from Chute mentioned *ante* ca 14 April 1761.

2. Not identified.

2a. Mr John L. Nevinson writes that he thinks this must be bobbin lace.

3. Perhaps the foot-stool on which Montagu rested his gouty foot, a conjecture strengthened by the reference to hassocks below.

4. William Gerard ('Single-speech') Hamilton (1729–96), Chief Secretary for Ireland 1761–4; Chancellor of the Irish Exchequer 1763–84.

5. Bushy Park, Middlesex, of which Lord Halifax was Ranger.

6. Of Guilford.

7. According to the story in Plutarch's *Moralia*, 'De Oraculorum Defectu,' 17, at the hour of the Crucifixion a cry of 'Great Pan is dead' swept across the sea in the hearing of certain mariners, and the oracles ceased. Possibly HW is punning on 'Pam.'

8. 3d D. of Argyll.

9. The Duke of Argyll had been the political leader and chief dispenser of patronage in Scotland.

10. He died 10 May.

his having Ward;[11] on Monday last proposed that Ward should be called in—and at night they owned they thought the mortification begun—it is not clear it is yet; at times he is in his senses, and entirely so, composed, clear and most rational; talks of his death, and but yesterday, after such a conversation with his brother,[11a] asked for a pencil to amuse himself with drawing. What parts, genius and agreeableness, thrown away at a hazard table, and not permitted the chance of being saved by the villainy of physicians!

You will be pleased with the following anacreontic, written by Lord Middlesex[12] upon Sir Harry Ballendine—I have not seen anything so antique for ages; it has all the fire, poetry, and simplicity of Horace.

> Ye sons of Bacchus, come and join
> In solemn dirge, while tapers shine
> Around the grape-embossed shrine
> Of honest Harry Bellendine.
>
> Pour the rich juice of Bourdeaux's vine,
> Mix'd with your falling tears of brine,
> In full libation o'er the shrine
> Of honest Harry Bellendine.
>
> Your brows let ivy chaplets twine,
> While you push round the sparkling wine,
> And let your table be the shrine
> Of honest Harry Bellendine.

He died in his vocation, of a high fever after the celebration of some orgies. Though but six hours in his senses, he gave a proof of his usual good humour, making it his last request to the sister Tuftons[13] to be reconciled—which they are.[14] His pretty villa[15] in my

11. Joshua Ward (1685–1761), quack doctor; his immense success made him especially unpopular with more reputable practitioners.

11a. George Edgcumbe (1721–95), 3d Bn Edgcumbe, 1761; cr. (1781) Vct Edgcumbe, (1789) E. of Mount Edgcumbe.

12. Charles Sackville (1711–69), styled E. of Middlesex; 2d D. of Dorset, 1765.

13. Lady Mary (1723–1806) and Lady Charlotte Tufton (1728–1803), daughters of 7th E. of Thanet (Collins, *Peerage*, 1812, iii.

446). Lady Mary m. (1763) Dr William Duncan (ca 1715–74), Bt, 1764; Physician in Ordinary to George III. See the account of her in Frances Burney, Mme d'Arblay, *Memoirs of Dr Burney*, 1832, ii. 119–20, iii. 345, which describes her as 'one of the most singular females of her day.'

14. The reason for the quarrel is not known.

15. From his will it appears that it was in Petersham, and was left to Lord Frederick Campbell (P.C.C. Cheslyn 159).

neighbourhood, I fancy, he has left to the new Lord Lorn.[16] I must tell you an admirable bon mot of George Selwyn, though not a new one; when there was a malicious report that the eldest Tufton was to marry Dr Duncan,[17] Selwyn said, 'How often she will repeat that line of Shakespear,

Wake, Duncan, with thy knocking—would thou couldst!'[18]

I enclose the receipt from your lawyer.[19] Adieu!

Yours ever
H. W.

From Montagu, ca Tuesday 21 April 1761

G.D. 15/8, No. 761.

Undated; postmarked (at London) 22 April; obviously written in 1761.
Address: To the Honourable Mr Walpole, Arlington Street, London. Free.
Postmark: Banbury 22 AP.

[Greatworth, ca April 21, 1761].

WHO tells you I shall not come amongst you before I go hence? Would you have me have been in town amongst all the cabals and violence of Lady Fanny[1] and her brother and drawn in to give my opinion and into a thousand scrapes?

I am delighted to hear I shall have a charming summer of my own to spend here. The halfpence of the winter months they are welcome to in Ireland.

I need not therefore be in any haste about my clothes, but may stay some months when their looms will be going for the public festivals.[2] I hope to put on my robes by the time the Strawberry Gallery[3] is fit for me to prance about.

16. John Campbell (1723–1806), styled M. of Lorne 1761–70; 5th D. of Argyll, 1770; his mother was Bellenden's sister.
17. See n. 13 above.
18. *Macbeth* II. ii. 74. For the double meaning of 'knock,' see John S. Farmer and William E. Henley, *Slang and its Analogues,* 1890–1904.
19. Missing; the lawyer is not identified.

———

1. Probably Lady Frances Montagu (d.

1788), sister of the E. of Halifax; m. (1739) Sir Roger Burgoyne, 6th Bt, of Sutton Park, Beds. The nature of the cabals and violence is not known; probably they had to do with Halifax's political manoeuvrings.
2. Attendant on the Coronation.
3. Begun in March 1761; perhaps discussed in a missing letter of HW's. It was not finished until Aug. 1763; see *SH Accounts* 109; *Works* ii. 461–8.

Most likely I shall come to you in May, a time you are not likely to be absent, but by no means disorder any schemes for me.

If you have any thoughts of seeing your Beauchamp again, for I cannot desire you to come and see me, I shall be most heartily glad you will call here.

I have had a thousand letters of congratulations and am indeed as happy as possible. Now I am a cardinal I take care of my health for I may be pope one of these days. It is worth living for, to be rich,[4] to throw away one's money, when one has set one's self clear, and to have one's old age pure [?][5] and comfortable. Adieu! Believe me always most faithfully yours,

G. Montagu

From Montagu, ca Sunday 26 April 1761

G.D. 15/8, No. 762.

Undated; postmarked (at London) 27 April; answered *post* 28 April 1761. *Address:* To the Honourable Mr Walpole, Arlington Street, London. Free. *Postmark:* 27 AP.

[Greatworth, ca April 26, 1761].

IT will be more agreeable and convenient to me to come to Strawberry in June than[a] May and before I come I shall certainly let you have timely notice.

There is a report here the Duke of Grafton is going abroad, having ruined himself at play. I conclude it is to recover his or the Duchess's health.[1]

---

4. In 1764 and 1766, the stated salary of Black Rod was £533 6s. 8d. (Ireland, House of Lords, *Journals*, Dublin, 1779–1800, iv. 312, 383); but Lord Hertford, offering the place to David Hume in 1765, said it was worth £800 to £900 (see John Hill Burton, *Life and Correspondence of David Hume*, Edinburgh, 1846, ii. 291). It was probably the same during Montagu's tenure. Montagu's other income is not definitely known. He had about £400 a year as Secretary to Lord North from 1767 till his death (*post* 8 Oct. 1767; *Court and City Register*). By his will he created a trust to pay his sister £200 a year out of his estate at Roel, Glos, left him by his

uncle, and out of five farms in Winchcombe and Sudeley, Glos, left him by his father. On her death his patrimony (value not disclosed) was devised to the Duke of Manchester for life, remainder to his 2d son, Montagu's godson, Lord Frederick Montagu. The remainder interest in Roel and the residue went to Frederick Montagu of Papplewick, who, HW says, got £500 a year (HW to Mason ca 14 May 1780).

5. The text is not clear.

---

a. Montagu wrote 'that.'
1. See HW's guarded reply *post* 28 April 1761, n. 9.

Pray tell Lord Dacre, when you see him,[2] the drawing he desired my sister Wetenhall to get done for him of Sir Lister Holt's[3] house is done, and she wants to know how and where he would have it sent.

My compliments to Mr Chute. I hope you are well during the cold weather we have had.

Adieu! Believe me always your most faithful

G. M.

To Montagu, Tuesday 28 April 1761

Arlington Street, April 28, 1761.

I AM glad you relish June for Strawberry. By that time I hope the weather will have recovered its temper. At present it is horridly cross and uncomfortable. I fear we shall have a cold season; we cannot eat our summer and have our summer.

There has been a terrible fire in the little traverse street at the upper end of Sackville Street.[1] Last Friday night between eleven and twelve I was sitting with Lord Digby[2] in the coffee-room at Arthur's. They told us there was a great fire somewhere about Burlington Gardens. I who am as constant at a fire as George Selwyn at an execution,

2. Lord Dacre seems to have been one of HW's close, life-long friends. Only a half-dozen letters have been recovered (1939), but this reference of Montagu's shows that HW saw him frequently in London. Dacre's presentation copies of *Royal and Noble Authors* and *Anecdotes* are now WSL. HW also gave him *Fugitive Pieces* and *Modern Gardening*.

3. Sir Lister Holte (ca 1721–70), 5th Bt, of Aston Hall, Warw. Aston Hall, 'which for beauty and state much exceedeth any in these parts,' was begun by the first baronet in 1618; see William Dugdale, *Antiquities of Warwickshire*, 1656, p. 639 and illustration. HW copied the 'embattled wall' shown in Dugdale for the North Wall at SH and paid for it 10 April 1761 (*SH Accounts* 8, 107).

1. According to *Lloyd's Evening Post* 25–7 April 1761, viii. 396, the fire began in the stable of the Sadler's Arms in Swallow Street, and spread from there to Glasshouse Street, HW's 'little traverse street' (now the eastern end of Vigo Street). The *Post* also reports that many persons of

distinction were present, who supplied the engines with water, and the populace with money and liquor, to encourage assistance; see also GM 1761, xxxi. 187–8, 233. No adequate means for providing water seem to have existed; see the letter of 'Atticus Police' in the *London Chronicle* 13–15 Jan. 1757, i. 51: '. . . the panic spreads, the fire plug is not to be found, the turn-cock is not at home, or perhaps drunk, the fire rages, the fireman stands gnawing his fingers, with his engine ready to play, and the general cry is for water . . . [would it not be better] instead of fire plugs, or in conjunction with them, to have fire cocks, in different streets, fixed to leaden pipes, which, joined to the main, might be brought up to the side of a house, cased over with wood, the key left behind the door of the said house, and upon the box of the said pipe to have wrote *Fire Cock?* . . . Who will do it? If the Insurance offices think it not worth their while, it ought to be a parochial expense, as I think fire plugs are.'

2. Henry Digby (1731–93), 7th Bn Digby; cr. (1790) E. Digby.

proposed to Lord Digby to go and see where it was. We found it within two doors of that pretty house of Fairfax, now General Waldegrave's;[3] I sent for the latter who was at Arthur's, and for the guard from St James's. Four houses were in flames, before they could find a drop of water; eight were burnt.[4] I went to my Lady Suffolk in Saville Row, and passed the whole night, till three in the morning, between her little hot bedchamber and the spot, up to my ankles in water, without catching cold. As the wind, which had sat towards Swallow Street, changed in the middle of the conflagration, I concluded the greatest part of Saville Row would be consumed. I persuaded her to prepare to transport her most valuable effects—*portantur avari Pygmalionis opes miserae*.[5] She behaved with great composure, and observed to me herself how much worse her deafness grew with the alarm. Half the people of fashion in town were in the streets all night, as it happened in such a quarter of distinction. In the crowd looking on with great tranquility I saw a Mr Jackson,[6] an Irish gentleman with whom I had dined this winter at Lord Hertford's. He seemed rather grave—I said, 'Sir, I hope you don't live anywhere hereabouts'—'Yes, sir,' said he, 'I lodged in that house that is just burnt.'

Last night there was a mighty ball at Bedford House; the royal Dukes and Princess Emily were there, your Lord Lieut[en]ant, the great lawyer-lords, and old Newcastle, whose teeth are tumbled out and his mouth tumbled in; hazard, very deep; loo, beauties, and the Wilton bridge[7] in sugar almost as big as the life. I am glad all these joys are near going out of town. The Graftons go abroad[8] for the Duchess's health. Another climate may mend that—I will not answer for more.[9] Adieu!

Yours ever
H. W.

3. Near the SE corner of Savile Row (*London Past & Present* iii. 211).

4. GM 1761, xxxi. 187–8 gives the number as 14; *Lloyd's Evening Post* 24–7 April 1761, viii. 396, agrees with HW; all but two were tradesmen's houses.

5. 'Portantur avari Pygmalionis opes pelago' (Virgil, *Æn.* i. 363–4).

6. Not identified.

7. A famous Palladian bridge at Wilton, built by the 9th Earl of Pembroke; see Emily J. Climenson, *Elizabeth Montagu, the Queen of the Blue-stockings*, 1906, i. 249; Arthur Young, *Six Weeks Tour Through the Southern Counties of England*, 1768, p. 164; A. Thornton Bishop, *Renaissance Architecture of England*, 1938, illustration p. 101. The Bedfords had used it before in glass (see HW to Bentley 6 May 1755).

8. They 'set out for Harwich to embark for Holland' 6 June (*London Chronicle* 13–16 June 1761, ix. 570).

9. An allusion to the incompatibility

TO MONTAGU, Tuesday 5 May 1761

Arlington Street, May 5th, 1761.

WE have lost a young genius, Sir William Williams;[1] an express from Belleisle,[2] arrived this morning, brings nothing but his death. He was shot very unnecessarily, riding too near a battery. In sum, he is a sacrifice to his own rashness,—and to ours—for what are we taking Belleisle? I rejoiced at the little loss we had on landing— for the glory, I leave it to the Common Council.[3] I am very willing to leave London to them too, and do pass half the week at Strawberry, where my two passions, lilacs and nightingales are in full bloom. I spent Sunday as if it was Apollo's birthday; Gray and Mason were with me, and we listened to the nightingales till one o'clock in the morning. Gray has translated two noble incantations[4] from the Lord knows who, a Danish Gray, who lived the Lord knows when. They are to be enchased in a history of English bards, which Mason and he are writing, but of which the former has not writ a word yet, and of which the latter, if he rides Pegasus at his usual foot-pace, will finish the first page two years hence[5]—but the true frantic œstrus re-

which ended in a separation and divorce; see HW to Hertford 27 Aug. and 3 Dec. 1764. A contributing cause was the Duchess's passion for gambling. See Rev. Frederic Barlow, *Complete English Peerage*, 1775, i. 86–7, discussing the Duke's affair with Nancy Parsons: 'The husband who finds no consolation at home, will seek it elsewhere. A violent itch for play in his first duchess gave rise to their bickerings, and when even her father advised her, with parental tenderness, to conquer so fatal a passion, she paid no attention to the salutary admonition.'

1. Sir William Peere Williams (ca 1730–61), 2d Bt, of Clapton, Northants; Gray wrote an epitaph on him (*Gray's Corr.* ii. 746).

2. The expedition against Belle Isle (off the southern coast of Brittany) had accomplished a successful landing 22 April; the citadel fell 8 June. For an account of the expedition and its effect in diverting French forces from the Rhine, see Julian S. Corbett, *England in the Seven Years' War*, 1907, ii. 160–70.

3. Of the City of London, which was at times rather chauvinistic.

4. *The Fatal Sisters* and *The Descent of Odin*, adaptations from the Icelandic; they were not published until 1768; see *Poems of Gray and Collins*, ed. Austin Lane Poole, 3d edn 1937, pp. 65–79.

5. Gray writes, in his advertisement to the above-mentioned poems (*Poems*, 1768, p. 75), 'The Author once had thoughts (in concert with a friend) of giving *the History of English Poetry:* in the Introduction to it he meant to have produced some specimens of the style that reigned in ancient times among the neighbouring nations, or those who had subdued the greater part of this island, and were our progenitors: the following three Imitations made a part of them. He has long since dropped his design, especially after he had heard, that it was already in the hands of a person well qualified to do it justice, both by his taste, and his researches into antiquity.' This 'person' was Thomas Warton; see *Gray's Corr.* iii. 1092–3, 1122–5.

sides at present with Mr Hogarth; I went t'other morning to see a portrait he is painting of Mr Fox[6]—Hogarth told me he had promised, if Mr Fox would sit as he liked, to make as good a picture as Vandyke or Rubens could. I was silent—'Why now,' said he, 'You think this very vain, but why should not one speak truth?' This *truth* was uttered in the face of his own Sigismonda,[7] which is exactly a maudlin whore tearing off the trinkets that her keeper had given her, to fling at his head. She has her father's picture in a bracelet on her arm, and her fingers are bloody with the heart, as if she had just bought a sheep's pluck in St James's market. As I was going, Hogarth put on a very grave face, and said, 'Mr Walpole, I want to speak to you'; I sat down, and said, I was ready to receive his commands. For shortness, I will mark this wonderful dialogue by initial letters.

H. I am told you are going to entertain the town with something in our way. W. Not very soon, Mr Hogarth. H. I wish you would let me have it, to correct; I should be sorry to have you expose yourself to censure. We painters must know more of those things than other people. W. Do you think nobody understands painting but painters? H. Oh! So far from it, there's Reynolds,[8] who certainly has genius; why, but t'other day he offered £100 for a picture that I would not hang in my cellar; and indeed, to say truth, I have generally found that persons who had studied painting least, were the best judges of it—but what I particularly wanted to say to you was about Sir James Thornhill[9] (you know he married Sir James's daughter) I would not

6. Now in the possession of Lord Ilchester at Holland House.

7. First exhibited in 1761; now in the National Gallery. Hogarth painted the picture to prove his thesis that he could equal the old masters. In *Anecdotes* iv. 78 (*Works* iii. 460–1), HW says of Sigismonda: 'Not to mention the wretchedness of the colouring, it was the representation of a maudlin strumpet just turned out of keeping, and with eyes red with rage and usquebaugh, tearing off the ornaments her keeper had given her. To add to the disgust raised by such vulgar expression, her fingers were bloodied by her lover's heart that lay before her like that of a sheep's for her dinner.' John Nichols, *Biographical Anecdotes of William Hogarth*, 1781, quotes this passage (p. 43) and states that, when he saw the picture, the fingers were

not bloodied, and adds in a note that HW's memory must have failed him. In HW's copy (now WSL), HW has written, 'It was so represented at first: Hogarth might correct or alter it, on its being so much censured as it was before his death, as appears from this very note.' HW then refers to p. 46 where it is shown in a note that Hogarth did alter it and adds at the bottom of that page, 'Here is a proof that it *was* altered, and probably after Mr W. saw it.' Nichols repeated his statement in his 1785 edition; but with the admission that the hands were originally blood-stained.

8. Joshua Reynolds (1723–92), Kt, 1769; P.R.A.

9. Sir James Thornhill (1675–1734), Kt, 1720; painter; his dau. Jane (ca 1709–89) m. (1729) William Hogarth.

have you say anything against him; there was a book published some time ago, abusing him,[10] and it gave great offence—he was the first that attempted history in England, and I assure you some Germans have said he was a very great painter. W. My work will go no lower than the year 1700, and I really have not considered whether Sir J. Thornhill will come within my plan or not; if he does, I fear you and I shall not agree upon his merits.[11] H. I wish you would let me correct it—besides, I am writing something of the same kind myself, I should be sorry we should clash. W. I believe it is not much known what my work is; very few persons have seen it. H. Why, it is a critical history of painting, is not it? W. No, it is an antiquarian history of it in England; I bought Mr Vertue's MSS, and I believe the work will not give much offence. Besides, if it does, I cannot help it: when I publish anything, I give it to the world to think of it as they please. H. Oh! if it is an antiquarian work, we shall not clash. Mine is a critical work; I don't know whether I shall ever publish it[12]—it is rather an apology for painters—I think it owing to the good sense of the English, that they have not painted better. W. My dear Mr Hogarth, I must take my leave of you, you now grow too wild—and I left him— if I had stayed, there remained nothing but for him to bite me. I give you my honour this conversation is literal, and perhaps, as long as you have known Englishmen and painters, you never met with anything so distracted. I had consecrated a line to his genius (I mean for wit) in my preface;[13] I shall not erase it, but I hope nobody will ask me if he was not mad. Adieu!

Yours ever

H. W.

To Montagu, Thursday 14 May 1761

Strawberry Hill, May 14, 1761.

AS I am here and know nothing of our poor heroes at Belleisle, who are combatting rocks, mines, famine, and Mr Pitt's obstinacy,[1] I will send you the victory of a heroine—but must preface it

10. Not identified.
11. HW's account of Thornhill (*Works* iii. 417–18) is matter-of-fact and uncritical.
12. He did not.
13. The only reference to Hogarth in the preface is, 'Mr Hogarth has received no honours, but universal admiration' (*Works* iii. 6).

1. In continuing the siege, which HW thought futile (*Mem. Geo. III* i. 43–4).

with an apology, as it was gained over a sort of relation of yours.[2] Jemmy Lumley last week had a party of whisk at his own house; the combatants, Lucy Southwell,[3] *that curtsies like a bear,* Mrs *Prujean,*[4] and a Mrs *Mackinsy.*[5] They played from six in the evening till twelve next day; Jemmy never winning one rubber, and rising a loser of two thousand pound. How it happened I know not, nor why his suspicions arrived so late, but he fancied himself cheated, and refused to pay. However *the bear* had no share in his evil surmises. On the contrary, a day or two afterwards he promised a dinner at Hampstead to Lucy and her virtuous sister.[6] As he went to the rendezvous, his chaise was stopped by somebody, who advised him not to proceed. Yet no whit daunted he advanced. In the garden he found the gentle conqueress Mrs *Mackinsy,* who accosted him in the most friendly manner. After a few compliments, she asked him if he did not intend to pay her—'No indeed, I shan't, I shan't, your servant, your servant' —'Shan't you?' said the fair virago—and taking a horsewhip from beneath her hoop, she fell upon him with as much vehemence, as the Empress-Queen would upon the King of Prussia if she could catch him alone in the garden at Hampstead—Jemmy cried out murder; his servants rushed in, rescued him from the jaws of the lioness, and carried him off in his chaise to town: The *Southwells,* who were already arrived, and descended on the noise of the fray, finding nobody to pay for the dinner, and fearing they must, set out for London too, without it, though I suppose they had prepared tin pockets to carry off all that should be left.[7] Mrs Mackinsy is immortal, and in the Crown Office.[8]

2. See *ante* 25 June 1745, n. 26.

3. Hon. Lucia Southwell (b. 1710), dau. of 1st Bn Southwell; apparently living in 1789 (Lodge, *Irish Peerage,* 1789, vi. 26).

4. Not identified.

5. Not identified except that her name was properly 'Mackenzie' (see below n. 8); the words appearing in italic were underlined in the original letter—why HW underscored them is not clear.

6. Hon. Frances Southwell (b. 1708), apparently also living 1789 (Lodge, loc. cit.).

7. Writing to the Duke of Newcastle 5 Nov. 1760, Chesterfield says that Frances Southwell's sole means of support for 12 years had been a pension he had procured her of £200 a year (Earl of Chesterfield, *Letters,* ed. Bonamy Dobrée, 1932, v. 2367).

8. 'Sure . . . some one has told you, how your *good friend,* Mr L. has been horsewhipped, trampled, bruised, and pissed upon, by a Mrs Mackenzie, a sturdy Scotch woman. It was done in an inn-yard at Hampstead in the face of day, and he has put her in the Crown-Office' (Gray to Wharton 23 June 1761, *Gray's Corr.* ii. 741–2, perhaps on information in a missing letter of HW's). The criminal business of the Court of King's Bench was called the 'crown side' or the 'crown office' (Sir William Blackstone, *Commentaries,* iv. *308). It does not appear that the Crown Office building was used as a prison (*London and its Environs Described,* 1761, ii. 206–7; it is not mentioned in John Howard, *State of the Prisons,* 1792). Doubtless

I can tell you two more quarrels, that have not ended quite so bloodily. Long Herbert[9] has lately made some alterations to his house in Berkeley Square: the workmen overturned three stone posts. Lady Mary Coke's servants disputed with his for the property, and she herself sent him a message about them,[10] to which he made this answer;

> What a pother you make about one single stone!
> Within a yard's[11] length I have two of mine own,
> Impaired by long standing, I fairly confess,
> And that yours is the larger, and mine are both less:
> That each may be gainers, do humbly propose,
> That I may use yours, and your Ladyship those.

The last battle in my military journal happened between the mother[12] of the last-mentioned dame, and Lord Vere. The Duchess, who always talks of Puss and Pug,[13] and who having lost her memory, forgets how often she tells the same story, had tired the company at Dorset House with the repetition of this narration; when the Duke's spaniel, reached up into her lap, and placed his nose as critically[14] as Herbert's epigram. 'See,' said she, 'see how fond all creatures are of me.' Lord Vere, who was at cards, and could not attend to them from her gossiping, said peevishly without turning round or seeing where the dog was, 'I suppose he smells puss.'—'What,' said the Duchess of Argyle in a passion, 'do you think my puss stinks?'—I believe you have not three better stories in Northamptonshire.

Don't imagine that my gallery will be *prance-about-in-able,* as you expect, by the beginning of June; I do not propose to finish it till

Gray and HW mean by 'in the Crown Office' that Lumley had filed an information against Mrs Mackenzie in the King's Bench. See Elizabeth, Duchess of Northumberland, *Diaries of a Duchess,* ed. James Greig, 1926, p. 42: 'January 10, 1762.—The cause between Jimmy Lumley and Mrs Mackenzie who horse-whipped him was to have come on before Lord Mansfield the 4th, but was compromised which prevented some excellent fun for both lawyers and spectators, for above 500 people went down to hear the decision.'
9. Probably Hon. Robert Sawyer Herbert (d. 1769), of Highclere, Hants; 2d son of 8th E. of Pembroke; M.P. Wilton 1722–68; held numerous offices; see Collins,

Peerage, 1812, iii. 141–2. His house was at the corner of Hill Street and Berkeley Square (rate-books of St George's Parish and his will). For other examples of his sense of humour, see Lord Chesterfield to Lady Suffolk, 2 Nov. and 24 Nov. 1734 (*Letters,* ed. Bonamy Dobrée, 1932, ii. 290, 310).
10. The rest of the paragraph and the verses have been omitted in previous editions.
11. 'The virile member' (OED).
12. Duchess of Argyll.
13. Pets; she called her dog 'Pug' (Coke, *Journals* i. 49).
14. Rest of sentence omitted in Toynbee.

next year—but you will see some glimpse of it—and for the rest of
Strawberry, it never was more beautiful. You must begin now to fix
your motions: I go to Lord Dacre's the end of this month, and to
Lord Ilchester's[15] the end of the next—between those periods I expect
you.

Saturday morning Arlington Street.

I came to town yesterday for a party at Bedford House made for
Princess Emily; the garden was open with French horns and clarinets,
and would have been charming with one single zephyr that had not
come from the north-east—however, the young ladies found it delightful. There was limited loo for the Princess, unlimited for the
Duchess of Grafton, to whom I belonged, a table of quinze and another of quadrille. The Princess had heard of our having cold meat
upon the loo-table, and would have some. A table was brought in,
she was served so, others rose by turns and went to the cold meat; in
the outward room were four little tables for the rest of the company.
Think if George the Second could have risen and seen his daughter
supping pellmell with men, as it were in a booth! The tables were
removed, the young people began to dance to a tabor and pipe; the
Princess sat down again, but to unlimited loo, we played till three,
and I won enough to help on the gallery. I am going back to it, to
give my nieces and their lords a dinner.

We were told there was a great victory come from Pondicherry,[16]
but it came from too far to divert us from liking our party better.
Poor George Monson[17] has lost his leg there. You know that Sir W.
Williams has made Fred. Montagu heir to his debts. Adieu!

Yours ever

H. W.

15. Stephen Fox (after 1758 Fox-Strangways) (1704–76), cr. (1741) Bn Ilchester;
(1756) E. of Ilchester. HW seems not to
have visited his seats at Redlynch, Somerset, and Melbury, Dorset, until July 1762;
see *Country Seats* 44, 47; HW to Ilchester
29 July 1762.

16. The French in Pondicherry, under
Lally, had capitulated 15 Jan. 1761; but
the victory of which news was received
overland in England 15 May was won 3

Sept. 1760, when a French sortie was repulsed; compare GM 1761, xxxi. 235, and
London Chronicle 14–16 May 1761, ix.
471, with Col. Harold C. Wylly, *Life of
Sir Eyre Coote*, Oxford, 1922, p. 95.

17. Hon. George Monson (1730–76), Brig.
Gen., 1763. His leg was only broken (ibid.
96). He was intimate with George Selwyn
and all his set, and became well known as
an opponent of Warren Hastings.

To MONTAGU, ca Monday 25 May 1761

Missing; date conjectural; answered by Montagu *post* ca 30 May 1761.

From MONTAGU, ca Saturday 30 May 1761

G.D. 15/8, No. 763.

Undated except for the day of the week. Preceded by a missing HW letter, and probably written before *post* 9 June 1761, since in this letter he is uncertain about his SH visit, while in that one he sets a date. Conjectural date assigned in the absence of information when Lord Halifax kissed hands.

Saturday, Greatworth [ca May 30, 1761].

THANKS, many thanks, for your information about my cousin.[1] I had a letter from Madam Osborn to tell me he had kissed hands and was to hold the lieutenancy *in commendam;* that is the best news for me for I have not yet had my pennyworths out of the kingdom nor truly he neither.

I had a letter from our General last post to tell me he was come to pack[2]; I expect him here in a few days and then shall be able to fix what I can do about my parties to your honour's Strawberry and Mr Chute's Vine, and then you shall again hear from me. I dread the heat but shall come like a thief in the night; I long more to see you than anything you have, though I have immortal longings[3] for them. I am brave and well, all life from the baldness of my crown to the gout in my foot, but am still your old faithful

G. MONTAGU

From MONTAGU, Tuesday 9 June 1761

G.D. 15/8, No. 764.

Greatworth, June 9, 1761.

PRAY tell me if next week you shall be at liberty for me to come and pass a few days at Strawberry. I hope this changeful weather has not disagreed with you; I have the rheumatism, which makes me

1. In HW's missing letter.
2. So apparently in MS; perhaps the sense is that he was about to pack for his return to England.

3. *Antony and Cleopatra* V. ii. 333.

hobble almost as bad as if I had the gout, and it depends upon the north-east wind to make it the gout in all its shapes. Be so good as to put your name to Charles's letter, and you will oblige your most faithful

G. M.

Pray send me word where Eckart lives.[1]

To Montagu, ca Friday 12 June 1761

Missing; answered *post* ca 16 June 1761.

From Montagu, ca Tuesday 16 June 1761

G.D. 15/8, No. 764.
Undated; answered by HW *post* 18 June 1761; in reply to a missing HW letter.

[Greatworth, ca June 16, 1761].

MONDAY the 22 will suit me very much and I shall like as well to meet Mr Chute as he can do to see me. I mean not to whisk away suddenly. Old Sir John Pelham[1] my great-grandfather, as all the *world* knows, used to ask people as soon as they sat down, 'Pray, for how long are you come to stay, that I may manage my civilities accordingly?' I, who never followed any of that kin, never tell how long I shall stay; but as I find the civilities, so I stay. Now you will begin your terrible conclusions, but to abridge I have always really stayed with you as long as my time would let me. I am to pass a day or two and take the oaths to my Viceroy at Bushey. I shall bring my brother John with me, who only proposes staying that day and the next and then goes to town on some business. I hope to find you in perfect health; our part of the world has been very feverish. You frighten me

---

1. In a list of 'Principal Painters now in London, 1761,' HW states that Eccardt lived in 'Newport street, house that was Reynolds's' (*Anecdotes of Painting*, ed. Frederick W. Hilles and Philip B. Daghlian, New Haven, 1937, pp. 3–4). HW states in *Anecdotes, Works* iii. 448–9 n. that on Eccardt's retirement he moved to Chelsea, but since he contributed to the exhibition of the Society of Artists, 1768, it may be assumed that he had not yet retired. Reynolds's house in Newport Street from 1753 to 1761 'when he removed to Leicester Fields' was No. 5 (*London Past & Present* ii. 597).

———

1. Sir John Pelham (ca 1623–1703), 3d Bt, of Halland in Laughton, Sussex.

about all the troubles and perils I am to go through in my Irish warfare;[2] be it as it will, it will be my welfare, and I enjoy every day the comforts of the affluence it will procure me and fancy I shall return only altered in my speech, not in my writing myself always most assuredly yours

G. MONTAGU

Do you know Prince Rupert invented mezzotinto?[3] And prince's metal.[4]

To MONTAGU, Thursday 18 June 1761

Strawberry Hill, June 18th, 1761.

I AM glad you will come on Monday, and hope you will arrive in a rainbow and pair, to signify that we are not to be totally drowned. It has rained incessantly, and floated all my new works; I seem rather to be building a pond than a gallery. My farm too is all under water, and what is vexatious, if Sunday had not thrust itself between, I could have got in my hay on Monday. As the parsons will let nobody else make hay on Sundays, I think they ought to make it on that day themselves.

By the papers I see Mrs Trevor Hampden[1] is dead of the smallpox. Will he be much concerned?

If you will stay with me a fortnight or three weeks, perhaps I may be able to carry you to a play of Mr Bentley's—you stare—but I am in earnest—nay, and *de par le roy*. In short, here is the history of it. You know the passion he always had for the Italian comedy. About two years ago he writ one, intending to get it offered to Rich—but without his name—he would have died to be supposed an author, and writing

---

2. In his missing letter, HW may have given Montagu an insight into Irish politics.

3. Though he was generally credited with the discovery, Prince Rupert (1619–82) did not invent mezzotint; but he introduced it into England (John Chaloner Smith, *British Mezzotinto Portraits*, 1883, i. pp. xxix, xxxiv). In his *Catalogue of Engravers* (*Works* iv. 63–7) HW gives the traditional story, recorded by Evelyn, of Prince Rupert's discovery, suggested by a sentry's rusty gun.

4. '[From Prince Rupert of the Rhine, who invented it]. An alloy of . . . copper and . . . zinc' (OED). Rupert is credited with its invention in Eva Scott, *Rupert Prince Palatine*, 1899, p. 337.

---

1. Constantia de Huybert (ca 1727–61), m. (1743) Hon. Robert Trevor (after 1754, Hampden), 4th Bn Trevor, 1764; cr. (1776) Vct Hampden.

for gain. I kept this a most inviolable secret. Judge then of my surprise when about a fortnight or three weeks ago I found my Lord Melcomb reading this very Bentleiad in a circle at my Lady Hervey's. Cumberland had carried it to him, with a recommendatory copy of verses, containing more incense to the King and my Lord Bute, than the Magi brought in their portmanteaus to Jerusalem. The idols were propitious, and to do them justice, there is a great deal of wit in the piece, which is called *The Wishes or Harlequin's Mouth Opened*.[2] A bank note of £200 was sent from the *Treasury* to the author, and the play ordered to be performed by the summer company. Foote was summoned to Lord Melcomb's, where Parnassus was composed of the peer himself, who, like Apollo as I am going to tell you, was dozing, the two Chief Justices[3] and Lord Bute. Bubo[4] read the play himself, *with handkerchief and orange by his side*.[5] But the curious part is a prologue which I never saw. It represents the god of verse fast asleep by the side of Helicon. The race of modern bards try to wake him, but the more they repeat of their works, the louder he snores. At last *Ruin seize thee ruthless King*[6] is heard, and the god starts from his trance. This is a good thought, but will offend the bards so much, that I think Dr Bentley's son will be abused at least as much as his father was. The prologue concludes with young Augustus, and how much he excels the ancient one, by the choice of his friend. Foote refused to act this prologue, and said it was too strong. 'Indeed,' said Augustus's friend, 'I think it is.' They have softened it a little, and I suppose it will be performed.[7] You may depend upon the truth of all this; but what is much more credible is, that the *comely young* author appears every night in the Mall in a milk-white coat with a blue cape, disclaims any benefit, and says he has done with the play now it is out of his own hands, and that Mrs Hannah Clio alias Bentley writ the best scenes in it. He is going to write a tragedy, and she, I suppose, is going—to court.

You will smile when I tell you that t'other day a party went to Westminster Abbey, and among the rest saw the ragged regiment.[8]

2. See *post* 28 July 1761.

3. Mansfield, and Sir John Willes (1685–1761), Chief Justice of Common Pleas, 1737.

4. The name by which Pope satirized Dodington.

5. Pope, 'Epistle to Dr Arbuthnot,' 228.

6. First line of Gray's 'The Bard.'

7. It was not; see *post* 28 July 1761.

8. The 'ragged regiment' was a miscellaneous collection of waxen effigies of prominent persons, which had been carried at their funerals. Since it included some English kings as remote as Edward

They inquired the names of the figures. 'I don't know them,' said the man, 'but if Mr Walpole was here he could tell you every one.'

Adieu! I expect Mr John and you with impatience.

Yours ever

H. W.

From Montagu, Monday 29 June 1761

G.D. 15/8, No. 767.

Dated by postmark and *post* 4 July 1761; written from Chute's house.
Address: The Honourable Mr Walpole, Strawberry Hill, Twickenham, Middlesex. Free. *Postmark:* 29 IV GC.

Berkeley Square, Monday [June 29, 1761].

MR CHUTE, which you will be glad to hear, is much better than I expected. He dined below and walks about his room a little and eat his dinner well and is in good spirits. I am well also and find your Mrs Mary Sturbridge¹ very obliging and handy. Mr Chute desires his compliments to you, I desire my best, am always most sincerely yours,

G. Montagu

From Montagu, ca Friday 3 July 1761

G.D. 15/8, No. 766.

Undated; answered by HW *post* 4 July 1761.

Berkeley Square [ca July 3, 1761].

DO excuse me waiting on you; I am uneasy till I get home. I am wellish but it is absolutely necessary for me to go through the land that flows with manna and salts and I do not care to postpone it a day. Mr Chute has been airing and I with him this afternoon, and presents his compliments to you. I wish you most truly your health

III, some of the specimens were in poor condition; hence the phrase; see Arthur P. Stanley, *Historical Memorials of Westminster Abbey,* 5th edn 1882, pp. 321–5. HW's familiarity with them was acquired during his researches for the *Anecdotes of Painting;* see *Works* iii. 50. They have re-

cently been cleaned and repaired and were (1939) on view in the Abbey.

———

1. Properly Jane Truebridge; not further identified. Montagu was staying at HW's house in Arlington Street, where she was housekeeper (see *post* 4 July 1761).

and all happiness and am much obliged to you for Mrs Mary Tru-
brige[1] and all her civilities and accommodations. I am most sincerely
yours,

G. MONTAGU

To MONTAGU, Saturday 4 July 1761

Misdated by HW; see postmark.
Address: To George Montagu Esq. at Greatworth near Brackley, Northamptonshire. Free Hor. Walpole. *Postmark:* Isleworth 4 IY.

Strawberry Hill, July 5th [4], 1761.

YOU are a pretty sort of person to come to one's house and get
sick, only to have an excuse for not returning to it. Your departure is so abrupt, that I don't know but I may expect to find that
Mrs *Jane* Truebridge, whom you commend so much and call Mrs
Mary, will prove Mrs *Hannah.*[1] Mrs Clive is still more disappointed;
she had proposed to play at quadrille with you from dinner to supper, and to sing old Purcell[2] to you from supper to breakfast next
morning. If you cannot trust yourself from Greatworth for a whole
fortnight, how will you do in Ireland for six months? Remember all
my preachments, and never be in spirits at supper. Seriously I am
sorry you are out of order, but am alarmed for you at Dublin, and
though all the bench of bishops should quaver Purcell's hymns, don't
let them warble you into a pint of wine—I wish you was going among
Catholic prelates, who would deny you the cup.[3] Think of me and
resist temptation. Adieu! Yours ever

H. W.

From MONTAGU, ca Tuesday 7 July 1761

G.D. 15/8, No. 770.
In reply to *ante* 4 July 1761; answered by HW *post* 10 July 1761.

[Greatworth, ca July 7, 1761].

I WILL give you and Mrs Clive who are well leave to be angry with
me who was growing too ill to return; I am but poorly now and I
dread always the being laid up abroad. I shall lay up in my mind

1. HW's housekeeper (see next letter).
———
1. That is, with child by Montagu.

2. Henry Purcell (1658?–95), composer.
3. HW makes another play on this doctrine *post* 26 Jan. 1762.

your friendly cautions and carry your letter of advice in my pocket as a charm to Dublin, as I have as many fears as you are kind and obliging to have for me; and hope I shall return to give you thanks, not in Twickenham church, for my deliverance from all the perils of my warfare. My brother John has had a little return of his fever, but is getting well again. I most truly wish you your health and all imaginable happiness.

I have had a very kind letter from my little Lord Dacre that has been most acceptable to me. Adieu! Yours most sincerely,

G. MONTAGU

To MONTAGU, Friday 10 July 1761

Strawberry Hill, Friday night, July 10th, 1761.

I DID not notify the King's marriage[1] to you yesterday, because I knew you would learn as much by the *Evening Post*,[2] as I could tell you. The solemn manner of summoning the council was very extraordinary: people little imagined that *the urgent and important business* in the rescript was to acquaint them that his Majesty was going to lose his maidenhead. You may choose what complexion you please for the new Queen: every colour under the sun is given to her. All I can tell you of truth is, that Lord Harcourt goes to fetch her, and comes back her Master of the Horse. She is to be here in August, and the Coronation certainly on the 22d of September. Think of the joy the women feel—there is not a Scotch peer in the Fleet that might not marry the greatest fortune in England between this and the 22d of September.[3] However the ceremony will lose its two brightest luminaries, my niece Waldegrave for beauty, and the Duchess of Grafton for figure. The first will be lying in,[4] the latter at Geneva— but I think she will come,[5] if she walks to it, as well as at it. I cannot recollect but Lady Kildare[6] and Lady Pembroke of great beauties.

1. An extraordinary meeting of the Privy Council was summoned to meet 8 July, when the King announced his intention to marry Charlotte Sophia (1744–1818), of Mecklenburg-Strelitz.

2. See *Lloyd's Evening Post* 8–10 July 1761, ix. 33.

3. So that she could take part in the Coronation ceremonies on that date.

4. See *post* 24 Oct. 1761, n. 17.

5. She did not; see HW to Mann 28 Sept. 1761.

6. Lady Emilia Mary Lennox (1731–1814), m. (1) (1747) James Fitzgerald, 20th E. of Kildare; cr. (1761) M. of Kildare, (1766) D. of Leinster; m. (2) (1774) William Ogilvie, a tutor in her household.

Mrs Bloodworth[7] and Mrs Robert Brudenel, Bedchamber Women; Miss Wrottesley[8] and Miss Meadows,[9] Maids of Honour, go to receive the Princess at Helvoet; what Lady I do not hear. Your cousin's Grace of Manchester, they say, is to be Chamberlain, and Mr Stone Treasurer—the Duchess of Ancaster[10] and Lady Bolinbroke[11] of her Bedchamber: these I do not know are certain, but hitherto all seems well chosen. Miss Molly Howe,[12] one of the pretty Bishops,[13] and a daughter of Lady Harry Beauclerc[14] are talked of for Maids of Honour. The great apartment at St James's is enlarging, and to be furnished with the pictures from Kensington: this does not portend a new palace.

In the midst of all this novelty and hurry, my mind is very differently employed. They expect every minute the news of a battle between Soubise and the Hereditary Prince.[15] Mr Conway is, I believe, in the latter's army; judge if I can be thinking much of espousals and coronations! It is terrible to be forced to sit still, expecting such an event—in one's own room one is not obliged to be a hero; consequently I tremble for one that is really a hero!

Mr your Secretary has been to see me today; I am quite ashamed

7. Margaret Bloodworth or Bludworth, Bedchamber-woman till her death in 1786 (*Court and City Register;* GM 1786, lvi pt i. 269).

8. Mary (d. 1769), dau. of Sir Richard Wrottesley, 7th Bt; see Maj. Gen. the Hon. George Wrottesley, *History of the Family of Wrottesley of Wrottesley,* 1903, pp. 348–51.

9. Frances (d. 1769), dau. of Sir Sidney Meadows; m. (1768) Capt. Alexander Campbell, Equerry to the D. of Cumberland (*London Magazine* 1769, xxxviii. 398; GM 1768, xxxviii. 446; 1773, xliii. 255).

10. Mary Panton (d. 1793), m. (1750) Peregrine Bertie, 3d D. of Ancaster; Mistress of the Robes to the Queen 1761–93. For a complete list of the Queen's household, see *Court and City Register for 1762,* pp. 99–100, and *A Treatise on The Prerogatives of a Queen Consort of England,* 1762, pp. 44–8 (HW's copy is now WSL).

11. Lady Diana Spencer (1734–1808), m. (1) (1757) Frederick St John, 2d Vct Bolingbroke, who divorced her; m. (2) (1768) Topham Beauclerk; Lady of the Bedcham-

ber 1761–8. She became a Twickenham neighbour of HW, who admired her artistic talents excessively.

12. Her name does not appear in either of the lists mentioned in n. 10, but Miss Bishopp and Miss Beauclerk do.

13. Frances (d. 1804), dau. of Sir Cecil Bishopp, Bt; m. (1764) Sir George Warren, K.B.; they were legally separated in 1772 after airing their differences in the Ecclesiastical Court, but were later reconciled; see *Annual Register* for 1804, xlvi. 468; GM 1801, lxxi pt ii. 861–2.

14. Diana Beauclerk (1741–1809), 'senior Maid of Honour' at her death (Collins, *Peerage,* 1812, i. 248; GM 1809, lxxix pt i. 190). She gave HW a picture of 'Johanna Lady Abergavenny' (sold SH xx. 76). She was engaged in 1768 to Lord Spencer Hamilton, a match which caused some stir in Lady Mary Coke's circle because she was 'extremely plain in her person and without a shilling of fortune,' but it apparently fell through (Coke, *Journals* ii. 185 and *passim*).

15. See *post* 22 July 1761.

not to have prevented him. I will go tomorrow with all the speeches I can muster.[16]

I am sorry neither you nor your brother are quite well, but shall be content if my Pythagorean sermons have any weight with you. You go to Ireland to make the rest of your life happy—don't go to fling the rest of it away! Good night!

Yours most faithfully

H. W.

Mr Chute is gone to his Chutehood.

To Montagu, Wednesday 22 July 1761

Strawberry Hill, July 22d, 1761.

FOR my part I believe Mademoiselle Scudéri drew the plan of this year—it is all royal marriages, coronations and victories; they come tumbling so over one another from distant parts of the globe, that it looks just like the handiwork of a lady romance-writer, whom it costs nothing but a little false geography to make the Great Mogul in love with a Princess of Mecklemburg, and defeat two Marshals of France as he rides post on an elephant to his nuptials. I don't know where I am! I had scarce found Mecklemburg-Strelitz with a magnifying glass,[1] before I am whisked to Pondicherri—well, I take it and raze it—I begin to grow acquainted with Colonel Coote[2] and to figure him packing up chests of diamonds and sending them to his wife against the King's wedding—thunder go the Tower guns, and behold Broglio[3] and Soubize are totally defeated—if the mob have not a much stronger head and quicker conceptions than I have, they will conclude my Lord Granby is become nabob. How the deuce in two days can one digest all this?[4] Why; is not Pondicherri in Westphalia? I don't know

16. Hamilton had doubtless come to see Montagu, and HW was going to apologize for failing to warn him Montagu had left.

1. Mecklenburg-Strelitz was one of the two ducal houses of Mecklenburg, in northern Germany; its territories lay to the east of, and were far inferior to, those of Mecklenburg-Schwerin; see Reginald Lane Poole, *Historical Atlas of Modern Europe*, Oxford, 1902, pl. 41.

2. Lt-Col. Eyre Coote (1726–83), K.B., 1771; Commander-in-chief in India 1769,

1777; took Pondicherry 15 Jan. 1761. The reference to his wife is fanciful, as he did not marry until 1763; see Col. Harold C. Wylly, *Life of Lieutenant-General Sir Eyre Coote, K.B.*, Oxford, 1922.

3. Victor-François (1718–1804), Duc de Broglie; Marshal of France, 1759; he and Soubise, who had joined their forces, blamed each other for the defeat; Broglie was exiled for three years (*Nouv. Biog. Gén.*). HW uses an antiquated spelling of Broglie.

4. The fall of Pondicherry was an-

how the Romans did, but I cannot support two victories every week. Well, but you will want to know the particulars: Broglio and Soubise being united, attacked our army on the 15th but were repulsed—the next day Prince Mahomet Alli Cawn[5]—no, no, I mean Prince Ferdinand returned the attack, the French threw down their arms, and fled,[6] run over my Lord Harcourt who was going to fetch the new Queen—in short, I don't know how it was, but Mr Conway is safe,[7] and I am as happy as Mr Pitt himself. We have only lost a Lieutenant-Colonel Keith[8]—a Colonel Marlay[9] and Harry Townshend[10] are wounded.

I could beat myself for not having a flag ready to display on my round tower and guns mounted on all my battlements. Instead of that I have been foolishly trying on my pictures upon my gallery—however, the oratory[11] of our Lady of Strawberries shall be dedicated next year on the anniversary of Mr Conway's safety[12]—think with his intrepidity, and delicacy of honour wounded,[12a] what I had to apprehend! You shall absolutely be here on the 16th of next July. Mr Hamilton tells me your King[13] does not set out for his new dominions till

nounced in a *London Gazette Extraordinary* 20 July; of Dominique in the regular *Gazette* of 18–21 July; and the victory of Kirch Denckern, 16 July, in another *Gazette Extraordinary* 22 July.

5. Muhammed 'Ali Walajah (ca 1717–95), established as Nawab of Arcot by the English in the unofficial hostilities between the English and French Companies which preceded the Seven Years' War; misgoverned his territories and deceived the English; accumulated great debts which were a never-ending source of corruption and embarrassment to the Indian government and provoked several Parliamentary inquiries; see *Cambridge History of the British Empire*, 1929–36, vol. iv, *British India 1497–1858*, ed. H. H. Dodwell. 'Cawn' is a corruption of 'Khan.'

6. This battle, called Kirch-Denckern in contemporary accounts, and Vellinghausen by modern writers, was not as decisive as first reports indicated; but it was important as showing that Ferdinand could hold in check a French force twice his strength; see Fortescue, *British Army* ii. 537–40.

7. He commanded a corps in the Allied force.

8. Robert Murray Keith (1730–95), K.B.,

1772; Lt-Gen.; M.P. Peebles 1775–80; diplomatist; in command of the 87th Foot at Vellinghausen. It was his major, Campbell, who was killed (*London Chronicle* 4–6 Aug. 1761, x. 121). See his account of the battle in *Memoirs and Correspondence . . . of Sir Robert Murray Keith*, 1849, i. 104.

9. Lt-Col. Thomas Marlay (d. 1784), of the 5th Foot; not in *Army Lists* after 1766; of Celbridge, co. Kildare, where Arthur Young visited him in 1776 (*Tour in Ireland*, 1780, pp. 10–11). He was a favourite uncle of Henry Grattan (see the latter's *Memoirs*, 1839–46, i. 39–41; *Marlay Letters*, ed. Richard Warwick Bond, 1937, table 5 at end).

10. Lt-Col. Henry Townshend, 3d son of Hon. Thomas Townshend; M.P. Eye 1758–60, 1761–2; killed at Wilhelmstahl, 1762 (Collins, *Peerage*, 1812, vi. 321).

11. At the entrance to the house; HW paid for it 6 May 1762 (*SH Accounts* 9, 112).

12. This did not happen, on account of the delay caused by strikes among the workers; see HW to Mann 1 July 1762.

12a. In the affair of the unsuccessful Rochefort expedition (*ante* 18 Oct. 1757; HW to Conway 13 Oct. 1757).

13. Lord Halifax.

the day after the Coronation—if you will come to it, I can give you a very good place for the procession—where, is a profound secret, because if known I should be teased to death, and none but my first friends shall be admitted.[14] I dined with your Secretary[15] yesterday; there were Garrick and a young Mr Burk,[16] who wrote a book in the style of Lord Bolinbroke[17] that was much admired. He is a sensible man, but has not worn off his authorism yet—and thinks there is nothing so charming as writers and to be one—he will know better one of these days. I like Hamilton's little Marly[18]—we walked in the great *allée*,[19] and drank tea in the arbor of *treillage;* they talked of Shakespear and Booth,[20] of Swift and my Lord Bath, and I was thinking of *Madame Sévigné*.[21] Good night—I have a dozen other letters to write;[22] I must tell my friends how happy I am—not as an Englishman, but as a cousin.

Yours ever
H. WALPOLE

From MONTAGU, Sunday 26 July 1761

G.D. 15/8, No. 769.

In reply to *ante* 22 July and answered *post* 28 July 1761.

Greatworth, Sunday [July 26, 1761].

I MOST heartily wish you joy of your German victory. I know what you have felt and what you must feel and am quite happy to hear you are so. I have so long valued General Conway and been

14. It was at the house in Palace Yard of HW's deputy Grosvenor Bedford; see HW to Bedford 23 Sept. 1761, HW to Conway 25 Sept. 1761.

15. William Gerard Hamilton.

16. Edmund Burke (1729–97), Hamilton's secretary at this time; the book was *Vindication of Natural Society in a Letter to Lord ——, by a late Noble Writer,* 1756, a satiric imitation of Bolingbroke.

17. Henry St John (1678–1751), cr. (1712) Vct Bolingbroke; statesman; Burke's satire was inspired by deistic portions of his *Works,* 1754.

18. A château built by Louis XIV, west of Paris; Mme de Sévigné records innumerable sojourns of the court there; it was apparently considered informal and

rustic, compared to Versailles; but see Pierre-Thomas-Nicolas Hurtaut and Magny, *Dictionnaire historique de la ville de Paris,* 1779, iii. 489–98. Hamilton's house was near Bushy Park, Hampton (*ante* 16 April 1761).

19. 'The chief glory of the park is the triple avenue (over a mile long) of horse-chestnuts and lime-trees, leading thence to Teddington, and originally planted by William III as an approach to Hampton Court Palace from the N.' Findlay Muirhead, *London and its Environs,* 1927, p. 480.

20. Barton Booth (1681–1733), actor.

21. Who had similar gardens at Les Rochers.

22. Only one other complete letter has been found, to Lord Strafford; HW added

in my little way anxious for him that I must light my farthing candle, at a distance indeed from your illumination, and much good may it do him.

A thousand thanks for the obliging offer of a place for the Coronation procession; it would involve me in going to Ireland in a great hurry with my cousin and I choose to go soberly before and to live soberly there before his entry. Take notice I do not request you in behalf of my brother John, though I know how comfortable it would be to him, for I am sensible how many other people you ought to oblige before it can come to his turn. I am glad you have been at Mr Hamilton's and to have your bon mots entered into their notebooks. 'Tis a mortifying title to be a wit; every fool thinks he has a right to your ear and I would lose both mine before I would pass a day with little Garrick. I am charming well and have been some time. I truly wish you so and am with great regard ever your most bounden

G. Montagu

To Montagu, Tuesday 28 July 1761

Arlington Street, July 28th, 1761.

NO, I shall never cease being a dupe, till I have been undeceived round by everything that calls itself a virtue. I came to town yesterday through clouds of dust to see *The Wishes*,[1] and went ac-

a postscript to a letter to Lady Ailesbury begun 20 July; on the 23d he wrote to Mann and Conway.

1. Bentley's 'play of the Wishes or Harlequin's Mouth Opened, was offered to Garrick and Rich the beginning of 1761, but was refused by both. His nephew Cumberland showed it to Lord Melcomb, who carried it to Lord Bute, with a compliment in verse to that Lord by Mr Cumberland. Lord Bute showed it to the King, who sent Bentley £200 and ordered the new summer company to play [it]. There was a prologue, flattering the King and Lord Bute which Foote refused to act. Two days before it was played, Cumberland wrote an anonymous pamphlet, addressed to Mr Bentley, and abusing Garrick, who had refused to act Cumberland's tragedy of Cicero's banishment, which he

printed this year [1761], unacted. The Wishes were played for the first time July 27th, 1761; the 2d 3d and part of the 4th, acts were much applauded, but the conclusion extremely hissed. The Epilogue concluded with a satire on Garrick. It was acted five nights. About the same time he wrote a tragedy called Philodamus, which he was to read to Garrick, but the latter was so angry at their treatment of him, that he declared against seeing Mr Bentley' (MS account by HW of Bentley's writings, in the collection of Lord Waldegrave at Chewton Priory). It was acted at Drury Lane; for other accounts and criticisms, all of which grant *The Wishes* some merit, see [John Genest], *Some Account of the English Stage*, Bath, 1832, iv. 617–19; Benjamin Victor, *History of the Theatres of London*, 1771, iii. 34–9; Thomas Davies, *Memoirs of the Life of Garrick*, 3d edn

tually feeling for Mr Bentley, and full of the emotions he must be suffering. What do [you] think in a house crowded was the first thing I saw! Mr and Madam Bentley perked up in the front boxes and acting audience at his own play—no, all the impudence of false patriotism never came up to it! Did one ever hear of an author that had courage to see his own first night in public? I don't believe Fielding or Foote himself ever did—and this was the modest bashful Mr Bentley, that died at the thought of being known for an author even by his own acquaintance! In the stage-box was Lady Bute, Lord Halifax and Lord Melcomb—I must say the two last entertained the house as much as the play—your King was prompter, and called out to the actors every minute to speak louder—the other went backwards and forwards behind the scenes, fetched the actors into the box, and was busier than Harlequin.[2] The *curious* prologue[3] was not spoken, the whole very ill-acted. It turned out just what I remembered it, the good parts extremely good, the rest very flat and vulgar—the genteel dialogue I believe might be written by Mrs Hannah. The audience were extremely fair. The first act they bore with patience, though it promised very ill—the second is admirable and was much applauded —so was the third—the fourth woeful—the beginning of the fifth it seemed expiring, but was revived by a delightful burlesque of the ancient chorus—which was followed by two dismal scenes, at which people yawned—but were awakened on a sudden by Harlequin's being drawn up to a gibbet nobody knew why or wherefore[4]—this raised a prodigious and continued hiss, Harlequin all the while suspended in the air—at last they were suffered to finish the play, but nobody attended to the conclusion—modesty and his lady all the while sat with the utmost indifference[5]—I suppose Lord Melcomb had fallen asleep

1781, i. 349–52; William Cooke, *Memoirs of Samuel Foote*, 1805, i. 114–17; Richard Cumberland, *Memoirs*, 1806, p. 162. It was apparently never printed; see Genest, loc. cit.; N&Q 1865, 3d ser. vii. 37. A probable reason for this is to be found in a letter from Bentley to Dodsley, printed in Cunningham iii. 462, in which Bentley with some hauteur says that Dodsley may take it or leave it at £100. There is a manuscript in the Huntington Library, San Marino, Calif., MS Larpent 5. M. (Allardyce Nicoll, *History of Late Eighteenth Century Drama 1750–1800*, Cambridge, 1927, p. 236).

2. The chief character in *The Wishes*.

3. Above n. 1; *ante* 18 June 1761.

4. The plot of *The Wishes* revolves around Harlequin's power to have three wishes come true; at this point he inadvertently wishes he may be hanged.

5. When this scene took place, Cumberland writes, 'my uncle, the author, then sitting by me, whispered in my ear—"If they don't damn this, they deserve to be damned themselves—" and whilst he was yet speaking the roar began, and *The Wishes* were irrevocably condemned' (Richard Cumberland, *Memoirs*, 1806, p. 162).

before he came to this scene and had never read it. The epilogue was about the King and new Queen, and ended with a personal satire on Garrick—not very kind on his own stage—to add to the judgment of this conduct, Cumberland two days ago published a pamphlet to abuse him.[6] It was given out for tonight with more claps than hisses, but I think will not do unless they reduce it to three acts.

I am sorry you will not come to the Coronation—the place I offered you I am not sure I can get for anybody else—I cannot explain it to you, because I am engaged to secrecy—if I can get it for your brother John, I will, but don't tell him of it, because it is not sure. Adieu!

Yours ever

H. W.

From MONTAGU, Saturday 15 August 1761

G.D. 15/8, No. 771.

Year determined by the contents.

Greatworth, August 15 [1761].

MONDAY 17th I leave Greatworth to begin my progress to Ireland. I intend staying about a week or ten days with my sister at Hankelow; as soon as I get to Dublin you shall hear from me, and I hope when you have a spare moment you will let me have the satisfaction of hearing from you. I am, thank God, well at present, and mean to set a sentinel at the door of my lips to confiscate every drop of claret that will be smuggled upon me. I expect you will pay this officer with, 'Well done, good and faithful servant!' I go to Ireland with as much anxiety as I did to Mr Hamilton's dinner; what am I not to suffer? Mr Miller[1] goes with me and stays a few days at the General's. 'Tis a pity he is in orders and cannot be my deputy. Adieu; believe me ever your most faithful and grateful

G. MONTAGU

6. Above n. 1; it was called *A Letter to R . . . B . . ., author of the new Comedy called the Wishes,* London, 1761 (BM Cat.); it is discussed and quoted in Thomas Davies, *Life of Garrick,* 3d edn 1781, i. 351–2.

1. Possibly Rev. James Miller (ca 1720–80), Vicar of Marston St Lawrence, Northants 1764–80; (?) B.A. of Brasenose, 1742. See Foster, *Alumni Oxon;* George Baker, *History . . . of Northampton,* 1822–41, i. 644.

To Montagu, Thursday 20 August 1761

Address: To George Montagu Esq. at Mr Wetenhall's at Hankelow, Cheshire. Free Hor. Walpole. *Postmark:* Isleworth 20 AV.

Strawberry Hill, Aug. 20, 1761.

A FEW lines before you go. Your resolutions are good, and give me great pleasure; bring them back unbroken. I have no mind to lose you—we have been acquainted these thirty years, and to give the devil his due, in all that time, I never knew a bad, a false, a mean or ill-natured thing in the devil—but don't tell him I say so—especially as I cannot say the same of myself. I am now doing a dirty thing, flattering you to preface a commission. Dicky Bateman[1] has picked up a whole cloister-full of old chairs in Herefordshire—he bought them one and one, here and there in farm-houses, for three and sixpence and a crown apiece. They are of wood, the seats triangular, the backs, arms, and legs loaded with turnery. A thousand to one but there are plenty up and down Cheshire too—if Mr or Mrs Wetenhall, as they ride or drive out, would now and then put up such a chair, it would oblige me greatly. Take notice, no two need be of the same pattern.

Keep it as the secret of your life, but if your brother John addresses himself to me a day or two before the Coronation, I can place him well to see the procession—when it is over, I will give you a particular reason why this must be such a mystery. I was extremely diverted t'other day with my mother's and my old milliner. She said she had a petition to me—'What is it, Mrs Burton?'[2]—'It is in behalf of two poor orphans'—I began to feel for my purse—'What can I do for them, Mrs Burton?'—'Only, if your honour would be so compassionate as to get them tickets for the Coronation'—I could not keep my countenance— and these distressed *orphans* are two and three and twenty!—Did you ever hear a more melancholy case?

The Queen is expected on Monday,[3] I go to town on Sunday— would these shows, and your Irish journey were over, and neither of us a day the poorer!

1. Richard Bateman (ca 1705–73), collector; about him and his chairs see COLE i. 90.

2. Not further identified.
3. She arrived Tuesday 25 Aug.; see HW to Strafford 25 Aug. 1761.

I am expecting Mr Chute to hold a chapter on the cabinet[4]—a barge-load of niches, window-frames and ribs is arrived. The cloister[5] is paving, the privy-garden making, painted glass adjusting to the windows on the backstairs[6]—with so many irons in the fire, you may imagine I have not much time to write. I wish you a safe and pleasant voyage.

Yours faithfully

H. W.

From MONTAGU, Monday September 14, 1761

G.D. 15/8, No. 772.

Address: To the Honourable Mr Walpole, Arlington Street, London. Free.
Postmark: Dublin 21 SE.

St Stephen's Green, Sept. 14, 1761.

I AM arrived safe and sound to St Stephen's Green after a fearful passage over the Welsh mountains and places that Gray has distributed to his Druids. Conway Castle[1] is as genteel as the General and the most charming place I ever saw; I, who am partial to the name, must have admired it had it belonged to my Gloucestershire enemy.[2] I have great civilities showed me here and on all the road for my cousin's sake; they seem disposed to be pleased with him, and I trust his reign will be happy. I cannot wish it long, for the sea and journey is most dreadful with sands one never passes soon enough. Had I not had Mr Miller to accompany and reason me out of my fears and hold me in leading strings I should have been wretched. The General is all kindness and attention, and I shall be as happy as possible till the day I embark again; the house he lives in is situated well and cheerfully

---

4. This is the room later known as the chapel, and finally as the Tribune; it was planned in 1758, and finished in 1763; see 'Genesis of SH' 76; *Des. of SH, Works* ii. 470–93; *SH Accounts* 114–16.

5. Illustrated COLE i. 90; paid for May 1762 (*SH Accounts* 9; *Des. of SH, Works* ii. 506).

6. Paid for May 1762 'Staircase by the Kitchen' (*SH Accounts* 9). 'The Window on the Staircase' is described in SH Sale Cat. xxiv. 55: 'The small window of fine

old stained glass, including the following subjects, Abraham and Isaac, Lot and his Brother separating, Isaac and Rebecca at the Well, and 4 others, the size 30 inches by 16.' It was sold to John Greathead, Esq., for £1. 15s.

---

1. Carnarvonshire; built by Edward I, 1284.

2. Possibly Montagu's opponent in his unsuccessful lawsuit *ante* ca 17 March 1761.

in a square bigger than Lincoln's Inn, and Dublin in general much handsomer than I had any idea of. Lord Hafford[3] went away with his family a few days before I came. Charles desires his compliments to you; I most truly wish you well and happy.

Believe me ever most truly and affectionately yours

G. MONTAGU

My compliments to Mr Chute.

To MONTAGU, Thursday 24 September 1761

Arlington Street, Sept. 24, 1761.

I AM glad you arrived safe in Dublin, and hitherto like it so well; but your trial is not begun yet; when your King comes, the plough-shares will be put into the fire. Bless your stars, that your King is not to be married or crowned: all the vines of Bourdeaux, and all the fumes of Irish brains cannot make a town so drunk as a royal wedding and coronation. I am going to let London cool, and will not venture my-self into [it] again this fortnight. Oh! the buzz, the prattle, the crowds, the noise, the hurry! Nay, people are so little come to their senses, that though the Coronation was but the day before yesterday, the Duke of Devonshire[1] had forty messages yesterday desiring tickets for a ball that they fancied was to be at court last night—People had sat up a night and a day and yet wanted to see a dance. If I was to entitle ages, I would call this *the Century of Crowds.* For the Coronation, if a puppet-show could be worth a million, that is. The multitudes, bal-conies, guards, and procession, made Palace-Yard the liveliest spec-tacle in the world; the Hall[2] was the most glorious. The blaze of lights, the richness and variety of habits, the ceremonial, the benches of peers and peeresses, *frequent and full,*[3] was as awful as a pageant can be—and yet for the King's sake—and my own I never wish to see another; nor am impatient to have my Lord Effingham's[4] promise ful-

---

3. Hertford.

1. Lord Chamberlain.
2. Westminster Hall, where the Corona-tion banquet was held; see *Annual Regis-ter* for 1761, iv. 215–42 for circumstantial accounts of the Coronation ceremonies and festivities.

3. Obsolete for well attended; often 'full and frequent'; see OED *sub* frequent.
4. Thomas Howard (ca 1714–63), 2d E. of Effingham; Deputy Earl Marshal for the Duke of Norfolk, who being a Catholic, was disqualified to act as Earl Marshal (until 1824, when Parliament removed the disability).

filled—the King complained that so few precedents were kept for their proceedings; Lord Effingham owned, the Earl Marshal's office had been strangely neglected; but he had taken such care for the future, that *next Coronation* would be regulated in the most exact manner imaginable. The number of peers and peeresses present was not very great—some of the latter, with no excuse in the world, appeared in Lord Lincoln's gallery,[5] and even walked about the hall indecently in the intervals of the procession. My Lady Harrington, covered with all the diamonds she could borrow, hire, or tease,[6] and with the air of Roxana, was the finest figure at a distance; she complained to George Selwyn, that she was to walk with Lady Portsmouth,[7] who would have a wig, and a stick—'Pho,' said he, 'you will only look as if you was taken up by the constable'—she told this everywhere, thinking the reflection was on my Lady Portsmouth. Lady Pembroke, alone at the head of the Countesses,[8] was the picture of majestic modesty;[9] the Duchess of Richmond, as pretty as nature and dress, with no pains of her own, could make her; Lady Spencer,[10] Lady Sutherland,[11] and Lady Northampton,[12] very pretty figures—Lady Kildare,[13] still beauty itself if not a little too large. The ancient peeresses were by no means the worst party—Lady Westmorland,[14] still handsome, and with more dignity than all; the Duchess of Queensberry looked well, though her locks milk-white; Lady Albemarle[15] very genteel; nay the middle-aged had some good representatives in Lady Holderness, Lady Rochford, and Lady Strafford,[16] the perfectest little figure of all. My Lady Suffolk ordered her robes and I dressed part of her head, as I made some

5. See *ante* 19 April 1760.

6. 'Seize' in previous editions; HW's habitual spelling was 'teize.'

7. Hon. Elizabeth Griffin (d. 1762), m. (1) Henry Grey; m. (2) (1741) John Wallop, cr. (1743) E. of Portsmouth.

8. Lady Pembroke was the fourth in order of countesses, following those of Shrewsbury, Derby, and Huntingdon (see *English Compendium*, 1753). Lord Huntingdon was a bachelor in 1761 and perhaps the Countesses of Shrewsbury and Derby were not in the procession (Miss E. G. Withycombe in N&Q 1939, clxxvii. 427). It is still not clear, however, why Lady Pembroke should walk 'alone.'

9. 'So she was; more modesty than majesty—as I remember' (Mrs Piozzi).

10. Margaret Georgiana Poyntz (1737–

1814), m. (1755) John Spencer, cr. (1761) Vct, and (1765) E. Spencer.

11. Mary Maxwell (ca 1740–66), m. (1761) William Sutherland, 18th E. of Sutherland.

12. Lady Anne Somerset (1741–63), m. (1759) Charles Compton, 7th E. of Northampton.

13. 'She was most admired' (Mrs Piozzi).

14. Mary Cavendish (1698–1778), m. (ca 1720) John Fane, 7th E. of Westmorland, 1736.

15. Lady Anne Lennox (1703–89), m. (1723) William Anne van Keppel, 2d E. of Albemarle.

16. Lady Anne Campbell (ca 1715–85), m. (1741) William Wentworth, 2d E. of Strafford.

of my Lord Hertford's dress, for you know, no profession comes amiss
to me, from a tribune of the people to a habit-maker. Don't imagine
that there were not figures as excellent on the other side:[17] old Exeter,[18] who told the King he was the handsomest young man she ever
saw, old Effingham,[19] and a Lady Say and Seal[20] with her hair powdered and her tresses[20a] black, were an excellent contrast to the handsome. Lord Bolinbroke put on rouge upon his wife and the Duchess
of Bedford[21] in the Painted Chamber;[22] the Duchess of Queensberry
told me of the latter, that she looked like an orange-peach, half red
and half yellow. The coronets of the peers and their robes disguised
them strangely; it required all the beauty of the Dukes of Richmond
and Marlborough to make them noticed. One there was, though of
another species, the noblest figure I ever saw; the High Constable of
Scotland, Lord Errol[23]—as one saw him in a space capable of containing him, one admired him. At the wedding, dressed in tissue, he
looked like one of the giants in Guildhall,[24] new-gilt. It added to the
energy of his person, that one considered him acting so considerable
a part in that very hall where so few years ago one saw his father Lord
Kilmarnock condemned to the block. The Champion[25] acted his part
admirably; and dashed down his gauntlet with proud defiance. His
associates, Lord Effingham, Lord Talbot, and the Duke of Bedford[26]
were woeful, yet the last, the least ridiculous of the three. Lord Talbot piqued himself on backing his horse down the Hall, and not
turning its rump towards the King, but he had taken such pains to
dress it to that duty, that it entered backwards;[27] and at his retreat the

17. Not handsome; see end of sentence.
18. Hannah Sophia Chambers (ca 1702–
65), m. (1724) Brownlow Cecil, 8th E. of
Exeter.
19. Annie Bristow (d. 1774), m. (1728)
Francis Howard, 7th Bn Howard; cr. (1731)
E. of Effingham.
20. Christobella Tyrrel (1695–1789), m.
(1) John Knapp; m. (2) John Pigott; m.
(3) (1753 or 1754) Richard Fiennes, 6th
Vct Saye and Sele.
20a. 'A plait or braid' (OED sb.1).
21. '[She] had on a great deal of rouge
(which became her vastly and made her
look like Lady Caroline [Russell])' (Elizabeth, Duchess of Northumberland, Diaries
of a Duchess, ed. James Greig, 1926, p. 36).
22. In Westminster Hall, where the procession assembled before going to the Abbey.

23. James Boyd (after 1758, Hay) (1726–
78), 15th E. of Erroll; see GEC for other
tributes to his appearance.
24. Gog and Magog at the entrance.
25. John Dymoke; see ante 21 May 1754,
n. 2. As Champion of England, he rode
into Westminster Hall armed cap-à-pie
and challenged anyone who disputed the
King's rights; see Annual Register for
1761, iv. 232–3; DNB, sub Dymoke, Sir John.
26. As Deputy Earl Marshal, Lord High
Steward, and Lord High Constable, respectively.
27. No other mention of the reverse entrance has been found; possibly the horse
merely spun around on entering the Hall.
A similar story of Wellington at the Coronation of George IV in 1821 is debated in
N&Q 1889, 7th ser. vii. 482, viii. 113, 175, 254,

spectators clapped, a terrible indecorum, but suitable to such Bartholomew Fair doings.[28] He put me in mind of some King's fool, that would not give his right hand to the King of Spain, because he wiped his backside with it. He had twenty *démêlés* and came out of none creditably. He had taken away the table of the Knights of the Bath, and was forced to admit two in their old place[29] and dine the others in the Court of Requests. Sir William Stanhope said, 'We are ill-treated, for *some of us* are gentlemen.' Beckford told the Earl, it was hard to refuse a table to the City of London, whom it would cost ten thousand pounds to banquet the King, and that his Lordship would repent it, if they had not a table in the Hall—they had. To the Barons of the Cinque Ports,[30] who made the same complaint, he said, 'If you come to me as Lord Steward, I tell you, it is impossible; if, as Lord Talbot, I am a match for any of you.' And then he said to Lord Bute, 'If I was a minister, thus I would talk to France, to Spain, to the Dutch—none of your half measures.' This has brought me to a melancholy topic—Bussy[31] goes tomorrow, a Spanish war is hanging in the air,[32] destruction is taking a new lease of mankind—of the remnant of mankind—I have no prospect of seeing Mr Conway! Adieu! I will not disturb you with my forebodings. You I shall see again in spite of war, and I trust, in spite of Ireland.

Yours ever

H. W.[33]

where it is concluded that the story was a garbled version of the present passage.

28. 'And the Duke of Cumberland the King's uncle laughed till he shook again' (Mrs Piozzi). Wilkes wrote a stinging commentary on this episode in the *North Briton* No. XII, 21 Aug. 1762, one of the attacks which led to his duel with Talbot. See also the admiring account in Elizabeth, Duchess of Northumberland, *Diaries of a Duchess,* ed. James Greig, 1926, p. 37; *Annual Register* for 1761, iv. 232.

29. The two junior Knights were seated above the judges to preserve their precedence for future affairs (ibid. 233–4).

30. There were thirty-two of them; they bore the canopies over the King and Queen in the procession (ibid. 223–4).

31. The Sieur, or Abbé, de Bussy, 'L'un des premiers commis des affaires étrangères' (Marquis d'Argenson, *Journal et Mémoires,* 1859–67, ix. 29) was sent to England as a Minister from Louis XV to discuss peace terms, while Hans Stanley went to France on a similar footing and mission (see [John Almon] *Anecdotes of . . . Earl Chatham,* 1792, iv. 53–7). Compare the flattering account of him in *Mem. Geo. III* i. 45 n. with d'Argenson, op. cit. iv. 314, v. 434, who abuses him as 'une âme basse et qui a fait toute sa vie le métier de délateur de ses maîtres,' and, at greater length, as a traitor and the nephew of a footman.

32. Though Spain had presented ultimatums to England through Bussy, and was clearly siding with France, only Pitt and Temple in the government favoured taking strong measures with her. Pitt resigned on that issue; continued hostility forced the government into war at the beginning of the next year; see *Mem. Geo. III.*

33. Gray attended the Coronation, and his letter of this date to Brown has so many parallels to this letter that it seems

I was much disappointed at not seeing your brother John; I kept a place for him to the last minute, but have heard nothing of him.

From Montagu, Thursday 1 October 1761

G.D. 15/8, No. 773.

In reply to *ante* 24 Sept. 1761.

[Dublin] Oct. ye 1st [1761].

A THOUSAND thanks to you, my dear sir, for your particular and entertaining account of the Coronation. I am much obliged to you for keeping a seat for my brother John, and quite grieved to think he did not make use of it, but to tell you the truth we expected you would have wrote an answer to say he might have it, for in the letter you wrote to me you said you had only one and, if I would not accept it, you begged that I might not mention it; and yet I trespassed so far as to desire my brother John might go in my stead, to which I never had a permission; so perhaps the letter miscarried.[1] However, I shall never let him know his loss, and it is none.

I am now, I hope, a little seasoned to this climate, and can but just begin to say so. Hitherto, though I have been feasted by all the primates and grandees, I have been indulged in drinking port and not pressed to bumpers; and I make no doubt but I shall have the same freedom from my cousin or else I will not attend and pretend sickness. The country about this city has great natural beauty, and, was the wood as fine as the river and sea, would be charming. It is sadly cultivated and slovenly, and a dull verdure in their meadows. The houses are most of them whitewashed, which adds much to the beauty of the scenery. I went one morning to see Mrs Delany,[2] a Granville that was. Her place is an absolute Sévigniade, her *chapelle, Notre*

---

probable that he and HW met after the ceremony (*Gray's Corr.* ii. 752–8).

1. *Ante* 20 Aug. 1761 missed Montagu at Hankelow, where it was addressed; he received it late in November at Dublin; see *post* 23 Nov. 1761.

2. Mary Granville (1700–88), m. (1) (1718) Alexander Pendarves; m. (2) (1743) Patrick Delany, Dean of Down. Their villa, Delville, just outside the city, is illustrated in Georgian Society, *Records of Eighteenth Century Domestic Architecture and Decoration in Ireland*, Dublin, 1909–13, v. pp. xvii, 1 (the earlier volumes are entitled *Records of Eighteenth Century Domestic Architecture and Decoration in Dublin*). She later became intimate with HW and left him a legacy (Delany, *Correspondence* vi. 489).

Dame des Roches,[3] all fitted up and painted by her own hand, the stucco composed of shells[4] and ears of corn the prettilyest disposed imaginable, and her way of life quite abstracted from the great world and given up to a few sensible friends. Tomorrow I go to Powerscourt,[5] the paragon of this kingdom. Lord Charlemont[6] is making an Abs Court farm[7] and casino[8] that promises to be very pretty.

The Provost's house[9] of the University is just finished after the plan of General Wade's,[10] but half the proportions and symmetry were lost at sea in coming over. There is a lying-in hospital near the city after Chiswick House,[11] but that has *miscarried*. Such a statue of General Blakeney[12] in Sackville Street as his fellows of the fleet would have erected to him at the bridge foot. The General is very kind and comfortable to mé, and sometimes we are permitted to have a Sabbath at home. We always meet at supper, I with my broth and he with his wine and water and the occurrences of the day.

As I see more I shall write more; at present receive my best wishes for your happiness and the good General Conway, who I must ever honour with my memory. Adieu; believe me ever your most faithful

G. MONTAGU

3. Mme de Sévigné built a chapel at the Sévigné seat in Brittany, Les Rochers; see her *Lettres*, ed. Monmerqué, 1862–6, ii. 272 et seq.

4. This shellwork is illustrated in *Mrs Delany at Court and among the Wits*, ed. R. Brimley Johnson, [1925] opp. p. 160.

5. Powerscourt House, co. Wicklow; illustrated and described in Georgian Society, op. cit. n. 2 above, v. pl. lxxi, p. 107; James N. Brewer, *Beauties of Ireland*, 1825–6, i. 287–90.

6. James Caulfeild (1728–99), 4th Vct of Charlemont, cr. (1763) E. of Charlemont, friend and correspondent of HW's.

7. Montagu was no doubt thinking of Apse Court Farm, Walton, Surrey; see Edward W. Brayley, *Topographical History of Surrey*, 1850, ii. 320.

8. At his seat Marino, near Clontarf. The casino was designed by Sir William Chambers (1726–96); see his *Treatise on . . . Civil Architecture*, 1759, plates opp. p. 79 and two described p. 85 which are variously placed in different copies; Georgian Society, op. cit. n. 2 above, v. 72, pl. cxx. Chambers apparently did not design

the house (ibid. 86). See Arthur Young, *Tour in Ireland*, 1780, p. 3; *post* 4 Nov. 1761, n. 4, for descriptions of it. A photograph of the casino is in William Rotch Ware, *The Georgian Period*, New York, 1923, iii. pl. 454.

9. Built by and for Francis Andrews (d. 1774); see William B. S. Taylor, *History of the University of Dublin*, 1845, pp. 88, 334; Georgian Society, op. cit. n. 2 above, iii. 51–6.

10. *Ante* 18 May 1748.

11. Probably the Lying-in Hospital in Great Britain Street, built 1751–7; see John J. M'Gregor, *New Picture of Dublin*, 1821, pp. 280–2; the illustration ibid. opp. p. 81 bears little resemblance to Chiswick; see also the large plate in James Malton, *Picturesque and Descriptive View of the City of Dublin*, [1794]. This is now called the Rotunda Hospital.

12. Gen. William Blakeney (1672–1761), cr. (1756) Bn Blakeney; defender of Minorca; the statue is by John Van Nost (d. 1780) (DNB; John T. Gilbert, *History of Dublin*, 1861, i. 20).

To Montagu, Thursday 8 October 1761

Arlington Street, Oct. 8, 1761.

I CANNOT swear I wrote to you again to offer your brother the place for the Coronation; but I was confident I did, nay, and think so still—my proofs are, the place remained empty, and I sent to old Richard to inquire if Mr John was not arrived. He had no great loss, as the procession returned in the dark.

Your King will have heard that Mr Pitt resigned last Monday.[1] Greater pains have been taken to recover him than were used to drive him out. He is inflexible, but mighty peaceable. Lord Egremont is to have the seals tomorrow. It is a most unhappy event—France and Spain will soon let us know we ought to think so. For your part, you will be invaded; a blacker rod[2] than you will be sent to Ireland. Would you believe that the town is a desert? The wedding filled it, the Coronation crammed it; Mr Pitt's resignation has not brought six people to London. As they could not hire a window and crowd one another to death to see him give up the Seals, it seems a matter of perfect indifference. If he will accuse a single man of checking our career of glory, all the world will come to see him hanged—but what signifies the ruin of a nation, if no particular man ruins it?

The Duchess of Marlborough[3] died the night before last.

Thank you for your descriptions. Pray continue them. Mrs Delany I know a little. Lord Charlemont's villa is in Chambers's book.[4]

I have nothing new to tell you; but the grain of mustard-seed sown on Monday will soon produce as large a tree as you can find in any prophecy. Adieu!

Yours ever

H. W.

PS. Lady Mary Wortley is arrived. If you could meet with ever a large prick very[5] cheap, you would make your court to her by it.

1. On the Cabinet's refusal to declare war against Spain.
2. Possibly the scourge of war.
3. Hon. Elizabeth Trevor (d. 1761), m. (1732) Charles Spencer, 2d D. of Marlborough; she was Montagu's second cousin on his mother's side.
4. See *ante* 1 Oct. 1761, n. 8. HW's copy (MS Cat. C.2.13) was sold SH viii. 3.
5. Nearly obliterated, but still decipherable.

From Montagu, Thursday 8 October 1761

G.D. 15/8, No. 774.

Stephen's Green, Dublin, Oct. 8th, 1761.

I AM sure for our sakes you will be glad to hear our cousin's excellence has charmed pit, box and galleries with his answers to the compliments of the Mayor,[1] who met him in his way from his landing to the castle,[2] in a pretty long speech; this had not been used to. The next day, when the Recorder[3] came and after him the University with their addresses, he replied to them paragraph by paragraph with great modesty, spirit and a most gentleman-like manner that did my Cudom good; in short, it was extremely well performed, and his behaviour has gained him a great deal of good will and made most favourable impressions. You are to know usually the replies were read or very short and stately.

We have a report here Lord Hertford has taken an house here for the winter for himself and family; I most heartily wish it may be so.[4]

I am now better acquainted with the Irish air and have established such an indulgence of sobriety that I am permitted my pint of port without murmuring, and I never accept of any invitation of supper. My Lord shows us both[5] the most cousinly distinctions and all the grandees treat us with a difference. This procures such a list of *repas* that I shall loathe the sight of three courses and a dessert as long as I live and wish for my tares and acorns in my own retreat. Mr Hamilton is very abstemious and so is some of the aide-de-camps, so that I am not ridiculously alone. My cousin too intends never to sup out or have company nor play high. He gets up by this means at seven, is cool, and will be healthy and active. Mr Hamilton, to pay his court to me, as he always does, speaks of you with the greatest esteem. Cliquetis does not come over, as the Primate[6] tells me, who has di-

1. Patrick Hamilton (d. 1780), Lord Mayor of Dublin 1761; knighted by Halifax 30 Oct. (GM 1780, l. 445; *Calendar of Ancient Records of Dublin,* ed. John T. Gilbert, Dublin, 1889–1913, xi. 478; William A. Shaw, *Knights of England,* 1906, ii. 291).
2. Halifax landed 6 Oct. (GM 1761, xxxi. 476).

3. James Grattan (d. 1766), Recorder of Dublin; M.P. Dublin 1761–6; see DNB *sub* his son, Henry Grattan.
4. It was apparently unfounded.
5. Montagu and his brother Charles.
6. George Stone (ca 1708–64), Abp of Armagh.

verted himself with me a whole afternoon with his remembrance of all his histories. We are to have a burletta as well as comedians and I hope a peaceable and agreeable winter. I wish I could entertain you with any accounts that would be worth sending; as I cannot, I will only present the General's compliments and my own best wishes for your health and happiness; assuring you I am most faithfully yours,

G. MONTAGU

To MONTAGU, Saturday 10 October 1761

Strawberry Hill, Oct. 10th, 1761.

PRAY, Sir, how does virtue sell in Ireland now? I think for a province, they have now and then given large prices. Have you a mind to know what the biggest virtue in the world is worth? If Cicero had been a Drawcansir[1] instead of a coward, and had carried the glory of Rome to as lofty an height as he did their eloquence, for how much do you think he would have sold all that reputation?—'Oh! sold it!' you will cry, 'Vanity was his predominant passion; he would have trampled on sesterces like dirt, and provided the tribes did but erect statues enough for him, he was content with a bit of Sabine mutton, and would have preferred his little Tusculan villa, or the flattery of Caius Allenius Atticus[2] at Baiae, to the wealth of Crassus, or to the luxurious banquets of Lucullus—Take care—there is not a Tory gentleman, if there is one left, who would not have laid the same wager twenty years ago on the disinterestedness of my Lord Bath[3]—come, you tremble; you are so incorrupt yourself, you would give the world Mr Pitt was so too—you adore him for what he has done for us; you bless him for placing England at the head of Europe, and you don't hate him for infusing as much spirit into us, as if a Montagu Earl of Salisbury[4] was still at the head of our armies—nothing could be more

1. Character in Buckingham's *The Rehearsal*, satirizing Dryden's Almanzor.

2. Titus Pomponius Atticus (110–33 B.C.), friend and correspondent of Cicero's. HW alludes to Ralph Allen (1694–1764), of Prior Park, Bath; philanthropist, postal reformer, and an intimate friend of Pitt.

3. Who accepted a peerage, after having been instrumental in overthrowing Sir Robert Walpole.

4. There were four Montagu Earls of Salisbury in the 14th and 15th centuries, of whom three were soldiers. The 18th-century Montagu families, the Dukes of Montagu and Manchester, and the Earls of Sandwich and Halifax, who had a common ancestor in Sir Edward Montagu (d. 1557), erroneously claimed descent from the Earls of Salisbury and from still earlier Montagu barons; see Collins, *Peerage*, 1812, ii. 42; GEC, *Peerage* ix. App. D.

just. We owe the recovery of our affairs to him, the splendour of our country, the conquest of Canada, Louisbourg, Guardaloupe, Africa and the East—nothing is too much for such services—accordingly, I hope you will not think the barony of Chatham and three thousand pounds a year for three lives too much for my Lady Esther. She has this pittance. Good night![5]

Yours ever

H. Walpole

PS. I told you falsely in my last that Lady Mary Wortley was arrived—I cannot help it if my Lady Denbigh[6] cannot read English in all these years, but mistakes Wrottesley for Wortley.

From Montagu, Monday 12 October 1761

G.D. 15/8, No. 775.

Dublin, Oct. 12 [1761].

MR HAMILTON has given me leave to have any packet of books or pamphlets or matters of that kind that you may have occasion to send me over directed to him, and I beg you will let me have any thing of your performances or what other matters you can spare by that method.

You will, I am sure, be glad to hear I get better and that my cousin is my kinsman *au pied de la lettre*. The many tokens of good will and respect he takes all occasions to bestow on us are most cordial and

5. For other outbursts of HW's provoked by Pitt's acceptance of a peerage for his wife and a pension for his family, see letters to Mann and Lady Ailesbury, 10 Oct., and to Conway, 12 Oct. 1761. At first public opinion generally seems to have been similarly outraged; but Pitt's defense of his actions quieted much of the opposition; see selections from newspapers and pamphlets in GM 1761, xxxi. 461–8, 513–21. The whole is a revealing commentary on 18th-century concepts of 'patriotism' and political 'virtue'; their exponents usually professed an unwavering independence of the court, and accordingly brought on themselves the contumely of political idealists like HW by

their acceptance of honours however reasonable. Thus Lord Holdernesse, an altogether undistinguished statesman, had shortly before received a pension of £4,000, without exciting any measurable opposition; but Pitt, who had won England an empire, was abused for not maintaining 'the exalted pitch of magnanimous independence, and utter disregard of sublunary interests' which his followers expected of him (Lord Brougham and Vaux, *Historical Sketches of Statesmen who flourished in the time of George III*, 1855–6, i. 45 [vol. iii of his *Works*]; *Mem. Geo. III* i. 63–7).

6. Who was Dutch by birth.

make us much considered here, so that my time will pass much to my satisfaction and vastly better than I expected.

I am to dine with your Mr Bourk[1] soon at the Bishop of Kildare's;[2] this is to be a private party and therefore I am happy. There were two young noblemen of the University in their laced gowns to wait on the young ladies,[3] that were the prettiest figures ever seen.

I find Charles Townshend would have liked being Secretary[4] had he not been better employed.[5] They report here Mr Rigby is in a bad state of health.

I am to go and see the Deanery of St Patrick's, where there are many remains of Swift's wit about the house. I don't wonder he disliked his situation, for from what appeared from the Archbishop's windows it was enough to turn a stronger wit than his to dullness or madness.

I hope I shall have divers entertaining accounts to give you when I have the pleasure to see you in our walks in your gallery, which and yourself I shall revisit with exceeding joy. Believe me ever with the sincerest attachment, etc., etc., ever yours,

G. MONTAGU

Pray put your name to my sister's letter.

Pray enclose me the catalogue of the Duke of Devonshire's pictures[6] if it is printed in a small sheet, to present to Mr Ponsonby,[7] our Speaker.

To MONTAGU, Saturday 24 October 1761

Strawberry Hill, Oct. 24, 1761.

I HAVE got two letters from you, and am sensibly pleased with your satisfaction. I love your cousin for his behaviour to you; he will never place his friendship better. His parts and dignity, I did not

1. Edmund Burke.
2. Richard Robinson (ca 1708–94), Bp of Killala, 1752; of Leightin and Ferns, 1759; of Kildare, 1761; Abp of Armagh, 1765; cr. (1777) Bn Rokeby.
3. Probably Lord Halifax's daughters, Lady Frances Montagu-Dunk (1743–64) (Collins, *Peerage*, 1768, v. 10); Lady Elizabeth (1745–68), m. (1766) John Montagu,

styled Vct Hinchingbrooke, 5th E. of Sandwich, 1792.
4. In Ireland.
5. He was Secretary-at-War.
6. See *post* 24 Oct. 1761.
7. John Ponsonby (1713–89), Irish politician; Speaker of Irish House of Commons, 1756.

doubt, would bear him out. I fear nothing but your spirits, and the frank openness of your heart; keep them within bounds, and you will return in health and with the serenity I wish you long to enjoy.

You have heard our politics—they do not mend. Sick of glory, without being tired of war, and surfeited with unanimity before it had finished its work, we are running into all kind of confusion. The City have bethought themselves, and have voted that they will still admire Mr Pitt[1]—consequently, he, without the check of seeming virtue, may do what he pleases. An address of thanks to him has been carried by 109 against 15; and the City are to instruct their members[2] —that is, because we are disappointed of a Spanish war, we will have one at home—merciful! How old I am grown! Here am I not liking a civil war! Do you know me? I am no longer that Gracchus, who when Mr Bentley told him something or other, I don't know what, would make a sect, answered quick, 'Will it make a party?' In short, I think, I am always to be in contradiction; now I am loving my country!

Worksop is burned down[3]—I don't know the circumstances; the Duke[4] and Duchess are at Bath; it has not been finished a month;[5] the last furniture was brought in for the Duke of York.[6] I have some comfort, that I had seen it, and except the bare chambers in which the Queen of Scots was lodged, nothing remained of ancient time.[7]

I am much obliged to Mr Hamilton's civilities; but I don't take too much to myself; yet it is no drawback to think that he sees and compliments your friendship for me. I shall use his permission of sending you anything that I think will bear the sea; but how must I send it; by what conveyance to the sea, and where deliver it? Pamphlets swarm already;[8] none very good, and chiefly grave; you would

---

1. 'At first the Common Council, which had been summoned to thank him for his services, dropped the intention and separated, after voting an address to Parliament for widening the streets' (*Mem. Geo. III* i. 66).

2. The Common Council instructed the City M.P.'s to prosecute the war vigorously (see GM 1761, xxxi. 461 n, 477–8).

3. On 20 Oct., with an estimated loss of £100,000; see GM 1761, xxxi. 477, 531–2; *Annual Register* for 1761, iv. 169.

4. Edward Howard (1686–1777), 9th D. of Norfolk.

5. It was built by Bess of Hardwick ca 1600, but 'upwards of £12,000 of late have

yearly been paid in wages to workmen who were constantly employed about the house' (GM 1761, xxxi. 532).

6. Who visited it 24 Aug. (*London Chronicle* 27–29 Aug. 1761, x. 205).

7. See HW to Bentley Aug. 1756.

8. HW preserved only two in his collection of 'Tracts of Geo. 3' (now WSL): *The Patriot Unmasked, or, a Word to his Defenders. By John Trott, Cheese-Monger and Statesman,* 1761. HW added in MS 'Oct. 21'; *A Letter to the Rt Hon. the Earl of B——, on a late important Resignation and its probable Consequences,* 1761. HW added the date, 'Octr.'

not have them. Mr Glover has published his long-hoarded *Medea*,[9] as an introduction to the House of Commons[10]—it had been more proper to usher him from school to the University. There are a few good lines, not much conduct, and a quantity of iambics, and trochaics, that scarce speak English, and yet have no rhyme to keep one another in countenance. If his chariot is stopped at Temple Bar, I suppose he will take it for the Straits of Thermopylae, and be delivered of his first speech before its time.

The catalogue of the Duke of Devonshire's collection is only in the six volumes of the Description of London.[11] I did print about a dozen, and gave them all away so totally, that on searching I find I had not reserved one for myself. When we are at leisure I will reprint a few more,[12] and you shall have one for your Speaker. I don't know who is to be ours; Prowse[13] they say has refused; Sir J. Cust[14] was the last I heard named—but I am here, and know nothing; sorry that I shall hear anything on Tuesday se'nnight.[15]

Pray pick me up any prints of Lords Lieutenants, Irish bishops, ladies—nay, or patriots: but I will not trouble you for a snuffbox or toothpick case, made of a bit of the Giant's Causey.

My *Anecdotes of Painting* will scarcely appear before Christmas.[16] My gallery and cabinet are at a full stop till spring—but I shall be sorry to leave it all in ten days; October, that scarce ever deceived one before, has exhibited a deluge; but it has recovered, and promised to behave well as long as it lives, like a dying sinner. Good night.

Yours ever

H. W.

9. It was not intended for the stage, but was acted in 1767.

10. Which he was entering as M.P. for Weymouth.

11. *London and its Environs Described,* Dodsley, 1761, ii. 225–32. HW's catalogue included lists of the pictures of Gen. John Guise and Sir Paul Methuen, from the same work; see *Journal of the Printing Office* 9, 37; *Country Seats* 29.

12. Only one copy has been located, at the BM, bequeathed by Brocklebank, 1799. A copy was sold SH iv. 168 and it seems to have reappeared at Sotheby's 1848 (Eyton Sale, lot 1143) and 1875 (?Hayes Sale). *Post* 8 Dec. 1761 suggests that it was reprinted.

13. Thomas Prowse (ca 1708–67), of Axbridge, Somerset; M.P. Somerset 1740–67, having been five times unanimously elected; see *Mem. Geo. III* i. 67–8. A letter from George Grenville offering the Speakership to Prowse, and his refusal on account of bad health, are in *Grenville Papers,* ed. William J. Smith, 1852–3, i. 398, 402.

14. Sir John Cust (1718–70), 3d Bt, of Stamford; Speaker 1761–70; about him see Lionel Cust, *Records of the Cust Family, Series III, Sir John Cust,* 1927.

15. 3 Nov., when Parliament opened.

16. See *post* 30 Dec. 1761.

PS. My niece lost the Coronation for only a daughter.[17]

It makes me smile, when I reflect that you are come into the world again, and that I have above half left it.

From Montagu, Saturday 24 October 1761

G.D. 15/8, No. 781.

Month determined by reference to Halifax's speech at the opening of Parliament, delivered 22 Oct. (GM 1761, xxxi. 511).

[Dublin] Saturday 24 [Oct. 1761].

I HERE enclose his Excellency's speech;[1] he spoke it gracefully and by heart. His figure before he was robed was noble and genteel; the robe itself, which by the way was the individual one that was wore by King James the Second, misbecame him much. Mr Hamilton gave the Commons a specimen of his eloquence, and acquitted himself well. He behaves very civilly and is at present much liked.

I have gone through my chief day's attendance, and for the future have no occasion to be in the House of Lords but when I please. Their adjournments are long and frequent. My cousin goes on pleasing by his manner and sobriety; the last quality they have never been used to: his old tutor, Dr Crane,[2] a very sensible staid person, is come to him and will be of service. The General presents his service to you; believe me ever most sincerely yours

G. Montagu

From Montagu, Wednesday 4 November 1761

G.D. 15/8, No. 776.

Dated by the postscript. In reply to ante 24 Oct. 1761.

[Dublin, Nov. 4, 1761].

I AM glad to hear you are well; I am now got quite acquainted with the air of this country and what you will call seasoned—I have had

17. Lady Charlotte Maria Waldegrave (11 Oct. 1761–1808), m. (1784) George Henry Fitzroy, styled E. of Euston; 4th D. of Grafton, 1811.

1. Missing; it is in GM 1761, xxxi. 511. 'A very brilliant composition. His graceful person, and impressive manner of delivery set it off to its best advantage' (Richard Cumberland, Memoirs, 1806, p. 164; Cumberland was Ulster Secretary).

2. Dr Edward Crane (ca 1696–1777), Rector of Sutton; Prebend of Westminster; became Halifax's chief chaplain; eulogized ibid. 157, 170–1; see Venn, Alumni Cantab.

the gout for two mornings. I lay it at the feet of the House of Lords—
thus it was—I stood the first day of the Parliament from eleven till
five, without once setting down. I was to introduce peers, Speaker,
and Commons, and the crowd so great I could not get a place. I was
taken very sick after dinner at home in the evening, put to bed, felt
pain, and the next morning could not walk down stairs without pain.
It went off in the middle of the day and made me just such a visit the
succeeding day, and I have never been so well since I came to Dublin
as this what-do-you-call-it has made me! I won't accept of congratulations on the occasion, for as it is a most treacherous attendant; it may
come back with seven more wicked spirits in spite of my care and ob-
servance and all you can say to me.

I was yesterday to see Mont Merion,[1] a villa of Lord Fitzwilliam's.[2]
He has built fine stables, and there is to be as fine an house. Nothing
near Naples can be more beautiful, with such a view of the sea and
Dublin as would even make your Thames blush for Richmond Hill
and Isleworth; and yet there is no wood to heat an oven, but such
ships, such mountains, such an hill of Hothe[3] as makes one not wish
for any other embellishment; add to this that Dublin is the worst
furnished with steeples and edifices of picturesque consequence of
any city in Europe; I can only say I know not how I was charmed, but
that I was so. We have balls here once a week, at which I attend for
a little while. We never sup out and are generally at home early. I
have been to see Lord Charlemont's villa: the situation of the house
beautiful, and the whole edifice finished in about twelve months.[4]
The design, by what I can judge of it, will be vastly pretty; there is
an old couchant lioness on one side of the landing-place extremely
well executed. The stone and artificers are from England and the
work is well performed. Perhaps it is in Chamber's book.[5]

I shall be able to pick up a few Irish worthies, but I will send you

1. Mount Merrion, co. Dublin; passed
to the Earls of Pembroke in the 19th century. Viscount Fitzwilliams's alterations of
the house, which included a new front,
were not particularly successful; see Francis Elrington Ball, *History of the County
of Dublin*, Dublin, pt ii (1903). 80–95,
which contains illustrations of both house
and stables.

2. Richard Fitzwilliam (1711–76), 6th
Vct Fitzwilliam.

3. Howth, a high peninsula on the
northeast side of Dublin Bay.

4. See *ante* 1 Oct. 1761; it is not clear
here whether Montagu is talking about
the house, the casino, or both, for according to DNB, the house was built in 1770,
and the casino was still unfinished in 1771
(see letters from Sir William Chambers to
Lord Charlemont in Historical Manuscripts Commission, 12th Rep. App. x,
Charlemont MSS, 1891, pp. 283 *et seq.*).

5. *Ante* 1 Oct. 1761.

their names lest they prove duplicates. I flatter myself all our business will be over by the end of February; judge how happy I shall be to return and see you, to whom I must ever wish the stock of my best wishes, sincerity, and esteem. I am most assuredly yours,

G. Montagu

November 4: this day we banquet with King William's ghost and every coach in Dublin parades round his statue and every man is drunk to the memory of old glorious, by six.[6]

Pray send me two prints of the view of Isleworth by Muntz.[7]

To Montagu, Saturday 7 November 1761

Arlington Street, Nov. 7, 1761.

YOU will rejoice to hear that your friend Mr Amyand is going to marry the Dowager Lady Northampton;[1] she has two thousand pounds a year and twenty thousand in money. Old Dunch[2] is dead, and Mrs Felton Hervey[3] was given over last night, but is still alive.

Sir John Cust is Speaker, and bating his nose,[4] the chair seems well filled.[5] There are so many new faces in this Parliament, that I am not at all acquainted with it.

The enclosed print[6] will divert you, especially the Baroness[7] in the right-hand corner—so ugly and so satisfied. The Athenian head was intended for Stewart,[8] but was so like, that Hogarth was forced to cut off the nose. Adieu!

Yours ever
H. W.

6. 4 Nov. was William III's birthday. The statue, in College Green, has often been the center of celebrations and riots; see John T. Gilbert, *History of the City of Dublin*, Dublin, 1861, iii. 40–56.

7. No copy of this print has been located. A drawing in pen and sepia wash by Müntz of a 'House on the River Bank' at Isleworth is now WSL.

———

1. Frances Payne (1719–1800), m. (1) (1748) George Compton, 6th E. of Northampton; m. (2) (26 Nov. 1761) Claudius Amyand.

2. Mrs Edmund Dunch.

3. Dorothy (d. 8 Nov. 1761), dau. of

Solomon Ashley; m. (1) Charles Pitfield; m. (2) Hon. Felton Hervey (Collins, *Peerage*, 1812, iv. 154).

4. Which was rather snub; see portrait in Arthur I. Dasent, *Speakers of the House of Commons*, 1911, opp. p. 274.

5. HW is less enthusiastic in *Mem. Geo. III* i. 68, 'the Favourite determined on Sir John Cust, who was a Tory, and had nothing but industry; he was indeed a very poor creature.'

6. Hogarth's 'Five Orders of Perriwigs,' just published.

7. Apparently, no specific Baroness was intended; see BM *Satiric Prints* iv. 14.

8. James ('Athenian') Stuart (1713–88),

From MONTAGU, Tuesday 17 November 1761

G.D. 15/8, No. 777.

In reply to *ante* 7 Nov. 1761.

Memoranda by HW:

Lord Mandevil [?]	
King	Queen
Duke of York	Lady Augusta
Prince William	Lady Susan Stewart
Prince Henry	Lady Egremont
Lord March	Lady Jane Stewart
Lord Bolingbroke	Lady Caroline Russel
Lord Northampton	Lady Bolinbroke
Lord Mandeville	Miss Bishop
Lord Suffolk	Miss Wrottesley
Lord Grey	Miss Keck
Lord Cantelupe	Miss Beauclerc
Lord R. Bertie	Miss Tryon
Lord Oxford	Miss Meadows
Lord Eglinton	

This is a rough pencilled list, reproduced more carefully, and with some changes, on *post* 19 Nov. 1761. It is no doubt the guests at the ball at court described *post* 28 Nov. 1761, and in a letter to Lady Ailesbury of the same date.

[Dublin] Nov. 17 [1761].

THANK you for your Perukes;[1] they have entertained me much. Our famous Money Bill[2] was carried last Saturday an hundred and seventy to forty-two. We now reassume our motto of *otium cum dignitate*.[3] Mr Bentley's play with alterations is in rehearsal for this kingdom.

Pray, when there is a list of the peers and peeresses that walked at the Coronation printed, send it me. Hamilton spoke extremely well.[4] We are all well, and I never better in all my life. My fiftieth year begins charmingly; my cousin behaves bravely to me and notices me as I could wish. Pray frank the good tidings I have sent to my sister.

---

painter and architect; the whole print was designed to ridicule his *Antiquities of Athens,* then about to appear, which gave dimensions of classical ruins in great, and, to Hogarth's mind, useless, detail (ibid. 11–15).

---

1. Hogarth's print, *ante* 7 Nov. 1761.

2. This Money Bill seems not to have been famous enough to attract the attention of historians.

3. Lord Halifax's motto.

4. The speech is printed in William Gerard Hamilton, *Parliamentary Logick* [ed. Edmond Malone] 1808, pp. 137–60.

The General desires his compliments to you.

I most truly wish you all happiness and am most faithfully yours,

G. Montagu

From Montagu, Thursday 19 November 1761

G.D. 15/8, No. 778.

From Dublin, therefore 1761.

Memoranda by HW:

King———————————	Queen
Duke of York	Lady Augusta
Prince William	Duchess of Ancaster
Prince Henry	Duchess of Hamilton
Prince Frederic	Lady Effingham
Lord March	Lady Egremont
Lord Eglinton	Lady Bolinbroke
Lord Huntingdon	Lady Caroline Russel
Lord Northampton	Lady Jane Stewart
Lord Mandeville	Lady Susan Stewart
Lord Suffolk	Miss Bishop
Lord Grey	Miss Wrottesley
Lord Cantelupe	Miss Keck
———————	Miss Beauclerc
Princess	Miss Tryon
Duchess of Bedford	Miss Meadows
Lady Bute	———————

This is probably a list of guests at the ball at court described *post* 28 Nov. 1761.

Dublin, Nov. 19 [1761].

SIR COMPTON DOMVILL,[1] Clerk of the Hanaper of this kingdom, is given over and cannot live. General Conway has the reversion of his place; I therefore give you notice of it.

The Usher of the Black of the same kingdom is in perfect health; nay, better for these last six weeks than he ever was in his life; two mornings' gout has set him up.

Our cousin is most popular and of course his kinsmen and friends are well received and happy.

I shall be glad to hear you are as well and as happy; I am most assuredly yours,

G. Montagu

1. Sir Compton Domvile (ca 1686–1768), 2d Bt, of Templeogue, co. Dublin.

From MONTAGU, Monday 23 November 1761

G.D. 15/8, No. 779.

Dublin, Nov. 23, 1761.

LAST post I received the letter you sent to me to my sister's, dated August the 20, in which you say there will be a place for my brother to see the Coronation. I could murder the postman—I shall never tell my brother and therefore be not surprised if he does not thank you when you see him, as you will do after Christmas at London. I am extreme well and not out of humour with my way of life.

Pray put your name to my sister's letter and believe me ever your most faithful

G. MONTAGU

From MONTAGU, Friday 27 November 1761

G.D. 15/8, No. 780.

Year obviously 1761.

Dublin, Nov. 27 [1761].

I HAVE enclosed a list from the picture shops;[1] mark those you will have and you shall have them when I come over. I have received the six views of Twickenham[2] and am obliged to you for them.

All things go on here most harmoniously, and I am perfectly well in my health, thanks to the gout.

We had the most magnificent of entertainments at the College, the room where we dined extreme elegant and well-lighted up, with a profusion of wax lights, claret, and scarlet gowns.[3]

I went to see St Patrick's, Swift's cathedral, old, large, and ugly, and but few monuments, his own very mean,[4] a large one for the first Earl of Cork.[5] There is only the cathedral of the Archbishops of Dublin[6]

1. Missing.
2. These are perhaps views by Müntz.
3. Doctors' gowns.
4. 'Dean Swift's monument consists of a plain slab of marble under his bust' (John J. M'Gregor, *New Picture of Dublin*, 1821, p. 89). The bust is frequently illustrated in books on Swift; the 'slab' bears the famous epitaph written by Swift himself.

5. Richard Boyle (1566–1643), cr. (1616) Bn Boyle; (1620) E. of Corke. The monument depicts sixteen members of his family; see John J. M'Gregor, *New Picture of Dublin*, 1821, p. 93.
6. Christ Church.

that deserves the name of a church. They are mean, modern buildings with a small hand-bell hung up to call the servants to dinner.

Mr Bourke that you saw at Mr Hamilton's at Hampton Court is
going to publish an history of Ireland,[7] and then you will know the
little that is to be known of this kingdom.

I wish you would tell me a little of that I have left; we have been
in mourning this week for Lady Cardigan, and yet I have not seen
her name in the papers.[8]

I hope you are very well and pass your time agreeably; my compliments to Mr Chute.

I am always your most faithful

G. Montagu

Be so good as to frank my brother's letter.

To Montagu, Saturday 28 November 1761

Arlington Street, Nov. 28, 1761.

I AM much obliged for the notice of Sir Compton's illness; if you
could send me word of peace too, I should be completely satisfied
on Mr Conway's account. He has been in the late action[1] and escaped,
at a time when I flattered myself the campaign was at an end. However, I trust it is now. You will have been concerned for young Courtney.[2] The war, we hear, is to be transferred to these islands; most
probably to yours—the Black Rod, I hope, like a herald, is a sacred
personage.

There has been no authentic account of the Coronation published; if there should be, I will send it. When I am at Strawberry, I
believe I can make you out a list of those that walked; but I have no
memorandums in town. If Mr Bentley's play is printed in Ireland, I
depend on your sending me two copies.

There has been a very private ball at court, consisting of not above

7. Burke seems never to have published
this work.
8. She was not dead.

———

1. No doubt an indecisive affair at
Escherhausen, 6–9 Nov. (GM 1761, xxxi.
530).
2. Charles Kellond Courtenay, nephew

of the Earl of Sandwich, was killed in Germany in 1761 (L. B. Namier, *Structure of
Politics at the Accession of George III*,
1929, ii. 378, n. 2; Collins, *Peerage*, 1812,
iii. 469). He was a Captain in the 20th
Foot (*Army List* for 1761), and was at Eton
in 1753 (R. A. Austen-Leigh, *Eton College
Register 1698–1752*, Eton, 1921).

twelve or thirteen couple;[3] some of the Lords of the Bedchamber, most of the Ladies, the Maids of Honour, and six strangers, Lady Caroline Russel,[4] Lady Jane Stewart,[5] Lord Suffolk,[6] Lord Northampton, Lord Mandeville and Lord Grey.[7] Nobody sat by, but the Princess, the Duchess of Bedford and Lady Bute. They began before seven, danced till one, and parted without a supper.

Lady Sarah Lenox has refused Lord Errol.[8] The Duke of Bedford is Privy Seal; Lord Thomond, Cofferer; Lord George Cavendish, Comptroller; George Pitt[9] goes Minister to Turin; and Mrs Speed must go thither, as she is marrying the Baron de Perrier,[10] Count Virry's[11] son. Adieu! commend me to your brother.

Yours ever

H. W.

3. See the list prefixed to *ante* 17 and 19 Nov. 1761.

4. Lady Caroline Russell (1743–1811), dau. of the 4th D. of Bedford; m. (1762) George Spencer, 3d D. of Marlborough.

5. Lady Jane Stuart (1742–1828), m. (1768) George Macartney, cr. (1776) Bn, (1792) Vct, and (1796) E. Macartney. Selwyn describes her at the time of her marriage as 'laide à faire peur' (Selwyn-Carlisle letters, Historical Manuscripts Commission, 15th Rep. App. vi, *Manuscripts of the Earl of Carlisle*, 1897, p. 229).

6. Henry Howard (1739–79), 12th E. of Suffolk.

7. George Harry Grey (1737–1819), styled Lord Grey; 5th E. of Stamford, 1768; cr. (1796) E. of Warrington.

8. 'Not Lord Errol surely; he married a very pretty woman afterwards—and she!! Sir Charles Bunbury! By her own choice! He is yet alive and so is her Ladyship in 1818' (Mrs Piozzi). 'Ajax [Lord Erroll], even the mighty Ajax, employ'd begging, prayer, kneeling, and even tears, to persuade me from my purpose, and I stood it all out for an hour. . . . I did not allow myself to be much moved, for all was in vain. . . . We are upon civil and friendly terms as if nothing had happened; that I like' (Lady Sarah Lennox to Lady Susan Fox-Strangways, 24 Oct. 1761, in *Life and Letters of Lady Sarah Lennox*, ed. Countess of Ilchester, 1901–2, i. 113–14).

9. George Pitt (1721–1803), cr. (1776) Bn Rivers.

10. Francesco Maria Giuseppe Giustino (1736–1813), Barone di La Perrière; Conte di Viry, 1766; Sardinian Ambassador to Holland, 1764; London, 1765; Madrid, 1769; Paris, 1773 (*Enciclopedia Storico-Nobiliare Italiana*, ed. Vittorio Spreti, Milano, 1928–36, vi. 924). See Gray to Wharton, 11 Jan. 1762: 'he is a very sober man; good-natured and honest' (*Gray's Corr.* ii. 770). Cf. Selwyn to Carlisle, 28 Feb. 1768: 'a stupid animal in appearance, this Viri' (Historical Manuscripts Commission, 15th Rep. App. vi, *Manuscripts of the Earl of Carlisle*, 1897, p. 247).

11. Francesco Giuseppe (d. 1766), Conte di Viry; of a Savoyard family, he entered the service of the King of Sardinia after quarrels with his family, and was Minister to Switzerland (1738), Holland (1749–54), England (1755–63), and Secretary of State for Foreign Affairs 1764–6. Louis Dutens knew him in London and Turin, and characterizes him at length in his *Memoirs of a Traveller*, 1806, ii. 18–22, 65–76 ('one of the most subtle politicians of Europe . . . he always had some secret to tell you, and that secret generally turned out to be nothing'). He played such an important *sub rosa* role in English politics at this time, as an intermediary between Bute, Newcastle, and Pitt, that the English government strongly protested and prevented his recall in 1758; see ibid.; Lewis B. Namier, *England in the Age of the American Revolution*, 1930, pp. 91–3 ('a peculiar intriguer, an ample talker, as-

To Montagu, Tuesday 8 December 1761

Arlington Street, Dec. 8th, 1761.

I RETURN you the list of prints and shall be glad you will bring me all to which I have affixed this mark X. The rest I have; yet the expense of the whole list would not ruin me. Lord Farnham,[1] who I believe departed this morning, brings you the list of the Duke of Devonshire's pictures.[2]

I had been told that Mr Bourk's history was of England, not of Ireland—I am glad it is the latter, for I am now in Mr Hume's England,[3] and would fain read no more—I not only know what has been written, but what would be written. Our story is so exhausted, that to make it new, they really *make* it *new*.[4] Mr Hume has exalted Edward II and depressed Edward III. The next historian, I suppose, will make James I a hero, and geld Charles II.

Fingal is come out[5]—I have not yet got through it—not but it is very fine—yet I cannot at once compass an epic poem now. It tires me to death to read how many ways a warrior is like the moon, or the sun, or a rock, or a lion, or the ocean. *Fingal* is a brave collection of similes, and will serve all the boys at Eton and Westminster for these twenty years. I will trust you with a secret, but you must not disclose it, I should be ruined with my Scotch friends—in short, I cannot believe it genuine—I cannot believe a regular poem of six books has been preserved, uncorrupted, by oral tradition, from times before Christianity was introduced into the island. What! Preserved unadul-

---

siduous, inscrutable, secretive, and yet plausible'); *Enciclopedia Storico-Nobiliare Italiana*, ed. Vittorio Spreti, Milano, 1928–36, vi. 924; La Chesnaye-Desbois and Badier, *Dictionnaire de la Noblesse*, 1863–76, xix. 883–4.

1. Robert Maxwell (d. 1779), 2d Bn Farnham, cr. (1760) Vct Farnham; cr. (1763) E. of Farnham. He was doubtless returning to his seat, Farnham, co. Cavan.

2. Apparently HW did reprint a few more, as he promised to do *ante* 24 Oct. 1761.

3. The last two volumes, in order of publication, of David Hume's (1711–76) six-volume *History of England* covered the

period from Julius Caesar to Henry VIII. Though the imprint date is 1762, their publication was announced in *London Chronicle* 12–14 Nov. 1761, x. 466. HW's copy, MS Cat. D.4, was sold SH v. 27 (4 vols only).

4. In seven years HW 'made it new' with his *Historic Doubts of Richard III*.

5. Ca 1 Dec. (*London Chronicle* 28 Nov.– 1 Dec. 1761, x. 528). HW's interest had been engaged by David Dalrymple and Gray and he had read part of *Fingal* in manuscript and had suggested improvements in form; see HW to Dalrymple 14 April 1761. At that time he wrote, 'My doubts of the genuineness are all vanished'; but see Cole ii. 206.

terated by savages dispersed among mountains, and so often driven from their dens, so wasted by wars civil and foreign! Has one man ever got all by heart? I doubt it. Were parts preserved by some, other parts by others? Mighty lucky, that the tradition was never interrupted, nor any part lost—not a verse, not a measure, not the sense! Luckier and luckier—I have been extremely qualified myself lately for this Scotch memory; we have had nothing but a coagulation of rain, fogs and frosts, and though they have clouded all understanding, I suppose if I had tried, I should have found that they thickened and gave great consistence to my remembrance.

You want news—I must make it if I send it. To change the dullness of the scene, I went t'other night to the play, where I had not been this winter. They are so crowded, that though I went before six I got no better place than a fifth row, where I heard very ill, and was pent for five hours without a soul near me that I knew. It was *Cymbeline*,[6] and appeared to me as long as if everybody in it went really to Italy in every act, and came back again. With a few pretty passages and a scene or [two,] it is so absurd and tiresome, that I am persuaded Garrick[7] . . .

From MONTAGU, ca Tuesday 15 December 1761

G.D. 15/8, No. 785.
Undated; answered by HW 23 Dec. 1761, immediately upon its receipt.

[Dublin, ca Dec. 15, 1761].

I SHALL get you some more prints and will bring you some Irish purple scollop shells.[1]

Yesterday Mr Cumberland gave me a copy of Mr Bentley's Epistle to Lord Melcomb in the Horatian Bentleian Cliquetis manner. There are some admirable lines, the whole spirited and really charming;[2] an

6. Considerably altered by Garrick; produced 28 Nov. 1761 and acted 16 times; see [John Genest], *Some Account of the English Stage*, Bath, 1832, iv. 635–7.

7. The rest of this letter is missing.

1. Perhaps a facetious reference to the late shell-grotto vogue.

2. Richard Cumberland also praises Bentley's 'Epistle to Lord Melcombe' in his *Memoirs*, 1806, pp. 162–3, but says that it was coolly received by Lord Melcombe and not published. However, it is in *St James's Magazine* March 1763, ii. 1–8, and the *New Foundling Hospital for Wit*, edn 1786, vi. 97–107.

(Lord Halifax)

elegant unexpected compliment to my cousin at the end after Gray,[3] but there is a piece of secret history that has put me to death:[4]

Even my COUSIN Rochester[5] but barren
From wholesome meat if you deduct the carrion!

Marry come up my dirty cousin! This must be an acquisition that Hanah has brought with her[6]—in short, a few copies[7] are to be printed, and you shall have one as soon as I get them.

Here is another list of personages;[8] you cannot imagine how incurious they are here, and how difficult I shall find it to please or oblige you.

We play upon velvet;[9] we are as gracious as when we first came over and have fresh graces conferred upon us. I am in the bloom of fifty; I have not been so well, so jolly, and so pleasant these ten years; I know if you was here you would scold me abominably.

I am to have *The Wishes* and the tragedy[10] lent me; you will wonder at all this; why I will tell you how it all came about.

I dined one day with Sangrenuntio;[11] I came in in the sort of spirits I used to have in the days of my youth; I battled for my cousin

3. The reference to Gray is on p. 5 of *St James's Magazine* March 1763:

'Soft Elegy has dried up all her tears,
And Gray composes once in seven years.'
The compliment to Halifax occupies the last eight lines.

4. Ibid. p. 8:
'E'en my good cousin ROCHESTER's but barren,
From wholesome meat if you deduct the carrion.'

5. John Wilmot (1647–80), 2d E. of Rochester; the poet.

6. Bentley's relationship to Rochester is explained *post* 23 Dec. 1761, n. 4.

7. No Dublin edition has been found.

8. This list of prints is missing.

9. According to John S. Farmer and William E. Henley, *Slang and its Analogues*, 1890–1904, vii. 273, to play on velvet is 'to gamble with winnings'; here, of course, Montagu refers to the success of the Vice-Regal party.

10. Bentley's *Philodamus;* see *post* ca 24 Dec. 1761. It was printed in 1767 by Dodsley, and produced at Covent Garden 14 Dec. 1782; see [John Genest], *Some Account of the English Stage*, Bath, 1832, vi. 265–6,

which accords it 'singular merit,' but considers it unfitted for the stage. According to David E. Baker, I. Reed, and S. Jones, *Biographica Dramatica*, 1812, iii. 145, it 'excited the laughter of the audience to so great a degree, that it was represented only one night.' They quote the *Biographica Britannica*, on the other hand, which states that Gray 'esteemed [it] . . . to be one of the most capital poems in the English language. Accordingly, Mr Gray wrote a laboured and elegant commentary upon it, which abounds with wit, and is one of his best productions' (*Biographica Britannica*, ed. Andrew Kippis, 2d edn 1778–93, ii. 247, on the authority of Richard Cumberland). This commentary, if it existed, seems to be unpublished. HW's copy of *Biographica Dramatica*, 1782 (now wsl), corrects two typographical slips in the articles on Bentley, *Philodamus*, and *The Wishes*, but makes no comment upon the text, thus tacitly acknowledging its accuracy.

11. Probably Archbishop Stone. The significance of 'Sangrenuntio' has not been discovered, nor what was the particular subject of Montagu's 'battle' for Hali-

against the prelate, so—well, shall I say? In short, I might have stripped the company of all they had for my pains; I asked for these things; indeed, I stayed till twelve at night, and you will think I earned them hard—I need never more stay anywhere, or open my lips; I am in vogue; this is as vain as 'my cousin Rochester,' but then it is an affinity you have been long acquainted with.

I must write no more for fear you will write no more to such a puppy; consider where I am and have been three months and you will not wonder I have catched the brogue. Adieu—I will meet you at Philippi in Arlington Street.

G. M.

My compliments to the poor invalid.[12]

From MONTAGU, ca Sunday 20 December 1761

One of the two letters mentioned *post* 30 Dec. 1761 as having been received between 23–30 Dec. is missing.

To MONTAGU, Wednesday 23 December 1761

Arlington Street, past midnight Dec. 23d, 1761.

I AM this minute come home and find such a delightful letter from you,[1] that I cannot help answering it and telling you so before I sleep. You need not affirm that your ancient wit and pleasantry are revived; your letter is but five and twenty, and I will forgive any vanity that is so honest and so well-founded. Ireland I see produces wonders of more sorts than one—if my Lord Anson was to go Lord Lieutenant, I suppose he would return a ravisher. How different am I from this state of revivification! Even such talents as I had, are far from blooming again, and while my friends, or cotemporaries, or predecessors, are rising to preside over the fame of this age, I seem a mere antediluvian, must live upon what little stock of reputation I had acquired, and indeed grow so indifferent, that I can only wonder how those whom I thought as old as myself, can interest themselves so much about a world, whose faces I hardly know. You recover your

---

fax. 'These things' must have been the MSS of *The Wishes* and *Philodamus;* Stone was a friend of Bentley's (*ante* 8 Oct. 1761).

12. Doubtless Chute, and a reference to the missing part of *ante* 8 Dec. 1761.

---

1. *Ante* ca 15 Dec. 1761.

spirits and wit, Rigby is grown a speaker,[2] Mr Bentley a poet, while I am nursing one or two gouty friends, and sometimes lamenting that I am likely to survive the few I have left. Nothing tempts me to launch out again; every day teaches me how much I was mistaken in my own parts, and I am in no danger now but of thinking I am grown too wise; for every period of life has its mistake.[3]

Mr Bentley's relation to Lord Rochester by the St Johns is not new to me,[4] and you had more reason to doubt of their affinity by the former *marrying* his *whore*, than to ascribe their consanguinity to it.[5] I shall be glad to see the Epistle: are not *The Wishes* to be acted? Remember me, if they are printed; and I shall thank you for this new list of prints.[6]

I have mentioned names enough in this letter, to lead me naturally to new ill-usage I have received. Just when I thought my book finished, my printer[7] ran away, and had left eighteen sheets in the middle of the book untouched, having amused[7a] me with sending proofs. He had got into debt and two girls with child—being two, he could not marry both Hannahs. You see my luck; I had been kind to this fellow—in short, if the faults of my life had been punished as severely as my merits have been, I should be the most unhappy of beings!— but let us talk of something else.

2. Judging from the reports in *Mem. Geo. II* and *Mem. Geo. III*, Rigby spoke fairly frequently, especially in the Irish Parliament when he was Chief Secretary there, but HW, while praising his parts, declares that he 'never shone in the Irish Parliament' (*Mem. Geo. II* iii. 246, passage finished in 1763 about events in 1759). A speech of his 19 Jan. 1762 is reported *Mem. Geo. III* i. 80, but no mention is made of its oratorical quality. Wraxall describes fully 'his manner, rough yet frank, bold and overbearing, if not insolent, but manly' in the House (*Memoirs* i. 421–2).

3. HW's depression was possibly caused by his printer's defection (see 2d paragraph below).

4. The closest relationship between Bentley and Rochester via the St Johns seems to be as follows: Bentley's mother's mother was Elizabeth, dau. of Chief Justice Oliver St John, great-grandson of the 1st Baron St John of Bletso. Rochester's mother was Anne, dau. of Sir John St John, Bt, of Lydiard Tregoze. The com-

mon ancestor of the Bletso and Lydiard Tregoze St Johns was Sir Oliver St John, d. 1437. Rochester and Bentley were seventh cousins twice removed (Thomas Wotton, *Baronetage of England*, 1741, iii pt ii. 365; DNB; GEC).

5. In the previous letter Montagu wondered if Bentley's relationship to Rochester was through his wife.

6. Missing.

7. Thomas Farmer, HW's printer 16 July 1759–2 Dec. 1761. HW wrote a circumstantial account of his actions in the days preceding his disappearance; see COLE i. 12; *Journal of the Printing Office* 81–2 and *passim*. The book whose printing was delayed was the *Anecdotes*. The 18 or 19 unprinted sheets (see *post* 30 Dec. 1761; *Journal of the Printing Office* 10), or most of them, printed by the new printer, can be identified by differences in the paper or presswork.

7a. 1817 is the latest example in OED of 'amuse' in this sense—to beguile ('the usual sense in 17–18th c.').

I have picked up at Mrs Dunch's auction[8] the sweetest Petitot[9] in the world—the very picture of James II[10] that he gave Mrs Godfrey— and I paid but six guineas and a half for it[11]—I will not tell you how vast a commission I had given;[12] but I will own, that about the hour of sale, I drove about the door[13] to find what likely bidders there were —the first coach I saw was the Chudleigh's. Could I help concluding that a maid of honour kept by a Duke,[14] would purchase the portrait of a Duke that kept a maid of honour—but I was mistaken. The Oxendens[15] reserved the best pictures;[16] the fine china and even the diamonds sold for nothing—for nobody has a shilling—we shall be beggars if we don't conquer Peru within this half year.

If you are acquainted with my Lady Barrimore,[17] pray tell her that in less than two hours t'other night the Duke of Cumberland lost 450 pounds at loo; Miss Pelham won three hundred,[18] and I the rest. However in general loo is extremely gone to decay;[19] I am to play at Princess Emily's tomorrow for the first time this winter, and it is with difficulty she has made a party.

My Lady Pomfret is dead[20] on the road to Bath—and unless the deluge stops, and the fogs disperse, I think we shall all die. A few days ago, on the cannon firing for the King going to the House, some-

8. On 10–11 Dec. 1761, when 115 pictures were sold by Prestage and Hobbs (Frits Lugt, *Répertoire des catalogues des ventes*, La Haye, 1938–, No. 1184).

9. Jean Petitot (1607–91), painter in enamel; see Ulrich Thieme and Felix Becker, *Allgemeines Lexikon der Bildenden Künstler*, Leipzig, 1907–. HW possessed a large number of his works.

10. 'James II when Duke of York; fine, by Petitot; bought at the sale of Mrs Dunch, daughter of his mistress, Mrs Godfrey' (*Des. of SH, Works* ii. 473). It was sold SH xiv. 41 to Miss Burdett Coutts for 75 gns and resold at the sale of W. Burdett-Coutts, Christie's, 11 May 1922, No. 417 for £283 10s (*The Connoisseur*, 1922, lxiii. 236).

11. In HW's copy of *Des. of SH* 1774 (now WSL) 'with the prices of such pieces as I can recollect,' HW has noted that he paid 8 gns for it.

12. To the agent whom he always employed to buy for him.

13. The location of the auction-rooms

of Prestage and Hobbs cannot at the present time (1940) be ascertained.

14. Of Kingston.

15. Mrs Dunch's dau. Elizabeth (d. 1779), m. (1720) Sir George Oxenden, 5th Bt, of Deane.

16. HW also had a Petitot of Mrs Godfrey (Mrs Dunch's mother), and an enamel by Boit of Mrs Godfrey's brother Admiral George Churchill, both of which had belonged to Mrs Dunch, and which HW presumably bought also at her sale; see *Des. of SH, Works* ii. 474; sold SH xiv. 44, 49.

17. Margaret Davys (d. 1788), m. (1738) James Barry, 5th E. of Barrymore (d. 1751); a zealous card-player (*post* 2 Jan. 1762).

18. She usually lost (*ante* ca 5 Oct. 1747, n. 7).

19. However, Mrs Lybbe Powys describes its popularity at an evening party at Eastbury in 1777 (Emily J. Climenson, *Passages from the Diaries of Mrs Philip Lybbe Powys*, 1899, p. 186).

20. 16 Dec., at Marlborough, Wilts.

body asked, what it was for? Monsieur de Choiseul[21] replied, 'Appa-remment, c'est qu'on voit le soleil.'

Shall I fill up the rest of my paper with some extempore lines that I wrote t'other night[22] on Lady Mary Coke having St Antony's fire[23] in her cheek? You will find nothing in them to contradict what I have said in the former part of my letter—they rather confirm it.

> No rouge you wear; nor can a dart
> From love's bright quiver wound your heart.
> And thought you, Cupid and his mother
> Would unreveng'd their anger smother?
> No, no—from heav'n they sent the fire,
> That boasts St Antony its sire;
> They pour'd it on one peccant part,
> Inflam'd your cheek, if not your heart.
> In vain—for see the crimson rise,
> And dart fresh lustre thro' your eyes;
> While ruddier drops and baffled pain
> Enhance the white they meant to stain.
> Ah! Nymph; on that unfading face
> With fruitless pencil Time shall trace
> His lines malignant, since Disease
> But gives you mightier pow'r to please.

Willes is dead, and Pratt[24] is to be Chief Justice; Mr Yorke, Attorney General—Solicitor, I don't know who.[25] Good night: the watchman cries, 'Past one!'

Yours ever

H. W.

PS. When you bring over the prints, pray roll them on a round stick, for the least crease is never to be effaced.

21. 'Governor' of Santo Domingo according to a quotation in Romney Sedgwick, *Letters from George III to Lord Bute*, 1939, p. 72, n. 3. He may be Charles-Antoine-Étienne (b. 1739), Marquis de Choiseul, who served in Santo Domingo (La Chesnaye-Desbois and Badier, *Dictionnaire de la Noblesse*, 1863–76, v. 665).

22. 20 Dec. ('Short Notes').

23. Erysipelas (OED *sub* fire A. 12).

24. Sir Charles Pratt (1714–94), Kt, 1761;

Chief Justice of Common Pleas; cr. (1765) Bn, and (1786) E. Camden; Lord Chancellor, 1766. According to *Mem. Geo. III* i. 99, he was made Chief Justice to get him out of the Commons and the Attorney-Generalship, to which Pitt had appointed him.

25. Fletcher Norton (1716–89), Kt and Solicitor-General, 1762; Attorney-General 1763–5; Speaker 1770–80; cr. (1782) Bn Grantley.

From MONTAGU, ca Thursday 24 December 1761

G.D. 15/8, No. 792.
Undated; answered by HW 30 Dec. 1761.

[Dublin, ca 24 Dec. 1761].

I HAVE finished Mr Bentley's tragedy;[1] 'tis Cliquetis all over dou-
ble-proof. There are a thousand pretty things in it, some really
fine, many conceited expressions, and no harmony at all. He seems to
affect to tear the ear to pieces instead of charming. Hanah appears in
more scenes than one, indeed, she is in good company: the Pitt, the
Bute, the K[ing] and Q[ueen], some of his friends, and his own self;[2]
it is much admired here by those who have seen it, my cousin particularly; I fancy, there is a great deal added of late to suit occasions.
I have been to see Lord Charlemont's collection. He has some charming things that would make a show even at Strawberry. His medals
are very fine, a charming Titian of Borgia,[3] two Carlo Marats,[4] a
Claude, two fine vases, a Queen Elizabeth, that he says was in Dr
Mead's collection,[5] three-quarters, carved in age, a lion skin of yellow
that serves for a veil, a brave collection of books, and an edition of a
voyage to Nubia printed at Copenhagen[6] that on comparison with
Baskerville[7] absolutely exceeds it. We have a burletta; the father

1. *Philodamus.*
2. It is hardly possible to detect the
characterizations that Montagu mentions,
especially since the play was not printed
till six years after he had seen it, and
might therefore have been much altered.
3. Arthur Young, in his *Tour of Ireland,* 1780, pt i. 2, also mentions a portrait
of Caesar Borgia at Charlemont House,
ascribing it to Titian. Standard works on
Titian do not specifically mention it; but
see Joseph A. Crowe and G. B. Cavalca-
selle, *Titian His Life and Times,* 1877, ii.
469: 'In the [Dublin International (ca
1874?)] exhibition, No. 67, was a portrait
of a man in a plumed cap and rich dress
called Cesar Borgia and assigned to Titian.
The picture is not genuine.' The critics do
not give the owner's name; see also Algernon Graves, *A Century of Loan Exhibi-
tions,* 1913–15, iii. 1322.
4. John Parker wrote Charlemont from
Rome in 1756 that he was sending him a
'boy of Maratti and Borgia' (Historical
Manuscripts Commission, 12th Rep. App.
x, *Charlemont Manuscripts,* 1891, p. 228).
5. By Valerio Vicentino. 'Dr Meade [Dr
Richard Mead (1673–1754), physician and
collector] had a fine bust of Queen Elizabeth on onyx, alto relievo in profile, and
very large, by the hand of this master'
(*Anecdotes, Works* iii. 138). 'Lord Charlemont bought it at Dr Meade's sale' (note,
ibid.). See *post* 30 Dec. 1761; *Museum
Meadianum . . .* 1755, p. 247, no. 1.
6. *Voyage d'Égypte et de Nubie,* Par Mr
Frederik Louis Norden, De L'Imprimerie
de la Maison Royale des Orphelins, Copenhagen, 1755, 2 vols folio (Frederik Lud-
vig Norden (1708–42), explorer; see DNB
and *Dansk Biografisk Leksikon,* ed. Bricka,
Kobenhavn, 1933–).
7. John Baskerville (1706–75), who had
first attracted public attention with his
'Virgil' in 1757.

Amicis and his daughter[8] are admirable, the rest of the company insupportable; it takes here much. Lord Farnham[8a] brought me the
catalogue[9] safe and I am obliged to you for it. He looks sadly.

The Lady Mayoress[10] has invited my Lord's daughters[11] to a Christmas Ale;[12] this is an unusual compliment.[13]

My cousin pleases as much as ever and is as good to us. I never was
better in my health in all my life, and really am not tired of the
country, I meet with such kindness and am so stout. Let me hear a
little how you do, and I pray you give as good an account of yourself.
Sir Compton Domevill is recovered, but in a miserable state of
health.

The General desires his compliments to you and joins with me in
wishing you all manner of good wishes.

I am always what I have so long been—most faithfully yours.

Lord Blayney[14] is in England, perhaps to return soon. Lord Dacre
will see him often and he will bring me any dab you will have ocu-
gion[15] to send me.

The books of painting may come in three parcels directed to Mr
Secretary Hamilton.

Pray frank the enclosed.

From Montagu, ca Saturday 26 December 1761

Missing; mentioned *post* 26 Jan. 1762; probably written before 29 Dec.; see
post 6 Feb. 1762.

8. Anna Lucia de Amicis (b. ca 1740),
singer, m. (1771) —— Buonsollazzi; first
appeared in London in 1762; still singing
1789 (Sir George Grove, *Dictionary of
Music; Gray's Corr.* ii. 812). Her father has
not been identified. The Amicis family
were engaged for burlettas in London in
1762. Anna de Amicis, says Burney, 'acted
and sung for the whole family; for by her
merits and good works, she covered the
multitude of their sins, which would otherwise have had no remission' (Charles Burney, *General History of Music*, 1776–89, iv.
479).

8a. See *ante* 8 Dec. 1761, n. 1.

9. Of the Duke of Devonshire's pictures
(*ante* 24 Oct. 1761, n. 11).

10. Sir Timothy Allen was Lord Mayor

(*Calendar of Ancient Records of Dublin*,
ed. John T. Gilbert and Lady Rosa M.
Gilbert, 1889–1913, xi. 478); his wife has
not been identified.

11. Lord Halifax's daughters (*ante* 12
Oct. 1761).

12. A descendant of the medieval was-
sail; see T. G. Crippen, *Christmas and
Christmas Lore*, [1923] pp. 99–104; W. T.
Marchant, *In Praise of Ale*, 1888, pp. 61–
86.

13. Presumably because there was ordinarily little social intercourse between the
Castle and the city.

14. Cadwallader Blayney (1720–75), 9th
Bn Blayney.

15. So in MS; perhaps an attempted
Iricism for 'occasion.'

To Montagu, Wednesday 30 December 1761

Arlington Street, Dec. 30th, 1761.

I HAVE received two more letters from you since I wrote last week,[1] and I like to find by them that you are so well and so happy. As nothing has happened of change[2] in my situation but a few more months passed, I have nothing to tell you new of myself. Time does not sharpen my passions or pursuits, and the experience I have had, by no means prompts me to make new connections. 'Tis a busy world, and well adapted to those who love to bustle in it—I loved it once, loved its very tempests—now I barely open my window, to view what course the storm takes. The town, who like the devil when one has once sold oneself to him, never permits one to have done playing the fool, believe I have a great hand in their amusements; but to write pamphlets, I mean, as a volunteer, one must love or hate, and I have the satisfaction of doing neither.[3] I would not be at the trouble of composing a distich, to achieve a revolution. 'Tis equal to me what names are on the scene. In the general view, the prospect is very dark; the Spanish war[4] added to the load, almost oversets our most sanguine heroism; and now we have an opportunity of conquering all the world, by being at war with all the world, we seem to doubt a little of our abilities. On a survey of our situation, I comfort myself with saying, well, what is it to me? A selfishness that is far from anxious, when it is the first thought in one's constitution—not so agreeable, when it is the last, and adopted by necessity alone.

You drive your expectations much too fast, in thinking my *Anecdotes of Painting* are ready to appear, and in demanding *three* volumes. You will see but *two,* and it will be February first.[5] True, I have written three, but I question whether the third will be published at all; certainly not soon; it is not a work of merit enough to cloy the town with a great deal at once. My printer ran away and left

---

1. One is missing.
2. HW's Gallicisms in this letter suggest that he had been recently reading or writing in French, although no letters in French have been discovered of this period.
3. It is not known which pamphlets HW was suspected of writing; but only a week before he had written his verses,

'Portrait of Lord Granville,' which had a wide circulation; see 'Short Notes' and *Horace Walpole's Fugitive Verses,* ed. W. S. Lewis, New York, 1931, p. 51.
4. The Spanish Ambassador left London 1 Jan., and war was declared 4 Jan. (*Mem. Geo. III* i. 100–2).
5. They were published 15 Feb. (*Journal of the Printing Office* 10).

a third part of the two first volumes unfinished—I suppose he is writing a tragedy himself, or an epistle to my Lord Melcomb, or a panegyric on my Lord Bute.[6]

Jemmy Pelham[7] is dead, and has left to his servants, what little his servants had left him. Lord Legonier was killed by the newspapers,[8] and wanted to prosecute them: his lawyer told him it was impossible —a tradesman indeed might prosecute, as such a report might affect his credit—'Well, then,' said the old man, 'I may prosecute too, for I can prove I have been hurt by this report; I was going to marry a great fortune, who thought I was but seventy-four; the newspapers have said I am eighty,[9] and she will not have me.'

Lord Charlemont's Queen Elizabeth I know perfectly; he outbid me for it. Is his villa finished? I am much pleased with the design in Chambers.[10] I have been *my out of town*[11] with Lord Waldgrave, Selwyn and Williams; it was melancholy the missing poor Edgcumbe, who was constantly of the Christmas and Easter parties. Did you see the charming picture Reynolds painted for me of him, Selwyn and Williams?[12] It is by far one of the best things he has executed. He has just finished a pretty whole length of Lady Elizabeth Keppel,[13] in the bride-maid's habit, sacrificing to Hymen.

6. A hit at Bentley.

7. Col. James Pelham (d. 27 Dec. 1761), of Crowhurst, Sussex; son of Sir Nicholas Pelham, of Catsfield Place; onetime Secretary to the Prince of Wales; Secretary to the Lord Chamberlain for 40 years; M.P. Newark 1722–41; Hastings 1741–61; relative, follower, and pensioner of Newcastle (GM 1761, xxxi. 604; John Comber, *Sussex Genealogies, Lewes Centre*, Cambridge, 1933, p. 211; Lewis B. Namier, *Structure of Politics at the Accession of George III*, 1929, ii. 523 n).

8. Which published a false report of his death: 'Yesterday morning died suddenly, at his house in North Audley Street, in the 80th year of his age, the Right Hon. John Lord Viscount Ligonier' (*London Chronicle* 15–17 Dec. 1761, x. 582; *Lloyd's Evening Post*, the only other paper seen, did not carry the report).

9. Which was correct.

10. *Treatise on . . . Civil Architecture*, ante 1 Oct. 1761, n. 8.

11. His semi-annual house party at SH.

12. It hung over the chimney-piece in the refectory or great parlour at SH. 'Richard second Lord Edgcumbe is seen drawing at a table, in the Library at Strawberry Hill; George James Williams is looking over him; George Augustus Selwyn stands on the other side, with a book in his hand' (*Des. of SH, Works* ii. 401). The picture was reproduced by Cunningham iii. 475 and in Jesse, *Selwyn* i. 1. It was sold SH xxi. 43 to J. M. Smith for 150 gns. It came into the possession of Henry Labouchere, 1st Baron Taunton, and passed from him to his son-in-law, Edward J. Stanley, M.P., who died in 1899 (Algernon Graves and W. V. Cronin, *History of the Works of Sir Joshua Reynolds*, 1899–1901, i. 276).

13. This picture is in the Duke of Bedford's collection at Woburn; see Algernon Graves and W. V. Cronin, ibid. ii. 548–9. It is reproduced in Countess of Ilchester, *Life and Letters of Lady Sarah Lennox*, 1901–2, i. 108.

If the Spaniards land in Ireland, shall you make the campaign? No, no, come back to England; you and I will not be patriots, till the Gauls are in the City, and we must take our great chairs and our fasces, and be knocked on the head with decorum in St James's market. Good night.

Yours ever

H. W.

PS. I am told that they bind in vellum better at Dublin than anywhere; pray bring me any one book of their binding, as well as it can be done, and I will not mind the price. If Mr Bourk's history appears before your return, let it be that.[14]

14. See *post* 25 Feb. 1762, n. 5.